MAITREYA'S MISSION

VOLUME THREE

BENJAMIN CREME

Share International Foundation
Amsterdam ♦ London

Cosmic Fire, *the painting by Benjamin Creme reproduced on the cover, was begun in January 1965 and substantially reworked in 1984. It represents the fiery nature of Cosmos, "Fire Electrical", from which issue all other fires. Our present day electricity is a physical-plane aspect of Cosmic Fire Electrical. The fiery element is contained in a variation of the 'Cosmic Egg'.*

This book is dedicated

with reverence and deep respect

to my Master Whose constant inspiration

has been its source.

As courtiers sit awaiting the entrance

of the King, do we await You, Maitreya.

Only, some do not sit but run hither

and thither, telling the glad tidings:

the Great Lord, chief among chieftains,

dismounts and approaches the gate.

Open it quickly, that He be not delayed.

Benjamin Creme

CONTENTS

PREFACE

Maitreya's Mission, Volume Three, looks forward to the future — the quality of life and consciousness which, gradually, will follow from Maitreya's appearance before the world.

Chapter 1 begins with an account of Maitreya's Priorities as given by my Master in His wonderful article — 'The Son of Man'— published in *Share International* in June 1984. My talk, given in 1995 at the Transmission Meditation conferences in San Francisco and The Netherlands, transcribed and edited, forms the commentary on Maitreya's priorities, hopefully throwing light on the inspiring range of possibilities envisioned by my Master.

Chapter 2 — The Challenge of the 21st Century — tackles the problems which currently face humanity. In interviews with journalist Patricia Pitchon, my Master, through me, clarifies these major concerns and dangers, nuclear and environmental; and emphasizes the need for Maitreya to act as the voice of humanity to ensure global response.

The chapter ends with an interview by George Catlin where I attempt to show some of the ways in which education in the new age will move in relation to our growing understanding of ourselves — and our children — as souls in incarnation.

Chapter 3 starts with an article by my Master — 'To Serve Anew' — followed by my commentary on His insights. The Master paints a moving and inspiring picture of humanity's experiences and reactions during Maitreya's overshadowing of their minds on the Day of Declaration. He presents to disciples the challenge of an enlargement of their service in educating the world in Maitreya's teachings.

Chapter 4 — The Ageless Wisdom Teachings — gives an overview of the esoteric lore which illuminates the mysteries of the evolutionary process. This includes a section on the Seven Rays which are further explored in **Chapter 5** — Artists and their Rays — a study of the Rays in relation to the achievement of ten famous artists of the past.

The Appendix brings together for the reader's convenience the ray structures of initiates already given in Volumes One and Two plus those published since 1993 in *Share International*.

The building of the Antahkarana — the bridge between the soul and its vehicle — provides the subject of **Chapter 6** and Transmission Meditation that of **Chapter 7**.

Maitreya's Mission, Volume Three, ends with **The Art of Waiting**, based on the first article written by my Master for *Share International* in January 1982. Here He postulates the non-existence of time which, He predicts, following our acceptance of the oneness of humanity, will one day be the common experience of all.

As usual, this book is the result of group work. I am indebted to the many people who have given unstintingly of their time and energy to make its publication possible. I am particularly indebted to Michiko Ishikawa for her organization of the mass of available material into book form.

Benjamin Creme
London, March 1997

Editor's note: Most of the articles, interviews, and questions and answers contained in this book were published originally in the monthly magazine *Share International*, during the period January/ February 1993 to February 1997. For ease of reading, they are arranged according to subject rather than by date of publication.

The date of first publication is given at the end of each question, unless the question was asked at a network conference discussion or interview.

'Share of the Air in print', a compilation of Monte Leach's interviews with Benjamin Creme (published in the July/August 1993 issue of *Share International*), is divided into separate parts and used mainly in Chapters 1 and 2 in order to supplement questions on varied topics published since 1993. These interview questions are indicated by the notation "July/August 1993" after each question.

Throughout the book, the term "billion" refers to an American billion, which equals one thousand million.

INTRODUCTION

THE EMERGENCE OF MAITREYA AND THE MASTERS OF WISDOM

New Age

Humanity today is living at a unique time in its history. The events that I submit are now under way will transform our lives, our world, in the most fundamental, radical fashion, within a relatively short number of years. We are at the end of a civilization, and therefore at the beginning of a new one: if we would have it so, this can be the most brilliant in our long history.

Most people will know that we are entering a new era, a new cosmic cycle. We call it the Age of Aquarius because of the particular relationship now being formed in space between our solar system and the constellation of Aquarius. In its cyclic movement around the heavens, our solar system has come into a definite energetic alignment with that constellation, which will continue for the next 2,350 years, more or less. This alignment causes the Earth to become saturated with the cosmic energies of Aquarius. Every civilization, beginning roughly every 2,000 years, is the result of this changing cosmic relationship.

As we near the end of the century, a powerful thoughtform of destruction is gripping the minds of millions of people. Throughout the world there is a 'doomsday complex'. As a result of misunderstanding the prognostications of people like Edgar Cayce, Nostradamus and others, people have the idea that towards the end of the century there will be some great catastrophic event in which the world will be physically changed: mountains will rise and many countries, perhaps continents, will sink under the sea. This belief is widespread and it comes largely from a misunderstanding of history and of scriptures which seem to point to such an apocalyptic end to the world.

As we enter a new age, everything changes. Political, economic, religious and social forms inevitably change under the impact of the new, powerful, cosmic energies that enter our lives. The foretold destruction I believe is altogether exaggerated. Countries will not go under the oceans. The oceans will not rise as mountains. The cataclysm which has been foretold by so many, emanating in the main from the astral planes — the planes of illusion — has little foundation in fact. Change there will be, but change for the better.

We are about to enter an era in which the innate spiritual nature of humanity will begin to express itself in a mass form. Countless millions throughout the world will awaken to the true purpose of their lives. A deeper, more soundly-based attitude to life will develop and people will recognize themselves as souls — souls in incarnation. They will come to understand the purpose of their incarnation, and, more and more, they will take a conscious part in their own evolution, creating modes of freedom and justice which this world has never before seen. Freedom and justice, and therefore peace, will allow the divine, spiritual aspect of humanity to come to the fore and be given expression, not only as a religious experience, but in every department of life. In politics, economics and education, in art and science, the inner awareness of our spiritual nature will increasingly be demonstrated. This will allow the discovery of a science, and the control over the forces of nature, which will give humanity unlimited power over its environment.

The Masters

All of this awaits us as we enter the new cycle. Far from destruction, we shall enter an era of unprecedented creativity and beauty of life. And this in large measure because of the re-entry into our lives of a group of men without fault, spiritual giants — from our point of view, perfected men. These are men who have gone ahead of us in evolution, and have completed the journey on which we are still engaged. They need no longer live on this planet, but accept the responsibility of remaining here to guide the rest of us to that same perfection.

For thousands of years in the Orient, the knowledge of the existence of these perfected men has been commonplace. They have many names: the Great White Brotherhood, the Society of Illumined Minds, the Elder Brothers of humanity, the Teachers, the Guides, the Mahatmas, the Masters of Wisdom and the Lords of Compassion. This group of spiritually illumined men have lived for millennia in the remote mountain and desert areas of the world, like the Himalayas, the Andes, and the Carpathians. From these mountain and desert retreats, they have beneficently overseen the evolution of humanity from the earliest times. Cycle after cycle, one of these Great Ones has come into the world to teach humanity the way forward, the next step in our evolution to perfection. These teachers are known historically, among others, as Hercules, Hermes, Rama, Mithra, Vyasa, Krishna, Confucius, Zoroaster, Shankaracharya, the Buddha, Christ, Mohammed.

Some 2,600 years ago, Gautama Buddha prophesied that at the beginning of this cycle there would come into the world another great teacher, a Buddha like Himself, by name Maitreya. Maitreya, He said, would inspire humanity to create a brilliant golden civilization based, as He put it, on Righteousness and Truth. For 2,600 years, Buddhists have awaited the coming of Maitreya Buddha. For the last 2,000 years, Christians have awaited the return of the Christ. The Christ is Maitreya, Who manifested Himself by overshadowing His disciple, Jesus, just as the Buddha overshadowed His disciple, the Prince Gautama. This is the age-old method for the manifestation of the Teacher. The Christ and the Lord Maitreya are one and the same individual; He is the Master of all the Masters, the Teacher alike, as Gautama Buddha called Him, of angels (devas) and of men.

The Masters of the Spiritual Hierarchy, of which the Lord Maitreya is the head, have known for over 500 years that sooner or later They would be required to re-enter the everyday world, known to us for what They are, living as men in the world. This return was inevitable. The only question in doubt was one of time: when would humanity be ready for the Masters' return to the everyday world? Until recently it was assumed it would be, perhaps, another 1,200 or 1,300 years before we would be ready for this event.

However, in June 1945 — significantly at the end of the Second World War — the Lord Maitreya made an extraordinary, most significant, announcement. The Lord Maitreya announced His intention to return to the world at the earliest possible moment, if humanity would take the first steps to put its house in order. He said He would come when a measure of peace had been restored to the world; when the principle of sharing was beginning to govern economic affairs; and when the energy of goodwill, the lowest aspect of love, was manifesting, and leading to the establishment of right human relationships. When these things were just beginning to take place, when our minds were at least moving in these directions, Maitreya said He would come without fail, and this time not alone, but with a very large group of His disciples, the Masters of Wisdom. This event would be the externalization of the activity of the Masters for the first time in nearly 100,000 years. For the first time in all those years, a large section of our Spiritual Hierarchy would be working openly in the world, with humanity, known to us for what They are.

Through Alice Bailey, the Master Djwhal Khul predicted that this event would begin around 1975. Precisely in 1975, five Masters did indeed come into the world — in New York, London, Geneva, Darjeeling, and Tokyo. These were quickly followed by two more Masters, one in Moscow and one in Rome.

When He made His announcement in 1945, the Lord Maitreya hoped that He could come in about five years, around 1950. It was hoped that the pain and suffering of humanity during the war would have chastened us and led to a change of direction. But not all the nations had suffered, nor equally, and the powers quickly went back to the old greedy, selfish, nationalistic, competitive ways of the past — the ways which had brought about the suffering of the war. In effect, as soon as the war was over, humanity set about repeating the whole, sad story once again. (Today, in many regards, the nations are even more set in their greed, selfishness, nationalism, and, above all, competition.)

Therefore, the coming of Maitreya was delayed until eventually, in July 1977, He announced that He was coming into the world whether we were ready or not. On the 8th of July, 1977, Maitreya descended from His mountain high in the Himalayas, where He has lived for thousands of years, and from where His consciousness overshadowed that of Jesus for three years, from the Baptism to the Crucifixion. Descending from His mountain, Maitreya stayed some days on the plains in Pakistan to acclimatize Himself. On the 19th of July 1977, Maitreya entered London, England, where He still lives as a member of the Asian community of that city. Since May 1982, He has been ready to appear openly in the world, if invited to do so.

Many people, when they hear this story, do not understand why Maitreya does not simply come forward and announce Himself, or do something extraordinary which will draw attention to Himself. But the free will of humanity is never infringed by any of the Masters; to Them, our free will is sacrosanct. In order not to infringe human free will, Maitreya insists that He must be invited to come forward.

Changing the world

While awaiting such an invitation, Maitreya has not been idle. Working behind the scenes, unknown to the vast majority, Maitreya has been changing the world. If we think only of the events of the last few years, we will be amazed at the transformation that has actually taken place. It was all so unexpected, and yet it has all happened so quickly that people now take it completely for granted. The Cold War is over. Since 1945, the Soviet Union and the United States of America, with their allies, have been facing each other across the oceans, ready to destroy the world. No one any longer expects that scenario to be enacted. Maitreya inspired Mr Gorbachev to go to America and bring about the end of the Cold War and the opening up of the Soviet Union. If someone had told us 10 years ago that the Cold War would end and that the Soviet Union would break up and become a federation of independent states, we would not have believed it possible. Yet so it is today.

If, just a few years ago, someone had said that Nelson Mandela, in prison for 27 years, a leader of an illegal organization (the ANC), would not only be released, but be elected President, the leader of a new society, ending for ever apartheid in South Africa, we would not have believed it possible. And yet that is what happened, against all expectations. Maitreya appeared to Nelson Mandela in his cell and inspired him to meet with President deKlerk and to create a new constitution in South Africa.

Only a few years ago, if someone had said that the Israeli army would withdraw from Gaza and the West Bank, that the Palestinians would have their homeland, we would not have believed it. It is taking place today. Maitreya made it happen, by appealing to the King of Jordan to give up sovereignty over the West Bank, and by inspiring Mr Arafat to accept the reality of the Israeli state.

If someone had said a few years ago that capitalist West Germany and communist East Germany would be reunited as one country, we would have said: "Not in our lifetime." These and many more such events have taken place in the shortest possible time. They were predicted by Maitreya. The predictions were published in our magazine, *Share International*, and issued as press releases to the world's media, from 1988.

One prophecy made by Maitreya has yet fully to be fulfilled. It is partly fulfilled, but still remains to work out. In 1988, Japan was one of the richest, most economically successful nations in the world. The Nikkei stock-market average stood at just under 40,000 points. In June 1988, Maitreya announced a world stock-market crash, which, He said, would begin in Japan. He said that the economy of Japan was a bubble that would inevitably burst, and would bring down the present economic structure. Immediately, the stock market of Japan began to fall, to about 14,000. It is hovering today at around 18,000–19,000. The US stock market, the Dow Jones Index, is at an all-time high. Historically, the major collapses of the US stock market (or any stock market, for that matter) occur when it is at its *highest-ever point*. The stock markets of the US and Britain are poised, now, for a major collapse, which will become world-wide, and will bring to an end this divisive economic system based on market forces and their corollary, commercialization.

Maitreya calls market forces "the forces of evil". They have inequality built in them, and benefit the few at the expense of the many. Market forces are based on a great deception: that every nation is trading on a 'level playing field', that all the nations are starting from the same point. Obviously, they are not. We cannot compare America, the European states, or Japan, with Tanzania, Zaire or any of the Third-World countries. And yet, through the pre-eminence of market forces, Third-World countries are forced to compete in the world's markets with countries like Japan, America, Germany and France. Maitreya calls commercialization, which is the tool, the agency, of market forces, more dangerous to the world than an atomic bomb. There is a place for market forces, but Maitreya says any government that *blindly* follows market forces is leading its nation to destruction. Commercialization — running life as if it were a business, whether in education or health care, for example — will bring this present civilization to the verge of disaster.

Today, the G7 nations, the seven richest, most industrialized nations, control the economy of the world, and see a high standard of living as their prerogative. They see life as supply and demand. Because they produce a lot, they demand much from what is produced, far more than they need or deserve. The developed world usurps and wastes three-quarters of the world's food, and 83 per cent of all other resources. Therefore, the so-called Third World, with three-quarters of the world's population, must make do with one-quarter of the world's food, and only 17 per cent of other resources. As a result, those in the Third World live in utter poverty and degradation, and die in their millions. The developed world sees this as their right to decide who will eat and live, and who will starve and therefore die. I say "they", but that is *us*. We are the developed world. *We* are the ones who are playing God, and deciding who will live and who will die. It is *our* greed, *our* selfishness, *our* complacency that makes possible a situation where millions of people starve to death in a world overflowing with food, a huge surplus per capita.

At the same time in the developed world, because of its worship at the altar of market forces, commercialization is reaching a point where more and more people are being made unemployed. Competition forces companies to cut their expenditure on everything, beginning with people. In every developed country of the world there is growing unemployment, growing crime, and a declining standard of living — less housing, more and more homeless people, and more poverty in the midst of plenty.

Spiritual crisis

Why do we do this? Why do we create such pain and suffering for ourselves and for our brothers and sisters in other countries? Maitreya would say because of complacency, which He says is the root of all evil. When we are complacent, we say: "I am all right, thank you very much. The rest of the world can look after itself."

This comes from the false idea that we are separate. This is the great illusion, the great heresy. Each one of us, whether we know it or not, is a soul in incarnation, a perfect, divine, spiritual Being in incarnation. On the soul plane, there is no such thing as a separate soul. Each soul is an individualized aspect of one great Oversoul. The sense, therefore, of being separate, is the great illusion. From that illusion stem all our problems, all our suffering. We do not know who we are.

Without recognizing it as such, humanity is undergoing a great spiritual crisis that is focused through the political and economic field. That spiritual crisis can only be resolved by the resolution of our political and economic problems, which are based on the false sense of separation. If we would evolve, develop as a race, we must realize our oneness, realize that we are brothers and sisters of one family, under the one Divine Source, and identical with that Source. What happens in a normal family? They share whatever they have. A mother will not feed one child better than another, give one child 17 per cent and another 83 per cent of the food. We have to realize that we

8

are one family, and therefore must share the resources of the world more equitably around the world. Maitreya puts it like this: "Sharing is divine. When you share, you recognize God in your brother." He also says: "The problems of humanity are real but solvable. The solution lies within your grasp. Take your brother's need as the measure for your action, and solve the problems of the world. There is no other course."

These sound like political or economic solutions. They are actually spiritual solutions, because the problem is a spiritual one. We do not know our true identity as souls, as brothers and sisters of the Kingdom of Souls. Maitreya has come, with His group of Masters, to teach us how to live correctly, as brothers and sisters of one humanity, creating therefore freedom for all, justice for all, and peace for everyone. If there is no sharing, there will never be justice in the world; if there is no justice, there will never be peace in the world; if there is no peace, there will be no world, because now we can destroy all life, human and subhuman alike.

Three practices

Those who await Maitreya as a religious teacher will probably not recognize Him. He has said: "I have not come to found a new religion; people should continue to evolve within their own tradition, whatever it is." Maitreya has not come to create followers. In fact, He says: "If you follow Me," in the sense of running after Him, claiming Him, trying to put Him in your pocket, "then you will lose Me."

Maitreya says He has come to teach humanity the art of Self- or God-realization. He equates humanity with the Self, and the Self with God. He says: "You are the Self, an immortal Being." Our pain, He says, our suffering, our problems, are the result of the fact that we identify with everything and anything other than the Self, the immortal Being of which we are a physical-plane reflection. He says: "Ask yourself: 'Who am I?'" You will find that you identify with the physical body. We look in the mirror and say: "That is me." In this way we are subject to all the limitations of the physical body. The physical body is mortal; it lives so long and then it dies, and we have to come back into incarnation in a new body. So we cannot be the physical body, it is only a vehicle.

Or we identify with our feelings, our sensations, our energies, our emotions. These are not us: they were not there yesterday, perhaps they will not be there tomorrow. They are unstable, never the same. If we are an immortal Being, they cannot be us. Or we identify with our mind, with the creations of our mind, our memory. We think we are Mr or Mrs So-and-so, with so many children. That is not us, that is our memory, the creation of our mind. We say we are Christian, Hindu, Muslim, or Buddhist. That is not us. That is a belief, an ideology. We are an immortal Being and therefore not subject to the limitations of the physical body, the emotional body, or the mind. We are not a fascist, a democrat, a Christian, or a Buddhist. These are all constructions of the mind. We are, above all these transient beliefs, an immortal Being.

How do we become that immortal Being here and now on the physical plane? Maitreya says His way is the most direct, the way of growing awareness. It involves the practice of three attitudes. One, honesty of mind. Almost no one has honesty of mind. It is not just being honest and not stealing other people's property. All of us think one thing, say something else, and do something else again. For honesty of mind, what we think, what we say, and what we do must be in a straight line. Two, sincerity of spirit — being who we are, distinct and individual. Not trying to be like somebody else, not imitating other people, but speaking from the heart to the heart. Not speaking to provide others with some false idea of ourselves, manipulating them so that they admire or like us. It is being honest in oneself, sincere. Few people are truly, inwardly sincere. The third attitude to practice is detachment. Detachment is the awareness that we are not the body, the feelings, or the mind — gradually detaching ourselves from that kind of identification. If we are attached to our emotions, for example, and someone plays a dirty trick on us, if our reaction is one of strong indignation and anger, then we are not detached. If we are detached, we will not react with indignation and anger at such a slight.

What we find in practice is that these three attitudes are mutually supportive. The more aware we become, the more honest we become, the more sincere. The more sincere we become, the more honest we manage to be. The more sincere and honest we become, the more detached we become. The more detached we become, the more sincere and the more honest. These three work together, like a yeast.

When Maitreya is teaching openly in the world, has declared Himself and begun His programme of stimulus and guidance in the political and economic field, He will also teach humanity the Art of Self-realization. The more we practise these three attitudes, the greater Self-awareness develops. The more Self-awareness develops, the more Self-realization becomes possible. Self-awareness leads to Self-realization. What is Self-realization? It is not a religion, an ideology, or a belief. It is the goal of life, which, when achieved, makes us a Master. All of the Masters are Self-realized Beings.

There are now 13 Masters in the world, plus Maitreya, the Master of all the Masters. Eventually, about 40 Masters will return and live openly among us. The Masters will guide and advise humanity; They have not come to take over the world. They are teachers, an advisory body that can prevent us from making too many and too terrible mistakes. Whatever we are ready for, They will teach. They will introduce a new science, the Technology of Light, which will give us unlimited power direct from the sun. This will solve all the energy needs of humanity; no one, ever again, will be able to corner the power of the world.

Obviously, after a world stock-exchange crash everything will be different. The crash will bring humanity face to face with reality for the first time. We blithely go on, day after day, year after year, believing that this divided world can continue to be divided and safe. This is no longer possible. The divisions in the world are so great, the tensions inherent in these divisions so intense, that they have within them the seeds of a Third World War. That war would be nuclear, and would destroy all life on this planet. But that war will not take place. Maitreya knows that humanity will accept the principle of sharing, if only because we have no alternative. Every other method has been tried and has failed, and has led inevitably to separation, misery, and war. We can no longer afford the luxury of another major war.

Miracles

In message number 10 of the 140 messages that Maitreya gave publicly through me at my London lectures, Maitreya says: "Those who search for signs will find them but My method of manifestation is more simple."

In June 1988, an associate in the Asian community of London where Maitreya lives, revealed: "The signs of Maitreya's presence in the world will continue to increase. He is going to flood the world with such happenings that the mind can never comprehend it."

For years now, the signs have been manifesting in abundance throughout the world. Visions of the Madonna and statues that weep tears or blood have appeared all over the Christian world. Icons in the holiest of holy churches likewise weep tears and blood. The people throng to these manifestations, are healed, and the Vatican keeps silence.

Crosses of light, up to 40 feet high, have appeared in homes and churches, many the source of miracle cures and healings.

For four days in September 1995, throughout the Hindu world, North and South, East and West, was enacted what must be the greatest world-wide miracle of all time: statues of the gods, made of stone, wood, brass, copper and bronze, appeared to drink the milk offerings presented by the priests and devotees. In India, Parliament closed, as did the shops. Hundreds of thousands of Hindus, many non-believers, queued for hours to offer milk to Ganesha, Siva and the other gods. Thousands of gallons of milk disappeared when offered. The television cameras of a fascinated and bewildered Western media showed these events to millions in the West. Did the statues really drink the milk? Of course not. They are made of stone, metal and wood. The milk was *made to disappear*, at the moment of offering, by Maitreya and a group of Masters, His disciples.

Around Christmas in 1996, a 50-foot-high image, in bright colour, of the Madonna and child, appeared on the windows of a downtown bank in Clearwater, Florida, USA. Half a million people have come to look and pray. This, and the other Marian manifestations, are created by the Master Who *was* Mary, Mother of Jesus, 2,000 years ago.

Almost weekly, Maitreya appears miraculously 'out of the blue' at fundamentalist, orthodox religious meetings around the world, always in a form that the group can recognize — if they are Hindus, as the people's idea of what Krishna will look like; if Jews, as their idea of the Messiah; if they are Muslims, as their idea of the Prophet, the Imam Mahdi or the Messiah; if Buddhists, their idea of Maitreya Buddha. He can change His appearance at will. He can be old or young, man or woman, fair or dark. In this way, everyone can identify with Him. He speaks to the gatherings in their own language, and then disappears again. He appeared in this way in June 1988 in Nairobi, Kenya, before 6,000 people who recognized Him as the Christ. The event, through photographs, was seen on CNN and BBC television and other world media.

At each such appearance, Maitreya magnetizes underground water sources with Cosmic (Aquarian) energy. Eventually there will be 777 such sources all over the world. Some have already been discovered, and the water, which in each case has phenomenal healing properties, used.

These miracles, now in extraordinary profusion, will continue until Maitreya reveals Himself, openly, to the world.

Day of Declaration

Maitreya has come for the whole of the coming Age of Aquarius — 2,500 years. Very soon we will see Him. He has been invited to appear on a major television network in America and also in Japan. This will lead, by appearances throughout the world, to the Day of Declaration.

When He declares Himself openly to the entire world, it will be an extraordinary experience for all. The television networks will be linked together by satellite for this event. At a given time (different in each time zone, of course), His face will appear on the television sets of the world. Maitreya is omniscient, omnipresent, and will mentally overshadow the minds of all humanity simultaneously. Each of us will hear Him, in our own language. I cannot tell you the details of that message, but no doubt He will outline who He is; where He came from; His group of Masters, the Spiritual Hierarchy and Their return to the world; the problems of the world and how they can be solved; the life ahead for humanity, an extraordinary vision of the future, the technology of the future, giving mastery over the forces of nature.

He will touch on the two great laws that dominate all life on this planet: the Law of Cause and Effect, or the Law of Karma as it is called in the East, and the Law of Rebirth, the *fact* of reincarnation as the method of evolution on this planet. He will give a vision of a better life for humanity, living more simply in correct relationship, not only to each other but to the planet of which we are a part. He will touch on the needs of the environment, the ecology of the planet, how we must conserve and correctly use the resources of the world. And He will show how a simpler life can be lived happily, more fulfillingly, when everyone is sharing the resources and living that life. Everything, however, will not change overnight. Changes will take place quickly, but with a minimum disruption of the existing social order.

While Maitreya is giving this message, this vision of the future, and outlining His role and that of the Masters in the future, His energy, the energy of love, will flow out in tremendous potency through the hearts of all humanity. This will evoke an intuitive, heartfelt response to the message.

Simultaneously on the physical plane, there will be hundreds of thousands of miracle cures, healings throughout the planet. Two things will determine who will be healed and who will not: the Law of Karma, and the faith of the individual. If the karma allows, and the faith is strong enough, that person will be healed.

This experience will give humanity a vision of its essential nature, bring it back to its true nature as souls, and give it a vision and purpose to go forward in life and to create the new civilization along better and more just lines. Our response to this experience will determine the entire future of this planet. Maitreya will present us with a choice: either we continue as we are now, in the old, greedy, selfish, complacent ways of the past, and destroy ourselves, or we accept the principle of sharing, accept that we are one, and begin the creation of a civilization such as this world has never yet seen. Maitreya knows already our answer, our choice. As He said in message number 11, given though me: "My heart tells me your answer, your choice, and is glad."

[The above article is an edited version of a lecture given by Benjamin Creme in Osaka, Japan, in 1996.]

CHAPTER 1

MAITREYA'S PRIORITIES

THE SON OF MAN

by the Master —, through Benjamin Creme

Many people await the return of the Christ with trepidation and fear. They sense that His appearance will promote great changes in all departments of life. His values, they rightly assume, will necessarily alter their ways of thinking and living and they blanch at such a prospect. Besides, so mystical has been the view of the Christ presented down the centuries by the churches that many fear His judgement and omnipotent power; they await Him as God come to punish the wicked and reward the faithful.

It is sadly to be regretted that such a distorted vision of the Christ should so have permeated human consciousness. No such being exists. In order to understand the true nature of the Christ it is necessary to see Him as one among equal Sons of God, each endowed with full divine potential, differing only in the degree of manifestation of that divinity.

That He has achieved the fullness of that divinity is His Glory, and well may we stand in reverence at this achievement. That this same achievement is rare indeed is also indisputably true. But the wonder of the Christ for men is that He was one of them. Naught there is, in the trials and sufferings of men, but He did know it. Each step of the path that men still tread has He painfully trod-den. Nothing is there, in the whole panorama of human experience, that He has not shared. Thus truly is He the Son of Man.

There can be little doubt that were He to appear unannounced in our midst few would recognize Him. So far from the general notion is He that He would pass unnoticed in the crowd. Thus it is today among His brothers as He awaits man's invitation to begin His mission. Many who see Him daily know Him not.

17

Others recognize Him but are afraid to speak. Still others wait and pray, hopeful that He may be the One for Whom they dare not hope. Only His Declaration before the world will establish Him in the sight and hearts of men.

While we await that Day of Days, let us clarify in our minds the reasons for His return. Let us understand the nature of the task which He has set Himself. To establish in our midst the fact of God, has He come. To recreate the Divine Mysteries, is He here. To teach men how to love, and love again, is He among us. To establish man's brotherhood does He walk the Earth once more. To keep faith with the Father and with man does He accept this burden. To usher in the new age has He returned. To consolidate the treasure of the past, to inspire the marvels of the future, to glorify God and man has He descended from His high mountain.

Let us look at His priorities: the establishment of peace; the inauguration of the system of sharing; the removal of guilt and fear — the cleansing of the hearts and minds of men; the education of mankind in the laws of life and love; an introduction to the Mysteries; the beautification of our cities; the removal of barriers to travel and interchange of peoples; the creation of a pool of knowledge accessible to all.

That such a task is not an easy one, not even for the Son of Man, is clear. Ancient habits of division and separation have strong roots, while fear and superstition cast their spell over millions of mankind. But never before, in the history of the world, has a Teacher come better equipped for His task. Maitreya has come to do battle with ignorance and fear, division and want. His weapons are spiritual understanding, knowledge and love; His shining armour is Truth Itself.

(*Share International*, June 1984)

18

MAITREYA'S PRIORITIES

The following article is an edited version of a talk by Benjamin Creme given at the 1995 Transmission Meditation Conferences in San Francisco, USA, and Kerkrade, the Netherlands, which relates to the above article by his Master.

In June 1984, my Master wrote an article for *Share International*, called 'The Son of Man'. In it my Master talked about Maitreya as the Christ, but also about His future work, and touched on the priorities which He would set Himself as aims or goals. No doubt these priorities are enumerated by the Master in some specific order, like tackling first things first. I cannot imagine it would be otherwise.

I thought it might be useful to acquaint ourselves with these priorities, and begin to think constructively about our relationship to them, both individually and as a group who have been involved in preparing the way for Maitreya. To prepare the way for Maitreya is, of course, to prepare the world. It is not just to alert people to the fact of His presence, but to have some knowledge of the way the world should go.

I am often asked: "What is going to happen? If we accept that Maitreya is in the world, that He is the Christ and that there are going to be Masters in the world, what is going to happen to us? How does this phenomenon — the externalization of the Hierarchy — affect the world?" Obviously, it will affect us profoundly, but in what ways? We may have no idea or we may have very fanciful ideas.

I think we should study what my Master, Who knows what these priorities are, has written. I am hoping by the end of this conference we shall have a better insight into what these priorities may mean. You will be building this New Age. It is yours to make what you will of it, especially the first 20, 30, 40 years; and you can help Maitreya to bring into being His priorities.

The Master's article shows very clearly the enormity of the task which Maitreya is taking on. We blithely think only of His coming into the world, His benefit to us, the healing waters, the crosses of light, the extraordinary uplifting experiences for everyone who meets Him, however briefly; how they cannot keep Him out of their minds, even if He is dressed as a beggar; and how the very sight of Maitreya or one of the Masters is enough for those acquainted with Their presence to feel better: uplifted, galvanized and, if they believe in the reality of the contact, grateful and blessed.

But obviously it is an extraordinary task. This world now holds between 5½ and 6 billion people, of whom one-fifth live in poverty beyond belief; millions starve to death. Others fight bitterly for a larger slice of the world's cake, larger than the one they now have, which might be already large enough. How does He unite all these different aspirations: some for more of the same — greater wealth, greater influence, greater power; and those exploited by them who look for a little to eat on a daily basis, for some shelter from the weather and hopefully an education for their children? How do we reconcile, and how can Maitreya help us to reconcile, these extraordinarily different levels of aspiration?

One of the plain facts which strikes me is that Christians, in the main, do not know much about the Christ. Above all people, they should know about the Christ's nature, and, of course, they do have an idea about it in their minds. It is so vague, however, and so obviously far from the truth, that one wonders what they are going to experience when they see Maitreya on television, when He comes to their homeland and they come close to Him.

The general view is that He is an omnipotent God come to punish the wicked and award the faithful. (That is probably one of the major reasons why most Christians await the Christ at the end of the world because they expect not to be around at that time.) They are scared even of their own Christ. They are scared of God, scared of punishment, and feel they are not worthy. They know they have been wicked in one way or another (even if it is not a very bad wickedness). They know, probably, that they are nasty and brutal at times; that they are sometimes unkind. Their huge sense of guilt, built over centuries by a powerful, influential, and cruel church, is probably the greatest barrier to a correct assessment of, and response to, the Christ when He shows Himself to the world. If I were an orthodox Christian, I am sure I would be terrified by the very idea that the Christ could be in the world.

So different is He from their idea of Him, of course, that they have nothing to fear. Nevertheless, millions of Christians today are waiting in a kind of suspended terror that the Christ might descend on His cloud into Jerusalem and the Second Coming might be at hand. They see the signs when there is trouble in the Middle East. They think: "It is Armageddon. That means the Christ is coming." When they hear about Maitreya from me, they say: "He is the Antichrist. That means that the Christ is near."

Everything points to this time as the time when the Christ could come into the world. Waiting for Armageddon is an added terror. But even without the expectation of Armageddon, just to be confronted with 'God' Himself — albeit in human form — with all the power, judgement and appetite for retribution which most people apply to God, is terrifying enough. Knowing nothing about the Laws of life and evolution, Cause and Effect, and Rebirth, they simply await punishment for every little so-called sin. They judge themselves so harshly that they are filled with little but negative expectation at the idea of the coming of the Christ.

The Master puts it in a restrained way that makes one almost smile: *"It is sadly to be regretted that such a distorted vision of the Christ should so have permeated human consciousness."* And yet it has. Everywhere in the world, the idea of the Teacher — whether He is called Christ, Buddha, Imam Mahdi, Messiah, or Krishna — is tainted with this distortion of the nature of the Teacher. Religions have presented the Teacher as an omnipotent God who comes to judge. If God judges, He will find something wrong, and if there is something wrong then inevitably there is punishment.

That is a general expectation in the West which will be very difficult to eradicate. When I paint the picture of a world transformed — living in harmony, if not total serenity, sharing the resources, at peace — I am again and again brought up against the orthodox belief in this wrathful, Jehovah-like figure of God. Jesus, on the other hand, has been presented in a rather sentimental way, as a nice, humourless, well-meaning, saintly individual who ran into difficulties at the end with the Romans.

The first and foremost task which Maitreya has set Himself is *"to establish in our midst the fact of God"*. What does the Master mean by that? How does Maitreya, or anyone else for that matter, establish in our midst the *fact* of God? Surely, this is something that the religious groups have been trying to do for thousands of years. Hindus, Buddhists, Muslims, Christians, Jains, and above all, probably, the Jews, have sought to establish the reality of God in our midst. It would seem that they have succeeded only too well, so that life for countless millions is a hide-and-seek game with God. They know He is up there watching everything they do, and most of the time they have to turn sideways on God so that He does not see what they are doing with their hand on the other side. All the time they are thinking: "I know God is there, but He surely cannot see all around," and so they do not let the right hand know what the left hand is doing. If the right hand knows what the left hand is doing, then God knows. If God knows, then God knows what is going to happen to you. The problem for most people is that they have a completely distorted idea of God as this wrathful punisher of the unworthy, the sinners. Born in sin, it is inevitable that we sin, so we must be punished, and that is God's pleasure.

"To establish in our midst the fact of God, has He come."
It surely cannot be to establish that same notion of God. It must be to establish some other notion, closer to the truth. He will establish the fact of the *spiritual* basis of life. At the core of every individual, every aspect of creation, is a spiritual dimension, a spiritual purpose, which is acting out through each aspect of which we can become conscious. Obviously, we are only touching creation in a very fragmented way; but if we see it as the outer expression of some great spiritual purpose which can bring it into being (and take it out of being), which can enlarge, expand it, and which can relate one aspect to another and so create nations, solar systems, galaxies, then God must be extraordinarily powerful.

In the Christian Bible, God is called *"a consuming fire"*. Fire, of course, is energy. I believe that Maitreya will talk about the fact of God in terms of the multiplicity of creative forces which make up that Life which we call God. There is but one Life informing the whole cosmos, giving expression to, and imminent in, every aspect of creation. The one Life, which we call God, expresses itself through a myriad forces and forms. The awareness of God, the knowledge of the nature of God, comes to us as we expand our consciousness, and therefore our sensitivity, to the various forces which together make God.

At the centre of the galaxy there is a Being who has that consciousness on a galactic level, which is so far above that of a solar system that one cannot even imagine it. The Logos of our solar system, for example, has an awareness, a consciousness, of an infinite variety of forces, an extraordinarily rich congruence of different fires, which in their interplay create the outer physical, astral, and mental planes of existence: all the forms on the physical plane which we see, all the etheric forms which most people do not see; and in so doing carries out a Plan of some Being greater even than the Solar Logos. We can think of the Planetary Logos carrying out the plan of the Solar Logos, and the Solar Logos carrying out the plan of the Galactic Logos — "The One About Whom Naught May Be Said", not because it would be irreverent to say anything about that Being, but because there is nothing we *can* say, there is nothing we could imagine to say about the Being at the centre of our galaxy.

I believe that Maitreya, in so far as He talks about God and establishes the fact of God in the world, will do so somewhat in these terms — in terms of energy, fire, relationship, and, of course, in terms of every human being. We are essentially gifted with all that. As we expand our consciousness, we can more and more know what it is that we call God. When we know what it is, can intuit it, feel it, not just as an idea, but the actual experience of it, we can gain control over these energies and therefore relate more and more to that nature.

The Masters are God-realized — Sons of God. When you become a Master, you have expanded your consciousness to include what we call the spiritual levels. That gives one the awareness of the energies of God and entry into the Mind of God, in our case as earthlings, into the mind of the Logos of our planet — but for a Master who has gone beyond that, more and more into the mind of the Solar Logos. There are Beings on the sun whose consciousness is expanding to include aspects of the One About Whom Naught May Be Said. We would only distort the nature of that Being if we even began to speculate about His nature.

To establish in our midst the fact of God is also to establish in our midst the Kingdom of God. The Kingdom of God is the Spiritual or Esoteric Hierarchy of which Maitreya is the head, the chief executive. By Their very presence, Maitreya and the Masters establish the fact of the Kingdom of God. He will talk, I believe, of the Hierarchy, His Ashram, as the Kingdom of God, when He is talking to Christians. He will have other terms for it when He is teaching in other parts of the world. For the Western Christian world, I believe, that is how He will demonstrate His awareness of our sense of God, as the Kingdom of God manifests in the world. As ordinary men and women find their way into the Ashram of the Christ, the Spiritual Hierarchy, through the first initiations, they enter the Kingdom of God. He will establish that idea openly in the world. I do not mean on the first day, but He will most probably touch on it briefly on the Day of Declaration.

"To recreate the Divine Mysteries is He here."
The Divine are the mysteries of initiation. The mysteries were established in various parts of the world in the ancient past as schools, training centres, for the initiates who entered one by one into the Kingdom of God. These will be reopened, re-established, some in the very places where they were in ancient times. Some will be built for the first time in countries which are relatively new. Candidates for initiation will go to these Mystery Schools. The plan is that by the end of the Age the bulk, some three-fifths, of humanity, will be within the Kingdom of God. They will have entered the Spiritual Hierarchy by taking at least the first initiation. Some who are now first-degree initiates will take the second and third.

Candidates will go for training in these schools; and the ancient mysteries of initiation will become the conscious goal of a large section of humanity. It may be extraordinary to think of this today, but the time is coming in the next 2,000 years when,

24

instead of simply aiming at a university degree, an MA or PhD, people will aim at initiation; consciously aim to go through the initiatory process. It is an extraordinary idea — that probably 3 to 4 billion people will consciously set out on that path. Of course, there are many going through the process now who have heard nothing about esotericism; who do not even know there is such a thing as initiation, because it takes place in sleep, out of the body. If you remember that over the next 2,500 years the inner ashrams of the Masters, where the training now takes place in sleep, will be established on the outer physical plane as well, you get an idea of the transformation of the world's goal which will have taken place.

People will know about initiation; it will become the goal of life for the majority of people; that must be different from the usual aim of getting a bigger house or car, and two holidays a year. There will be such a shift in consciousness as the result of the presence of the Masters that we cannot really take it in.

"To teach men how to love, and love again, is He among us. To establish man's brotherhood does He walk the Earth once more."
That is the difficult one. If He could teach men how to love then He would have established man's brotherhood, because what prevents the establishment of the brotherhood and sisterhood of men and women is that there is little or no expression of love. Love is difficult, we all know; it is difficult to love. Some people find it easy, but even those who find it easy to love, whose nature it is to love, given a little resistance to that love turn obdurate. The love stops flowing. It is easy to love when there is no resistance to it. But when you love somebody who does something that you do not like, it is difficult to go on loving. In other words, we have reactive love, even if it is a kind of love.

This is very different from the love of a Master. If we had the love of a Master, we would be Masters. The fact that we are not Masters is because we do not demonstrate Their total, unqualified, unconditional love. The nature of the Master is to love, and the nature of Maitreya is to love as the Lord of Love. He embodies the Love of God, the Christ Principle. That love aspect of God is embodied by a man on earth. That is His

25

extraordinary achievement. As the Master says: *"That He has achieved the fullness of that divinity is His Glory, and well may we stand in reverence at this achievement. That this same achievement is rare indeed is also indisputably true."* How many Christs, how many Buddhas have been created even in our solar system? There are planets more evolved than ours that have not yet created a Christ. The creation of a Christ is an extraordinary achievement. It is rare indeed, not only on this planet but on any planet.

The nature of God's love is such that it is one of the greatest possible achievements to *embody* it at a planetary level. We can express affection, a reactive love, we can love those who love us. But to love totally, unrequitedly and consistently would be a major achievement by humanity. That will be one of the major tasks of the Christ — to establish the nature of God's love, in its true sense, as the energy which He embodies. He does it by example, and by the spiritual nourishing of our being which it is His pleasure to do.

By the outflow of the Christ Principle through the hearts of humanity He is teaching us, whether we know it or not, whether we can actually respond to it or not, not only the nature of God and the nature of love, but the *ability* to love. The more the energy of the Christ Principle is active in us, the more we are able to love.

Love is a powerful, active, magnetic force which draws together all the fragmented building bricks of cosmos and holds them together, without which it would all fall asunder. Our solar system, the galaxies, would disappear without that magnetic, attracting force which we call love.

Maitreya establishes that in the world, through embodying it in His own Being. He is so pure, so advanced, that He has achieved this incredibly rare achievement of embodying the Christ Principle at a planetary level. That is a major achievement among the planets of our solar system. He is more exalted and more to be reverenced than, probably, we imagine. Although in our hearts we believe in His value and level, it is impossible for anyone less than His level to recognize what that level really means. By His release of the Christ Principle, He establishes in the world the ability to love. He galvanizes humanity through the power of that love to transform the world. This is precisely what He is doing now, from behind the scenes, and what He will do openly as He appears before the world.

Love is an active force which transforms. Love which does not act is hardly love at all. Love in action is the essence of love. It is an ability to love the world and all that is in it which is the capacity of Maitreya. The deepest desire of the heart of the One who can do that is to unify all. He looks into the world and sees 5.6 billion people: suffering, striving, competing, all the different actions, some positive, some deeply negative. He sees all of that and His urge, His deepest desire, the outflow of His spiritual heart's need, is to bring all of that together, to unify it all. He is a Planetary Life. He has entered into the consciousness of the Logos at the highest level; He has two further levels of cosmic consciousness; and overshadowed by the Spirit of Peace and the Avatar of Synthesis, sharing the consciousness of the Buddha, this is enlarged to a degree beyond our imagination. There has never been an Avatar better equipped for His task than Maitreya. There has never been a need for such an Avatar, but this world is now so complex, so divided, so riddled with both good and bad, positive and negative, that all of these forces have to be reconciled. This is His aim, this longing in the heart of the Christ for unity, for using His powers, His insights, to establish His nature, which is love, in the world. In this way He teaches us how to love and, as the Master says, *"love again."* To love again is not to love in a normal, reactive sense, but to love totally, unconditionally, in the way that the Masters do. This will establish the brotherhood of man.

But it takes more than that. We have to look at the different stages of the establishment of brotherhood in the world. First of all, there has to be peace. Without peace, there is no world. The first priority for Maitreya is the establishment of true peace in the world: the abandonment by humanity of war and the competition that leads to war. This can only be achieved by fulfilling the needs of all the people.

Most wars are wars of aggrandizement. You see something you want, and you take it. If you have to go to war to take it, you go to war. That has happened in Bosnia. The Serbian adventurers saw the opportunity to use the natural aspiration of the Serbian people for their national identity to establish a Greater Serbia, to fulfil their own personal desires. Unless all peoples everywhere see an end to their sufferings and hopelessness, their inferior position in the world — in a word, until the developing world can eat and grow and live decent, civilized lives like everyone else, there will never be peace in the world. The first requirement for establishing peace is the sharing of the world's resources.

The inauguration of the system of sharing is probably the easiest of all to accomplish. It is difficult to teach men to love. It is difficult to establish the brotherhood of humanity. But it is easy to share the resources of the world; it is a question of distribution, nothing else. The resources are there; the science and technology are there. No one need go without. Humanity has to accept a degree of oneness that will make it a normal and self-evident truth that the only way to peace is to share the resources of the world.

Everyone will feel better for it. The people of the Third World will, of course. But the developed world will also feel better: in their health, in their consciousness, and they will feel a great deal less guilty. There will be less crime and drug abuse. Cities will be much healthier and better to live in, and freer from the fear of muggings and murders. Sharing is a priority because unless we can do it we will destroy the world. The tensions are so great today; the adventuring demagogues so adept at mobilizing nationalistic aspirations and forces; the ever more powerful and sophisticated weapons so easily obtainable from all the developed nations, that the problem of isolating even small wars becomes significantly more difficult and hazardous.

The United Nations found this to be the case in Bosnia as the result of their indifference of three-and-a-half years, their lack of political will to do what was obviously right: to raise enough money to create the right military strength for a United Nations army to go into Bosnia and end the adventurism of people like Milosevic and Karadzic. If the UN had acted in the beginning, they could have prevented the Bosnian war from developing. It has proved enormously difficult but now a start is being made for peace. It needs the political will to build a truly United Nations force with the armour, planes, and generals, and with the will to stop such wars. The Masters believe in peace. No one can demonstrate the function of peace as well as a Master. But the Masters are realists. They know that the only thing which could have prevented the extermination of so many of the people of Bosnia, the raping of their country by the Serbs, was a United Nations force sufficiently armed to end that conflict.

"The removal of guilt and fear — the cleansing of the hearts and minds of men"

So wrong, so distorted have been the teachings of all the religious groups for centuries that vast numbers live in guilt and fear. Two thousand years of Christian teaching, thousands of years before that of Jewish, Hindu, and Buddhist teaching, has filled humanity with fear, superstition, and guilt. There is hardly a person in the world today who is untouched by this disease. Everyone is prone to fear.

Guilt is the result of fear, is inculcated through fear. If you are taught that God is watching your every action, that practically everything you do from the cradle onwards is wrong, fear and guilt are inevitable. "Do not do this, and do not do that. That is naughty, good children do not do that. Good Christian children believe this and do not believe that. Good Hindu children do this, do not do that, and do not believe that. God will punish you if you do that or do not believe that."

This imposition of ideologies and beliefs creates, at the same time, punishment expectations which go with those beliefs. In this way all the religious groups throughout the centuries have controlled the minds of their followers. It is an age-old method that always works. That is why it is age-old. It means that always there will be one group of people in control of other groups. They may be in intellectual, financial or political control, but they are always in control. They are always exploiting the inferior position of other groups. The history of European Christianity alone is a history of unbelievable cruelty — based on fear, the dogmatic imposition of ideas, lack of liberty, financial dependence and poverty.

These various totalitarianisms are now beginning to break down, but they have been working for thousands of years. Political totalitarianism means that millions of people are kept under surveillance and ground into submission and denial of free will. Economic totalitarianism does the same today for countless millions. Twelve hundred million people live in official absolute poverty. Even in the US, 33 million people, and one in four children, live in poverty.

This ability to exploit: in religious terms through people's minds and hearts; in economic terms, on the physical plane; politically, through the imposition of power over the actions of people, all of these tyrannies have to go — and are beginning to go. One of the greatest benefits conferred on the world by the new energies of Maitreya, His presence, the return of Hierarchy, is the growing awareness by humanity of what it needs to do, the growing action of the New Group of World Servers, known and unknown. All of this is showing humanity that we are coming to an end of tyranny. The coming into the world of Maitreya is both the lever of this ending and will bring to an end that tyranny. The establishment of true peace needs the ending of all tyranny: political, economic, religious, and social. That, gradually, will happen, and free us from guilt and fear.

The religious groups have presented a picture of God as an omnipotent, vengeful, wrathful, Jehovah-type figure demanding an eye for an eye and a tooth for a tooth; who is out with a big stick to punish anybody who does anything other than what they are told by the priests or the political rulers, by the king and the king's agents. These tyrannies have kept humanity in thrall for, literally, millions of years. Historically, there has never been a time when these tyrannies did not exist. The world's history is the history of tyranny, of exploitation, of totalitarianism in one form or another. All of that will come to an end and remove fear and guilt from humanity.

Human beings will wake up gradually to the idea presented by Maitreya and the Masters, and those through whom They work, that humanity is really sound, that we are spiritual Beings, that there is nothing wrong with us. There is no need to be guilt-ridden or fear-ridden. We are not going to be punished if we do not believe what the priests say. Who are the priests to say what anybody should believe? The priests are almost always wrong. They were profoundly wrong in Palestine 2,000 years ago when they got rid of the best man among them — Jesus, the Messiah, who, they now say, is a wonder, a great gift to the world, the one and only Son of God. He was put to death. They hated the very sight of Him and His ideas that men were free and divine, that there was a soul in every human body. The notion that Jesus brought that people should love one another, stop fighting, stop exalting notions of separation and greed, did not go down well with the priests of His time. That is why they got rid of Him. Maitreya will remove the guilt and fear. That is *"the cleansing of the hearts and minds of men."*

"The education of mankind in the laws of life and love"
The laws of life are few but very powerful. No one pays them much attention. That is why we have our problems. The major law of life is the Law of Cause and Effect; it dominates all life on this planet. It used to be expressed as "an eye for an eye and a tooth for a tooth", which is a very inadequate expression of the Law of Cause and Effect. Jesus put it very simply: "As you sow, so shall you reap." It is so simple that people have forgotten it or do not take it in. Whatever you sow, you reap. If you sow corn, you reap corn. If you sow oats, you reap oats. If you sow bad corn, you do not get much of a crop. We are all sowers. Every thought, every action that we have, sows seeds. They create causes. The effects stemming from the causes make our lives. We are all doing it all the time, making our own lives and the life of humanity.

We are all responsible for what happens in the world, for what happens in and through the human race, because we are all part of that race. We all create thoughtforms. These thoughtforms are real. Every time we have a destructive thought, we are destroying a bit of our system. *The well-being of the planet depends on the well-being of our thoughts.* If our thoughts are full of greed, selfishness, destructiveness, that is what we will create. When enough people are doing this (and enough people are always doing this), we have the problems of the world. Every one of us is doing this. We are not living in a vacuum where everything stays within the ring-pass-not of our own selves. It would be easier if we could keep our destructive thoughts and actions to ourselves. Then we would reap directly. Unfortunately, it does not work that way. Our thoughts stream out from us in all directions. They impinge on the astral planes

31

and create the astral mirage. They enter the mental planes and create or destroy on these. We are always destroying and sometimes creating, continually. Multiply this process 5½ billion times, the number of people in incarnation now, and you will see the power behind this capacity of humanity to think.

We are the Sons of Mind. We think. That is what distinguishes us from the animal kingdom and is responsible for the creation of the human kingdom. Sooner or later humanity will realize that it is not at the top of the ladder, but a transitional kingdom between the animal kingdom and the Kingdom of God or the Spiritual Kingdom. As we progress through the initiatory process we enter that kingdom. There is an aspect of oneself that is a member of, and lives in, that kingdom: the human soul. Eventually that becomes a totally conscious experience. The soul impresses its consciousness so powerfully on its reflection, that the man or woman can indeed act as a member of that kingdom.

At this time, few understand the Law of Cause and Effect, practically. Few live as if they understood it. Most people (in these groups) have read Alice Bailey or the Theosophical teachings, and accept this Law, but until we actually put it into effect as a moment-to-moment reality in our lives, we will go on creating disorder.

We have to see the utter necessity for harmlessness. As soon as we understand that Law in the deepest sense, as soon as we really become aware of it as a revelation in our hearts, in our minds, and not simply as an intellectual idea of which we can see the justice, as soon as it is a definite experiential reality in our lives, we cease to create disorder, we cease to create that imbalance wrought by destructive action.

The nearest we can come to it *en masse* is an expression of goodwill. Maitreya will emphasize the need for goodwill in all relationships. Goodwill is the lowest aspect of the energy of love expressible by the bulk of humanity. Loving in the real sense is very difficult. The expression of goodwill is the next stage on the onward path of evolution which we will achieve. This creates right human relations.

Goodwill is attainable. It is the level of the energy of love that should not be too difficult for humanity to express. In fact, many millions of people do indeed feel and express goodwill. That is not just being nice, tolerant and decent; all of these are the result. Goodwill is an active force. It is the will aspect allied with the love aspect. When the love aspect informs the will aspect, you get goodwill. If you think "good", meaning love, and "will", meaning purpose, you get good purpose, loving purpose. That loving purpose has to imbue our lives and create right human relations. Right human relations will free us from guilt and fear, will share the resources in the world and create peace. Right human relations is a priority of humanity, and Maitreya will make that one of His major concerns. The laws of love mean right relationship. The laws of life mean right thinking, right acting. When you get a combination of right acting, right thinking, and goodwill, you have the kind of free, tolerant, harmless society to which we should be aiming. Harmlessness must inform all our actions, and this is difficult. It is difficult to be harmless. What I am talking about is not an easy thing which, after the Day of Declaration, will demonstrate by itself. When people really acknowledge Maitreya, when they open themselves to Him, and to His energy, His advice, His principles, His vision, they will see the necessity of harmlessness.

It is easy to appear to be harmless, but actually to be harmless is very difficult. Everyone is selfish, everyone wants their own way, their will satisfied and given form. If people are strong-minded, intolerant and greedy enough, they go on and on until they get their way. Some people are anything but harmless, whether they are smiling sweetly or not.

"The laws of life and love" — honesty of mind, sincerity of spirit, and detachment. These are the three ways that will lead to the correct expression of the laws of life and love. Detachment releases us from the glamours of which I have been speaking — the fear, the guilt, the twisted, greedy expressions, and also the cover of these, the smiling hypocrisy of the world.

"An introduction to the Mysteries"

Maitreya will, even on the Day of Declaration, touch on the mysteries of initiation. He will, however briefly, talk about the re-entry of the Masters into the world, and relate His coming to the establishment of the ancient mystery schools. Just what He will say, I cannot tell you, but He will touch on it and in due

33

course introduce the mysteries. The mysteries of initiation remain mysteries until you are initiate. Many people like mysteries, and the whole idea of initiation is surrounded by glamour. On the other hand, there are many people who hate and fear mysteries. Mystery means there is something they do not know, do not understand.

People have limited consciousness and limited energy to expand their consciousness. They are badly educated, and life itself is hard and limiting. This is one of the problems for Maitreya. The minds of most people are pretty closed. They do not easily expand and learn new things. So the transformations must necessarily go at a more leisurely pace than many might want. It is difficult to expand the consciousness of humanity quickly, because when many people come to about age 25, their minds stop expanding. Most people settle for that degree of knowledge, experience, and understanding which they have acquired through childhood, their early and later youth, and their early man- or womanhood. When they have taken up jobs in the world, they are not very concerned about expansion of consciousness, but about the expansion of their ability to compete in the world, and that is something quite different. They use their brains in a manipulative war of attrition with everyone else around them: in their jobs, their profession, in whatever area of life they are. They are competing all the time, and such consciousness as they demonstrate is brain consciousness — to gain and retain the upper hand in any competitive situation in which they find themselves. I generalize, of course, and perhaps exaggerate, but this is broadly the case world-wide.

Unfortunately, most of life today is based on competition, which is why we have such commercialization of society. Commercialization, according to Maitreya, is now coming to an end. It cannot do so soon enough. The collapse of the present economic system will end it and competition will be replaced by co-operation. The idea of co-operation itself begins to release one's consciousness. When people begin to think in terms of co-operation, they begin to read more books, to study teachings which, up until then, they have never studied. Their minds expand to accommodate the teaching. The bulk of humanity are too tired, too jaded, too limited in their experience of life, in their capacity to create, to have any chance of expanding their consciousness. Millions never open a book from birth to death. Millions of people never expand their consciousness beyond what it was as a child. You can see, therefore, the educational task which lies ahead for humanity. Maitreya will try to expand human consciousness at a rate which will allow the changes to take place very quickly, as quickly as possible. But, necessarily, some of these changes will be delayed as humanity itself lacks the capacity to understand the need.

The distribution of resources, on the other hand, will be relatively easy. That could be done tomorrow through a United Nations agency acceptable to all. That is the easiest of all to do, and the most pressing. That would establish justice and peace. Once justice and peace are established, the rest gradually follows.

We are talking about difficult concepts. The laws of life and love, put that way, are very difficult ideas. Maitreya is adept in making the profound clear. That is why He is a World Teacher. When you see Him you will find a teacher whose simplicity appeals to humanity. Maitreya can make the profoundest statement of truth in the simplest possible way, which touches the heart and understanding, and therefore the intuition, of quite average people. In the Asian community of London, at the present time, that is exactly what He often does. Many people who are not very well educated are awakening to His teaching. The Asian community is full of bright, intelligent, well-educated professional people. But the vast majority have come to earn a better living. They are engaged in commerce and only their Hindu or Muslim background keeps them in touch with the ideas Maitreya is expressing. Nevertheless, they find what He has to say extraordinarily enlightening.

I know a man who has met Maitreya many times, and listened to Him talk. He says quite frankly: "You, Mr Creme, use a lot of words." (He never understands what I have to say. He asks me what Maitreya means, but he never understands what I say in response; he hardly listens.) "But with Maitreya," he says, "you do not really need to listen. Maitreya speaks in such a way that it touches you inside." It automatically opens up your consciousness. You believe it because you see that it is real.

Imagine teaching in that manner to the simplest people throughout the world. Gradually they will make contact with the ideas of Maitreya which they will absorb almost subliminally, as if subconsciously they are being transformed. Their consciousness — through the heart — will be opened to more and more of reality, of aspiration. In this way, they will be educated very quickly, directly, in a way which has never happened before.

"The beautification of our cities"

Parts of New York, London, Cleveland, Detroit, Birmingham, Düsseldorf, Osaka, Calcutta — dozens of huge cities — sprawl for miles with hardly a decent building to be seen. They make life in our cities one long stressful grind and transportation a nightmare. Our cities certainly need beautifying and reorganizing. There is a group of Masters who are great architects, and they will inspire the architects of the immediate future with the concepts of the new cities.

Architecture is always the art which defines a particular era and culture. It sets the tone for all other art — painting, music, and so on. Architecture is the biggest and heaviest, the most material; buildings, not just ideas, but ideas embodied in stone, concrete, brick. That takes time and it needs the 7th ray of Ceremonial Order or Ritual. A piece of architecture is really a ritual: organized space. A well-planned city is ritualized architecture.

Certain parts of the new cities will be set aside as sanctified areas. These — etheric centres — will be near water and the site of temples, for worship and prayer. All cities will eventually have this kind of sanctuary. The best of these buildings will be built under the inspiration of the Masters. Necessarily, these will be 7th-ray Masters the ray which concretizes the spiritual ideal on the physical plane. These new buildings will be quite different in shape from the buildings of the past. Some of them, by their very shape, will focus and accumulate particular energies. They will have 'shape power'. The tetrahedron, which we use in Transmission Meditation, is used because of its particular shape which focuses mental energy. In the same way, these buildings will focus different energies. In relationship, they will create the area of sanctified land for all the people.

Cities will have to reduce in size. Mexico City has a population of some 20-22 million people. To live in, it must be very difficult, although a very interesting city to visit. The slums of Mexico City are amongst the worst in the world. The slums of London, parts of New York and Calcutta, likewise. These have to go. No one should be expected to live in slums in the future cities of the world.

The new architecture will cover these different levels — that which is part of the sanctuary area, large civic buildings for the various institutions, and residential areas for ordinary habitation. The beautification of our cities must also allow the city dweller access to nature, not necessarily "in the raw", but nature. Land will be made over to parks and recreation areas when the slums are erased. These will add a large dimension to the beautification of our cities, and will be a priority for those engaged in transforming city life. Teams of architects, national and international, will meet and discuss these ideas. With the advice of the Masters, consensus along these lines will be achieved. Gradually, the worst areas of slums and decayed buildings in the major cities will go. They will be replaced by recreational parkland, and by ordinary housing, on a human scale, interspersed with parks and shopping areas.

Transport will be completely transformed. A new form of public transport will replace the motorcar. I do not mean that this is going to happen tomorrow, or even the day after the Day of Declaration, but, gradually, transportation systems will be devised which will be so silent, so apparently motionless, that travel fatigue will completely disappear. We will end a journey, even if hours long, completely refreshed. Transportation will become one of the major advancements. Access from cities to countryside will be enhanced, and from one part of a city to another.

Areas will be defined; each will have its own particular quality. People will choose to live in one rather than another depending on their own requirements and priorities, and so a very interesting mix of city life will be inculcated. This will give visual beauty to the life of the city, but also an experiential beauty. It will be a pleasure rather than a chore to live in a built-up area.

Today, city life is becoming more and more stressful, and this will increase until these changes take place. It will probably take 50 years to get rid of the worst aspects of today's major cities, but with the right advice, with goodwill and the energy of the right people, all of this will be achieved. The cities of the world will become what they should be — places for the interchange of ideas, for the growth of culture, and the creative expression of all groups of people.

"The removal of barriers to travel and interchange of peoples"
One of the major needs of humanity today is to know other parts of the world. As we say, "travel broadens the mind". It can also narrow the mind, but it depends on who does the travelling. Anyone who travels in the right spirit learns that people have other ideas, other ways of doing things. This can be either interesting or irritating depending on the type of mind. Travel between peoples should be enlivening and interesting. It should be enriching to the human consciousness. Just to learn that everyone needs the same things will be a revelation to many people. Whether you live in China or Chinatown, in Tibet or Syria, you need pretty well the same things: enough food, shelter, health care, and education — the basics. You might also need to listen to music, to have variety in your food. As you travel, you certainly get variety in your food. That may be one of the irritations. When you travel, you do not find your own food wherever you go. It teaches you (or may teach you) tolerance, broad-mindedness. Obviously, the more people who travel, the more we will know about the world in which we live. There are many barriers to travel — most of all lack of cash and lack of seats on planes. The removal of barriers means the ability to travel at rates which are not prohibitive, the accessibility of seats in planes and trains, and the removal of barriers in the form of visas or passports.

"The creation of a pool of knowledge accessible to all"
This is beginning to happen. It is called the Internet. It is building up throughout the world a great source, not of

knowledge, not of awareness, but of facts. If you turn up such a page, find a certain site, you will get all these facts. You can build a boat, a bomb, you can do lots of things from exploring the Internet. You can learn to make liquor of every kind, or read pornographic literature all by yourself.

It certainly has grown tremendously, eating its way into everyone's home. This Internet triffid is going to take over the world, and build a great monster called "The Fact". The fact will be taken for knowledge, the knowledge for insight, and insight for wisdom. The wisdom will be so corrupted by facts that you will not recognize it as other than 'gobbledegook'. This is what is happening with the Internet. It is going to be so stuffed with unusable, unworkable, and useless information that the whole thing will have to be reorganized and vetted by some committee of wise men representing consensus opinion among the nations.

However, "the creation of a pool of knowledge accessible to all" is a very different thing from the Internet. What is visualized by the Masters is an electronic library which embodies the highest thoughts, ideas, and information of a kind useful to humanity. The Internet, as it is now, is open to abuse. Everything of worth we quickly abuse. We abuse every aspect of our life so why not the electronic world as well?

However, a true body of knowledge will be built up which will be electronically relayed, and give us access to all the useful information in the world. It will create a unity of science, of ideas. Each part of the world, very quickly and easily, will have access to the knowledge of every other part. You can imagine the response of people in the Third World who have access now to the Internet, and what they have learned about the developed world. This is completely changing their expectation of life. Therefore, how urgent it is to transform the world economically, and make it possible for the whole of humanity to take part in this revolution — a revolution of consciousness — which will result when everyone is keyed into this body of knowledge.

That covers, if inadequately, the priorities of Maitreya. He has much to do. Maitreya is here; He is here to stay, and is awaiting His opportunity to come forward and declare Himself openly to the world and begin His task.

(*Share International* January/February 1996)

THE RARITY OF A CHRIST IN OUR SYSTEM

Can you clarify the interrelation between the son of man and the son of God?

Every single one of us is a son of God. The Son of Man is that person who began as a man and advanced to the point where He could embody the Christ principle. That is the marvel of Maitreya. The interrelation between the two is one of history. He *evolved* to be a Son of God, but He is the Son of Man because He comes not just from God, but from humanity too. The Christ Principle demonstrates when that which is human and that which is divine come together. The human is the highest aspect of all that is below it. Eventually, the man stands free as a Son of God, totally at one with the divine aspect of himself. Nothing can touch him; nothing of the vibration of matter has any hold or pull on the Master from that time. One day, everyone will achieve that state of being.

Why do we have a Christ on this non-sacred planet, and why is it so rare? Does it relate to the fact that this is a 3rd-ray planet?

It is rare because it is so difficult to achieve. It is a tremendous achievement to embody a divine principle of which we know three: the principles of will, love, and wisdom. To *embody* any one of these is a major achievement. It is not simply a question of experiencing and channelling it; it is to *be* it; something entirely different from being sensitive enough to channel it, while it is not essentially your nature. It is the *nature* of Maitreya to be the Christ, to embody the Christ Principle. That is an extraordinarily rare achievement, and this planet is not even a sacred planet.

Why do we have one? Because we are very fortunate. We have a Buddha who embodies the Wisdom aspect at the cosmic level; He was a man. We have Maitreya, who embodies the Love aspect; He was a man. This is the marvel: these two brothers from early Atlantean times have gone through that long journey of evolution and in so doing have made these extraordinary, rare achievements.

40

Does it relate to the 3rd ray of the planet? No, it has nothing to do with the ray of the planet but with the particular gifts of these two great Beings. From the earliest times, They were destined for this. Eventually every Master has to make His choice of further evolution, in relation to His intuition of His destiny. That great decision a Master makes at the sixth initiation. He has to find His destined path, which, for Maitreya, is to be a Cosmic Christ. That is the path of Absolute Sonship.

Which other planets have created a Christ?
There are seven sacred planets and only five of them have created a Christ. But the Christ Principle is not the only quality that planetary Logoi can express. The Christ is one particular, an embodiment of the love aspect. There are others of equal stature on other planets, but a Christ is a very rare event in the system. Five out of the seven sacred planets have created Christs, not once but several times. But this is the only non-sacred planet which has created a Christ. Two of the sacred planets have not yet done so; they may not have that destiny. We are dealing with cosmic purpose, cosmic law, cosmic sacrifice. It is very complex.

So there are beings a lot more evolved than, for instance, Maitreya, but they do not necessarily embody that aspect of God on that planet?
On the non-sacred planets, there are no beings more evolved than Maitreya (except for Avatars outside their evolution). They have not yet produced a being of that stature. There are other aspects which are being developed on other planets, but not higher than Maitreya on the non-sacred planets.

Can you tell me whether Maitreya is Christ returned, or was Christ his disciple? (December 1996)
In Palestine 2,000 years ago, Maitreya used the normal mode for the appearance of the Teacher at any cycle: overshadowing. The process of Jesus' overshadowing started when Jesus was 12 (which is why he could discuss profound theological ideas with the rabbis). When Jesus was 24 the process was more or less

complete. From the age of 30 to 33 — that is from the baptism until the crucifixion — Maitreya totally overshadowed Jesus. Sometimes, Maitreya was working through that body alone; at other times Jesus was working in it alone; at still other times both Maitreya's consciousness and Jesus' consciousness were working through that body. So Maitreya did the teaching, and Jesus was the observer of all that took place through him.

Jesus is a Disciple of Maitreya Who is the Master of all the Masters.

When Christ was here before, He went through a cycle of events, and was crucified and killed. What is to prevent that from happening again? (April 1994)

It is very difficult to crucify someone whom you cannot see, and Maitreya can appear and disappear at will. You could fire a cannon at Him, an 18-inch shell, and it would just bounce off Him and fall to the ground. He created His own body, and if you can create your own body you can keep it intact. He is inviolable.

So He is transcending the laws of matter? (April 1994)

He is not transcending the laws of matter — He knows the laws of matter that we do not even see or understand.

Since Sai Baba entered the world in the usual, human way, why did Maitreya do it differently? (June 1995)

Maitreya could have used the body of a disciple (the usual method for the appearance of the World Teacher) as He did through Jesus, but His purpose this time is different. He is here as head of our Planetary Hierarchy and as leader of His Group, Who are also emerging, and so comes Himself. Also, He will remain with humanity for 2,500 years. This requires a very special vehicle: one equal to the strain of living at our level in a body still sensitive to His (cosmic) spiritual consciousness to do His work as the mayavirupa Christ — and to convince us that He is Who He is. This has involved the creation of the mayavirupa in which He now appears. Sai Baba will die in the normal way and return for a third incarnation early next century.

So really rather than a human being He is a sort of manifestation of God, in the sense that He has powers that normal people do not have. (March 1995)

Normal people do have exactly these powers but they have not yet achieved the demonstration of them. Nothing which He does is abnormal — there is no abnormality: there is simply an extension of what we call normal until it surpasses the average and so appears to us as abnormal. He expresses divine powers still potential in us all.

One day we will be able, by thought, to go to Australia without that 26-hour journey — we will just think ourselves to Sydney, or wherever, and back again.

Is Maitreya omniscient — I mean, can He see the future? (December 1996)

Yes. He has made, from 1988 to 1991, a series of the most remarkable and accurate predictions of world events which have been published, as given, in *Share International*. They have also been sent to the world's media as press releases. I would say these predictions of Maitreya constitute the most extraordinary, widest ranging, and most accurate series of forecasts ever given to the world. *Share International* publishes an ongoing report called 'Facts and Forecasts' which shows the implementation of Maitreya's predictions in the everyday world.

You stated in **Maitreya's Mission, Volume One** *that Melchizedek is another name for the Christ. However, this is in contradiction to the claim made in the book* **The Destiny of the Nations** *by Alice. A Bailey, which clearly indicates that this is but another name for the Ancient of Days — Sanat Kumara, the Ruler of the Holy City, also known as Shamballa. Could you please clarify further?* (November 1994)

Far be it from me to contradict the Master DK (Who gave *The Destiny of the Nations* through Alice Bailey) and, to the further confusion of the 'nit-picking' mind, let me say that there is no contradiction in our two statements. Hierarchy, of which Maitreya (the Christ) is the Head and Representative, is the Representative of Shamballa and of Sanat Kumara, the Lord of

43

the World. For many centuries, therefore, Maitreya has been seen as the Representative of Shamballa and given the name of Melchizedek.

In the Letters on Living Ethics — introduction to Agni Yoga — I found a sentence which puzzles me. It is written there that Maitreya and the Archangel Michael are identical. Is this true? (April 1993)

If you mean are Maitreya and the Archangel Michael the same identical individual, then the answer is no. They are two quite separate individualities. If you mean are They at the same point in evolution, then the answer is yes.

Is Maitreya the Son of Yahweh? (October 1994)

No.

Is Maitreya also known as Soraya? (June 1995)

No. The names which you can call Maitreya are: Maitreya, Maitreya Buddha (awaited by Buddhists), the Christ (by Christians — He embodies the Christ Principle), the Imam Mahdi or the Messiah (awaited by the Muslims), the Messiah (awaited by the Jews — although the Master Jesus is really the Messiah of the Jews, and they will have to recognize Jesus as the Messiah before they accept Maitreya as the World Teacher); He is also Krishna, or Kalki Avatar, to the Hindus. All these are names to which He could reasonably respond, although He does say such names are all man-made and bring about confusion — if He is the Christ for Christians, what about the Buddhists, the Muslims, the Imam Mahdi and so on? So He wishes to be called, simply: "The Teacher".

Did Maitreya have the same people around Him 2,000 years ago when He overshadowed Jesus? (March 1996)

Some of the people around Maitreya were around Jesus in Palestine. The Master Morya, a very well-known Master, was St Peter. John the Beloved is now the Master Koot Hoomi. The disciple who came after Jesus, St Paul, who created 'churchianity' and called it 'Christianity', is also now one of the

Masters, Hilarion. We will see Them very shortly. The Master Jesus, the best-known Master of all, is already in the world, and has been living in the outskirts of Rome for about seven years. Very soon after we see Maitreya, we will see the Master Jesus and Maitreya side-by-side. People see Them together now in all sorts of different guises. As readers of *Share International* know, we publish accounts of people's experiences with Maitreya and the Master Jesus.

Does Maitreya belong to the White Brotherhood? (November 1996)
Yes. Our planetary Spiritual Hierarchy, of which Maitreya is the Head, is a Lodge of the (cosmic) Great White Brotherhood.

Does humanity know Maitreya's name when He was an ordinary man like us? (November 1995)
No. He would, of course, have had a succession of names during His various incarnations. It is so long ago that they are lost to us.

Is Maitreya still living in London, now in 1996? (December 1996)
Yes; His base is in the Asian community of London but He moves around the world, by thought, all the time.

Is He materially here and materially somewhere else at the same time? (December 1996)
Yes; He can send out reflections of Himself all over the world, while He remains in London.

(1) When you say that Maitreya has been here since 19 July 1977 and that the Master Jesus is in Rome, do you mean in a physical body? (2) Are the Teachers really seen as men? (October 1994)
(1)Yes. (2) Yes.

Does Maitreya eat, and everything, like a normal person? (July/August 1995)

No. He does not need to eat. He can eat if the social circumstances demand it; a little bit of rice, for example. He lives in the Asian community of London. He is, as it were, a member of that community, and many of them identify with Him as one of themselves — only an extraordinary man, obviously. He can appear and disappear at will, which He does all the time. He can be in any part of the world by thought, He can appear in different places simultaneously. He is omniscient, omnipresent — so He can know what a person is feeling (someone perhaps connected with one of the groups with which I am associated) and He will appear to them to bring them solace or encouragement.

Does Maitreya have papers — a passport? (July/August 1995)

Yes. He came from the Himalayas, where He has lived for thousands of years. He came down on 8 July 1977, and stayed some days on the plains in Pakistan to acclimatize the body which He has created for Himself (it is not an ordinary body; He has no mother or father) by an act of will. It allows Him to live at our level, as an apparently ordinary man, and at the same time to bring in enough of His consciousness as the Christ to do His work as the Christ — to be the World Teacher, not only for Christians but for all groups everywhere in the world.

Has Maitreya ever been married? (April 1994)

No.

What is Maitreya doing as employment to pay for His food, for the flat or house where He lives, to pay for His travels and clothes? (December 1993)

He does not eat, or sleep; He creates His own clothes, and travels, by thought; and lives as one of a community in a house which is also a Temple. He needs no money. When He first came to London and lived in the Brick Lane area, He did have a job as a night-porter in a hospital.

What precisely is Maitreya going to do? Ridding the world of starvation, physically bettering, sharing of comforts — all that is *not saying what **we** are becoming. What does Maitreya do for us that we cannot do for ourselves?* (October 1995)

Maitreya will not rid the world of starvation but inspire *us* to do so for ourselves. Maitreya embodies what we call the Christ Consciousness — the energy of love — and it is this energy, as it manifests through us, that will change the world. Maitreya will inspire in us a "change of heart" to create justice — and therefore peace — in the world.

He will take those who are ready through the process of the first and second initiations, and bring a new revelation of the nature of God (the Logos), and therefore of ourselves. He comes, He says, to teach humanity the art of Self- (or God-) realization — the goal of our lives.

You say that Maitreya comes as a teacher — does He come with a system that we should follow? (December 1996)

No. He will not present the world with an ideology, a belief system, or a new religion. An ideology is simply a belief structure. Maitreya has come to teach humanity the art of Self- (or God-) realization which is not a belief, a religion, or an ideology; it is the very basis and purpose of our lives.

THE FACT OF GOD

Will Maitreya inspire us to worship God? (September 1993)

No, I do not think He will. He has said: Do not worship Me. If you worship Me you are putting yourself below Me, whereas you are on the same level.

There is only one Divinity — we all share it. The only difference between Maitreya and you or me is that He is a tremendously advanced human being who has several degrees of cosmic consciousness, and we have barely the beginnings of mental consciousness. There is a difference in the degree to which we manifest that Divinity, but the Divinity is the same in everyone.

You will find that the approach to God will change dramatically. When a Teacher has come before, the groups to whom He has given His teachings have made Him a God, have put Him up in Heaven, and one day a week they worship Him — (if they are from Islam they worship Him every day, several times a day). More and more, people will begin to realize that *they are God*, that what we call God, what we call Nature and what we call humanity are one and the same, there is no division. We are God in incarnation. We are Divinity Itself. Maitreya says the Self alone matters — you are that Self, an immortal Being. If you realize yourself as God, as Divinity Itself, *who is there to worship?*

Worship will change into invocation. There will be a new religion — Maitreya said: "I have not come to found a new religion." But we have to call it something, so let us for convenience call it a religion — a new religion which is esoteric in basis, which is a science, the science of evolution, of which the Masters are the custodians. They know the path of evolution scientifically — not as a vague, devotional hope that 'something nice will happen to me today' from God.

We shall come to know God as an ever-present reality, not someone up in the sky whom we worship, but something which *we are,* which every one is. What will change is the approach to God through worship to the approach to God *by invoking the energy which is God*. In the Christian Bible it says: "God is a consuming fire" — that fire is energy.

Our present most potent idea of God is the solar system, at the centre of which is a great Being who ensouls it, whose body of manifestation this solar system is — that is God. But our solar system itself is only one of billions of suns in the galaxy at the centre of which is another great Being about Whom we can know nothing.

So God is energy. The laws governing this energy make the qualities of God, and these can be invoked by humanity as a whole, particularly at the three Spring Spiritual Festivals and at the nine other full moons throughout the year. This mass approach will transform the attitude to, and understanding of, what we call God.

Who or what is it that we call "God" — the Galactic Logos? (January/February 1997)

This planet is the body of expression of a great Cosmic Being, a Heavenly Man. He reflects Himself at the etheric-physical level as Sanat Kumara, Lord of the World, on Shamballa. Sanat Kumara has been on this planet for 18½ million years, coming originally from the planet Venus, and is the etheric physical-plane expression of the Logos of our planet. He is not the Logos but the reflection of the Logos. He is "The Ancient of Days" of the Bible, the "Youth of Endless Summers", the Jewish "Jehovah" or "Our Father in Heaven".

What is meant by "mother of the world"? (1) Is this an Avatar? (2) A being from another planet? (3) A highly evolved entity? (4) Is she in visible human form? (5) What is her role? (6) What is her relationship with Sanat Kumara? (7) What is the difference between: "the Divine Mother", "the Mother of the World" and "Mother Earth"? (June 1996)

(1) No. (2) Originally, yes. (3) Yes. (4) No. (5) She embodies the Mother or nurturing aspect. (6) She is His Shakti. (7) They are the same.

It is well known that in other names for teaching there is no reference to a God, only to gods in the various heaven worlds. Will all Buddhists need to revise their beliefs on this point as they eventually become aware of the fact of Maitreya's mission and teaching? (January/February 1994)

No, I would not have thought so at all. Buddhism, in my estimation, is the closest to the esoteric teaching of Hierarchy on this point. It is important to remember that Maitreya is not "God" nor will He claim to be God, but a divine Messenger come to show us the divine nature.

When asked about whether or not God exists, the Buddha answered to the effect that if you do not know who and what you are (as a man) how can you know about God. Leave that question alone, therefore, He said, until you know yourself.

Could you elaborate your description of the relationship between Lord Maitreya and God? (December 1996)

Let me say right away that Maitreya is not God. He is a representative, an expression, a messenger, of God. He has, as a moment-to-moment experience, realized His complete identity with God or the Self, the Lord. He is so evolved, and so pure, that He can, in *His own Being*, embody that aspect of God's nature we call Love, the Christ Principle.

I am a Catholic and I believe in one God, and I disagree with what you've been saying about Maitreya. (October 1996)

I am not saying Maitreya is God; He is a teacher, just as Jesus was a teacher. You would say Jesus was God: I would not agree. I would say Jesus was a God-like man; Maitreya is a God-like man. Eventually you, too, will be a God-like man. It is in every single one of us to be like Jesus, Maitreya, Krishna, or Buddha, but I agree with you that there is only one Source from which we all come: that is what we call God.

Is there any specific practice that Maitreya advocates to know God? (October 1994)

Maitreya advocates the cultivation of these three: honesty of mind; sincerity of spirit; and detachment — that is, detachment from identifying with the body, the feelings and sensations, and with the mind. These are the vehicles of the Self and should not be mistaken for the Self. He also advocates the use of the New Age Prayer to achieve Self-awareness.

You say in your books that the force of evil (the Antichrist) was released at certain times in history, for example during the Roman empire and during the world wars this century. May I ask by whom? God, I presume, but God in the involutionary or evolutionary aspect? (June 1995)

By Sanat Kumara, the Lord of the World on Shamballa. God is always evolutionary. The involutionary aspect — spirit descending into matter — is part of God's evolutionary creative process.

Does heaven exist? (January/February 1994)

"Heaven" is an inner state of Being or consciousness. "The Kingdom of Heaven is within," as Jesus Himself said. The Kingdom of Heaven is the Spiritual Kingdom, the Kingdom of Souls, the Spiritual Hierarchy of Masters and Initiates, the kingdom immediately above the human. It is entered into through the door of Initiation. It is the consciousness which results from the union of soul and human personality. The mode of achieving that union is meditation which is the means by which the true Being, the Higher self or soul and its reflection — the man or woman in incarnation — are fused together in the soul-infused personality.

There is also another meaning of "heaven". Souls not in incarnation spend a greater or lesser length of 'time' (time is a physical-plane concept of the human brain) in *Devachan*, a state of unending bliss, while awaiting the call to reincarnate. The Christian concept of heaven, while somewhat distorted, relates to this experience.

If a God of Love created the world why is there so much suffering? (June 1994)

In creating humanity, the Creator gave us free will, without which we would never develop into responsible, right-

51

intentioned co-workers with the Divine. Our suffering is the result of the action of the Law of Cause and Effect (the Law of Karma). If — as we do — we misuse our divine free will, we suffer, and will continue to suffer, until we learn harmlessness.

What is correct — the Big Bang theory or the Steady State theory, or other, for the origin of the universe? (September 1993)

The Big Bang theory comes closest to the esoteric teaching, ie that the universe is the result of a great explosion or 'outbreathing' in which the polar opposites, spirit and matter, are united. In that union matter becomes spiritualized. There follows the phase of 'inbreathing' of all that has been created and the whole process repeats eternally at a higher turn of the spiral.

PRAYER — INVOCATION

Is prayer a way to invoke Maitreya? (March 1993)

Yes, indeed. All the Masters respond to prayer — that is how prayer is answered, not by people sitting up in heaven, there is no such place. Heaven is a state of Being, and that, the heavenly kingdom, is the Kingdom of Souls.

The Masters are wide awake, They never sleep, and They hear every prayer. Whether They can answer that prayer depends on the strength of the invocation, on what proportion of emotional or mental matter the prayer is wrapped in. The higher and the more mental the matter in which the prayer is wrapped, the more impact it makes on the minds of the Masters, because They work on the mental not the emotional planes. There are plenty of beings on the astral planes who respond to astral-type prayers, but the Masters Themselves respond on the mental and super-mental planes, the soul or spiritual planes. So the higher you can make your invocation through prayer the better. More important even than that is karma. The Law of Karma controls the action even of Masters in relation to prayer.

Certain invocations have been released to the world by the Masters as prayers. Maitreya Himself has released a World Prayer for the New Age to bring about one's sense of oneself as divine, as the 'creator of the universe', as identifying with God. It goes like this:

> *"I am the creator of the universe.*
> *I am the father and mother of the universe.*
> *Everything comes from me.*
> *Everything shall return to me.*
> *Mind, spirit and body are my temples,*
> *for the Self to realize in them*
> *my Supreme Being and Becoming."*

In this coming age humanity will gradually recognize its identity with the Self or God. Seeing God not only as 'up there', but immanent in every aspect of creation — that there is no

53

separation whatsoever between God, nature and humanity. Everything interrelates.

Of course, many prayers are answered but the answer is often unrecognized as such. The answer might well be an unsought gift of stimulus or opportunity presented rather than the expected answer to felt need which was asked for.

When using the New Age Prayer given by Maitreya, should one identify with the soul or with the Monad (as much as one can at this point of evolution)? (April 1993)

One should identify, in so far as one can, with the soul. You are lucky if you can identify with the soul during any form of meditation, affirmation or mantram. The New Age Prayer, of course, is an affirmation. For most people, the soul is unknown, not unattainable, but generally speaking unknown. The Monad is as yet simply an idea in the minds of most disciples.

Has the Master given any visualization for Maitreya's Prayer for the New Age? We had visualizations which were very helpful for the Great Invocation, and I wondered if the Master would be kind enough to provide any for the new Prayer? (December 1993)

No, He has not.

What is the effect of prayers addressed to Saints who have already reincarnated? Can they be as effective as if they were addressed to the souls of Saints out of incarnation? (January/February 1995)

There is no difference. Most of the Saints of the past, moreover, are now Masters.

I have heard a version of the Great Invocation in which it had been changed to include the feminine. Is this right? (January/February 1996)

No, it is not right. The Great Invocation was worded precisely as it is by the Masters. It is not just a set of ideas, but ideas embodied in mantric form. When you say it as it is, the mantram works. When you dilute it by all sorts of changes, as many groups do for simple, personal reasons — their own prejudices — you change what has been given at the highest level by Hierarchy, diminishing the effectiveness of the mantram. Maitreya's Messages, given through me, are likewise mantric in effect. Again and again, Maitreya says "brothers", "men"; He doesn't say: "men and women." He could, but it would break up the mantric rhythm of the text. So one should not change these things.

Every one should know that the Masters are people who, like us, have been man and woman throughout Their evolutionary history. For Them there is no separation, no difference between men and women. It is absolutely essential that women take their full place in every aspect of life in this coming age, the age of the Tara, or Mother, in which the nourishing, mother aspect comes to the fore. That does not mean a domination of the female over the male. On the contrary: it is a perfect balance between male and female, both contributing equally, but each remembering that they have been male and female over and over again throughout their evolutionary experience. So every denial of freedom that women feel today they, too, have contributed to in the past.

(1) Should the Great Invocation always be said in English or can the various groups around the world translate it into their own language? (2) Are there 'official' translations into other languages? (3) If so, what languages and who has provided the translations? (4) Would the mantric/invocatory qualities be compromised through translations undertaken by persons other than the Masters? (November 1994)

Already the Great Invocation has been translated into many languages and is used in these various languages by groups and individuals around the world. There is no obligation to use the English version. In my experience, there are several translations in some languages, and, according to my information, they differ somewhat in quality and 'style' — the more devotional people translate the Invocation more devotionally, for example — but it still works perfectly well as far as Hierarchy is concerned, which, after all, is what matters.

More importantly, many groups and individuals change the wording, and, therefore, the meaning, to suit their own prejudices and beliefs. This I believe to be a profound mistake and misuse of the Invocation. For example, many 'new-age' people do not believe in the existence of evil on the planet and change the line: "And may it seal the door where evil dwells", or leave it out altogether, as if, by ignoring the fact of evil, it will just not manifest. The "evil" meant in this line is that wrought by the Lords of Materiality whose role is the upholding of the matter aspect of the planet — that is their domain. "Sealing the door" ensures the restriction of these Lords of Matter to that domain alone. This is the "chaining down of the Beast" (in the *Book of Revelation*) "for a time and half a time".

Other than the first version in English given through Alice Bailey, the Masters Themselves do not make translations of the Invocation.

THE FACT OF THE KINGDOM OF GOD

The Spiritual Hierarchy

Who is Maitreya's 'boss' — is He the real boss of the whole Hierarchy? (July/August 1996)

The Hierarchy is His Ashram, and He is the Head of the Hierarchy, the Master of all the Masters. They look up to Him as Their Master as we would look up to the Masters as ours.

There are three major 'posts' in the Hierarchy, filled by three Great Lords: the Manu — the exemplar of the race, the Master Who embodies the racial goal in its perfection; the Bodhisattva or Christ — the World Teacher, the Lord Maitreya; and the Lord of Civilization. These Lords form a triumvirate at the head of the Hierarchy.

There are three departments under these Great Lords: one under the 1st ray of Power; one under the 2nd ray of Love-Wisdom, the Christ ray; one under the 3rd ray of Active Intelligence or Adaptability. From the 3rd ray comes four other rays — 4, 5, 6 and 7 — and 49 Ashrams altogether dealing with the total work of the Hierarchy. So it is a huge organization, and there is constant interchange between these three departments and the 49 Ashrams.

Maitreya's Teacher is Sanat Kumara, the Lord of the World. He has many other names: the One Initiator, the Youth of Endless Summers, the King, and when we talk about "Our Father in Heaven" that is Who we mean; He is the Jewish Jehovah, of the Bible. Sanat Kumara dwells on Shamballa, a Centre in etheric matter in the Gobi desert.

He is a 'young' man; He came from the planet Venus some 18.5 million years ago, bringing the energy of Mind — we are the sons of Mind.

Is the Hierarchy under Maitreya totally constituted as to names, personnel etc? (July/August 1996)

The Hierarchy is made up of 49 Ashrams: there are seven major Ashrams with a 6th-degree Master, called a Chohan, at the head of each, and from these stem six other Ashrams — so there are seven lines of seven Ashrams, making 49 in all. The personnel of all these Ashrams are not in place as yet.

In your book **The Reappearance of the Christ and the Masters of Wisdom***, pages 30 and 31, you state " . . . the Planetary Hierarchy of Masters ... have reached a point in Their own evolution which necessitates a re-enaction, this time in group formation, of physical-plane life experience. This is the fundamental reason behind the planned and imminent re-emergence . . . "*

My questions are: (1) Is the primary reason of Maitreya's re-emergence to benefit the Hierarchy of Masters and is this still true? (2) Given that the Masters are of great help to humanity, does the description of Their authority structure as being a hierarchy mean an aristocratic top-down rule? (3) Is this truly democratic? (4) Is this really altruistic? (5) Does this mean humanity is only of secondary importance? (6) Should humanity know humility and not so arrogantly request primary importance? (July/August 1993)

(1) The statements from my book which you quote refer to the re-emergence of the Hierarchy as a whole, not only that of Maitreya. His re-emergence does not benefit the Masters (He is always with Them) but He emerges *as one of Them*, at Their Head, as Their Leader. It is the externalization of the Hierarchy which is the most important event, not simply the aiding of humanity, however beneficial to us that undoubtedly is. This remains the case.

(2) No. The Spiritual Hierarchy of Masters and Initiates constitutes a Kingdom — the Kingdom of Souls (or the Kingdom of God, in Christian terminology). Its structure is the opposite of *autocratic* or *authoritarian* but is based rather on the reality of Spiritual relationship. All its members (as is humanity as a whole) are recognized as being equal, and equally divine, but also as expressing that divinity to different degrees, depending on the evolution achieved. It is the reality of this fact which *automatically* (and this is true throughout cosmos) determines the initiatory status of any member. There are Initiates of many different degrees within the Hierarchy, the less

58

advanced learning from those more advanced. All look to the Christ, the Lord Maitreya, for guidance (not orders or commands) as the most advanced and experienced.

(3) The Hierarchy functions within a synthesis of democratic and hierarchical modes. Each Master has democratic right of input on any general matter under discussion but inevitably, because of superior knowledge and experience, final decisions must come from the most advanced members. However, consensus decisions form the majority.

(4) Yes, completely and totally; the Masters have no *personal* desires whatsoever.

(5) No. Humanity forms but one kingdom in the total Scheme and Plan but is of major importance.

(6) Yes.

(1) In the new world society in which everyone shares, will there still be a hierarchical system (just as there apparently is at the level your Master inhabits according to esoteric philosophy); and (2) if so, how will there not be the same difficulties connected with inequality? (December 1994)

The Hierarchy of which the Masters and Their disciples are members should be understood to be based on spiritual evolution and not on authority or privilege. To the Masters, all are equal but at differing stages in the expression of divinity; the divinity itself is one and indivisible. In any new economic/political system, it is up to humanity itself to regulate the degree of participation and democracy it would see as necessary and fair. All is in our own hands; no system will ever be imposed on us by the Hierarchy of Masters.

Have The Masters any obvious bodily markings which would set Them apart from other people? (July/August 1996)

One thing, which is not a birth 'mark' but is part of their birth right, is that They are perfect, men without faults. They know only total, unconditional love. They are the senior members of the Centre where the Love of God is expressed. This is true for all the Masters, whatever Their ray. Some demonstrate other qualities as well: Power, Purpose, Intelligence of different kinds;

some stimulate the scientists of the world, some the educational groups, some the politicians, the economic thinkers, etc. As men, They are as varied as are men. They are full of grace, kindliness, ready to serve and save unceasingly. They are radiant in a way few can imagine. Their intelligence and wisdom cuts through to the heart of every problem; They have a spiritual force which can galvanize whole groups of disciples into action.

Do the Masters possess the power of destruction as well as of healing? (July/August 1996)

Creation is a process of creation and destruction. That is carried out by the Logos of any particular planet, of a solar system, or of a galaxy. When the Logos decides that His work of creation has gone 'out' a certain 'distance' and wishes to bring it back into Himself, which is what happens, then the destructive phase takes place.

The Masters, of Themselves, are not destructive, but They understand the laws of creation, which include the laws of destruction. Certain of the Masters will be called upon, especially Those on the 1st ray of Purpose or Will, which is often called the destructive ray. The Masters along that line work at destroying the old forms, the old structures, to prepare for the new life which comes in as the new energy, thus generating new forms.

(1) Could you please explain why Masters still have astral bodies? (2) Of what use is an astral body once the second initiation has been taken? (3) How does the astral body relate to the creative imagination? (July/August 1995)

(1) In the Master the astral vehicle exists as a sensitive, feeling apparatus and a mirror of Buddhi. (2) It is the sensitive, feeling apparatus for *all* humanity. It simply begins to come under *control* when the second initiation can be taken. (3) The astral imagination usually contributes a large measure of energy to the creative act. The more evolved the person the less is this the case.

How long will it be before Masters appear in female bodies, since our evolution might be speeded up by the presence of the Christ in the world? (March 1996)

250-350 years.

Why is the existence of a Spiritual Hierarchy only mentioned in the esoteric teachings of the West and not in the teachings of all the great sages and Avatars of India (Ramakrishna, Vivekananda, Sri Aurobindo, Premananda, Sai Baba)? (December 1995)

Because it is precisely in the West that the idea of the existence of great spiritual Teachers has been lost or abandoned. Also, Avatars are not actually members of this planet's Spiritual Hierarchy. They 'come in' from outside the planet.

The group of Masters involved with the Western world are members of the Trans Himalayan Lodge. Unlike the members of the separate, South Indian Lodge, these Masters do not work openly, hence the need for teachings about them.

Master Jesus

Where is the Master Jesus and what is His relationship to Maitreya? (July/August 1993)

The Master Jesus, as He is known in the Hierarchy of Masters, has been living in the outskirts of Rome since 1989. He is one of the first group of Masters to come into the world with the Christ.

The Christ and Jesus are not the same individual. The Lord Maitreya embodies, in His own Being, what we call the Christ Principle, the Christ Consciousness, the second aspect of the Christian trinity, the energy of love. He overshadowed and worked through His disciple Jesus for three years, from the baptism to crucifixion. For these three years, the disciple Jesus became Jesus the Christ or Messiah. Nearly 600 years earlier, the Buddha overshadowed His disciple, the Prince Gautama, who, at age 29, became Gautama Buddha. This is the age-old way for the appearance of the Teacher in the world, which is a cyclic event. What we are witnessing today is the return, according to cyclic law, of the Teacher, this time in His own full physical presence, not overshadowing a disciple as has been the case up until now.

How will Maitreya and the Master Jesus work together? (October 1995)

These two Great Ones have worked closely together for many centuries. According to the Master DK (Who gave the Alice Bailey Teachings), the Master Jesus seeks to save the time and effort of Maitreya whenever possible. This collaboration, no doubt, will continue. In the Christian Churches, the energy of the Master Jesus or of Maitreya Himself magnetizes the wafers at every Eucharist service.

The responsibility for the Christian Church lies with the Master Jesus. His task will be to purify the teachings of the man-made dogmas and doctrines which condition it today. Without doubt, Maitreya will aid Him in every way.

The function of the Church has been to teach and to heal. In my opinion, it has taught badly and healed little. This will change under the inspiration of both Maitreya and the Master Jesus, and a path to initiation will be created — the true religious path.

Who will come first, the Master Jesus or Maitreya? (October 1995)

Both Maitreya and the Master Jesus are *already* in the world: Maitreya in London and the Master Jesus in Rome. The Master Jesus and the other Masters (there are at present 13 in the world) will make Themselves known only *after* Maitreya's Declaration.

It is generally admitted that the Master Jesus and Apollonius of Tyana were contemporary — or at least very close to being. Is this true? (July 1994)

No. Jesus went out of incarnation at the crucifixion and returned as Apollonius seven years later. He became a Master in that life as Apollonius.

In the 650 or so years that the Master Jesus has been incarnate on the physical plane, has He ever done work that has become publicly known in the world, or has He been relatively hidden all these years? (May 1995)

The question shows some misunderstanding. The body in which the Master Jesus now appears is the third such since His incarnation as Jesus. The others were also physical manifestations. Like the other Masters He works mainly through inspiring *disciples* to make changes. A very good example of this is the beginning of the Ecumenical Movement which He initiated through Pope John 23rd. He is also the Master behind *A Course in Miracles*, which was given through a disciple on the inner planes who then dictated it to Dr Helen Schucman.

Buddha and Other Masters

What part does the Buddha have to play in the reappearance of the Christ? (June 1993)

He has a very powerful part to play, which is not generally known. He works with, and in a sense stands behind, Maitreya all the time. He is no longer in the physical body, but has given that up to be on the highest spiritual Centre of our planet, Shamballa, an energetic Centre in the Gobi Desert. There dwells the Lord of the World (Sanat Kumara), a group of Kumaras around Him and various very evolved individuals like the Buddha (not Gautama Buddha but the One Who worked through Gautama; the Prince Gautama is no longer in this solar system; He is on Sirius).

The Buddha stands behind the Christ, and affects His thinking in relation to the East. There is an ancient Eastern teaching about what are called "the vestures of the Buddha", at present safely hidden, but which will be taken up by the Christ, the 'Coming One'. These 'vestures' are the sum-total of the Buddha's emotional-intuitive nature and the sum-total of His knowledge and thought, ie the astral and mental bodies of the Buddha. They augment the emotional and mental equipment of the Christ Himself.

The Buddha embodies the energy of wisdom, Maitreya the energy of love. In relation to the East, Maitreya thus gains the experience of the Buddha, and through the use of the Buddha's emotional-mental equipment is able to enter into the consciousness of the Eastern mind, presumably to a deeper extent than would otherwise be possible.

The Buddha now embodies the wisdom aspect from cosmic levels and He transmits this energy through Maitreya into the world.

(1) Is the Tibetan figure Gesar, whom Tibetans expect to return as a teacher and enlightener, another name for Maitreya? (2) Does Tibetan Buddhism also look for the return of Maitreya Buddha, knowing Him as Maitreya?

Recently the relics and birthplace of Gautama Buddha were found in Nepal, and are now officially recognized as such. (3) Was it planned (by Hierarchy?) that the Buddha's birthplace should come to light now to coincide with the public appearance of Maitreya Buddha?

(4) Is it part of Tibet's karmic role to keep sacred and protected the more esoteric knowledge and ancient mysteries; to preserve intact ageless wisdom which might otherwise have been lost or damaged? (5) Tibet seems to have a very particular role to play and contribution to make to the world community, does it not? (June 1996)

(1) Yes. (2) Yes. (3) No. (4) No. (5) Yes, but not as the preserver of ancient mysteries. It is an example of extraordinary long-suffering patience and loving understanding in the face of difficulties.

Did Buddha overshadow any teachers other than Gautama? (June 1993)

Yes: Mithra in ancient Persia and Memnon in later Egyptian times.

Could you please tell me in what period Memnon, who was overshadowed by the Buddha, and who is mentioned in connection with the Trojan War, actually lived? (November 1994)

Around 6,000 BC. The Trojan War occurred around 2,500 BC and I know of no connection of Memnon with that event. I think the questioner must be thinking of King Agamemnon, who indeed was very much involved in that war.

*Swami Satyeswarananda, the Himalayan Yogi Vedantist, in his book **Babaji: The Divine Himalayan Yogi**, says that, in October 1974, at Dunagiri Hill in the Himalayas, a man who Satyeswarananda says "looked like the Lord Jesus" mysteriously appeared to convey a message to Satyeswarananda. Satyeswarananda identifies him only as "M". "M" said that he had "approached Babaji for the needs of the West; he told me to inform you of this message: 'Wake up and follow me'". This was three years before Maitreya left the Himalayas for London. Obviously the question is: (1) Was "M" Maitreya? (2) It seems that Babaji is slowly allowing his work to become more exoteric? (3) What will be Babaji's future role? (4) What is the nature of his co-operation with Maitreya?* (September 1993)

(1) Yes, "M" was indeed Maitreya. (2) No, that is not the case. (3) As at present, a divine Avatar upholding the Earth. (4) Adviser.

Where are Rama, Hercules and Hermes and what is their present mission? (July 1994)

I can say nothing about Their respective missions but Rama and Hercules are on Sirius and Hermes is on the Council of the Lord of the World on Shamballa.

Is Hermes (7000 BC) identical to Hermes Trismegistus? (November 1994)

Yes.

Do you know where the entity is who was Krishna? (October 1994)

Krishna is on Sirius. He was overshadowed in his incarnation as Krishna by the Lord Maitreya.

Where is Lao-tse today? (October 1994)

On Sirius.

Could you tell us what became of the initiate St Francis of Assisi? (January/February 1995)

He is now a Master of the fifth degree and resides in the Italian Alps.

Can you tell us the name of the prophet who is now in Madrid? (November 1995)

He is not a prophet but one of the Masters. His name is not being revealed as yet.

Will the Masters who were once Sri Krishna, Moses and Mohammed, after Declaration Day, rouse people to reform Hinduism, Judaism and Islam? (June 1994)

No, not personally. A Master is already at work in the Islamic world to try to reform Islam.

You have stated that the Prophet Mohammed (AD570-632) was taught by Jesus just as Jesus had been taught by the Christ. (1) For how long was Mohammed overshadowed by Jesus? (2) Did Mohammed know during his life that he was being overshadowed by Jesus? He is reported to have told his followers that the Archangel Gabriel revealed the messages of the Quran to him, and this appears to be confirmed by the Quran itself. (December 1995)

(1) For four years. Mohammed was not "taught" by Jesus but overshadowed by Him. (2) Yes. The Archangel Gabriel was not involved.

(1) Is the Master who will be the German Master already in the outer world and active? What is his name and in which town does he have his Ashram? (2) Am I subject to glamour when I believe that I could be part of his Ashram? (July/August 1996)

(1) No. (2) Yes.

I read that St Germain said he and Maitreya were one and the same. (June 1995)

I do not believe that that came from "St Germain". There is a huge body of teaching coming out of the astral planes claiming to be from St Germain — He does not work under that name any more. This is total glamour and illusion, coming through what is called 'channelling' from the astral planes. None of that is from the Masters Themselves. On the astral planes there are facsimiles of the Masters, put there by humanity itself as astral thoughtforms, created by disciples who respond to the true teachings from the Masters. The authentic Hierarchical teachings are the Alice Bailey teachings, the teachings of H. P. Blavatsky (who knew the Masters and worked with Them) and the Agni Yoga teachings from Helena Roerich.

There was an extraordinary Being who was known in the courts of Europe throughout the 18th century under various names but mainly as the Comte de St Germain. He 'died' at the end of that century. He was born as a Prince in the family of the Rakoczis in Budapest. He 'died' as Prince Rakoczi, but when the coffin was disinterred it was empty. He is very much alive: He is the Master Rakoczi (the "Master R") and the Regent of Europe. He is based in the Carpathians. He is a sixth-degree initiate — a Chohan of the 7th ray, an ascended Master, and since the 7th ray is coming into incarnation He will *act* as the Lord of Civilization for this coming time. He is totally separate from, and is a disciple of, Maitreya.

Is the Master Who is supposed to come to Paris now there? (June 1994)

Yes, in the outskirts.

(1) Was Moses a previous incarnation of the Master Morya as some people think? (2) If not, where is Moses now and what is his point of evolution? (June 1996)

(1) No. (2) He is on Sirius (the Master Morya is, of course, on Earth). If Moses were in this solar system He would be an eighth-degree Initiate.

I have a doubt about the Holy prophet Zarathustra (Zoroaster), whether he was a former incarnation of Buddha or Maitreya? (December 1994)

Neither. He was overshadowed by Hermes.

Avatars

What is Kalki Avatar? (June 1996)

Kalki Avatar, for Hindus, is the Avatar for this coming age or Yuga, and is synonymous with Krishna. Hindus expect an Avatar — they have the doctrine of Avatars who come cyclically, age after age. In the West Jesus is seen as a 'one-off' event: God made flesh, who came specifically for a particular group. In fact, there has never been an age without an Avatar. Hindus await a reincarnation of Krishna. Maitreya overshadowed Krishna, so as far as Hindus are concerned, Maitreya is Kalki Avatar, the Avatar for this coming age, the "age of righteousness", which indeed it will be. It is the age in which for the first time on a mass scale the spiritual essence of humanity demonstrates; in which humanity realizes, experiences itself, as one, and therefore creates structures which will demonstrate that oneness. It will also see itself not only as one but as whole, intrinsically part of its environment. There will come a time when humanity will see that humanity, God, and nature are one and the same; there is no separation between any of these. That sense of wholeness, eventually, humanity *en masse* will know, not just as an intellectual idea but as direct experience. Krishna, or Kalki Avatar, comes at the end of this "dark age", Kali Yuga. Though not everyone would agree that Kali Yuga, the "dark age", has ended, the great Teacher, Sai Baba, in south India, has said that the dark age is over; Swami Premananda has said the same thing; my Master has confirmed that it is now ending. So it is now possible for Kalki Avatar, "the rider on the White Horse", to come.

In a book about Sai Baba it says He is the third fully divine Avatar, the other two being Rama and Krishna (who were also Himself). Does this mean that Maitreya is not fully divine? (June 1995)

I do not know from which of the scores of books written about Sai Baba the above information is taken, but it is obviously written by a devotee who believes (as many do) that *every* Avatar throughout history is a manifestation of Sai Baba, who, they believe, created all things.

With the greatest respect and reverence for Sai Baba, I have to say that I think the above quote to be nonsense. Of course, there are many different types and levels of Avatar, but all of them are at least sixth-degree initiates by Earth standards. All the Masters of our Hierarchy are fifth-degree or higher and, by Earth standards, are all "fully divine" (whatever is meant by that). Sai Baba was not "also" Rama and Krishna. Rama was the vehicle for Hercules (Himself such a vehicle 2,000 years earlier) while Krishna was the vehicle for Maitreya, 3,000 years before Jesus. As a seventh-degree initiate, Maitreya is, by Earth standards, eminently "fully divine" and could be anywhere He chose in our System.

If people must measure the divinity of these God-men then I would say that Sai Baba is not the third but the *most* "fully divine" Being to grace this planet with His presence.

In relation to evolutionary attainment, at what level does the Avatar of Synthesis, Who overshadows Maitreya, reside? (May 1996)

This Avatar embodies in His Being the first three aspects of God that we know — the Intelligence, the Love and the Will aspects — plus a further aspect for which, as yet, we have no name. What level is this Cosmic Entity? It would stagger you if you could know. Maitreya is a seventh-degree initiate. That means that, as far as this solar system is concerned, He has two levels of cosmic consciousness. The Avatar of Synthesis has 12 levels of cosmic consciousness.

Is Sai Baba the Avatar of Synthesis? (May 1996)
No.

(1) Is Mataji, referred to in Yogananda's autobiography, currently in incarnation? (2) Is she an Avatar? (May 1995)
(1) Yes. (2) Yes.

(1) Do highly evolved beings in female bodies anchor some "female energy" on our planet? (2) Are there female Avatars although there are no female Masters? (May 1995)

(1) Energy but not "female energy". (2) Yes.

Editions Amrita, in France, present a video cassette entitled: **Swami Premananda or the joy of loving**, *in which one finds a new Master of Wisdom who not only has a physical appearance close to that of Sai Baba, but whose work is the same. One can see Swami Premananda materialize, from his mouth, before thousands of people, five stone lingams. (1) Who is Swami Premananda? (2) Are his activities complementary to those of Sai Baba or different?* (June 1994)

(1) Swami Premananda, according to my information, is an Avatar (for an interview with Swami Premananda see *Share International* April 1983), who is continuing, to some extent, the work of Sai Baba; for example, for some years now, He has produced the lingams mentioned in the question, once produced by Sai Baba, at the annual Shivaratri Ceremony. (2) His work is complementary to that of Sai Baba.

TREASURE OF THE PAST, MARVELS OF THE FUTURE

Please elaborate on the phrase "consolidate the treasure of the past and inspire the marvels of the future" in the Master's article, 'The Son of Man.'

Many today cannot really tolerate the modern world. Everything that happens — politically, economically, religiously, socially, scientifically, culturally — is abhorrent to them. Either they are longing for the far-distant past, or for some as-yet-unrealized future. They are not living in the present. Their notion of change is to sweep away everything and create an entirely new world. The attraction for them of so-called New Age groups is precisely because these groups tend to see the world in those terms. For many, economics is just having money or not having money. If you have money, you do not talk about it. You only talk about money when you do not have it. Or, society is so corrupt and decayed that they want to sweep the whole thing away. Some people would really like to get rid of most of humanity except for their friends, sweep all that away, start afresh with their friends, and build a new world.

Many people have precisely that thoughtform. It is so strong that they have the confirmation of it from their 'guides' on the astral plane. How many times have you read so-called communications from 'Masters' (which are really from some astral entity or even their own subconscious), through mediums, which say: the starships are waiting. There is going to be a colossal upheaval on earth. Everything is going to be destroyed. Most people are going to be killed, but there are 144,000 who are going to be lifted up and kept secure in the starships until everything is purified and the world has settled down again: the oceans have gone down, the new lands have come up, it is all dried out, and everything is waiting for them. Then they will be brought down and life will begin again — with them and their friends. That is a very powerful thoughtform, and you surely know the groups who perpetuate it. There are books in every esoteric book shop which tell exactly that story.

This is a dream of people who want to get rid of the world because they do not like the world. They do not like humanity.

71

They do not like the way people think, talk, or smell. They do not like anything about other people. There are only a few people that they get on with — people who believe the same thing. This is a very powerful syndrome — to sweep everything away except what you believe in.

The New Age is not going to be like that at all. If we were to get rid of everything in the world, we would get rid of 18½ million years of evolution. What is the sense in that? There is an enormous inheritance from the past, and, were we to reject it, we would lose immeasurably. Maitreya calls it the "treasure of the past". "Consolidate the treasure of the past, inspire the marvels of the future." It is not as if *everything* in life today is wrong or corrupt or basically at variance to future needs — on the contrary. Our educational systems are inadequate, but millions of children go to school.

The Master DK writes, through Alice Bailey, that an average educated child of 14 today has the equivalent consciousness of a scholar of the Middle Ages. A scholar in the Middle Ages had the PhD of the time. He could speak Latin and Greek, interpret the philosophies, and probably do all sorts of alchemical and so-called scientific experiments. A scholar of the Middle Ages had the consciousness of a 14-year-old educated child today. That is phenomenal progress.

Are we going to get rid of the educational system, throw everything out, so that we do not have any books, teachers, any inherited knowledge and wisdom? Are we going to get rid of all the scientific laboratories of the world? Will there be no more technology, no more transport systems in the future? Of course there will be. There is an enormous need in the world for the things we have, but we overdo it. We have too many of the same things. Or some of us have.

The treasure of the past is always of use. The great universities, the great libraries, surely must continue. How much richer this world would be if the library of Alexandria had not been destroyed. Can you imagine the teaching, the esoteric lore, the philosophical experience, which, along with probably a lot of rubbish, stood in the library of Alexandria and which is now lost to the world? If people had access to the library of the Vatican, you would be surprised at the teaching which could be revealed.

What is it doing in the Vatican? Why is it not made available to humanity? We need the past. We do not come from nowhere. This present incarnation, with our present ray structure, present ideas, hopes and fears, is a result of our past. No one has no past. Almost every one has a past so long, so distant, that we cannot even remember it. Because we cannot remember it, we do not believe that it existed.

We must retain the present treasures — the best aspects of life today, the things that we have built up, like our educational process (not the present educational ideas, but the educational *process*), transport systems, communication systems like radio and television but advanced to a degree that you would hardly call it the same invention. Everything comes out of something. Before electricity we had gas; before gas, candles; before candles, rush tapers, and we had to keep a fire going all the time otherwise we had no light. Following electricity will be another form, using energy directly from the sun. We will have all the power we need. That is only possible on the basis of what we already have. Technology stems from technology which stems from previous technology. Science is knowing. You do not throw away what you know until you have acquired something new.

We will come to understand the power of psychic energy, inherent in every human being. Consider a photograph of Maitreya in Nairobi. A second before that was taken, He was not there. Suddenly He is there. That is a marvel. Then He disappears again. That is another marvel. It is not a one-off marvel but a capacity, a way of being able to act, totally within the laws of life, and demonstrable on a wide scale.

If we want to go to Australia, we will just think ourselves there — and think ourselves back again. We will move around the world in this marvellous fashion, saving time and energy.

We have a big, heavy suitcase and we want to move it from A to B. We just remove gravity from it and we can bounce it like a ball. Everything that is imaginable in the world is possible. We will demonstrate abilities like that. These are divine powers, not tricks. When Sai Baba makes *vibhuti*, or a ring or bracelet, it is not a trick. People who do not believe in this quality of human life say it is a trick. But He does it because He is demonstrating the divine powers. He is not divine in any different way from you and me; we all have these same powers. They are potential in every human being and will one day be demonstrated by everyone.

The quality of our lives will depend on our adaptability to the necessity to change, and the direction that change takes. Our idea of science will broaden. You cannot have science without religion, for example. By religion, I do not mean a set of beliefs but an understanding of the laws of life and love. That is what religion is. It is not taught by the churches because they do not understand it. They think that religion is to do with belief but it is the science of the human spirit. Science means knowing, and it is the knowledge of the qualities of the divine life in humanity that creates what we call science and religion. They are one and the same.

The new science will depend on the religious understanding of the laws of life and love. The new religion will depend on what we would more exoterically call science. The split between the two is artificial, and was in fact brought about by the religious groups because the growing science seemed to question the validity of the religious outlook on life. It only questions religion in so far as the religion is based on belief. But it should not be based on belief but on knowing the laws of life and love. Science is to do with the implementation of the laws of life and love. When these two come together, we will have the marvels of the future.

Would you like to enlarge on the construction of the new civilization? (January/February 1994)
It will come as a result of the transformation in humanity of the sense of who we are: the development of the sense of interdependence, and the correct distribution of the energy of the Will — in particular of the Will to Good, which creates right human relations.

The new civilization, based on right relationship, is the next predestined, planned advance for humanity, on every level — politically, internationally, socially, scientifically, culturally, in education, and so on. Eventually, the education of the young will go forward in a very systematized way. The science of the antahkarana will be an intrinsic part of the new education which will create the culture from which the civilization stems.

You do not have a civilization and then on top of that build a culture. We build a culture through the work of the disciples and initiates of the world: from their ideas and the ideals stemming from them, the civilization is built. The 'ideas-people' are the initiates and the disciples of the Kingdom of God, of the Hierarchy. They do the initial work of promoting the ideas and ideals which are gradually stepped down until they reach the level of the educational institutions and so on, and a whole new civilization is created. And it can be in a relatively very short period of time.

If we knew the scientific, educational and religious endeavour of the coming age we would say: "How can we possibly bring humanity, as we are now, to that stage?" But if you think about it, we take for granted ideas and concepts which 150 years ago would have been unthinkable, would never have entered the mind of any but the most advanced thinker. Everything that we know and think and talk about today is relatively new, and so it is with the New Age concepts, ideas and relationships. The next 150 years will see a transformation in these departments which would stagger the imagination of anyone living today.

When you come into incarnation at that time, you will find a changed world — not just changed in the outer sense, politically and economically, but in the sense that humanity will already have reached the stage where vast numbers are consciously creating the antahkarana, the bridge between the personality and the soul: this will become the ideal for every individual, so deeply will the scientific idea of connectedness go, with the Christ and the Masters in the world, teaching along these lines. All these ideas which seem so abstract today will become powerfully anchored on the physical plane. The incoming 7th-ray energy and the fact of the Christ's presence and that of the Masters will make this so.

Sai Baba says that before every birth there has to be a death; before every new age there has to be the death of the old age — *can you explain this?* (October 1993)

Everything evolves and dies and is reborn; this happens throughout the whole process of evolution. We come into incarnation, grow up, evolve a bit, die, then come back again and evolve a bit more. We do this hundreds of thousands of times until we are ready for the five initiations which lead to Mastery. Every time we come into incarnation we start again at the point reached in the last life. The soul creates a new body round the one permanent atom, physical, astral and mental, which remains from life to life. These atoms vibrate at exactly the rate that the individual reached in the previous incarnation.

This is true for all living things — nothing stands still in the whole of cosmos. From all that has been created and perfected in this solar system another solar system, the third of three, will be created at a higher turn of the spiral.

This is the nature of all being: there cannot be life without the death of the one before it — death is simply a process of renewal. We have to understand that death is only the death of the physical, and that is renewable. We have all had countless physical incarnations to come to the point where we are now, and we will have a great many more to become Masters. The process is inevitable, however long we take over it. Likewise, each new civilization is built on the ruins of the preceding one. Old forms become crystallized, bereft of energy, and necessarily die. New energies come with each new age and need new forms through which to express themselves. Humanity responds to the new energies and ideas and remakes the culture and civilization, age after age.

WORLD PEACE AND BROTHERHOOD

United Nations

What does the building of the temple in the city of Jerusalem really mean? (January/February 1996)

This question came up when I was on a radio programme with a Roman Catholic priest, a fundamentalist Baptist minister, and a rabbi. The rabbi took it as the building of the temple, literally, in Jerusalem, and when that was built the Messiah would come. There are plans already made in the hands of the Israeli Government for the rebuilding of the temple. The blueprints are ready, they could go to work tomorrow. They want to make sure that Jerusalem means the head of the Jewish state and only the Jewish state. This is why they have not gone forward. They know it would be a real *faux pas* in the present situation. They are waiting until gentler times to do it, but they could start tomorrow.

Nobody seemed to know too well what the building of the temple was, so I put in my penny's worth. I said that the building of the temple was a symbolic statement. It does not involve the rebuilding of the physical temple. Jerusalem means "the city of peace." When the world is at peace, the Messiah comes, the Christ returns to the world. That is what Maitreya said in 1945: when a measure of peace had been restored, He would return. World peace had been established, even if later threatened by the Cold War. But in a world sense, peace had come. There are still many small wars today, but they do not on the whole, except in the Middle East, threaten world peace. With the ending of the Cold War, even that threat has receded. The building of the temple is the building of the Body of Christ; when the Christ Principle is manifesting through all people, whether they call it the Christ Principle or not. When that energy, embodied by Maitreya, flowing through the hearts of all humanity, creates peace in the world, we have the building of the temple in the city of peace.

Does Hierarchy have a plan for World Government? (September 1993)

World government is not an aim of Hierarchy for this world. The aim (we already have it in embryo) is for the United Nations to be the debating chamber and the arbiter for the world, so that all disputes, on every level, can be aired, debated and resolved without war. It should, for the moment, be the 'police force' of the world, and collect enough money, troops, military wherewithal, to make sure that peace is kept in all the dangerous pockets of the world. This is essential, because the most destructive weapons of war are so freely available now to 'adventurers' and demagogues.

Do you think that the United Nations will be replaced by another organization for peace? (June 1994)

No, I do not, nor do I believe it necessary. The United Nations is slowly coming into its own as the maintainer of peace in the world. At present, it is reluctant to accept the role of world policeman, and governments everywhere balk at the cost involved. But until world peace is assured through sharing and the implementation of justice, such a responsibility must be accepted. Its future role is to become, not a world government, but the world parliament, where problems can be discussed and resolved peacefully.

Do you think the UN should become more involved in the internal affairs of countries like the former Yugoslavia to help halt the bloodshed there, as they did in Somalia? (July/August 1993)

Very much so. I believe that the UN has a very definite role to play. I am appalled and deeply aggrieved that the UN and Europe stood by and watched the fratricide that has occurred in Croatia and again in Bosnia. The atrocities could have been prevented by a more positive stance by the UN. The UN and the Europeans should have been in there in the very beginning, forcing the Serbs to toe the line and bring about a peaceful solution to what are real problems — independence, minority peoples, and so on. These problems should be talked out in the context of the UN. That is its role. The UN has to grasp that and make it a reality. It has very much missed the bus on this.

(1) Will the United Nations be the governing body of the world, or (2) will there be another organization and (3) will Maitreya 'head up' this organization? (November 1995)

(1) There are no plans for a one-world government. The UN will become (as it is now to some extent) a debating chamber to air and settle international problems. (2) No other such organization is planned. (3) Maitreya will not 'head up' any organization but will act only in His capacity as World Teacher.

Where has the United Nations gone wrong in trying to solve the Bosnian crisis — how would Hierarchy solve it? (April 1995)

My Master wrote an article, 'The Mantle of Power' (*Share International,* June 1993), which we sent as a press release to media around the world. He called for the creation of a United Nations which had 'teeth', a military potential which could cope with situations like Bosnia, Rwanda, and those arising in the Soviet Union. Without a strong United Nations we will have a series of such wars.

Men like Milosevic in Serbia and Karajdic in Bosnia are adventurers who see opportunities in the weakness of the United Nations and the various imbalances in the world to create situations in which they can gain territory and power — power-hungry men. They have taken advantage of the breakup of the Soviet Union, which has released a tide of nationalism and an aspiration towards self-expression in the various peoples, to gain that power. They are authoritarian, fascist-type dictators, not really concerned with the national aspirations of the people.

The only way to counter that is to have a United Nations with an army powerful enough, supported by all the nations, who must give enough men and armaments. They would not have to fight a war, they would simply have to be there and be ready to act and so prevent these particular situations arising, which otherwise will continue to arise around the world.

It is not without importance that when the United Nations threatened to bomb the Bosnian Serb forces on the slopes around

Sarajevo the Serbs withdrew, and Sarajevo suddenly became a "safe" area. That could have happened all over Bosnia, but the powers — the British, French and the Germans in particular — are too concerned with their own petty, political problems, their own economies. The last thing they are prepared to do is put in the money and the forces which would allow a correct reaction to the adventure of the Serbs in Bosnia.

The United Nations has to be powerful enough to act in the name of humanity. The dangers are too great today — only one of these adventurers needs a nuclear bomb, which can be bought cheaply in the Soviet Union, for the situation to become very dangerous indeed.

Editor's note: For the reader's convenience, we print here the aforementioned article by Benjamin Creme's Master.

The Mantle of Power
by the Master —, through Benjamin Creme

There are many today who fear that an escalation of the fighting in former Yugoslavia will lead, inevitably, to a third and catastrophic world conflict. The Balkans has replaced the Middle East as the key to Armageddon in the thinking of those who, interpreting wrongly their scriptures, hold such expectations before the world. Did they but realize how inadequate is their understanding of the forces now at work throughout the planet they would save themselves and those who heed them much heartache and worry.

Fear of such an eventuality is behind the present inaction, however rationalized, of many nations, particularly the United States. Such fear paralyses decision-making and leads to confusion and doubt.

Needed now is leadership, firm and clear. The Assembly of Nations, hesitant and divided, should voice aloud the concern of all peoples for the victims of fratricide and authorize the economic and military measures which will bring it to an end. Nothing is to be gained by further delay. Sanctions, alone, will not be sufficient to force the issue and halt the momentum of carnage; military forces, commensurate with the task, should be made available and ready for use. Only thus will the power-hungry leaders call a halt to the slaughter. Only thus will their counterparts around the world, riding on the aspirations of their peoples, take pause for thought.

Soon, the nations will come to realize the necessity for corporate action in solving the many problems which beset the world from day to day. Little as it may have seemed likely in the recent past, it is these shared problems and anxieties which are drawing the nations together in mutual preservation. So dangerous, now, are the forces available to errant groups and individuals that only concerted action by the nations can hold them in check.

Gradually, slowly, step by hesitant step, the United Nations is coming into its own, donning bravely the responsible mantle of power. It represents the rallying point for the highest aspirations of men for justice and peace and must be prepared to act to ensure their preservation. Nothing less will guarantee a future free from the threat of fratricidal war. War, today, must be made illegal and the instigators answerable to Law. The nations must be prepared to enforce the law and to accept the price of action. Until true and lasting peace is assured such policing of the world remains the sole recourse.

Changes

Meanwhile, much of good pertains among the mayhem. Far-reaching changes are making their presence felt in all areas, and a new realism is gradually dawning in the minds of governments and peoples. The old glamours, though strong, are gradually losing their grip, and a healthier sense of purpose colours the new approach to the pressing problems of the time. That these problems will be solved is not in doubt.

(*Share International,* June 1993)

Change in Political Structure

Do you see different types of political structures evolving in the coming time to meet the growing needs of the people for self-

81

determination, participation, and political freedom? (July/ August 1993)

We have witnessed the end of imposed 'communism'. I do not believe that true communism was ever tried; in the Soviet Union they had a form of state capitalism. Naturally, people objected to it because they saw the bosses, the élite of the Communist Party, a tiny minority, enjoying a standard of life which nobody else had. People were envious, and only too glad to see the end of it. They were straitened in their circumstances, living drab, colourless lives without variety. You must have colour and variety in life. They did not have it, and they are not going to have it under the regime of Mr Yeltsin. He is imposing a programme based on market forces which has failed in the West.

We are in the middle of a major economic crisis in the West which is going to reflect itself in the former Soviet Union. The Russian people are now feeling the pains of a market forces economy. Like people everywhere, they are seeking the freedom to express their livingness, and this they are not getting. They will not get it through capitalism any more than through communism. It will come through a blending of the best of capitalism and of communism — a social democracy or democratic socialism in which that which pertains to the community as a whole is owned and administered by the community as a whole, and that which pertains to the individual is left to the private enterprise of the individual to develop to the best of his ability. It is not either/or; it is a fusion of these two.

You mentioned George Bush and his 'new world order', which I have always taken to mean a world government with a central banking system. Would Maitreya's new world order involve anything central like that, such as a Federal Europe, or a decentralization of government and money control? (November 1996)

The aim of Hierarchy will be to inspire humanity. They will not put into place any kind of organization or government or economic system; it is up to us to do that. They will advise and guide. Among Their disciples are some who have been taught the best means of producing the best results, and by the normal democratic processes these people will be voted into positions of authority and power. So the changes will take place through humanity but the original concept will have come, through those disciples, from Hierarchy. In this way humanity's free will is not infringed.

The aim, you will find, will be the greatest degree of decentralization rather than centralization, and the greatest possible participation of all the people in their own government. It is participation that makes true democracy. In the world today there is no true democracy; we have elected governments but there is no true participation of the people except by putting a vote in a box. The aim in Europe is to centralize and create a federal state. This is not advised by Hierarchy. The Common Market of Europe has the nod of approval of Hierarchy but not as a federated state of Europe. Maitreya forecast that just as the Soviet Union would break up and become a federation of individual sovereign states (which it did), the United States is moving in the same direction, and more power will accrue to the individual states and less to central government.

In this world, small is beautiful, truly, and we have to simplify our way of life. Decentralization by its very nature will lead to a more human type of organization on a scale more related to the needs of people, because only people know what they need. Most governments pay very little attention to the true needs of the people — but to what they visualize as the needs of the *nation,* mainly for power and prestige. The needs of the people are seldom met, not even in the most democratic countries, because there is no participation. The tendency, therefore, will be towards decentralization and participation.

Do you see a shift toward decentralization occurring in various parts of the world and, if so, how does that coincide with the globalization of problems and the need for global approaches to solving them? (July/August 1993)

I would not say that this is occurring, but that it is the ideal towards which we should move. The role of governments is to create conditions in which people can live in peace with enough food, adequate shelter, health care, education, and so on. It is not the role of governments to impose one ideology on the people. That has been the case up to now, whether that ideology was communism, democracy, capitalism, or fascism. That time is past. We are seeing the end of political indoctrination and totalitarianism. The need of people for freedom, self-advancement and self-determination should be worked out on a local level through participation in local government. The only way that people can influence the events of their life on a national scale is through influencing local government. You have to have a level of government in which people actually can be involved.

Most people in so-called democratic countries vote for local and national representatives. But if people are really participating on a local level, their needs can be met locally. The national government should not interfere on the local level. Here the more conservative governments have the answer, in that they do not want to get involved in the day-to-day managing of local affairs, at least theoretically. In practice, the opposite tends to be the case, for political reasons. In the UK, our present Conservative government is the most centralizing we have had, certainly this century; local government is strapped by the central government in almost every aspect of its action. There is almost no local government *per se*, almost no participation. Without participation, there can be no self-determination. Self-determination, self-expression in determining how one's life will be lived, which is true liberty, does not exist in any real sense anywhere in the world.

Will participation be a key to the future types of political structures? (July/August 1993)

I think it is essential. Without it, there can be no liberty. Liberty and freedom are dependent on participation. It does not take professionals, alone, to run the country. It does not take professionals to run local affairs. The people themselves know what kind of local government they need for housing, health care, education, and so on. The role of national government is to organize itself in relation to other nations, to oversee defence, transport, and the overall well-being of the nation, and so create the conditions in which local government can get on with the job of realizing the potential of people locally.

Will we see more non-politicians like Vaclav Havel coming to power? He was the playwright who became President of Czechoslovakia. (July/August 1993)

I believe we shall. It is precisely from the non-professional politicians that we will find the leaders of the people. The people have enormous untapped resources but have never been given an opportunity to express this potential. If you create the structures on a local level which are sufficiently open to allow all types — artists, writers, housewives, teachers, engineers, playwrights, and so on — to speak for the people as a whole, the needs of the people will be given expression. In parliamentary government, the political and economic laws laid down will allow the people's needs to be given expression on a national scale. You need two tiers of government, local and national. Both are essential. One should not be seen as more important than the other.

Will we be more involved in local communities, wherever we live, and more human energy be directed to the arts? (May 1994)

There will be greater leisure for humanity, and so a greater awareness of who and what we are as souls, and a very strong impulse to demonstrate in one way or another the divinity of which we have become aware. This means, of course, a huge educational programme throughout the world, to lift the billions of uneducated and under-educated people to a level where they can really take themselves seriously, see their worth, see that every single person is unique and has a part to play. You will find a growing participation at all levels in not only government but the general administration of life in every country; and a flowering of the arts, especially as the 4th ray of Harmony comes into 'incarnation' early next century.

(1) With a growing recognition and acceptance of Maitreya's presence in the world, will there be a growing acceptance of

liberal ideas (Liberalism) which will be followed over time by a turn towards a peaceful and more spiritualized form of that body of ideas called Anarchist-Communism or Libertarian Socialism such as that teaching now being given out by individuals such as Noam Chomsky (born 7 December 1928 in Philadelphia, USA)? (2) If they are to be related to any 'ism' at all (and I know that He doesn't approve of 'isms'), will Maitreya's political, economic and social teachings primarily resemble most closely those of Anarchist-Communism (or Libertarian Socialism)? (November 1995)

One of the most pressing problems in the political/economic life of humanity is the growing polarization between 'right' and 'left' political parties. The capitalistic right is being forced to change and adapt to the changing world situation in which the recognition of our essential interdependence is growing apace, and when governments are losing control of their currencies (and therefore of their economic viability) to a group of international financial gamblers. "Market forces" dominate the thinking of those administrators in charge of social services like health care, education, cultural activities and recreation. The *quality* of life is ebbing away in the name of business efficiency.

The communistic left, on the other hand, with the demise of the Soviet Union, is at present rudderless and unsure of itself, with no clear answers to the activities of the rapacious states and individuals who now run the economic world. There is no future for humanity in the present situation. No political party, left or right, by itself can remedy the present crisis. I believe that Maitreya will align Himself with no party, no 'ism'. As He has put it, a cart needs two wheels to move. In political/economic terms that means the bringing together of the best of capitalism and the best of socialism — a new social democracy or democratic socialism.

It should be remembered, however, that Hierarchy has no intention of imposing a one-world system. There will probably be many variants of a general structure as individual nations make their own choices.

What is the future of nation states? Are they going on or will they perish from the earth? (September 1996)

A nation, like an individual person, is an entity with particular purposes and ray structure. As such, they will continue to exist but serving the greater cause of world harmony and interdependence rather than, as now, their own self-interests.

Will Europe become one nation? (October 1993)

No, I do not believe it will. Each nation will keep its own particular identity, ray structure (energetic structure), and its own occult purpose.

Certain nations have important parts to play in the evolution of humanity, and one of those is the United Kingdom. Britain is a base where a great experiment in relationships among different ethnic groups is under way; the plan is that they should (eventually) live together in total harmony but as distinct ethnic groups — not, as in America, through intermarriage, becoming one very interesting and varied non-ethnic entity which we call 'America'. In America, the experiment is that of many races mixing together.

In Russia the experiment was that of separate nations living together as one but retaining their autonomy, to form the Soviet Union. The experiment will continue in a different way now, and the Soviet Union will be replaced by another Union — it has already been called a "Commonwealth" of states, and it will continue as a Commonwealth — recent events are simply a hiccup in the evolution of that great country. Many problems still face the Russian people, in particular in the growth towards democracy.

Do you think the European Union is a good political change? (November 1994)

All that aims towards unity is a good thing in the long term, but it depends on the basis. If it is simply a businessman's club as for many, for example, in the UK, it would appear to be, then I do not think it has any great value. If it is a way of uniting Britain and the other countries of Europe, in particular Germany and France who have been at war over and over again for a century, and is a guarantee of peace in Europe, then it could be a good thing. But the principle of sharing has to pertain; as it is, it is of no value to the world. It is greedy and selfish — producing butter, cheese and meat mountains through huge subsidies to the French, Dutch and Danish farmers, but doing nothing for the people of Bangladesh, Rwanda or Somalia. It has done nothing for Bosnia. If it had acted as a political, not just an economic, union, there would not have been the horrors of Bosnia: the hundreds of thousands of deaths and rapes, the displacement of peoples, the millions of refugees now all over Europe. It has done nothing of any consequence in that regard.

Is French Guyana a nation, a future nation, or a part of France for ever? (April 1994)

A nation and, one day, a free, independent nation.

In the Third World a lot of the countries have been administered by the Western World in times gone by, and now they can't arrange their own government to suit the people. How can Maitreya make them alter their administration? (May 1995)

Maitreya will not 'make' anyone do anything. He does not even make those closest to Him announce His presence. There are people around Maitreya who know as well as I do that He is in the world but they do not come out and say so, perhaps because they do not want the publicity, the encroachment on their lives that would follow. It is very disturbing to have the media intruding in your life, which would be the direct result of their making their experience known. If some of the people who are around Him today did speak out, He would be known tomorrow.

Maitreya will show us what is wrong and stimulate us to make the changes; but we have to *want* these changes. They have to be made *gladly* by us because we see that that is the only thing to do, not because a superman tells us what to do. Anyone who has that notion of Maitreya is totally wrong. He is a teacher, an adviser; we have to save ourselves through the acceptance of the teachings. And put them into effect.

If we in the developed world are reluctant to make the sacrifices necessary for all people everywhere to live decent, civilized lives, then we will destroy ourselves. Not as punishment, but the direct result of the Law of Cause and Effect. If we do the right thing, we will transform the world; if we continue as we are, and do not see or accept the need for the changes, then they will not happen.

Maitreya says: "Nothing happens by itself." We have talked about 'brotherhood' for thousands of years, but it is only a vague ideal, still sitting up there on the astral plane — lovely, beautiful ideas of Love, Brotherhood, Justice. The *reality* is separation, greed, misery, pain, suffering, by millions of humanity; the vision is real but not until it comes down onto the physical plane and we make it real. "Man must act and implement his will," Maitreya says (Message No. 31); so it is up to us. Everything is up to us.

Are you saying that the power in essence will be from the people, and not from any teacher like Maitreya? (July/August 1993)

Exactly. Maitreya does not come with power. He comes with the power of inspiration and guidance, but not with autocratic power. He says that from now on governments everywhere will be by the people, for the people. We are already witnessing it. Look at what has happened in the former Soviet Union. It is chaos at the moment, but who brought down the Berlin Wall? Who opened up the Soviet Union to *glasnost*? Mr Gorbachev was mainly responsible for ending the Cold War and for *glasnost* in the Soviet Union. Of all the world leaders, he is the one most responsive to the mental impress of the Lord Maitreya.

We are witnessing the galvanizing of humanity, the people of the world, to take upon themselves responsibility for their own lives. Over the last few years, that has been happening all over the world. The dictatorships of the world are going. That is why the Soviet Union broke up — not from the collapse of communism, but from the collapse of political totalitarianism, which is something else.

We have certainly heard the people's voice in the last few years, perhaps most dramatically in Eastern Europe and the former Soviet Union. But at the same time the people's voice has been muted, if you will, in many areas — Yugoslavia, Somalia,

Liberia and Haiti come to mind — where the social and political order has broken down. How are we to interpret these seemingly contradictory trends in world affairs today? (July/August 1993)

Everything that we are seeing is the result of our response to great energies, mainly cosmic in source, which are playing upon humanity. These energies call forth various responses; humanity does not respond uniformly. Each one of us responds, conditioned by our own separate interests, ambitions and desires, individual and/or nationalistic. Hence, you have the plethora of nationalistic movements and ethnic demands now coming to the fore.

Looked at from the point of view of Maitreya, and the Spiritual Hierarchy of which He is the head, these movements and demands are legitimate but distorted reactions to the incoming energies. The energies are engendering a desire for freedom which now permeates the world. This desire is applauded when acted upon to overthrow an oppressive political regime as in the Soviet Union, China, Romania, and so on. But it is condemned, and of course rightly so, as the instigator of atrocities, fratricide and war in Yugoslavia and elsewhere. The same energies produce different responses.

Would it be safe to say that, given these new influences, the general political trend in the world is a positive one? Are we headed in the right direction? (July/August 1993)

In the short term, no; in the longer term, yes. If we had no outside help, humanity would be in dire straits because nearly everything that we are doing — politically, economically, and socially — is headed in the wrong direction. Our actions are leading inevitably to a breakdown of this civilization. All of our structures — political, economic, and social — are increasingly based on commercialization, whose agency is market forces. The major 'god' of the present day world is the market, that is, competition, which is based on greed. This approach is bringing humanity and this civilization to the very verge of self-destruction. But for the presence in the world of the Lord Maitreya and His group of Masters, I would fear a very bleak future indeed for humanity. I posit a very positive future for us, not because we are so wise, but because the Masters are wise.

It seems that in the very recent past, with the end of the Cold War and so on, the political situation looked so positive. What has happened? (July/August 1993)

It is not the political pressure; it is the economic pressure. The major divisions in the world today are economic. We are witnessing the end of three great totalitarianisms: political, economic, and eventually, religious. We have seen the beginning of the demise of political totalitarianism with the opening of the former Soviet Union by President Gorbachev's programmes of *glasnost* and *perestroika* (under, I may say, the inspiration and guidance of the Lord Maitreya). This has created an entirely new situation in the world, and has inspired other groups to try to emulate that gesture towards freedom. This is the beginning of the end of political totalitarianism.

Economic totalitarianism still has the world in its grip. The major exponents of this totalitarianism are the G7, industrialized nations with the United States at their head. The developed countries usurp and greedily waste three-quarters of the world's food and 83 per cent of all other resources. The developing world, the so-called Third World, where almost three-quarters of the world's population live, must make do with one quarter of the world's food and not more than 17 per cent of the rest of the world's resources. We cannot expect three-quarters of the world's population to put up with that situation for ever. This economic imbalance is leading the world to the verge of economic destruction.

With governments — especially the US Government — in concert with, and acting on behalf of, the monied interests engineering and perpetuating wars, and with poverty and involution actually attacking progressive 'Third World' countries, what does Maitreya suggest as correct action by the rest of us — I am a US citizen — who are equally at the mercy of these criminals? (January/February 1994)

I have no information on Maitreya's view of this but I am sure He would suggest that you exercise your democratic right and vote-in a more just administration. You should also make known, through the available media resources, your non-acceptance of the particular governmental acts with which you disagree. In other words, get more involved, participate. Broadly speaking, in a democratic society, we get the governments we deserve who reach and retain power if only through our neglect of our democratic rights.

Has the Master who has recently come into Cairo had anything to do with the new, very positive moves for peace between the Arabs and Israelis? (October 1993)

Yes, indeed. It is largely His influence (some of those involved in the negotiations, at least on the Arab side, are His disciples) on the minds and hearts of both sides, which has brought about the present breakthrough in attitude and the abandonment of the hitherto fixed positions. This has made sane and necessary compromise possible. There is a long way to go yet before peaceful coexistence is a reality, but the first (and probably the most difficult) steps have been taken.

The newspapers say there might be a cease-fire in Sri Lanka. Is this due to the work of Maitreya or one of the Masters? (March 1995)

Neither. It is the logical outcome of a long-drawn-out effort to end a totally useless war. It is the response of the Sri Lanka Government, the Tamil population and "the Tigers", as they are called, to the energy which brings about co-operation and compromise — the same energy which has brought about other agreements like that between Sinn Fein and the British, the Palestinians and the Israelis, the East and West Germans, black and white South Africans, and so on.

This is the energy of equilibrium which Maitreya radiates into the world. It comes from a great Cosmic Avatar called The Spirit of Peace or Equilibrium. He works with the law of action and reaction which, as you may know, are opposite and equal. The effect of this energy is to transform the violence, discord and turmoil in the world into its opposite, so that we will enter a period of tranquillity, peace and poise — mental and emotional — in exact proportion to the existing turmoil, violence and hatred. People are responding to this energy. It is not that Maitreya is directing His attention to them; they are reacting to an energy which has been pouring into the world for many years.

President Bush changed course significantly when he offered to supply approximately 30,000 US troops as part of a UN-sponsored military operation in Somalia. (1) Was this dramatic change perhaps inspired by Maitreya (2) If so, in what way did this inspiration take place? (3) Has Maitreya given experiences to any of the Somali 'warlords' to encourage a peaceful solution to the problems in Somalia? (January/February 1993)

(1) No. It was inspired, I believe, by Mr Bush's desire to be remembered for at least one positive, humanitarian action. It is significant that he waited until the presidential election was lost and won before taking any action at all. That left him with everything to gain and nothing to risk or lose by committing the US troops to the UN operation in Somalia. (3) No.

Since the Earth Summit in Rio in 1992, there have been many international conferences on global issues, including the Cairo Population Conference, and most recently the Social Development Summit in Copenhagen. From the Hierarchical point of view, are such gatherings useful for solving global problems, or do they just amount to a lot of speeches? (September 1995)

Yes, they are very useful — and indications that humanity is itself seeking solutions.

I was most interested in reading the Editorial in the latest (September) **Share International** *regarding Sarajevo, where Mr Creme's Master's call for "economic and military measures" parallels the Master DK's belief when writing through Alice Bailey in the early years of the Second World War.*

My questions are: (1) Can this belief be applied to the Tibetan people who have heeded the Dalai Lama's teaching for over 40 years in not taking up arms against the Chinese? The

93

Master DK's words "... the forces of evil do not understand gentle measures" would certainly seem to be relevant to the brutality of the Chinese occupation. (2) Given the decades of suffering, can the Dalai Lama's argument for passive resistance be sustainable? (October 1993)

(1) Most certainly this belief can be (and, to my mind, in 1959 should have been) applied to the tragic Tibetan situation. It is to our shame that not one significant international voice was raised to condemn the invasion of Tibet by the Chinese in 1959. Very quickly, the maps of the world showed Tibet as a province of China; the UN remained silent and inert. Since then, every attempted uprising or demonstration by the courageous Tibetan people has been ruthlessly repressed by the Chinese military.

However, it is not a call for military heroics, much in evidence already, by the Bosnian majority in the face of Serbian aggression which my Master has given, but a call to the United Nations to accept the responsibility for the necessary economic and military action which alone will end this conflict with justice and, most importantly, prevent its repetition in other parts of the world.

(2) There is no way in which 5-6 million unarmed Tibetans, spread across one of the most inhospitable areas on earth, can engage in serious contention with the powerful Chinese army now occupying Tibet. Only international action by the UN on a huge scale could effectively intervene. It would be wishful thinking to expect such action at this time. In these circumstances the only *practical* action for the Tibetan people at present is passive resistance as advocated by the Dalai Lama. Change must (and I believe will) come from transformations within China, and, I am certain, from Maitreya's public emergence.

Will Britain finally leave Ireland? (March 1994)

Maitreya, through one of His associates, has said that the British army will withdraw from Northern Ireland. When you say "Britain" I think you have to say "the British army", because the Ulster people will not leave Ireland; they are Ulster people living in the Five Counties, and will for the most part want to remain there, as part of Britain.

I see reunification of Ireland in the long term, but my Master has said that it will not happen in the short term. (He said this before the present approaches.) I think it will be some time before the diehards of both sides find the ability to compromise. It will take Maitreya to cut a way through the terrible, bigoted, intolerant situation. But it is happening in the Middle East; if it can happen there, it can happen anywhere.

You can imagine the impact Maitreya, accepted as the World Teacher by all nations and all religious organizations, will have on the problems of the world. It will be very difficult for the men of anger and the gun to continue their killing.

Is the British Royal Family going to be demolished? (September 1995)

If the British people demolish it, it will be demolished. As far as the Hierarchy are concerned, They have no hand in it. The Masters do not rule our lives. They do not come to take over the world and to put even a better world in its place. They come to inspire humanity with the needs of the world for sharing, justice, correct human relationship, the manifestation of love — but it is up to us: we have free will. The speed of change is entirely in our hands, and that includes monarchies — or not monarchies. Whatever we want, we make.

Every nation, like every individual, is governed by certain energies called Rays, as souls and as personalities. The soul ray of a nation is demonstrated by the initiates of the nation and the personality by the mass of people in the nation. That gives the individual identity, colour, the uniqueness, to each nation, and that will be preserved: if we want it one way we will keep it that way, if we want it changed we will change it. The free will of humanity is never infringed by Hierarchy — even if we would like it to be so. They will never do that because we would not grow. Maitreya says: "Do not let anyone take away your free will; it is a divine gift. Use it and manifest it." The trouble is, we *misuse* it. Our troubles in the world are due to a misuse of our free will.

95

Can I ask for equitable treatment of North Korea (re its nuclear potential) and not have to listen to the (US) media speculate on a strike against their plant? (July 1994)

You can ask. In a democracy the responsibility lies with the people.

When will we see a break in the storm of current events? (July/August 1993)

We are coming to a point of crisis. Very soon that crisis will reach its peak, and we will see the denouement. From that tremendous critical manifestation will emerge a new society, a new life for humanity, based on entirely new and more spiritual ideas.

There has been much talk of forgiveness and demanding apologies from former enemies for atrocities committed during the Second World War. (1) Should we forgive and forget? (2) Should former enemies be expected to apologize? (3) What is an appropriate attitude towards countries, now often economic allies but once deadly enemies? (4) Is it possible to put the blame on one section of humanity? (5) Surely we, as still evolving beings, share our honour and dishonour? (October 1995)

(1) Yes. (2) No. (3) Forgiving and forgetting. (4) No. (5) Yes.

If Masters were present throughout history, how could They stand by and watch happenings like the Holocaust, wars, the Inquisition, the decimation of humanity in many different ways, without helping? (January/February 1996)

They did not stand by and watch it happen. There has never been a war, a holocaust, pain or suffering of any group in which the Masters did not help that group to the greatest extent allowed by the Law of Karma. They are not allowed simply to take away the results of humanity's actions. The Law of Cause and Effect, which is the Law of Karma, binds the Masters as it binds us.

We have the power, individually and as a group — as humanity — to change the way we act. It is we who create holocausts and wars, who involve whole groups in assassination, murder, rape, pillage and the rest. We created the Inquisition —

the cruelty of the Inquisition is the cruelty of humanity itself. It came out of the fanaticism which is the direct result of the misuse of the energies of Pisces. The fanatical belief in their own ideal created the Holocaust, the Inquisition, and almost every war. Some wars have been for gain, but the wars which involved an ideology were the result of a fanatical belief that a particular ideal was the only one fit for humanity. That has nothing to do with the Masters.

The Masters are perfect. Their involvement with us is by grace: They do not have to be here, They have finished with this world and are here simply to serve the Plan of Evolution, which involves us. But we are not the only part of that evolution — there is the animal kingdom, the vegetable and mineral kingdoms, the great angelic or devic evolution, so that what the Masters have to do vis-à-vis humanity is only a tiny fraction of Their work. In so far as They are able — under law — to intervene and prevent suffering of humanity, so They do.

Since He is so concerned about hunger in the world, what was Maitreya doing while six million Jews were dying in gas chambers? (October 1994)
Throughout the war (1914-1945) — from the point of view of Hierarchy that is one war, which went underground in 1918 and re-emerged in 1939 — Maitreya and His group of Masters aided in every way, *within the law governing human free will*, the Allied forces against the Axis powers. His decision to emerge into the world was arrived at and announced in 1945, precisely *because* the Axis powers had been defeated with His help.

MAITREYA'S VIEW: THE POLITICS OF THE NEW AGE

Interview with Maitreya's Associate
by Patricia Pitchon

During a discussion in September 1993 with Patricia Pitchon, Maitreya's associate explained Maitreya's views on the politics of the New Age, as well as impending changes in world affairs.

The Politics of the New Age — Power politics will give way to the politics of food, shelter and protection. This will spread the world over. Socialism and capitalism will converge. They are the two wheels which are essential. Politics cannot function with only one wheel.

The UK — Although we may not realize it fully, the political spectrum is now changing. The old models cannot provide the answers. There will be a more pragmatic 'mix' at local levels to try to solve the problems of people in the area.

The implication here is that confrontational or old-style adversarial attitudes and hard ideologies will give way to consensus-building among a variety of political tendencies at local levels. Indeed, this is already happening in a striking manner in some local councils where co-operation of this type yields better results in solving local problems.

Northern Ireland — Despite all appearances to the contrary, there will be changes. Current processes leading to positive changes are not reported in the media. There will be greater autonomy and communities will take greater control of local affairs in a more satisfactory way. Although the UK will be responsible for overall defence, its influence in other areas will lessen. At the local level, the people will be represented in a type of regional Parliament in which both Protestants and Catholics will be represented. Better links between them will develop. Regional representation in a Parliament will also develop in Wales and Scotland.

Russia — In Russia both Boris Yeltsin and the forces opposing him will have to work together. The politics of confrontation will have to give way to the politics of food, shelter and protection for the Russian people. Boris Yeltsin cannot rule by force and by decrees. Many in the military are behind him only up to a certain point. Boris Yeltsin has put his faith and trust in the armed forces but there is a law in creation which will compel him to give up rule by force. The moment the armed forces realize that these are nothing but dictatorial attitudes their support will begin to fade away.

At the end of the day the representatives of the people and the Government itself will give priority to food, shelter and protection, which will be the politics of Russia. The same scenario will begin to develop elsewhere, including the West in its scope.

Yeltsin will be removed from his present position. He cannot fight the machinery of opposition within Russia. With "masked faces", elements of the old regime will come in through the back door. It will not be the old communism, but socialism with a blend of capitalism, modelled on the current pattern of political and economic evolution of China. In this connection Maitreya's view is: "If a person has been born in a jungle and you take him out of his environment into 'society', you can change him over years but not overnight." The implication here is that changes which are too sudden cannot be digested adequately, and this is true of Russia.

According to Maitreya's associate, the countries of Eastern Europe will find a way of evolving more in line with their own values and not by trying to be carbon copies of Western-style democracies. There will be, eventually, a better balance of socialist and capitalist elements.

The Maastricht Treaty — This treaty cannot work. The French will remain French; the British will remain British, and so on. The nations will retain their sacred individuality. But food, shelter and protection must be given priority so that the seeds of destructive nationalism and racism cannot grow.

Free trade is not the same as the abolishing of all border controls. To abolish these is to allow the drug business to flourish. If we allow this, the national identities will suffer. This suffering itself gives rise to nationalism and racism, which are the seeds of destruction.

Once the identity is destroyed there is darkness. Identity is the space between the Self and the Lord. Without identity there is no life.

The sacredness of nations — The current European experiment (ie ever-closer political and economic union) has not worked. There can be a convergence along certain lines, but the identity of a nation remains sacred. Human ideologues cannot destroy it.

The US — Just as the 80 regions of the Russian Federation are seeking greater autonomy, the same process is occurring in the United States. Each state wants a greater say in managing its own affairs (education, health, housing, police forces, etc). Each state is willing to pay its due share of taxes to central government, but at present the feeling is that too great a share goes to the centre, leaving insufficient funds for local management of local affairs. There will be a change of policy. Central government will concern itself with defence and national priorities.

The Middle East — Countries which were considered belligerent will gradually be accepted by the Arab nations as a whole, and then by the international community. Iraq is no superpower, and the awareness of the Iraqi people is growing all the time. The Government there will gradually allow the people to express themselves more. The same will be true of Iran. Even in Syria, the Government will not continue in its present form. Israelis and Palestinians will live alongside each other in greater harmony despite all the difficulties they have faced, and a greater sharing of wealth in the region will take place.

Iran and Iraq — Despite outward appearances, fast changes are taking place at ground level in both countries. In Iran the religious leaders will not be able to rule the masses as they have done until now. They are trying to bring in 'younger blood' so that they can continue to hold on to power, but the old political faces will go.

Governments everywhere will evolve towards a variety of forms which reflect "government for the people, by the people".

Yugoslavia — The war in Yugoslavia has been called a civil war but this is really the butchery of humanity without even the rules of war.

According to Maitreya, power does not bring happiness. Politicians and leaders who have failed to understand what awareness is in life cannot lead the masses. Man's 'second nature' (ie his conditioned nature) can evolve into awareness through honesty of mind, sincerity of spirit and detachment. But if the environment (the circumstances people find themselves in) fails, the second nature is like a blind man walking the streets.

Bosnia is a tragic legacy for political leaders West and East, and for the United Nations Security Council. They have failed to protect the innocent, leaving the conscientious few to venture into the war-torn arena to feed, shelter and nurture the people. Defenceless people here, in the estimation of all these leaders, are worth less than the oil wells in Kuwait. Present-day politics are sheer hypocrisy.

Japan — Japan is entering a phase where much corruption, the darker side of Japanese life, is opening up and will bring to an end the era of more and more money-making. There is much family disintegration even in Japan (due to the pressures created by the excessive competition and daily struggle, themselves the products of an excessively commercialized world). Market forces are the antithesis of freedom and salvation.

Public servants — Those in power must see themselves as public servants. The change in world politics, leading to emphasis on food, shelter and protection, leaves no place for power struggles as they exist now.

China — China is on the way to being a very powerful country. For the present it will have capitalism as an aspect but it will still retain values of life pertinent to its civilization, unlike Russia where the values of life have been destroyed. Capitalism on its own cannot survive in the world. Socialism on its own cannot survive either. China's economy will become very strong: it will "match the dollars".

Violent human actions disturb the Earth's balance — On 12 July, 1993 Maitreya's associate sent a letter to American President Bill Clinton. In the last paragraph, referring to

Yugoslavia, Maitreya's associate pointed out that the forces which have been triggered and unleashed upon humanity, imposing murderous sufferings, "will now reverberate in terms of major earthquakes and disastrous floodings and aerodynamic failures. Let your generals and scientists now watch and analyse the happenings."

Maitreya's associate pointed out that shortly afterwards there were floods in several parts of the world, among other natural disturbances; the event which the West focused on was the disastrous flood when the Mississippi River burst its banks.

The associate offered the information that Maitreya enabled a small group of people to experience these events vividly "as if they were there", *in advance* of the physical occurrence.

Maitreya's associate and a few others have written to a number of political leaders in a variety of countries, detailing these trends and events. The letters refer to Maitreya as "The World Teacher", and more generally try to develop a wider understanding of the Laws of Cause and Effect, thus linking the violence of events such as those in Yugoslavia and elsewhere to subsequent natural disasters which can and do affect people not directly involved, but who nevertheless have to endure the consequences of a disturbed planet.

Knowing these laws enables Maitreya to foresee the effects of the causes we ourselves have set in motion. Understandably, Maitreya's communications (whether directly to groups around the world or indirectly through those who willingly assist Him) are designed to raise awareness of that for which we ourselves are responsible. A growing understanding of these laws will in itself lead to strengthened collective preventative action on the part of peoples and governments.

Extra-planetary help — Already, there are beings from more evolved planets in our solar system living on Earth. In the United Nations there are records of the fact that they are acting in some instances as advisers in government circles in various countries. Much inspiration is being given in the medical field also, particularly with reference to the Technology of Light.

Enlightened beings can control this Technology of Light but they do not misuse it. In important instances, they have prevented its misuse. Their role is protective and inspirational. (*Share International*, October and November 1993)

ECONOMIC INJUSTICE — A THREAT TO WORLD PEACE

There are about 1,000 million people throughout the developing world living in absolute poverty. In the developed world, economic recession and crime are pervasive. What are we doing wrong? What's the problem? (July/August 1993)

The major problem is the fact that we have come to the end of our civilization. We are witnessing the break-up of the civilization of the last 2,000-odd years and the beginnings of the process of creating a new civilization. This is why Maitreya is in the world, to inspire and guide us, to educate us in the creation of the correct structures — political, economic, and social — which will allow us to go forward in our evolution on the right premises.

At the moment we see a super-division of the world, a separation into major groups — the developed and the developing world. The developed world usurps and wastes three-quarters of the world's food and 83 per cent of the resources. The Third World, as it is called, has to make do with the rest. As a result, 38 million people are, at this moment, starving to death in a world with a huge surplus of food. We have a 10 per cent per capita surplus of food in the world, so no one need starve.

What is required is a reassessment of who and what we are in our relationship to each other. Maitreya says the first step we have to take to address these problems is to see ourselves as one, brothers and sisters of one humanity. We have to get that sense of globality, that we are one people, one group — and therefore the food, raw materials, energy, scientific know-how and educational facilities of the world belong to everyone. These resources are given so that all people may evolve correctly according to the Plan which underlies our evolutionary process. As a result, we must share these resources more equitably. When we share, Maitreya says, we will create justice in the world, and when we create justice, and only then, will we have peace. He has come to show us how to have peace. If we do not accept the process towards peace, there will be no world, because we can now destroy all life on this planet many times over. We have the nuclear arsenal to do this.

So the major threat to world peace is not nuclear arms per se, it is the tension which underlies the economic situation. (July/August 1993)

According to Maitreya, what He calls the "engines of war" have been switched off. The Cold War is over. No one any longer believes that the US and Russia are going to destroy each other in a nuclear holocaust. But the energy which sent the planes into the sky and the tanks and troops into the battlefield does not just disappear. It is a destructive force which He says has been going around the world looking for a new home. He says it has found a "new womb". That "new womb" is commercialization based on market forces, which, He says, are based on human greed. Maitreya calls market forces the "forces of evil" because they have inequality built into their very structure. They help a few to achieve a better standard of living, but at the expense of millions who suffer a lower one. Commercialization is gripping every nation in the world as the market forces concept begins to dominate even in the previously communist bloc. We are finding a situation where the rise in tension is so great it has within it the seeds of a third world war, and that war would destroy all life.

How does that relate to what you were talking about in terms of sharing? (July/August 1993)

Unless we share the resources rather than compete for them, we cannot create that new situation. We have enough food and resources in the world for the needs of all people, but the major nations — the US, the European states, Japan and one or two others — completely dominate the scene and usurp and misuse most of these resources. So there is not enough for others at a price that they can afford to pay. The Third World is strapped for its very existence. That is why there are 38 million people starving there.

If we had a drought in California, Florida, Britain or France, for example, we would be able to buy food grown elsewhere. The reason why millions die is not from drought but because they do not have the finances to replenish that which is lost through drought. If you have an economic system which is not based on competition, greed and self-service, which is what market forces are about, then you can redress this whole situation.

Maitreya says that any government which follows market forces blindly is leading its nation to destruction. He says this civilization is literally at the end of its tether. It is coming to a halt. What we are witnessing today is not simply a recession or slowdown of production. We are witnessing the death throes of the current civilization because it is based on wrong premises.

Market forces assume that everyone starts at the same point. But everyone does not start at the same point. No two nations start at the same point. No two individuals within those nations start at the same point. There are extraordinary discrepancies in living standards. How many people imagine that the world can go on indefinitely in this hideous situation? For how long do people imagine that the people of the Third World will put up with this state of affairs? The answer is sharing, a sharing of resources.

In other words, the current system will collapse. (July/August 1993)

Maitreya says we are witnessing its collapse. He says it is inevitable, and that there will be a world stock-market crash which will begin in Japan. Maitreya said this in 1988, and since then the stock market of Japan has lost nearly 60 per cent of its value. Maitreya says it is a bubble; it will burst inevitably. How it bursts depends on ourselves, but it has to burst and let out all the corruption and inequality which prevents the demonstration, as He would say, of the true inner spiritual nature of humanity. We are wasting the resources of countless millions in the world by condemning them to an enforced poverty and degradation, and the misery of undernourishment and starvation.

You are saying it will literally take a collapse for the changes that you are recommending to be made, and nothing short of that will be enough. Perhaps we can see the error of our ways. (July/August 1993)

Many people see the error of our ways. I am not alone in pointing these out. But governments, and people who keep the governments in power — enormous vested interests in the world in all sectors, the simple greed, the self-protective mechanism of humanity — prevent these changes from taking place. Almost everybody would admit these changes would be useful, but may be impractical to implement. Maitreya says if they do not take place, we will destroy ourselves. He says that it will take the collapse of our economic system, as we have known it, to bring us to a sense of reality, to realize that we cannot go on indefinitely in a world where one-third of the population uses three-quarters of the world's food and 83 per cent of the other resources. The crime, drug addiction and social unrest in the developed world are a direct result of this imbalance in the world's resources. Even the distortion of the world's long-established weather patterns is the direct result of this disequilibrium created by man's disharmonic thought patterns.

It is obvious that humanity needs to change direction. We need a radical change in every aspect of life. How can we change the system? How can we canalize the energy from Aquarius to realize that change? (June 1994)

According to Maitreya — The World Teacher — such change needs only the acceptance of the principle of sharing. This alone would transform the world. He has said: "Take your brother's need as the measure for your action and solve the problems of the world. There is no other course." "Take your place by My side and together shall we make all things new."

Since the power in the world remains with the rich and the powerful, is it up to the rest of us to wait until they change their minds? (October 1996)

No; we will wait for ever for that to happen. Few rich and powerful people will give up their power or riches unless they have to. The mechanics of the change is a world stock-market crash. Maitreya has predicted many, many things which have come true. He has also predicted a world stock-market crash which He said would begin in Japan. He made that prediction in 1988, and immediately the stock market of Japan began to collapse. As far as Japan is concerned, everyone knows that the 'bubble', as He called it, has burst. This stock-market crash will end the present distorted and unjust economic structures.

Speculation is seen by Hierarchy as a disease. At present, over 90 per cent of all stock-market transactions are currency speculations. The markets have become what Maitreya calls "gambling casinos"; they have no part to play in a rational economic structure based on justice.

You say the present economic and financial order is going to break down — what do we do? Do I take my money out tomorrow? (March 1995)

What we do is share the resources of the world. The major gambling in the world is in currency and in 'futures'. The value of any currency bears little relation to the industrial base of the country to which it belongs. This is true for all the developed nations. Each of us puts an exaggerated value on our currency in relation to our industrial potential. This is true even of Japan, which makes the yen extremely valuable in relation to the dollar and other currencies.

There are Japanese who are working every day but they do not take any pay, because their business cannot afford to pay them. They work on, perhaps for two or three years, living, rather sparingly, on their savings, in the hope that things will change and they will get paid once again. There are many more who are unemployed but they go every day to the factory, because it is not acknowledged that there is no work for them there. Where 10 men were working before, perhaps three or four are working today.

Millions of people are unemployed and are not counted as unemployed because they are women — they have simply been made redundant and go back into the home; in Japan, as women, they are just taking up their natural abode. About three million people are registered and admitted by the Japanese Government as unemployed, but actually the true figure, as in the UK, is many times that.

The value of the stock exchange in Japan is based on unreal land values, which is traditional to Japan. Until recently this has been accepted as collateral for billions of yens-worth of share and currency gambling. Now the banks are calling in the losses on the exchange (which has lost 60 per cent of its value since 1988). This is transforming the reality of financial life in Japan. If it happens in Japan — which underwrites by 25 per cent the national debt of America, and the dollar is falling — then it is obvious that a totally destabilizing situation exists.

This has nothing to do with your own personal situation — unless you have bonds and shares and do the gambling yourself. If that is what you do, my advice is: "Get out tomorrow!" But if you simply have your wages on a weekly or monthly or yearly basis in the bank, you are going to survive in the normal way, but your life will change because the life of everyone will change. We in the developed world cannot any longer continue to destroy the resources of the world — they are finite. If we want our children to live half-decent lives we have to preserve these resources. That means we have to create a *sustainable* economy — which is perfectly possible. For years, groups throughout the world have been advocating such an economy. There are various measures by which this can be done — mainly a simplification of our living habits and styles.

Is it not a wrong delineation of Maitreya's teachings to emphasize the negative aspects of human life? Surely there are positive things that we have done, otherwise we would not have arrived at where we are? (December 1995)

I quite agree, but to come to a point of readiness for change we have to think of the pain and suffering caused by the wrong thoughts and actions of humanity. Just think about what is happening today in Bosnia, in Rwanda; the fact that one-fifth of the world's population is living in absolute poverty; that 38 million people are starving to death and that millions more die from malnutrition; that we have wars, and that many hurricanes and earthquakes occur quite unnecessarily as the result of our wrong thought and action. If I or others were not to point out these things we would have no idea of what lies behind these destructive events in the world. We have it in our own hands to change it. People see these destructive events, like earthquakes and violence of all kinds, as "acts of God". They are not acts of

God. Some of them are natural; some earthquakes, for instance, are the result of the movement of the earth's plates, but the majority of earthquakes are caused by underground nuclear explosions and our wrong, destructive thinking. We could halve the incidence of earthquakes; we could transform our world if we did not think always in terms of competition, if we were not so greedy. This negative thought and action is bringing humanity to the verge of self-destruction. To put it in a positive sense, what you will hear Maitreya say is that "you are Gods"; "you are not necessarily destructive beings. What you have created is destruction, but you are literally Gods in incarnation and I have come to show you the way to become the Gods that you are, to demonstrate your inner Divinity." That requires the relinquishment of our destructive thought and action.

Stock-market Crash

In 1994 you predicted that the stock market would collapse by the end of 1994. How do you account for the fact that it hasn't happened? (April 1995)

I am not aware of making such a firm "prediction" but only that it was my personal expectation. However, as far as the Masters are concerned, and as far as the Japanese people are concerned, the stock market has already collapsed. The world's stock markets have not yet crashed but the Japanese market certainly has. It is being artificially supported by the Japanese Government with the infusion of enormous sums of money, and by the extreme discipline of Japanese industrialists who do as they are told by government. If the Japanese stock-market fall — 60 per cent — had been in America, for example, the industrialists and financiers would have been jumping out of high windows long ago. We would recognize what the Japanese recognize: that there *has* been a stock-market crash. We are witnessing a process, the end of which is a collapse of the markets as a whole.

From the Hierarchy's perspective, has the predicted stock-market crash already occurred? (June 1996)
Yes.

I am sure that I am not alone in being baffled by the above response that, from the Hierarchy's perspective, the predicted stock-market crash has already occurred.

*For a number of years, each **Share International** issue has included the statement "A major event, which, Maitreya says, we may expect to see in the near future and which He announced as early as 1988: an international stock-market crash, beginning in Japan." If the crash has already occurred, why has each issue indicated that the crash is still to come?* (July/August 1996)

Hierarchy sees ahead, already precipitated, the events which, from our point of view, have not as yet materialized. A straight answer to a straight question — it was not meant to confuse but to illuminate.

It is generally recognized that brokers in share-dealing profit whether the market goes up or down; a quiet, stable market would generally, therefore, be 'bad for business' for brokers. This being so, is it the case that brokers artificially manipulate 'sentiment' to cause a marked rise or fall in the world's markets? (May 1995)

Strange as it may seem in this profit-oriented business, this does not actually happen on a major scale. The opportunities for brokers to manipulate the market in this way are limited.

Is the Third World debt going to be cancelled before the stock market crashes? (January/February 1995)

Whether or not it precedes the stock-market crash, it is inevitable that the majority of the Third World debt has to be written off. There is no possibility that these nations can repay what they owe, but in fact they have repaid it over and over again in interest on the loans. It is not 'aid' that the Third World countries receive, although that is what it is called; it is really 'usury'. Some 80 per cent of the aid given to Third World countries returns to the developed world from which it came in repayment of, and interest on, the loans — so they can never become solvent. They are having to compete, through market forces, with the developed Western countries in order to receive the aid in the first place. It would be far better if they could withstand the

111

blandishments and refuse the aid from the World Bank, the International Monetary Fund and the Western banks who have squeezed them dry for years.

Could you say more about the effect of the change in the stock market? (March 1994)

Obviously if the stock markets collapse the present economic structure collapses with them — it is already collapsing. What we have today are the G7 nations, the seven major industrialized countries, dominating the world's economy, determining how the world as a whole will live, even though they comprise only one-third of the world's population. They impose on the other two-thirds their structure, their *modus operandi*, which is commercialization, "competition" biased in their favour, the action of market forces, and so on. This is grinding the world to its knees, everywhere, even in the developed world, so you can imagine what it is like in the developing world. This is economic totalitarianism and must come to an end. It is based on the lie that we all start equal; we do not. The new economic structure will be based on the best of capitalism and the best of socialism. According to Maitreya, the symbol for this is the unification of Germany. Capitalist West Germany and Communist East Germany have come together (30 or 40 years ahead of any expectation) through the action of Maitreya. Eventually, the general political form will be Democratic Socialism, or Social Democracy.

To me the G7 nations, into which I have done a lot of research and on which I lecture, are headed by a secret organization under about 12 extremely powerful families. How are they going to give up their wealth? (March 1994)

It is not a question of people giving up; they are going to lose. When the stock exchanges crash this particular economic structure crashes with them. That power and wealth will go too. The priorities of all governments then will change.

There are plenty of people who, right now, know about Maitreya and resist the transformation, maybe the very people of whom you speak, although personally I do not believe that there are 12 families behind this whole 'conspiracy' — I do not believe there is a conspiracy. I believe there is deep involvement in the greed and selfishness of humanity, but when humanity is up against it, which the economic crash will bring about, it will see its interdependence. We can only go forward interdependently, or not at all. It is that, or complete destruction of life on this planet: that is our choice, and Maitreya will spell it out very clearly.

What will the conditions be like immediately following the predicted economic collapse? (December 1993)
Obviously, very chaotic indeed, although every effort has been, and will be made to reduce such chaos to a minimum. Were humanity to respond to the teaching of Maitreya and share resources now, the effect of the stock-market crash world-wide would be considerably reduced. Maitreya is concerned to appear openly as soon as possible to mitigate, as far as can be, the inevitable disruption which will ensue.

What happens after that? (July/August 1993)
Maitreya says when that happens the priorities of all governments will change. He says the number one priority of all governments will become the provision of correct, adequate food for all the people: it is the number one necessity; two, the provision of adequate shelter for all the people; three, the provision of adequate health care; and four, educational facilities for all the people. These are the basics which do not seem too much to ask for — enough food, shelter, health care, and education. Yet there is no country in the world — not even the US, the most powerful militarily, and once the richest, country in the world — not anywhere do these four requirements pertain as a universal right. He says that when they do, they will transform the world.

The first step is the sharing of the world's resources, because if we do not do this we will destroy ourselves. It is as simple as that. We have free will. Maitreya is not going to interfere and make sure that we do not destroy ourselves. He is going to present us with these alternatives: carry on as we are today in the

113

old, greedy, selfish, competitive ways of the past and destroy ourselves, or else accept that we are one, accept the principle of sharing; implement it, create justice in the world, and therefore peace, and begin the construction under His inspiration of a most brilliant and wonderful civilization such as this world has never known.

Establishment of a System of Sharing

Is Maitreya going to inspire us to action, such as with sharing, based on an experience He will give us of our oneness? Otherwise, will humanity be motivated to share? (January/February 1996)

The answer to that is yes and no. Maitreya is not going to force anyone to share, but He is going to talk about the necessity of sharing as the only way to produce a rational economic system which will create justice. It is the injustice of the present system which is bringing it to its knees. It is ending because the age which brought it into being has ended. It is a decaying, corrupt, crystallized form which does good to a few and to the many a great deal of harm. Of course it also does harm to the few to whom it seems to be doing good. It is poisoning, dividing, and threatening the world, so it has to go. All of this will be spelled out by Maitreya. If that does not inspire us with the idea of sharing, then nothing will.

Maitreya will also release His energy — the Christ Principle — in tremendous potency. As Maitreya Himself has said: "It will be as if I embrace the world. People will feel it even physically." If that energy flowing through us, plus the words of Maitreya analyzing the economic situation and the harm which it is doing to planetary life, do not motivate us to share, then nothing else will. If it does not motivate humanity, then we will not learn to share and we will destroy the world. We have it in our own hands.

This questioner obviously does not have too much faith in the rest of humanity. "Otherwise, will humanity be motivated to share?" Humanity will be motivated to share by the analysis by Maitreya of what will happen if we do not, and also by the experience of the Christ Principle. That is the experience which He will give us. The Christ Principle embodies the sense of oneness. It is the magnetic energy of love whose nature is oneness. Love is, above all, the inclusive energy. It is that which unites, draws together, the building blocks of creation and holds them magnetically in oneness.

How will it work in practice? Will the changes occur on a national basis? For instance, in the US, will we say: "We need to change our priorities?" Or will it happen internationally through the UN or some other forum? (July/August 1993)

I would suggest it is a combination of both. The UN will become the major debating chamber of the world. All world problems will be debated there and resolutions passed which will implement the new system. An entirely new UN agency will be set up specifically to oversee the process of sharing the world's resources. But I must emphasize that we have free will; nothing will be forced on humanity. When humanity of its own free will accepts the principle of sharing and asks Maitreya and His group of Masters, how do we do this, how do we set about sharing, then we will find that the plan is already there. There is a group of high initiates who have worked out with the Masters over many years a whole series of interrelated plans which will solve the redistribution problems which today are at the heart of the economic problems. It is really a problem of redistribution of resources.

That redistribution results from a change of consciousness. Humanity is approaching a point where it is undergoing a great shift in consciousness, beginning to recognize itself in relation to each other and to cosmos, to nature, to what we generally call God, in an entirely new way. Maitreya says that everything, every single thing in cosmos, is interconnected. There is no break at any point. What we do to ourselves, we do to nature. What we do to nature, we are doing to ourselves as God, because we are reflections, points of consciousness of that total consciousness that we call God.

Throughout the whole of cosmos this process is enacted and re-enacted; every thought, every action is setting into motion a

115

cause. The effects stemming from these causes make our lives. If we have an underground nuclear explosion, for example, we will certainly have an earthquake. Every effect streams from a cause.

Maitreya will emphasize — and we ought to know it by now, we have had thousands of years to understand it — that everything in life obeys the Law of Cause and Effect. We cannot go on creating wrong conditions and expect there will be no effects. If we create conditions of imbalance in a nation, inevitably we get crime. Just making a stronger police force or army will not solve the problem. We have to combat the source of the crime — inequality, imbalance. The whole process of evolution is moving towards oneness, fusion, synthesis. Market forces, which are based on division, separation and competition, act against the evolutionary process. That is why Maitreya calls them "the forces of evil". They have their place, but only a very limited place. When they are followed blindly, they lead inevitably to destruction.

Will Maitreya be openly advising humanity? (July/August 1993)

Maitreya will be openly advising. He will come forward as the World Teacher for all groups, religious and non-religious alike. He will be looked towards by religious groups as their expected Teacher — the Christ for Christians, Maitreya Buddha for Buddhists, the Messiah of the Jews and the Muslims, Krishna for the Hindus — but in fact He is really a teacher, an educator, for the whole of humanity, showing us how to become what we are, spiritual beings, and therefore how to create the environment in which that spirituality can be expressed. It cannot be expressed in the midst of these divisions and separations, this competition based on market forces.

Will the Christ need to take over the United Nations and put down the countries that stop their people from having the aid that is sent? (January/February 1995)

No. That would be a tremendous infringement of human free will, and neither the Christ nor any of the many Masters who live on this planet will, under any circumstances, infringe human free will. It is sacrosanct. Everything, every transformation, every change, we must do for ourselves, from our willing acceptance of the need. Nothing will ever be imposed on the world by the Spiritual Hierarchy of our planet — were that not the case you could not call it a Spiritual Hierarchy.

Eventually a new agency will be formed, by us, as part of the United Nations, which will oversee the redistribution of the resources of the world. It will be done by humanity but under the guidance and with the advice of the Masters.

I worry that one has almost to subjugate one's will and blindly follow Maitreya? (April 1996)

Not at all; the very opposite is the case. Unless humanity, *of its own free will*, willingly, gladly, accepts the need for transformation, the transformation, the changes, will not take place. Nothing is ever imposed by Hierarchy on humanity; to Them our free will is sacrosanct. We impose on each other's free will all the time, but the Masters never.

(1) The idea of sharing is a two-way thing. What will the "haves" gain by giving to the "have-nots"? (2) Will the pleasure received by giving in itself be enough in the new world society? (November 1996)

(1) Not only the "haves" but the whole world will gain by sharing. In this way — the only way — will be created justice, and, following from that, world peace. Without sharing, there is no safe future for anyone. (2) It is not a question of receiving pleasure by giving — that is open to anyone at any time — but the creation of economic structures that will ensure peace between all peoples.

It is said that if we distribute the food and the benefits all over the world to the people who are starving, till they are not starving, they will expect it the next time. What message can we give to go with it? (May 1994)

The message is that if you are starving you need food today but you also need it tomorrow and the next day and the next — until you are strong enough to plant and grow it for yourself. It is not a lack of desire to work which makes people starve, it is sheer poverty. If, for example, there were a drought in the UK and we were facing starvation, what would we do? We would simply import more food from Europe or America or wherever, because we have money to pay for it. The only reason that the people in the Third World do not do that is that they have no money — because we keep them poor. The G7 nations organize the world's economy in such a way that they are rich and the Third World lives in poverty; the gap between the two is getting wider every day. We give 'aid', so called, to the Third World, that is not aid but usury. More money flows, by billions, from the Third World to the developed world in repayment and servicing of loans than goes to the Third World in new aid. No Third World country can get out of this impasse, in which it remains solidly, fixedly, poor.

Maitreya will inaugurate a climate of service-for-the-world, in which people will dedicate themselves to carrying the food into the Third World, until the people are ready to plant and cultivate their land and become self-reliant. But you cannot become self-reliant from a position of starvation overnight. A programme way above anything we have so far tried will be set in place; we are only nibbling at the problem today.

You talk about the starving children in the world. We have thousands of people from Third World countries — which have palaces and gold mines, etc — living in the UK: why don't they send money back to the poor people in their own countries? (September 1996)

In my experience they do. A large proportion of the income of people from Third World countries who are working here goes back to their original countries to help their own families. They can only do what they can do in an individual way, otherwise their families here would be starving. I do not think too many Third World citizens have palaces and gold mines.

If I am a farmer in the US, for instance, if I am growing food and I put a lot of hard labour into it, should I not reap the benefits of doing that work? Sharing sounds great, but will we actually implement it when the time comes? (July/August 1993)

According to Maitreya, we shall. He knows already that humanity is ready for sharing and will accept the principle of sharing. That is why He can be here.

Of course, the farmer in the US producing food should reap the benefit of his labour, but the poor peasant in Zaire or Zambia should also reap the benefit of his hard labour. That does not pertain today. In the developed world, we produce so much that we dominate the world's markets. We lay down the price of our goods and, because of our resources, the price of the goods of the Third World also. We demand from the Third World countries the raw materials and products at a price which leaves them able to live only at a very low level, with 1,000 million people living below the poverty line and 38 million actually starving. Yet we demand for our resources, for our production, the top value that we can demand on the world market so that we can maintain what is a very artificial level of living. People in the US, Europe and Japan live on the backs of the Third World. This is the reality. The reason that we do not see it is simply our complacency. Maitreya calls complacency "the source of all evil".

Yet many people here in the US would say we are not complacent. When there is a crisis in Africa or elsewhere, we are right there responding with food and aid. (July/August 1993)

Of course, but these are individual reactions. In every country you will find those whose hearts respond to human need. But it is an on-again, off-again affair. Humanity as a whole, through its agencies, the governments of the world, does not address these problems on a global scale. We would not put into power, perhaps, a government whose number one priority was the saving of the starving millions if it meant the reduction of the living standards of our own nation. Nobody can win votes on that basis, or so the politicians think. The time is coming when they will not win any votes at all unless they put that issue at the forefront of their priorities.

What we are going to witness is the creation, by Maitreya, of a world public opinion focused, galvanized, centred on sharing as a divine right. Maitreya says: "When you share, you recognize

119

God in your brother." He says "the problems of mankind are real, but solvable." The solution lies within our grasp. He says: "Take your brother's need as the measure for your action and solve the problems of the world. There is no other course." He will galvanize and potentize world public opinion which, when so organized, no government on earth can withstand. It is that world public opinion which eventually will force all the governments in the world to accept the principle of sharing because it will be seen that we have no alternative. We either share or we die. It is as simple as that.

In this new civilization, are we talking about the Third World coming up to Western European and North American standards of living, or are we talking about the planet generally having a simpler, more sustainable lifestyle? (May 1994)

What we will have to aim at is a simpler and sustainable economy, based on need. Today the economies are based on the pressures of commercialization, of market forces. All the developed countries are producing — and over-producing — goods that they cannot sell, because each has and creates the same things. The only people who could really buy the produce of the developed world as it exists today are the people in the Third World, but they cannot because we do not pay fair prices for their produce and rig the markets against them. The Masters will show that a satisfying and creative life can be lived which will be full and rich but on a simpler level, using the resources of the world in a sustainable way.

Could you explain the difference between a good system of trade and commerce and commercialization? (September 1993)

Any fair system would have to take account of the differences in living standards, industrial potential and available resources between developed and developing countries. This necessarily requires co-operation and therefore a sense of interdependence, sadly lacking in the present competitive commercial system. A sophisticated form of barter will replace the present economic system.

Have you a view on the current measures to barcode all goods and all people in the world in anticipation of a cashless society? (May 1994)

Instinctively, I do not like the idea of barcoding individuals — you can barcode goods if you like — but you will find that a new United Nations agency will be set up (under the guidance of either a Master or at least a third-degree initiate) which will oversee the redistribution of resources. Whether that would involve barcoding or not is up to us, but as far as I understand it, that is not the method which has been adopted in the various blueprints already formulated.

The commercialization of our life seems to grow worse every day. Have we seen the peak of market forces yet, or are they still on the increase? Will their decline start only from the Day of Declaration onwards? (September 1996)

They are still on the increase which will continue until after the Day of Declaration.

Poverty, Crime and Self-esteem: the Crucial Connection

The problem of crime, particularly violent crime, is certainly on the rise throughout the developed world today, with the US the most violent among all industrialized nations. The traditional approaches to this problem, such as more prisons and police and longer prison sentences, do not seem to be working. Why are we experiencing this increase in crime, and how do we begin to understand why people are committing such acts? (July/August 1993)

There are a number of reasons for this phenomenon, but the most important is that we are entering a new cosmic cycle. New energies are making themselves felt. In particular, a new energy now pervading the planet, the energy of equilibrium (which involves the Law of Action and Reaction), flushes out all the negative forces. Under the influence of this energy, more and more people will revolt because the old habits and ways of thinking, the centuries-old codes imposed on the mind, must be broken. People will no longer accept the old, imposed solutions.

121

Society as a whole is attempting to emerge from this age-old bondage. The eruption of crime, corruption, drugs, and violence is the inevitable prelude to this change. It occurs mainly in the inner cities, where what Maitreya calls "crime combustion" occurs, where people are addicted to drugs, sexual violence, murder, and other crimes. This process of combustion, He says, brings the dirt up to the surface, and neither the police nor the military will be able adequately to control the outbreak of crime now occurring.

How can we begin to break this cycle of crime? (July/August 1993)

Maitreya says we have to understand the causes. The domain of the problem, He says, cannot be limited to the crimes themselves, because the solutions then will be simply reactive, dealing only with effects. To increase the police forces, build more prisons, put more people in prison, deals with an effect and not a cause.

To understand the genesis of the violence, it is necessary to acquire a more detailed, overall picture of the pattern of people's lives so as to redirect their energy. This crime is the result of a rising energy, wrongly directed, that needs to be more constructively channelled.

Maitreya says, for example, that politicians have a responsibility for the desperation of those addicted to drugs. People go to drugs, Maitreya says, because they are suffering from spiritual starvation. If people are so straitened in their lives that they cannot even eat properly, they will lead desperate lives. They will sell their bodies. They will steal, and end up in prison. If they are deprived of nourishment, if they are deprived of a future, if there seems no hope, they turn to drugs to help them forget their desperation. From drugs, it is not far to crime, even murder. People who take drugs generally commit the greatest number of crimes because they are desperate for money for drugs. They lose all restraint, and lash out in any direction to get what they want.

You are saying that there are new energies coming into the world now, and these are producing changes, not always for the better? (July/August 1993)

That is the major reason. These changes are definitely for the better in the long run. But in the short term they raise to the surface all the corruption and violence which has been repressed and suppressed for centuries. Once this energy of equilibrium galvanizes them, that repression becomes aggression, leading to an increase in crime and violence in this disjointed and divisive society. Crime occurs when we have extreme wealth next door to extreme poverty. In a more equitable society there would be less crime.

You talked about the connection between drug addiction and crime. A recent study found that heroin addicts committed 15-20 times as many robberies and burglaries as criminals who did not use drugs. It is also reported that approximately 70 per cent of the people in US prisons have abused drugs. (July/August 1993)

Drugs loosen the fabric of behaviour patterns. Drug addicts get desperate and lose all sense of restraint; they need money for their 'fix'. The average criminal works almost as a professional. He knows the limits to which he can go without ending up in prison. But the drug abuser loses this sense of proportion. Because of this, he does not have any expertise in avoiding arrest, and inevitably ends up in prison.

Can you say what proportion of crime in the UK is the result of drug use? (May 1993)

According to my information 68 per cent of present crime in the UK is drug-related. In the US the percentage is 85 per cent. This is now the primary social problem in the US.

Why are cocaine-addicted babies born? How should they be taken care of? (September 1993)

Because more and more people are becoming addicted to drugs, including cocaine. This is a world-wide happening in response to social stress caused by separation, division, poverty, imbalance and commercialization. The addicted babies need, of course, to be detoxified, preferably by homoeopathic means.

Could you explain what Maitreya means by "spiritual starvation" when referring to those who take drugs, and how that starvation can be cured? (July/August 1993)

Spiritual starvation is a very extreme form of self-alienation. People do not know who they are. Life, therefore, becomes totally purposeless. People want to end their life; they commit slow suicide by taking drugs.

If you present a future without purpose and hope to people with enormous disadvantages, who live in inner cities in a dreary environment, with no jobs and no prospects, they are going to avoid work altogether and therefore commit crime to live, or give up and take drugs. But they need money for the drugs. It becomes a vicious cycle.

A drug addict has inwardly divorced himself from life. He has given in. The way to restore hope is to restore meaning to his life: he has to gain a new view of himself, a sense of his own worth. The first thing is to help him raise his self-respect. Self-respect gradually becomes self-awareness and eventually, according to Maitreya, Self-realization, which is the aim of all life. If people are not aware of themselves, if they think they are useless, worthless and powerless, with no place in society, then suicide is an inevitable result, whether it is immediate or slow, by drug abuse.

We cannot solve the problem by putting drug addicts into prison or just by strengthening the laws or by preaching ideologies or religion. As Maitreya says, if you lecture a prostitute or thief, they will reject your words as ideology. But if you say, "whatever you are doing, whether thieving, prostitution, or taking drugs, be yourself, be honest, be sincere, be detached," then the person can experience himself as he is and feel what Maitreya calls the "observer within". The observer within is not a limited, finite person; it is infinite. People call it divinity. When the person experiences himself as this infinite divinity, then he grows in self-respect. That is how he can get out of this vicious cycle of crime and drug addiction.

*I read a recent **New York Times** article that reported a drug rehabilitation effort in one of the New York City prisons, Rikkers Island. This effort has proved quite effective in curbing not only drug addiction but crime and violence as well. Is this the type of approach that you believe could be effective on a wide scale?* (July/August 1993)

In a prison environment, very much so. Maitreya says the only effective way to deal with the individual's internal world, his sense of self-alienation, is through his environment. If he is in prison, it has to be the prison environment. If he is in the outer world, it has to be the environment of the city in which he lives.

According to Maitreya, it is through the power of the environment that self-awareness is created. For example, when an individual enters a church, he feels peaceful and tranquil. The Self experiences this and the mind is no longer in confusion and turmoil. But the mind of someone living in the bleak, depressing conditions of run-down inner city housing will be desperate, and the person will reach for drugs to find escape. If there is no stress or strain in the surroundings, then there is no need for drugs. Maitreya says that within the human body is the most powerful drug known to humanity — detachment. Detachment can emerge only within a sane, clean, and peaceful environment.

In the New York prison experiment, they have changed the environment. The prisoners, for instance, live in dormitories. They do not have single, isolated cells. They can move about. They wear ordinary clothes. They can talk to each other and exchange ideas. They have a kind of group communication in the broadest sense, a group therapy where they can discuss their problems both individually and as a group, and in this way rehabilitate themselves. They grow in self-awareness because they are growing daily in self-esteem and self-respect. This is certainly the way forward.

I understand that Maitreya is training certain people to achieve this type of self-esteem and self-awareness that you were talking about. (July/August 1993)

Yes. As I understand it, in London, Maitreya teaches and trains a group of holy men from India, swamis, who organize groups of young people from broken homes, displaced persons, people who are caught in the cycle of drug and alcohol abuse and criminality. They are taught self-respect. At one point in the process, they are given a simple breathing exercise which for a moment allows Maitreya to give them the experience of themselves as the Self. That sense of themselves as the Self, the observer, frees them more and more from their addictive situation. They gain self-respect, and then work by themselves to get out of the seemingly endless cycle of drug addiction, crime, and alienation. These programmes are gradually being put into effect in the United Kingdom.

Could you comment on how poverty contributes to this cycle of crime and drug abuse? (July/August 1993)

I have no doubt that poverty is one of the main factors in the growing incidence of crime. This increase has been taking place in the richest countries of the developed world. That is no accident. With wealth tends to come complacency which Maitreya calls the root of all evil. Divisions create envy and therefore crime.

Modern wealth has been created mainly through the action of market forces which now dominate the whole of the industrial world. It is based on the false premise that we all start at an equal point. Of course, nobody starts at the same point. Market forces help a few to become very wealthy at the expense of the many who become poorer. This is taking place all over the world. There is an increasing number of hungry and desperate people living in utter poverty. Yet there are more millionaires of all nationalities throughout the developed world. Market forces are inevitably divisive because they separate one section of society from another. For this reason Maitreya calls market forces the forces of evil.

This is what creates the cycle of crime, and therefore prison as the only alternative. At the moment prison *is* the only alternative for violent and dangerous criminals. The prison population is growing all the time but has reached a point where it can hardly grow any more because the prisoners are revolting. They, too, are responding to the new energy of equilibrium.

They will not put up with the excess of rules and regulations necessary to keep them quiet.

Paradoxically, to create a society based on the free play of market forces, there must be a very strict control over the economy to ensure "business efficiency". This is the 'poison' of commercialization, as Maitreya calls it. It imposes restrictions on the natural needs of society. When the needs of society are not being met by the politicians, the people revolt. When the people's voice is not heard, there will inevitably be revolution. Part of that revolution is the growing incidence of crime.

Are crimes of protest, like the 1992 Los Angeles riots, ever justified? (July/August 1993)

They are understandable. They are also inevitable. As soon as there is injustice on a large scale, there will be a flaring up of violence. It has always occurred, and it will occur more and more violently as people lose control, as drug abuse increases, as people under the influence of drugs take part in the protests. But the violent protests are not the result of drug-taking. They are the result of the imbalance of our society — too great wealth side by side with too great poverty. The only answer to this problem is the implementation of the principle of sharing. That is why Maitreya puts the principle of sharing as the cornerstone of everything He has to say about social change.

Commercialization, based on market forces, is now gripping all the nations of the world. The West is even encouraging this system in the former Soviet Union. It will work no better there than it does anywhere else in the world. There is a place for market forces, but blindly followed, they will bring this present society and its economic system to the verge of destruction.

Do you really believe that with the advent of the Age of Aquarius the world of persecution, hatred and domination will become a world of respect and charity? (June 1994)

Yes, indeed. The quality of the energy of Aquarius is that of Synthesis. That will blend and fuse humanity into an experience of oneness. With the presence of Maitreya and His group of Masters physically among us I have no doubt that we will build, under Their inspiration and guidance, a civilization worthy of our divine origin — a Golden Age is in the making.

There are also personal and spiritual reasons that people take drugs and commit crimes. It sounds like there are no easy solutions. Would a combination of economic reform and personal/spiritual counselling for the individuals involved be of help? (July/August 1993)

That is part of the answer. Remember that the new energy of equilibrium has been released into the world and this energy counteracts the negative forces. When general world tension begins to decrease, when the principle of sharing begins to be implemented through a variety of social, economic and political reforms, people will feel less threatened and there will be less and less crime.

There have been (at least) two well-publicized events in the US recently in which individuals claiming to be Christ created havoc in their communities (one in Waco, Texas, one in southern California). These events took place within a couple of days of the bombing of the World Trade Center in New York, apparently by a Muslim fundamentalist. What's happening here? (1) Is Maitreya now pouring more energy into America? (2) Are these events occurring as unstable individuals unconsciously respond with resistance to that energy? (3) Will we see more of these events around the world as we approach the Day of Declaration? (April 1993)

(1) There is no connection between these events and Maitreya's actions. (2) These events occur as unstable individuals respond, not with resistance, but in a distorted fashion, to the energies now saturating the world. (3) Probably.

(1) Given that Sai Baba and a "mayavirupa" of Maitreya are both in India and India has the reputation of being a very spiritual country, how can we account for such horrendous practices as bride burning, selling girls of 11 or 12 to old men from other countries and also aborting babies if female, to mention only some of the horrors? (2) Why does Sai Baba spend time giving rings and such like to rich Americans while these

evils exist? Why doesn't He, and Maitreya, do something to improve things in India? (March 1993)

There are many reasons for the existence of such social evils not only in India, it should be realized, but also in China, South America, Thailand and other Eastern countries. Although not the only one, endemic poverty is the main cause of these atrocities. In poverty-stricken countries, a female child is often experienced as a drawback, a liability, who, if sold (usually into more or less slavery or prostitution), can realize at least some money to feed the other family members. This pressure, allied to ancient devaluation of the female role in society in general, easily escalates to the appalling practices to which the reader refers. I do not believe that most poor families *enjoy* selling or killing off their female children. (2) It is a common mistake to assume that the purifying of our lives and redressing of social evils is the responsibility of Avatars or Masters. The responsibility for ending these man-made evils rests with humanity; we are all responsible. We have free will and if we choose to misuse it, by karmic law (cause and effect) we will suffer. At the same time, however, Sai Baba, Maitreya and other Masters work unceasingly to ameliorate conditions in India (and elsewhere) within the limits of karmic law.

At this time, we have a strong interest in human rights in the world and many occasions to discuss the abolition of the death penalty. I am very sorry, but in my opinion we must execute in a very few cases, such as when a criminal has done something so evil we can hardly imagine it possible. For example, a criminal (here in Japan) raped many children, killed them and ate some of the bodies. What do you think of this problem? (April 1993)

Firstly, I think a person who commits such actions is not really a criminal but is profoundly ill and requires treatment, even if they have to be separated from society as a whole. I do not believe that the death penalty is ever a deterrent to such unbalanced individuals. It is therefore simply an act of vengeance and degrades the society which takes such retribution. Besides, one never knows the karmic reasons which might lie behind these acts of insane violence.

RELIGION AND FUNDAMENTALISM

Religion

Normally our morals are based on religion. Will there be a new morality and how will it equate with the new economic situation? (June 1993)

The morality which has come to us through the different religious traditions is as different as the ideologies, so that, for instance, in one part of the world it is immoral to have more than one wife; in another religion, in another part of the world, it is perfectly moral to have four wives. Morality is relative, man-made. What is not man-made is the spiritual essence of humanity, living ethics.

When humanity recognizes its spiritual basis it will realize that each one of us is a potential God. Spirituality is the essential nature of our being, simply needing demonstration in outer forms. Whatever we can conceive of as human activity can be, in fact must be, spiritual. True morality is not to do with a code of values which humanity evolves to suit a certain society or a certain religious belief, but something which is intrinsic in our spirituality.

When we create an economic system based on co-operation and sharing rather than on competition and market forces, we will create a more moral economic structure. When the stock exchanges collapse, humanity will be brought face to face with its illusions about the nature of reality. At the moment we are worshipping mammon — in the 'temple' of the stock exchange. Politics and economics are the major dominating forces in the world today, which is why they are so important. There are many so-called spiritual groups who dislike talk of economics, for whom politics is a dirty word, because many politicians are corrupt. Humanity is really going through a great spiritual crisis, but that crisis is focused through the political and the economic fields and can only be resolved in these fields. If we cannot resolve it there we will destroy all life on the planet. To share the resources of the world is a spiritual decision; to create democracy in a nation is a moral, a spiritual, decision: We need to separate morality from religious belief and place it where it really belongs — in spirituality itself.

I have difficulty in finding the right system: is it Christianity, is it Buddhism or whatever else? (December 1996)

The reason you find it difficult to choose between different systems is because you already have the enlightenment which cannot tie itself to a fixed dogma or doctrine.

Within all the religions of the world are great initiates, but they are not initiates because they are in a particular religion. They are in that religion because they are initiates, and can benefit the religion in which they act.

Maitreya has come to show humanity that we are one, brothers and sisters of one humanity, stemming from the One Divine Source. Maitreya has come to make sure that we do not destroy ourselves — not by holding up a divine hand and saying: "It will not happen. God says it will not happen." He is not God. He is divine but then we, too, are divine. The only difference between us and Maitreya is that He has demonstrated His divinity, He is aware of it moment-to-moment, as an on-going process, while we have not to any great extent done so. Our problem is that we do not know how best to do it. We will respond to Him, I believe, and He will show us the way to be ourselves, not by following other people or a particular religion because it makes us feel happier. Maitreya calls religion a ladder: it helps you to get onto the roof; but once on the roof you can throw the ladder away. A religion itself is not the truth, though it may help you to find the truth.

If you don't believe in the religious presentation of reality, how can you be an initiate of any degree? (May 1996)

Because the religious path is only one path. You can carry out the greatest work for the world as a scientist, an artist, a politician, an economist, without having anything to do with religion at all. These are all spiritual activities. The religious groups have monopolized the idea of spirituality, and you, in your question, have demonstrated what Marx said — that religion is the opiate of the people. Marx was a disciple of the

Master Jesus, carrying out a very important work. The fact that he was not religious left him open to see the new ways. If you are locked in the old you find it very difficult to create anything new. I do not believe that religion is necessarily an opiate, certainly not always, or in all ways, but I know what Marx meant.

Does religion have a value for us today? (January/February 1994)

Religions remind humanity of the interconnectedness of humanity and God — even if they define God as an old man with a beard upstairs who watches everything you do; and does not like most of what you do. It is a simplistic view, but it reminds humanity that we are not alone, that there is more to life than the immediate needs of the physical body, that life has a spiritual basis and is to be lived always on a higher and higher turn of the spiral. That is the strength and value of the organized religious groups. They protect the young. I do not mean little children but the young souls who otherwise might waste many incarnations in useless, not to say dangerously destructive, lives. That framework protects, even if there comes a point when it is outgrown. The protective mechanism of mother- or father-church is eventually outgrown; it is no longer needed. The person usually revolts; he may give up the entire idea of God for years, until by himself, through meditation, he makes the connecting link with the soul. The process of building the antahkarana begins, even if he has never heard the word antahkarana. For esotericists on the path, that process is totally conscious.

A number of times you have mentioned the breakdown of religions — how will this come about? (March 1994)

No, I did not talk about the breakdown of religions, but about the ending of religious totalitarianism. There is nothing wrong with religion itself — the fault is in those who administer the religions: the priests of different religions who impose their dogmatic beliefs on the people. That is totalitarianism. They even go so far as to tell people how to live and how not to live. For instance if you are a priest in the Catholic church you may not get married; in the Anglican church you can get married. The same is true of teaching on contraception. These are impositions. The evil is in the *imposition* of the ideology, the belief structure.

When the 'New Age' does come, how are we to convince people who already have a fixed idea? (September 1996)

There are millions of people in the world who believe in a particular religion — Catholicism, Buddhism, Hinduism and so on — and they have an absolute right to believe in it. They are neither right nor wrong in their beliefs. It is more a question of fine-focusing. Every religion has an element of the truth and can be expanded in a way which will give it a greater aspect of that truth.

Jesus demonstrated the Love of God in its perfection for the first time, and He did so because He was overshadowed by the Lord Maitreya Who embodies that quality of Love. I do not find that a problem, but others have a problem because they think I am talking about Maitreya as God, and about many different Gods.

Maitreya Himself has said: "Many will follow Me and see Me as their guide. Many will know Me not." (Message No. 10) I believe it will take a long time before every convinced Christian, Hindu, Buddhist, Muslim, Jew, Rastafarian, or whatever, can accept Maitreya as the World Teacher. And it does not really matter. If they are Christian, they will probably accept the Master Jesus much more quickly than Maitreya, but there is no difference between the ideas of Maitreya and those of the Master Jesus: the Hierarchy have one (group) consciousness. They all demonstrate the same qualities to a greater or lesser extent. Maitreya, because He is more evolved than the others, is the Leader of that group, but all of the Masters demonstrate the Love of God. Whatever other qualities They demonstrate, They will first and foremost demonstrate the Love aspect of God.

I think those in fixed, rigid religious traditions today will find someone in the Hierarchy to follow and believe in. They will eventually come to follow Maitreya, because He will be seen as the Hope of Humanity. Countless millions will give Him their credence and will ask for His advice and guidance, and eventually it will be unpopular not to do so; people will find it difficult to stand against this tide of acceptance.

When Maitreya talks on television, transmitted via satellite, and everyone in the world understands what He is talking about, what role do you see for the existing religious leaders — Pope John Paul, for example? (June 1995)

That is up to him if he survives the shock. The Master Jesus has been living in Rome for over four years, and He will take over the throne of St Peter. He will not become the Pope, but the true apostolic succession will begin from that time.

The Master Jesus is, now, in charge of the Christian churches. Maitreya is the World Teacher for all groups, religious and non-religious alike, and the inspirer of all the different evolutionary endeavours on the planet. In the light of the new dispensation, when the Master Jesus, the Master Who was St Paul, the one Who was St Peter, the Master Who was St John the Beloved, and other disciples who were around Jesus are seen openly and acknowledge Themselves to be who they are, it will completely transform the thinking of intelligent Christian people. The shock to the Christian Church will be immense, of course. Theologians will have to rewrite their theology.

Every teaching that has been handed down has come, in the beginning, by word of mouth, taking centuries for its dissemination. Inevitably, every teaching is distorted, more or less, with the result that the teachings in some cases bear little relation to the original. There is enough of it to grip the imagination and the spiritual aspiration of the masses, but the details alienate one teaching from another. All the teachings come from the same source, the Spiritual Hierarchy, and all are in total agreement but with slight differences — given for certain peoples at specific times. The distortions have led to the divisions which we see between nations and religions.

The task of the Master Jesus is to rid the Christian Church of all its man-made dogmas and doctrines which today befuddle, and I would say bedevil, the minds of countless millions of Christians who otherwise would be ready for this event. They are told it cannot happen until the end of the world; it is happening *now*. We have the same situation now as there was 2,000 years ago in Palestine, when the Sanhedrin was expecting 'a warrior king' to rid them of Roman rule. When Jesus came they did not recognize Him. The Christian, Muslim and other fundamentalist religious leaders will probably be among the last to recognize the Christ, the World Teacher, for Who and what He is.

What does the Vatican know about the return of Maitreya, and what is its (or the Pope's) reaction? (December 1995)
The Vatican is very well informed about the content of my information regarding Maitreya's presence — the reports and queries flow in from Catholic groups all over the world. Needless to say, they are at great pains to deny its validity and to limit its influence. In his recently published book, the Pope himself goes out of his way to point out that any new Buddha claimed by Buddhists must not be confused with, or taken to be, the Christian Christ. They have much to learn and a painful awakening awaits them — especially when they see the Master Jesus, two of Whose disciples are among the cardinals in the Curia, the group around the Pope who actually run Vatican affairs.

When Maitreya overshadowed Jesus did he realize that He would be creating another religion? (October 1994)
I do not think that Jesus did create a religion. His followers did. I am sure Maitreya knew — experience would tell Him that that was probably what would happen. But the hope always is that the teaching will be followed — and of course many enlightened men, through the Christian tradition, have become disciples, then initiates, and are now Masters. Religion is not 'wrong'. It is not religion but fanaticism, exclusiveness, that causes wars: it is believing that *your* ideology, *your* religion, *your* concept of life, *your* idea of God, is the one and only for the whole world.

For the past 2,000 years up to the present day people have awaited the return of one called Jesus as the Saviour of the World. This was demonstrated recently when people of many lands took part in the 'Walk for Jesus'. You say that Jesus has returned and is now in Rome at this very time. What do you think people's reaction will be when one called Maitreya declares himself as the "World Teacher"? Do you think people will still regard Jesus as the promised one? (December 1994)

For a time, it may well be that very orthodox Christians — in particular fundamentalists — will reject both Maitreya *and* the Master Jesus, now in Rome. He has not come "on a cloud at the end of the world" as they expect, nor does He have holes in His hands and feet. But gradually, many Christians will find it easier to accept the Master Jesus as the returned Christ (at least the name is the same) rather than Maitreya, and the Master Jesus is in charge of the Christian Church world-wide. Eventually, however, I believe that most people, Christian and otherwise, will accept that Maitreya is indeed the Christ, Messiah, Krishna — World Teacher for all.

(1) Is it "OK" if Christians just think of Maitreya as a teacher, keeping Jesus "higher" in their minds? (2) Or will that retard their evolution? (November 1996)

(1) Yes. I imagine it will be impossible for many, older, Christians to stop thinking of Jesus as the "One and only Son of God". (2) No. Maitreya has said expressly: "Do not worship Me."

The Christian Bible states very clearly that the path to spiritual salvation and everlasting life can be achieved only through recognizing Jesus Christ as our Saviour. Where does this leave those who are not essentially "reborn" Christians? (October 1995)

First of all, I do not accept that the Bible states (clearly or otherwise) that such is the case; and if it were true it would certainly exclude the majority of humanity from salvation. This, surely, must be seen as an exaggerated and over-exclusive claim, made, it should be noted, not by Jesus Himself, but by St Paul, the over-zealous Christian-baiter turned over-zealous Christian promotion officer, who never met Jesus or heard Him speak.

The path to salvation, I suggest, does not consist in recognition of any Teacher or Guru, now, or in the past, but in the recognition that each one of us is an expression of the Divine, and in the ability, eventually, to *demonstrate* that Divinity in all Its fullness.

What will happen to the religious fundamentalists who think Maitreya is the Antichrist? (November 1996)
Nothing will "happen" to them. Eventually, they will realize that the love, wisdom and mission of Maitreya is also for them, and will gradually accept that the Antichrist manifestatation (through Hitler and his group) is behind us, and has cleared the ground, so to speak, for the return to the world, not only of Maitreya, but of the Spiritual Hierarchy of which He is the Head. Perhaps it will take the presence of the Master Jesus to convince them. He is in charge of the Christian Churches.

I have become involved in a large spirit-filled fundamentalist church, and find myself often singing that "Jesus Christ is the ONLY Name and Way to God". Is it proper to continue all this in an esoteric manner, or am I accidentally misrepresenting Maitreya? (June 1993)
You can be certain that Maitreya does not feel "misrepresented". It is the fundamentalist and orthodox Christians who have the problem of separating Maitreya and "the Christ", not esotericism. It is the *Christ Principle*, embodied by Maitreya, and manifested through Jesus for the last three years of His mission, that is the Way to God.

*I feel that the following question may have relevance to many Christians who believe in Maitreya's presence in the world, and who seek to follow His teachings: Maitreya says (**Maitreya's Mission, Volume Two**, p. 243): "I have not come to create followers . . . Each of you should continue to develop within your own religious tradition. A real disciple is one who will respect the traditions ..." As a Christian in a Church that one would think would be more open than any other to the return of the World Teacher, I was surprised by the total lack of interest or even open-mindedness about this issue. It became clear that such an idea was frowned on by the 'orthodoxy', and that if I* *continued to affirm this, not only would my path to the priesthood be made difficult, but also my membership of the Church untenable. I must have brothers and sisters in far more 'orthodox' mainstream Churches who have even greater difficulties with a 'blinkered' orthodoxy; the response to the suggestion of Christ's return would be ridicule, fear and even anger, I would imagine.*

*In the light of experience, continuing "to develop within your own religious tradition" at the present time can be made very difficult, if not impossible, by totalitarian orthodoxies unready to accept Maitreya the World Teacher. (1) What does one do in this situation? (2) Are you aware of **any** sacramental Christian Churches now open-minded enough to accept His presence in the world and the changes in thought and practice that must ensue as a result? (3) Can you give me the names of any Christian Churches, groups or associations who openly accept His presence in the world, or who show the **readiness** to do so? I would like to get in touch with them! If not, Christian readers of **Share International** might consider forming an association . . .* (April 1994)

(1) Wait. (2) No. (3) No. The statement by Maitreya, quoted above, refers not so much to this period of preparation as to the activities of religious people in general after the Day of Declaration. He is really saying that no one should try to 'claim' Him.

What is your view of the ordination of women in the Anglican Church? (June 1994)

Personally, I don't know what all the fuss and resistance to women priests is about. Of course, I can see how many male priests would consider it an unwelcome invasion of their private domain. That is predictable. I find it more difficult to understand the reaction of many *women*, some of whom have left the Anglican Church for the Roman Catholic as a result. Why on earth should there not be women priests — the priestesses of ancient times were held in great respect; far greater, indeed, than the average male priest of today commands (or probably deserves).

*What is the reason for the rise in **old** religions — Wicca, Druid, Goddess-based and indigenous? Are they much related? Organized religions fear and vilify them. Why?* (October 1994)

Under the influence of new and powerful energies streaming into our planet, a great spiritual revival is going on throughout the world. This manifests not only in the religious sphere but in all areas of life. In the religious field, as in others, the old structures and forms are breaking down under the impact of these energies and millions, especially in the West, have left the crystallized Churches of their youth. They have, rather romantically to my mind, looked backwards to more ancient forms of worship in a search for greater meaning than that provided by the current organized religions. An acute awareness of, and identification with, the Earth and "nature" is a common thread running through all these ancient forms of worship — a much needed awareness in the age ahead if we are to restore the planet to health and live in right relation to each other and to the environment.

The organized religions fear these older forms because they are older and are seen therefore as inferior; because they involve practices which seem to Churchmen to be little short of devil-worship; and because they attract many people away from the 'true' Church, their own. And, of course, they vilify them *because* they fear them.

If the 7th ray is coming in, which is to do with ceremonial order, why is there such an attack on Freemasonry? (June 1993)

I think there are two reasons for this: because Freemasonry is misunderstood, and also because it is corrupt. It is the oldest society in the world, and at the basis of its rituals are hidden some of the mysteries of initiation. When it has been cleansed of the accretions of the last 8,000 years it will become one of the major paths to initiation. I think it is under attack today because it is sensed that there is something secret going on of which we are not aware, and 'people should not have secrets'. They do not attack the CIA, or the other intelligence services around the world — MI.5, MI.6 — and *they* live on secrets. But since Freemasonry seems to be, and today largely is, a 'club' of people who are mutually self-interested and who simply help other

Masons, there is an opening for corruption. I call that a corruption of Freemasonry — it is not an attack on Freemasons *per se* but on the corruption.

What do you think about the present mission of the Real Rosicrucians in the world and their task concerning Maitreya's Emergence? (September 1993)

Everyone and every group can be involved in helping the emergence of Maitreya by making known that He is in the world. So far as I am aware, the Rosicrucian groups have not become involved in this work.

Where does the story of Noah fit into the esoteric tradition? (November 1994)

The story of Noah relates to a period about 15,500 years ago at the time of the biblical flood, when the island of Poseidonis went down, leaving only the mountains which today make up the islands of the Azores. North Africa and Spain, which were once joined, were separated by the floods and the Mediterranean was created. Forty days of rain is a purely symbolic expression. Noah did not build an 'ark' into which two of every animal came; that, too, is a symbolic statement. Noah was a Master; He knew what was coming and warned the people, telling them to take their families and animals to high ground and so escape the flood. The area of the Middle East and the Mediterranean basin was affected but there were large land masses elsewhere which were not affected.

Are the battles as described in the first chapters of the "Gita" symbolic or real battles? (March 1993)

Symbolic.

*In the List of Initiates in the book **Maitreya's Mission, Volume One**, Moses is described as a 2.3-degree initiate. That seems very advanced for the 12th century BC. Does this mean (1) he was actually able to part the Red Sea, (2) talk to God on a regular basis, and (3) receive the Ten Commandments on two stone tablets from God on Mount Sinai?* (July 1994)

2.3-degree initiate status was indeed unusually advanced for the time. Moses, however, was not an ordinary man but a (human) Avatar. Nevertheless, he did not part the Red Sea, talk to God (but to his Master) nor receive any stone tablets from God or anyone else on Mount Sinai. He simply passed on what he had inwardly heard. The Old Testament is no more to be taken literally than is the New Testament; they are both couched in symbolic language.

How do the Hindu Gods, like Siva, Ganesha and Muruga, fit into the Hierarchy? (January/February 1994)

They don't. The Hindu Gods are concepts of embodied energies: the energy is invoked when the God is invoked. The Hierarchy consists of those men and women who have made the evolutionary advance into some level of the Spiritual Kingdom — as first-degree initiates up to Planetary Lives like Maitreya.

Jesus and Bible Stories

Did Jesus fail in His mission when He died on the cross? (October 1995)

No, He triumphed completely. The mission of Jesus in Palestine was to act as the vehicle for the Christ, the Messiah. He came as a Jew as the Messiah of the Jews, and they did not recognize Him because the fundamentalists of the time put out a wrong teaching, just as they do today. They were talking for generations about the coming of the Messiah, but said the Messiah would come as a warrior King who would free the Jews from the Romans. When Jesus came He did nothing of the kind, so they got rid of Him. He came as the World Teacher for that time — or rather, to allow Maitreya, as the World Teacher, to use His vehicle for three years. That was a great gift that Jesus gave. He also learnt to be a Master, by acting as the vehicle for a Master. Jesus is now a sixth-degree Master, a "Chohan".

What do you really think about the Bible? (January/February 1993)

I believe that the Bible is a profound esoteric work of prophecy and truth, but it is not one solid, homogeneous work. The teachings, both in the Old Testament and the New Testament, and especially the teachings of Jesus as we have been given them, however distorted, are very enlightening indeed. However, they are wrapped up in symbol; they are not, I believe, meant to be taken literally. The Bible is so symbolic, so arcane and esoteric, that great truths are hidden in what appear to be very straightforward accounts but which are not that at all. I find the Resurrection, for example, perfectly acceptable; true, but wrapped up in symbol. The Gospel story is true in its broad general outlines; but in detail, no.

(1) What will happen to the Christian Bible in the future? (2) Is the Bible accurate? (January/February 1994)

It is obvious that the advent not only of Maitreya, the Christ, but also of the Master Jesus and a large group of other Masters (some of Whom were disciples of Jesus in Palestine) will have enormous repercussions for Christian groups of rigid, orthodox belief. It will have a similar impact on the fundamentalists of *all* the religions. The Master Jesus is in charge of the Christian Churches and has the task of purifying them and removing the man-made dogmas and doctrines which condition the minds of these groups today. A similar purification will take place in the other religious groups. Some rewriting of the Bible and the Eastern scriptures will therefore take place in the light of the new dispensation. The true *symbolic* nature of these scriptures will gradually be accepted. (2) As I have suggested above, the teaching of the Bible is largely symbolic.

Could you please comment on Matthew 24: "And immediately after the affliction of those days, the sun will be darkened and the moon will not give her light, and the stars will fall from the heavens, and the powers of the heavens will be shaken." (Matthew 24:29) (1) I suppose that all this has already taken place? (2) Is it true that by "the darkening of the sun and the moon not giving light" is meant the dropping of the atomic bombs on Hiroshima and Nagasaki? (December 1995)

(1) Yes. The quotation refers — symbolically — to the period of the world war(s) 1914-1945 (from the viewpoint of Hierarchy that is one war which went underground in 1918 and came above ground again in 1939). (2) Not specifically. It refers to the general chaos and destruction of that war — really a war between the forces of light and darkness — which had been going on (on astral levels) since the destruction of Atlantis around 95,000 years ago.

Did the disciples at the Last Supper see the Lord Maitreya overshadowing Jesus? (July/August 1996)

My information is that most of them did not, but they did see the light of Maitreya around Jesus. Three of the close disciples knew Jesus' role — that He was overshadowed by Maitreya — and they saw Jesus transfigured in the way that the three disciples had seen Him transfigured on the Mount, but the bulk of the disciples did not know the whole of the truth. The Transfiguration on the Mount was a symbol of the Third Initiation, which Jesus had taken in a previous life.

*At the birth of Jesus a large bright star appeared, leading the Three Wise Men to Him. More recently, one week before Maitreya miraculously appeared in Nairobi (June 1988), Job Mutungi reported in the **Kenya Times** that a "big bright star was sighted above the city". (1) Were they really stars, and if not what were they? (2) Does this happen with the advent of every new Teacher? (3) Who were the Three Wise Men? (4) Was Jesus really born in a stable?* (April 1996)

(1) They were UFOs. (2) No. (3) They were three initiates. (4) No. He was born in a house, "small but adequate", according to my Master.

I know that 25 December is an old pagan festival date and not the birth date of the Master Jesus in Palestine. Can you tell me the real date of Jesus' birth? (June 1993)

The disciple Jesus (as He was then) was born on 15 March, 24 BC.

(1) Was Jesus truly crucified? (2) And did He actually die on the cross? (October 1994)

(1) Yes. (2) Yes.

I find it confusing with the two St Johns. People refer to John and it isn't clear if it is John the Baptist or John the Beloved. (1) Why did Jesus particularly love John? (2) Which Master was John the Beloved and which was John the Baptist? (January/February 1997)

(1) John the Beloved was one of the more advanced of the Disciples around Jesus and one of the "inner three". (2) He is now the Master Koot Hoomi, Chohan of the Second-Ray Ashram in the Spiritual Hierarchy. John the Baptist is now on Sirius.

Is it true that Jesus lived near Shrinigar, Kashmir, in His later years, and even had children? Many local Kashmiri residents believe this. (June 1993)

No. It was Apollonius who went to Kashmir and is buried there. He was the same *Being* as Jesus but one incarnation later. He became a Master in that life. Jesus did not have children and died at 33 years.

(1) Did the Apostle Thomas and Apollonius (who was Jesus) actually meet each other in India? (2) What was the ray structure and point of evolution of Thomas (1st century)? (January/February 1993)

(1) Yes, several times, and sometimes for long periods. (2) Soul 2; personality 5, sub-ray 6; mental body 3, sub-ray 6; astral body 4, sub-ray 6; physical body 7, sub-ray 3. He was 2.0 degrees initiate.

If the correct name of Jesus was Jehoshua Ben Pandira (or Panthera), (1) what was his relationship to a Roman soldier named Panthera? (2) Could this soldier be the biological father of Jesus? (3) Did Joseph know Mary's lover? (4) Is it possible that Joseph adopted Jesus? (July 1994)

(1) No relation at all. (2) No. (3) Mary did not have a lover. (4) He had no need to — Jesus was the natural son of Joseph (Pandira).

*As related by H. P. Blavatsky in **Isis Unveiled II**, p.386, a virgin, called Mariana (St Mary), betrothed to a young man Iohanan, conceived from another man, Joseph Panthera. When Iohanan learned about Mary's condition, he left her, so says the old Kabbalistic work **Sepher Toldos** (or **Toledoth**) **Jeshu**. The child which was born, Joshua (or Jesus), was taken by his uncle, Rabbi Jehozhua and was initiated to the secret doctrine, first by Rabbi Elhanan, a Kabbalist, and after that by the Egyptian priests, who consecrated him for his great mystic gifts as High Priest of the Universal Secret Doctrine. (1) Could it be that a man, Iohanan, though not actually Mary's lover, indeed was her fiancé? (2) Was Jesus High Priest of the Secret Doctrine (Ageless Wisdom)?* (October 1994)

(1) Yes. (2) Yes.

Recently in Germany there has been much interest in the exhibition in the Cathedral of Trier of a 'seamless' robe believed to have been worn by Jesus. Please could you confirm whether it really belonged to Jesus? (October 1996)

No, it has no connection with Jesus.

You mentioned the overshadowing of Jesus by Maitreya up until His crucifixion. In the biblical story, who then was the so-called Risen Christ — and why was He sometimes not recognized as Jesus? (November 1993)

Jesus went out of incarnation at the crucifixion; He was then a fourth-degree initiate. The body of a fourth-degree initiate is three-quarters light — one-quarter atomic, three-quarters sub-atomic. Jesus' body was laid in the tomb and on the third day Maitreya entered into it and took total control of it. In so doing the downflow of energy as He entered the body transformed the one-quarter of atomic structure into light. So there was a body of light, a Master's body — all the Masters are in such bodies, all of Them resurrected in the occult sense of the word. They are free of the pull of matter for ever.

Jesus was out of incarnation, and Maitreya used the body for "40 days", according to the Gospel story. He was seen by the disciples, sometimes recognized and sometimes not.

The disciples saw the *body* of Jesus but not as they had last seen it: battered and bruised and bleeding on the cross, the face resembling that on the Turin Shroud. In its resurrected state all blemishes would have been restored to normality, all injuries healed. It is quite to be expected that the resurrected body of Jesus, inhabited now by Maitreya, would not be immediately recognizable. Moreover, most of the disciples did not expect to see Jesus again — except in heaven.

The Gospel story is correct in its broad general outlines, but in its details purely symbolic and/or distorted. Nevertheless He was recognized from time to time by certain of the disciples. The story of Thomas putting his finger in the side is symbolic — it did not happen that way, but is given to emphasize the need for faith.

After "40 days" Maitreya destroyed the body and returned the particles, the tiny Devic lives (Solar Pitris) which made it up, to the sun from which they came.

The record of all this is in the Turin Shroud, the authentic burial shroud of Jesus, which eventually He will claim as His own. What we see on the Shroud is a negative photograph created by the downflow of energy into the body of Jesus and which ionized it — the same principle as used in photography today.

Although some of the Dead Sea Scrolls have been made public, a great deal of controversy still exists among scholars regarding their meaning. (1) Is it possible to say who wrote the scrolls, and (2) when, and (3) for what purpose? (4) Do references to a "Pierced Messiah" and a "Teacher of Righteousness" who will some day vanquish the "sons of Darkness" refer to the Christ? (5) Are there any other scrolls or parchments yet to be discovered which will shed more light on the Christ's mission in Palestine? (May 1994)

(1) No. (2) 2nd Century AD. (3) As records of historical events. (4) The "Pierced Messiah" refers to the Master Jesus. The "Teacher of Righteousness" refers to Maitreya. (5) Yes.

The Dead Sea Scrolls are a more accurate account of the events surrounding the life of Jesus than are the biblical texts. Their discovery in 1947 and those of the Nag Hammadi Scrolls in 1945 were inspired by the Master Jesus to shed a clearer light on the events of that time in preparation for the Christ's return today.

Did "the Teacher of Righteousness" himself write the "Hymns of Thanksgiving" quoted in the article on the Dead Sea Scrolls? (July/August 1996)
Maitreya, through Jesus, voiced and dictated some of the hymns which were written down by a scribe. Some are of later date.

Some scholars say that "the Teacher of Righteousness" mentioned by the Essenes in the Dead Sea Scrolls is John the Baptist. Is this correct? (July/August 1996)
No. "The Teacher of Righteousness" is Maitreya, overshadowing Jesus.

Isaiah is generally considered to be the wisest of all the prophets of the Old Testament. Although scholars consider the book in the Old Testament bearing his name was by the hand of more than one author, was there such a figure and, if so, what was his ray structure and point in evolution? (December 1993)
Yes, Isaiah was a real historical figure, the most inspired of all the prophets. His ray structure was: Soul 4; personality 6, sub-ray 6; mental body 3, sub-ray 7; astral body 4, sub-ray 6; physical body 7, sub-ray 3. He was 2.3 degrees initiate (very advanced for that time).

EDUCATION IN THE LAWS OF LIFE AND LOVE

Will we have an education system for adults in the future?

Yes. There is a huge educational need in the world. I would say the major problem of the future 50, 60, to 100 years is education. First of all, the physical changes, like the introduction of the principle of sharing, the reorganization of distribution. Political and economic change will be the first outer manifestation of the New Age. But concurrently with that, and the only thing that will bring it about, is an expansion of the educational system. The education of everyone, adults and children, has to go forward with the greatest possible speed.

In some parts of the world there is little or no education, so everyone who does not at present have an education must be educated. Educational standards have to be raised throughout the world. Those who have none must have the basics, nothing less. Those who have the basics must have more. Throughout the world, energy and effort must pour into education to create the possibility of changing society. We will not get change without education.

When we talk about education, we have to know what that means. It does not mean only education about arithmetic, French, Dutch or English. It means that too, of course, but it also means education about the nature of life, the laws of love and life, the need to transform the political and economic structures. This, in the first place, is largely the work of Maitreya, the Masters, and the senior disciples. But it is on-going.

People have to learn to live more simply. They are not going to do it overnight, just because Maitreya says: "My advice is to live more simply. That way, there will be enough to go around." That is not enough, even if Maitreya says it. People have to see it. They have to say: "Of course! It is an absolutely common-sense necessity. Everybody can see it."

Why does everyone not see it today? Because there is no common sense. The chief quality lacking in people's lives is common sense. So many things are self-evident, it seems to me. It is self-evident that the political and economic structures of the past and present do not work. They do not work if millions are outside them, unemployed, starving, living under appalling conditions of poverty. We have to devise a system that works. That is the number one necessity. If we are not going to impose it, we have to do it by democratic means. If we do it by democratic means, there has to be an educated world public opinion. People will not do it from themselves, just wake up one morning and say: "I am going to put in a new system that will be more equitable, fairer, more just." It has to be agreed upon, and to be agreed upon it has to be seen to be right. That needs education.

Starting from the Day of Declaration-plus-one there must be a major education of humanity, by Maitreya, by the other Masters, by the disciples all over the world, by the various groups, about the laws of love and life.

Children seem to be unhappy with the school system. In what way will Maitreya's education of mankind in the laws of life and love have an effect on the present school system of the Western world?

It will in so far as it has an effect on the entire school curriculum: teachers' consciousness, the consciousness of parents and their expectations for their children, their demands on the school system for a richer and truer education, and the effect of transformation in the world. When the base materialism of today is overcome, and replaced by a truer relationship between living on the planet and what we need to live on the planet — in other words, when we are living more simply, in material terms, then education will be seen as crucial to the development of a sane, loving humanity, demonstrating goodwill. Goodwill will take its place as a *sine qua non*. Everyone will be 'into' goodwill, until we so take it for granted that we are demonstrating it.

When this takes place, we will see that the present educational system is relatively inadequate. It does not take care of the true Being. It is not true to say that the present educational system does not develop consciousness; it does. But it is consciousness along rather narrow lines. Largely, it is brain and mind consciousness. That is fine; we all need to know how to cross roads, do arithmetic, and so on. We have to know how to go to an airport and buy a ticket. We have to learn to do things correctly on the physical plane. There are many things that children need to know just to become reasonably sensible, efficient adults in the present or future world. But that is a different thing from the development of consciousness. The new education will be concerned precisely with the development of inner consciousness. That means development of contact with the source of consciousness, the soul.

The soul nature of the child has to be recognized. The point in evolution and the ray structure must be known, so that the correct teaching can be given to prepare the child to be what he/she is. The Masters will be training educators to give this information. That does not mean to say that children will not have the general training in living efficiency which everyone needs. But over and above that, the major part of the curriculum will be the specific type of education that that child requires at his/her point in evolution.

If the child is 0.5 degrees initiate, it will not be the same as if he/she were 1.5 or 2.5. (If it is 2.5, the child will tell you the type of education he/she needs!) Most 2.5 individuals, even as young children, are able to exert their influence on their environment. This is one of the facts of discipleship. A disciple is someone who is in control of his environment. The initiate is known by his impact on the world, the demonstration of his service in the world. A child who is nearing the third initiation, and is going to have a major impact in the world, can demonstrate at 2.5 his or her needs. There is an inner knowledge, awareness, and very often an outer demonstration.

Giotto, the great Italian painter, was a shepherd boy, and he used to sit and draw his father's sheep. One day through the field where he was sitting, drawing with a flint on a stone, came Cimabue, a great and established painter, very famous. He came over and looked at the boy, and said: "This is a wonderful drawing of sheep. Can you draw anything else?" Giotto took his flint and drew "a round and perfect circle". Seeing him draw a perfect circle, Cimabue said: "Ah! This boy is a genius. Come with me. I will take you to your father." (Giotto was 2.0, at six or seven years old.) Cimabue said to the father: "You have a genius for a child. If you will let me train and prepare him, come into my studio, I will make a great artist of him. He will be lauded throughout Italy." And so it was.

What about education on the ecological problems of the world?
Since we are polluting our planet with nuclear radiation, gasses of all kinds, fertilizers, pouring the most obnoxious chemicals into our rivers, reservoirs and land, and making the air practically unbreathable in major cities by the exhaust of cars, then it is obvious we must get rid of the pollution.

Everyone, without exception, is suffering to a greater or lesser degree, depending on their constitution, from pollution. There is a growing incidence of diseases throughout the planet — mainly skin, heart, and lung. That is a huge problem facing humanity, and it has to be tackled right away. The nuclear power plants must be wound down. The polluting of our rivers must be seen as a crime against society. At the moment, it is an easy way to get rid of effluents. It is criminal to poison the rivers, on which much drinking water depends. It is criminal to pour into the seas chemical effluents which kill off many fish. For the Japanese, and others, for example, this is a major problem, because they live mainly on fish — or they did until very recently.

My Master has said that, after the redistribution of resources, the number one priority is to tackle the ecological problems of the world. Maitreya has said this is something that engages everyone. No one is too young or too old, He says, to take part in this. Whether it is wasting a little piece of paper or burning an entire forest to make way for grazing cattle for beef, we have to change.

This cannot be done overnight, and it can only be done by consensus. Consensus will take place only when the need is seen. When the need is seen, the way towards it will be found. This will result from the acceptance of the principle of sharing. When we accept the principle of sharing, we are accepting that we can no longer destroy the environment. We have to change the distribution process, and we have to learn to live with less. That does not mean with not enough; there is enough for everybody if it is distributed more equitably. This will be done.

People will recognize that the Christ is right. It is the only sane, common-sense thing to do. As soon as we do that, we will see that we do not need this or that. When we remove competition, the blind following of market forces which drive people to competition, we ease the pressure on the environment. We will see the need for an economy which is sustainable long-term. The present economy is not and is poisoning the planet at the same time. What happens when we have burned all the forests and there is no more oxygen? We are absolutely dependent on the vegetable kingdom for the oxygen which we breathe.

We are so wrong-thinking because we do not think as a whole. We do not think as a planetary thinker, with a planetary voice. We think as independent nations, each doing our own thing — and within nations, independent groups and individuals each doing his or her own thing. Everyone is working in this isolated, although interrelated, individualistic way. We have to recognize that the world is one, and that the goods of the world belong to everyone. They must be shared and properly used.

In the very immediate future the present petrol or gas engine will be replaced by an electric engine. We could have electric engines on motor cars now. This is perfectly feasible, and it may be that as a transitional measure the electric car will become the norm. They will be replaced by more efficient public transport.

We have to deal with the ecological problem, and because we have to, we will. It may be that the major technological aspects of it will never touch any of us, but day-to-day questions will touch everyone, whether it is making do with produce which is less well-wrapped than it used to be: only one outer wrapper instead of three — it takes 10 minutes to open a bar of soap today — or economizing in energy use of all kinds.

Many of us are prepared to work in education after the Masters emerge. What do the Masters have planned in education so we may work most effectively with Their plan in the immediate future in approaching public education in schools and adult education?

Read *Education in the New Age*, by the Master DK through Alice A. Bailey (Lucis Trust). The direction of education in the future will be along the lines of soul realization. Every child will be seen as a soul with a particular ray structure, which will determine his/her particular bent and direction, at a given point in evolution. This knowledge will determine how much and what he/she can absorb, the degree to which the child should be stimulated along certain lines.

Soul education is the new psychology. This is the way forward for psychology. In *Esoteric Psychology I* and *Esoteric Psychology II*, by the Master DK, you can read about the rays. Each ray has its own psychological quality, or colour. This conditions the way a person demonstrates as a soul, personality, type of mind, brain, and so on. All are dependent on the ray make-up.

The new psychology, and the new education, therefore, will work with that knowledge. Introduce that into the new educational programmes at the level that it can be understood and used, and you will be setting out on the right path. It takes time. The educational curricula in schools and colleges always come a good deal after the thinkers, the ideas-men, the psychologists, the educators. Gradually the ideas are formed into a programme that can be utilized in a school.

Teaching itself will change from simply the imparting of knowledge to the elucidation of the quality and purpose of the individual. It is fitting individuals for life, not for particular jobs, which is what 'education' largely does today, well or badly. It is fitting individuals for their life destiny, coming from the nature, the purpose, of the soul. All of this needs to be understood if we are going to make an individual package or educational programme for any child.

After the Masters emerge, I could say, as an educator, regarding the global sharing of resources: "Sure, look for it. There is a blueprint." And people will go to work in that area. As an educator, I can go up to the school systems and say: "I know some of the ABCs. I am not capable of determining a person's ray qualities or point in evolution." Will I just say: "I do not know when it is going to be coming", or is there some kind of blueprint?

There is not a blueprint. There is a body of ideas set out in *Education for the New Age* by the Master DK. It might take another 50 to 100 years to implement. But the direction has been shown. If you call yourself an educator, it is up to you to implement it. You do not have to know the ray structure of every child in the class in order to bring into their education some of the ideas of DK. You are seeing it as if it were one perfect body of knowledge which you must have before you do anything. It is a stage-by-stage process. We are making enormous steps forward in consciousness, and therefore in educational possibilities. The time ahead will only speed up that process, but it will not happen overnight.

Will the structure of the family be outmoded in the new age? If so, what will replace it? (October 1994)

No. The family is the basic unit which provides the best conditions and karmic situation for correct evolution. It cannot, with impunity, be replaced.

What role do parents and family have in the ultimate restoration of individuals and the human race at large? (November 1996)

The role of parents and family is crucial in the education of young people in right human relationships. It is precisely the family — the building brick of society — that provides the arena for the interplay and resolution of karmic forces which, in time, create right relationships.

Since parents inevitably pass on their own experiences and mode of upbringing, good or bad, it is obvious that an enormous educational programme is needed to limit the worst cruelties — physical, emotional and mental — which today (and for centuries past) are inflicted by ignorant parents on their children. A family dedicated to the creation of right relationship within itself — through the inculcation of goodwill — is preparing its members for living in right relationship to that larger aspect of the human family, community.

*I read an article which your Master wrote some time ago called 'Leisure is the key' (**Share International**, November 1986), in which He said that most people in the world live a stressed-out, uncreative, mechanical sort of existence and that humanity needs time to develop to become self-realizing in leisure. Presumably, after the world economic systems collapse and a new way of life emerges, that will become possible. Is this something that your Master envisages in the next 15, 20, 30, 100 years?* (March 1996)

Fifteen to 20 years from now this world will be transformed. In the next five years it is going to be changed dramatically, so fundamental, so basic are the changes which will take place through the redistribution of the world's resources. Eventually, factories will be built with machinery programmed to create all we need. This will free humanity for the exploration of its own nature. The resultant leisure will give to everyone what today is the privilege of a tiny minority, of a few gifted people who can make enough money to indulge their gifts — artists, singers, writers, composers and so on, some scientists who can work for a few large organizations. Eventually all the artifacts of the world will be created by machinery, and, in time, much of that machinery will be created by man's thought.

This is how the Masters create. They can take, say, a microphone, and turn it into the most extraordinary instrument. They could probably make it into a 'radiator' to dispense spiritual energy around the planet. Certainly 10-15 years from now we will know a different world. Those who are really young today will grow up in a world such as we have never known before, created by man himself under the inspiration of the Masters.

There have been wonderful, brilliant civilizations, with science far more evolved than we have today, in the distant past, but these were created by the Masters and given to the humanity of the time. This new way of life will be created by humanity, who is now adult and able to do it, in response to, and in conjunction with, the Masters.

GOODWILL, HARMLESSNESS AND DETACHMENT

Please discuss harmlessness and goodwill. How are they different? Is one usually learned and practised before the other?

Goodwill necessarily comes before harmlessness. Harmlessness has gradually to be evolved, but anyone can have goodwill which every child is born with. It is the nature of the human psyche to have goodwill. It is the will to good, and every individual comes into incarnation with it; it is human nature. It can be stamped out of the individual quite early on if a child is ill-treated. A child can be warped psychologically and his/her innate goodwill transformed into an undying hatred which brings about the violence that is being expressed around the world.

The distortion of the innate goodwill of humanity is probably the greatest cruelty perpetrated in the world. The cruelty of parents to their children is unbelievable and is done usually quite unconsciously. They are simply passing on to the child the cruelty, the behaviour, by which they themselves were raised. That is passed on, over and over again, generation after generation. The result in some cases is the destruction of the individual's goodwill. That individual becomes, sometimes, a murderer, not because there is anything innate in their make-up that makes them a murderer, but because their goodwill has been thwarted and strangled in their early years. The first five to seven years of life, especially the first five years, are crucial in the creation of a harmless individual. If a person from birth is treated harmlessly, that person usually becomes harmless in their turn. If they are treated cruelly and abused in one way or another, they perpetuate that cruelty. That is the sad story of our present civilization.

First of all, keep the goodwill of the children intact by not harming it, by not implanting your idea of what that person is and should be, thus stamping out their spontaneity, their originality, their own very special free will. Everyone infringes the free will of everyone else. Only the Masters do not infringe free will. Infringement of free will very quickly leads to the end of goodwill. When you have free will and correctly use it, you inevitably have goodwill.

The world is going to be changed, above all, by the countless millions of people, men and women everywhere, of goodwill. It is precisely the people of goodwill who, in the first place, will respond to Maitreya. He will potentize that goodwill. He will confirm in them their attitude to life and will so potentize it that He will build a world public opinion against which no government on earth can stand.

In this way, through an educated, correctly led, potentized goodwill of the masses, the changes in the world will take place. That will eventually lead, when we have correct political, economic, social, and religious structures, to the manifestation of harmlessness. When people become more attuned to their own Being, their Self, their own soul, they will inevitably become more harmless. The nature of the soul is harmlessness. When Maitreya speaks and shows the need for harmlessness in all human relations, you can see how that will quickly catch on and excite the imagination of more and more people. They will see the need for harmlessness.

When they really understand the Law of Cause and Effect, which most people understand only vaguely, they will see the need for harmlessness. They will know that every thought and action has an effect, and that the effects make their lives; that there is no such thing as good or bad luck but the outer result of previous actions. It is not only what is way back in one's youth or past life that is to be considered. It is actions moment to moment, right now, just a moment ago. All of that determines the life which is spreading out ahead of us, which we are creating moment to moment. Thus the need for detachment which inevitably leads to harmlessness. This is why Maitreya puts detachment at the very root of the transformational process of Self-awareness which becomes Self-realization.

Why are we harmful? It seems so much a part of our make-up. What is the root of this problem?

Why are we harmful? Because we are greedy and selfish — in a word, egotistical. Ego is the root of the problem. We are harmful because we are incomplete, imperfect. Anything imperfect demonstrates the opposite of perfection, which is limitation of some kind. We are harmful because we do not recognize the need for harmlessness, and because all of us are deeply, profoundly egotistical. We want what we want and when we want it. It is the desire principle at the basis of all personality life which has to be overcome. That is the problem for all humanity. It is the overcoming of separatism, the personality's sense of itself as separate.

The personality is used by the principle of desire to bring about individuality. Without that desire principle, there would be no evolution. As personalities we evolve to a point where the soul can begin to infuse us with its higher spiritual energies. But it cannot do that until the vibrational rate of the vehicles of the soul — the physical, astral, and mental bodies of the personality — are vibrating at a more synchronous rate. That allows the soul to invest its reflection with its own nature. We have to become active, potent individuals that the soul can use. The soul cannot use a personality which is feeble, unstructured, and fragmented. The reconstruction only takes place as that individual nears the first initiation.

How does one approach being harmless in one's relationships? How does this relate to detachment?
It relates completely to detachment. Harmlessness proceeds stage by stage as detachment proceeds. Through the evolutionary process, we develop detachment. That is what evolution of consciousness is about. As we detach from the results of the physical, emotional, and mental experience, the soul can express its harmless nature through the personality. The more detached, the more harmless. The less detached, the more harmful, inevitably. Attachment is an overdeveloped sense of the separate personality, the ego. The more you detach yourself from the experience of the personality, which is really the experience of the soul in incarnation, and detach from identifying with the vehicles, and more and more identify with the soul and its purpose, the more harmless you become. It is the soul in form which incarnates. It is the soul expression which produces harmlessness.

Personalities can be taught, and one of the powerful means will be Maitreya's teaching about the nature of the Self in relation to its vehicles — physical, astral and mental — and the need for detachment from identifying with these vehicles. This will be central to Maitreya's teaching about the nature of life. The nature of life is the nature of the Self, as far as we are concerned. The need for harmlessness will become more and more clear even on the personality level.

Relate that to a growing understanding of the great Law of Cause and Effect. This law determines the results of all our actions: what we think, what we do, sets in motion causes. The effects stemming from those causes make our lives. That will be harmful or harmless depending on the nature of the causes which we set in motion. So we can see the need for harmlessness. Harmlessness can be inculcated when we know that it is necessary. Maitreya will set in motion a schooling of humanity in the need for harmlessness in a day-to-day way. That does not mean that everyone will be harmless by the next day, but He will set it in motion in people's consciousness. When we see the need, then, gradually, we can change.

If one is truly detached from a specific vice, do you not only refrain from indulging it but become free from the pull of that vice altogether? Many people who give up vices or addictions such as alcoholism, drugs, overeating, etc, spend lifetimes fighting the desire to indulge them again.

I understand that if a person dedicates himself to service, practises meditation and develops aspiration, they eventually develop Self-awareness. Wouldn't this Self-awareness bring about an overall sense of detachment rather than just detachment from specific vices one at a time? (May 1993)

The problem is not so much detaching from specific addictions one by one as that of cultivating a general attitude of detachment. If a person is *truly* detached, the problem of "fighting the desire" does not arise. The attitude of fighting creates conflict and increases the problem. Detachment is the result of withdrawing attention (and therefore energy) from the effort of overcoming the addiction. The aim is to find out who is attached.

Self-awareness is the result of a growing detachment rather than the other way round.

Does Maitreya have in mind any end-purpose to life? (January/February 1994)

He says the meaning and purpose and goal of life is the achievement of Self-realization — that is what we are here for — and He has come to teach the "art", as He calls it, of Self-realization. He says that it is not a religion, an ideology or a belief but is something which is the goal of our life. When you are Self-realized you are also illumined, enlightened, and become a Master; then you are free to leave this planet, if that is your destiny.

(1) What is Self-realization, and (2) how does it manifest in one's being? (November 1993)

(1) Self-realization is the same as God-realization. When unity or at-one-ment has been established between the individual in incarnation and his or her soul, and through the soul with the Monad (in Theosophical terminology) or Spark of God, Self- or God-realization takes place. The soul is then no longer required as the Divine Intermediary and is reabsorbed into the Monad (of which it is the reflection). The Self can then manifest directly through the reflection of its reflection, the physical-plane personality, now totally soul-infused. (2) The manifestation is that of the perfected Master with consciousness and control on all planes of this planet. Maitreya has said: "The Self alone matters. You are that Self, an Immortal Being."

When Maitreya says "Self" and "spirit" what does He mean? (May 1993)

By the Self Maitreya means the Monad or the Spark of God, the Absolute, that which stands back of creation, which reflects itself on the soul plane as the individual human soul. The Self is impersonal. There is only Self, which is everybody. It is untouched by creation, but experiences or observes creation through the Soul and the reflection of the Soul — the man or woman in incarnation.

Is forgiveness part of Maitreya's teachings? (October 1994)

Yes. The basis of His teaching, I would say, is the cultivation of detachment. Forgiveness becomes possible only through a growing detachment and correct identification.

How is the World Teacher going to prevent the 'botching up' of His teaching — will He remain in incarnation for the rest of humanity's evolution? (May 1996)

We may not 'botch it up' too much, because we either make it work or we destroy ourselves. In the first place it is a political-economic transformation, but basically it is a spiritual rejuvenation of the world. Maitreya will ensure that His teaching stays intact by remaining in the world, not till the end of the world but till the end of the Age of Aquarius, which will be, as far as He is concerned, 2,500 years from now. Every time we come into incarnation during that time we will find Him at the centre of our planetary life, inspiring and teaching, and acting as the Initiator at the first two of the five initiations which make one a Master.

In the very near future, after the Day of Declaration, He will set out on an itinerary round the world, so that all countries will see Him close-to — He will be on television and so on — and people will have the opportunity to ask Him all sorts of questions. As far as the overseeing of humanity's response is concerned, this is something which at the top level He will do, but which at a somewhat lesser level certain Masters will do; They have trained a large group of initiates and disciples to help in that work. Humanity cannot simply be 'imposed on'. The transformation will be made by humanity itself — in the main led by the disciples and initiates trained by the Masters in the different departments: political, economic, religious, social, scientific, and so on.

What will happen to people who do not go along with Maitreya's teachings when He comes out? (October 1995)

There is a huge misunderstanding underlying this question. Maitreya's teachings will be given for humanity to consider and accept or reject as people wish. No infringement of our free will

will ever be made by Maitreya and His group of Masters. Nothing will "happen" to anyone who dislikes or disagrees with Maitreya's ideas and advice — except that they will probably hold up their own evolution by their inability to make the shift in consciousness required to share and so create justice and peace in the world.

ON AWARENESS, KNOWLEDGE AND WISDOM

Interview with Maitreya's Associate
by Patricia Pitchon

During a talk with Maitreya's associate on 30 August 1993 we discussed Maitreya's views on knowledge, wisdom and awareness. His views are particularly relevant because our society places a high premium on knowledge. Maitreya's associate explained that when the phrase "knowledge and wisdom" is used in this context, what is meant by knowledge is "that which gets stored", whereas wisdom here means "knowledge which is experienced." In the associate's words: knowledge becomes wisdom when it has been experienced. If you do not experience it, then it remains as a role model. The image that comes to mind is a library. Even what you experience can remain stacked up there. The moment you act with detachment awareness takes charge of you.

According to Maitreya: "You want to achieve salvation from the cycle of birth and death. This means you want to be free of the 'Big Bang's' influence. But knowledge and wisdom on their own will not help you. It is awareness which guides the true Self." In Maitreya's view, this awareness *is* freedom and salvation. Awareness arises as a result of detachment.

Maitreya's associate illustrated the importance of Maitreya's continual emphasis on detachment by discussing the Bible story of Adam and Eve: the moment the "fruit of the tree of knowledge" was eaten, Adam and Eve became conscious of the things around them. The point here is that knowledge, without detachment, entraps you. It becomes one of the bondages of life.

In Maitreya's view: "The body needs bathing every day. You also need to bathe your mind and spirit. Your spirit is the source of energy. Your spirit can become exhausted. You need the water of detachment."

Going forward, not back

The entire creation came from the Big Bang. Does this mean you have to go back to the Big Bang? No. You want to move on.

163

Maitreya's associate described a recent scenario where there was a gathering of people after religious ceremonies. A person came from India, hired a boat, and charges for two-week stays on this boat. He takes the money back to India to spend on charity. He also lectures on Indian religious scriptures, especially the *Ramayana*.

The boat was full of people and someone asked: "Why has this lecture been repeated over and over and yet we don't see transformations in India or in any part of the world?" Maitreya's associate explained that many questions were asked and the saints and swamis at this gathering had no answer for this type of question.

A saint there described Ram's predicament: "Ram was born in a royal family and was destined to sit on the throne. He went into the forest because of political upheavals and returned only after 14 years. His wife Sita was taken away by Ravanna and was no longer in the palace. She had two sons. Ram was still in the forest and wondered whether these were his sons. Sita said if he had doubts, then she would not stay with him." Someone at the gathering asked: "Why, if Rama is supposed to be God, did he have doubts?" Maitreya's associate added: this is a good question. Maitreya teaches that when you are detached and therefore aware, you are one with God. Your doubts disappear.

Maitreya's associate commented: if you teach that Ram is God without understanding, this creates confusion in young minds. How many youngsters go to temples? Some are there, taken by their parents. But today knowledge and wisdom are necessary in order to face the problems of life, rather than the past.

Referring to the story of Jesus, the associate said: before Jesus was put on the Cross He was crowned with thorns and was powerless to prevent it. At some point He appeared to have doubts. But the experience given to Him on the Cross made Him say: "Father, forgive them, for they know not what they do." Jesus was freed from the bondage of knowledge and wisdom. He realized that in awareness He was one with God.

Maitreya says: "You can control knowledge and wisdom. You can use it positively. But it should not take charge of your

Self. It should not master you. The moment you are detached from it you master it."
(*Share International*, October 1993)

THE NEW ARCHITECTURE

The Temple of Solomon symbolizes initiation. With the new architecture, will there be a building built which actually facilitates this process?

Yes, there will be temples set up in various parts of the world. There will be two here in the United States, a preparatory and a more advanced school, which will prepare initiates for initiation. But initiation is always a self-initiating process. It does not mean that teachers there will give set rules. They will give various lines of thought and books to read. They will probably give fields of service, and in this way people will learn to become candidates for initiation. But it is life itself, and the relationships which come out of life itself, which lead you to initiation. When you master the devas of your physical, astral, and mental bodies, you take the first three initiations. When you take the first three, you do not need me to tell you how to take the fourth and fifth. It becomes clear as you go along.

Some of these sacred temples are of ancient origin, and will be reactivated; others will be new. Maitreya will go from country to country and the first two initiations will be conducted outwardly on the physical plane in those temples by Maitreya and two Masters. The energy from the Great Rod of Initiation, the Flaming Diamond, transferred to the Lesser Rod, which Maitreya uses at the first two initiations, is directed into the chakras of the initiate.

Initiation, up until now, has always taken place out of the body. That is why, for the most part, people do not remember it. They may remember something, but they do not remember the actual ceremony which puts the seal on what has already been achieved. You are initiate before you take initiation. Your chakras must be vibrating at the required rate, so that when the energy from the Rod of Initiation is directed to them by Maitreya you do not die. Otherwise, you would certainly die. Initiation — the first two — will take place on the outer physical plane from now on, when Maitreya inaugurates the process. In certain temples, energized precisely for this, the initiatory process will go on throughout the world.

What makes possible the Masters' return to the world is that there are three-to-four million people who are on the threshold of the first initiation. The ashrams of the Masters will be replicated on the physical plane in large groups around the world.

Will we be able to participate in the future beautification of our cities?

The beautification of our cities is for the architects and city planners, but with input from every individual. Everyone has the need to, and the possibility of, participating in the creation of the New Age. This will not be done by experts and then imposed on humanity but arrived at by consensus, clearly indicated, first of all, perhaps, by Masters, and then by trained men and women in their various fields. At the highest level inspired, probably, by the Masters, and at the lower levels carrying out the plans of these higher disciples. We can all be involved in such beautification.

When you were talking about the transformation of the cities, you said something about areas being defined on the basis of different qualities, where people will choose where they want to live. Can you say anything more about that? Is that related to the rays?

No, the make-up of different areas of the city has nothing to do with the ray make-up of the people. It refers to different qualities of city life — some more, some less, urbanized. Today, we have cities with a very congested city centre, inner suburbs, and outer suburbs. Some like the outer suburbs, and hate to travel in. Others like the leafy suburbs, to see green around but do not like to be too far out, so they are in the inner suburbs. Others like the day-to-day congruence of people, shops, restaurants, cinemas, art galleries. They like to be in an urbanized town.

These different areas will be of those different types. There will be those which are heavily urbanized, but small. There will be larger areas in which there is a combination of houses, shops, shopping centres, and certain kinds of light industry. There will be outer suburbs which are pretty well country. They will, in the same way as today, accommodate the needs of different types of people, but in a much more mixed way than today. For instance, there will probably be no area which will be without a real park, an area of green with water for sailing, for bathing, given the right climate. On the other hand, the actual built-up areas of a town will be altogether much smaller than they are today. Industry will be largely taken out of the town except on a rather small scale, and a very light type. Not so very different in some respects from the underlying notion in our towns now, only much smaller, much more accessible to all different parts, and without the congestion of traffic.

You said that architecture is the expression of the 7th ray. Can you go more into that?
The 7th ray concretizes the spiritual idea on the physical plane. A spiritual concept needs the 7th-ray energy actually to bring it down to earth and create it on the physical plane. The structure which embodies any idea is the result of ritualized action. An action performed over and over again gradually creates a structure, a form. The 7th ray does precisely that. The ritualistic quality of the 7th ray makes the continuity, the succession of movements which ultimately are sounds which concretize the spiritual idea into a form.

The 7th ray is coming into incarnation now in a very powerful way. Together with the 4th ray, which is coming in around 2025, we will have the flourishing of art forms of all kinds. The highest type of art is always created by the combination of the 4th and 7th rays. Although there are artists on every ray, the highest type of artist, almost always, has these two rays in abundance. Leonardo da Vinci had *only* 4 and 7, for example. The combination of these two will make a new art form in which architecture becomes the kind of exemplary form. It is the biggest, it is public. The new architecture will be very strongly influenced by the 7th ray, which structures. The 4th ray gives the quality of colour, life, expression, and of melody, if it is music. The 7th ray gives the structure of the music, the painting, what painters call "composition", the underlying form which allows the melody, the colour, to act out its expressive role. A 4th-ray artist, for instance, without much 7th ray, may have a very eloquent colour expression but will lack form, cohesion, and be weaker, therefore, perhaps making very nice colour relationships of which we soon tire. We tire less of the structure which gives form to that type of colour or melodic sensitivity.

Not everyone is going to be a painter, an architect, or musician, but everyone, under the influence of these two rays, will begin to colour their life along the lines that an artist might do in his painting, or a musician in his music. It will change the quality of life.

People will make their life a work of art, and this will find expression in the architectural field with the creation of new structures, many of which will be extraordinarily beautiful and new. Those strictly related to the devotional life of humanity, the religious expression, will embody, hold, and radiate particular energies, and will be the sanctuaries, the places set apart, usually in the centre of every town, where people will go for their particular kind of devotion. There will be churches and temples of all kinds. But instead of just being square blocks of concrete, they will be formed out of shapes which themselves are energetic, which attract and radiate particular energies. For the rest of it, the actual civic architecture, clarity of design, beauty of form, and elegance of expression will come more and more to the fore. As the 7th and 4th rays work together, we will get, probably, the greatest architecture that this world has seen — perhaps since Atlantean times.

Do the new schools of geomancy have any value in the creation of the new architecture and life forms?

No. They are really the resurgence of old forms. The Masters will seek to inspire a growing sensitivity of each person's psychic mechanism. That is something quite different from geomancy. Magic is out. I know that the 7th ray is called the Ray of Ritual or Ceremonial Order or Magic. This is true, but magic is always seen as magic of the physical plane and making things appear and disappear. The magic of consciousness is something quite different — the broadening, the expansion of

169

consciousness which allows more and more of the innate, divine attributes to demonstrate.

It is a question not of geomancy but of the power which comes to an individual when they no longer impede the flow of energy through them. When a person expands his or her consciousness to a point of such awareness that they are acting with the life, and with the various energies and forces of the life, they can become an instrument by which that life does the creation. The person does not do it, the life does it. They simply become a more sensitive instrument because they are more aware of that life. It is really the expansion of awareness, which is an organ of sensitivity. Such a person can perform all sorts of miracles. But it is not the person who is performing the miracles. It is the life that is performing the miracle because they are not impeding the flow of energy.

I was talking about principles such as Feng Shui which deals with the siting and orientation of buildings, and has specifically to do with objects in the dwelling.

There is an enormous glamour at the basis of those, too. It is based on superstition and fear. It is true there are natural forces which are detrimental to human health. As people become more and more aware in the sense in which I am talking, by an expansion of consciousness rather than the development of geomancy, they will learn to site their buildings in the correct place.

The Masters can place objects which earth energy. There are many places in the world which are earthed by the Masters, so that these energies no longer harm the people in the country or city where they are. They place objects all over the world — magnets — which radiate beneficial energy. Sometimes they are discovered, but for long ages they may be totally undiscovered. I know of one special one in Japan which was placed there about a century and a half ago. It was discovered very recently when an image of Maitreya appeared in a house on a glass door. The people moved it, and built a shrine outside in a part of the garden. They had to dig up everything, and found this huge circular "something". They did not know if it was stone or metal.

That was placed, according to my Master, about a century and a half ago by another Master. It is a magnet. If you put your hand to the outside of the building, you feel the radiation from it. Gold dust appears on the outside of the building. People come from all over Japan. We reported it in *Share International* (April 1993). But the knowledge which the Masters use is not geomancy. It is the awareness that comes from expansion of consciousness. It is like intuition, but it is different in function from intuition.

NEW FORMS OF TRAVEL

Are the blueprints for the new forms of travel already in existence?

Yes and no. In the minds of the Masters, the blueprints are already in existence. Some of them have been impressed on the minds of certain disciples, but it would be untrue to say that even these disciples have set down what we could call blueprints for new forms of travel. What it amounts to is that certain disciples have ideas. They may not know where the ideas come from. They probably do not know anything about Masters; they have no sense of being impressed, but they are tuning into the thoughtforms which the Masters place as clichés in the mindbelt, and are responding to that. They are thinking up (it seems to be from themselves) new forms of travel; inventions which will facilitate travel; new means of locomotion — using very simple forms that do not use many parts and therefore not much fuel or material; and investigating the use of lighter metals that will be strong but easy to project with minimal power. All of these ideas are circulating within the minds of various disciples around the world. But so far it would not be true to say that there are blueprints set down ready to be put into effect as soon as humanity gives the word. That is not the case. There are such blueprints in respect to the process of sharing, redistributing the resources of the world. Various such blueprints are ready to be implemented when humanity sees and accepts the need.

How long will it take to implement these changes in travel?

Ten to 15 years to implement the new advanced forms of travel which are basically quite conventional in relation to existing methods. For the implementation of entirely new modes of travel, the kind I was referring to in the keynote talk, from about 10 or 15 years up to about 50 years. You will see a beginning of these changes over the next few years in theory, and this will lead, in 10 to 15 years, to the actual reconstruction of existing forms of travel along better lines. They will be changed as the new energies, the new approach to living, really begins to hold sway.

POOL OF KNOWLEDGE

What will be the form of "the pool of knowledge accessible to all" which the Master refers to in His article, 'The Son of Man'?
This body of knowledge will be largely, but not exclusively, scientific and technological. Throughout the world, scientists and technicians inspired by Hierarchy will publish their work in a way accessible to all. Gone for ever will be the scientist selling his discoveries to the highest bidder. Gone for ever will be the time when great corporations can buy up technological masterpieces and put them on a shelf so that their existing products can go on and on. We have lived through a period of a tragic waste of the world's resources. That has to stop. All knowledge will go into the computer system. You can call it the Internet, the World Knowledge Bank, the World Wisdom Bank, where the wisdom, the accumulated thoughts and knowledge of thousands of years of inspired writings will be available. The up-to-date inventions, the scientific knowledge which will speed up the invention process, will go on to this same Bank which anyone, anywhere in the world, can access.

Today, scientific discoveries are very often sitting in manuscript form in the scientist's study, never taken up by industry or whoever. These discoveries will be taken up because the information will be readily accessible. Knowledge from all over the world will be funnelled into this bank and be immediately accessible. Then a scientist in Japan might say: "This information that came into the knowledge bank today has given me the key I was looking for, towards which my studies were moving. I need precisely that key to fulfil this." In the relationship of one area of study to another, tremendously quick advances will be made in science and technology of all kinds. We can separate pure science and technological science, but both are needed, both are parts of the same expansion of consciousness of humanity. Great discoveries will be made and placed in the knowledge bank and become inspiring insights for groups of technicians who may not have the concept, but immediately are stimulated to produce the technology which can make use of the concept. In this way the new technology will develop.

More and more, we will develop machines which will create the artifacts which we use in everyday life, so the need for human beings in factories will increasingly disappear. Then will come a time when these same technological inventions will be created by mind, programmed by mind, with a very clear end-result already foreseen by the creator of the technology.

I am moving a bit ahead now, but this is how the Masters work. They Themselves create wonderful artifacts, instruments, apparatuses of all kinds, which do Their work, which They use in the radiation of energy, experiments of all kinds. The Masters do not think that They know everything. They are experimenting all the time, exploring the planet, experimenting with energy, with what happens when energy, for example, leaves in the form of a thought made by one person and is picked up by another. All of this is under constant experimental attention by the Masters. We ourselves will develop, more and more, this kind of approach.

All of this is dependent on a realization that we live in an energetic universe, that the world is made of energy, that what we call God, the One Life, is energy differentiated into myriad forms. We are entering an age in which God, Creation, the Nature of Being, will be seen as energy and studied in every aspect. The next aspects to be studied are the etheric planes, of which there are four. When the etheric planes become a reality for the scientists they will become a reality for everyone. Initially, scientists will probably study the fourth and third, and then the two higher etheric planes. Then they will be able to study thought itself emanating from the astral plane, or the lower and higher levels of the mental plane. Thought will be seen as energy, and that energy conforms itself to thought. This is the basic occult axiom. Then we shall be able to use the power of thought to move objects and to travel instantaneously around the world.

How can the Internet be transformed into a pool of knowledge? What is the difference between facts and knowledge?

Facts are the basis on which knowledge is gained. A body of facts is meaningless without the insight of the mind, the intelligence and understanding. When the mind, the intelligence, and the understanding look at the facts and relate them, you have knowledge. Facts in relationship produce what we call knowledge. They need insight and understanding to produce useful knowledge. There is a great deal of knowledge which is not useful.

On the Internet, today, there is a great deal of useless knowledge. "How to make a bomb." "How to become an urban guerrilla fighter." This is useless knowledge. They give you the facts to make agencies of destruction. What use is that? We are talking about a bank of useful knowledge, accumulated discoveries, technologies, sciences which can inspire the workers in these fields simply by using their computers. They do not have to hope that someone somewhere will come up with that fragment which is missing from their knowledge. There it will be. When we share this body of knowledge, when everyone who has any use for it has access to it, the whole process of discovery, science, technology, will speed up amazingly. Because it will not be conditioned by commercialization, market forces, it cannot be cornered by those who make a particular brand of computer, where you have to buy the programme to make it work for you. It will do away with commercial competition. Mainly, it is a bank to which anybody can go freely and withdraw the knowledge which is lying there for the taking. You do not even have to have a bank account.

CHAPTER 2

THE CHALLENGE OF
THE 21ST CENTURY

THE ECOLOGICAL BALANCE OF THE WORLD

Interview with Benjamin Creme's Master
(through Benjamin Creme)
by Patricia Pitchon

The great challenges of the next few decades, according to British historian Paul Kennedy, are: a population explosion, environmental hazards, and technology-driven change. The way these three factors could interact and their possible effects are examined in his book *Preparing for the Twenty-First Century* (Random House, New York, 1993).

Currently we are facing population explosions in countries which can least afford them. As more people cut down more trees for firewood in rural areas, for example, soil erosion caused by this deforestation leads to increasing desertification. People who cannot make a living in the countryside head for the cities, where the pressure on resources such as transport, housing, health care, water and electricity leads to partial collapse and in some areas total collapse of services. This is the picture in many Third World cities today.

As a country becomes more urbanized the population stabilizes, but that time is not yet for many poor countries. Sweeping technological changes are often poorly co-ordinated and throw hundreds of thousands out of work. Additionally, environmental hazards affect the entire globe. Great challenges require great changes, not least in the economic sphere.

Benjamin Creme's Master kindly agreed to answer questions on these topics.

Is the demographic analysis made in Paul Kennedy's book **Preparing for the Twenty-First Century** *accurate?*

The Master: Yes and no. If nothing were done it would be accurate. But, as seen by Hierarchy, the changes planned, if implemented, would to a large extent prove these assumptions false, and happily so for humanity.

Could you give an indication of the changes required?

The Master: The main assumption in these forecasts is that the population will inevitably grow and this is not the case. It is true that many nations are expanding their populations to an alarming degree. This is a temporary situation (in the current political and economic climate) and is, paradoxically, the result both of poverty and of growing prosperity. This is the case in Egypt, for example, which is seeing the growth of richness within a basically poor nation.

The major change in population growth will come as a result of the sharing of world resources. When implemented, this will change the perceptions for many millions of people. The old notion that children are guarantors of security for people in their old age will change. A new sense of well-being and prosperity will create the conditions in which the world population will drop dramatically, as is proved time after time in movements from underdeveloped to developed nations.

This is not to say that there will not continue to be a crisis in the ecological balance of the world, which itself threatens the well-being of even a reduced population, and it is this imbalance which must be tackled as a priority. With ecological equilibrium and a sane goal of living standards this planet can comfortably sustain roughly 3-3.5 billion people. The current population is about 5.5 billion. This assumes the use of the world's resources at a sustainable rate.

What are the major hazards now?

The Master: Pollution of the air, seas and soil. This is the number one hazard for humanity and is responsible for the ill health of millions and the premature deaths of countless thousands. A slow poisoning of the world's population is taking place throughout the world and only the extraordinary resilience of the human biosystem allows humanity to sustain itself even at the present level.

Secondly there is the decimation of the forests of the world. The results of desertification are well-documented. This has a major effect. Desertification is adding to the problem of pollution because with every tree that is lost oxygen is lost to the atmosphere. The third hazard is the warming up of the atmosphere, the so-called greenhouse effect. This will have short-term and long-term effects on the quality of life, including climate. The main factor is the increase of deserts in the world. As the climatic changes take place they affect the forests, and would require movements of large sections of the population from one area to another in a very short period of time.

What are the main steps to limit this greenhouse effect?
The Master: The realization that this is truly a global problem and must be tackled not independently but as one affecting all peoples without exception, and therefore requiring UN Assembly recognition of the importance of the threat to humanity. Every nation must contribute.

Was the Rio Summit a step on the way?
The Master: Yes, but with the obvious exception of lack of co-operation of some of the major nations who refused to back resolutions which would have begun to tackle these problems in a realistic way. Some of these nations, moreover, are the worst offenders.

A second urgent step is a drastic reduction of the waste of the resources of the planet, which means a complete transformation of the economic structure of the world as we know it today.

This will be possible only when the nations as a whole accept the just redistribution of resources, thus implementing the principle of sharing. Then it will be found that the true needs of all — albeit for a simpler lifestyle — can be met without the continued reduction of the planet's viability. This itself can lead to the reduction of the world's population and so to a sustainable level of the world's ecological base.

Is any of this likely to happen without the emergence of Maitreya?

The Master: To be realistic, no. Humanity at the present time is too selfish, too divided and too narrow in its outlook for these changes to be accepted. But more and more, the climate of perception is changing as the ecological threat is borne home on the nations. The problem today is that powerful vested interests, together with the complacency of humanity in general, prevent the political will for change being exercised. An educational programme is required which will face humanity with the horrors which would inevitably ensue were the present practices allowed to continue.

That education, it must be admitted, would require a powerful voice and only Maitreya, accepted and honoured as a World Teacher, would have the requisite authority and persuasion. Under His guidance, the nations will begin the task, firstly of amelioration (thus providing a breathing space), and then of cure for the present ill health of Planet Earth. A simpler and saner lifestyle is the key to this cure. The present profligate misuse of resources cannot be allowed to continue unchecked.

When humanity truly realizes this, the necessary steps will be taken to reduce the consumption of resources and so lead to a regeneration and stabilization of the globe.

The volatility of the stock market has been noted. The 24-hour-a-day trading is essentially a transnational force over which sovereign nations have less and less control. Daily foreign exchange flows amount to one trillion dollars. By the late 1980s more than 90 per cent of this trading in the world's foreign exchanges was unrelated to trade or capital investment. Millions of investors, companies and banks speculate in currencies. Nowadays countries are afraid to make the necessary changes which "alarm international investors", even though raising funds for local needs is a priority. As historian Paul Kennedy puts it in his book: "The market per se is accountable to no one," and since the controls are inadequate, "financial meltdown" is always possible.

Is the shock of a stock-market crash likely to jolt the consciousness of humanity because of the hardship that will ensue?

The Master: Verily, verily! Humanity has for long suffered from the disease of speculation. The symptoms of this disease are world poverty, crime, drug abuse, violence and war. The basic cause is age-old human greed based on separation and fear. Under the leadership of the Christ (the Lord Maitreya) the Masters will help humanity to see this and evoke from them a greater sense of their interdependence. The very presence of Maitreya, known to all, will go far to make this transformation possible.

When humanity gains that sense of interdependence it will lose its fear and thus its greed. Naturally this will not take place overnight but nor will it be too long delayed. The economic collapse and the transformation which will ensue will prove a potent teacher. The relative strictures of a transformed economy will bring to humanity a new sense of reality, and in this way the changes will be logical and acceptable.

The countries of the former Soviet Union, since the collapse of Communism, now face a variety of localized ethnic conflicts, internal movements of refugee populations arising from these conflicts, ageing and dangerous nuclear reactors, heavy air and water pollution in many areas, disrupted trade flows, collapsing health services, inadequate food distribution networks and rising unemployment. Are these countries going to be affected also if there is a stock-market crash?

The Master: The major impact will be on the developed nations of the world. The stock market is not developed extensively in the countries of the former Soviet Union so they will be much less affected.

However, the overall effects in the world will affect these countries. There is, here, a paradox: despite the collapse of the system which held them together as a nation, if they can avoid ethnic conflicts they are in an advantageous situation in relation to the new dispensation. They have inbuilt in their consciousness (even if not fully implemented in practice) the concept of justice, and the transition to a world in which that divine aspect becomes paramount they will find no difficulty in accepting.

What kinds of steps can they take now to mitigate ethnic conflict?

The Master: Many forces are at work in the world which lead large groups of people to seek to enforce their self-identity. This is a transitional phase. However painful it may be in the short term, it will lead to a new sense of cultural individuality which enriches the many-coloured tapestry of humanity. It is only in the short term that the nationalistic element is uppermost in the minds of the people — this under the influence of certain ambitious and power-hungry leaders. The same problem can be seen working out in former Yugoslavia, in parts of Africa, the Middle East and elsewhere.

What are the major issues the United States should be confronting right now?

The Master: The major task for the United States at the present time is to discover its soul, and with it its need to serve, rather than dominate, the world. So focused today is the United States in its personality expression that little of true service is demonstrated in its decisions. Separatism, selfishness and greed still condition much of the action of that great country. The demise of the Soviet Union as a rival in world affairs has only contributed to these glamours (illusions). The way forward for the United States is to put its manifold resources, talents and energies at the disposal of the world community and so lead the nations into the creation of a new and more viable world. The world waits for such a consummation of purpose. However, it is not unlikely that this much-to-be-desired action will await the appearance and the acceptance of the Christ.

What can we do at the present time to further the awareness of the presence of Maitreya?

The Master: Use every channel open to you. Many know and speak not. Many are afraid of the laughter of others, but nothing is to be gained by holding back this precious and most welcome news. See it as a gift and a privilege of service to make known to all who will listen that the Great Teacher walks once more among His brothers, ready to guide and to sustain all those who love the world.

(*Share International*, September 1993)

CLOSING NUCLEAR REACTORS
AND DISCOVERING NEW ENERGIES

Interview with Benjamin Creme's Master
(through Benjamin Creme)
by Patricia Pitchon

During a wide-ranging discussion I had with Mr Creme on 4 August 1994 about major problems of land, air and sea pollution, Mr Creme's Master kindly agreed to answer questions on these topics. The Master underlined the urgency of dealing with dangerous nuclear reactors as an absolute priority. He also provided a fascinating picture of forthcoming discoveries.

Currently the nuclear industry in various parts of Western Europe is promoting itself as the clean form of energy. The main problems, however, refer to storage. Nuclear reactors in the major industrialized countries now operating or being built will produce thousands of cubic metres of high-level waste. The problem of a long-term repository for high-level wastes remains unsolved. High-level wastes are stored in stainless steel tanks, but there have been leaks. A process to solidify waste in glass (vitrification) is being studied, but the danger is that the glass blocks may disintegrate later on. As for underground sites, the search for stable geological sites has not been successful, and we cannot predict future geological movements; earthquakes mean there are no guarantees. Intermediate and low-level wastes are buried in shallow grounds in the US and in the UK, but in the US three sites were closed down several years ago due to contamination. Low-level waste has also been dumped into the sea.

This panorama is made infinitely worse by the fact that in Eastern Europe the dangers multiply with a large number of ageing and dangerous nuclear reactors. The entrepreneur Edward Goldsmith estimated in a recent book that there are at least 41 disasters of the Chernobyl type waiting to happen in Eastern Europe.

What is the Master's view on these dangers?

The Master: Our advice is to close down all nuclear fission reactors *without delay*. They are a major source of deadly pollution. Life on this planet would be utter misery were it not for the help of our Space Brothers who neutralize this pollution and render it harmless within karmic limits. Fleets of Their space ships, using implosion devices, do this on a daily basis.

Within how many years does the Master think we will manage to do this?

The Master: One of the first things Maitreya will advise is the closing down of nuclear reactors and ending all representation of nuclear fission as being a more efficient way of producing energy. From the politicians' point of view, there is power, prestige and commercial gain from nuclear energy. The average person's mind is confused by all the scientific jargon; his voice is not properly heard in the realms of power. But the voice of the people is about to become more articulate: one of the many aspects of Maitreya's mission is to act as the voice of the people, to address the problems of peace and war, and starvation in the midst of plenty; to galvanize the will of the people to force politicians to address these issues. Government, today, is about power and the wielding of power, rather than about service. The problem is to shift the emphasis. What is required is the appearance of Maitreya, *which is very imminent indeed*. These questions have to be addressed by humanity itself, with Maitreya as a guide.

Increasingly we are becoming aware of the hazards of toxic chemicals in the form of sulphur oxides, nitrogen oxides and volatile hydrocarbons; the various sources of pollution include industry, motor vehicles, household waste, etc. What are the dangers here?

The Master: The *interaction* of the three types of chemical is serious; there is a poisonous relationship between them. There is even more danger to nature than to human beings — ie the trees, the plants, the soil. Even 'organic' vegetables are contaminated. The water, the air we breathe, is contaminated. This is one of the

185

greatest causes of skin rashes, eczemas and allergies. It is impossible to eat pollutant-free food.

(Benjamin Creme at this point added that there is a high rate of eczema in Japan, and much of its origin is due to fish polluted with mercury and other toxins.)

What about the water itself?

The Master: Water at the moment contains much aluminium, mercury and zinc. Aluminium is a very toxic ingredient, and many people also cook in aluminium. This is a health hazard. It is the source of stomach diseases, ulcers, fatigue — a general toxic condition of the body. It is a miracle that people are not more ill; only their extraordinary resilience explains it.

According to reports this summer in London, unusual summer heat combined with ozone from car emissions trapped at ground level to make the air difficult to breathe, and a recent report on Inner London schools indicates that one in every five children has asthma. Are catalytic converters which reduce the level of lead important?

The Master: Yes. In Japan, where controls are strict, there have been major improvements. Already many individuals, groups and agencies have warned and informed governments; a Master need add nothing to this. Instead of putting more and more cars on the road, public transport can be made more efficient, more regular and consistent. In time, governments will restrict the use of cars to the countryside. A new technology will lead to a more sophisticated form of public transport which will alleviate pollution. It will be silent, apparently motionless and will vibrate very little. Travel fatigue will disappear. It will be the perfect means of transport of large numbers of people between countries and between cities.

What timespan are we talking about?

The Master: Within five to 20 years, more and more sophisticated use of this technology will transform and beautify the cities. Men have not envisaged, not even in the imagination of science fiction writers (because until now there has been no blueprint), how the light of the sun will become the fuel.

This will provide the energy for all human needs. It will be clean, without waste, and there will be an inexhaustible supply to every home in every city in the world. Help is being given to scientists in Russia and in the United States by our Space Brothers.

Do governments know?
The Master: Some members in both governments know.

Where do the Space Brothers come from?
The Master: Most of the space vehicles are from Mars and Venus. The Martians are the greatest space engineers.

I worry about the economy of countries like Nigeria, where 90 per cent of its revenue consists of oil exports. What is going to happen to countries which have been so dependent on oil, when the new solar fuel becomes available?
The Master: No one will be able to 'corner the market' on this technology. It will become freely available to all.

What is the Master's view about the ozone layer in the stratosphere? Is there an ozone hole over the Antarctic?
(Benjamin Creme at this point noted that Maitreya has already said that it does not exist. It is an illusion, caused by the fact that light does not stream in a direct line: imagine that you are in the dark, and there is a tennis ball. If you shine a light on it, you get the impression of a hole behind it, due to the refraction.)

The Master: There is, however, a general thinning of the ozone layer all over the earth.

At the conclusion of the interview the Master added the following:
In restoring the planet, salvation is a collective effort. Maitreya will make it clear that this is the case. I estimate that within three to five years from the moment of Maitreya's appearance an enormous transformation will be taking place. Starvation on the

planet will be tackled: mass progress for the starving millions is the aim, and on a scale which we have never contemplated. That achieved, we will tackle the problems of the environment around us. The top priority is the complete transformation of our mode of living towards one that is sustainable.

We will see the end of the current economy based on unbridled growth. Men everywhere will be able to eat and live and preserve the resources of the environment.

(*Share International*, October, 1994)

THE ENVIRONMENT —
WHAT THE SCIENTISTS MAY BE OVERLOOKING

Restoring the Environment

Many people believe that it is too late to restore the environment, that there is little hope for a sustainable, healthy future. Do you subscribe to that view, or do you think there is still time to turn it around? (July/August 1993)

I think there is still time. It is not just my opinion because that would be no better than anyone else's. But it is certainly the view of Maitreya that there is time to turn this dangerous situation around.

Following a crash programme of aid for the starving millions of the world and the implementation of the principle of sharing, will be the saving, protection, and healing of the environment. This involves everybody; we all use the environment.

Maitreya says there are two environments, an inner and an outer. The outer reflects the inner. If the inner is disturbed, the outer also is disturbed. We are witnessing this today. Because we are so disturbed in our inner environment, not recognizing ourselves as spiritual beings related to each other, we rape, pillage and despoil. We inflict our greed and aggression on each other in wars and all sorts of aggressive actions and reap the results: a gradual erosion of the very environment which keeps us in being as a species. If we do not address this problem, the human and sub-human kingdoms of this planet will die out.

Many ecologists recognize this fact. The 'Green' agencies have been talking about this for years, trying to impress on governments the need for change. But at the Earth Summit in Brazil in June 1992, some major nations, most notably the United States, refused to sign the very resolutions which would address these urgent problems. The atmosphere is heating up, the air, the rivers and seas of the world are becoming so polluted that we are poisoning ourselves all the time. It is simply the extraordinary resilience of the human body, mind, and spirit that has prevented our destruction before this time.

How is the damage already perpetrated against the earth going to be healed? (August/September 1994)

When the Lord Maitreya works openly, this will set in motion a dynamism which is presently lacking in the approach to these problems. The nations have known for half a century about world hunger — the non-governmental agencies bring this question before humanity over and over again and little or nothing is done about it. At the same time, scientists show the nations the damage we are doing to the planet, the ecological damage resulting from the over-use and misuse of resources: the poisoning of the land, the rivers, the oceans and the air we breathe.

The number one priority immediately following the Appearance and acceptance by humanity will be the saving of the starving millions of the world; Maitreya will advocate a crash programme of aid. After that, the number one priority will be the saving of the planet — the changing of our political and economic structures which will enable a sustainable economy to be created — for example, the world's primeval forests, on which we depend for our very oxygen let alone the medicinal plants which are 'stolen' by the pharmaceutical industries today, will be maintained. Every man, woman and child on the planet, I would say above four years of age, has to be engaged in this. Maitreya will recommend — and there are groups now all over the world responding to this idea — a *sustainable* economy: we will have to live more simply so that all of us can live, and so that our children's children, on into the future, can live on Planet Earth. The Earth can sustain approximately 3.5 billion people with comfort. At the moment we have 5.5 billion and will have an estimated 10 billion in a very few years. With the transformation of the economic structure, when people will have the ability to live decent, civilized, dignified lives — the kind of life *we* take for granted — we will find that the incidence of large families will diminish, even in the Third World, where it is mainly an insurance for old age.

Will this be in time? (August/September 1994)

Yes. You can be sure Maitreya has not delayed too long. He is here to help us and show us the way. We have to agree to do it, but you can be sure He is here in the nick of time to save the planet.

What changes will the Earth itself, as an organism, go through? (August/September 1994)

If you read many of the books which are in the 'New Age' bookshops, if you believe in the messages which are 'channelled' in all countries, you would believe that this world is going to be more or less destroyed, that tremendous, catastrophic world changes will take place. This is a fantasy, put into the astral planes by what we call the 'forces of evil'. It is meant to frighten humanity, and that is what it does to large numbers of people. There is no truth in these predictions — and people should refrain from giving them energy by repeating them.

The world is now suffering profoundly from the misuse of resources. We have polluted our planet so much that there is no person in the world today, probably — except a Master — who is free from the pollution created by ourselves: the air, the earth, the oceans of the world are polluted to an extent that we are really endangering our own species and the sub-human kingdoms. This is the way that the Earth is really suffering, these are the changes which have to be righted, the changes which are taking place in our immune system as a result of these polluting agencies. The husbandry of the world needs complete transformation — that is the change which will take place.

Today's weather changes, which are real and dramatic, are to do with the destructive thoughtforms of humanity itself; we affect the very weather. The political, economic, and social imbalances in the world create imbalances in the devic, elemental forces whose work it is to control the weather. When we go out of equilibrium, they go out of equilibrium. When, by right relationships, we bring about the end of war and the sharing of the world's resources, we will create justice in the world. When we create justice we will create peace, and when we create peace we will create harmony, equilibrium. When we create equilibrium, the elementals controlling the weather will themselves come back into equilibrium. It will rain occasionally, of course, but not at weekends!

The environment is so polluted now; we have the greenhouse effect and other major problems. How can we come to terms with this situation? (July/August 1993)

The Masters of our Spiritual Hierarchy, Who are coming into the world with Maitreya, have the technology to neutralize the greenhouse effect, the pollution of the atmosphere, even the effects of nuclear radiation. We have to wind down the fission process of creating energy. What I am not advocating, or even suggesting, is returning to the old days — humanity living in pastoral conditions, and so on. We will still have a prosperous, well-balanced, modern lifestyle, with all the technology which we are capable of inventing. We shall be given the blueprints of technology which at the moment we cannot even begin to imagine. It would boggle the mind of the most advanced scientist.

But we are not going to be waiting for Maitreya and the Masters to give us the technology to make these changes. We cannot just sit back and say: "They are going to give us the technology to clean up the planet, so we do not have to do anything." (July/August 1993)

When we accept the principle of sharing, and when that process is actually working out in the world, we will be given the gift of new technologies. I do not mean that we will be given an instrument and shown how to use it. We will be given the secrets of how to create this technology. Then our advanced scientists will develop it.

There is a new technology — the cold fusion process — that is in the offing. I would say that in a very few years from now cold fusion will produce a rather large proportion of the earth's energy needs. But after that there is another technology which Maitreya calls the Technology of Light which will provide unlimited energy for all our needs.

Factories will be run by robots. We think of robots which make cars in factories today as being very sophisticated, but compared with those of the future, these are the primitive beginnings of that technology. By thought alone we will create the machines which will make the artifacts of our daily living. This will allow man the time for the investigation of his own nature, for recreational and creative pursuits and so on. An entirely new and highly sophisticated technological world will be created, but only when we see ourselves as one humanity. If that technology were given now, we would destroy the world with it. We almost destroyed the world with nuclear weapons. Nuclear fission is the most dangerous way to tap the energy in the atom. That same energy streams to us from the sun. The Technology of Light will use energy direct from the sun. It will even be applied medically, and with our growing genetic experimentation will allow us to create new organs in the body as needed.

Is there no truth in the prophecies of what will happen if we don't change our ways? (August/September 1994)

If we do not change direction, we will destroy *everything* in this world. Our greed, selfishness, complacency, our over-production for profit rather than production for a sustainable economy, is creating a situation in which the very planet on which we live is collapsing under us. Unless we change, we will create a situation in which there will be no life, human or sub-human.

Many of the traditional American Indians would like to see everything destroyed so that something new will come out of it . . . ? (August/September 1994)

I do not believe that the earth itself needs to be destroyed in order to create something good. Humanity needs to reorganize the way it relates to each other and to the earth, and to use the earth in such a way that it provides for everyone. There is an over-production of almost everything but we in the developed world hoard and greedily waste while three-quarters of the world's population have to do without. It is the *imbalances* which endanger the world.

Will Europe become a desert in the future? (March 1994)
No.

Will Africa become a desert in the future? (January/February 1993)

Some parts will, but much new land will become fertile.

Is this due to evolution and planetary changes? (January/February 1993)

This will be due to short-term disturbances of world weather patterns.

Is there any esoteric reason why so many creatures and plants are becoming extinct — or is it simply humanity's misuse of the planet? (December 1996)

Many plants are indeed becoming — or are already — extinct as a result of the massive environmental damage caused by humanity in its misuse of resources. Huge areas of tropical forest, for example, no longer exist to provide the natural habitat for innumerable species. This is increasingly so for many animals, too, large and small.

With the animals, however, another, esoteric, factor is involved: some are being deliberately taken out of incarnation under the (benevolent) destructive agency of the 1st ray of Will or Power. The rhinoceros, crocodile and alligator, many of the great cats, all ancient and basically untamable, too primitive for access by, and response to, the human mind (the mechanism for animal evolution of consciousness) are doomed to extinction.

Those animals — cats, dogs, camels, elephants, cattle, horses, etc — who have been domesticated, more or less, by man will respond more and more to the energy of the human mind, preparing them for a closer relationship with the human kingdom and (eventual) individualization as humans.

Underground Nuclear Testing and Earthquakes

How does underground nuclear testing affect the environment? (July/August 1993)

It is impossible to have an underground nuclear test without creating an earthquake — not necessarily in the immediate vicinity but anywhere in the world. Of every 30 major earthquakes, some 21 or 22 follow a nuclear explosion. There are other reasons for earthquakes, but the vast majority are the result of underground nuclear testing. We need not test nuclear bombs. The scientists involved in nuclear testing are trying to maintain their jobs by producing refinements of the existing mechanisms of the various bombs. Just as in the commercial fields companies are producing more and more prettier-packaged goods to keep their products going, so the scientists are producing refinements of their technology simply to keep the technology going, and with it their jobs. Self-interest is causing these earthquakes.

And that is having a devastating effect. (July/August 1993)

Yes. As I have said, you cannot produce an underground nuclear explosion without creating an earthquake. Also, you cannot produce an underground nuclear explosion without throwing into the atmosphere thousands of tons of dust saturated with nuclear radiation which eventually falls into the oceans, rivers, and reservoirs of the world. We are all taking in nuclear radiation every time we breathe and drink.

*Maitreya has said that underground nuclear tests interfere with the equilibrium of creation and result in earthquakes. (**Share International,** October 1988). Have the recent earthquakes in Turkey, Peru and Japan any connection with the resumption of French underground tests in the Pacific?* (November 1995)

Until now, no. That is not to say that future tests will not result in earthquakes.

What do you think was the cause of the recent (January 1995) Japanese earthquake? (1) Was it underground nuclear explosions? (2) Could Maitreya not have prevented it? (March 1995)

(1) No. Its cause was natural — the result of the movement of the earth's tectonic plates. (2) Some degree of intervention by Maitreya was possible under karmic law. Otherwise, the earthquake would have been even more destructive — 8 or even higher, instead of 7.2 as it was, on the Richter scale. As the disaster took place and for many days afterwards, Maitreya spent

195

much time in Kobe saving many people from death or greater injury and easing the passing of the dying.

In Patricia Pitchon's interview with Maitreya's associate (see page 106), he said he had "sent a letter to American President Bill Clinton" and political leaders in other countries regarding current events including Yugoslavia and the natural havoc caused in terms of "major earthquakes and disastrous floodings". (1) Did President Clinton, or any of the other leaders, actually read these letters, and if so, are any of them responding positively to the possibility of Maitreya's presence and His teachings? (2) Was the major earthquake in India such an earthquake mentioned in the letter? (January/February 1994)

(1) No. (2) No. It was the result of underground nuclear testing.

Weather

Can you comment on the effect of humanity's actions on the world's weather patterns? (July/August 1993)

We have a direct effect on our environment. Very soon, under the tuition of Maitreya and the Masters around Him, humanity will come to understand that what we call God, what we call nature, our environment, and what we call humanity are one. There is no separation between these. Everything, according to Maitreya, is interconnected. Every atom, every particle within every atom, is related to every other particle throughout cosmos. Therefore, what happens in one aspect of creation inevitably has an effect on another. Humanity is part of its everyday environment; we call it nature. The destructive thoughtforms of humanity create the conditions of imbalance and tension in the world. The imbalance between the developed world and the Third World — the poverty and suffering which ensues from that imbalance — and therefore the thoughtforms of pain, agony and of destruction, pour into the mindbelt of the world. They affect what are called the devic elementals whose work it is to control the weather patterns of the world.

What are the devic elementals? (July/August 1993)

They are elemental forces which control and organize the patterns of nature. They are energy forces and respond to human thought. When our thoughts are in equilibrium, they are in equilibrium. When our thoughts are destructive and chaotic, as today, the devas go out of equilibrium. This has resulted in the complete distortion of the world's weather. For instance, we see floods, major earthquakes, volcanic eruptions, torrential rain where they have never been known, lack of rain where it was normal, hurricanes. All of these phenomena have been with us since we can remember but in controlled patterns. All of that has gone. There is no set pattern in the world's weather today. When we come into equilibrium by creating the conditions of equilibrium — living together in peace, sharing the resources of the world, creating, thereby, harmony in the world — the devas will return to their preordained forms and patterns and create equilibrium once again. They respond directly to human thought.

On Palm Sunday 27 March 1994, a series of tornadoes and storms swept through the southern United States killing at least 40. One caved in the roof of a Methodist church killing 20 people, including the minister's daughter, and injuring 90. In our local paper one headline asked: "Why?" and another said: "Tornado shakes foundation of congregation's faith". (1) Could you tell us why the twisters singled out and flattened this and other churches at just that time? (2) Is this a manifestation of the incoming 7th-ray energy causing the destruction of the crystallized 6th-ray religious institutions? (3) or was it due to the karma of the people involved? (August/September 1994)

(1) The churches were not "singled out" for destruction; their size and shape made them likely obstacles to the force of the tornadoes, hence the damage. (2) No. The tornadoes are a result of the destructive thoughtforms of humanity which affect the elemental forces controlling climate and weather. (3) The fact that certain people were killed or injured is a result of their individual karmic situation, not because they represent crystallized religious institutions.

AQUARIAN TECHNOLOGY

What are the qualities of the Aquarian Age? (October 1995)

The outstanding quality of the Aquarian energy is synthesis. We shall find, as that energy grows in potency in our lives, a coming together, a fusing and blending of human thought and consciousness which will lead to the demonstration of Brotherhood and Sisterhood on a world scale. Right human relations will be no longer simply an ideal, but an established fact in our communities. The key to this achievement is the realization that humanity is one and the creation, therefore, of justice and peace through the sharing of resources.

Is there any connection between our modern technology and the Age of Aquarius? (June 1996)

The Age of Aquarius brings in a particular energy called the 7th ray of Ceremonial Order, or Magic, or Ritual, or Organization, and our modern technology is 'modern magic'. Ancient Atlantean magic was governed by this energy, and the modern counterpart is the precipitation of that same magical method of ritual on to the electrical and mechanistic field.

Our technology is literally magical — not in the sense that it is irrational; it results from a growing knowledge of the relationship between matter and energy. It is the basic occult axiom that in the whole of the manifested universe there is only energy vibrating at various frequencies; the nature of the frequencies determines the form that the energy will take. We too are energy.

Everything that we can see and think of is energy, which can be activated and directed if you have the 'magic' — the technology — to do it. A modern computing system, our ability to send a spaceship to Mars, is the result of the magical use of the 7th ray of ritual, magic, or organization. If you make a sound and ritualize it — repeat and repeat it many times — you create an energy field; by that same energy you can make things disappear or float up in the air. (Years ago a small model airship was made to rise by someone playing a violin.) One day in the not-too-distant future we will be able to shift 30-ton blocks of stone by the use of sound. This is done by reversing gravity, by the ritual of the 7th ray of ceremonial order.

This ray is daily becoming more potent in our lives, while the 6th ray of idealism is receding. Our problem is that our structures are still 6th-ray while the incoming energy is 7th-ray. The 7th ray has the effect of drawing humanity together, it synthesizes, and it is the most practical of all the rays. It works on the dense physical field, relating the spiritual ideal to matter. Science, today, is revealing more about the nature of reality than religion has done in 2,000 years. The schism between science and religion is an artificial one, created by the religious groups at the end of the 19th century because they felt threatened by the revelations of the then growing science.

In the technology ahead of us we will create instruments by thought which will be programmed to create all the artifacts of our everyday life. This will free humanity for the investigation of its own nature.

Is it part of the Plan that the Technology of Light will arrive before the precession of the equinox which accounts for some form of physiological disaster? (August/September 1994)
The first, small beginnings of the Technology of Light are likely to come in about five years' time, and will gradually be developed over the succeeding years. It is an ongoing process. There is no end to the Technology of Light; it is not one simple technology which once we have, we have. This technology will eventually give us control over the forces of the universe.

*In one of your books you write that humanity will be able to take photographs of our etheric bodies. I am very interested in the subject of etheric and astral bodies, in particular in their separation from the physical body, and I have purchased a book which delivers the scientific proof that not only is our structure made up entirely of atoms but that really we only consist of light of the highest order. (1) Is this book (**Biophotons — The Light in our Cells**, by Marco Bishof) the beginning of the research into our subtle bodies? (2) Is the biophotonic research one of the building blocks of the New Age?* (September 1996)

199

(1) No. There is already much research. (2) Yes.

This past year, especially during the last three months, we have seen an astonishing number of apparently quite significant breakthroughs in the scientific world: in the realm of nuclear fusion, superconductivity, and gene research in particular. Is this a result of efforts on the part of those Masters who inspire and impress some scientists? Or are these scientists' insights stimulated by the increased energies pouring into the world prior to Maitreya's wider appearance? Or is it simply that long years of hard work are finally paying off, coincidentally at the same general time? (March 1994)

All three of these factors are at work simultaneously.

Will computers play any part in the new world order? (November 1993)

Computers will play an extraordinary part in the new civilization. Today, millions of people work in factories, producing vast amounts of goods. In the future, with the development of the human mind (which has barely begun to manifest itself), we will create computers *par excellence*, which will respond to human thought — scientists are already beginning to do this. They will respond so completely that they can be programmed to make all the artifacts that we use in everyday life. This will free humanity for leisure and for an exploration of our own nature and creativity. Today's robots are as nothing compared to the unbelievable sophistication which will characterize the computers of the future, computers which will be programmed, by thought, to create in the way that we create.

Why is it that the Hierarchy, after prompting the Allies to discover atomic energy uses ahead of the Axis powers, allows the current abuses to remain unchecked? (July 1994)

Because humanity has free will which is never infringed by Hierarchy.

(1) What do the Masters teach regarding the use of nuclear energy? (2) If nuclear energy is not to be used by mankind, then what will be the disposition of our nuclear materials? Who will have control of the plutonium and enriched uranium produced on this planet? (June 1996)

(1) In the Masters' view, nuclear fission reactors are highly dangerous and should, without exception, be shut down. The fusion process of nuclear energy is perfectly feasible today and would provide a safe method in the interim period before the Technology of Light — the science of the future — makes all such technology redundant. (2) A UN panel of experts, supervised by an initiate recommended by the Masters.

Nine atoms of anti-matter have just been created in the CERN laboratories in Geneva, Switzerland. Could you please explain what anti-matter is, from the esoteric point of view? Is it the same as etheric energy? (March 1996)

There is really no such thing as "anti-matter". It is (usually) invisible matter of a finer kind than dense physical — namely etheric.

Every human person is different because of genetic variables. Does the new order foresee a new 'make' of person through some sort of genetic engineering? (December 1994)

Each human body is different because of genetic variables, but each person is different and unique because each is an individualized soul in incarnation. No amount of genetic engineering could alter that spiritual reality (except in science fiction films).

HEALTH CARE

Ensuring Health Care as a Universal Right

Health care is certainly one of the most basic of all human rights, yet in the developed world we see health costs skyrocketing, most dramatically perhaps in the US where millions of people cannot afford adequate care. Throughout the developing world there are severe shortages of even the most basic care. How can we begin to guarantee health care as a universal right, and how do we pay for it? (July/August 1993)

It depends on a restructuring of our society, in particular of our economic structures. We are living today in a world dominated by market forces, and there is not much profit to be made out of providing health care for those who need it most. People at the receiving end of health care are not seen as producing much of benefit to society. Therefore, health has a very low priority in the eyes of most governments in both developed and developing countries.

The solution will come as a result of the breakdown of the present economic system, which is on its last legs. This recession which we hear so much about is more than a recession. It is really a collapse of the economic system of the last hundreds of years.

This will bring a new sense of reality to humanity, and the priorities of all governments will change. These will become the provision of adequate food, of shelter, of health care and education for all people, as a universal right. This will be paid for from an economic restructuring and the redirection of the countless billions a year now spent on armaments.

The basic problem is that health care is primarily in the realm of market forces, and, speaking generally, is based on profit rather than the need of people. (July/August 1993)

It is not seen as a priority. The number one priority in the world would seem to be the provision of arms. That keeps the major countries in a very powerful military position. They also sell the surplus to the less wealthy countries, who sell to Third World countries who can ill afford any arms at all. There is profit in arms and no profit to be had in health.

How does that change? (July/August 1993)

We have to change our values. The priorities of life lie first of all in the continuance of the planet Earth as a viable being in the solar system. Therefore, the environment must be one of our fundamental concerns. We will come to see that there is an interconnection between nature and humanity, between all life.

The energy of equilibrium now pervades the planet. People and nature will respond constructively to this new influence and, as a result, humanity will live in closer contact with nature; there will be greater harmony. When there is greater harmony, there will be improved health. Much of the ill health of the planet is the result of stress. Heredity is another factor. Also, for countless aeons, we have buried our dead, with all their diseases, in the earth. These diseases seep out into the vegetable kingdom, which is eaten by the animal kingdom; people eat the animals, and the cycle goes on age after age. We have been eating the same diseased food from time immemorial. Until we recognize cremation as the only hygienic way to restore the physical body to the earth after death, we will carry on that pattern of ill health from generation to generation.

How can we develop a new approach to health that is more effective? (July/August 1993)

Most people put up with very limited health, and are relatively unhealthy. For those living in crowded inner cities, it cannot be otherwise.

Throughout the 19th century with the industrial revolution, the growth of cities took place, and with it all the diseases which rose to the surface during that time. Many of these diseases have gradually been conquered, as in the developed world people of the inner cities moved out into more salubrious suburbs where there are trees, sunshine and restful surroundings. The incidence of disease among the more well-off groups has dropped dramatically. But it still exists among the poor who live in the inner cities.

If you put too many rats into a confined space, they go mad and start killing each other. In a less restricted environment, that same number of rats live together in complete harmony. In the same way, a great many of the social evils, violence and discord in the inner cities is due to overpopulation. There are people who live 10 or 12 to a room. That is not a thing of the past except in the most developed areas of the developed world. Throughout the under-developed world, and in many parts of the developed world, especially in the poor inner city areas, it is the norm. Ill health is the natural result. These are problems we have to address and redress.

You mentioned adequate food as a priority. Would you say that would be a contributor to health as well? (July/August 1993)

Indeed. One of the problems today is that even people who eat sufficient volumes of food remain unhealthy because the food itself is denatured. Through chemical fertilizers we have denatured the very soil on which food is grown. It is not the bulk of food that matters; it is the vitamin energy in the food which keeps us healthy and guards against disease. No amount of vitamin supplements can make up for that energy direct from the sun. When food is denatured by chemical farming methods, the bulk of the food that we eat has little or no effect in nourishing the body. A return to more traditional organic methods of farming will restore the vitality of food.

It is said that genetic engineering can solve the world's hunger problems by creating crops suitable to different soils and climates and by delaying the rotting process. Some such foods are already on sale in supermarkets. What is your opinion of this technology? (January/February 1995)

There is no doubt that through genetic engineering of crops the quality of agriculture can be raised world-wide, but the problem of hunger can only be solved through the *sharing* of the world's food. Already, there is a surplus of some 10 per cent per capita yet millions starve.

The food markets all over the world are being swept more and more by genetically engineered food products. There are many people who consider such food, where the natural borderlines between different species — even between plants and animals — are broken, as poisonous and as a bigger threat to the survival of mankind than nuclear power plants and nuclear weapons. Does the Hierarchy share this view? (January/February 1997)

No. One must discriminate. Some are beneficial.

The media report more and more about gene-manipulated foods. The effects on human beings are not yet known — for example, whether or not enzymes are allergy-producing. Direct changes in inherited characteristics in domestic animals and plants are observed: fruit resists rotting, and plants gain immunity to pests. Gene-manipulated micro-organisms like yeast fungi and enzymes are used in the production of food. (1) Is this progress for us humans? (2) Is it possible to help starving people in this way? (July/August 1993)

(1) Potentially yes, but much rather dubious experimentation is being carried out at present. In the long run, a great improvement in quality of plants and other produce will be achieved. (2) Yes, but there is no shortage of food per capita at present. It is simply not distributed equally enough to prevent starvation in developing countries.

Does Hierarchy hold in its hands any kind of instrument of technology to 'reverse' genetically engineered plants, in the same way as Hierarchy seems to control a technology for cleaning up radioactive pollution? (January/February 1997)

No.

The edition of the **Evening Standard**, *a London newspaper, dated 4 January 1996, featured an article on the potential fluoridation of London's water supply. Local health authorities and the government are considering the introduction of such a programme.*

According to my information, fluoride has a significant detrimental effect on a particular part of the physical brain in human beings. Outside this, common sense would counsel against adding chemicals to anything which will be consumed internally. It would be useful if Mr Creme's Master could clarify the following: (1) Does fluoridation have any significant effects, beneficial or detrimental, on the dense physical vehicle? (2) Do any effects manifest restrict the ability of the dense physical brain's etheric counterpart to transmit energies and forces? (3) Similarly, would any such effects impair the ability of the mental vehicle to function through the dense physical brain? (April 1996)

(1) Yes. It has a detrimental effect, particularly on the cells of the brain. (2) Yes. (3) Yes.

Fluoridation of drinking water has a marked beneficial effect on children's teeth — if they need it; a lack of fluoride leads to weak, spongy teeth. However, the mass poisoning of everyone else is clearly unacceptable. Individual treatment of those children lacking fluoride can easily be given safely and effectively by homoeopathic potencies of fluoride. This proposal for water-poisoning should be resisted by mass protests.

*The April 1996 **Share International** contained information on the detrimental effects of fluoride on the body, particularly the brain. Could Mr Creme's Master say if high potency homoeopathic doses of fluoride, say 1M, 10M, or CM, help to remove the residue? Would homoeopathic Tlacote tablets help?* (June 1996)

No, they would be of no avail. Tlacote water tablets would strengthen the body's cellular structure.

It was reported recently that in Greater London, for example, there are over a thousand sufferers of tinnitus (continuous hissing in one or both ears). Is this the modern name for a centuries-old malady which has always been known, or is this at present untreatable problem a consequence of modern, perhaps stressful, living conditions? (January/February 1994)

It is entirely the result of the stress of modern conditions, increasing all the time through the growing commercialization of our political/economic/social life.

What is tinnitus — has it a spiritual dimension? (June 1996)

Tinnitus, for those who do not know the term, is a buzzing, a sound of various different notes, in one's ears, which comes about in different ways. Tinnitus is to do with the nervous system, and is the result mainly of stress and strain. It may have some relation to other imbalances in the physical body, in the inner ear for example, which produce the typical tinnitus sound.

Some people with tinnitus say the sounds they hear are almost like voices — they are not voices, but they are so complex that it is almost as if they were hearing words. (This is different from people who actually do hear voices.)

Tinnitus, being the result of stress and strain, can often be helped by rest and, I believe, some homoeopathic treatment; sometimes acupuncture, skilfully done, will reduce if not cure it altogether.

Tinnitus should not be confused with the interior sound of the movement of the chakras in the head. There are many people who think they may have tinnitus who may simply be hearing the energy vibrating through the head chakras.

A recent British governmental investigation confirmed — though there is no conclusive proof — that there is a link between cancer in children and their fathers' exposure to radiation while employees at nuclear power stations. When will the new Science of Light be available to neutralize harmful radioactivity affecting such workers? (January/February 1994)

In about five years.

Is there a danger of getting cancer from the high electromagnetic activity from things like hairdryers, microwave ovens, cellular phones or power lines? (May 1993)

No. The problem (not real danger) rests in the large output of positive ions from such sources. These include computers and word-processors.

Some years ago there was a debate about the safety of cellular mobile phones. There was concern about the proximity of the tiny aerial on the phone being too close to the head, which might cause brain cancer. Is this true? (June 1996)

No.

A British judge has recently ruled that RSI, Repetitive Strain Injury, is not a medical condition but purely psychological-emotional in origin, only suffered by "eggshell personalities". Can you throw some light on this troublesome illness which is affecting more and more people? (December 1993)

Most professional physiotherapists must be amazed at this judge's misunderstanding of what is becoming a most troublesome illness, arising out of the commercialization of our lives. People are being technologically conditioned to the extent that their physical bodies are protesting at this 'robotization'. Long hours spent at computers, repeating the same gestures ad infinitum, affect the muscles, sinews and joints and can lead to severe impairment of mobility. It is an illness, even if not yet written up in medical books.

I think we should adopt the Japanese practice of exercises before work and at regular intervals through the day. Many people — not necessarily "eggshell personalities", whatever they are — sit tensely before their computers and are therefore predisposed to RSI.

We usually give morphine products to our terminally ill and dying patients who are in pain. My opinion is that these products also have some side-effects, maybe hallucinations? If so, is there any other effective painkiller with less negative results? (April 1996)

At the moment, no. I am informed that a substitute for morphine will be discovered before long — two years at the most.

Can you comment on whether BSE or 'mad cow disease' can really be transferred to humans as Creutzfeldt-Jacob disease (CJD)? (May 1996)

I refer readers to *Share International* Vol 9, no.6 (July/August 1990), where this subject is discussed: "Market forces are the source of the 'mad cow disease', currently causing the death of thousands of cows in the United Kingdom. Degrading milk by feeding cattle contaminated food and giving injections of artificial chemicals can only lead to trouble. The disease is already affecting human beings," said the associate. "The symptoms are loss of memory, awareness and consciousness."

By now, March 1996, 26 people have died from CJD; some were diagnosed as suffering from Alzheimer's disease.

I recall reading a comment by Maitreya's associate some years ago about the feeding of dead animal tissue to cattle in this country (UK). He warned then that there would be dreadful health consequences for such an unnatural practice carried out for purely commercial reasons.

Some experts have predicted that we could be facing an AIDS-proportion epidemic over the coming decades, resulting in as many as 100,000 deaths a year in the UK. (1) Is this true? (2) Will the Tlacote water tablets be effective in treating people who succumb to Creutzfeld-Jacob disease? (3) What will be the long-term effects on the farming industry in Britain? (May 1996)

(1) Probably that is an overestimate but we might well have tens of thousands over the years. (2) Many people will be helped by Tlacote and other water magnetized by Maitreya. A vaccine will also be developed to limit the disease. (3) It will recover in time with better (more sane) farming methods.

(1) Is it safe to consume products (milk, cheese, etc) from cows who are infected with BSE? (2) If it is not safe, what more can we do apart from not eating these products? (July/August 1996)

(1) No. (2) Eat only organically grown food.

Some years ago I had an attack of chronic depression which resulted in electro-convulsive therapy (ECT). Would this have any lasting adverse effect on my spiritual well-being and progress? (January/February 1995)

No, although I must say that ECT is a very heavy, clumsy way to deal with depression.

Recently, in the USA, a child who had been diagnosed as HIV-positive since birth has now been tested as HIV-negative. Please can you explain how this can happen? (September 1995)

It happens fairly frequently. It is the result of the resurgence of the child's immune system which overcomes the HIV virus. It requires a basically strong system to bring it about.

Why is there such a large percentage of men over 45 affected by enlargement of the prostate gland? Is stress a major factor? (November 1995)

No. The major factor in the rising incidence of this complaint is water pollution. The use of filtered water is therefore strongly indicated.

The hormone known as melatonin, taken as a food supplement, is currently being touted in America and elsewhere as an anti-ageing drug which can prevent cancer, extend life and boost the immune system. As melatonin is produced by the body's pineal gland, which is related to the etheric body, can ingesting melatonin actually be harmful to the dense physical and etheric bodies? (January/February 1996)

No, it is unlikely to harm the etheric or dense physical bodies. On the other hand, claims that it can prevent cancer should not be accepted at face value. That may, or may not, be the case in individual situations.

There has been a resurgence of interest in recent years in the USA in the 'Kombucha' or 'Manchurian Mushroom', from which a yeast enzyme tea is made to be consumed as a daily tonic. Many people say it helps increase energy, strengthen the immune system, eliminate toxins, promote longevity and in general has rejuvenating effects. I have been using it for nearly a year now and really cannot tell if it has benefited me or not. Is it beneficial only to some, or is it in fact not beneficial to anyone? (December 1996)

It is hallucinogenic and not particularly beneficial to anyone.

Does the DNA of a person carry the soul properties? (December 1994)

No. The DNA carries the vibration of the individual's body in their last incarnation. When a person dies the physical body disintegrates, but there is one permanent physical atom, one permanent astral or emotional atom, and one permanent mental atom left. Round these permanent atoms the soul forms a new body, taking the vibrational rate of the three permanent atoms as the key for the vibrational rate of the body which is being created. The soul magically forms this new body, first of all on the etheric physical level which is then precipitated down to the dense physical. You start in your next incarnation at *exactly* the point you reached when you died in the previous incarnation. That is carried through the permanent atoms and forms what today we call the DNA.

The nervous systems, sympathetic and parasympathetic, are the keys to the contact between the soul, on its level, and the human personality. Through the nervous systems flows a nerve gas, unknown to present-day science, which carries the energy of the soul and the life principle. There is a life-thread connected to the heart and a consciousness-thread connected to the centre of the brain. Through these two 'threads' the soul stimulates and nourishes the person in incarnation. When a person dies it is because the soul has snapped the life-thread; it may have snapped the consciousness-thread before that and then the person becomes a kind of living vegetable, but when the life-thread is snapped the person dies.

*In a recent article in **The Sunday Times**, a woman who had had a heart and lung transplant in 1988 claims that since the operation she is experiencing quite significant personality changes. She says that she has taken on habits and preferences of the donor, which she clearly did not have before. Apparently other organ transplant patients have experienced similar changes but don't talk about it for fear of ridicule. Doctors say that this is not possible; that organs have no capacity for memory, all memory is in the brain only.*

(1) Is this case "supporting evidence" of your view that in the long term artificial organs will be developed, to avoid such mix-ups (and of course the karmic consequences)? (2) Or are these patients just imagining things? (October 1996)

(1) Yes. Every atom of a body is imprinted with the consciousness of the individual. In theory a transplanted organ can indeed influence the recipient's personality. (2) No.

Is it right to mix the vibrations of the animal and human kingdoms through the use of animal organ transplants in humans? (June 1996)

No. Artificial organs can be developed.

Could you please explain the phenomenon of twins? Why are people born as twins, both identical and non-identical; is it purely physiological or is it also related to the individuals' karmic relationship? Does it denote an especially strong bond? Does it indicate a particular soul-purpose for that life? (June 1996)

It is mainly (nine times out of 10) purely physiological. There are, however, at times, twins who for karmic reasons are born such. The reasons may vary: to produce a strong, supportive bond, or to ensure close relationship through life, or other.

*In **Esoteric Healing** by Alice Bailey, p568, the Master DK states that rheumatism is "the result of the inability of the soul to produce an expression of 'the true' within the man, the instrument of the soul in the three worlds." (1) Can you elucidate this? (2) Does this statement also apply to rheumatoid arthritis? (3) Why does rheumatoid arthritis affect mostly women? (4) Can meditation exacerbate this condition? (5) Is there any hope of a cure on the horizon for the millions who suffer from this unrelenting disease?* (April 1996)

(1) This statement by DK could well be applied to every disease. Its specific application to rheumatism stems from that disease's relation to the astral/emotional body. Rheumatism is basically the result of selfishness and separation. These basic glamours prevent the expression of "the true", that is, the soul's

inclusiveness and altruism, on the physical plane. (2) Yes. (3) On the whole, women are more emotionally oriented than men, less given to abstract mental thought, and so are more subject to diseases of an underlying emotional cause. (4) No — on the contrary, it should help. (5) There will be various types of amelioration of this condition, from drugs and vaccines to magnetized water. Cure will result from the gradual release from misuse of soul energy as individuals become increasingly mentally polarized.

You talk about the neurosis of disciples. Is there any difference compared to the neurosis of an average person? (April 1994)

Neurosis in disciples comes about as a result of the wrong (or non-) use of the soul's energy contacted by meditation. If not used in service (the purpose of the soul) the contacted energy can turn inward and produce stasis. This stasis can manifest as neurosis or physical-plane illness. Hence the need for service to accompany meditation. The neurosis may be no different from that of "an average person" except, perhaps, in intensity.

What has the growth of homosexuality to do with this new era? (April 1994)

Two things. The growth of homosexuality is the result of the incarnation of a group of individuals who, back in the Lemurian race (which was the first race, before the Atlantean), through a misuse of the sex function, developed monsters, giants, pygmies, all sorts of physical abnormalities — and homosexuality. A large group from that time is in incarnation again, so there is an influx of people with that long-standing tendency and rhythm. The Masters say that very few people are actually born homosexual — it is mainly, according to the Masters, a result of imitation, as children, of the mother or the father (when it should be the opposite), and that, throughout childhood, repressive sexual mores in various parts of the world, particularly in the UK and America, have led to a large homosexual population.

The other thing is that homosexuals have always been here but today people are more relaxed and open-minded, responding to the energies of freedom released into the world by Maitreya, and therefore a more humane and tolerant attitude to homosexuality is prevalent — that means more and more people are 'coming out'. There have been homosexuals in the world for countless thousands of years.

What would Maitreya say about the eating of meat? (November 1994)

He would say that if you eat meat you are not really standing in correct relation to the animal kingdom. But if everyone had to give up eating meat under law — some people who would like this actually advocate it as a measure of legislation — then whole peoples would die out. There would be no Eskimos, for example. But for the advancing initiate the eating of meat is really unwise, because it is holding up his evolution. So Maitreya would probably say: it depends at what point in evolution you are. For average humanity it does no particular harm, but as soon as you enter the path of discipleship, and later the path of initiation, then the eating of meat holds you back. The vibration of the meat, in particular of the blood, is pulling you down whereas you are (or should be) trying to heighten the quality of your vibration. But you will find that Maitreya is the least fanatical of anyone you know; none of the Masters are fanatical — it is the fanatics who do the damage.

Was the creation of the recovery group Alcoholics Anonymous inspired by a Master? (October 1995)

Yes, by the Master Jesus.

Abortion

What is the attitude of Hierarchy to abortion, especially in the light of the militant anti-abortion group which has recently come over to the UK from America? (July/August 1993)

Hierarchy is made up of very intelligent, very wise people. They are Masters because They have mastered life and They have control over all aspects of life open to us on this planet.

Being intelligent and wise, They do not take narrow views on anything, so They would not take the fanatical anti-abortion stance of the fundamentalist Christians in America, of whom the group who have come to England seem to be representatives. These groups are becoming more vociferous in the United States as President Clinton has promised to ease the laws relating to abortion.

The Masters of the Hierarchy know that there are pros and cons on most issues; not only that but They know the inner meaning and purpose of life. They know that the purpose behind the creation of a foetus is to serve as the vehicle for an incarnating soul. They also know that at this time there are more foetuses created than are necessary for incoming souls. Therefore, there are a large number of souls of a not very advanced grade drawn into incarnation because of the plethora of foetuses created through the misuse of the sex function.

The Hierarchy are not 'for' abortion — to Them any killing of life at any time is to be regretted — but very often They will see abortion as the lesser of two evils. It is also evil to bring into incarnation a Being who is unwanted and unloved, and there are many foetuses who grow up unwanted, unloved and uncared for. Many are born with only one parent, in situations where they would be far better not incarnating ahead of their time, drawn in by the magnetic force of the created foetus. In some cases, therefore, the Masters would advise against abortion; at other times They would recommend that it go ahead. In that case it should, if possible, take place before the fourth week of pregnancy. Between the fourth and fifth week the soul actually begins to grip its vehicle, so any abortion that takes place should preferably be done before the fourth-to-fifth week.

What happens to the soul of a foetus that is terminated after then? (July/August 1993)
The later the termination occurs, the worse it is for the woman: the abortion itself may be technically more difficult and the psychological effect and the physical changes more pronounced. For the incoming entity, it may be glad not to incarnate — who knows? Each soul is individualized; it comes in with purpose, but it can be drawn in, magnetically, ahead of its purpose.

Could you please say whether the use of contraceptive pills (for females) has (1) any adverse effect on their health? (2) a: whether it can cause imbalance or disturbance in the endocrine system, and b: therefore, esoterically speaking, would influence the state of the chakras in the etheric body? (3) Are such pills and other medicines which act on the hormonal system better avoided? (4) In the case of young, still immature girls in their very early teens should the pill be avoided for health reasons? (5) Is their use linked to cancer of the breast and uterus? (6) Should hysterectomies be avoided for similar reasons? (7) Surely all this type of medical (chemical or surgical) intervention plays havoc with the endocrine system? (July/August 1995)

(1) It can and does in many (but not all) cases. (2) a: Yes. b: No, the influence is of the chakras on the endocrine system, not the other way round. (3) In the main, yes. (4) Yes. (5) Frequently, yes. (6) Not necessarily. Sometimes an operation is essential. (7) Yes, but we live in — as yet — an imperfect world.

Can you tell us what is the Hierarchy's view of surrogate motherhood? (May 1993)

On the whole They are not in favour of surrogacy, but the Masters seldom take rigid views on these matters. One of the main problems involved in surrogacy is that it completely confuses the karmic pattern of the baby involved, bringing in three (one not necessarily related in any way) different karmic strains and heredity.

(1) Is there such a thing as the "right age" for teenagers to begin having sexual intercourse? While most countries have a legally stated minimum age of consent, there seems to be a climate of peer pressure, on the one hand, and societal tolerance bordering on indifference, on the other hand, which almost makes early sexual experience inevitable. Parents of teenagers are very aware of the dangers of AIDS but at a loss as to how to advise their offspring. Free will and a person's right to make his/her own mistakes is paramount but parents are also morally and legally responsible for their children's well-being. (2) How does the Hierarchy envisage or advise dealing with this problem

now that the threat of AIDS (and not only unwanted pregnancies) hangs over such young lives? (3) Will education in future address such issues? (4) Can the innate aspiration, which often blossoms along with puberty, be stimulated so as possibly to help the teenager use his/her energy creatively in other directions? (July/August 1995)

(1) No. It depends on the child, his or her background, upbringing, physical body, race, karma. (2) This question is too complex in scope to be dealt with adequately here. Maitreya Himself will address it publicly in due course. (3) Yes. (4) Yes, indeed.

Healing Waters

How does healing work? (July/August 1995)

There is no simple answer to potentially as inexhaustible a question as that.

To summarize: in the etheric body — the body of finer-than-solid but still physical matter — there is a group of chakras or energy centres, including seven major ones in the spine, through which our energies flow. The energy that we receive comes from cosmos, the solar system, our own planet and our soul, entering the system we call 'ourselves'. If the chakras are working in a balanced way we get equilibrium in the energetic system. If from wrong use of soul energy (the major factor in dis-ease) we have produced a stasis, or dislocation of the flow, some of the chakras will not be functioning as they should. This results in an imbalance in the energy streaming through the body.

Related to the chakras is our endocrine system, the glands in the physical body. The health of the glands depends entirely on the correct flow of energy in the etheric body through the chakras, while the health of the physical body depends on the correct functioning relationship between the glands.

We are souls in incarnation. The energy which galvanizes our life is coming from the soul. As we evolve we can come more and more into touch with the soul, but if we do not use the energy in the correct way we produce dis-ease, disequilibrium. Healing brings to bear a degree of higher or stronger energy, to create a balance. That might be total and permanent, or in many cases temporary.

The best way to produce correct health is (a) to treat the body with respect and (b) to use the energy of the soul *in service*. The soul knows only service, it wants only to serve; that is why it comes into incarnation. If a person meditates, for example, and brings in energy from the soul but does not use it in service, then one may get the problems of disease, neurosis, emotional imbalance and so on.

In the New Age, shall we have a longer span of life, and instead of physically dying will we transmute our body into something else? (July 1994)

It depends at what level we are. The Masters do not die — They have already transmuted the physical matter of the body into light. Theirs is a resurrected body — that is what the Resurrection story in the Christian gospel is about — and Easter will become the major festival of the Christian calendar, the major festival in the West.

Resurrection is the result of the gradual transformation of the physical atomic matter of the body into sub-atomic matter, or light. This takes place through the evolutionary process. A Master is released from the pull of matter for ever, He is resurrected, He has conquered death — some of the Masters are thousands of years old.

When we become Masters, of course, we will do the same, but the healthy lifespan of humanity will gradually be lengthened with the use of the healing waters (777 of them) around the world and with the Technology of Light which will restore individual organs, all within the Karmic Law. The healing of humanity will progress to an extraordinary extent; people will definitely live longer, and with greater vitality. With the advent of the Masters in the world people will see that death does not exist. Reincarnation will be understood to be a fact in our life. When our body 'runs out of steam', which is all that is happening at death, the soul makes another body — with luck a better, stronger body, that will last longer if taken care of. People will gradually lose the fear of death.

Shall we become more healthy and live longer? (November 1996)

In the main I would say yes. The Waters of Life created by Maitreya all over the planet (777 eventually) — sources of practically inexhaustible water charged by the energy of Aquarius — will vastly increase the health of humanity. They strengthen the cellular structure of the body and act as a general tonic. It almost does not matter what the disease is: if your karma allows it the cure or amelioration will take place and on a wider margin of karma than would normally be the case.

There are other healing wells — for example at Lourdes, and so on, created by the Master Who was the Madonna. They have healing power but nothing to compare with the healing power of the Aquarian waters which Maitreya has created. These will increase tremendously the quality of physical, emotional and mental health. This will inevitably give people longer lives but just the lessening of stress in the world will allow people to live longer.

Most people suffer and die from stress. You can imagine that when the resources of the world are shared, when there is no more war, when the world is living in harmony and peace, people will respond with greater relaxation, and their health will improve.

Do you have any other comments you would like to make in terms of the overview of health and healing, and what we can expect to see in the coming time? (July/August 1993)

The stress which exists in the world today is a result of competition and fear — the fear of failure, disease, death, war, calamity, and economic disruption. The pressure that these fears put on humanity inevitably results in psychosomatic diseases. The cure lies in a re-establishing of equilibrium. When we establish equilibrium in our lives through a restructuring of our political, economic and social institutions, we will find that the health of humanity will improve dramatically. We will not have to spend enormous sums of money maintaining health. In fact, illness prevention will become the norm. Disease can generally be prevented more easily than it can be cured.

For some time I have been using Tlacote water ointment to treat non-malignant skin cancer spots (keratosis) on both hands. Usually, the spots become red and slightly inflamed before shrinking. One spot, on the top of my right wrist, became very inflamed. After moving my gold wrist-watch to my right wrist, and continuing to apply the cream, the inflammation began to reduce within a day. After a week, the spot had completely disappeared leaving a small white scar. Did the gold in the watch speed up the healing process? (December 1994)

Yes. The gold of the watch *focused* the energy in the ointment and so speeded up the healing.

(1) Does it have any effect on the unborn baby if a pregnant woman is taking Tlacote medicine? (2) After the baby is born, can she still go on taking these Tlacote tablets while she is breast-feeding? (September 1996)

(1) A positive effect, yes. (2) Yes.

Do you know how many people suffering from HIV and AIDS have been cured by drinking the healing water charged by Maitreya at Tlacote, Mexico? (January/February 1995)

As of January 1995 — full-blown AIDS: 56; HIV: 70-80.

Some people seem to respond more dramatically to the taking of Tlacote water itself rather than the homoeopathic potencies derived from it. Is there any difference in effect between the water itself and the homoeopathic potencies? (November 1993)

It would seem that there is a psychological factor at work. Some people believe that taking the water direct is somehow better, purer (and therefore stronger in action) than the potencies; very many people do not know about, or believe in, homoeopathy. Actually, the potencies *increase* the effectiveness of the water and, of course, make it more generally available.

Is it my imagination, or would it be true to say that Tlacote water (or tablets) seems to work at a very deep level and bring to the surface 'long buried', old constitutional problems? Is it a question of getting worse before getting better? (April 1993)

This is certainly true in some cases though not uniformly so. In very many cases there is an immediate or gradual improvement of the condition. Tlacote water (this is equally the case with the Nordenau and other waters) has a deep purifying effect and this sometimes results in a temporary intensification of the symptoms. For this reason, amounts taken at one time should be small: one teaspoon to one tablespoon (depending on the illness) one to three times daily, as a (very) general rule.

Argentina has banned the importation of "holy water" from Tlacote in Mexico because of possible cholera contamination. (1) Should people drinking Tlacote water boil it as a precaution, and if so, for how long? (2) Does boiling the water have any effect on the energetic properties of the water? (3) Does the fact that the water is cosmically charged 'protect' it from contamination by bacteria? (November 1993)

The Argentinian authorities have a low opinion of the quality (purity) of Mexican water. Whether this is justified or not, it is certainly not so in relation to the water issuing at Tlacote as the result of Maitreya's action. So pure is this water that the US (with extremely rigorous purity controls) makes no difficulties in the importation of Tlacote water. (1) There is no need to boil this water, charged as it is, cosmically, by Maitreya. (2) No. (3) Yes. If stored, it should be kept in *sterile* glass bottles, in a cool place, preferably refrigerated.

Ainsworths Homoeopathic Pharmacy has four potencies of Tlacote water. Can you advise on the appropriate potencies and frequencies for treating various ailments? (October 1995)

Tlacote water is water which was magnetized by Maitreya with energy from Aquarius, and appeared as a well which suddenly flowed out of the ground in Tlacote, near Mexico City. Maitreya is creating similar wells all over the world, four of which have so far been discovered. Thousands of people come daily to collect the water.

We have had the water homoeopathically potentized by Ainsworths Homoeopathic Pharmacy. I had it potentized in 6

221

and 30 potencies. Other people have had it potentized up to 200 and 1m.

We *do not* give prescriptions for the use of Tlacote or other water potentized by Maitreya. If you wish to use the homoeopathic potency from Ainsworths, ask the chemist there for their idea of how you should use it.

We are a small group, stretched to the limit already. We are not doctors and cannot be responsible for the health of the world; we cannot give prescriptions for the hundreds of people who otherwise would be phoning every day.

[For the reader's convenience, Ainsworth Homoeopathic Pharmacy's address is: 36 New Cavendish Street, London, W1M 7LH, U.K. Web: www.Ainsworths.com]

Does high potency homoeopathic medication interfere with karma? (July 1994)

Neither high nor low potency homoeopathic remedies interfere with karma. In either case, they are ameliorative only.

We have heard that some homoeopathic pharmacies (for example one in Zürich, Switzerland) are using the "magnetic vibrations" method of potentizing remedies rather than the usual manual method. Is there any loss in the quality of the remedies by using the "magnetic vibrations" method? (September 1995)

According to my Master the loss in potency is 50 per cent. This method is, therefore, not recommended.

Is cymatic therapy (healing by sound vibration) one of the healing sciences of the future? (September 1996)

Yes.

A documentary in the UK recently explored the use of colour therapy in helping autistic children. Most of the 'experts' interviewed for comment believed the practice to be just another unscientific trendy therapy, but the children seemed to benefit from it. Is this the beginnings of a useful treatment in this area? They used coloured lights which flashed intermittently at the children's faces. Does it have wider applications? (December 1996)

Colour therapy, properly and scientifically used, far from being "just another unscientific trendy therapy", is destined to be one of the future healing sciences. (The trouble with so-called 'scientific experts' is that they tend to call unscientific any science which they do not understand.)

Every colour is, essentially, an energy vibrating at a particular frequency. Different organs and areas of the body can be stimulated and enhanced in activity by exposure to the relevant coloured light. The better way to apply the light is in a darkened, black-painted room (large or small) in which the patient (for all manner of ailments) can be "steeped" in the coloured light for the required time. The science, of course, must involve a knowledge of which colours affect which organs and areas of the body — in effect, which chakras, and the necessary time of exposure to the coloured light.

Tlacote water is fascinating. In effect we are imbibing the energies of Aquarius, made accessible through water charged by Maitreya, the Christ, are we not? Can you explain, does this mean that we are thus provided with a means of not only curing present illnesses but are making a profound change to the quality of our bodies (cured or not), present and possibly future? (March 1996)

Yes.

Healing in the New Age

What new healing techniques can we expect to see in the future? (July/August 1993)

Maitreya has talked about a new technology which He calls the Technology of Light which uses energy directly from the sun. This will give us energy for all our needs — industry, transportation, heating — and healing. In fact, He says that as far as healing is concerned, with an advance in our present genetic engineering, organs can be rebuilt. Instead of going to a hospital and having an organ removed or receiving a transplant, we will have the organ remade through this technology. This will be a tremendous fillip to the health of humanity.

When can we expect to see some of this technology? (July/August 1993)

There is already a town in Russia where all the energy for heating and lighting comes directly from the sun through a satellite. In general, I would say that in the very near future, perhaps 10-15 years from now, the Technology of Light will be used in its first elementary stages.

Can we expect to see increasing co-operation among healers who use different approaches to healing? (July/August 1993)

Yes, indeed. Specialization has brought enormous advances along certain lines, but a specialist along one line may be quite blind in others. Groups of technicians — doctors, consultants, specialists, healers of all kinds — will work together. This is already happening to a small extent in England, but it will become pretty much the norm around the world. You may have a surgeon, for example, working with a homoeopath and an expert in acupuncture, as well as with someone who might be called a faith healer, and someone else who is an expert on the chakras, the energy centres up the spine which exist on the etheric physical plane. The health of the physical body depends entirely on the correct functioning of the endocrine system, which in turn depends on the correct energy balance in the chakras.

Scientists are on the point of discovering the existence of the etheric planes of matter. When these subtler planes are discovered, we will be able to practise all sorts of healing techniques which we cannot do today.

In the absorption of spiritual or healing energies does the nature of our clothes have any part to play — I mean, are some materials more or less absorbent than others? (April 1996)

Very much so. The most absorbent — therefore limiting to some extent the reception of the energies by the physical body — are: wool (30-40 per cent, depending on the weight and thickness of the wool); cotton (30-35 per cent); linen (25-30 per cent); silk

(15-25 per cent). The most resistant to the energies — thus directing them away from the physical — are the man-made materials, acrylic, nylon and polyester, which can block off 60-80 per cent of the energies.

If we eat meat do we prevent the reception of the Christ's energies? (October 1994)
No.

What is your opinion on gene therapy? (April 1995)
The present exploration of genes and genetic engineering, as we call it today, is only in its infancy, but even so is making very fast strides, some of them in a wrong direction. To create babies, for example, through gene therapy, and to give women who cannot, in the normal way, become pregnant, babies in test-tubes, especially from unknown or arbitrarily selected donors, is unwise. We come into incarnation in groups — a father becomes a son, a cousin, a daughter, a mother, an aunt — over and over again. We have been, in our incarnational cycles, men and women, husbands or wives, children and parents of our children and parents. In this way those groups incarnate and share a karma together. If, through genetic engineering, you bring in genes from some other group which has no incarnational relation to your group, you are upsetting the Law of Cause and Effect — which is basic, fundamental to our evolution. The Law of Rebirth, in relation to the Law of Cause and Effect, dominates life on this planet, and to interfere with it in this way makes the work of the Lords of Karma that much more difficult.

When we have set to rights the world and live together in peace and harmony, the Technology of Light will be given to humanity. By its means all energy will come to us direct from the sun. It can also be applied to genetic technology and the creation of new organs. This will happen, not tomorrow, but not far in the future. Genetic engineering is part of this science, but at the moment it is in the wrong direction, especially when it involves experimentation in uniting different species — the human and the animal kingdoms, for example. That is a monstrosity but is taking place behind closed doors in many of the clinics in the world today.

I used to practise "Network Chiropractic" which involves releasing meningeal tension in the nervous system. On a lot of people it releases a psychosomatic wave and a respiratory wave. One goes up the spine and one down the spine. Many people call that the kundalini. Many of the people receiving "network" have some wild experiences and some of it is upsetting. I got a bad feeling about doing it so I am weeding it out of my practice, but some people love it. A few patients had it released while still out of alignment and it is unpleasant. Can you give some insight on this phenomenon? I do not feel comfortable doing the treatments any more because I know it is not good to tamper with the kundalini. I need some higher information on this situation. (July/August 1993)

What is being released is not Kundalini but pent-up nervous energy 'locked', over a long period, in the spine and nervous system generally, by stressful and inhibiting life conditions and situations. The problem lies in the sudden, *uncontrolled* release of the chronically inhibited energy and the process, according to my Master, is not to be recommended.

I introduce myself to others as: "Magnetist-astrologist-fortune-teller", but also as "an adviser in esoteric matters and a guide on the path of evolution and initiation". I find the second part rather pretentious and try to find a more humble way to indicate my interest in these matters. Could you recommend to me something else? What would you say about: "Maitreya's little mate"? (January/February 1997)

I would say that was even more pretentious.

I practise magnetism myself, but mainly on photographs, which gives me the opportunity to treat well-known persons like actors, athletes, and so on, who suffer from diseases, or to increase their performance, without their knowledge. A friend of mine claims that this influences their karma and also my own. What is your opinion in this matter? (January/February 1997)

Your friend is partly right. This unasked-for 'healing' infringes peoples' free will and it is you, not they, who are creating negative karma for yourself.

Whenever I come into contact with sick people (I visit hospitals regularly and also have senile and handicapped acquaintances) I feel as if all my energy has been drained from me. It feels as if my "batteries are flat"; I get tired, irritable and exhausted. I want to be able to serve those I meet. What should I do? Should I try to avoid contact with such people? Should I 'protect' myself and if so how? Has this feeling of having no energy anything to do with years of Transmitting (I also do TM)? (November 1995)

The questioner needs to gain more control of the astral vehicle. He/she is too attached to the feelings for those visited in hospital. A more detached attitude should be cultivated. This reaction has nothing to do with Transmission Meditation, which would only recharge the 'batteries'.

Could you please explain how we take in prana? (1) Is it through breathing, or directly and automatically through the etheric body? (2) Can we improve our health by learning to absorb more prana, or rather by absorbing it correctly? (3) Does cooking or cooking food in a particular way (eg in microwave units) destroy prana? (4) Are there certain localities which are richer in prana than others — mountains, at the seaside, in forests, for instance? (5) Can negative emotional states hinder our correct assimilation of prana? (December 1995)

(1) Through the etheric body and also by breathing. (2) Yes. (3) Yes. Prana is the vitality in "vitamins" and much is lost in cooking. (4) The mountains. (5) Yes.

In cases where mediumistic healers appear to give 'psychic guidance' and healing, often to large enthusiastic audiences, would you say that, by and large, those experiencing healing are (1) only temporarily healed, (2) hypnotized, (3) being carried along on a current of emotional response? Amazing claims are made, if not by the healer, then by his or her followers as to the source of their apparent powers. (4) Does actual, lasting healing take place? (5) If the Masters only heal "within the Law of Karma" this throws some doubt on the claims made by and about certain types of healers. (May 1995)

(1) Yes. (2) Yes. (3) Yes. (4) Yes, sometimes. (5) Precisely. Many illnesses are of a psychosomatic nature and it is these which most readily respond to this type of healing suggestion. They take no account of Karma, however, and may not last.

Death and Dying

Related to the entire question of health is the issue of death and dying. Most of us are afraid of the prospect of death. How can we develop a new approach to death and dying that is more positive, and less fear-inducing? (July/August 1993)

It is a gradual process of realization that death is not the end. I would have thought that the work of the various spiritualistic societies in the 19th century and the earlier part of this century proved to any open-minded person that there is life after death, that some form of consciousness continues after death. This realization will gradually gain acceptance when more and more people begin to experience it, and this is happening already. Many people are having near-death experiences, and many books now exist about these.

Under hypnosis people have been taken back through their life experience to their previous death and beyond that to previous incarnations. I am not sure whether this *proves* the doctrine of reincarnation (of which I personally have no doubt), but it certainly does prove the existence of continuity of consciousness after death. When this knowledge is widespread enough, it will become respectable, and people will gradually lose their fear of death.

Do you believe that after our death we are aware, or are we only aware when we are in incarnation? (October 1995)

Out of incarnation, after death, we are more aware than we ever are in this life, because we do not have the limitations of the physical body and brain. The physical brain dies with the body. Eventually the etheric sheath which is part of the physical body dissipates, usually in about three days. Then the astral body gradually dissipates; then the mental body. The soul reincarnates and creates a new body with these three vehicles, physical, astral, and mental. Out of the body, we have a clarity of perception, a vividness of experience, which is altogether more conscious, more aware, more interesting, more rich than anything — except perhaps profound meditation — which we might experience here.

What happens to the soul when the body dies? (July/August 1996)
The soul causes death by cutting two threads — one to the head, the consciousness thread, and one to the heart, the life thread. When the soul decides that an incarnation serves no further purpose, even if the person is not particularly old, it will cut the life thread and the person dies. While the life thread is kept intact the heart is kept beating; while the thread to the head is kept intact the consciousness remains.

The soul has a seat — at the right side of the chest — in the subtle, etheric, physical body, and it is there that the Christ Principle or Consciousness is awakened. (On the Day of Declaration people will feel this energy pervade the whole of their body while Maitreya is speaking, telepathically, to them.)

The soul, on its own plane, prepares a body, in due course, for its next incarnation, bringing together the various ray influences to continue its purposes of evolution on the physical plane.

What is it that people experience when they breathe their last breath (immediately before dying), when their faces contort and show an expression of pain and/or anguish? (April 1996)
People do not invariably express pain or anguish at the moment of death. As often as not they "slip quietly away" as it is often expressed. When there is facial contortion and apparent pain, it is the result of the shock of the severing of the life thread (from the soul) in the heart.

Are near-death experiences real — that is, is this really what happens to us all after we die (Beings of light, dark tunnels, personal identity in the spirit world, etc)? (January/February 1995)

In a general sense, this is the usual experience of those quitting (or nearly quitting) the earth plane. For others, more advanced, the movement upward to the mental or spiritual planes is direct and unencumbered with such experiences of an astral nature.

EDUCATION IN THE NEW AGE

Interview with Benjamin Creme
by George Catlin

Our topic is education in the New Age, so perhaps the best place to begin is with some clarification of exactly what you mean by education. What does that term mean to you?

To me, education is every activity that fits a man, woman, or child for the fullest expression of their potential. Coming into incarnation at a certain stage in development, carrying on from a previous life, we have a given potential in terms of soul expression, intelligence, and physical equipment, whatever that brings into this life. Education is the preparation of a man, woman, or child, on physical, emotional, mental, and spiritual planes, to bring out their potential in any given life.

So you're taking education quite broadly then. Would you say that parents are educators?

In the sense that every child imitates its parents from the word go, then indeed every parent is an educator, for good or ill. If the behaviour of the parent is restrictive, authoritarian, then it is bad education. If the parent surrounds the child with love and patience, and seeks to enhance its expression in any given area, then it is taking an essential part in the education of the child. But most of us pass on to our children what we received from our own parents. If that is 'full of holes', then that is what we pass on. Most of us receive, and endow our children with, much harmful 'garbage'. I do not call that education but conditioning.

Outside the home and formal schools, would you see places like the workplace as having a potential for education?

Very much so. In fact, I would see in the education of the future a closer relationship between formal schoolroom situations and the outer workplace and community in general. And I would see, as part of education, a growing need to involve children at a young age in full-blown community activities so that they see

231

themselves from the very beginning as part of a community, wider than the family and different from the school — not to replace the school, but to enhance what the school can bring to life.

Given your mention of the future, and the potential for communities emerging in the child's awareness, maybe this is a good time to get into the question of what the New Age is. Could you explain that?

The New Age is the result of the cyclic activity of certain great cosmic energies that impose themselves on the life of our solar system. As it moves around the heavens, our system comes into direct energetic relationship with each constellation of the zodiac in turn. These constellations embody powerful cosmic energies with particular qualities which dominate the life of the cycle for as long as it lasts — roughly 2,150 years per cycle. We are emerging out of the Piscean experience and entering the new age in which the Aquarian energies, which are very different from those of Pisces, will influence us, and create a new culture and civilization as we respond to them. These energies embody certain great ideas which become our ideals; as we put the ideals into effect, so our culture and civilization grows.

Does one age end at a particular moment and a new age begin?

One ends and one begins, but not at a particular moment. There is a transitional phase of roughly 200-300 years. For example, the energies of Pisces began to recede, as our sun moved away from their sphere of influence, around 1625. The energies of Aquarius began to come in 50 years later, around 1675. Every day since 1675 has seen the energies of Aquarius mounting in potency. This they will do until they reach a zenith and then there will be a gradual declining as the sun moves away from their influence and enters that of Capricorn. That will take roughly 2,350 years.

To get some perspective on the challenges of education as we move into the Aquarian Age, I wonder if you would say something about the state of human consciousness at the dawn of the Piscean Age 2,000 years ago.

It was dark. We have a very clear example of this. A great man, one of the greatest Beings who has ever graced this Earth, namely Jesus, lived, worked and carried out a three-year mission in a little country called Palestine. It is extraordinary that a man Who exemplified in Himself the quality of Love, and to a degree that had never been shown in a man before, could be sent to His death — crucified.

This happened because there was no education. People were benighted. There were a few individuals — in this case, the priests — who could read and probably write. They were the teachers, the rabbis, who controlled the others. You can multiply that across the world. A few people read and the rest were totally uneducated. They were peasants, shepherds, fishermen, tool makers, and so on, with no education at all. They simply did as they were told. This relationship had gone on from the earliest times.

In the Atlantean civilizations, which are said to have ended about 95,000 years ago, there were a few people, priests and kings, who could read, were educated. The rest of the people simply obeyed, did what they were told. The Master Djwhal Khul, writing through Alice Bailey, says that a scholar of the Middle Ages had a consciousness equal to that of a 14-year-old child of the present.

In every age, in every century, there have been those individuals who stood out; for instance, among the Greeks, Aristotle, Pythagoras, Plato, Socrates, Euclid and all the other extraordinary minds who have given us the embryonic beginnings of the science and philosophy of today. But they were the exception. We have to remember, too, that the "glory that was Greece" was built on slave labour.

The exceptions certainly dominate our sense of history, but at the time of Jesus, what was the average person, the man or woman in the street, able to do and think? Can you describe their consciousness in any way?

They could not think. They could certainly be stimulated and made to act in a certain direction. But it was purely an emotional reaction to excitement. It was in no sense thinking for themselves. Otherwise, for example, Jesus would not have been killed. The populace was whipped up by the priests to get rid of Jesus.

Would you say that we can think now?
We are beginning to think.

Is that the result of the energies of Pisces?
The energies of Pisces have brought out humanity's individuality. This is a great step forward in the evolution of the human race. We have come out of the herd; we were really intelligent animals in the human herd. Broadly speaking, people today are individual in a very real sense, quite distinct from what pertained 2,000 years ago. This is the result of the energy of Pisces. Also, the quality of idealism, the aspiration and vision so prevalent today, has been responsible for the growth of the ideologies and religions. People are now ready to die for their beliefs. This would have seemed unthinkable 2,000 years ago. This is an extraordinary, self-sacrificing view of life, visionary, and fundamentally spiritual.

Is it inevitable that we progress in a certain way as a result of the energies of a particular age?
If we handle them correctly then we do progress. Each energy gives to humanity the ability to unfold a further aspect of our potential, divine nature. Individually, we can slip back, of course, but each age confers on humanity, in an upward spiral, the enhancement of the quality of its consciousness. There is not an equal response by all people because we are not all at the same level of evolution. In relation to our point in evolution, so will we respond to these energies, and they will enhance our ability to develop our fuller potential with each age.

Is there choice involved in that? Have we maximized the opportunity of Pisces? Could things have developed differently? Have we done all that we could have achieved through Pisces?

I doubt it. Separativeness, which has also been a result of the energies of Pisces, has hindered the development of humanity and created great negative karma, both personal and racial. We have hindered ourselves tremendously. Separativeness, of course, is the great hindrance to evolution. There is no separation; this is the heresy of heresies. We are souls in incarnation; there is no such thing as a separate soul.

The fundamental need of any new approach to education will be the understanding, the realization as a fact in life, of the soul.

Given that soul realization would be the overall aim of evolution, what particular aspect will Aquarius draw forth? What energies does Aquarius bring?

Above all, the energy of synthesis. You can already see the effect of the energy of synthesis if you look at almost anything in life, certainly education.

Synthesis has to do with relationships — for instance, the relationship of ideas. Through philosophical investigation you can broaden the consciousness until what seemed the most distant can be seen as standing side by side. Not only complementing and completing each other, but throwing light on each other. It is this ability to synthesize that inevitably broadens the consciousness of humanity and makes correct human relationships possible.

These energies of Aquarius, with their synthesizing quality, will broaden the individualistic consciousness until it can embrace the one humanity. So that we can stand fully individual, unique, and at the same time as one part of this great group which we call humanity.

Even in the abstract that sounds like a huge step forward for human consciousness. How do you imagine that playing out in more concrete terms, in terms of institutions and forms of daily living?

This is a difficult one because the forms are not yet there. Experimentation is going on throughout the world, in some countries more than others. It will make for a growing group consciousness. People will see themselves more and more as part of a group.

In educational establishments, in business, in every aspect of life, you will find groups forming. People who want to make their voices heard in the political field, for instance, form, or join, parties. A party is simply a big group. That group can make known its general ideology, beliefs, intentions, hopes and aspirations in a more powerful way than can the individual.

In this way the world gradually becomes more unified because we find that, although people are individual, they all need the same things. Everybody needs enough food, shelter, housing, clothes, health care and education. These requirements, which are common to every man, woman and child on the planet, will more and more become the accepted norm. When they are seen to be the basic requirements for all, we will see global consciousness become a fact.

Unfortunately, up until now, education in most countries has been very nationalistic. People have been taught the history of their nation, usually in a very biased form: everything that nation did was good, and everything other nations did was bad. This has given a very jaundiced, and quite incorrect, vision of the world to the developing child.

I would say that education, in the first place, has to show the child that it is a member of a world family. The synthesizing energy of Aquarius must be used to create this global consciousness. Children need to be shown that we are not living alone in one large or small country, but in a world shared by 5.7 billion people. The child, above all, should be taught that this is the fundamental position of his/her life on Earth: that they are one of a group, a family. Just as a family shares the resources that come into the household, so the human family should share the resources that are given by Divine Providence for that purpose.

It is hard for me to see consciousness, individuals, and education moving in that direction. In the face of world need, people seem to be getting ever more individualistic.

We have the expression, today, probably, of the greatest greed that we can imagine, although compared with what one knows about Atlantis, we do not know what greed is. They had the greatest greed that has ever been: rich people who bathed in milk; kings who stored gold by the ton, and some castles which were actually made of gold. Everyone else lived little better than animals: they thought like animals (if you could call it thinking), they emoted like animals, they obeyed like animals. Those above them, the kings and chiefs who could think, completely dominated all life. For most people, life was very brutish.

Today, we have growing wealth and growing greed around the world, as the mechanism for making money becomes more and more refined. The techniques of making money are now so exquisite that people can make a life out of doing just that. At the same time, more and more people are realizing the needs of the one humanity. They realize that millions of people are starving to death, and countless millions more are living in utter poverty, degradation, misery and want. That gap, the discrepancy between the rich and poor, is the real problem.

This cannot go on for ever. There is a growing awareness that things have to change. The very speed of the advance of greed through market forces and competition is forcing us to the edge of a precipice. This will suddenly bring us face to face with reality. There are various portents of breakdown in our economic structure, collapse of the stock exchanges of the world. When such events occur, they will transform the present economic system, probably for ever.

You have spent most of your recent life emphasizing that, soon, and potentially shortly after this kind of economic readjustment, the externalization of the Spiritual Hierarchy will complete itself and that the Masters will emerge into public view led by the Christ. How is that going to affect education?

The fundamental purpose of education, as I see it, is to equip people to demonstrate their divine potential as souls in incarnation. The externalization of the work of the Masters will have an enormous physical, emotional, mental, and psychological impact on humanity. We will come to realize that the soul really does exist. They, the Masters, are the Kingdom of Souls. People like Jesus will be talking to the people daily. He is alive and well and, if you can believe me, has been living in Rome for the last seven years. The Master of all the Masters, the Lord Maitreya, has been living in London (although moving around the world at will) since 1977. If these are facts, then the fact of the Hierarchy will also demonstrate the fact of the soul. People will say: "That was Saint John", or "That was Saint Peter." But today He is the Master Koot Hoomi or the Master Morya.

It will become clear that reincarnation is a fact of life. This will transform human thinking about the reason for our being on the Earth. We will come to know the answers to the age-old questions: "Why are we here? Who are we? What is the purpose of life? Where are we going to?" It will become clear that we are here for a certain purpose: the evolution of the soul in incarnation, carrying out the evolutionary process.

Every soul comes into incarnation with a given set of purposes. Each person's education should be geared to facilitate that process, the working out of the soul's purpose in life. This means that teachers, the educators, whether in school or out of school, must know the point in evolution of any given child. They must know the focus of their consciousness, what really commands their greatest attention, the polarization, as it is called, of their consciousness. Is it on the physical plane? (I do not think any human being is polarized on the physical plane today.) Is it on the astral, the mental, or the spiritual plane?

With the vast majority of people, it will be found that their polarization, the seat of their consciousness, is the astral/emotional plane. That being so, the point of education for these people will be to lift their consciousness onto the mental plane. If they are mentally polarized, then the educational aim will be the raising of consciousness from the mental to the spiritual level, so that they become spiritually polarized.

How will teachers be able to assess that? Is that something that one can be trained to perceive?

With the Masters working openly in the world, They will train Their disciples. Today we have school teachers. A school teacher is trained to teach children to read, write, do arithmetic, and so on. It is a very limited range of ideas which a teacher is called upon to evoke from the pupil. In most cases it is not even that; it is a limited set of ideas which the teacher is instructed to teach the child by rote to adhere to and accept. That, to my mind, is not education at all.

Education should be the evocation of the potential, whether emotional, mental, or spiritual, of each individual child. Teachers need to be equipped with the new psychology, which is soul psychology. They have to know the point in evolution of the child. They have to know the seat of consciousness, where the child is polarized. And they have to know the governing energies, or rays, of each individual child.

Every individual is governed on all levels — soul, personality, mental, emotional, and physical — by certain rays, streams of energy, seven in number. You can have one of each of these rays or just a few. The personality, mental, astral/emotional and physical rays can change from life to life while the soul ray remains the same for a world cycle, which is an immeasurably long period of time. When these rays are known, the propensities, the lines of greater or lesser resistance for any individual child will be known. This will help the educator to teach the child the best way to proceed to bring out its talents — to go along the line of least resistance when that is the right thing to do, or to tackle a line of greater resistance when that might evoke a trait which is trying hard to express itself and finding it difficult.

It is one thing to understand the rays in the abstract, but it is quite another to be able to assess that in an individual. Will that be the result of specific training that teachers will receive?

Yes. People will have specific training. It is not so very difficult to recognize the rays. If you really study them and make it a daily habit of mind — looking at people and visualizing them in terms of their rays — it is relatively easy for intelligent people who are interested in the subject to become pretty accurate in the delineation of a person's ray structure.

This will move education out of the classroom. When we think of teachers, we usually think of one teacher in the class. I do not see any reason why a much richer kind of education could not be given. Instead of one teacher, they could have a series of teachers from outside who are educators. They might be artists, scientists, esotericists, policemen, doctors, who will give them the benefit of their life experience, which is what students need.

They do not need simply specific teaching, as it is given today, along a subject line only. They need that too, of course. But you can broaden the consciousness of a child. Most children find that what they later think of as their best education came from inspiring parents, uncles, teachers, friends — people who have caught their imagination in life.

If the community really took education seriously, which I am sure it will eventually do, days could be set aside for meetings with philosophers, scientists, and so on, who will donate a day, a week, or whatever, to come into colleges and schools and give the benefit of their experience along their own line of work. In this way the gifts of unusual, and unusually gifted, people can be better put at the service of the growing population.

Earlier you mentioned "lines of least and greater resistance." Could you expand on that a little bit? What is a line of least resistance and why shouldn't one just follow it wherever it leads?

It is sometimes better to do what is hardest for us. That brings out qualities of self-discipline that are very necessary. I am not talking about discipline imposed, but self-discipline, which is probably the most important thing we can do, as long as it is correctly managed. Just to discipline oneself for no reason, as many ascetics do, especially religious ascetics who beat themselves, does nothing but harden the nature and turn one against the world and life.

If your line of least resistance is to be rather lazy, take life easy, not try very hard, it could well be an impediment to progress from the soul's point of view in that life. You may well need to tackle the things you do not like doing, the things that are difficult. If you can do that, discipline yourself in these ways, you can become more disciplined in the bigger ways, the ways that really matter.

I think education is also about: the disciplining of the individual in the management of his or her life, and his or her potential, given by the rays. Anybody with a 3rd-ray mind has a very active mind, creative, lively, full of ideas. They could, however, be overactive and manipulative, never learning to sit still, to look inwards and find the meaning of life. Then there are other rays, like the 6th, which is very idealistic and yearning for the higher vision and the higher inner life. People dominated by the 6th ray can be often very unpractical on the outer physical plane. The same is true of the 2nd ray, which is very inturned. It finds that the way into the soul is very easy, a line of no resistance. But the way outward, in relation to the outer physical world and all its demands, is something which is often very difficult for the 2nd-ray personality.

If you can discipline yourself and use your qualities intelligently (which is not easy to do) you can strengthen your weak points and modify your strong points so that — although they will still dominate — they need not obliterate the other aspects of yourself. You strengthen the weak points in the beginning in small ways by little disciplines, until they add up to a strong disciplining will. That is education — self-education — in terms of handling your ray structure, which is really handling life.

Inherent in what you just said is the idea that the problems come in two directions, essentially. One is handling life on the outer plane and knowing how to cope with the external world, and the other is this inner movement toward the soul.

This is the crux of the matter. Up until a certain point in evolution, you are either one or the other: either introverted or extroverted in any given life. That is the path of discipleship, in which you are learning to handle these energies which are driving you inward to soul life and also outward to personality life, sequentially. A whole life can be introverted to the soul, or extroverted to the outer world. The individual in each case has an inner unhappiness because he realizes this, but he really cannot do much about it. When a certain balance has been reached, and when the person has integrated the physical, emotional, and mental vehicles, he or she becomes initiate. The sign of the initiate is that he/she can go inward, be introverted at will, but also go out and relate perfectly easily to the outer world, at will.

It would seem that our present education is mostly geared toward relating to the outer world. We are primarily taught skills designed to help one fit into society. What about the developments that might come in the future toward the inner side?

Today, most education, for what it is worth, is education for jobs. People are simply fitted to make their living in the outer commercial world under the whip of competition. This will change. Competition has to give way to co-operation. Above all, it is competition, which is based on greed and fear, that holds humanity back in its most important expression of its oneness, its sense of being part of one group. This has to change. When it does, people will realize, and the Masters will exemplify, the fact of the soul. People will realize that they are souls and will turn to the soul. Then the education for the life of the soul, and the psychology of the soul, will become more and more the norm in our educational system.

I do not mean that we will have only religious education. I am not talking about religion at all. The religious path, as seen by the Masters, is only one of many paths to the demonstration of our innate divinity. God does not reside in the religion, although the religion might help you to realize that divinity. Every aspect of life — politics, economics, religion, art, culture, science, education — can be lived in such a way that what we call God can be known and expressed.

The divine becomes a moment-to-moment experience. That is in fact what it is. It is not a man with a beard sitting up in the sky watching that you are not stealing, lying, or cheating. It is inside you; it is your sense of the divine inside that gradually changes you from lying, cheating, and stealing to not doing these things. Not because somebody is telling you that it is bad, but because you instinctively know that that is not the right way to live with your fellow human beings.

Whatever injures or harms another person is intuitively, instinctively, wrong. A change in behaviour comes about by self-observation and self-determination. These things fall away as you become more aware of, and imbued with, the quality of the soul. That will happen on a wider and wider scale as humanity ceases to compete and learns to co-operate — in the family, in the community, nationally and internationally.

In regard to getting to the state of being able to co-operate and beginning to sense the soul and its values and mission, the World Teacher, the Lord Maitreya, has been quoted as saying that without self-esteem nothing can be done. Is this a first step in that direction? Is that something parents, teachers and schools should be thinking about?

Very much so. One of the saddening things about present education is the way children are put down, told that they are wrong, told not to do that, that is naughty. This inhibition of the child that goes on all the time has nothing to do with naughtiness. The child has no concept of naughtiness. The child has only desires, instincts, and a looking for adventure. If they were allowed to do that without always being told that they are naughty and wrong, they would grow up without these inhibitions, this lack of self-esteem. They would feel loved, feel that their parents really cared about them, had patience for them, were ready to listen to them, speak with them, and so on. That would give an inner confidence which reflects itself in an ability to make the best of any opportunity presented by life.

What holds most people back is a lack of confidence. That is mainly the result of continual nagging by parents, putting the child down. "You're only a child", or: "How could you know?" Everything a child says is sneered at and belittled. I do not mean in every family, but in many. Even among otherwise intelligent and educated people you will find the same kind of down-putting, derision of their children.

Children should never, ever, be derided. It is only a convenience for parents to inhibit the child so that they can keep them under moderate control. People are so overworked and tired, their nervous systems so taut, that they cannot bear the presence and demands of their own children. That is a tragedy for them, for the children and for society as a whole.

Self-esteem is a fundamental need in every human being. The lack of it is what drives people to crime, drug-taking, all the abuses, even suicide. All of that is a direct result of the inability of many parents to inculcate a sense of love and understanding, to treat them with a warm, patient, readiness to help, to listen and relate to the child, and give them that essential confidence.

It seems at present that most teachers spend about 50 per cent of their time and energy in school trying just to cope with the problem of discipline, trying to keep children within bounds, in some sense. Are you saying that if the child is well-parented, given this love, that won't be such a problem?

Absolutely. My Master has written for *Share International* that it really is not a problem of discipline at all. It is a question of freedom. It is a matter of seeing the validity of the child, the need of the child for self-expression.

Each child, at whatever level it comes into incarnation, comes into the world with its own set of purposes. A main purpose is to learn to live in peace and harmony with the rest of us, all the people with whom he or she comes into relationship. The actual possibility to do this is rare today. You are a very exceptional individual if you come into life in a family, a school situation, a national community, where everything you need to work out your life purposes as a soul is available to you.

We need to recognize that all young people are unique. They are sons of God evolving towards the manifestation of that divinity and sonship. How many people see an individual child in that way?

Many parents love their child, but you can love a child and not respect it. To say that you really respect its uniqueness and validity at every turn, I think is a huge claim. Not many people meet that need of the child.

We have the Year of the Child, but that is playing at the game, this giving respect to the child. The very fact that we have the Year of the Child, however, even if it is only a non-active slogan, means that we are beginning to see the validity of the child and the need to respect it.

A child at any point of evolution comes into incarnation with all its past achievements. There is a wonderful child today, aged 11, who paints pictures that are said to be like Picasso, Matisse, or Chagall — obviously a tremendously gifted child. She is Romanian, living in America, and already fantastically successful. This child is allowed to paint. She is a genius, and is allowed to be a genius. And she does it. Instead of going out to play, she paints these great big canvases and covers them with the most interesting and beautiful ideas.

Children should be introduced to all that they need to further their talents. This is to do with respecting the child as a soul. If you respect each child as a soul, and see that they have all of that behind them, give them the scope in which that can come out, marvels of creativity will come forth.

Do you imagine special kinds of schools for special kinds of development?

I see special kinds of education for specially gifted children — not necessarily special schools. It can be in the same school. But there have to be different departments that will accommodate, enhance and develop the gifts of specially gifted children. Otherwise, the race will suffer.

Today, if you are a specially gifted child, usually sooner or later these gifts show themselves, whatever the circumstances. But a tremendous amount of time may be lost in the process. Some demonstrate only a fragment of their potential because it was not noted when the person most needed it. That will mean training teachers at higher and higher levels. As far as education is concerned, it will only be as good as the quality of the teachers. Training of teachers, I would say, is the fundamental first step in all new educational needs.

There's some writing, particularly by the Master DK, about the possibility of schools starting to become focused more on the problem of reaching beyond the mind to the soul. Do you envision that happening?

Yes, absolutely. Obviously, you need to discipline the instincts. You need to enhance and develop the intellect, the mind and the brain. And you need to evoke the intuition. These are higher and higher steps. The more advanced the individual, the more the intuition will play a role. The bridge to it, the antahkarana, which is created by meditation and service, will become known as a definite part of the educational curriculum. You have to build the bridge. Meditation, therefore, at a certain point in the educational system, will have to come in as the way, par excellence, to create the bridge to the soul.

It is interesting you mention meditation and service. Many schools are already instituting service components of their education. Many colleges have that as part of their requirements for a degree. It is nice to think that is already happening.

Yes. The more the child is related to the community at an early age, the more service will become normal and natural.

In that same vein, are you suggesting that meditation will be taught in our schools or colleges?

Yes. It should never be imposed at an early stage. I do not believe in making young children meditate, but the beginnings of meditation are beneficial. We discussed the problems of discipline. If the children were to start the day by just sitting quietly for five minutes and taking a few deep breaths, just quietly thinking about themselves and maybe what they are going to do for the rest of the day, just letting these breaths quiet them down, you could have a completely different atmosphere in the school.

And then for older children the more technical training in meditation?

Indeed, the beginnings of meditation, or light meditation, in which the concentration is focused. You have to learn to concentrate, to use the mind, and to meditate and build the bridge to the soul. There are times for doing this. I am not going to set down ages because children vary enormously depending on their point in evolution. Those who are more evolved can start at an earlier age than those less evolved.

I have one last topic that you might address: television and its effect on children.

I would say that television has one of the greatest negative effects on children. It is not the fault of the children but of the type of television. I have found that meditators in America, for example, have very little concentration. Their attention span is very limited. I think it is largely due to the breakup of attention from a very early age, through watching commercial television. It is convenient to let you go and get a cup of coffee, or whatever, but it breaks up the attention in the middle of any programme. Your interest is held for a certain point and then suddenly you have a break, which goes on for almost longer than the preceding episode of the programme you were watching. That is terrible for the concentration.

If it is bad for adults, it is also very bad for children. Children's television is no better in that respect. They have their own set of nasty advertisements telling them to get their parents to buy this, that and the other. This is a social thing. It is to do with competition, greed, the wrong economic systems in the world, which will change when co-operation and sharing replace the present competitive system.

Children have to be taught to concentrate. It does not always come naturally. With some it does: the more evolved, of course, can usually concentrate. Yet there are many gifted children who cannot concentrate at all.

Do you imagine television eventually playing a more positive role?

Yes, indeed. Television will become the great teacher in the world, but it will have to change dramatically in its content, its substance. You can imagine television screens in every home, where the children can be taught about history in the real sense

— global history, not nationalistic, chauvinistic history, but the history of humankind throughout the ages — and relate themselves to it. The Masters can project onto the television screens a view of life in the far, far distant past, in Atlantean days, and forward into the future, showing visions of what can be. There will be wonderful programmes for children projected onto the screens by the Masters. Television will be the key tool by which Maitreya and the Masters teach humanity.

(*Share International,* July/August 1997)

CHAPTER 3

TO SERVE ANEW

TO SERVE ANEW

by the Master —, through Benjamin Creme

Since the time is short indeed till mankind sees the Christ, it would be wise to consider, somewhat, the likely repercussions of that momentous event. Firstly, men will awaken to a new situation, one altogether unfamiliar and strange: nothing similar will have been the experience of anyone alive; no one, anywhere, will have heard before the thoughts broadcast on that day of days. Never, before, will men have heard the call to their divinity, the challenge to their presence here on Earth. Each, singly, and solemnly alone, will know for that time the purpose and meaning of their lives, will experience anew the grace of childhood, the purity of aspiration cleansed of self. For these precious minutes, men will know afresh the joy of full participation in the realities of Life, will feel connected one to another, like the memory of a distant past.

Suddenly, men will realize that their life till now was a shallow thing, lacking, for the majority, all that makes life dear: brotherhood and justice, creativeness and love. Many will know for the first time that they count, that they matter in the scheme of things. An unfamiliar sense of self-esteem will replace their present hopelessness; drugs of all kinds will cease their hold on men. Quietly, men's tears will flow in humble gratitude and longing for the good.

From that time forwards, a new spirit of sanctity will prevail upon the Earth; men will walk on tip-toe for a time. Soon, however, men will realize that the changes needed in the world are vast, manifold, requiring patience and dedication, imagination and trust. Before long, men everywhere will engage themselves in the work of reconstruction, the rehabilitation of the world. Succour for the poor and hungry will take pride of place, and so will end for ever a blasphemy in men's midst: millions will know for the first time the quiet happiness of satisfied need — no more will the dying forms of the starving disgrace the screens of the affluent; no longer will men watch their brothers dying before their eyes. So will end a dark chapter in the history of the race.

Onslaught

Changes, unequalled in extent, will engage men's minds and hearts; naught but the finest of the past will prevail against the onslaught of the new. Daily, the transformations will be recorded for men to compare and admire; a new world will be constructed in the blazing light of day. All will, in their way, participate, each will add his vision and contribute to the whole.

Problem

For many, the very presence of the Christ will constitute a problem — their long-held beliefs will be shaken to their core. For them, a period of heartsearching will be inevitable as they seek to understand the meaning of the new dispensation; ancient beliefs die hard and hurt bitterly in the process. Nevertheless, millions will respond with a glad heart, happy to accept the Teacher in their midst. Few, in time, will stand against the common acknowledgment that the Christ, in the person of Maitreya, walks once more upon the Earth.

Educational

Those relatively few who have led the way in preparation for this time will find themselves offered another field of service: an educational endeavour vast in scope. From all sides will come the queries; a long-felt hunger for knowledge will, like a dammed-up river, overflow and burst its banks. Many will seek to know the background and history of this event; for others, the immediate future will be the chief concern. Still others will feel the need to analyse and to question every explanation, unsatisfied in the end with aught but their own beliefs. Persuasion and tact, therefore, must be the order of the day, so to avoid the charge of bigotry and pride.

Societies, world-wide, will play their part, assuring the broad dissemination of the needed teachings. Much remains to be given, but, already, much remains unopened and unread in the hands of men. Endeavour, the counsel is, to inculcate the habit of reading much, thus to inform and guide the seekers on the way. Systematic study of the teachings, and earnest attempts to live the precepts of Maitreya, will give the needed balance and authority with which to teach. Each one, thus equipped, can avail themselves of this opportunity to serve anew. Seize it, the counsel is, with alacrity and humble pride.

(*Share International*, August/September 1994)

TO SERVE ANEW

The following article is an edited version of the talk by Benjamin Creme given at the July 1994 Transmission Meditation Conferences in San Francisco, USA, and in September in Kerkrade, the Netherlands.

[The talk was based on the above article by Benjamin Creme's Master, 'To Serve Anew'.]

Kali Yuga

"Firstly, men will awaken to a new situation, one altogether unfamiliar and strange: nothing similar will have been the experience of anyone alive."

I do not know whether you have thought of it, but this is manifestly true. When Maitreya speaks as the World Teacher for the new age, enlightening humanity with certain ideas that, as students of the esoteric tradition, we take for granted and with which we have familiarized ourselves in the process of making known His presence, most people are going to have an extraordinary revelation. The world as a whole does not know that Hierarchy exists. They have heard that the Christ exists, but living up in heaven in some remote place in the sky — waiting until the end of the world to return on a cloud. That, as you know, is the general expectation of orthodox Christians. The other religions have their equally unlikely scenarios for the coming of the Teacher into our midst. Muslims are awaiting the Imam Mahdi who, likewise, can only come on Judgement Day, again at the end of the world; and into Damascus, the "centre of the world", at noon, when He will appear suddenly and say: "I have come. Give Me bread. Give Me clothes." Hindus have their own interpretation, awaiting Kalki Avatar or the return of Krishna, at the end of Kali Yuga.

I heard the other day that Sai Baba had announced recently that Kali Yuga had ended, was coming now to an end. I thought that He had said that several years ago, and we published it in *Share International*, but we are always ahead of events! My

Master affirmed, as did Swami Premananda, that Kali Yuga was indeed ending and we published that at the same time.

However, there has been a rumour, as always, coming from Puttaparti, that Sai Baba has said that Kali Yuga has now ended, and that this week, from Monday 18 to today Friday 22 July 1994, was a most important period in the life of this Earth. He did not, as far as I know, go on to explain why it was important, why it was so crucial. I have checked up, of course, with my own source of information. Indeed, what Sai Baba appears to have been referring to is that this week is the culmination of a great period of trial and testing for the Earth, and that the Earth has come through it — that is, mainly humanity, although not only humanity — safely.

For example, a great battle has been going on, on Cosmic levels, between the forces of Light, under Maitreya, and certain evil Cosmic forces. That has culminated recently in a triumph for our Spiritual Hierarchy. Maitreya has been waiting for just such a time to emerge into the open. As you know, at other times, in particular in 1985 when Maitreya was ready to come forward to a group of journalists meeting in London, there was a great battle fought, again on Cosmic levels, between these forces and our own planetary Hierarchy. This, too, ended in a triumph for our Hierarchy, but at the expense of the coming forward of Maitreya. It took all the combined efforts of Hierarchy to contain the assault which was launched.

I know the signs. I know that during such a period when cosmic battles are going on, about which humanity hears nothing, my Master becomes very remote indeed. I can sense His remoteness. Although He will respond and will answer questions, it is as if His answers are coming through a series of filters and barriers. All the Masters were totally focused, meditating. The same thing happened in the two or three months before July 1977, when Maitreya came down from His retreat in the Himalayas.

Having accepted the invitation to appear on a major US network, He has been waiting for the best possible moment in which to do it. That would be when the spiritual energies in the world were at their highest, when a reservoir had been built up which would guarantee (as far as that can ever be guaranteed) a correct response from humanity. So that it would not be wasted, that the maximum response of a good kind, positive and welcoming, would come from such a broadcast.

During the Three Spiritual Festivals in April, May and June, powerful energies were poured into the world — the Spirit of Peace, the Buddha, the Avatar of Synthesis, the energies from Aquarius focused through Maitreya, and so on. All of this has been building up in tremendous potency. The Avatar of Synthesis, in particular, I have experienced as never before, coming also with the Shamballa force, which is unusual; it is usually one or the other. This has built up a barrier against these Cosmic forces which have been levelled against us, a last ditch stand, if you like, of these materialistic forces, trying to prevent the manifestation of our Spiritual Hierarchy openly in the world.

They have not succeeded, they will not succeed, and the way is now clear for the open manifestation of Maitreya and the other Masters. I believe that is what Sai Baba meant when He said that the period from 18-22 July will be of major import. It has turned the wheel. We are now in the Age of Aquarius. I know Maitreya said that when the earth was slowed down in its revolution, brought symbolically closer to the sun, that was the turning of the wheel. That was the beginning of a process which has culminated now. We are at the end of Kali Yuga, and at the end of Kali Yuga the Kalki Avatar can come. Maitreya is, of course, the Kalki Avatar.

Even on the Day of Declaration, I doubt very much that Maitreya will say: "I am the Christ." He will probably say something like: "Many millions await Me as the Christ, and it is to fulfil their expectations that I come." Something of that nature.

He will introduce to the world as a whole the fact that He has been living in the Himalayas, rather than in "heaven", this past 2,000 years and more; that He is the head of a large group of similarly, if not equally, advanced men, and that They too, in growing numbers, will be in the world. Already a large number, 14 including Maitreya, are among us.

This will be a revelation for humanity. There is one thing on which I disagree with the Master DK. I find it very difficult to agree when He says that the idea of Hierarchy has filtered right down to "the man in the street". I would have thought that probably everyone in California today has heard of the Masters. But Kansas City? Cleveland? Detroit? I doubt it. Manchester? Birmingham? Bremen? Yokohama? No, I think that there are many places in the world, most of them in fact, where the idea of Hierarchy has never entered into the consciousness of the people.

Yet they are going to hear about it for the first time on the Day of Declaration. And they are going to hear about it from the One who knows about it, who leads the whole group of Masters, and in this miraculous way by their minds being overshadowed. As the Master put it, "singly, and solemnly alone" they will hear this voice in their hearts. Can you imagine the experience this will be for the bulk of humanity, who have never before heard of Masters or a Christ who isn't up in heaven; a great teacher who is actually there on a television screen speaking for the first time to the whole of humanity in this extraordinary way? Can you imagine what that will mean, the shock to the consciousness of the vast body of humanity, probably most of the 5½ billion people who live in the world.

I have never yet grasped the immensity of this event. I have said it so many times, but never until this moment, and probably not at this moment, have I been able to grasp the enormous impact of that, the enormity, the newness, uniqueness, of this event. For the first time in history, there will be a world telepathic contact. The whole world will be in contact with one man, hearing His words enter their minds in their own language, speaking directly to them, "singly, and solemnly alone". Every individual will be watching the screen. They will turn to each other to ask: "Are you hearing what I am hearing?" Because of the tone of the voice, as it were, the tone of the thought, the solemnity of the ideas, the vastness of these concepts, people will be experiencing what they have never experienced in their lives. That is phenomenal. We are standing at a unique moment in the history of this planet.

"Altogether unfamiliar". That is the understatement of the year. *"Altogether unfamiliar and strange."* A new situation. Suddenly, people will know that we do not have to wait for UFOs to descend to have enlightened Beings in our midst. We will know that 'that' man is the most enlightened Being we are likely to meet. And He is not alone; He has a large group of similarly enlightened men who are going to live among us, who are going to be accessible: to know, to learn from, to guide and advise humanity. That must mean a phenomenal lifting of the weight of anxiety and depression. You can imagine what effect that will have when humanity, living largely in stress and anxiety, hears His words of hope and concern.

Most people, whether they are starving to death or multi-millionaires, are living under stress. Anyone living today who is half-way sensitive must be living under conditions of strain, of tension: of inward expectation because of their sensitivity as souls, but perhaps not knowing what is taking place, responding to the energies perhaps negatively, finding them simply an imposition, trying to drive them in directions in which they do not want to go. Others gladly accept these energies, and, without knowing that they are there, bring out the constructive ideas which will give form to the experience of the energies. People are going to have these different reactions, not only to the energies, but to the One who carries these energies, the Water Carrier. Whether He will call Himself the Water Carrier on that day, I do not know. My guess is that He will.

"No one, anywhere, will have heard before the thoughts broadcast on that day of days. Never before will men have heard the call to their divinity, the challenge to their presence here on earth."

It is a challenge. Maitreya will present to the world a choice: to continue as we are, in the old, greedy, selfish, very human ways, and destroy ourselves, or to demonstrate at last the divine potential in every person by grasping the realities of life: the fact of the oneness of the soul; of the oneness, therefore, of humanity as a group of souls in incarnation. This will be a revelation for most of humanity.

Millions of people already believe in the soul, believe in the idea of the soul, but have very little notion, it seems to me, of what the soul really is. For most Christians, and not only Christians, the soul is a very wonderful, beautiful, powerful, divine entity who lives up in heaven and who, when we die, we come before and know for the first time. And that is the end of it; we go on then as souls with a harp if we like. And one day at the end of the world the Christ will descend, and there will be a great rapture in "heaven".

It is a beautiful idea, but it is a mystical idea. The truth is even more beautiful, more wonderful: that divinity can be, is scheduled, planned to be, manifest on the physical plane. That is a greater mystery and a greater beauty than any rapture in "heaven". To bring the reality of the soul, that divinity, onto the physical plane and to demonstrate it as a Master, or a Krishnamurti, or a Leonardo da Vinci, is, it seems to me, a far greater mystery and beauty than the mystical idea of union in "heaven".

That will be a sudden revelation for humanity. We will know that we are souls. It will be presented to us in such a way that we will immediately grasp its reality and will feel this divinity in ourselves. The Christ Principle, the energy which Maitreya embodies, will flow out, as He has said, in tremendous potency. It will be as if, He says, "I embrace the whole of humanity". That will be an extraordinary experience for all of us.

Purpose and meaning

"For these precious minutes," the Master says, *"Each, singly, and solemnly alone, will know for that time the purpose and meaning of their lives."* For the first time we will grasp, during this overshadowing, hearing the words of Maitreya, the outline of the reality of our spiritual structure as spirit, reflected as souls, involved on the physical plane as the human personality. That will become clear, grasped suddenly, if not completely understood, by millions of people for the first time — a tremendous event for most people, hearing ideas which those interested in the esoteric teachings have taken as a matter of

course, even if they do not actually understand and experience them as a reality.

Each one *"singly, and solemnly alone"* will know this for that little time, when Maitreya is overshadowing the world, maybe half an hour, 35 minutes, at the most. For that time the world will stand still. Nothing else can be done, everyone will be listening, experiencing the ideas, looking at themselves as He speaks from heart to heart, so that their attention is focused in their reality, in their Beingness in the heart, not in their sense of themselves as Mr Smith or Mrs Johnson or whatever. Suddenly, during that time, humanity will experience itself for what we really are, souls in incarnation, divine beings.

Then, having given us the sense of our divinity, He will present the challenge to that divinity. He will talk about the needs of the world: the fact of the starving millions, *"a blasphemy in men's midst"*, as the Master calls it. He will show that problem to be the first priority awaiting a renewed and regenerated humanity. He will show that without addressing the problem of hunger and starvation in the midst of plenty we will never take one step forward in the demonstration of the divinity of which He is giving people a sense, perhaps for the first time. As we are listening we will feel ourselves to be divine. We will know ourselves to be quite different from what we thought. We will remember our childhood feelings. The Master puts it so beautifully: *"Each, singly, and solemnly alone, will know for that time the purpose and meaning of their lives, will experience anew the grace of childhood, the purity of aspiration cleansed of self."*

The beauty of the child is that it has all the aspiration of a soul in incarnation. Not in the slightest way sullied with scepticism, with cynicism. It knows that this is what is best for the world. It says: "If there is illness in the world, it should be 'magicked' away. Would it not be wonderful if we could magic away all the ills of the world?" Every child wants, and uses the idea of magic, to get rid of the ills of the world — a totally unselfish aspiration. When the heart speaks, when the energy of the Christ, flowing through the hearts of humanity, awakens in each one of us that early, pure aspiration, the world will turn to Him.

Joy

"For these precious minutes, men will know afresh the joy of full participation in the realities of life; will feel connected one to another, like the memory of a distant past."

People will realize for the first time that, up till then, they have only played at life. They have never really touched the core of what life is really about; perhaps as children, yes, but never with that simple, direct, spontaneous experience of what is, what life actually is at this moment, in a way the child automatically, instinctively does. Everything of that full, rich, total absorption in, concentration on, the moment-to-moment experience of life as it is, is covered up by tensions, by 'busy-nesses', by all the worries and the problems which surround every adult human being in the world. Few can, for long, experience total enjoyment of the beauty of life, total absorption in that reality.

For that time, for that half hour, or whatever it is, the whole of humanity will experience that childhood joy of being truly alive. And of being *alive*, not simply a physical aliveness, a sense of well-being, of good health, but a sense of being whole, connected to the reality of life on all its different levels. That is new, and yet people will feel: "That's it, and it is to do with everybody." They will feel connected to one another even though they do not see one another because they will know that everyone in the world is undergoing the same experience. Some, of course, to a greater and some to a lesser extent. Some will be worried with everything they hear. Others will open their hearts and drink it in and experience it for the bliss which it is.

"Like the memory of a distant past." People have, at the very seat of their consciousness, the sense of past lives, past experiences, of soul experience, of life out of the body, as well as life on the physical plane. That lies at the core of the consciousness of every single being. And at that moment, they will experience a connectedness with all their previous experience as a person, and that contact they will know to be the reality for everyone. We are all parts of one great Oversoul. On

the physical plane that fact gives the sense of brotherhood, of connectedness, and in the case of most people, "like the memory of a distant past", something from way, way back will register and they will say: "Yes, that's the truth! That's how it is." The truth of what Maitreya is saying will in an energetic, and also in a consciousness, and a memory sense, become one experience. The words, the meaning of the words, the information, and the actual experience of the Christ Principle will awaken all of that in everybody.

"Suddenly, men will realize that their life till now was a shallow thing, lacking, for the majority, all that makes life dear: brotherhood and justice, creativeness and love."

Few there are who know what brotherhood is, and justice is a dream dreamt by many, struggled for by many, and, so far, never achieved on a world scale. Some have achieved a relative degree of justice: trade unions have fought for justice in their industrial life; people have fought for political justice, for economic justice. For ever, it seems, most people have been struggling for justice, because it is the number one concept in the human mind. It means right relationship; that is the meaning of justice. People know instinctively at their best and highest moment that the meaning of life is to demonstrate right relationship. But how can we, when there is not justice?

Some people are strongly fired and motivated by injustice. Others suffer injustice for a long time before they react. But everyone, at the core of their being, longs for justice. I cannot imagine anyone who, just for the sake of it, would like injustice. They may go along with it, they may actually bring it about by their selfish actions, but no one puts it forward as the best possible relationship we could have. They would not be so stupid; they would know that no one would believe them. Justice is taken, like love is taken, as an expression of the nature of our divine being. And it is indivisible. There is only one justice, one love, one freedom, and that is what people long for. They long for justice, even though they may do the opposite. People long, very often, for what they themselves are the least able to demonstrate. But because of that, they long for it. They long for what they know is badly expressed in their behaviour, in their nature. It is the basis of guilt. It can also be the basis of great revolutionary endeavour.

"Many will know for the first time that they count, that they matter in the scheme of things."

Most people, everywhere, have the idea that they are not worth anything unless they are born into a rich family or into a powerful situation. Unless they are equipped with a powerful brain and a large ambition and the drive, the energy, to bring fulfilment of their desire, they think that they do not count. They feel like 'also-rans'. For centuries our unjust political and economic structures have created this illusion that most people have: that they do not count. They are just nobodies, peons, peasants, "the workers", drones, there for the benefit of others.

If you are born into a powerful situation, if your father is rich, if he can leave you a lot of money, or a position of power, if you can start from such a situation, the tendency, unless you are a remarkably advanced individual, is to indulge yourself in that situation — to take advantage of the injustices which that creates and to strengthen them. The desire principle of the personality (I do not mean in every case of course; there have been wonderful reformers) has been used to further the advantages which the powerful already possess. That is why the world changes so slowly. There are many powerful people in the world who know the changes that the world needs, but who never seek to put them into effect. On the contrary, they often tend to strengthen the disadvantages for others which they clearly see. They tend to make their fortunes grow greater, their positions stronger. It is for them a self-defensive process. They are maintaining, or are trying to maintain, the status quo. The status quo is about to change in every aspect of life; the time has come to manifest these changes. For this very reason alone, much that Maitreya will say will be very unpleasant hearing for a great many presently powerful and privileged individuals.

Self-esteem

"An unfamiliar sense of self-esteem will replace their present hopelessness. Drugs of all kinds will cease their hold on men."

Most people take to drugs because they have a sense of hopelessness. They are suffering, as Maitreya says, from "spiritual starvation". They see no hope, no future. Nothing that they do ever seems to work. They are often so low in the social scale that there is no possibility that they could achieve what probably they are longing for: power, riches, admiration, love, affection, all the things that everyone longs for but which few people really achieve. It takes a lot of energy, a lot of what is called 'luck', and a lot of hard work to achieve the ambitions which many people on drugs have, but cannot possibly attain. They know they do not have the energy, the advantages. Unless they can get off the drugs, there is no hope whatsoever. Being on drugs, they do not have the ambition, only the *idea* of the ambition. Above all, they do not have the *will* to get out of that situation. If the will is not applied to the situation, nothing can change. But when a sense of self-esteem takes the place of the hopelessness, then everything is possible. And when the social, political, and economic changes go along with this new-found self-esteem, and establish a norm in which everyone has a place, in which everyone counts, we will have an entirely new society.

"Quietly, men's tears will flow in humble gratitude and longing for the good."

People are cynical, but inwardly they are not really cynical. Most people, the vast majority of people everywhere, long for the good. They long for the good because they know it is the only thing that is worth having. They know that what we call right relationship, right human relations, is not only the next predestined achievement of humanity, but that it is good, something to look forward to, something which is needed.

Everyone longs for love, for affection, for harmony, for the establishment of conditions in which their creativeness can manifest. For most people this is not available. For most people, creativeness is a dream, something that died in childhood, before they even had a chance to be creative. That is the reality for most of the 5½ billion people in the world. People who have the opportunity, the education, and the background, financial or otherwise, to be creative are the relatively few; they are the lucky ones. It is not because they are superior, it is because of a coming together of various circumstances which determine whether some people will have that kind of 'luck' or whether they will be relegated to the dustbin.

It is mainly a political/economic problem. It is a spiritual crisis through which humanity is going today: we do not know who we are. We have forgotten the reality of our being. That spiritual crisis is focused through the political and economic fields, and unless we can create *spiritual* political and economic institutions, we will not know peace or justice, and the human evolution would cease on this planet. That is the nature of the crisis: to discover who we are.

In these minutes, in that half hour, people will realize who we are. Each individual, as he or she experiences this overshadowing by Maitreya, experiences the Christ Principle, and awakens to what He is saying, and to the reality of their own spiritual nature, will say: "Yes, that's it! I want this! I want it because it is the good. This is what I have always wanted. I remember when I was a little boy, a little girl, I would dream of this for the world. And I have forgotten it. I haven't given it a thought in all these 30, 40, 50 years." People will awaken anew to their early aspiration for right relationship. People want this between themselves and others. They long for it, they know it is right. Everyone inwardly longs for that sense of justice, of goodness, of right relationship, of freedom for everyone. And the *"tears will flow in humble gratitude."* It will be a very wet afternoon.

"From that time onwards, a new spirit of sanctity will prevail upon the earth."

From that moment, and for a time, this sense will carry forward. This day, this experience of half an hour, or however long it is, will carry on in people's hearts. They will feel refreshed as never before. They will feel: "Oh, it must be wonderful to be like this all the time. I remember, this is how I felt when I was a child."

People will feel again that freshness and vitality and uplifted spirit, blitheness, which children have, but which most adults have lost. Because they go around with their worries: "How am I going to pay the rent, the school fees, the doctor's bills?" People are worried to death. They are worried out of life. It is called commercialization. Commercialization has taken over from real life. That is why Maitreya calls it "more dangerous than an atomic bomb." It steals life from the people. It takes their life until every drop is out, like a squeezed lemon.

"Men will walk on tip-toe for a time."
Isn't that beautiful? Men will walk on tip-toe. Don't make too much noise, it might break this marvel. Keep your voices down. Don't shout. Let me keep this in my heart. People will not know what to do with themselves. They will want to keep this feeling, which, of course, will not last for ever. But it will last for some time, and this sense that they have touched divinity will remain.

Spirit of sanctity

"A new spirit of sanctity will prevail upon the earth."
When they see Maitreya, and when you see Maitreya, you will know what the Master means. I would say, above all, the quality surrounding Maitreya is holiness, sanctity. He embodies, to my mind, everything that you can imagine about God. He is not God, of course (except in the sense that we are all God), but He is imbued with the holiness, the sanctity of God; pure love and will and wisdom surround Him as an aura. That is what radiates and will radiate out on that day. He will evoke that same sense in all the people, or most of the people, listening to Him and experiencing His energy on Declaration Day.

The sense that life is sacred will be renewed in people's minds and hearts. For a time, no one will want to disturb the feeling that we have seen life in a new way, that it is sacred, sanctified, and it is up to us to demonstrate that: to get rid of all the mess that prevents that sanctity from demonstrating. Maitreya will tie together the political, economic and social problems with the demonstration of the sanctity of life. People will grasp that, and will *"walk on tip-toe for a time."* It is beautiful.

Soon, however, men will realize that it is not so easy; the problems will still be there. Just because the Christ is in the world, you cannot turn away from the problems, which are real. We are living on the physical plane, and though, for a time, people will experience divine sanctity and know that to be the true quality of life, they will also know that to demonstrate that sanctity, life on the physical plane must be changed. No longer can we watch millions of people slaughtering each other, or starving to death in the midst of plenty.

"Men will realize that the changes needed in the world are vast, manifold", very complex indeed, and very many of them, "requiring patience and dedication, imagination and trust."

People will have to believe that Maitreya and the Masters know what They are talking about. They have to take on trust that these changes will really transform their life. They have to realize that the major obstacles to the continuous demonstration of that divinity, which, for half an hour, they experienced, are the old political and economic divisions in the world — with millions starving, others living no better than animals. They have to see that though they are far away, in Africa, India, or South America, not next door, these problems must be tackled. And people will wake up to the reality of life.

Rehabilitation

"Before long men everywhere will engage themselves in the work of reconstruction, the rehabilitation of the world."

The Masters will galvanize, with Their spiritual energy, all around Them. Their insight into the problems and into their solution will be clear-cut and logical. Their disciples, men and women everywhere, will be elected into positions of influence and power — by the democratic method — and they will put into effect the needed changes.

People everywhere will engage themselves in this work. *"Succour for the poor and hungry will take pride of place."* Maitreya says that the number one priority is to rid the world for ever of starvation. *"And so will end for ever a blasphemy in men's midst."* The ending of starvation, the feeding of the hungry, the rehabilitation of the poor, is the number one priority after the Day of Declaration. It has to be tackled on a major scale. A new United Nations agency will be set up to deal with this. At its head will be a Master, or at least a third-degree initiate, and it will, through its actions, reconstruct the world; the sharing of the world's produce will go forward apace.

Humanity, of course, has to accept this. Our free will will never be infringed. Governments will turn to Maitreya, and the other Masters when They have become known, and ask: "What do we do, what is your advice?" Because of the vastness of the problems, and the urgency of the need, all resources will be galvanized. The efforts of the aid agencies up until now will be as drops in the ocean compared to what will be achieved in the first months and year or two after the Day of Declaration.

"Millions will know for the first time the quiet happiness of satisfied need."
When we are hungry we buy something to eat. We go to a restaurant or we look in the refrigerator. Quiet satisfaction, we do not think twice about it. But if you are living in the Third World, if you are one of the 1,300 million people who live in *absolute poverty*, if you are one of the 38 million who are literally starving to death, you cannot do that.

So will end what the Master calls *"this dark chapter in the history of the race."* *"No more will the dying forms of the starving disgrace the screens of the affluent. No longer will men watch their brothers dying before their eyes."* That is a tragedy which has gone on for so many years, for as long as I can remember.

"Changes, unequalled in extent, will engage men's minds and hearts; naught but the finest of the past will prevail against the onslaught of the new."
Whatever stands in the way of the new energies, the new structures which these energies will create — to do with synthesis, sharing, justice, freedom for all, in every country

without exception — whatever stands in the way of that achievement, will go down, will not prevail.

"Only the finest of the past ..." Of course, there is always good at the end of every age. The achievements of the age, the aspirations of the millions, the readiness to share, the aid agencies, organizations like the United Nations and the various international groupings which, behind the scenes, unite people with people and give a sense of internationalism and co-operation, will be maintained and will grow; they can only flourish in the new situation. But those which stand in the way, those narrow, nationalistic structures based on competition, market forces and greed, will find it impossible to stand against the *"onslaught of the new"*, the ideas of the new time.

First to go will be the world's stock markets. They are, as Maitreya has said, about to crash. They will come down because they stand in the way of right relationship. They really bear no relation to the needs even of trade between countries. They are an anachronism, what Maitreya calls, very accurately, "gambling casinos which have no part to play in the future time, at least in their present form.

"Daily, the transformations will be recorded for men to compare and admire."
Instead of watching all these soap operas and sitcoms, you will switch on and see what is happening in Rome, Moscow, Tel Aviv, and Seattle. What new marvel has been achieved in the world, what new record has been broken in achieving parity, justice and right relationship? This will be recorded and shown on a daily basis. People will register this and compare, and say: "We have not done that yet. We have to do that." This is the kind of competition and rivalry which will be a very positive stimulus to securing these goals. People will say: "If they can do it, we can do it." And so up will go the score cards every day: achieved ending of hunger in such in such and such and such. People in so and so rehabilitated, rehoused, and so on. All of this will be recorded, so everyone will be kept informed of the

transformations which are taking place. *"A new world will be constructed in the blazing light of day."*

"For many, the very presence of the Christ will constitute a problem." There are many people who hate this whole idea, who do not want change. *"Their long-held beliefs will be shaken to the core."* When the Christ comes on television and overshadows them and says: "I am the World Teacher, I am the one you are awaiting." Perhaps He will say something like this, I do not know. In some way He will make it known that He is the One expected by everyone, even though they do not know they are expecting Him.

Some will have a very difficult time. *"For them, a period of heartsearching will be inevitable as they seek to understand the meaning of the new dispensation; ancient beliefs die hard and hurt bitterly in the process."* If you are a fundamentalist Christian, Hindu, Buddhist, Muslim or whatever (and for those people, to be fair, their religion is serious; they hold these beliefs in a very serious, if fanatical, way), this is going to be very disturbing. Many of them believe, now, that Maitreya is the Antichrist. They are really going to be shaken when they see what they think is the Antichrist speaking to them with a beautiful, wonderful vision of the future. And they will not know whether to believe it or not.

They will have the same experience, they will feel His energy, they will know that this man is embodying the energy and it does not feel bad. It feels good, actually, it is like when they go to church, only better, more so. They are going to have a problem.

Then they will see all the changes in the world. Eventually, so many people will be involved in the changes, so respectable will this whole experience become, that they will find it more and more difficult to stand against it. It will be a sad time for fundamentalists because they will see the end of their beliefs. They will have to replace them with all these New Age ideas. They will have to accept that those "New Age" types were telling the truth, talking sense, that it was not some attack, a conspiracy, which was going to be imposed on humanity by the Antichrist.

"Ancient beliefs die hard" — and they have had them for hundreds of years — *"and hurt bitterly in the process. Nevertheless, millions will respond with a glad heart, happy to accept the Teacher in their midst. Few, in time, will stand against the common acknowledgment"* — the obviousness, the demonstration in their midst — *"that the Christ, in the person of Maitreya, walks once more upon the Earth."*

What a realization for humanity. If you are prepared in advance, you do not experience it. We are going to miss out in a way, because we know about this. We have run through this scenario already, we have lived it. There will be plenty of revelations but we will miss out on this sudden new awakening to a reality which we take for granted — although the actual experience of it will be such as you cannot begin to imagine. When you feel His energy pouring through your heart chakra, when you hear His words in your head in your own language, you will say: "I never thought it would be like this. I never imagined it could be so powerful and so transforming."

"Those relatively few who have led the way in preparation for this time will find themselves offered another field of service: an educational endeavour vast in scope."

Do you realize what it means? The vast majority of humanity do not know anything about this, and will want to know. They will ask: "Who is Maitreya?" "Where does He come from?" "What is the historical background to all of this?" "And, if what He says is true and the world is going to be changed in all these ways, where do I stand? What is going to happen to my stocks and shares? What about my job?" It is going to be traumatic for most of us.

"An educational endeavour vast in scope. From all sides will come the queries." We shall become an information booth. *"A long-felt hunger for knowledge will, like a dammed-up river, overflow and burst its banks."*

People are hungry for knowledge. People who will not give much time to this information now will suddenly discover that they have an appetite for information such as they never knew. They will not be able to get enough, and they will not be able to digest what they get, so they will want more and more.

"Many will seek to know the background and history of this event. For others, the immediate future will be the chief concern."

How will this work out? What has Maitreya, or the Masters, to say about this? What do you think is going to happen? How will it be? What task can I do? What should I learn? How should I develop myself?

"Societies, world-wide, will play their part, assuring the broad dissemination of the needed teachings."

We are not the only group in the world who knows the esoteric teachings. We share this knowledge with many societies and groups, some of them far older than ours, who have long played a part in informing humanity about the reality of Hierarchy, of the evolutionary process, the human spiritual constitution, and so on.

The most important piece of knowledge that everyone needs, I believe, is the knowledge of the spiritual constitution of humanity. Everyone needs to know that they are the Monad, the Spark of God, the Divine Self, which reflects itself on the soul plane as the individualized human soul (part of one great Oversoul) which incarnates — through the Law of Rebirth in relation to the Law of Karma — over and over again until it has completed the evolutionary journey and is perfected. That is the fundamental information which, I believe, every single man and woman needs to know. When they do, that alone will give them a grasp of the true relationship between each other and between them and God. From there, the educational work can proceed. Meditation, as the means of reuniting these separated units, will become the aim of many. But people have to be educated, have to learn to do these things, to see the reality of them. That is an on-going educational task.

Many societies will play their part, the Master says, *"assuring the broad dissemination of the teachings."* He says: *"Much remains to be given."* Maitreya will teach, probably on a daily basis, I do not know, but frequently. He has already given a body of teachings which were published in *Share International*. This teaching will go on both from Maitreya and from certain of the Masters. But the Master says: *"Much already remains unopened and unread in the hands of men."* There is a vast body of teachings — the Theosophical teachings, the Agni Yoga teachings, the Alice Bailey teachings — which is largely unread, even by those who know about them.

I am astonished by people's lack of interest in the information, which is available to them in, for example, the Alice Bailey teachings. People ask me questions which are easily answered if they would just turn to the right book. But people are lazy, they want me to give it to them. I am amazed at the lack of reading of the existing material. You have to read in order to know, and you have to digest what you read. So you have to read it with care.

How can you know anything if you do not study it? You have to learn to study. You have to do what the Master says: "Systematic study of the teachings and earnest attempts to live the precepts of Maitreya, will give the needed balance and authority with which to teach." How can you possibly teach others if you do not know yourself? You have to learn, yourself, in order to pass it on to other people.

Also, *"earnest attempts to live the precepts of Maitreya".* Nothing convinces so much as the authority of experience. If you have already experienced something, you can talk about it. Even if you have difficulty putting that experience into words, the words you do say to describe your experience of a lived knowledge will communicate itself to the listener in a way that nothing else could do. No amount of simple book learning can take the place of living. Anyone can read a book. But only if you have lived the precepts, tried to put, to the best of your endeavour, the precepts of Maitreya into effect in your life will it have that persuasiveness, that energy of true livingness which you want the teaching to convey. The teaching will only mean something to people if it is living, and it is only living if it is part of your true experience, not simply out of a book. If it has affected and changed your life, then you can talk about it, you can make it real and living to other people in a way which otherwise is impossible.

Humble pride

"Each one, thus equipped, can avail themselves of this opportunity to serve anew. Seize it," the Master says. *"Seize it, the counsel is, with alacrity and humble pride."* That is lovely. Humble pride. That is the way forward for the groups. If you wish to serve in the new way after the Day of Declaration, you will find a world out there longing for information, for experience: longing to participate, to know what meditation is and how they can be involved, longing to know what the experience of others has been, how they entered it, and how it has changed them.

They will want to know because everyone after that day, Declaration Day, will realize that the world will never be the same again. A new world, a new dispensation, a new civilization, will gradually grow. What, till now, we have taken for granted will be swept away. I do not mean the first day, but fast. People will demand the new insights, the new teaching, the new revelations. They will come, of course, mainly from Maitreya and the Masters. But everyone who has any claim to discipleship has a part to play, can put their energy into spreading the teachings. As needed, as they are called for.

(*Share International*, January/February 1995)

As far as studying goes, how can we avoid the danger of having too much information and not integrating it, having spiritual indigestion? Is there any practical way to avoid this? (January/ February 1995)

The way to avoid spiritual indigestion and to make best use of the information that you are learning, is to practise it. For it to have any value in your life you have to put it into effect, actually practise the teachings.

The precepts are given to set the ground plan for the correct use of the teachings. There are people who know the Alice Bailey teachings like some people know the Bible, chapter and verse. They could quote almost any page of the books by heart. But they do not necessarily live the teachings, except to a limited extent. It is to them like an academic body of knowledge, which has its value, but it is not a major value. You could know nothing about the teachings, but actually live them daily. This science is also not something you can read up in a book and apply; it is not applied science in that sense. It is a science which is also an art. It is an understanding of the nature of the universe, which is an understanding of the nature of life.

You can only understand life in the macro-cosmic sense if you have experienced it in the microcosm. As above, so below. You can know what the greater is if you experience it in you, the smaller, because there is only one life. Life manifests as solar systems and also as the human being. It is exactly the same life. That is why Sai Baba can say: "Yes, I am God. But you, too, are God. There is only God, that is all there is, so how could you be other than God?" The difference is, of course, that He knows He is God and, what is more important, He demonstrates it, while we do not. We do not know it, and do not demonstrate it. Even if we knew it, theoretically, we would not necessarily demonstrate it. You have to know it in the sense of 'being' it to demonstrate it.

To invoke the intuition, you have to fill out the requirements of the lower mind. So these teachings are given in a particular way, and they are difficult. They are not made difficult expressly, but they are difficult because the Master DK had the task of bringing down His intuitive, Buddhic, knowledge of all that He is talking about to a level where it will mean something to our lower concrete mind — and invoke our intuition. To say you understand the teachings by intuition means that the soul is involved. By invoking the intuition, which comes from the soul, you are making contact with the soul. The more the teachings become an everyday part of your consciousness, not something that you have to look up, but to do with everyday reality, the more the intuition will flow, the more your intuitive understanding of the teachings will occur. If your intuitive understanding is such, so will your life be. That radiates outward, because it is the nature of the soul to radiate. As that becomes part of your everyday, living awareness, it radiates out and communicates. Then you get the creativity of the disciple. It is not something just to look up in a book. You can do that for ever.

As far as priorities for studying are concerned, should we start with Maitreya's teachings, the Bailey books, or your books?
I would say, because they are the simplest and the most direct, and the closest to you, the teachings of Maitreya in so far as they have been given out through His associate. That is the first step; perhaps the most difficult but the most easy of access, because this is how Maitreya will talk to the world — bringing it down to the very simplest level. He will be talking to the whole world, which has to change in consciousness. He is not going to say: "Do this meditation or that meditation, then align this chakra with that chakra, then build the bridge", and so on. He will not do anything of that at all.

He will talk about honesty of mind, sincerity of spirit, and detachment. These are the three. He gives them as three very potent forces of evolution. They are potent because they are the essentials. They are the essentials because only in growing detachment can you advance to the point of being a Master, of being Self-realized. Only through honesty of mind and sincerity of spirit can you become detached. Unless you become detached, you cannot do the others. Unless you do the others, you cannot become detached.

Life is really about detachment. Without detachment, you cannot make one step forward in evolution. A growing detachment, by its very nature, frees you from identification with your body, your emotions, your mental concepts. That is how the steps are taken. I would say, read Maitreya's teachings and put them into practice. Read Krishnamurti and put it into practice. It is not simply a question of reading and knowing; it is a question of putting it into practice. They are talking about exactly the same thing, the same process — detachment.

MAITREYA'S EMERGENCE

Television Appearance

Has Maitreya determined the most auspicious date when He will accept the American invitation to appear on television? (April 1995)

No, He has not. He has, however, determined a most auspicious time (although in my experience there have been several such which have come and gone). My understanding is that He has an arrangement with the network whereby He can give them just a few days' notice. He watches the cosmic energies which are changing all the time; sometimes they are more favourable, and at others more unfavourable, to His emergence. He also watches humanity to assess our responses — we must be *eagerly* responsive. He watches the state of the world, what we are doing for ourselves: are we ready to hear this extraordinary message which is a challenge to our humanity? It is a challenge to every individual who hears it: are we ready to be true human beings, to share, to create the conditions in which every one, without exception, has the right to develop their potential, a spiritual potential in the deepest sense of that word: to make their life better on the physical plane, on the emotional, the mental, and the spiritual planes. To live out and manifest that for which they came into incarnation in the first place. It is largely our corrupt political, economic and social structures which prevent us from doing this. That needs a change of heart — and that, I believe, is taking place, otherwise He could not be here — which will be stimulated by Maitreya when He speaks openly.

I am curious to know how the media will introduce Maitreya. (June 1994)

The problem for the media anywhere is how to present Maitreya. There are many stations, especially in the US, who have given me an open invitation for Maitreya to appear on their programme but who are not sufficiently national, and certainly not international, to allow Him to do so. But even when they are international, they have the problem of how to present Him

275

impersonally — not to say: this is the Christ; this is the Messiah. One of the reasons why the major networks have not presented Him so far, although they know of His existence, is that they do not want to take upon themselves this responsibility. Who do they say He is; how do they present Him to a sceptical world? They know how sceptical *they* are so they know how sceptical the world is in general.

We have provided the media with a formula by which they can present Him in a neutral way — as an extraordinary man but not in His true status as the Christ. I, too, am interested to see how they handle it.

If the BBC asked Him would He come forward? (May 1993)
If the BBC *at the highest level* invited Him to speak He would come forward. They offered to do so in 1986 and went back on their promise. Since 1986, there could have been an end to war, and the resources of the world would already be shared; there would be no people starving in the world — it could have started all those years ago. The media do not understand at all their role in this process of emergence.

Why does Maitreya have to involve the media when Sai Baba does not need that or anybody's help to make Himself known? (January/February 1994)
Sai Baba is known to thousands of devotees around the world but has no direct influence on the actions of governments or peoples and has no plans to make Himself known to the everyday world in that way. As World Teacher, Maitreya requires the use of the communication networks, not only to become known, but to teach humanity over the next 2,500 years of Aquarius. Their roles are entirely different.

Day of Declaration

How long will there be between Maitreya's first television appearance in America and the Day of Declaration? (September 1995)

That depends on us: it depends on the response of humanity, of the media of the world, which allows us to hear Him, and on the forces which are against this. Why do you think it has taken so long to get to this point? Because there are very powerful vested interests against this manifestation. They are not only what we call "the forces of evil", but the forces of ingrained selfishness, greed, separatism and ignorance, both at the level of extreme power and also of the ordinary uneducated masses. I believe, from what I have been told by my Master, that it will be very quick. But when a Master says "soon" he does not mean "tomorrow", as we might think. "Forthwith", which was the Master's latest statement about Maitreya's appearance, can mean "anything up to a year", and "soon" or "very soon" could be anything up to a few years. The Masters are working in 2,000-year cycles — a few years are nothing to Them.

If Maitreya is going to communicate with everyone in a broadcast without speaking, is He already putting out Transmissions from where He is, for those who are open to this form of impression? (June 1994)

One of His major ways of appearing in the world is by impressing the minds of disciples. That is what happens with people like Gorbachev, like Nelson Mandela, for example.

Maitreya is the World Teacher, so advanced in consciousness that we cannot imagine it, and for Him to impress or overshadow the average person would be difficult. The happening on the Day of Declaration is a unique event — it will probably last for about half-an-hour; it could not be sustained for longer. But, as reported in a reader's letter published in the April 1994 issue of *Share International*, He impressed an identical message on the minds of five individuals simultaneously last year in a church in Glastonbury, UK. He will repeat that on a wider scale on the minds of more and more people; if that is what the questioner means, then the answer is yes. But more than that, no.

Is Maitreya putting out thoughtforms for us to respond to? (June 1994)

The Hierarchy are putting out thoughtforms all the time — the mindbelt of the world is saturated with thoughtforms, many of no value at all, created by humanity; but some are major ideas to which the sensitive minds of the race tune in. Suddenly, all over the world, a group of scientists, for instance, have the same idea, which was placed there by a Master, or even by Maitreya. The Masters see the need for a certain step forward to be taken, a certain technology, for example, to be discovered. They are the inspirers, the 'muses', of the world. Behind all the great teachers, scientists, painters and artists of all kinds have stood the Hierarchy, down through the centuries. Rembrandt is Rembrandt because he was a third-degree initiate, inspired by his Master; likewise Titian and Mozart. Leonardo was 4.4 degrees initiate, practically a Master. All the culture of the world has been created by the initiates of the world, sent to stimulate humanity in the gradual expansion of consciousness which is evolution.

Is it only the Masters who can receive thoughtforms from Maitreya? (June 1994)
No. The bulk of humanity cannot tune in at a high enough level to the thoughtforms of the Masters and so the culture of any civilization is created by the initiates of the time; they are the ones who are inspired. That is gradually absorbed and put into effect and the civilization grows out of the culture: the culture comes first.

Have I understood correctly that on the Day of Declaration it will be possible to see Maitreya on television even if it is switched off? (July/August 1995)
The Day of Declaration will be a day of many miracles but that is not one of them. If your television set is switched off you will, of course, see nothing, but you will still *hear* Maitreya's appeal to the world inwardly, telepathically, in your own language.

If Maitreya's appearance, on the Day of Declaration, is videotaped, will the telepathic overshadowing still take place when the tape is played? (September 1995)

The energy which is released — the Christ Principle in this case — would be magnetized on to the tape, so every time you played the video you would see the face of Maitreya and feel His energy once again, but you would not hear the message, because it occurred only in your head — an inner, telepathic, experience.

On the Day of Declaration, below what age will children not be telepathically contacted? (January/February 1995)

Around 12. It will vary from child to child, but somewhere between 12 and 14. With some it will be 14, and at the lower end around 12. There might be the odd one of 11, but mainly between 12 and 14. Above 14, everyone.

And then the outflowing of the Christ Principle energy as if He were embracing us; will the younger children have an experience of that or not? (January/February 1995)

To a limited degree. Maitreya Himself knows exactly the point in evolution of any child and the state of its chakras, what it can absorb, what would be safe. It is so complex that I could not answer that. Everyone's state of health, age, and so on, will be taken into consideration. This is the miracle of the omnipresent overshadowing.

I have difficulty in understanding what the position of Maitreya will be after He emerges. Will He appear on television and in front of huge crowds? (November 1995)

After the Day of Declaration, Maitreya will begin a tour of the world, appearing on television and to large crowds in all the countries. Thereafter, He will work through groups of disciples in public life who will reveal and interpret Maitreya's ideas and advice to the mass of people. In this way, the needed changes will take place through the democratic process, without the infringement of human free will.

With regard to a television appearance by Maitreya, isn't there a bias towards the Western world — what about the vast majority who have no access to television? (May 1994)

With respect, it is not true that the vast majority has no access to television, even if only in a local, communal sense. There are only a relatively small number of people in the world who have absolutely no access to television — these are remote tribes up in the mountains, in the deserts, and so on; but even in Third World countries, desperately poor, there is communal television and radio — there is an extraordinary awareness of what goes on in the developed world. It is this communication, above all, perhaps, which makes it imperative to transform the world. People are no longer content to live in poverty, degradation and misery in a world where they know unbelievable wealth is being wasted. They know this through radio and television. Besides, the television appearance acts only as a control. The actual communication, the call for justice and sharing as the only way to peace, will be heard inwardly, telepathically, with or without the television.

Is it true that Maitreya will be speaking through all of humanity? (June 1996)

Maitreya will not be 'speaking' through humanity, but will work in terms of changing the world *through* humanity. In so far as the Christ Principle is awakened in your heart, He can work through you; He can stimulate and galvanize you to the degree that that Principle is manifest in you, so that what you do is the result of your response to His teaching, His energy, His ideas — but you do the actual work. The more you act in relation to the world and for the world, the more that energy will flow to you: if you take one step to Him, He will take 12 steps to you.

That process will continue for the next 2,500 years of the Age of Aquarius. Then Maitreya will be finished with His work for humanity at this time, and He will go on to higher work. His place will be taken by another of the Masters Who is being trained for this work. Maitreya will be the first of the Teachers to be a World Teacher for two succeeding ages — the Age of Pisces, through Jesus, and the Age of Aquarius which He is doing now as Himself.

Make Known His Presence

Mr Creme, with due respect, I heard you say the same thing as you are saying now, 12 years ago on television — that the World Teacher was going to appear on television ... (August/September 1994)

Precisely so. Any time since the end of May 1982 Maitreya has been ready to appear before the whole world in the way in which I have announced — on invitation from humanity. The only thing that has withheld that appearance has been a lack of interest from the media, which reflects the lack of interest from humanity as a whole. If those who saw me on television had made a noise, and got their media to act on this, Maitreya could have been known any time since 1982. Every one who has heard this story, who more or less believes it, and who has done nothing about it, is at fault in this regard. It is not Maitreya's fault, it is not my fault. Maitreya works according to the law — the law governing our free will. The World Teacher Himself cannot come on the media networks of the world and speak to the whole world as He needs to do, *without an invitation*. If Maitreya can speak directly to the minds of all humanity on the Day of Declaration, as He will do, He can do that at any time, but He will not do it without an invitation — anything less would be an infringement of our free will. That is the only reason you have not seen the Lord Maitreya to date.

What can I do? — I have been waiting for Him for 13 years ... (August/September 1994)

Make it known! If you believe that what I say is true, make it known by every means at your disposal. If you have 100 per cent conviction, as I have, make it known at that level; if it is only 50 per cent, then at that level; if you have a minuscule, 5 per cent conviction that it might possibly be true, then make it known at that level. Whatever you do is of value. In that way you will help to create the 'climate of hope', of expectancy, which allows Him, under law, to come forward openly.

You say your task is to "help create a climate of hope and expectancy into which Maitreya can emerge without infringing

281

our free will." Does this mean that Maitreya will not emerge until it is possible to do so without infringing our free will? (November 1996)

Yes. To Maitreya and the Masters, our free will is sacrosanct and must never be infringed. I have found great difficulty in getting the public, and especially the media, to understand this major law governing Maitreya's approach to humanity.

(1) With Maitreya's perfectly developed awareness, what message in a few words will He give that results in healings and convinces the world that Love has spoken through the Christ? (2) Can we speak the same to ourselves and our neighbour now, without waiting for Maitreya? (January/February 1994)

(1) In a few words, you can say: Share and save the world. That is the message, in the first place, of Maitreya. The healings which will take place on Declaration Day will not be the result of the message but of the energies and will of Maitreya. (2) Try it.

What can we do now to help Maitreya? (January/February 1997)

First and foremost, if you believe, even as a possibility, that Maitreya is in the world, make it known, in every way, to all who will listen: through speech, radio, television, press, letters, etc. In this way you help to create the climate of hope and expectancy for His advent which will allow Him to enter our lives — without infringing humanity's free will. Advocate sharing and justice in the world, as the only way to true peace — and try to live His teachings.

Maitreya, the Lord of Love, said that we have to make it known, as a top priority, that He is in the world. Would this help us, along our evolutionary path, to grow more spiritually — for instance in meditation? (September 1993)

Maitreya has said that the most important thing you can do at the present time is to make His presence known. It is the number one priority for all spiritual groups who can believe it at any level — either as total, or even as 5 per cent, conviction that it is true. Then you are helping Maitreya, and yes, indeed, helping your own evolution: there is, inevitably, a karmic benefit from every spiritual action you make.

Now that the timing for the emergence of Maitreya (on television) has been set, according to your Master, what purpose is to be served by our continuing "to make it known", your continuing lectures, and so forth? It would seem that the objective, as you have explained it, would have been met. (October 1996)

It is true that the timing (but not the date) of Maitreya's first appearance on television has been "determined", but it is equally true that many millions have not yet heard that such an event is planned or even that Maitreya is in the world. At every lecture I give abroad, the vast majority (often up to 90 per cent of the audience) are hearing the information for the first time. This means that a huge educational effort by those who do believe in Maitreya's presence must continue up to, and beyond, the Day of Declaration. Providing the background to, and purpose behind, Maitreya's emergence, and some interpretation of His teachings and aims, remains, therefore, the ongoing work of all those who accept this "gift of service".

Do you think it will be a problem that only a small amount of the world population have heard your message? (June 1994)

That is not as true as you might think. Outside the UK (a prophet in his own country is not listened to), especially throughout the United States of America, this message is known. I have given literally hundreds of media interviews in the US, and I would say that millions of people there know this story. The same is true in Japan and many other parts of the world. This country [the UK] is benighted — we have the media we deserve!

Are you the only one speaking about the appearance of Maitreya? (October 1995)

Originally, five disciples were asked to make this approach to the public about the reappearance: one in New York; myself in London; one in Geneva; one in Darjeeling; and one in Tokyo. Unfortunately, I am the only one who has taken up this work publicly. The disciple in New York (working in the New Thought movement) does not believe in the Christ's *physical* presence. Likewise, the disciple in Geneva does not believe my story. The disciple in Darjeeling is still "asleep", while the one in Tokyo — a woman — believes that *she* is Maitreya! So, in a sense, I am alone in presenting this information to the world, but I am courageously aided by very many men and women all over the world. We work very much as an extended group, in close communication all the time. These — autonomous — groups in each country make themselves responsible for disseminating this information in their area.

I love basketball and my dream is to be an NBA player. But now that I have heard your talk I don't know if that way I am going to help humanity and God? (November 1996)

I am happy that my talk has inspired your aspiration to serve humanity but I am sure you could still do that *and* become a great basketball player. These two roles are not necessarily mutually exclusive. In fact you could inspire a whole generation of young sportsmen and women to serve the needs of humanity too.

What single piece of material would you recommend for someone like myself — new to this information — to become familiar with to be able to pass it on in a meaningful way? (November 1995)

There are books, a newspaper, a magazine, a booklet summary of the Ageless Wisdom teachings. If you want to propagate the ideas quickly among a mass of people who are otherwise totally uninformed, I would say our newspaper, *The Emergence Quarterly*, is probably the most accessible. We distribute it freely in the Third World, and it is available very cheaply here. It contains articles taken from the magazine S*hare International*, and it presents the story in a simple yet rather potent way. Any single issue of *The Emergence Quarterly*, if distributed widely, would enable a large number of people to know what is happening in the world. Whether they believe it is another matter, but they would be informed — not necessarily deeply, but to a degree that would enable them to take a further interest; perhaps subscribe to *Share International* and get a month-by-month update; and perhaps one of the books — the best book from the point of view of Maitreya's teachings, thoughts and ideas is *Maitreya's Mission, Volume Two*. But your own conviction will be the most telling thing of all.

Is there usually one particular Master with whom we are more closely associated and whom we can best help in His particular field of service? If so, is this governed by our ray structures for any particular incarnation? (October 1994)

The Hierarchy is organized into seven-times-seven — 49 — related Ashrams, each line of seven being along one or other of the seven rays. The ray of our soul determines to which line we gravitate when we are advanced enough to be considered for entry into a Master's group.

Realistically speaking, if Maitreya does appear, there are going to be people who will want to get rid of him. (January/February 1995)

"Realistically speaking" there will be many people who will want to get rid of Him. There are people who always want to get rid of anyone who is doing good for the world — like Martin Luther King, or President Kennedy; it always happens — Abraham Lincoln was assassinated because he had a vision of right relationships for humanity. They can try, but they will fail. How do you get rid of someone if you cannot even see Him, if He can disappear at will; Who is omniscient, omnipresent, Who has created a body and can recreate it a moment later?

(1) Will at least half of the world recognize Maitreya for who He is? (2) Will people argue about it? (November 1996)

Immediately, no; eventually many more than half. (2) Yes.

Will Maitreya be accepted by Christians? (December 1996)

Most Christians, I think, will find it easier to accept and follow the Master Jesus rather than the Lord Maitreya. Jesus 'stood in' for the Lord Maitreya. As far as Jews are concerned, the Master

Jesus is the Messiah, though they have yet to recognize Him as such. He came to them, as a Jew, to end the Jewish dispensation and prepare the way for Christendom.

No one knows for sure, but my feeling is that the vast majority of open-minded Christians will accept Maitreya and the Master Jesus, Whom they will see side-by-side. Maitreya will introduce the Master Jesus and other Masters to the world after the Day of Declaration. The Master Jesus has a special task in that He is in charge of the Christian Churches, and very many Christians will look to Him for guidance and teaching.

Will it not be that the political and economic powers will surely resist the emergence of Maitreya? (March 1995)
Maitreya, you will find, will be the mouthpiece for the countless millions of ordinary people in the world, and through them He will create a unified, educated, articulate world public opinion against which no institution or government can stand. Maitreya has said: "Many will follow Me and see Me as their guide. Many will know Me not." (Message No. 10)

There are many fundamentalists — Christian and others — who see my information as a travesty of the truth, and who will reject Maitreya in the first place, but not for ever. It may be that Christians will accept the Master Jesus before they accept Maitreya, but it could well be that they will not even accept the Master Jesus. The name is right, but He does not have holes in His hands and feet any more. He is in the third body since that time, a totally perfected (ascended) Master, and people will realize that the presence of the Masters creates a new situation in the world.

People will see the *normality* of Maitreya and the Masters. They are normal, human men. The difference between Them and us is that They have no faults. They are perfected, faultless, filled with the love of God and able to demonstrate that love and to radiate it into the world. They will *galvanize*, through Their energy, groups of people who will be inspired by the words of Maitreya on the Day of Declaration.

Maitreya's Appearances to Fundamentalist Groups and Various Individuals

Can you comment on Maitreya's appearances to groups around the world? (November 1993)

Maitreya has been making a series of appearances round the world to large groups of fundamentalists of all religions over a number of years now. It started on 11 June 1988, when He appeared, miraculously, in Nairobi, Kenya, at a regular open-air prayer-healing meeting run by Mary Akatsa. Suddenly He appeared, literally out of nowhere, dressed in a long white garment, and the crowd of 6,000 people instantly recognized Him as their idea, their inner thoughtform, of the Christ. They called Him Christ, beat their chests, fell down, wept, shouted "Halleluiah!", and so on. He spoke to them in perfect Swahili for 15 or so minutes, and then disappeared as amazingly as He had come, leaving some 30 or 40 people in the area where He had stood completely cured of their various and many terrible diseases.

He was photographed, the story was reported in the *Kenya Times* and went out over the wires. It was shown on CNN television around the world, was taken up by the BBC, appeared in *The Guardian* (UK) and various other newspapers, and in Japan. It was a two-day wonder around the world.

Maitreya has appeared again and again, in this way, all over the world. In the vicinity of the town in question, He charges a stream or well of water which then has extraordinary healing properties. Gradually these will be discovered and will significantly improve human health. Some have already been discovered. He appears also to groups (of which I have no details) in North Africa, the Middle East, India and Pakistan, to Hindus, Muslims, Jews, Jains, Sikhs — people of all the religions of the East and Near East are receiving the same kind of extraordinary appearances. They are all fundamentalist groups, deeply orthodox, with their own idea of what the World Teacher will do and how He will appear. He is 'softening them up' before the Day of Declaration.

[For a list of Maitreya's appearances world-wide, see the end of this section.]

Why, if Maitreya appears before 600 or even more people at a meeting of a religious group in Britain — as in Edinburgh and York — do we see nothing about it in the media? (March 1994)

The people before whom He appears are in every case fundamentalist Christians of one persuasion or another; denominationally they vary tremendously but the consistent factor is that they are all extremely dogmatic in their beliefs. Maitreya appears to them to 'soften them up'. These are the groups from whom, throughout the world, He expects the major opposition and rejection. If He appears as the World Teacher and they are expecting the Teacher in their own terms — as the Christ, Maitreya Buddha, Krishna, the Imam Mahdi, the Messiah — with their very fixed views they would be inclined to reject Him.

The most important thing is the creation of the healing waters, which is done first. When Maitreya has magnetized the waters, in due course — it might take a few weeks — He finds a group of fundamentalists in a town nearby and appears before them. He speaks to them in their own language and many healings take place during the process. He does not say: "I am Maitreya"; "I am the Christ"; or "I am the Imam Mahdi." He just appears 'out of the blue' but in a form which they will recognize — as He did in Nairobi in Kenya, on 11 June 1988, an appearance of which we have photographs.

Maitreya leaves it to the groups, in the thoughtform in which He has appeared to them, to recognize Him or not. Some of them will say: "Beware, it could be the Antichrist: before the Christ comes, the Antichrist is coming." That is why they do not speak out, and if they do not speak the media does not speak. Occasionally at these meetings there have been representatives of religious newspapers who do not write about it. Why not? I think they *do not know what to do* with this information: it is too 'hot'. Either they believe it is the Christ or they believe it is the Antichrist; or they are mystified because He has not said who He is. Perhaps 80 per cent of the people believe they had an experience of the Christ, or the Mahdi, or the Messiah — whomever it happened to be — and they are perfectly content to accept that and just wait for something more to happen in connection with it. That must do something to their awareness, even if they do not talk about it except among themselves. When eventually they see Maitreya on television they will say: "That's the one who appeared to us — perhaps he is all right after all; perhaps he is not the Antichrist."

The appearance in Nairobi was reported and photographed because the editor of the Swahili edition of the *Kenya Times* was present and wrote it up. It was picked up by various media and was a two-day wonder around the world. The media in general, as ordinary men and women, are deeply, profoundly sceptical, and professionally, not only sceptical, but cynical in the extreme.

When Maitreya appears to fundamentalist groups (East and West) does He say who He is (the Christ, Maitreya Buddha, Krishna, and so on)? (May 1993)

No. He appears to the different religious groups in a form that they can recognize as the "expected one" but does not give Himself a name or title.

*(1) Does Maitreya operate His London mayavirupa (His body of manifestation) simultaneously with His other appearances in the world? (2) Does Maitreya ever dematerialize His London mayavirupa, or put it to sleep? (3) When Jesus appears in various male and female bodies (See **Share International**, Letters to the Editor) what kind of bodies are these? (4) What state is Jesus' Rome body in during His other appearances?* (May 1997)

(1) Yes. (2) Dematerialize it, yes. Put to sleep, no. (3) Materialized thoughtforms. (4) Its normal state.

At some point will somebody come forward and say that they have been at a meeting where Maitreya appeared? Is that what He hopes will occur? (July/August 1993)

That is part of it. The main goal is 'softening up' the fundamentalists. But as these visitations to different groups

289

continue — and there have been a great many of them now: well over 10,000 people, not counting the 6,000 in Nairobi in 1988, have experienced the Christ — this extraordinary experience cannot but change their whole view of things, and when they do talk about it, the media will eventually take note. The discovery of the healing waters which He has created in connection with most of these appearances will reinforce the fact of His presence there, and bring media to investigate this subject.

(My recent information is that there have been newspaper reports of some of these appearances: two of Christian, five of Muslim, three of Hindu and four of Sikh communities.)

Why do you give only the name of the country, and not the town, when you first tell us where Maitreya has addressed a meeting? (April 1995)

To give the people to whom He appears the opportunity to make it known, for themselves, so that their free will to do, or not do, this is not infringed.

You say that Maitreya has appeared in different parts of the world and created wells for healing. Why has He not appeared in Rwanda where the fighting and appalling refugee crisis is going on? (November 1994)

He has done so and continues to do so. He moves around among the refugees and heals and helps all the time, but the Law of Karma (the Law of Cause and Effect) determines how much a Master, even of Maitreya's status, may interfere in our self-made suffering and problems.

Why have Maitreya's reported appearances been primarily in Europe? What of China, India, the rest of Asia, South America, Australia, etc? (December 1993)

We have already reported in *Share International* that besides the named appearances of Maitreya there have been many such appearances in North Africa, the Middle East, India and Pakistan. He has also appeared in other parts of Asia. I have not been given specific details of these very numerous appearances. Mexico City has had two appearances and, in due course, in

China, Japan, Australia, New Zealand and most other areas of the world, groups will be visited — at least up to the Day of Declaration — and the healing waters will be created.

When Maitreya appears to groups does He always look the same? (January/February 1997)
No. He changes His appearance to fit the inner thoughtform of expectation held by the particular religious group.

Has Maitreya made appearances to people who are working for peace in Northern Ireland? (January/February 1994)
Yes, many.

Can we know how many appearances to such religious groups around the world Maitreya has made so far? (April 1994)
300.

In the photograph of Maitreya as He appeared in Nairobi He is wearing a gold chain with a medallion or relic. Can you please give us more detailed information about this relic? (January/February 1997)
It is a medallion which belonged to Jesus in Palestine.

(1) Have any world leaders heard your lecture? (2) Are any of them aware of the awakening taking place? (October 1995)
(1) No. (2) Yes, several world leaders, including Mr Gorbachev and Nelson Mandela, are keenly aware of present happenings.

Have the current Pope and other religious leaders met Maitreya? (October 1995)
According to my information the present Pope has not met Maitreya although he knows of Maitreya's reported existence. Many other religious leaders, Christian, Buddhist, Muslim and Hindu, have met with Maitreya, some of them several times. Maitreya works with a large group of Hindu Swamis and Muslim leaders in London, for example. He also appeared, years ago, to Pope John 23rd.

291

It is common knowledge in the Mormon Church, though not published, that the Christ appeared to the President of the Church, in the late 1970s, in the hallway of the Tabernacle in Washington DC. Was this Maitreya? (October 1994)

No. It was the Master Jesus.

A recent newsletter from the Ramala Centre in Glastonbury, England, stated that somebody had asked Sai Baba about "those people who said that Christ(s) had appeared in Toronto and Jerusalem". It was reported that Sai Baba had said that this was not authentic. (1) Is Sai Baba deliberately saying that such appearances are not authentic so as not to infringe our free will? or (2) has the questioner got his question wrong so that Baba can deny it? Some Sai Baba devotees are taking this news-sheet information as evidence that Sai Baba is not authenticating your information. (November 1995)

(1) I do not think that Sai Baba made any references at all to reported appearances of Christ(s) in Toronto or Jerusalem. I think the report is a fabrication — one of many, to try to discredit my information. In fact, Sai Baba has recommended UK visitors to His Ashram to attend my lectures. In any case, I have not said that Maitreya appeared in either Toronto or Jerusalem. He may do so in the future but, to my knowledge, has not so far. (2) Probably.

Is Maitreya your Master? (September 1995)

No. Maitreya is the Master of all the Masters, including my Master. I am a disciple of one of the Masters, who lives in the Himalayas and works very closely with Maitreya. I may not give you His name at the present time. It has been 'under wraps' for the last 20 years and it will have to remain so for a little while longer — there are very good reasons for that.

How often does Maitreya appear to you? (July/August 1996)

Never. I first started this work in January 1959 and it was not until August 1977 (Maitreya came into London in July 1977) that I was taken before Him (out of the body) on several occasions. He asked me if I would take, publicly, the Messages which I had been receiving privately for some time. I said I would try, do my best, and the 140 messages which He then gave at my London lectures began on 6 September 1977. These are published in book form as *Messages from Maitreya, the Christ.*

I know where Maitreya is, I could go and see Him any day but I am asked not to. Occasionally I know in advance where He will be, but if I do this work without seeing Him before other people, there is for me a karmic benefit which is shared by all those who work with me. If they need to see Him to believe He exists, I can arrange for that, but they will lose the karmic benefit which accrues if they work for Him without this confirmation. Their intuition tells them that He exists; their reading of the signs, their experience with me, the energies, tell them. For most people who work with me that is enough, but if they need to see Him badly enough to forgo the karmic benefit, then I can arrange it and they will see Him. He has, of course, appeared in many different guises to many of the people in the various groups around the world with which I work.

List of Maitreya's Appearances World-Wide

The list on the following pages contains Maitreya's miraculous appearances to orthodox religious groups world-wide does not include those in North Africa, the Middle East, India and Pakistan, of which no details are available. Unless otherwise noted, a water source in the area of each appearance was charged by Maitreya with cosmic energy before the appearance, causing the water to possess extraordinary healing properties. In addition, at each appearance, some of those in attendance were healed of their illnesses.

This information is given to Benjamin Creme by his Master, and published monthly in *Share International* magazine.

Maitreya's Appearances World-Wide

Date	Place	Audience (approx.)	Minutes	Response/comments (if known)
1988				
11 Jun	Nairobi, *Kenya*	6,000 Christians at a prayer gathering	15	Many recognized Him as the Christ. Dozens of healings took place. (Footnote 1)
29 Sep	Mexico City, *Mexico*	500-600 Christians	20	The initial response was profound and heartfelt but, soon, the people became divided into two groups, more or less equal: those who believed Him to be the Christ and those who feared He may be the Antichrist. (Footnote 2)
1992				
26 Jan	Mexico City, *Mexico*	800 Christians	25	The reception was particularly good — people listened spellbound. The division of opinion was 70 per cent acceptance that they had seen the Christ and 30 per cent advising caution.
1 Mar	Moscow, *Russia*	600 Russian Orthodox Christians	37	The people divided 500-100 in favour of acceptance that they had seen the Christ.
22 Mar	Leipzig, *Germany*	950 Christians	34	Divided roughly 800-150 in favour of the belief that they had seen the Christ.
5 Apr	Hanover, *Germany*	800 Christians	35	700-plus people were confident that they had witnessed the Christ.
26 Apr	Düsseldorf, *Germany*	650 orthodox Christians	16	500 people present were convinced they had seen the Christ.
24 May	Geneva, *Switzerland*	600 Christians	—	—
28 Jun	Zürich, *Switzerland*	700 Christians	—	—

19 Jul	Vienna, *Austria*	900 Catholics	—	—
16 Aug	Prague, *Czech Republic*	600-700 Eastern Orthodox Christians	18	—
13 Sep	Bratislava, *Slovakia*	400-500 Eastern Orthodox Christians	15	—
27 Sep	St Petersburg, *Russia*	800-900 Russian Orthodox Christians	—	Water not charged.
18 Oct	Tbilisi, *Georgia*	500-600 orthodox Christians	15	—
8 Nov	Belgrade, *Serbia*	—	—	(Footnote 3)
13 Dec	Edinburgh, *Scotland*	600 Christians including clergy	—	—
27 Dec	Bucharest, *Romania*	800-900 Eastern Orthodox Christians	—	
1993				
17 Jan	Oslo, *Norway*	600-700 Lutheran Christians	—	—
7 Feb	Bucharest, *Romania*	Large group at a religious convention	—	—
28 Feb	Richmond, Virginia, *USA*	500-600 fundamentalist Christians	—	(Footnote 4)
21 Mar	San Antonio, Texas, *USA*	400-500 Southern Baptists	18	70 per cent believed they had seen the Christ.
4 Apr	Yakutsk, Eastern Siberia, *Russia*	300-400 people	17	80 per cent believed they had seen the Christ.

Date	Location	Audience	No.	Response
25 Apr	Tashkent, *Uzbekistan*	800 Muslims	15	90 per cent accepted that they had heard a Messenger from Allah.
23 May	Tashkent, *Uzbekistan*	800 Muslims	18	Very enthusiastic reception; 95 per cent were convinced they had witnessed a Messenger from Allah.
13 June	Kabul, *Afghanistan*	1,800 Muslims	20	80-90 per cent positive response.
27 June	Rome, *Italy*	900 Catholics	18	85 per cent were sure they had seen the Christ.
18 July	Sarajevo, *Bosnia*	—	—	(Footnote 5)
25 July	Brussels, *Belgium*	400-500 Catholics	18	75 per cent positive response.
8 Aug	Sofia, *Bulgaria*	800 Eastern Orthodox Christians	—	Very enthusiastic response.
22 Aug	Sofia, *Bulgaria*	Similar group to previous appearance in Sofia	—	—
5 Sept	Pietermaritzburg, *South Africa*	800 Catholics (mainly white)	15	Around 700 believed they had seen the Christ.
19 Sept	Rome, *Italy*	600 Catholics	19	—
3 Oct	Warsaw, *Poland*	800 Catholics	16	A very emotional, enthusiastic response.
17 Oct	Copenhagen, *Denmark*	500-600 orthodox Christians	16	—
31 Oct	Nicosia, *Cyprus*	800-900 Greek Orthodox Christians	17	—
21 Nov	York, *England*	600-700 orthodox Christians	15	—
12 Dec	Johannesburg, *South Africa*	400-500 orthodox Christians (mainly white)	15	—

1994			
2 Jan	Bloemfontein, *South Africa*	600-700 orthodox Christians	18	Water not charged this time.
9 Jan	Kampala, *Uganda*	500-600 Christians	14	—
16 Jan	Port of Spain, *Trinidad*	600 fundamentalist Christians	16	—
30 Jan	Stockholm, *Sweden*	300-400 Lutheran Christians	—	—
6 Feb	Helsinki, *Finland*	600-700 fundamentalist Christians	17	—
13 Feb	Bangkok, *Thailand*	600 Buddhists	18	—
6 Mar	Nairobi, *Kenya*	400-500 fundamentalist Christians in their tabernacle	16	—
13 Mar	Montreal, *Canada*	600 fundamentalist Christians	16	—
27 Mar	St Petersburg, *Russia*	700 Russian Orthodox Christians	20	Water charged this time.
10 Apr	Palermo, Sicily, *Italy*	300-400 Catholics	20	—
24 Apr	Orleans, *France*	500 Catholics	16	—
1 May	Barcelona, *Spain*	600-700 Catholics	18	85 per cent recognized Him as the Christ.
29 May	*The Philippines*	300-400 Christians	16	85 per cent believed they had seen the Christ.
5 Jun	Paris, *France*	700-800 Catholics	15	70 per cent believed they had seen the Christ.

19 June	Istanbul, *Turkey*	600-700 Eastern Orthodox Christians	18	—
24 July	Kingston, *Jamaica*	400-500 Christians	14	—
31 July	South London, *UK*	300-400 Christians	17	—
14 Aug	Copenhagen, *Denmark*	300 orthodox Christians	15	—
21 Aug	Cracow, *Poland*	600 Catholics	16	Particularly excited response; no water was charged.
28 Aug	Seoul, *South Korea*	700 Buddhist priests	16	No water was charged.
11 Sep	Wellington, *New Zealand*	600 orthodox Christians	18	—
9 Oct	Athens, *Greece*	800-900 Greek Orthodox Christians	18	—
6 Nov	Ottawa, *Canada*	600 fundamentalist Christians	16	—
4 Dec	Cardiff, *Wales, UK*	300-400 Christians	16	—
11 Dec	Frankfurt, *Germany*	600-700 Catholics	18	—
18 Dec	Baghdad, *Iraq*	800 Muslims	20	—
25 Dec	Rome, *Italy*	400-500 Catholics	16	—
1995				
1 Jan	Dublin, *Ireland*	600-700 Catholics at a seminary	20	Completely mystified by His appearance.
8 Jan	Stockholm, *Sweden*	300-400 Lutheran Christians	18.5	70 per cent positive reaction.
29 Jan	Osaka, *Japan*	300-400 Buddhists	16 1/2	—
5 Feb	Istanbul, *Turkey*	600-700 Muslims	18	—
12 Feb	Helsinki, *Finland*	100-200 fundamentalist Christians	15	—

Date	Location	Audience		Reaction
	Amsterdam, *Holland*	400 Baptist Christians	18	Listened in respectful silence without obvious belief or disbelief.
26 Feb				
5 Mar	Palermo, Sicily, *Italy*	400-500 Roman Catholics	18	Those present listened in stunned silence.
12 Mar	Ioánnina, *Greece*	300-400 Greek Orthodox Christians	18	—
26 Mar	Paris, *France*	300 Roman Catholics	15	—
9 Apr	Phoenix, Arizona, *USA*	600-700 people	18	—
16 Apr	Aberdeen, *Scotland*	300-400 Christians	17-18	Crowd was silent.
23 Apr	Ulan Bator, *Mongolia*	300-400 Buddhists	18	Appearance was taken very seriously.
30 Apr	Moscow, *Russia*	300 Russian Orthodox Christians	17	Reaction good.
14 May	Santander, *Spain*	600-700 Catholics	15	Reaction mixed.
21 May	Volsk, *Russia*	300-400 orthodox Christians	17-18	Reaction mixed.
28 May	Sydney, *Australia*	300 fundamentalist Christians	18	Very frightened reaction.
4 June	Kansas City, *USA*	—	—	—
11 Jun	Antananarivo, *Madagascar*	200-300 Christians	18	—
25 Jun	Caracas, *Venezuela*	400 Baptist Christians	20	Quite open reception.
9 Jul	Marrakesh, *Morocco*	300-400 Muslims	18	Quite good reaction.
23 Jul	Vladivostok, *Russia*	600-700 orthodox Christians	—	Good reception.
6 Aug	Beijing, *China*	600-700 Buddhists	17-18	—
13 Aug	Dodoma, *Tanzania*	400-500 Christians	18	Very good response.

27 Aug	Lahore, *Pakistan*	900 Muslims	Nearly 30	—
17 Sept	Durban, *South Africa*	300-400 fundamentalist Christians	18	Fairly good reception.
24 Sept	La Coruna, *Spain*	300 fundamentalist Catholics	17	Rather fearful response.
1 Oct	Saskatoon, Saskatchewan, *Canada*	200 fundamentalist Christians	17-18	Unexpectedly open response.
15 Oct	Liverpool, *England*	600 Christians	16	Surprisingly open response.
22 Oct	Buenos Aires, *Argentina*	300-400 Catholics	18	Very good reception.
29 Oct	Lisbon, *Portugal*	300-400 Catholics	16	Tentatively open response.
5 Nov	Vancouver, *Canada*	300 Christians	18	Rather positive response.
19 Nov	*Kazakhstan*	200-300 Muslims	18	A very good response.
26 Nov	Oporto, *Portugal*	600 Catholics at a seminary	20	Respectful, numb silence.
17 Dec	Zanzibar, *Tanzania*	300 Muslims	16-17	Silent, rapt attention; quite good reaction.
1996				
7 Jan	Rome, *Italy*	300 Catholics (including many Church dignitaries)	17	He was listened to in stunned silence.
14 Jan	Ankara, *Turkey*	400-500 Muslims	18	—
28 Jan	Elko, Nevada, *USA*	200-300 Christians (Mormons)	17	Cautious but interested response.
4 Feb	Ljubljana, *Slovenia*	300 Christians	17	Reasonably positive reaction.

25 Feb	Denver, Colorado, *USA*	200-300 fundamentalist Christians	17	Doubtful response.
10 Mar	Lyons, *France*	250 Catholics	17	Fairly open reaction.
17 Mar	Mozambique, *Mozambique*	200 Christians	18	A rather positive response.
24 Mar	Washington, DC (Maryland), *USA*	600 fundamentalist Christians	17.5	Very negative and fearful response.
14 Apr	Cairo, *Egypt*	800 Muslims	16	Mixed reception.
28 Apr	Uppsala, *Sweden*	300 Lutheran Christians	18	Very fearful reaction.
5 May	Flagstaff, Arizona, *USA*	200 fundamentalist Christians	17	Very mixed response.
26 May	Bouânane, Figuig (edge of the Sahara Desert), *Morocco*	200-300 Muslims	16	Reasonably open response.
2 June	Volgograd, *Russia*	800 Muslims	18	Reasonably good response.
9 June	Quito, *Ecuador*	300 Catholics	20	Good, open reception.
23 June	Chicago, Illinois, *USA*	200-300 fundamentalist Christians	18	Not too negative reaction.
30 June	Charlotte, North Carolina, *USA*	200-300 Christians	16	Awed reception.
28 July	Detroit, Michigan, *USA*	300 fundamentalist Christians	16	Silent awe and suspicion.
11 Aug	Novgorod, *Russia*	150 Russian Orthodox Christians	15	Quite a good reception.

Date	Location	Audience		Response
1 Sept	Baie St Paul, Quebec, Canada	200 Catholics	17	Reasonably open response.
8 Sept	Chungking, China	300 Christians	16	Awed, silent response.
29 Sept	Kuopio, Finland	200 Christians	17	Rapt attention; most people thought He was an Angel from God.
6 Oct	Ashland, Maine, USA	250 Christians	16	Serious silence.
27 Oct	Edmonton, Alberta, Canada	65 fundamentalist Christians	14	Stunned silence.
3 Nov	Kabul, Afghanistan	400 Muslims	18	Reasonable response.
17 Nov	Seoul, South Korea	450 Buddhists	18	Thoughtful, interested audience.
1 Dec	Mogadishu, Somalia	300 Muslims	17	Reasonably good reception.
8 Dec	Mbabane, Swaziland	300 Christians	16	Stunned silence.
15 Dec	Ayaguz, Kazakhstan	200 Muslims	17	Silent crowd.
22 Dec	San Fernando, Venezuela	300 Catholics	18	Very good reception.
29 Dec	Kobe, Japan	400 Buddhists	18	Quite a good reception.
1997				
5 Jan	Lima, Peru	500 Christians	20	Quite good, open reception.
19 Jan	Shanghai, China	250 Christians	17	Surprisingly good reaction.
2 Feb	Bogota, Colombia	500 Christians	20	Quite open reception.
16 Feb	Iasi, Romania	300 Christians	17	Quite good, positive reaction.
2 Mar	La Paz, Bolivia	250 Catholics	17	Quite a good reception.
9 Mar	San Miguel de Tucuman, Argentina	400 Catholics	17	Reasonably good reaction.
6 Apr	Salt Lake City Utah, USA	300 Mormons	17	—

13 Apr	Rabat, *Morocco*	600 Muslims	18	"Silent wonderment".
20 Apr	Kracow, *Poland*	300 Christians	18	—
27 Apr	Vrsac, *Serbia*	250-300 Eastern Orthodox Christians	17	"Rather positive" reaction.
4 May	Ust Kut in central *Russia*	300 Muslims	17	Very good, open reception.
11 May	Brasov, *Romania*	250 Eastern Orthodox Christians.	17	A reasonably open reception..
18 May	Varna, *Bulgaria*	300-400 Eastern Orthodox Christians.	18 1/2	Reasonably open reception.
25 May	Cairo, *Egypt*	Over 1,000 Muslims	25	Quite good reaction.
8 June	*Venezuela*	200-300 Christians	18	Numb silence.
6 July	Guayaquil, *Equador*	300 Catholics	18	The response was not unfavourable but cautious.
13 July	Puerto Natales, *Chile*	350 Catholics	20	Stunned silence.
27 July	Amiens, *France*	200 Christians	20	Quite a good reception.
3 Aug	Mwanza, *Tanzania*	400-500 Christians	18	Response was very good.
10 Aug	*Chechnya*	200 Christians	18	Respectful silence.
17 Aug	Kisangani, *Zaire*	300 Christians	18	Stunned silence.
31 Aug	Port of Spain, *Trinidad*	250 Christians	19	Quite a good reaction.
7 Sept	Montevideo, *Uruguay*	300 Christians	17	Respectful silence.
21 Sept	Phrae, *Thailand*	150 Buddhist monks	19	A very good response. Many saw Him as Maitreya Buddha.
5 Oct	Mendoza, *Argentina*	100 Christians	15	A silent, awed response.
12 Oct	Kano, *Nigeria*	400 Christians	18	Respectful silence.
9 Nov	Nagasaki, *Japan*	300 Buddhists	16	Quite a good reception.
30 Nov	Oporto, *Portugal*	200 Christians	18	Silent awe.

1998				
4 Jan	Portland, Oregon, USA	300-400 Christians	14	—
25 Jan	Melo, *Uruguay*	200 Christians	18	Listened in silence.
8 Feb	Bahia Blanca, *Argentina*	600 Christians	20	—
15 Feb	Ouargla, *Algeria*	100 Muslims	18	—
1 Mar	Edmonton, *Canada*	2-300 Christians	18	—
22 Mar	Graz, *Austria*	3-400 Christians	17	—
5 Apr	Villahermosa, *Mexico*	200 Christians	16	—
12 Apr	Zaozhuang, *China*	300 Christians	17	—
19 Apr	Quebec, *Canada*	200-300 Christians	17	—
17 May	Omsk, *Russia*	150 Russian Orthodox Christians	17	—
31 May	Neuquén, *Argentina*	200 Christians	17	—
21 June	Mercedes, *Uruguay*	150 Christians	16	—
5 July	Medellin, *Colombia*	200 Christians	16	—
26 July	Mbuji-Mayi, *Democratic Republic of the Congo (Zaire)*	200 Christians	15	—
9 Aug	Thessaloniki, *Greece*	200 Greek Orthodox Christians	18	—
30 Aug	Quandahar, *Afghanistan*	200-300 Muslims	18	—
6 Sept	Oruro, *Bolivia*	250 Christians	—	—
20 Sept	São Paulo, *Brazil*	150 Christians	18	Awed silence.
27 Sept	Hermosillo, *Mexico*	150 Christians	19	—
25 Oct	Kazan, *Russia*	300 Christians	17	Quite a good reception.

1 Nov	Lagos, *Nigeria*	200 Muslims	17	Awed silence.
8 Nov	San Juan, *Argentina*	200 Christians	18	—
29 Nov	Reykjavík, *Iceland*	120 Christians	18	—
27 Dec	Limassol, *Cyprus*	200 Christians	17	—
1999				
10 Jan	Izmir (Smyrna), *Turkey*	200 Christians	15	
7 Feb	Annapolis, Maryland, *USA*	100 Christians	18	"Astonished" gathering.
14 Feb	Fès, *Morocco*	300 Muslims	18	—
21 Feb	Biel, *Switzerland*	150 Christians	18	—
7 Mar	Jackson, Mississippi, *USA*	200 fundamentalist Christians	18	Stunned silence.
14 Mar	Malmberget, *Sweden*	120 Christians	17	—
18 Apr	San Cristobal, *Venezuela*	200 Christians.	19	An awed silence.
25 Apr	Chicago, Illinois, *USA*	500 fundamentalist Christians	18	—
23 May	Khartoum, *Sudan*	150 Muslims	18	—
24 July	Lublin, *Poland*	150 Christians	17	—
1 Aug	Zhengzhou (Chengchow), *China*	200 Muslims	17	—
22 Aug	Zagreb, *Croatia*	100 Christians (Orthodox)	18	—
12 Sept	Baden, *Switzerland*	100 Christians	19	—
19 Sept	Regina, *Canada*	100 Christians	18	—
26 Sept	Silesia (Slask), *Poland*	100 Christians	18	—
10 Oct	Kiev, *Ukraine*	100 Orthodox Christians	18	—

17 Oct	Asmara, *Eritrea*	60 Christians	17	—
24 Oct	Christchurch, *New Zealand*	50 Christians	18	—
31 Oct	Odessa, *Ukraine*	400 Orthodox Christians	18	—
20 Nov	Haidar Khel, *Afghanistan*	250 Moslems	20	—
28 Nov	Zittau, *Germany*	100 Christians	18	—
5 Dec	Zanzibar, *Tanzania*	200 Christians	20	—
2000				
30 Jan	Canberra, *Australia*	150 Christians	17	—
13 Feb	Bucaramanga, *Colombia*	160 Christians	17	—
20 Feb	Samarkand, *Uzbekistan*	250 Muslims	17	—
12 Mar	Barcelona, *Venezuela*	120 Christians	16	—
19 Mar	Managua, *Nicaragua*	25 Christians	17	—
26 Mar	Phitsanulok, *Thailand*	300 Buddhists	17	—
2 Apr	Quesnel, British Columbia, *Canada*	80 Christians	18	—
30 Apr	Bahia Blanca, *Argentina*	200 Christians	18	—
28 May	Tabora, *Tanzania*	250 Christians	17	—
4 June	Banjul, *Gambia*	—	17	—
2 July	*Bahrain*	300 Muslims	18	—
23 July	Xiangtan, *China*	200 Christians	17	—
3 Sept	Osijek, *Croatia*	150 Christians	18	—
24 Sept	Laval, Quebec, *Canada*	150 Christians	18	—
29 Oct	Libreville, *Gabon*	150 Christians	20	—
5 Nov	Birmingham, Alabama, *USA*	250 Christians	18	—

Date	Location		Age	
12 Nov	Peshawar, *Pakistan*	150 Christians	19	—
3 Dec	Atlanta, Georgia, *USA*.	250 Christians	16	—
10 Dec	Vaslui, *Romania*	180 Russian Orthodox Christians	17	—
24 Dec	Perth, *Australian*	200 Christians	18	—
2001				
14 Jan	Kyoto, *Japan*	50 Christians	17	—
11 Feb	Auckland, *New Zealand*	150 Christians	17	—
4 Mar	Tangshan, *China*	120 Buddhists	18	—
11 Mar	Seidice, *Poland*	150 Christians	17	—
25 Mar	Lucknow, *India*	200 Christians	18	—
8 Apr	Rio de Janeiro, *Brazil*	400 Christians	18	—
10 June	La Paz, *Argentina*	150 Christians	—	—
24 June	El Progresso, *Honduras*	100 Christians	17	—
1 July	Porto Novo, *Benin (Africa)*	150 Muslims	18	—
8 July	Lubeck, *Germany*	200 Christians	17	—
15 July	León, *Nicaragua*	150 Christians	18	—
16 Sept	Lensk, Southern Siberia, *Russia*	100 Russian Orthodox Christians	17	—
23 Sept	Sapporo, Hokkaido, *Japan*	100 Buddhists	17	—
30 Sept	Luxor, *Egypt*	200 Muslims	17	—
7 Oct	Rabat, *Morocco*	200 Muslims	18	—
21 Oct	Lloydminster, *Canada*	100 Christians	18	—
4 Nov	Pisa, *Italy*	150 Christians	18	—
25 Nov	Recife, *Brazil*	150 Christians	16 1/2	—

2002			
24 Feb	Asunción, *Paraguay*	200 Christians	18	—

FOOTNOTES:

1 For more information on Maitreya's June 1988 appearance in Nairobi, Kenya, see *Maitreya's Mission, Volume Two* and *Share International* magazine September 1988 and July/August 1994.

2 A book mentioning Maitreya as the Antichrist was commissioned by the Catholic Church and published just before Benjamin Creme's visit to Mexico in 1991.

3 8 Nov 1992 — Belgrade, *Serbia* — Maitreya appealed to those present to use their influence with their leaders to end the fighting in Bosnia-Herzegovina.

4 28 Feb 1993 — Richmond, Virginia, *USA* — According to Benjamin Creme's Master, there was some symbolic purpose in choosing Virginia as the first group appearance in the U.S.

5 18 July 1993 — Sarajevo, *Bosnia* — Maitreya planned to appear at a large gathering of Muslims, but the meeting was cancelled at the last moment due to fears of shelling from the military activity around the city. Water in the area had been charged in June.

THE AGE OF MIRACLES HAS NO END

Visions of Virgin Mary

The question 'Do you believe in miracles?' was the title of a recent cover story in **Life** *magazine which acknowledged the thousands of unexplained or miraculous phenomena that have been occurring world-wide. Other sources, such as* **Time** *magazine and the* **Washington Post**, *have also reported on such phenomena as, of course, has* **Share International**. *To list a few of these unexplained events: we have had reports of visions or personal experiences of the Christ; visions of the Virgin Mary; weeping and bleeding statues of the Virgin Mary; crosses of light suddenly appearing in people's windows; healing water discovered in Mexico and elsewhere; reports of a mysterious hitchhiker who appears in people's cars and says the Christ is in the world and then disappears; an increase in UFO sightings; crop circle formations appearing in farm fields around the world; and so on. Speaking generally, should people be taking such reports seriously, or can most of them be written off as the product of people's imagination, as hoaxes, or as events which could be explained scientifically?* (July/August 1993)

I have no doubt that there are some hoaxes of crop circles, certainly in England. But the vast majority of the various phenomena you have described should be taken very seriously indeed. These events are occurring on a world-wide scale, and are part of the signs which people expect and look for in connection with the reappearance of the Christ today.

You see these as signs of the reappearance of the Christ? (July/August 1993)

Yes, indeed. They are signs that we have come to the end of one era and the beginning of a new one, and that the Christ has returned to the world to inaugurate this new cycle. These signs are given to uphold people's faith and hope in the future and in a spiritual basis to life, to keep them aware that we are in a world which is constantly changing, and that the days of miracles are not over. The miracles of the Bible, for example, and also of earlier times, are being repeated now daily, almost hourly, across the world. These events add up to very definite evidence to humanity that the time is nigh for the appearance of the Christ openly in the world.

*I would like to ask you specifically about some of the various phenomena that have been reported. There have been reports that people have had visions or personal experiences of the Christ. In fact, a counsellor in Minneapolis, Minnesota, named G. Scott Sparrow, has written a book called **Witness to His Return** in which he interviewed a number of people who said that they have had personal encounters with the Christ. Can you comment on such reports?* (July/August 1993)

Certainly I would accept this. These experiences are part of the manifestations surrounding His return. Maitreya appears to people in three ways. Many people recount having had a vivid and powerful dream, usually associated with some great spiritual, uplifting experience, in which they feel they have seen the Christ. That is the most common way in which He makes Himself known to humanity.

Another, less common, way is to give people visions. These experiences are waking visions, not solid physical presence. People see or experience the Christ as light or a kind of transparent form. Their accounts vary as to how He appears. That is the second mode of Maitreya's contact with people.

There are also direct physical appearances in which He appears to people individually, and in groups, all over the world. I know of many people who have experienced Maitreya in this way.

Share International has published several photographs of the Christ, the Lord Maitreya, as He appeared suddenly 'out of the blue' in Nairobi, Kenya, on 11 June 1988 before 6,000 people. The crowd instantly recognized Him as the Christ and called Him by that name. He talked to them in their own language, Swahili, for 10 or 15 minutes, and then disappeared as amazingly as He had come, leaving in the vicinity of where He had stood some 30 or 40 people completely cured of all their ailments. Photographs show Him dressed in what looks like Arab costume, pure white with a blue headband and carrying a fly whisk in one hand. Standing beside Him is the woman who normally runs these regular healing gatherings, Mary Akatsa. These photographs appeared on CNN, the BBC, and went out over the wire services throughout the world.

***Share International** has for some time now reported on what it calls "miracles" — signs of the presence of the Christ. Can you clarify — do you use the word miracles to indicate astounding events which our present science would not be able to explain and the general population would see as therefore being "miraculous"? I had thought that Theosophy and subsequent bodies of teachings had sought to explain the realities underlying what may seem to be miraculous or inexplicable? In other words, the editors of **Share International** understand how the "miracles" are performed. We see from the history of our development that what was "miraculous" to one century becomes commonplace to the next.* (March 1996)

Precisely. We call "miraculous" these events which seem to defy "natural law", even though we know that it is our ignorance of laws governing energy and matter which make them *appear* to be "unnatural" or supernatural.

We have also had reports of visions of the Virgin Mary and weeping statues as well. Are these reports to be believed? (July/August 1993)

Most of them, yes. They are occurring world-wide and in enormous numbers. The visions of the Virgin Mary are created as thoughtforms by the Master who was the Madonna, the mother of Jesus, 2,000 years ago. This Master creates these visions of the Madonna which are always seen by more than one person.

There are also visions created by the fervent aspiration and desire of people, perhaps afraid of world events, who are looking for some reassurance and security. They create for themselves visions of the Madonna which are purely astral and have nothing to do with that Master at all. These are seen only by the individual concerned, the one who has created them. These I discount, but even they are part of the process by which the thoughtform of the return of the Christ is given expression. The very fact that so many are occurring in this way is a sign that the time is now ripe for the presence of the Christ. But the visions seen by more than one person, the weeping statues, the moving statues, the statues which bleed real blood, and so on, are created by the Master who was the Mother of Jesus.

I recently read a news story about a young boy in the Philippines who has been having visions of the Virgin Mary since 1989. There are also two statues of the Virgin Mary in this area that reportedly are crying tears of blood. (1) Are these manifestations created by the Master who was the Madonna? (2) Are the tears on the Virgin Mary statues actually turning to blood? (3) Why is she crying? (April 1993)

(1) Yes. (2) Yes. (3) For the pain of suffering humanity.

How do all the events which have been predicted in **Share International** *relate to the events of Fatima and the appearances of the Blessed Mother (the Madonna) in the world?* (August/September 1994)

The appearances are not really of the Madonna at all — the Madonna is a Master. The woman who was the Madonna 2,000 years ago, then a second-degree initiate, is now a great Master, a very high level (sixth-degree) initiate, Who is the creator of the thoughtforms which are appearing as the Madonna all over the world. That Master is also responsible for the statues of the Madonna which weep real tears or blood. These appearances, so prevalent today, are among "the signs" of Maitreya's presence. They are signs for the Catholic Christian world, because Catholics relate more to the Madonna than they do to Jesus — even though they love Jesus, and see Him as God. In response to that adoration these appearances take place for the faithful. They show them that God is concerned with humanity. They are indications, for those who can understand, that there is a Plan, and that God never forgets about the world. If you are a devout Catholic you will see that in religious terms.

The Master Jesus, likewise, is hard at work appearing to people — for instance, to Sister Anna from Kenya (see *Share International,* April 1994), who held a press conference on 15 February this year and introduced a book in which she states that "Jesus Christ" appears to her "every Thursday" and He allowed her to take photographs of Him, two of which appear in her book. In one of them, He is crying blood, and every Wednesday night Sister Anna's face becomes congested and she too weeps blood.

These are signs. Maitreya said, in one of His Messages (No. 10): "Those who search for signs will find them, but My method of manifestation is more simple". Maitreya does not need the signs, but humanity needs, loves, calls for, signs — 'if He is the Christ, then there must be signs'. Among the signs are crosses of light which have appeared in windows all over the world, as reported many times in *Share International.* These, again, are signs for those who need them. For those who need the political, outer signs, they are there; for those who need the mystical signs, they, too, are there.

Share International is able to make predictions because we were given the information, sometimes several years in advance of the events. Only Maitreya can do that. He is not looking into a crystal ball and by clairvoyance seeing these events. He knows by His total understanding of the Law of Cause and Effect that if we continue to do so-and-so then such-and-such will happen; if we change direction, then something else will happen. (He does use a certain amount of clairvoyance, but mainly it is an understanding of the Law of Cause and Effect.)

I am wondering if an appearance of the Virgin Mary on the side of a mountain at a small community in southern Queensland "Woombye" some two years ago may have been inspired by Maitreya. The lady who witnessed the event described what she saw as wearing "a cream dress with a green sash. To the side of her were beautiful pink roses". At first this lady saw a beautiful white light high up a tree and began to pray to Our Lady. She is a Roman Catholic. Then the 'appearance' occurred. It has had some publicity — television and other media, and is attracting

314

100 pilgrims monthly, with healings taking place. There is an altar set up at the site and Mass is said there. One pilgrim saying the Rosary reported that the links between the rosary beads changed from silver to a beautiful gold colour. (September 1993)

This was an authentic appearance of the 'Madonna'. It was created not by Maitreya but by the Master Who was the Mother of Jesus in Palestine 2,000 years ago. It is (was) a thoughtform.

Dutch television viewers have recently seen films of a weeping statue in a house in the town of Brunssum (Province of Limburg). Only one eye appears to be weeping blood. Investigators into this particular case claim that the substance is not real blood and assert that the wax, which is said to have been used to 'glue' in the eyes of the statue, is melting in the unusually warm weather. Could you please say whether this is the case or whether this is another genuine sign created by the Master who was the Mother of Jesus? (A logical response to the investigators' conclusions is that if it is caused by wax melting why is the "bleeding" restricted to only one eye?) (September 1995)

Precisely. The phenomenon is a genuine sign created by the Master Who was Mary, Mother of Jesus.

Would the fact that the weeping statues phenomenon is caused by a Master account for the fact that DNA testing proves the blood to be male? Would the Master involved tend to reproduce his own blood type — type 'O' positive, for example — in such cases? (September 1995)

No.

I have heard of a Dominican nun from Kenya who has had many visions of and messages from — she claims — Jesus. Her name is Sister Anna Ali, and a book has been published detailing her experiences. Would your Master please comment on whether it is in fact the Master Jesus who has been in contact with her? (May 1993)

The contacts, since 1987, are indeed with the Master Jesus, but the communications, as related in her book *The Divine Call,* are

315

mainly astral. Actual messages from the Master Jesus at these appearances have been very rare indeed, brief, and relatively 'neutral' in tone. In other words, the long communications published in Sister Anna's book are — largely — the result of her own astral imagination. This is not unusual in this kind of contact — the Masters often say nothing, but the recipient expects (and supplies) some form of message, warning or teaching. Hence the confusion.

What causes the phenomenon of the stigmata — where people's hands and/or feet bleed — very often at Easter? (July/August 1993)

There are many well authenticated instances of this phenomenon — one thinks of Father Pio in Italy and Therese Neumann in Germany for example — and I am sure many quite unknown people experience various degrees of these happenings.

They are brought about, I believe, by an intense emotional identification with the assumed suffering of Jesus on the cross. So one-pointed does that devotional identification become in these cases that there is a precipitation on to the physical plane of these powerful astral feelings. Sometimes the bleeding is more or less constant but very often regularly intermittent or occurring only at particular times, as the questioner suggests — at Easter, for example.

Would it be true to say that in the many instances (now being reported on fairly frequently in the media) of experiences of angels that often the 'angel' seen or sensed is Maitreya Himself or one of the Masters? I'm referring to recent polls which indicate that a very high percentage of Americans not only believe in angels but have had experience of divine help or intervention of some kind. (May 1995)

The "Angels" are always one or other of the Masters and often Maitreya Himself.

More and more people are reporting encounters with 'angels' — some recognizing these 'angels' to be Masters taking many different guises. Could you please give a rough percentage of people in the world who have been fortunate enough to experience such a visitation (in the physical sense or in a dream)? (March 1996)

About 80 per cent.

I heard that someone in Holland had seen a CNN International News programme in which a young girl of seven or eight years, living in North London, UK, spoke about a 'Messiah'-like man who had appeared to her. Do you know anything about this and was it Maitreya? (May 1993)

Yes, a friend called me from Holland about this news report. We tried all means to gain more information from CNN in London and at their headquarters in Atlanta, Georgia. CNN representatives to whom we spoke claimed to have no knowledge of this broadcast. We are still trying to trace the source of the story. My Master has confirmed that it was, indeed, Maitreya who appeared to the young girl.

Hindu Milk Miracle

*Having read the article on the Hindu 'milk miracles' (**Share International** November 1995), I can't help feeling a more useful miracle might have been a better idea. However, I suppose if there is a totally useless miracle at least it is obvious that no one has a vested interest. Why was this phenomenon chosen?* (January/February 1996)

When the questioner knows more about the Masters and Their methods of working, he/she will realize that nothing which They initiate could possibly be described as useless or ill-conceived. No action, however seemingly trivial from our ignorant perspective, is made by Them without due consideration and multi-faceted judgement. That does not mean that everything They set in motion and inspire inevitably succeeds; They must rely on humanity's response and actions in implementing Their efforts, and many wonderful beginnings have petered out through our failings.

The "milk miracle" is seen by the Masters, however, as one of Their most successful attempts to alert modern humanity to the major phenomenon in our midst: the presence of Maitreya. To Hindus, such miracles mean that a Great Soul, a Teacher or Avatar, is among us or "descending" now. Many millions of Hindus, world-wide, have thus been alerted and made expectant, while millions more non-Hindus have shared, through media coverage, in this major manifestation — thus being prepared to associate it with Maitreya when they see Him.

In the Hindu Temples milk miracle, did the statues of the gods really drink the milk? (November 1995)

No. The milk was made to *disappear* by Maitreya and a group of Masters Who specialize in these kinds of phenomena.

Miracle Waters

*Has the "manifestation" of Maitreya referred to in your Master's article, 'The People's Voice' (**Share International** July/August 1992) yet happened? Could it be the miracle water of Tlacote, Mexico?* (January/February 1993)

Yes. Indeed. The miracle water of Tlacote is but one of the many miracles with which Maitreya is now benefiting the world. At every appearance of which we have knowledge, except that at St Petersburg in Russia, Maitreya has charged water in the vicinity, always before, sometimes many months before, His miraculous appearance. Having charged the well or underground stream, He sometimes has to wait a long time for a group, to whom He can usefully appear, to gather in a town reasonably near the water source.

One after the other, these healing waters will be discovered. Already, that at Nordenau, the district of Schmalenberg associated with Maitreya's appearance in Düsseldorf in April 1992, and a well near New Delhi, India, which attracts 20,000 people daily to its healing waters, have been discovered. At the same time, a significant number of healing springs, charged not by Maitreya but by the Master Who was the mother of Jesus in Palestine, have suddenly appeared. These may be compared to the well at Lourdes, charged by the same Master. The difference is that the energy used by Maitreya to charge the waters is cosmic and therefore more powerful.

Are the waters which Maitreya is charging in different places anything to do with the 'waters of Aquarius'? (November 1993)

Yes, indeed. Maitreya goes all over the world creating healing waters. The most important thing is that a network is being created throughout the world, energetically linked together — a network of "the Waters of Life". In the Bible, Jesus said: "I am come that men might have life, and that life more abundantly." Maitreya has repeated that statement, and the "life more abundantly" is, precisely, the Waters of Life of Aquarius. These flow on the physical plane through these wells and water sources, on the emotional-astral planes, the mental planes and the spiritual planes. Maitreya said in one of His many Messages: "On all the planes this Life will flow, reaching the hearts and souls and bodies of men, bringing them nearer to the Source of Life itself" (Message No. 42), thus creating new life and new experience for humanity, inevitably bringing about tremendous changes in consciousness, and also curing the physical ills, strengthening the physical body, of humanity. Our bodies are weakened at the present time by pollution, a number one disease-producing factor. Pollution of the air, the waters and the soil is slowly poisoning humanity, and there will be change only when we end the misuse of the resources of the planet, implement the principle of sharing and so create new balance, equilibrium, in the world.

How does Maitreya choose sites for energizing water around the world? (June 1994)

On the basis of the availability of very long-term, more or less inexhaustible, underground supplies.

How many waters/wells have so far been magnetized? (April 1994)

286.

Is there a final number which will be aimed at? (April 1994)

777.

Will the water from these wells be used for the whole of the Age of Aquarius? (April 1994)

Yes. As the age proceeds the magnetization charge will gradually be increased in potency.

Can one help people to find the healing waters created by Maitreya more quickly? (April 1994)

No. The water is discovered in a definite, lawful rotation. Maitreya brings about the finding. They appear to be found by chance, but someone is always impressed to find the water. It is useless, therefore, for groups of people to organize searches for these healing waters. It all takes place under law.

In 1990, in Dokkum, Friesland (the Netherlands), a child was healed of whooping cough when dipped into water at the well of St Bonifatius, which has long been a place of pilgrimage. There is a chapel over the well for pilgrims. Legend has it that at the spot where St Bonifatius tapped the ground with his staff a healing spring would bubble up. Since 1990, there have been more than 60 reported cases of healing connected with the water in Dokkum. Was the water charged by Maitreya or the Master Jesus which would explain its healing powers? (The parish priest who served there for over six years has now gone into retreat to write a book about his experiences at the St Bonifatius chapel. He believes the place to have special powers but not necessarily the water.) (July/August 1995)

The Master Jesus.

*I have heard it said that you or **Share International** has sent a water-tanker to Nordenau to collect 20,000 gallons of healing water there — presumably to sell. Is there any truth in this story?* (December 1993)

Absolutely none whatsoever. Not only do we not need to collect this water but we would not dream of selling water charged by Maitreya.

Recently I attended a workshop entitled 'Tlacote Healing Water'. The presenter had been to Tlacote and brought back some of the water. Those planning to attend the workshop were urged to bring a gallon of regular drinking water with them to the meeting. The workshop flyer stated: "You will be shown how to use the water from the original spring to activate your own, so you will have a never-ending supply." The activation process was explained as follows:

1. The presenter poured one to two tablespoons of the original water into each participant's gallon of regular water.

2. After 72 hours the regular water would be as potent as the original Tlacote water.

3. The activated Tlacote water could then be used to activate additional water, ad infinitum.

In the Southwest US this type of activation process is referred to as a "sourdough starter phenomenon", referring to the way sourdough yeast was used and promulgated on the frontier before the advent of refrigeration.

Is it true that regular water can be potentized by small amounts of Tlacote water? If so, please describe the process we should use. (April 1993)

No, no, a thousand times no! The presenters of the "workshop" should be warned that they are misinformed and are doing a disservice to others. This is not the method of homoeopathic potentization. They are simply diluting the potency (and effect) of the Tlacote water. Regular water goes bad, so they are risking water poisoning at the same time.

The Tlacote and Nordenau waters (and other such waters as they are discovered) should be used neat, straight, *as they come* from the source, or in homoeopathic potency 6c, 12c or 30c in tablets or pillules.

Would it be a good idea to get scientists to do research on the Tlacote water and the water in Germany, because it is very interesting what happened to the weight and the structure of the water, and it also would draw attention to this miracle, to this phenomenon? (April 1993)

The answer is 'yes', if they are interested, but it is not our business. There is nothing to prevent any scientist in the world, if he is interested, in making an investigation into the water from Tlacote or the other places that have been discovered, but it is not the work of this group to find such scientists, to introduce it to them or to try to get them involved. Scientists, like everybody else, have free will; the facts have been made known and they can follow it up or not as they see fit. The purpose of this group is to make known Maitreya's presence and concerns for the world, not to publicize these healing waters — even though Maitreya has charged them.

Crosses of Light

People in southern California and elsewhere around the world have reported crosses of light appearing in their windows. How is that explained? (July/August 1993)

They first appeared in El Monte, California, a part of Los Angeles, in May 1988. In April of that year, my Master said that very soon Maitreya would create so many crosses of light around the world that people would not be able to ignore them. No one would know where they come from, or how they came about. There are now 20 or 30 such crosses in the El Monte area. They have also appeared in various parts of the world. I received a letter recently from a woman in New Jersey who had a cross appear miraculously in her apartment window.

The crosses appear suddenly; they were not there previously. They are 'activated' by Maitreya, and have a great effect on the people around them. They draw thousands of people to see them and some people have extraordinary healing and spiritual experiences. The whole society in El Monte has been transformed, both individually and as a community, since the first appearance of a cross of light in the bathroom window of a Hispanic family there.

The family in whose window the first cross appeared took the glass to their local church, because there were so many people coming to see the cross. But the cross promptly disappeared and nothing they tried could bring the cross back. Reluctantly, they took the glass to be put back in the house. The cross immediately reappeared on the glass.

Editor's note: In November 1995, 40-foot high crosses appeared in the windows of a Baptist church near Knoxville, Tennessee. Many healings have been attributed to these crosses. See *Share International*, July/August 1996.

It is interesting that the crosses appeared in a low-income community in southern California. Is there any significance to that? (July/August 1993)

The Christ has said: "Look for Me in the dark places, where hunger and strife abound. Know Me as the brother of the poor, the rejected of the world." (From Message No. 128) It is as a spokesperson for the poor and dispossessed that He comes. There are some 1,200 million people living in conditions of official, absolute poverty, which means they have an income of less than US$100 per year. Half of these have nothing at all, and a large proportion of them, many millions, are literally starving to death — in a world with a huge surplus of food per capita. It is because Maitreya can no longer stand aside and watch what He calls "this blasphemy", "this slaughter", "this crime" of starvation in the midst of plenty that He has now returned to the world.

In the small town of Eisenberg in Austria, near the Hungarian border, there is a cross on the grass of a garden of a farm belonging to Aloisia Lex and her husband. It has been there since 6 September 1956. The arms of the cross are about 1 metre long. Aloisia had a vision of Jesus there and there is also a strange, inexplicable light on the spot. Church authorities and scientific analysis, both chemical and biological, could find no natural reason for the unusual brightness. Miracles take place there. The church has not yet officially recognized this case.

Aloisia Lex had visions of Jesus and the Holy Mother, Mary, until her death in 1984. Now, one of her daughters, Anna Maria, also has visions. Aloisia spoke only in the local dialect yet the messages from Jesus and Mary were always spoken and immediately written down by Aloisia in perfect German. According to Aloisia the cross was made by an angel. Now, 40 years after it first appeared, the cross is still clearly visible in the grass.

(1) Was the cross made by an angel? (2) What is the function of such phenomena? (3) Were the visions and messages from the Master Jesus? (4) Would the cross have healing powers? (June 1995)

(1) No; by the Master Jesus. (2) To kindle faith. (3) Yes. (4) No.

THE SOLAR SYSTEM

Crop Circles

Could you comment on increased UFO sightings and the appearance of crop circles that have been reported? (July/August 1993)

Aside from the few hoaxes, the crop circle patterns are certainly real, but not directly connected with Maitreya. They are created by our brothers of the nearest planets, Mars and Venus. The crop circles have appeared all over the world. We have had hundreds of them in England, and they have appeared in Canada, the US, across Europe, Japan and elsewhere. The crop circle patterns are created by the space vehicles that we call UFOs. They are part of a process of energization of the Earth, and are duplicating on the physical plane many of the vortices of the network of magnetic energy which surrounds the Earth. These formations will become 'batteries of energy' for humanity in connection with a new energy source, part of the science of light which lies just ahead for humanity.

There seem to be fewer reports of crop circle sightings recently. Some people say that their disappearance is connected to the fact that the crop circles had become commercialized by the locals in Britain, many of whom profited from them. Can you comment on this, and why there seem to be fewer crop circle patterns forming? (October 1993)

My information is that there are still a great many crop circles being formed, only slightly fewer than in recent years, as this particular manifestation of the Space Brothers' activity is being phased out gradually. Certainly there have been many in England and elsewhere in Europe. One reason for the apparent lack of activity is that there has been a diminished interest in them by the media and therefore fewer reports. It is characteristic of media to drop a subject, however interesting or important, if no obvious explanation, purpose or outcome can be ascertained. Moreover, two men have come forward with the claim that they had hoaxed the world by creating all the crop circles since 1978.

A ridiculous claim but one eagerly accepted by the media — one 'rag' newspaper having paid the men a large sum of money for their story.

I do not understand the reference to commercialization of the crop circles by "locals" (unless is meant the two men mentioned here in Britain, or the appearance of some successful books on the subject by serious researchers).

Recently, I stood in the centre of a large corn-circle (a circle with a little 'comma', like a capital 'Q') in Wiltshire in England. I have visited, and gathered some corn from, many circles in the last two years or so and I believe I can recognize differences in the energies in them. This one struck me as being different from any I have ever experienced. I know you have written that the circles are made by spacecraft from Mars and Venus respectively. I wonder if you can throw any light on this very different one? (October 1993)

This circle was made by craft from *both* Mars and Venus; the circle by a Martian and the 'comma' by a Venusian ship. What you felt was a blend (together yet separate) of the two energies. Why a Q? The Q stands for: "Question — what is different about this one?" — an example of Venusian, not Martian, humour!

Are the various stone circles in the south of England and elsewhere based on ancient corn circles observed by the people of the time? (June 1993)

No. The stone circles are of ancient origin. The corn circles are a recent phenomenon.

Can you say something about the real significance of Silbury Hill and Avebury in southern England? Are they special energetic or magnetic centres of some kind, for example? (June 1993)

Many individuals and groups in the UK impart great mystical significance to these ancient monuments. I do not, however, subscribe to that view. Silbury Hill is a burial mound, I believe, and nothing more. Avebury (and Stonehenge, another such stone circle which is even more dramatic) is part of the ancient Druidic religious tradition of England and Europe in pre-Christian and pre-Roman times. They functioned as calendars to determine the major solstices. I do not believe they had (or have) special energetic significance.

UFOs and the Space Brothers

Does the Plan of the Logos include contact with other solar systems? (October 1996)

In the short term, it certainly entails contact (which it already has) with the other planets of our own solar system, and with our nearest solar system, Sirius. Many of the Masters, when They become Masters, go directly from Earth to Sirius. People like Gautama, who "stood in" for the Buddha, Leonardo da Vinci, Michelangelo, or John the Baptist are all on Sirius. Jesus is here, but John the Baptist, who prepared the way for Him, is actually on Sirius. If He were here He would be more evolved than Jesus because the evolution on Sirius is fantastically fast.

The Hierarchies of all the planets are in communication all the time. This solar system evolves as a system, not just as separate planets going their own way. The Logoi of the various planets know the Plan, to a greater or lesser extent, of the Solar Logos, Who is 'God' for this solar system. Their work is the fulfilling of the plan of the Solar Logos for Their particular planet. Eventually this contact and communication will become the common heritage of all of us. At the moment it is restricted to the Masters and senior initiates, but eventually, through what we call the UFO phenomenon (coming mainly from Mars and Venus), the reality of this interrelation between the planets will become known to everyone.

Do you think there is any threat from the people on other planets? (October 1996)

Absolutely not. Their intention is totally beneficial — in fact, without their help this planet would not be liveable in at this point. We owe them an enormous karmic debt.

Will Space Brothers work more openly in the world in the future? (October 1995)

Yes; the process is already beginning.

Do you know of a connection between the White Brotherhood, UFO people and Maitreya? (October 1994)

Maitreya is the Head of our planetary Spiritual or Esoteric Hierarchy which is a branch of the Cosmic Great White Brotherhood. The Hierarchies of all the planets in our system are in constant contact. The "UFO people" come, in the main, from Mars and Venus with the full knowledge and co-operation of our Hierarchy.

On radio two years ago you said you had met beings who had taken you on a spaceship to Mars and Venus. Can you tell us about that? (September 1995)

You have it a little bit wrong: I did not say that I had been taken to Mars or Venus, but in spaceships — yes, many times. UFOs, as we call them, are real. They come in the main from these two planets; most of them are made on Mars, many are designed on Venus but made on Mars — Mars is the great 'factory planet'. They are made by thought and guided by a combination of thought and very high technology, far beyond anything we know about. They have visited this planet for countless millennia, and are very closely concerned with the externalization of our Spiritual Hierarchy into the world.

Are the people who are your hosts when you go up in spacecraft Masters? (September 1995)

We would see them as Masters, very evolved beings. Every planet has seven 'rounds', lasting millions of years; we are in the middle of the fourth round, so we are not very evolved as a planet. There are seven sacred planets; we are one of the non-sacred planets. Mars, too, is a non-sacred planet, but it is much more advanced in technology than ours. Venus is in its last round, so I cannot call the people on Venus Masters; they are more like Gods. The relationship between Venus and this planet is the same as between the soul and the personality: Venus is the alter-ego of this planet.

Are the Space Brothers who come to assist our Earth Hierarchy also Masters within the Hierarchies of the planets they come from? Or are the visitors from space simply very evolved beings on their planets? (July/August 1995)

In many cases, yes. They are at various stages.

What would Maitreya say about the belief that there is a 'conspiracy theory' — that there are bad guys out there as well as good guys going round in spaceships? (September 1995)

There is a belief, especially in America, that there are abductions going on by 'nasty' space beings of people in the world. My information is that there is absolutely no truth in abductions whatsoever. No one is abducted by the Space Brothers. There is total control in this solar system by the Hierarchies of the higher planets. There are many people who *claim* that they have been abducted and have been experimented on; my information is that this is 100 per cent astral glamour. The people involved believe it is true, just as when you are in the middle of a dream you believe it is true. These claims stem from hysterical, astral fantasies, believed to be real.

(1) Is there any truth whatsoever in the various claims made by people that they have been kidnapped by, raped by, operated and experimented on by Space Brothers? Recent documentaries showed interviews with many people who appeared in all other respects to be normal, or at least not extremely neurotic. Some viewers found these people quite plausible. (2) The key question might be: how can one distinguish between real contact with the Space Brothers (such as in Adamski's case) and hysterical fantasy? (April 1995)

(1) No. (2) Discrimination is difficult to acquire. Astral-type experiences such as these *seem* very real to the one experiencing them — as do our dreams. Nevertheless, they are no more real. True contacts with the Space People are always positive in nature.

The Mars Observer probe from the US recently lost contact with the earth just before it reached orbit around Mars. Scientists speculate that the spacecraft malfunctioned in some way. Was this simply a malfunction of the spacecraft or were other factors at work? (October 1993)

I suppose the questioner really means: was there some deliberate interference (by Martians or others) which made for the loss of contact. My information is that there was no such interference; it was simply the result of technological malfunction.

You said that all the planets of our system are inhabited, without exception, but the material in which the bodies are created is vibrating at a different rate from our own, and so if we went there they would be invisible. Are the Western governments aware of this? (November 1996)

Some, yes; others probably not. There may be individuals in governments who have read my books, or who themselves have come to this knowledge. The Space Brothers — those who work from the other planets, and who use the UFO vehicles as their means of entry to our planet — have contacts all over the world. I am sure that in many governments there are those who are secretly in contact with, or knowledgeable about, the UFO phenomenon, mainly in the airforces and the defence ministries. In fact the Defence Ministry of the UK pays farmers to obliterate crop circles to prevent people from connecting them with UFO activity.

(1) Is the meteor being investigated by scientists for signs of life really from Mars? (2) Was there dense physical-plane life on Mars in the past? (October 1996)

(1) Yes. (2) Yes.

*(1) You have said that only on planet Earth can human beings exist with gross physical bodies. Is this the reason planet Earth was chosen to express the physical body of the great Third Ray Life (see page 99 of **Esoteric Psychology, Volume Two**)? (2) Does the above make us particularly vulnerable to the influence*

of the Lords of Materiality? (3) Does the Earth humanity have a special role in spiritualizing matter? (May 1995)

(1) Yes. (2) No. (3) No. The inhabitants of all planets have the role of spiritualizing matter (at its various levels). Earth humanity does this at the dense physical level also.

Can we make contact with entities outside our solar system? (March 1993)

Despite the many claims to the contrary, the answer is no. For the Masters, of course, there is no such limitation.

Can beings from other solar systems contact ordinary mortals (and do they want to)? (March 1993)

From certain systems, yes, but there is no reason for them to do so. (Again despite the claims to the contrary).

Do the many drawings, models and descriptions of Beings from other planets tally with the reality? Or are they just representations of astral glamours? (March 1993)

Some, George Adamski's for example, are very accurate. Most are the result of over-heated astral imagination.

Is it possible that people claiming contact with Beings from Sirius, for example, are really, by chance, contacting Beings from other planets (known or unknown) in our system? (March 1993)

It is possible but *very* unlikely. Contact with Beings from other planets does not depend on "chance" and is *always* initiated by them.

You have said that all the planets in our solar system are inhabited by people. (1) How, then, are the people of Jupiter affected by the colliding comet fragments; and (2) how are we affected here on Earth? (January/February 1995)

(1) Not at all. The inhabitants of Jupiter live on the various moons orbiting the planet. (2) Not at all.

331

*You say: "The inhabitants of Jupiter live on the various moons orbiting the planet." Yet in the Alice Bailey book **Treatise on Cosmic Fire**, pp. 794-795, it says: "Every moon is occultly a point of corruption." On page 1,178 of the same book, it describes Jupiter as "The School of Beneficent Magicians", and its halls "The Palace of Opulence". How could "The Palace of Opulence" exist on a "point of corruption"? (May 1995)*

It does not. Three of Jupiter's 12 moons are artificial — man-made. It is on these that the population of Jupiter — a sacred, and one of the most advanced, planets of our system — resides.

What effect will the crash of the comet fragments on the surface of Jupiter have on the Earth? (October 1994)

None that we could measure.

You indicated that the comet fragments hitting Jupiter a few months ago had no effect on humanity. However, was there a connection with the attack from Cosmic levels in the same period which you referred to in your article 'To serve anew'? (September 1995)

No.

I believe you have said that comets deposit their energies within the magnetic fields of the planets they pass. Does each comet have an ensouling Logos? (June 1994)

No. Only solar systems and planets have Logoi.

A Japanese astronomer has found a new comet coming from deep space. Called Hyakutake, it is at this moment visible at night. (1) Has this comet a relationship with the Reappearance of Maitreya? (2) A French observatory made public that the comet has broken in three parts. Is this a coincidence? (May 1996)

(1) No. (2) Yes.

Is an asteroid belt really the remains of a planet which has been destroyed? (March 1996)

No.

Recently the media have shown a NASA photo of a face on the surface of Mars. Please comment as to who, what, when, how and why it is there. (January/February 1994)

If the photograph meant here is the one I have seen, it is nothing more than the effect of light on large rocks. It is not a photograph of a face.

CHAPTER 4

THE AGELESS WISDOM TEACHINGS

Interview with Benjamin Creme
by Rollin Olson

The Ageless Wisdom teachings were first made available to the general public around 1875 by Helena Petrovna Blavatsky in her seminal works: *The Secret Doctrine* and *Isis Unveiled*. Blavatsky established the Theosophical Society to introduce this 'new' perspective on history and human evolution. The intermediate phase of the teaching was revealed by Alice Bailey who, from 1919 to 1949, collaborated with a Master of Wisdom known as "the Tibetan". Through a process of telepathic overshadowing, the Master Djwhal Khul communicated a vast body of information about the world and its future.

Since 1974, British artist Benjamin Creme has been the source of further revelations concerning the Ageless Wisdom and, in particular, about the reappearance of Maitreya, the Christ and World Teacher for the coming age — information which Creme receives through his moment-to-moment telepathic contact with a Master of Wisdom.

The following article gives an overview of the basic tenets of the Ageless Wisdom teachings. It is based on an interview with Benjamin Creme which took place in November 1994. For readers who are new to this subject, we have provided a glossary of esoteric terms at the end of the book.

Innate Divinity

Every day it seems people are talking about how things are out of control — corruption ruining countries, economies in collapse, people losing their jobs, some becoming homeless, the family unit breaking down. A lot of people see no purpose in life any more. Others keep hoping for a turn-around. Do you see any hope for the future?

Very much so. I think that before humanity lies a civilization more brilliant than anything this world has ever seen.

But how, given the problems we have today?
I think these problems are really temporary. They are the result of the fact that tremendous new cosmic energies are influencing our world and creating the present — temporary — turmoil and chaos. Our innate divinity, potential in every human being, is sufficient, I believe, to show us a way out of these problems and to create the conditions which will ensure, not only the continuance of humanity, but the creation of a civilization which will fulfil our every aspiration.

You say "innate divinity". Who are we, really?
We are really gods in incarnation. We need to recognize our threefold constitution: We are a spark of God; every religion has postulated this and has kept the idea of our divinity before humanity for thousands of years. But it can be seen more scientifically and still correctly. Speaking as an esotericist, I would say that the divine spark is so refined in vibration that it cannot manifest directly on the physical plane. It reflects itself, therefore, as the individualized human soul. The soul in its turn, reflects itself in the human personality, with its physical, emotional, and mental bodies. Through the physical plane personality, the soul enacts its reincarnational process, until finally the individual on the physical plane, the man or woman, reflects perfectly the quality of the soul, which is the divine quality of the spark of God.

What's getting in the way of expressing this divinity right now?
The main thing is that at the coarse physical-plane level there is a resistance, a limitation of expression of our divinity. Hence, the expression of selfishness by most of humanity. We then create conditions — political, economic and social — which further prevent our divinity from expressing itself. When the changes, which are now under way, go further and reflect the essential spiritual nature of humanity, we will create conditions —

political, economic, religious, social and scientific — which will allow the innate divinity of all people to manifest.

If we're divine innately, then what is our purpose; what goal are we shooting for as a race?

As a race, our purpose is to spiritualize matter. We are spirit in matter, in incarnation at this relatively low level (although from the mineral, the vegetable or the animal point of view it is a relatively high level). From the point of view of spirit, the human being, with a physical, an emotional and a mental body, is not a very clear expression of divinity. The evolutionary process, therefore, is that by which we spiritualize the matter of our own bodies and, thus, matter itself. That is why we are here: to spiritualize matter, to inform the matter of our physical, emotional, and mental bodies with the qualities of the soul, which is perfect; perfect spirit reflected from the spark of God.

People routinely talk about their physical body, about their emotions, their thoughts. You are saying there is an actual body which is the emotions, a body which is the mind, in addition to the dense physical body?

Yes, indeed. These are vehicles for the spirit aspect, working through the soul, to express itself at this level. Gradually, through the process of incarnation and reincarnation, we do, indeed, create a body through which the spirit aspect can, to a very full degree, manifest. When that happens we become perfected Masters.

It seems that what you're describing is not strictly in the department of religion. Am I right in assessing it as a kind of broader view of things?

Indeed, it is a synthesizing teaching. The Ageless Wisdom teachings, or esotericism as it is often called, is not a religion. It is not, strictly speaking, a philosophy; it is not an art or a science, but it has something of all of these.

You might say that esotericism is the philosophy, or the science, of the evolutionary process, as it pertains to the human and the subhuman kingdoms. But it is about the evolution of consciousness, not of the physical form. If you want to know about the evolution of the physical form, turn to Darwin — he has pretty well summed up the nature of evolution as regards the form of the animal and the human kingdoms. But in terms of the evolution of consciousness, you have to turn to the esoteric — esoteric only so far; for that which is esoteric gradually becomes exoteric. Nothing which humanity can safely use is ever withheld, so it is up to us how much of this teaching is given at any time.

Let me clarify a couple of terms before we go on. What is the difference between 'esoteric' and 'occult' — terms that are often used synonymously?

They both mean 'hidden'. That is, hidden for a given time, not for all time — but hidden because, at this point in the evolution of the race, it is largely unknown and unacceptable to all but a relatively small number of initiates and disciples of those who give the teachings. To humanity in general it is unknown, therefore esoteric or occult. The word 'occult' has been given, by various religious groups, a rather bad connotation: it is seen as something dark, evil, to do with nefarious practices, devil worship, and so on. This is a complete misunderstanding of the word occult. Occult simply means hidden, and specifically the hidden knowledge or science of the energies behind the evolutionary process. Esotericism might be seen more as the philosophy of the evolutionary process and occultism as the science of the energies which bring that process about.

Source of the Teachings

What is the source of this information you are giving us?

The Ageless Wisdom teachings are as old as humanity itself. These are the teachings of a group of men who have gone beyond the strictly human stage and have entered the next kingdom, the Spiritual Kingdom. They are the Masters of Wisdom and the Lords of Compassion. They are men and women like us who have expanded their consciousness to include the spiritual levels. There are a large number of these

Enlightened men on our planet, Who have been living in the remote mountain and desert areas for countless thousands of years. From time to time They release aspects of Their teachings, in so far as we can absorb and use them, to enlighten us.

In modern times the major expression of these teachings was given through Helena Petrovna Blavatsky, one of the founders of the Theosophical Society, between 1875 and 1890. Her book *The Secret Doctrine* is the preparatory phase of the teachings given for the new cosmic cycle which we are now entering — we call it the Age of Aquarius. A later phase was given through an English disciple, Alice Bailey, between 1919 and 1949, by a Tibetan Master, Djwhal Khul, and this is seen as the intermediate phase of the teachings. Between 1924 and 1939, a further body of teachings — the Agni Yoga teachings — was given through another Russian disciple, Helena Roerich. These Ageless Wisdom teachings are the means by which humanity is kept informed of its essential divinity and of its journey of evolution toward perfection.

How did Blavatsky and Bailey get their information?
As far as Madame Blavatsky was concerned, she received it from a group of Masters with whom she lived for some years in the Himalayas. The Masters have gone through this evolutionary process in which we are still engaged and have learned how it works, what evolution is about. They are Masters not in any authoritarian sense, but masters of Themselves and the forces of nature. They have full consciousness and complete control on all planes of this planet.

And I would assume that it's from this level of human accomplishment that the greatest teachers of all the ages have come.
Indeed. Every new cosmic cycle — we are entering a new one now, the Age of Aquarius — brings into the world a teacher. People like Hercules and Hermes, Rama, Mithra, Vyasa, Zoroaster, Confucius, Krishna, Shankaracharya, the Buddha, the Christ, Mohammed — these are all Masters who have come from the same spiritual centre of the planet, called the Spiritual, or

Esoteric, Hierarchy, which is made up of the Masters and Their initiates and disciples of various degrees. It is also known as the Kingdom of God or the Kingdom of Souls.

So this is a state of being as opposed to a place?
Yes. Christians are waiting for the Kingdom of God to descend on the earth when we are good enough to receive it. Actually it has always been here, behind the scenes, made up of those men and women who have fitted Themselves, through the expansion of Their consciousness (and therefore the demonstration of Their divinity).

Is this what the scripture relating to "the kingdom of heaven in our midst" is about?
Christ, through Jesus, said the Kingdom of Heaven is within you. Don't look outside or up to heaven. It is within you. And indeed it is, as consciousness. If you have that consciousness, you are in the Kingdom of God.

God

What about God? Who is He? Where is He? How does He relate to the Spiritual Hierarchy and us?
God, in the esoteric meaning, is the sum total of all the Laws and all the energies governed by these Laws in the manifested and unmanifested universe. So God is impersonal. Nevertheless, that transcendent God is manifest in every aspect of creation, including ourselves. We are not separate from that creation — from God. Every human being has the potential of the knowledge, the awareness, of all in creation that we can think of as meaning God.

The Masters are God-realized, which is a very specific state, in that They have brought Their consciousness, in terms of the divine spark, the Absolute, the Self, into complete at-one-ment with Themselves as men on the physical plane — the personality and the divine aspect are totally integrated.

What about God who is not in the body?

God is also the great Cosmic Being who ensouls this planet. For all its solidity, its cities and aeroplanes and television studios and the like, this planet is really the body of expression of a Cosmic Being who gives the planet its life, and who has a plan of evolution for all the kingdoms in nature, including the human kingdom. What is really happening is that we, at our different levels, from the mineral kingdom up to the Kingdom of God itself, are carrying out an evolutionary process, which, in its summation, will make this planet a perfect expression of the thoughtform in the mind of the creating Logos.

You mentioned God ensouling this planet. Is there another God or higher level of consciousness beyond that?
Indeed. There is the God who ensouls the solar system. Our Planetary Logos is only a part, a centre in the body of the Solar Logos, Who in turn is a centre in the body of the Galactic Logos. And on and on, galaxy after galaxy. There is no end to God; it is transcendent and also immanent in every part of creation. Every aspect of God, including ourselves, has the potential one day to know all and be all of that, and to work with the energies which create the universe.

God is everything that exists, and all space between that which exists, between you and me, and around us, around everything. All of that is God. God manifests through Its creation, which is made of energies at particular vibrational rates. The form depends on the particular frequency of the nucleus and the electrons of these forms. Modern science has been able to break down cellular structures and show that at the centre of every atom is a nucleus with electrons around it, vibrating at a specific rate, and that every atom in the universe is made in the same way. There is nothing but energy in all of the manifested universe. The difference between that totally scientific view and that which an esotericist would hold is that the esotericist goes further and says, indeed, all is energy, but energy follows thought, is acted upon by thought. Thought is the agency by which creation takes place.

Energies

Can you give us a practical example?

The Great Pyramid at Giza was created by thought. The blocks of stone were actually moved by thought. It is very simple when you understand how to do it. You create a formula, like $E=mc^2$, the great formula of Einstein which has transformed our whole concept of both energy and matter: energy equals mass times the speed of light squared, the speed of light being 186,000 miles a second. That formula has transformed our physics, and so we see matter and energy as interchangeable. When you recognize this, you can create a mantram. That formula, $E=mc^2$, can be changed into a mantram. When you enunciate the mantram in the correct way, you can move objects to wherever you want. You bring the energy of mind to bear on what is simply free etheric energy, surrounding every block of stone and every human being, every fish, and so on. All of that is a precipitation of etheric energy. The stones likewise can be made to have no weight, because the weight is to do with the inert mass and gravity. But when you create the mantram out of the formula and enunciate it, then you can move the stone from here to there. We shall do this in the very near future.

What would you say is the major benefit in understanding that energy underlies all things?

It gives us control over the universe, over matter. It makes it possible, by thought, to be anywhere in the world in seconds. It makes possible modes of communication which are instantaneous, like telepathy. It is the knowledge of energy that makes all of this possible.

So these things are not just tricks.

Not tricks, no. They are the natural ability of all people, only they have to be developed.

And those who have developed these abilities are on the cutting edge of where all of us are destined to go?

Precisely. Telepathy is a natural faculty of human beings. Most people experience it at times; a mother and a child might have a very close telepathic rapport. That does not mean that they know word for word what the other is thinking, but if something is happening to a child, the mother will instantly know. She will feel that child is in danger and act accordingly. This is something we share with the animal kingdom. Animals have that same kind of emotional, instinctual, telepathic contact. When this is brought up to the mental level you have direct mind-to-mind communication. A Master communicates with His disciples by telepathy; He does not usually appear physically. He could be in the Himalayas or the Andes or the Rockies or wherever, with His disciple in New York or London or Geneva, and still be able to talk moment-to-moment.

I know, from having seen Kirlian photographs of the energies around the physical body, that science has made some strides in being able to demonstrate or measure these energies. What about at the levels of emotion, mind, thought? Can this energy also be measured?

It is something which will come. But, at the moment, what we are really measuring is that level of energy which science as yet has not demonstrated, the etheric levels of physical energy. Our modern science recognizes only three levels: physical, liquid, and gaseous matter. But above gas there are four further states of matter which are, strictly speaking, material — each one finer than the one below. These etheric planes of matter are the next phase of the material world to be researched and finally demonstrated by modern science. Then the etheric planes will become a reality and more and more people will be born with the ability to see the etheric planes of matter. This is really to do with a certain vitality and with a double focus: you see the physical; you change the focus and you see the etheric. Both are there. The physical is really a precipitation, downwards, from the etheric.

If energy follows thought, where does the initial thought come from? Is it a soul activity which we record mentally and then manifest through language? (May 1995)

It depends on the nature of the thought and the point reached in evolution. For the vast majority, the thought originates in the lowest of the four mental planes and, through the mental body, finds concrete expression in the brain. More evolved individuals may contact a growing degree of abstract thought emanating from the manasic level of the soul. This, likewise, finds expression in the brain. On a yet higher level, intuition or intuitive thought — thought without thinking — stems from the Buddhic level of consciousness of the soul.

The mind-belt of the world is filled with thoughtforms to which people respond on one or other level depending on their point of evolution.

Is energy a result of consciousness? (May 1996)

No. Consciousness is an aspect of energy. All is energy, and what we call consciousness is a particular quality of energy; that which is embodied by the soul. Everything you can see, or might see or imagine as being seen, is energy. The whole of creation is really energy vibrating at different rates. The rates determine the form which it takes.

Consciousness you cannot see, but you can see the results of its presence. Consciousness comes to us from our soul, and the more we are ensouled, the more we are conscious. A Master has a tremendous level of consciousness compared to us because He is totally soul-infused.

How do you control energy to make it more powerful? (May 1996)

Energy is free but it can be manipulated by thought. We can think, so we can take "mind energy" and by a destructive thought destroy, by a creative thought create; it is in our own hands. The problem for the world is that we cannot control our thought. If we can really control our thought we can create a better world. But this is a matter of growth, of consciousness, of evolution. The Master can control His thought, totally and absolutely; He only uses thought as it is needed at the moment. He does not have a stream of thoughts flowing from His subconscious as most people do; He has no subconscious. So how correctly, creatively, you can manipulate thought is a question of how evolved you are. A writer, a poet, an artist, a great scientist, an innovator of some kind, uses thought creatively in the creation of various forms.

The Seven Rays

What about energies from, let's say, higher planes or higher levels?

Esoteric science postulates seven streams of energy, or rays, whose interaction, at every conceivable frequency, creates everything in Cosmos. Each ray is the expression of a great cosmic Life, cyclically demonstrating its unique energetic quality through the vehicles in which it manifests — whether it be a grain of sand, a man or a solar system. To say that a man or a nation or a planet is 'on' the 1st or 2nd ray, for example, is to say that they are controlled by, and express the quality of, that ray.

The idea of the septenate is found at many levels and in many branches of our lives: the seven colours of the rainbow, the seven notes of the musical scale, the seven planes of existence, the seven sacred planets, etc. And, in keeping with this scheme, there are seven ray-types of people.

How do you describe these rays?

There are three primary rays, or rays of aspect, and four secondary rays of attribute. They are usually expressed as follows:

Rays of Aspect:
1st ray of Power, Will or Purpose
2nd ray of Love-Wisdom
3rd ray of Active, Creative Intelligence

Rays of Attribute:

4th ray of Harmony through Conflict, or Beauty, or Art

5th ray of Concrete Science or Knowledge

6th ray of Abstract Idealism or Devotion

7th ray of Ceremonial Order or Magic or Ritual or Organization.

How do these rays affect the average person?

All of us are governed basically by five ray forces: the ray of the soul, which remains the same for countless aeons; the personality ray, which varies from life to life until all the qualities are developed; the ray governing the mental body; that governing the astral-emotional equipment; and the ray of the physical body, including the brain. These all vary cyclically. Each ray works primarily through one centre (or chakra), and together they determine the physical structure and appearance, the astral-emotional nature, and the quality of the mental unit. They predispose us to certain attitudes of mind and certain strengths and weaknesses, which we call the virtues and vices of the rays.

For example, the 1st ray of will or power has strength, perseverance and breadth of viewpoint. Its vices, however, include pride, ambition, wilfulness and the desire to control others. The 2nd ray of love-wisdom has the qualities of love, empathy, the ability to see the other person's point of view. Alternatively, it can produce indifference to others, selfishness and suspicion — according to the vehicle through which it is expressing.

The soul expresses only the virtues of the ray, while the imperfect personality expresses, more or less, the vices. The evolutionary aim is to transmute the vice of the ray into its higher (virtue) aspect.

What would be the value in knowing what rays are manifesting through us?

A knowledge of one's rays provides an insight into one's strengths and limitations, one's line of least resistance in this life, and also an understanding of the bridges and the barriers between oneself and others. Those on similar rays tend to see things from the same point of view, to have the same approach to life, while those on disparate rays find it difficult to come to an understanding of each other's attitudes and meaning. It will be obvious how this factor conditions, for example, the quality of married life or how one relates to one's children.

This sounds like a new approach to psychology.

Indeed. Our present science of psychology is only in its infancy. It seeks to understand the workings of the human psyche and to alleviate the symptoms of stress and disorder. But until it is understood that man is a soul in incarnation, governed by certain ray influences, much will remain obscure. It is the soul which determines the rays of the personality and its vehicles. The new psychology, as yet esoteric, will begin from that premise.

You have said that the rays manifest through everything in creation. How would this work out at a level greater than a human being?

Well, as an example, every nation is governed by two rays: the soul ray, expressing the highest, if as yet unmanifested, ideals of the nation; and the lower personality ray, governing the people's selfish national desires.

To view history from an understanding of the rays governing the nations and races is to see it in an entirely new light. It becomes obvious why certain nations are allies, while others have little in common and are traditionally hostile towards each other. Or why particular ideas, movements and religions flourish at one period and fall into decay at another; why some countries emerge for a time and become dominant influences in the world while others lie fallow, so to speak, awaiting their time of awakening through the stimulus of an incoming ray.

What do you mean by an 'incoming ray'?

Like everything in Cosmos, the rays have periods of activity and inactivity, ebb and flow. In the case of the rays, these cycles cover thousands of years and are determined by the Plan of the Logos.

Which ray or rays are manifesting now, and what effect does that have on humanity?

The 7th ray of Ceremonial Order or Ritual is (since 1675) coming into manifestation. The 6th ray of Abstract Idealism or Devotion is (since 1625) gradually passing out. Our present problems are the result of the fact that these two highly potent energies are functioning simultaneously, and in roughly equal potency.

As a consequence, the world is divided politically, economically, religiously and socially into two main groups; and these groups are in confrontation throughout the world. On the one hand, there are the exponents of the 6th-ray approach who, from love of the old forms, are holding on to the outworn structures, fighting a last-ditch stand for their preservation. This group forms the conservative and reactionary forces in all fields throughout the world. The other, the progressive forces, are those who are able to respond to the new incoming 7th-ray energies, who sense the need for the new, more living forms through which the new age civilization can manifest. The most impatient would sweep everything away, the good as well as the bad, and need the restraining hand of Hierarchy to produce ordered change.

Under the divine Plan, each ray prepares the way for its successor. The 7th ray relates spirit to matter, thus synthesizing these opposites. Through its exponents, it will bring into expression, as a physical-plane reality, the ideals and visions of the previous cycles.

Rebirth and Reincarnation

Earlier you mentioned that the goal of human life is to become God-realized. Obviously we don't accomplish this in the span of one lifetime. Do we get another chance at it?

Evolutionary progress is based on the process of rebirth; reincarnation is the method of our evolution of consciousness.

How does it work?

Groups of souls are brought into incarnation through two great Laws: the Law of Rebirth and the Law of Cause and Effect. The dominating law is the Law of Cause and Effect, and this can be seen in a number of ways. Scientifically, you can say it is the Law of Action and Reaction, which are, as you know, opposite and equal. In religious terms it is seen, in the Old Testament, as God demanding "an eye for an eye and a tooth for a tooth" — very rigid and very cold and implacable, and a bit nasty. But in the Christian Gospel, the Christ — as Jesus — called it very simply the process by which you reap what you sow; so simple that people forget it.

Every thought, every action that we have, under this law, sets in motion a cause; we are creating causes all the time. The effects stemming from these causes make our lives, for good or for ill. At this moment, we are making the rest of this life and our next life. We are receiving what is called karma. The Law of Karma is the Law of Cause and Effect. The effects from our previous deeds, good and bad, create the conditions of our life today, and the results of our deeds today create the conditions of the next period of life, either now or when we return in our next body.

The soul magically creates a series of bodies through which it can, eventually, really demonstrate itself as a soul. At that point we are well on the way towards the end of the evolutionary process. It takes hundreds of thousands of incarnations, but once that point is reached and the soul, looking at its reflection (the man or woman in incarnation), sees that it is beginning to respond to its (the soul's) quality and is becoming more divine — more unselfish, more altruistic, more concerned for other people and not just for the satisfaction of its own desires — it stimulates the vehicle and begins a process which ends the evolutionary journey — the process of initiation.

Initiation has been brought into life to speed up the evolutionary process. It is not essential, we could evolve without it, but it would take millions and millions more years to get to the point where we are today. There are five great planetary initiations to perfection.

We tend to associate reincarnation only with Eastern religions. Why didn't it get into Western religion?

It did, but it was pushed out. Jesus taught it, and those around Him took it for granted. There are passages in the Christian Bible where it is quite clear that His disciples understood and accepted reincarnation.

Such as?

Talking about John the Baptist, the disciples asked Jesus: "Who is John? Who is this extraordinary man who is preaching in the wilderness?" And Jesus said: "Don't you remember what I told you? He is Elias come again." Another time, when He healed a man of blindness, they said: "Who sinned, that child or his father, that the child was born blind?" In other words, was it the karma of the father, who from some misdeed in a previous life had to have a child who was blind, or was it the karma, some misdeed, of the child, in a previous life, that required him to be born blind? Many of the early Church Fathers — for example, Origen — taught about reincarnation.

What happened to it?

The Emperor Justinius and his wife did not like it, so they forced the Church Fathers to get rid of it. In the 6th century it was taken out of the Bible, except for these few instances which were overlooked.

But even in the East there is a very uncertain view of reincarnation. Buddhists accept it; Hindus accept it. All the Eastern religions accept reincarnation as a fact. But they see it in a very fatalistic way. If you are born into a very poor family, if you are an 'untouchable' in India, for example, it is because of your misdeeds in a previous life, and there is nothing that can be done about it. You are an untouchable for life, you are poverty-stricken for life, and we will exploit you all the more because you were meant to be poor. So it is as if there should be no change; they accept it totally as a punishment, as the result of misdeeds. It is not punishment. There is no punishment. It is the action of the Law of Cause and Effect; it is impersonal. Social change could end the poverty and suffering irrespective of individual karma.

If we get these repeated chances at life to work our way up the evolutionary ladder, what happens to us in between? What happens to us upon death?

It depends at what point we are in evolution. If we are not very evolved (and the vast majority of humanity is not very evolved), then we quickly come back into incarnation. The great magnet of evolution brings us into incarnation over and over again. Because we have a lot to learn, we need frequent teaching — the experience of life, over and over again, to make any progress at all. If we are rather more evolved, we come into incarnation in groups — family and extended family groups. We have all been mother, father, brother, sister, child, grandfather, etc — in relation to one another — over and over. In this way we create karmic ties. These karmic ties hold the groups together, and they also allow us to work out, in a relatively restricted circle, our karmic debts — until we resolve them. When we learn to be harmless, we overcome karma. There comes a time when the soul is manifesting so powerfully through its reflection, the man or woman in incarnation, that he or she ceases to make too much karma of a negative nature, and becomes more and more harmless. We can see, therefore, the need for harmlessness in all human relationships. By being destructive we create negative karma, which means we have to work it off. We come in with this karma, and all the misfortune of our life, the pain, the suffering, is put down to bad luck. It is not bad luck but the direct result of our karma.

You talked about the soul and the body. What mechanically happens to each of those in between these incarnations? When we die, for example, does the soul go off to one place and the body to another?

Yes, the body returns to dust. Except that one permanent atom of the physical body remains, along with one permanent atom of both the emotional and mental vehicles. Around these three permanent atoms the soul will create the next body — on the physical, the emotional and the mental planes. We come into incarnation at exactly the same level, the same rate of vibration, where we left off, which is that of these three permanent atoms.

But what about in between lifetimes?

That again depends on how advanced we are. If we are not very advanced, we do not have much time out of incarnation. We are in and out rather quickly. If we are rather more advanced we have a relatively longer period in what is called pralaya. Pralaya is something like the Christian idea of paradise. Nothing happens, you do not make any advance, but it is a state of unending bliss which is interrupted from time to time as your 'number' comes up and you are called into incarnation again.

If there is this process of reincarnation and the body, as you say, goes back to dust, what about the different forms of treating the body at death — burial versus cremation?

The only scientific and hygienic way to dispense with the body is cremation, to burn it. Everybody comes into incarnation with a long history of the illnesses of humanity, and some of these go back to the very earliest times. Through the practice of burial, these illnesses, like cancer, syphilis and tuberculosis, are leached out into the earth, enter the food chain and are reabsorbed by animals and humans alike. This has gone on for so many thousands of years that these illnesses are endemic and will take several hundreds of years to overcome completely. Cremation is a first, major step in this process.

We are part of the fifth root race. The first truly human root race was the Lemurian, which lasted about six million years. (There were two earlier races not in dense physical bodies.) That was followed by the Atlantean root race, which lasted about 12 million years. Our root race, the Aryan (nothing to do with Hitler's notion of Aryan man), has been about 100,000 years in the making, so it is in the very early stages. Each root race has the task to perfect one or other body. The Lemurian race had the task of perfecting the physical vehicle. The Atlantean had the task of perfecting the astral-emotional vehicle. It did this so well that it is man's strongest vehicle, and the vast majority of humanity today are still at an Atlantean state of consciousness, 'polarized' on the astral or emotional plane.

The Aryan race, our race, has the task of perfecting the mental vehicle. We are only using the lowest aspect of the mental planes. There are four mental planes, according to esotericism. The highest of these is called the causal plane, on which is found the body of the soul, the causal body. The soul uses the causal body for most of its incarnational experience, up to the fourth initiation, when it is dispensed with. In this way, the races are brought forward, evolve. Each race has seven sub-races; the Europeans and Americans today are the fifth sub-race of the Aryan root race.

Is there another category for people on other continents?

Yes, there are various sub-races. Today, there are people who are really Atlantean in the physical body, like all the Mongolian type peoples — the Chinese, Japanese, American Indians, the Eskimo, South American Indians — these all have Atlantean bodies, but the people in those bodies are, of course, of the Aryan race.

There's a lot of folklore out there, I guess, about what happens to us in reincarnation; for example, do we switch bodies with animals?

No. Transmigration of souls does not happen. The fantasy about reincarnation in the East is that you can do nothing about it; however low in life you are, you just have to accept it; there is no social change to better yourself. In the West, some people believe that you go back and forth between the animal and human kingdoms. You do not. Once you are a human being, you go on being a human being until you become a super-human being, a Master.

But you can come in either as a man, or as a woman.

Everybody has incarnations as both men and women. Not necessarily alternately, you might have two or three incarnations as a man, and then three or four as a woman, then one or two as a man, and so on.

Is there a tendency to come back in certain group relationships?

Indeed. We come into incarnation in groups, and these are usually family groups. There are exceptions, of course; there are always new people coming into the family. In the reincarnational cycle, people come into families who bring in different energy, a different quality, different experience, but then are part of that family, and make karmic ties and undo karmic knots together. The whole thing is about working out, within the family, the knots of karma which we have created by our selfishness, our egotism.

What about reincarnating in different races?

We might be in the same race for a large number of incarnations, or we might have a succession of different experiences over half a dozen races. Or we might be restricted only to one race. We might never incarnate in the East if we are in the West, and never in the West if we are in the East; or we might flip between one and another for many incarnations. It is to do with individual destiny.

So, you can learn the lessons, repeat the experiences or gain the experience you need to reach this point of perfection through different races or racial combinations.

Yes. We are all human beings. We are all God's children; and we all have the same potential.

Why don't we remember our earlier lives?

When we have continuity of consciousness we will remember, but we do not have continuity of consciousness, even from the sleeping to the waking state. We might remember a few dreams, but that is really the activity of the astral-emotional body in shallow sleep. In deep sleep we do not dream at all; it is only as our sleep gets more shallow, as we are emerging out of deep sleep, that we begin to dream, and these dreams we may remember. For the most part we do not remember what happens during deep sleep. Likewise, we do not remember from life to death to life again. Eventually, we will enter the death state completely consciously, know who and what we are and why we are there and what we are doing, and then come back, equally consciously. As you become more advanced in the evolutionary process, this is what happens.

At the end of the evolutionary process, the initiates of the world, who are consciously undergoing the process of evolution, eventually develop continuity of consciousness. They come in because they know the Plan of evolution. They come in to carry out that Plan, and not only because of karmic necessity — although there will be some karmic necessity.

The Law of Cause and Effect

If people understand, and respect, the Law of Cause and Effect, does that mean they can consciously change their future by what they do right now?

Absolutely. That is the essence of it. When you know that every thought and every action creates a reaction which impinges on other people, and of course on yourself, then you see the need for harmlessness. When we really understand this basic law of existence it will transform our world.

So are we the only ones who determine what our karma is going to be?

No, there are four great Lords of Karma — They are not on this planet, not even in this system — Who administer and organize the manifold differentials of this Law of Karma for the 5½ billion people who are in incarnation right now, and the other 55 billion who are not in incarnation. There are about 60 billion souls potentially able to incarnate on this planet. So this is a major work of the Lords of Karma.

So there's a degree to which we can determine the future by changing our thoughts and actions, but you're saying that there are already certain things set in motion for the planet as a whole that — no matter how hard we try — we cannot undo until they are worked out.

The point is that this planet is not very evolved — not even in our solar system. It is still a 'non-sacred' planet; there are seven sacred planets and we are not one of them. That is why we have all the problems. Humanity itself is not at a very evolved stage, in terms of its future evolution. Even our solar system is not all that evolved. It is probably a quite insignificant solar system, at the edge of the galaxy.

Humanity, from its very inception — and this is put at 18½ million years ago in the esoteric teaching — has been creating karma, good and bad. Let me make it clear: according to the esoteric teaching, there is actually more good karma than bad karma, but we only notice the bad karma. When our karma is good, and much of it is good, we just take it as our norm, our right. When it is bad karma we think: "I don't know why I'm suffering this." But of course it is still our karma. This has been going on for 18½ million years, so there is a huge planetary karmic debt. Every human being is involved not only with his or her own karma, individually-created, but also with the karma of the human race as a whole. It is not simple. The Lords of Karma, working from Their unbelievably exalted state of consciousness, can administer not just our individual karma, but our relation to world karma. The Masters act as agents in this respect. A Master can, if He sees fit and the law allows, mitigate the effects of individual karma. It is divine intervention, if you like.

So correct me if I'm wrong, but what you're saying is that, with this world karma, the people who happen to be very fortunate in this life — have all the resources that they need, and who don't pay attention to the problems going on in the rest of the world — ultimately will still have to face them.

Yes, indeed, but that is called complacency. It has nothing to do with karma. Complacency and good karma are two separate things. Nobody is free from the karma of the world. If you live your life, as millions today do, as if the poor did not exist, as if there were no poor nations, as if it was God's gift to the world that the developed world, the G7 nations, should live at the high standard of life that we demand and take for granted as our right, and totally ignore the fact that three-quarters of the world are living in poverty and millions are starving to death in a world of plenty, that is complacency. If we accept that, we are not living in right relationship. The next step forward for the human race is the creation of right human relationships. The Masters say we either do this or we die. We either create right human relationships, or we destroy all life on the planet. That is our choice.

How does free will enter into this set of conditions with reincarnation and the Law of Cause and Effect?
We have limited free will. Our free will goes only so far. Inevitably, the 'cosmic magnet' draws us back into incarnation. Occasionally people write to me and say: "Please, Mr Creme, would you ask your Master to free me from the need to incarnate at all. I don't like it; I don't want it. I want to get out of life altogether. But I know that, if I die, I'll just come back. So is there some law that will cancel the need to reincarnate any more?" Of course there is not; you do not have the free will to do that. When you are in life, you have the free will to continue or to end your own life; everyone has that right. But you cannot do it without some reverse. If you take your own life, you have to come back and face the same situation.

So you don't escape ...
There is no escape until you have learned to be perfect. I do not mean perfect in the religious sense: being 'good' and believing this and not believing that, and doing this and not doing that. I mean being perfect in the sense that the Masters are perfect, which is having complete control of your physical, emotional, mental and spiritual nature.

What's the best way to avoid making bad karma?
Harmlessness. To recognize and accept that harmlessness in relation to others is the key to the evolutionary process. When we really create harmlessness, we create right human relations.

But why harmlessness? Does it have to do with the inner divinity that you talked about?
It is because the nature of divinity is altruism. The ego is the harmful aspect. The ego pertains only to the personality. The

personality needs ego; it needs the desire principle to get to a certain point. If it did not have ego, it would not get to that point; it would not create its individuality; it would be a useless thing for the soul to use. Eventually, a point is reached when the soul can really 'grasp' that powerful, individualized human being, and turn it into a god — which the soul already is. The soul recreates that divinity on the physical plane, as the man or woman, and reflects itself through that. This can only be done when the individual personality reflects the quality of the soul, which is totally altruistic. It is the selfishness, even if, up to a point, a necessary selfishness, which in the end has to be relinquished.

Once a person learns about reincarnation and develops some conviction or comfort level with it, does it have any effect upon their attitude towards death?

Profoundly. If you really believe in reincarnation, if it is part of your consciousness — rather than an idea which you think is reasonable to accept — if you take it quite seriously, it removes the fear of death to a large extent. You may be afraid of the final moments, but the idea of death no longer has the terror that it has for most people who see death as the end of everything and who cannot imagine themselves, this conscious, thinking being, continuing. And yet, after death you have an expansion of consciousness. You are the same being, but your consciousness is immeasurably expanded, because it is freed from the limitations of the physical body. Out of the body, there is freedom and knowledge, joy and experience of love, and you meet again people who had died before you. In fact, it is easier to die than to be born!

I was going to say, it almost sounds like being in incarnation is something of a liability.

It is not a liability but an opportunity for service, for the expansion of our consciousness and the evolution of our being. But to be born is often more fraught with problems and pain than to die.

I have met people who say: "I don't want to come back." They do not want to believe in reincarnation because they do not want to come back and have to do this all over again. Of course we do not do 'this' all over again. We are not the same person because usually we have no memory of ourselves in the previous incarnation. So we do not have all this 'baggage' behind us, thinking: "Well, last time it was much easier," or "I'm all right! Last time was much more difficult." We do not have that sense.

If we do something to set a negative cause into motion, is there any way to mitigate the effects of it?

Yes, you can make restitution, and you can serve to an extent that will counterbalance the effect of that negativity. This is one of the great results of the Law of Service, that it 'burns up' karma.

Looking at karma from a much broader perspective — groups of people, nations, even people of the whole world — are there certain things that we as large groups of people set into motion that affect life on the planet?

Yes indeed, we do this all the time. Governments do it all the time. People like Hitler, for example, set in motion wars which devastate life on the planet for years on end. The events in Bosnia were set in motion by the head of the rebel Serbian groups and the President of Serbia. These two men have an enormous karmic debt to repay to hundreds of thousands of Bosnians and Croatians who have suffered at their hands. Millions starve in the Third World through the actions of the developed nations. Some 40 wars are going on in the world as we speak. These can only continue while the rich nations sell the arms to fight them.

What about altering life on the planet in other ways?

Well, for example, we affect the weather very considerably. Our destructive thoughts affect the elemental forces which govern the climate and weather patterns in the world. If our thoughts are, as they very much are today, in disequilibrium, these elemental forces go out of equilibrium. The result is earthquakes, storms, tornadoes, tremendous floods, and so on, which devastate large areas of the world continuously. This is our own doing. We call them acts of God, but they are really acts of humanity, through its wrong thought and action, setting out of trim the elemental forces. When we eventually come into equilibrium, these forces too will come back into equilibrium, and the climates will return to their normal patterns.

So there are good reasons for right actions?
Goodwill 'pays off'. It is the essential nature of our being to express goodwill. If we express bad will, we reap the karma of that bad will. Goodwill is the lowest aspect of the energy of love that humanity as a whole can demonstrate. It is essential that we grasp this and manifest it as much as we possibly can. Not only that, as I say: to the individual it 'pays off' handsomely.

But it sounds also like it pays off for society and the world at large.
Of course, very much so. Goodwill generates goodwill and is the first step towards manifesting love.

The Plan of Evolution

Where is this plan of evolution going for humanity as a whole? You've talked about what it means in terms of individual perfection. What about the world?
This world is in process of change. It is going through a temporary period of extreme trouble and violence and manifested hatreds. But new energies are pouring into the planet all the time, particularly a great energy from a cosmic Avatar called the Spirit of Peace or Equilibrium. This Avatar works precisely with the Law of Action and Reaction, which we call the Law of Karma. Under this law, action and reaction are opposite and equal. Out of the present violence and discord, hatred and turbulence, we will enter an era of tranquillity and peace, mental and emotional poise, and an established harmony, which will transform the whole world — and in exact proportion to the discord and disharmony of today.

Where did this plan come from? Is there some place or being or level of authority where it says: "This is the plan for humanity, and here's where it's going to end up"?

Essentially, the Plan issues from the Logos of our planet; the Heavenly Man who is ensouling the planet. He reflects Himself as the Lord of the World on a very high etheric centre in the Gobi Desert, called Shamballa. The Plan of God issues from Shamballa. It is brought from Shamballa to the Masters of our Spiritual Hierarchy by the Buddha. The Masters seek to carry out the Plan through humanity. They give aspects of the Plan to Their various initiates and disciples, men and women in the world, to carry out, and so the transformations take place; the Plan works out. The Masters are also the custodians of the spiritual energies entering the planet. They release them in such a way as to further the Plan. Humanity responds to these energies, even though they do not know that they exist. These energies are embodied by certain great ideas which become our ideals. As we put the ideals into effect, the plan of evolution works out, age after age, cycle after cycle.

How do the scriptures of the world figure in this evolutionary plan?

The scriptures relate to it, but they are usually (although not always) given in a more exoteric manner, in a way that can be understood by the least educated, the simplest of humanity, in a very direct way. They have mainly an emotional appeal for the masses. Over and above that emotional appeal is a very mental and spiritually oriented body of teachings given by the Masters specifically for the initiates and the disciples of the world, which acquaints them with the Plan, with their possible part in that Plan, and invites them to take part in the implementation of the Plan.

People seem to argue endlessly about the interpretation of scriptures. How does one know who has got it right?

The scriptures, if taken literally, very often make a kind of nonsense. But understood in their more esoteric meaning, as metaphor and symbol, the scriptures of all religions keep trust with humanity, keep that relationship between what we call God, the Logos of our planet, and His expression, humanity and the lower kingdoms. They keep us informed that there is a relationship, that there is a Plan of evolution, that this is not the end, that we will go on until we create perfection on the planet — perfection being the total working out of the Plan of the Logos, in all of its varied manifestations. Another problem with these ancient scriptures is that they have all, more or less, become distorted in their slow dissemination over the centuries.

I think one thing I had behind that question about scriptures is the sense that this evolution must be happening in certain steps and that each step has some new revelation behind it?

Indeed, there is a continuity of revelation. Some teaching, like that of Christian groups, does in fact state categorically that Jesus came and gave the top teaching, the end of all the teaching, which revealed suddenly the nature of God to humanity. They leave out of the picture this continuity of revelation, which has continued from the very earliest days of humanity's existence on the planet, and will continue until we are perfected. I believe it is a misunderstanding on the part of the Christian groups to assume that kind of superiority vis-à-vis the other religions.

Could you explain something about devas and their evolution? (December 1993)

'Devas' is the Eastern name, the Sanskrit term, for 'Angels'. The Christian and Judaic Bible contains many references to angels and "angelic hosts". Many of the prophets were visited by angels who are seen as messengers or intermediaries, imparting information, or, in the Old Testament, for instance, staying the hand of Abraham as he was about to sacrifice his son Isaac.

The angels, or devas, are a separate evolution from the human, and parallel to it. The modern world largely dismisses the idea of angels as it dismisses the fairy tales of children, but there are devas who are fairies; there are, literally, fairies at the bottom of our gardens. There are many different kinds and categories: elves, goblins, fairies, sprites. They are the sub-human builders on the evolutionary arc. Devas exist on both the involutionary and the evolutionary arc. They are responsible for the creation of the matter of the trees, vegetation, etc. The devas control the forces of climate and weather and inhabit the springs and rivers; all of that is kept moving and in correct relationship in matter by the devic evolution.

It is prophesied in the Christian Bible that when the Christ returns He will be accompanied by "a host of angels"; that is literally true; it has actually taken place. Maitreya is called, both by the Buddha (in His prophecy of the coming of Maitreya Buddha) and by St Paul: "the Teacher alike of angels and of men" (the Buddha said "of devas and of men"). Maitreya is the World Teacher of both humanity and the devic evolution which are immensely varied and numerous.

Humanity is the kingdom through which everything passes. Everything is becoming human, is human or has been human and gone beyond the human. Our physical bodies are created from the life activity of the devas. Our astral-emotional and mental bodies, likewise, result from the activity of devas of these planes.

The soul body, the causal body, is created by devas from the sun — Solar Pitris, as they are called, while the devas of the earth (lunar pitris) create our physical, astral and mental bodies.

Most people cannot see the devas, but very often children do and are told they don't exist. But the fairy tales of the world are the result of the knowledge of their presence in our lives. They do not do all the things they are reported to do in the stories, but without their action there would be no forests, nothing would grow. When we are out of equilibrium our disturbed thought-patterns influence the devic evolution, and so you get distorted patterns of weather, climate and so on. When we come back into a sane evolutionary equilibrium, they will do likewise. The long-term evolutionary plan, millions of years ahead, is for the coming together of the human kingdom and the devic, or angel, evolution, and then will be created "the Divine Hermaphrodite", half human, half angel.

There are, therefore, angels who are sub-human, angels who have been human and have gone beyond the human, and also great angels, 'Archangels', as they are called, very evolved beings like Masters and higher than Masters.

(1) Do devas reach a particular stage in their evolution and then individualize or incarnate as people? (2) Or do you mean that some devas are in effect human because they are our Solar Angels? (March 1996)

All life is in process of becoming human, is human, or has gone beyond the human stage. (1) Yes, if they are sub-human. (2) No. Solar Angels, our souls, incarnate in human bodies. Essentially, they are emanations of the Divine Spark of God.

(1) Have members of the Angelic or Devic evolution developed their own technologies such as achievements in physics, mathematics, etc? (2) Do They use the Technology of Light? (November 1994)

(1) No. (2) No. They evolve through the development of feeling.

Evolution and Initiation

Evolution is a term that most of us tend to associate with Darwin and physical change. In esotericism, are you talking about evolution in a bigger context?

I am talking about the evolution of consciousness. We take for granted that Darwin has shown the evolution of the form aspect of nature, the physical body of the animal kingdom, out of which grew the human kingdom. The human being is not simply an animal but is the point where spirit and matter meet. The individualized human soul has taken incarnation, 18½ million years ago, according to the teaching, to enable a higher aspect to manifest.

Each kingdom grows out of the kingdom below it. First is the mineral kingdom, the densest. From that grew the vegetable kingdom. From the vegetable grew the animal kingdom. From the animal kingdom has grown the human kingdom; we owe our body to the animal kingdom. Out of the human kingdom has been growing another kingdom (which we do not even recognize, unless we are esotericists), which is the spiritual kingdom, made up of the Masters and initiates. The spiritual kingdom, or Kingdom of Souls, is the kingdom immediately above the human kingdom; you enter it through the human kingdom. As you evolve to a point where the soul really begins to demonstrate itself through its reflection, the man or woman on the physical plane, you enter the spiritual kingdom through the 'door' of initiation. There are five doors through which you pass to become a Master. All of the Masters have achieved these five initiations. Eventually everybody will become perfect in that same way.

And what are the five steps?
The first step is the birth of the Christ Principle. The whole thing is re-enacted in the Gospel story, the life of Jesus symbolizing this path of initiation. (Of course, it is much older than Christianity. It is almost as old as humanity itself, and it has been presented to humanity over and over again, in different ways, in the past.) In the gospel story, the birth of Jesus at Bethlehem is the symbol for the first initiation, which is called 'The Birth at Bethlehem', the birth of the Christ in the cave of the heart. That takes the man or woman into the Spiritual Hierarchy for the first time, and demonstrates control over the physical body.

The second initiation is called 'The Baptism', and is symbolized by the baptism of Jesus at Jordan by John the Baptist. This demonstrates control over the emotional-astral vehicle.

The third initiation is called 'The Transfiguration', and is symbolized by the transfiguration of Jesus on the Mount of Olives. For the initiate, this is the culmination of the lower process that integrates the three lower vehicles — physical, astral, and mental. From the Masters' point of view this is really the first initiation, because it is the first soul initiation.

Then you go on to the fourth initiation, which is symbolized by Jesus dying on the cross. It is called 'The Crucifixion'. In the East it is called 'The Great Renunciation', where everything is renounced, even life itself if necessary, to demonstrate the lifting of the initiate out of matter into the radiance of the light of Spirit. Jesus went through it on the cross to demonstrate it for us, physically to set this great experience of renunciation before the world.

This is followed by 'The Resurrection'. The resurrection of the body of Jesus on the third day symbolizes the Resurrection initiation in which the man, now a Master, is freed from the pull of matter for ever. The Master is in a body which is totally resurrected — a body of light. Every initiation confers on the initiate more and more energy of sub-atomic particles. By the time he or she is taking the fourth initiation, three quarters of that body is literally light. It looks perfectly normal, just like anybody else's, but seen occultly, esoterically, it is radiating light; only one quarter of that body's atomic structure is truly atomic, the rest is sub-atomic. This is completed at the fifth initiation. The Master stands free from the physical planet; He no longer has to incarnate; He is now in a body which is totally transfigured and resurrected in the esoteric sense of the word. Many Masters do, in fact, stay on the planet to oversee the evolution of the rest of us, but many go on to higher planets or even out of this system altogether.

What are the prerequisites for beginning the initiatory process?
The soul sees that the person is beginning to reflect its qualities on the physical plane, the emotional-astral plane and the mental plane, and is becoming more altruistic, that its actions are no longer totally governed by his or her personal desires. The personality becomes 'negative' to the soul, and seeks to carry out soul purpose, even though it might not know it is a soul. Then we see a beneficent person who is rather altruistic, who is really looking for, and working towards, the betterment of humanity; he will have some mode of service, and put others, evolution, and society as a whole somewhat higher than his or her own self.

How long does it take to ascend to this point of Mastery, once you begin the process?
It takes hundreds of thousands of incarnations to come to the first initiation. Once that is taken, it can take anything from two to 15 or 18 lives between the first and the second initiation. The average is around six or seven lives. Once the second initiation, which is said to be the most difficult, is taken, showing the control of the astral or emotional elemental which is so powerful

in humanity, the whole thing speeds up, and you could take the third initiation in the same life or the immediate next life, the fourth in the life after that, or even the same life, and the fifth in the life after that, if that is your destiny. There are certain conditions which are too abstruse to go into, but generally speaking the last few incarnations quickly finish the evolutionary process.

And at the finish, a person becomes, as you said, a master of himself, a master over life.

Yes. With consciousness on all planes, and control on all planes, which is another thing altogether. We all have consciousness on the physical plane; it is a reality to us. But few people have control on that plane. There are 5½ billion people in incarnation at the moment, and around 850,000 people in incarnation who have taken the first initiation and therefore demonstrate this control.

That's not a lot.

No, not very many. About 240,000 people in incarnation have taken the second initiation, and about 2,300-2,400 have taken the third initiation. About 450 only, of those in incarnation, have taken the fourth initiation.

How many have taken the fifth?

Connected with the human evolution, there are 63 Masters. But there are many more Masters, Who are working with the sub-human evolutions: the animal, the vegetable and the mineral kingdoms. There are also many Masters involved with the angelic or Deva evolutions, which are vast in numbers.

The Masters of Wisdom

What is the relationship of the Masters to us?

They are our 'elder brothers'. They have gone ahead of us and, having finished the evolutionary journey on which we are still engaged, have taken upon Themselves the responsibility of overseeing our evolution. They know the way, the hazards, the possibilities. They know the steps which are the best to take, because there are many blind alleys, many pitfalls on the path, and They teach the correct way. The correct way is the way of selflessness, lack of ego. This is the hard way. It is slow because we are all so egotistical.

Do any of these Masters have names that we'd recognize?

One of them everybody knows, the Master Jesus. Jesus in Palestine was a very advanced disciple, a fourth-degree initiate, just short of a Master. He took the fourth initiation, the Crucifixion, openly, on the outer plane. Normally you are not expected to die on a cross when you take the fourth initiation. He did that to symbolize for us, dramatically, that great experience of renunciation. He is now a Master, having become a Master in His immediate next life as Apollonius of Tyana, who opened an ashram in north India, where He is buried. From that fact has come the legend that somehow Jesus did not die on the cross, that He was secreted out of Palestine and went to India and is buried there. It was the Being who was Jesus, but in His next incarnation as Apollonius. Jesus is now a very advanced Master. In the seventh to eighth century He went to America and taught the Indian populations, then went out into the Pacific and taught the Polynesians. They all have the legend of a white man who came and taught, and the names are all related to the word 'Jesus'. He taught that another great teacher would come from the East, who would teach the Indians again. So, of course, when the Spaniards came, Cortez and his men, they were welcomed with open arms by Montezuma and his people, who were slaughtered for their efforts, as we know.

You mentioned Jesus. Are there other names that might be familiar?

One, very well known, is the Tibetan Master Djwhal Khul. Between 1919 and 1949, He dictated, by mental telepathy, a series of 19 books through Alice Bailey. (Bailey herself wrote five additional volumes.) These 19 very profound, and to my mind very practical, teachings are the intermediate phase of the teachings given out by the Masters for the new Age of Aquarius now beginning. *The Secret Doctrine* was the preparatory phase of the teachings, given through Madame Helena Petrovna Blavatsky, who lived and worked for some years with a group of Masters in the Himalayas. One of them was the Master Morya, her own Master, and another the Master Koot Hoomi, both very advanced Masters. These two Masters are deeply involved with humanity and, with the Master Jesus, will be the inaugurators of a world religion which eventually will develop: a very scientific religion based on the process of initiation which we have been talking about.

These names you've mentioned of Masters are all men. Are there no women Masters?

There are no Masters in female bodies at the present time. The Masters, in a sense, are neither male nor female. They have brought both of these aspects into total equilibrium. On the soul plane, there is no sex, no male or female. There is simply one energy with two poles: one positive, one negative, as in electricity. They are the same energy in polarity. The Masters are perfected souls, so They have brought both into equilibrium, but when They take a physical body, which not all do (some two-thirds of the Masters today, that is about 40, are in dense physical bodies), They take a male body at this time to anchor powerfully, in the world, the energy with which They are so strongly endowed, the male or spirit aspect, to relate to the much greater matter aspect as it manifests in the world today. This is to do with the point in evolution reached by this planet. In about 350 to 400 years this will change, and then Masters will come in female bodies until there is a balance between Masters in male bodies and Masters in female bodies.

It has nothing to do with any kind of bias against women, or the female aspect. On the contrary, the Masters are the stimulus behind the women's liberation movement. They see it as essential that women take their full place in total equality with men in this new age, the age, as it will come to be known, of Tara, the Mother. The Age of Maitreya is the age in which the Mother aspect manifests. The female is the Mother, the nourishing aspect; it nourishes the child, the family, the civilization. Nations are also male or female, and nations which are female may become the seat of a civilization. And so it is essential that women play their full part with equal status in the life of humanity. In the West this is becoming very largely a fact, but in large areas in the East this is sadly very far from being the case. Women are often seen as little more than chattels. A great change has to take place. That is why the women's liberation movement was inspired by the Masters.

How does a Master's body compare to our physical bodies?

He looks the same — better-looking — but His body is perfect; it is a body of light and He can disappear and appear again at will. He can walk through walls and travel instantaneously by thought.

Disease-free?

Absolutely. They do not die; They do not grow old. A Master can be thousands of years old, in the same body. People will soon see the Master Jesus , Who is in a body over 650 years old. Some are in the bodies in which They became Masters. Others are in bodies which are literally thousands of years old. They do not sleep or eat. They live directly off prana, energy direct from the sun. They are spotless in Their robes or, if They wear Western clothes, very well-cut suits. But they create them by thought.

Where does humanity fit into the overall scheme of Hierarchy?

There are three great centres, and I have mentioned two of them: the centre which I called Shamballa, a great etheric centre in the Gobi Desert. That is the centre where the Will and the Plan — the Plan of evolution — of the ensouling Deity is known. That works out through the agency of the second centre, the Spiritual Hierarchy of Masters and initiates, the centre where the Love of God is expressed. The third centre is humanity itself, the centre where the intelligence of God manifests. They are separate today but, through the evolutionary process, they will be united. Just as the spark of God, the 'Monad' in Theosophical terminology, reflects itself as the soul, which again reflects itself in the human personality, which are both reunited by the evolutionary process, so in the outer scheme of things humanity will unite with Hierarchy. When humanity is ready, when there are enough disciples in the world creating a link with Hierarchy, the centre which we call humanity will be one and the same with the centre where the Love of God is expressed, the Spiritual Hierarchy. That will be united eventually with Shamballa, the centre where the Will of God is known. The Masters are aiming to link up with Shamballa, as we, whether we know it or not, are aiming to unite with Hierarchy. Eventually all three will be linked together, and the evolutionary process will be complete.

Do the Masters work independently or as a group? Do They have a leader? How is Hierarchy structured?

They share a consciousness; They have no separate consciousness as personalities. They can never say 'I', because They have no sense of I. They are a group with group consciousness. At Their head is the Master of all the Masters, whose personal name is Maitreya. He was foretold to come now, by the Buddha: 2,500 years ago Gautama Buddha made a prophecy that at this time would come another great Teacher, a Buddha like Himself, Maitreya by name, who would inspire humanity to create a new and brilliant, golden civilization, based on righteousness and truth. There are 60 Masters, and three Great Lords, as They are called. Maitreya is one of these three. Maitreya holds the office of World Teacher, and embodies the energy we call the Christ Principle or Consciousness, the second aspect of the Christian trinity. Two thousand years ago He overshadowed His disciple Jesus for three years, and Jesus became Jesus the Messiah, or, translated into the Greek, Jesus the Christ. The Christ Himself is Maitreya. His consciousness, from the baptism to the crucifixion, manifested through Jesus and inaugurated the Piscean Age which is now coming to an end. Maitreya has come back into the world now to carry on what He began through Jesus, and will complete in the Age of Aquarius which is now beginning.

You mentioned Maitreya and Jesus. What is their relationship with the other teachers throughout history, like Buddha, Krishna, Mohammed?

Jesus taught through Mohammed. As Maitreya had taught through Him, so He taught through Mohammed. The Buddha taught through the Prince Gautama and Mithra, and Maitreya also taught through Krishna and Shankaracharya at previous times.

The Christ

How would you compare the Christ, as He actually functions, with orthodox religious views?

The orthodox view is that He is the one and only Son of God. Actually, there is no such person; there never has been and never will be such a person. Every single man, woman and child in the world is a son or daughter of God. Every one of us has, in potential, that divinity. There is only one divinity, and we all share it. The only difference between the Christ and ourselves, the Buddha or Krishna and ourselves, is that They have manifested Their divinity. They know that They are Sons of God, and They demonstrate it. We do not know that we are sons of God. We are taught otherwise by the churches: we are taught that we are born in sin and only through the agency of Jesus can we know God.

In fact, God can be known by anyone, moment to moment. You do not have to be a Christian or a Hindu or a Buddhist or a Muslim to know God. You can know God whether you are religious or an atheist, whether you believe in God or not. It has nothing to do with belief, but with direct experience. Because you are God, because you are divine, whatever your belief or non-belief, you can know God as an immediate experience in your life — in the way every child automatically, instinctively, does when it comes into the world, without having heard that it is born into a Christian or a Buddhist or a Muslim or a Hindu family. It is not concerned with that but with its experience.

God is not concerned with whether you are a Buddhist or a Hindu or a Christian. These are temporary manifestations in time

372

and place, and the accident of birth — where you happen to be born. If you are born in the West you are more likely to be Christian. If you are born in the East you are more likely to be Hindu or Buddhist. If you are born in the Middle East, you will probably be Jewish or Muslim. The more fanatical exponents of Christianity, Islam, Hinduism, of Judaism and Buddhism, and so forth, have made these totally artificial separations in the world. This has hindered the evolution of humanity. It holds us back. It prevents the creation of right human relationships. Right relationship is the next step forward for humanity, so anything that holds it back is not something to be welcomed.

You mentioned the "next step forward for humanity". Does that have something to do with why Maitreya is here now?

Yes, very much so. It is a new age that we are entering, the Age of Aquarius, and of course this is an astronomical, not an astrological event. It is to do with the relationship now being formed in cosmos between our solar system and the constellation of Aquarius. For the next 2,500 or so years we will be absorbing the cosmic energy of Aquarius, which will transform all life on the planet. It is a synthesizing energy: it draws together, fuses and blends, while the energy of Pisces, the Age now ending, has separated and divided the world. This process will go forward for 2,500 years and, gradually, humanity will understand the reality of its spiritual nature.

This has enabled the Masters to begin to come into the world. It is due to the fact that so many disciples are nearing the first initiation, and therefore entering the Hierarchy, that sets up a magnetic pull, a conduit, through which the Masters are magnetically drawn into the world. They have been ready to do this for over 500 years; the only question has been when would it be possible. It was thought probable that it would be another 12 or 13 hundred years. But in 1945, at the end of the war, Maitreya announced His intention to return at the earliest moment and to bring His group, the Masters, into the world with Him. That is what is happening now.

It's an incredible thing to imagine teachers like this, not just one but many, being among us. Why are They all coming out at this point?

We have reached the end of the age, an age in which humanity has become so divided but has taken a big step forward. We have developed individuality; we have an idealism which, correctly developed, can take us far forward in evolution. Also, as I said, so many have become disciples and are drawing the Hierarchy into the world. But essentially, They have come to an end of a cycle in Their own evolution, quite apart from the human, which requires Their return to the world. Each Master has done this individually, but now They must show, in group formation, Their ability to function simultaneously on all planes, from the dense physical to the highest spiritual.

If the wisdom of the ages will no longer need to be interpreted through various people, what becomes of religions?

They will go on, but purified. It is obvious that, with the return of the Masters to the world, a transformation in consciousness is taking place and will continue to take place. The emphasis of religions will change. Essentially they are nurturing stations, to keep alive the reality of the spiritual behind everyday life, and to protect young souls, so that they are kept on a spiritual path. They allow, in that way, a measure of control and of self-regulation of individuals who can, having established that discipline in their own lives, enter the esoteric path and continue their evolution more consciously, as disciples.

Will there be new religious forms or structures?

The Master Djwhal Khul, who gave the teachings through Alice Bailey, has predicted a future world religion which will be very scientific. It will be based on the esoteric process of evolution, of initiation as central to that path, and the first two initiations will become the goal for the mass of humanity. There will be special schools in which preparation for initiation will be made — it is not something you can teach — which will enable people to take the first and second initiations. Maitreya is the initiator at the first two initiations, and will go around the world initiating hundreds of thousands of people into this deeper aspect of our life. Every initiation confers on the initiate a deeper insight into the mind of the creating Logos, so that you become aware of more and more of the Plan of evolution. If you are aware of the Plan, and of your part in that Plan, you can act much more consciously and, therefore, much more effectively. And so the service aspect of the disciple is reinforced.

The Antichrist

If Maitreya is the Christ, then who or what is the Antichrist?

There is a tremendous misunderstanding about the Antichrist, certainly among Christian groups. They expect the Christ "at the end of the world". Actually, He came at the end of the age, not the end of the world. At the end of the world, when the whole world is disintegrating, they expect Him to come down on a cloud into Jerusalem. They think He is sitting up in 'heaven', but the Christ has been no nearer heaven than the high Himalayas, 17,500 feet up, for the last thousands of years. And it is from there that He comes into the world, not from this mythical heaven. Heaven is a state of being. The Kingdom of Heaven is within, as Jesus Himself taught. It is the Spiritual Hierarchy, of which He is a member.

The Antichrist is not a man, as Christians believe, who will come out before the Christ, and could even be mistaken for the Christ. The idea comes from the Revelation of St John: the Beast, 666, is unchained for a time, and then chained down for a time and half a time. This refers to the release of the energy we call the Antichrist. It is not a man but an energy, a destructive force which is deliberately released to break down the old order, the old civilization. It was released in John's own day, through the Emperor Nero, to bring about the end of the Roman dispensation, to prepare the way for Christendom. It was released again in our time through Hitler, a group of equally evil men around him in Nazi Germany, together with a group of militarists in Japan and a further group around Mussolini in Italy. These three groups, the Axis powers in the war from 1939 to 1945, embodied the energy we call the Antichrist. That destructive force was released to prepare the way for the return of the Christ to the world now. And it was, indeed, in June 1945, precisely at the end of the war, that Maitreya announced His intention to return at the earliest possible moment, and this time to bring His group, the Masters of the Spiritual Hierarchy, back into the world — in Their case for the first time in some 95,000 years.

The Antichrist is behind us; it has done its destructive work; it has gone. Now it has to be "chained down for a time and half a time". This means sealed off to its own domain for the Age of Aquarius — that is "the time" — and half the following age, the Age of Capricorn, when it will be released again. In the middle of the Age of Capricorn the 'Beast' will be released once more, there will be another great war, this time fought out on the mental planes. That will be the third phase of the manifestation of the Antichrist. It was the war between the forces of light and the forces of evil, as we call them (the forces of materiality as they are called by the Masters), which destroyed the ancient Atlantean civilization some 100,000 years ago. For the last 100,000 years that war has been waged on the astral planes. It was precipitated onto the physical plane in 1939 by Hitler and his group, along with the Italians and the Japanese groups, thus manifesting, for this time, the Antichrist. Now it has to be sealed off to its own domain.

The forces of materiality have a role to play: the upholding of the matter aspect of the planet. If they would do only that, there would be no evil involved. But they do not restrict their activity to the involutionary arc, which is their natural sphere of activity. Their work overflows onto the evolutionary arc, where we are, and is inimical to our spiritual progress; it has, therefore, to be countered. The Antichrist forces are sealed off to their own domain by lifting humanity above the level where they can be used, contacted, influenced, by these materialistic forces. That is the work of the Christ and the Masters in the Age of Aquarius which is now beginning.

In popular culture, and certainly to a degree in religions, the Antichrist, Satan, Lucifer, are personified. It makes for great drama, of course. But what is the esoteric view of Satan, Lucifer?

Satan is what we call the Antichrist. I just mentioned the forces of materiality. These have the role of upholding the matter of the planet.

Lucifer is seen by Christian groups as the devil. It is nothing of the kind! Lucifer is really the name of the great angel who ensouls the human kingdom. Every human soul is an individualized part of one great Oversoul. The name of that great Oversoul, which is divine, is Lucifer.

So who is the devil?

There is not an individual who is the devil. You could say the opposite of good is the devil, and that is in every one of us. It is just the selfish, greedy personality expression of individuals. But in esoteric terms, deeply, profoundly, the devil, or the forces of evil, or the forces of materiality, have the role of looking after the fires of the planet. This planet is a living, breathing entity. These fires are controlled scientifically, otherwise they would explode and the planet would be destroyed. The whole thing works under law. The Lords of Materiality, having the role of upholding the matter of the planet, work with the sub-human devic evolution, the elementals on the involutionary arc, to carry out that work. They are not content with that but overflow onto the evolutionary arc, and that is where the evil comes in.

So, does Hierarchy have to deal with them?

They have to deal with them, and They do deal with them by protecting humanity from too great an overflow of evil, which we could not handle. We are well protected.

From the standpoint of a benign and purposeful creation, why do bad things exist? Why does danger and evil exist in the planet, outside the human race? (April 1996)

What exists is perfection and imperfection. Evil is the manifestation of that aspect of creation which is not yet perfect. But all is moving towards perfection.

The Earth is not a very evolved planet; there are planets which are far more evolved in our own solar system — for example, Venus, Jupiter, Mercury, Vulcan, Saturn, Uranus, Neptune. Each planet has what is called a "round", an incarnational experience, rather like the human incarnational experience (only much longer) and incarnates seven times. Our planet is in the middle of the fourth incarnation, or round, so we are only half way to perfection. If we were evolved enough to live on Venus, for example, we would have no evil; we would be aware of cosmic evil and be able to counter it, but there would be no manifestation of evil on our planet.

The Masters are aware of cosmic evil and They counter it, but the planet itself, being imperfect, naturally is able to demonstrate aspects of that evil. Every human being is evolving, from the lowest to the highest. We are spiritual Beings, literally gods, who reflect themselves on the soul-plane as the human soul, which acts as an intermediary between that divinity and the personality on the physical plane. For as long as is needed, the soul acts in this way, and gradually more and more of the soul's divinity demonstrates through the man or woman. Until it does so perfectly, that man or woman will still demonstrate what you have called "badness", or imperfection.

At what time did the world go astray? (December 1994)

The world "went astray" during the time of Atlantis. There was a point about 95,000–100,000 years ago, towards the end of the 12-million-year-long Atlantean civilization, when a series of wars developed between the Hierarchy of Light (the Masters of Wisdom) and the Lords of Materiality, or the "forces of evil" as we call them. Each sought to work with humanity — the one for good, along the evolutionary line, and the other to enthrall and imprison humanity. That war culminated in the destruction of the Atlantean civilization and a large part of the Atlantean continent which went under the ocean (the Atlantic Ocean is named after Atlantis).

That war continued on the astral-emotional planes until Hitler and his groups in Germany, Japan and Italy precipitated it onto the physical plane in 1939 (it actually began in 1914, went underground in 1918 and came above ground again in 1939). This war ended in the defeat, but not the destruction, of the forces of materiality in the overcoming of the Axis powers by the Allies in 1945.

Do the Lords of Materiality ever assume human form? (December 1994)

No, but they do manifest through humans — one very well-known example of this was Adolf Hitler. He was literally obsessed by two of these beings, of which there are 12 — six in the occident and six in the orient. Through him they precipitated the War — from 1939 to 1945 — onto the physical plane, a war — between the forces of light and the forces of darkness — which had been waged on the astral planes since Atlantean times.

The Master DK predicts, through Alice Bailey, that there will occur the true Armageddon, in the middle of the Age of Capricorn, which will be worse than the world war we have known this century. (1) Will this war be fought at physical level? (2) If not, what form will it take? (3) Will the Beast, the Lords of Matter, be released back into interchange with humanity at that time? I know it's a long time away from now, but perhaps it's best to be prepared for the issues involved? (January/February 1995)

(1) No. (2) It will take place on mental levels. (3) That is not really the way to describe the situation then. The energy of the Lords of Matter, the involutionary force (the energy of the Antichrist as we call it) will be released once again. The war will end in the complete destruction of the forces of evil on this planet.

If evil is going to be eliminated from the planet in 3,000-4,000 years — and this is truly known so far in advance — what is the purpose of requiring us to work to achieve this? (April 1993)

Because it would not be eliminated if we did not change. The process is one of restricting the activity and influence of the forces of evil — the Lords of Materiality — to their own domain: upholding the matter aspect of the planet. This is achieved by lifting humanity — spiritually — above the level where they can be used and influenced by these forces. This requires that we work on ourselves to heighten our consciousness. Otherwise the situation would remain the same; there would be no evolution.

The Origin of Man

How did this get so misinterpreted?

Because of the symbolic nature of its presentation in the Bible story of Adam and Eve. Early animal man, not quite truly human, but no longer simply animal, had reached a certain point in his evolution, with a strong, co-ordinated physical body, a sentient or feeling astral body, and the germ of mind, an incipient mind that would later form the nucleus of a mental body. When that point was reached 18½ million years ago, the human souls, waiting on the soul plane for just this moment in evolution, incarnated for the first time in these early animal men. That is the 'fall from paradise' of Adam and Eve.

It was a metaphor.

Indeed. The whole thing is a metaphor. It was not a fall from grace but a deliberate part of the Plan of evolution, that the human souls had to give up 'paradise', living in pralaya, a wonderful paradisaical state of endless bliss, and "eat of the fruit of the tree of knowledge" — take incarnation on the physical plane in these as-yet-animal men. That is what happened, and that has been misinterpreted as a fall from grace: that Lucifer was a great angel but he rebelled against God and thought he was as good as God, and so was put out of heaven. It is a story, only a story, and totally misinterpreted. It is really the story of the incarnation of the human evolution.

Meditation and Service

Is there anything we can do as individuals to help us move through evolution faster?

Evolution is speeded up through meditation and service. These are the two levers of the evolutionary process. Nothing moves you forward faster than correct, scientific meditation and powerful, altruistic service to the world.

The soul comes into incarnation in the first place to serve the Plan of evolution. It is aware of the Plan of the Logos of the planet and it seeks in every way to carry out that Plan. The major aspect of that Plan is the spiritualization of matter, which the soul does by entering into incarnation. On its own plane, the soul is perfect, but in incarnation it has to go through all the limitations of our miserable lives: the selfishness and greed, the misshapen thoughts that we project around us that create the Bosnias, the Rwandas and other terrible situations in Africa — starving millions in a world of plenty.

What does meditation do that propels a person forward?
It co-ordinates the vehicles and it brings one into contact with the soul. Meditation is a method, more or less scientific depending on the meditation, of bringing a person into contact with his or her own soul; and eventually into total at-one-ment with the soul. It is given for this purpose. Once that is established, the person uses meditation as a means of going higher and deeper into the nature of the soul, because the soul is really threefold. It is a reflection of the spark of God, which has three aspects: atma, buddhi and manas. The manasic focuses the Intelligence aspect; the buddhic focuses the Love-Wisdom aspect; and the atmic focuses the Will aspect. Gradually, through meditation and service, the Intelligence, the Love-Wisdom, and finally the Will of God is contacted and known, and becomes part of the nature of the disciple.

What is the difference between meditation and prayer?
Prayer is often a largely emotional supplication for help, but at its highest is a heart communion with deity. Meditation is the method, more or less scientific, of contacting the soul and achieving union with the soul. There is no emotion involved. Prayer eventually will change and become invocation. God will be seen as consciousness, demonstrating as energy, which can be

invoked. This will be central to a new, world religion, which the Master Djwhal Khul said will gradually evolve. People will move away from strictly emotional appealing, into the scientific invocation of what we know to be God: the energies, the spiritual nature of God, which is then demonstrated in the world.

You yourself have brought something into the world known as Transmission Meditation, which you have said is meditation and service combined. How so?

My Master introduced Transmission Meditation in March 1974 when the first group was set up in London. There are now hundreds of groups all over the world. It is designed to give to the modern, busy, active disciple a field of both service and meditation which, in its effect on the world, is very powerful.

How does it work?

The Masters are the custodians of all the energies entering the planet. Many of these energies are cosmic and, if sent directly into the world, would be too high and would simply bounce off the mass of people. So Transmission Meditation groups have been set up through whom the energies can be stepped down. The energies are sent through the chakras, the force centres, in the spine of the individuals in the group. This automatically transforms the energy to a level where it can be readily absorbed by humanity. These are the great transforming energies which change the world as humanity responds to them.

The work is done in such a way as to give the disciples a field of service — powerful, effective — but requiring very little time and energy; and at the same time it stimulates the evolution of the disciples. It is not possible to have these powerful cosmic and solar energies scientifically transmitted through one without the chakras being galvanized. So that when you enter a Transmission Meditation group you are entering a kind of hothouse, a forcing process, which speeds up the evolution of the individuals concerned.

Spirituality

Some people would say that intelligence is not expressing itself very well through humanity.

It is not lack of intelligence but a lack of spiritual will. We have great ideals, but we tend to think that having the ideal is enough, that somehow it will implement itself. We have to do it. What is needed is applied, practical spirituality. For the last 2,000 years we have had many ideals: of brotherhood and sisterhood, a recognition that we are all God's children, a desire for peace on earth, goodwill to all men, and so on. We enunciate it every Christmas, once a year, and repeat it at Easter, perhaps. But in fact, in our day-to-day lives, we are as corrupt as we can be. This is because we have only a notion of spirituality. The religious groups are largely to blame for this. Their task has been to teach and to heal. They have taught, to my mind, very badly, and healed practically not at all. And this has separated humanity from its own spiritual nature. The Master Djwhal Khul says categorically that one of the greatest triumphs for the forces of evil, the forces of materiality, is the fact that the religious groups have monopolized the idea of spirituality: whatever is religious is automatically spiritual (whether in fact it is or not) and everything else can be as corrupt as we like. Business is corrupt; politics is corrupt; economic systems are corrupt. But religion is thought to be exempt from this corruption; that is 'spiritual'. We have to understand that the word spiritual means the active betterment of life for all people, for most people. Spiritual is anything which brings a man or woman to a higher state of life, whether that is on the physical, the emotional-astral, the mental, or on the spiritual or soul plane. Anything which is towards the betterment of humanity is fundamentally spiritual; it is not only a religious thing. The religious path is only one path. So we have to create structures — political, economic, and social — which are fundamentally spiritual in intent.

So would you say that the essential role of all religions is to teach right living, as opposed to deifying some figure?

Absolutely. That is what the central teaching of the great Teachers has been. Every Teacher has come, given His teaching to a small group, then has apparently disappeared from the planet. He has been put up in heaven, or nirvana, well out of the way, separated from humanity, and that has left us under the control of the priests. They have interpreted (or misinterpreted) the teaching to keep themselves in power, for the most part. They are the interpreters, they are the link between man and God. Well, man does not need these links. Man has God within him. The church leaders have always taught that God is 'up there', and you must watch what you say and do because God is listening. Whereas, in fact, the God within is the God that really counts, the God who is taking you forward on the path of evolution, and which you have to learn to demonstrate in Its real nature, which is altruism, love, generosity, caring, and so on.

How does one cultivate spirituality?

Maitreya says to cultivate three things: honesty of mind, sincerity of spirit, and detachment. These sound easy, but they are very difficult, otherwise we would all do them, of course. We all think one thing, say something else, and do something else again; we have little honesty of mind. We have to inculcate, and practise, honesty of mind. This allows us to become detached. Practise detachment and that allows us to have honesty of mind. It also involves sincerity of spirit. Hardly anybody is who they really are. We imitate all the time. We want people to think that we are this rather than that, that we are nice, that we are good, that we are honest, that we are whatever ideals we seek to present to the world. It is rare to find people who sincerely and honestly are who they are. This produces a state of speaking from the heart and, in this way, the spiritual nature of a person can be conveyed to somebody else, and they can respond. It is a 'heart to heart' relationship which you seek to establish. Then you are who you are. It is like registering and expressing your own identity, sincerely and totally. Again, this produces detachment. These three work together: detachment produces honesty and sincerity, which produce more and more detachment. Maitreya says: "The Self alone matters" (the Self meaning the divine aspect, the Lord). "You are that Self, an immortal Being." And, He says, our pain, our suffering, our problems, are due to the fact that we identify with everything and anything other than that Self. He says, ask yourself: "Who am I?" If you do so, you will find you are identified with this physical body, which lasts only for one life at a time and is renewed successively, so it cannot be the eternal Self.

Or you identify with your emotions, your feelings, your energy sensations, which are transient — one day you feel one thing, another day you feel another. They are not the Self. Or you identify with the constructions of the mind, with your beliefs, ideology, whether you are Christian or Buddhist or Hindu or whatever, and with all the traditions that go with that. It does not matter to the Self for one instant whether you are a Christian or a Buddhist or a Muslim or a Hindu, or of no religion at all; what matters is that you register yourself as the Self, that you identify with the Self, which is the same as God. Self-realization is God-realization. If you practise right identification and detachment, you come inevitably to Self-awareness, which leads to Self-realization. It is not a belief, not a religion, not an ideology, but something which benefits all people and is, in fact, the goal of all life.

You say people also develop spiritually through service. Is there a right form of service that people should look for?

The right form of service is that which you can do to your utmost at the given moment. Of course there are different levels of service. Mother Teresa serves day in and day out, helping the poor and dying in Calcutta and elsewhere; others serve as prime ministers and presidents of great nations, either well or badly, but they serve; others serve as religious advisers, as counsellors; others serve as teachers, as artists, and so on. There are many forms of service, but they are all to do with altruism. Service is not service unless it is altruistically undertaken.

Future Changes

Tell me a little bit about what changes you see ahead of us, and how they're going to be brought about.

There will be a new technology called the 'technology of light'. We will begin to use light directly from the sun. All forms of power used today will become obsolete. This new energy will supply every energetic need of humanity. And, of course, it cannot be cornered by any individuals or groups. It is everywhere, free to all, and is endless in its ramifications. It will also have medical applications in connection with a more advanced aspect of the genetic engineering in which humanity is already engaged. Whole organs will be recreated. Instead of having heart, liver, kidney transplants, you will simply go to a clinic for a few hours and, with this genetic engineering technique and the technology of light, a new organ will be built into the body without surgery. I do not know how many times, but perhaps once or twice per life.

Transport will become so apparently motionless, so silent, vibrationless, that fatigue will disappear, and we will be able to go on long journeys without feeling tired.

Also, a time is coming when humanity, just by thought, as the Masters do now, will be able to place themselves anywhere in the world. So if you want to go to Australia, think yourself there and back again.

Do we have to do something to deserve all this?

We have to become decent human beings and recognize that we are one, brothers and sisters of one humanity, and therefore that the food, the raw materials, the energy, the scientific knowledge, the technology, the educational systems, the health care of the world, belong to everybody, and must be redistributed more equitably around the world: so that we create the reality of the one humanity, the brotherhood of man. And, in this way, we will create the right conditions to deserve all these technological advances.

CHAPTER 5

ARTISTS AND THEIR RAYS

The following article is an edited version of lectures given by Benjamin Creme in San Francisco, USA, and Ubbergen, Holland in 1986. During the lectures, Mr Creme showed slides of the various paintings discussed. Unfortunately, we are not able to reproduce these slides in this book. However, we hope that readers will find value in this unique commentary on the work of some of the world's greatest artists, given by another artist, Benjamin Creme.

This article is about painting, but from an unusual standpoint. I will discuss certain painters, all of them famous old masters, from the point of view of their ray structures. Readers might then get an insight into the role played by the rays in the style and quality of particular painters. There is another reason for choosing these particular painters: they are, without exception, now Masters, not necessarily working in this world on the physical plane, but on higher levels.

At the time they were working, the painters we will discuss were inspired by Masters. When we talk about initiates of their level, we literally mean inspired by their Master. Not in a vague way, but inspiration as meaning a particular relationship between disciple and Master. It is the term for the end-stage of that relationship. Initially, the disciple is held at a distance and never really allowed to come close, "the chelah on the thread" as it is called. The disciple is gradually brought closer until he is within the Master's aura. He is brought closer still until the "blending of the lights" occurs: the Master's and the disciples mind are as one. Whatever the Master needs the disciple to know, he instantaneously knows. There is a blending of the light of the two minds. That is where inspiration takes place. It is the result of overshadowing to the point of inspiration where the Master is really working through the disciple. The stages leading up to this relationship involve simply mental impression.

The Master DK has written (through Alice Bailey) that artists are to be found on all the rays but that the combination of 7th and 4th ray makes for the highest type of artist. Those who have studied the list of over 600 initiates in *Maitreya's Mission, Volume One,* will find, almost without exception, that the rays 4 and 7 are outstanding in the ray structures of all the painters.

It is interesting also, when looking at these painters, to note the influence on their work of the rays of the nations in which they were born. The rays of the nation always influence the work of an artist or musician, whatever their individual rays might be. Remember also that it is not the rays themselves which make someone great or small, it is the point in evolution which is relevant, and the consequent use of the rays.

CIMABUE (1240-1302)

For his time, Cimabue was very advanced: 2.35 degrees initiate. Today, that would be the equivalent of an advanced working disciple — someone like a top statesman with a large group of people working under him.

Cimabue's ray structure was interesting:

	Soul	Personality	Mental	Astral	Physical
Rays	6	6	4	6	7
Sub-rays		6	4	2	7

He had a 6th-ray soul which was common in the 13th century among initiates. A great many Italian painters have 6th and 4th rays prominently in their make-up. What one has to remember in the case of initiates is that they represent the soul aspect of their country, in this case the 6th ray of idealism and devotion. The masses as a whole express the personality ray, which with Italy is the 4th.

Although he was working away from it, Cimabue was influenced by the Byzantine tradition: highly stylized, unrealistic, almost no perspective; one can just see the beginning of perspective in some of his work. There are four 6th rays in Cimabue's structure and if that doesn't make one a devotee, nothing on earth will! Together with a large number of 6th rays (which give Cimabue's painting its particular devotional quality) he also has two 4th rays and two 7th rays, which make him one of the highest types of artist.

The quality of devotion is obvious in his paintings, for example, of the Madonna and Child — they are really icons, visions of a divine, and very abstract, idea of the Virgin with the child usually surrounded by angels. They are more objects of worship than paintings simply to be looked at, and, of course, they were originally painted for churches. Even today, in Greek and Russian Orthodox churches, the icon is carried round for the people to kiss. It is believed to be charged with divine energy because it is the image of a divine being. Exactly the same thing would be expected of a Cimabue painting — an icon radiating divine energy into the church and focusing the aspiration of the people. Only a 6th-ray, devotional, painter could express the particular abstract idealism which his paintings demonstrate. Cimabue is now a highly evolved (sixth-degree) Master, an ascended Master. He works on one of the seven higher globes of this earth.

No reproduction can give adequate expression of the extraordinary power of Cimabue's paintings. The power comes partly from their size, but also from the intense concentration of 6th-ray energy so that the whole picture radiates the devotional worship characteristic of this great initiate.

GIOTTO (1267-1337)

Giotto was the major pupil of Cimabue, whose work overlapped from the 13th to the 14th century. One being the teacher of the other, there is a stylistic resemblance, reflecting the same artistic conventions typical of the time in which they both lived.

Giotto had almost identical rays to his teacher (but in different positions) and this, of course, is what drew them together. Looking at their paintings, we might see that this different positioning of the rays accounts for the differences in the quality, feeling and flavour of their work.

Giotto's ray structure is as follows:

	Soul	Personality	Mental	Astral	Physical
Rays	*6*	*4*	*6*	*2*	*7*
Sub-rays		*4*	*6*	*4*	*7*

Cimabue's paintings are large, abstract, remote and powerfully devotional. Giotto's are devotional, not so abstract, and they have the beginnings in art of a humanistic radiance which is more immediate, much less remote. Giotto was 2.4 degrees initiate, again almost the same as Cimabue, and he is now also a sixth-degree initiate.

Instead of Cimabue's double 6 personality, here we have the required (double) 4s of the painter. With Giotto, although he was still closely tied to the Italian 'primitive' style from Byzantium, we have a much more humanistic and narrational style — he is telling a story. Giotto's double 4th-ray personality makes him need to communicate, to express his awareness, in this case, of the Christian story and ideas. As his work evolved it became more and more humanistic and less abstract. He is the great forerunner of the humanistic art to come.

REMBRANDT (1606-1669)

Rembrandt van Rijn is one of the best-known Dutchmen of all time. He was a third-degree initiate working from 1606 to 1669. He came in as a second-degree initiate and ended up with both feet on the third rung of Hierarchy. His ray structure was as follows:

	Soul	Personality	Mental	Astral	Physical
Rays	*2*	*4*	*3*	*4*	*7*
Sub-rays		*6*	*1*	*4*	*3*

Rembrandt had one 7th ray and three 4th rays. A preponderence of 4th rays goes with a love of colour as well as a desire to communicate with and move out towards the audience. The 4th ray confers radiance, the beauty of colour and light in a painter, or melody in a musician. The 7th ray, on the other hand, gives the artist an ability to draw, to design, to organize the architecture of the work.

Rembrandt very quickly became fashionable when he went to Amsterdam from Leiden where he was born. During a later period of his life, Rembrandt became bankrupt, mainly through his own extravagance (probably as a result of the three 4th rays in his make-up). Add to this his acquisitive, 3rd-ray mental and he could not help but collect things. At this time, his marvellous collection of paintings, jewels, swords, armour and precious costumes were publicly sold for a pittance. He had to leave his big, beautiful house in the fashionable part of Amsterdam and go to a very poor quarter. His original, fine house is now open to view.

He dressed his subjects in oriental costumes, weapons and armour to give a rich, romantic and mysterious radiance to his paintings. At the same time he was a very down-to-earth Dutchman with a passion for reality. His art is the synthesis of a tremendous attraction to reality, with a need to draw things as they really were, and a desire for the exotic, the dramatic, the radiant, the unusual and the mysterious. As a third-degree initiate these were qualities he saw in the world of meaning. His 2nd-ray soul was really dominating other aspects of his nature. The essence of the 2nd ray in its highest expression is the quality of magnetic love which draws everything to itself, creating a unifying synthesis. This enabled Rembrandt to synthesize all the disparate qualities in his own make-up: realism, romanticism, religious devotion, drama. I see this as one of the major reasons why Rembrandt has become a symbol to all people everywhere of the great artist. People always recognize the quality of love which draws them magnetically.

Rembrandt painted many self-portraits. This was not out of vanity; he saw them as a way of gaining insight into what made him 'tick', and as a measure of the passage of life in time. In his mature work, the empathetic quality of love and ability to identify with the other is exemplified in all his paintings. The third-degree initiate is already a God-expressing individual. The soul is infusing the personality and this can be seen in the self-portrait which is in the Frick collection in New York. It is a very mature painting, done about 1658. Here is a man who has just been made bankrupt, who has lost everything: his reputation, his possessions, his house, and who died later in poverty, buried in a pauper's grave. What does the portrait show? We see a man of extraordinary power, resilience and nobility. He expresses a quiet calm and self-esteem which is the hallmark of someone who knows who he is, what he is doing, where he comes from, without any outer show. It is a very simple pose, with Rembrandt sitting in a chair holding a stick and looking straight out quietly, impassively, at the spectator, allowing who and what he *is* to demonstrate.

He seemed to have the ability to see into the hearts of his sitters. Rembrandt could paint a beggar and make him look like a saint. Not by idealizing, but, maintaining full realism, by conferring on his subjects without exception his own beautiful, loving, 2nd-ray soul-nature. *The Jewish Bride*, in Amsterdam, is arguably one of the greatest demonstrations of tender love in all painting. There is no way one can learn to paint anatomy as such an articulate vehicle of emotion as in the extraordinary tenderness conveyed here. Only a few painters have this capacity to paint reality as if it were actually happening — it is in the imagination and not in the eye. Perhaps he did not deliberately set out to create a painting full of love and tenderness. He probably got totally involved in the technical problems of realizing the inner vision of his 2nd-ray soul.

His colour in his mature style is extremely restricted, selected from a narrow range of browns and yellows with touches of red and gold. Yet despite using very simple colours he could achieve a radiance in all his work. In fact, with three 4th rays in his make-up, he could not help being a marvellous colourist.

In *The Night Watch*, again in Amsterdam, we have the feeling of communication: that something dramatic is happening before our very eyes. This scene of a company of guards painted as a group portrait was very popular in Rembrandt's day. The only other Dutch painter who could do anything at all with the subject was Frans Hals, who did it several times and rather well. But the conventions prevailing at the time were for such a group portrait to consist of an inert line of figures which was boring in the extreme. Rembrandt, tackling this subject, sees it as a dramatic event but also as an entirely realistic everyday occurrence.

The painting shows the end of a night watch as the company of guards emerges into the morning sun. The light is used to highlight the faces in a natural but highly dramatic, effective and lively way. The naturalness of the scene is accentuated by extraneous figures moving through the group, such as a girl on her way to market, a little dog exploring, etc. It was probably the most ambitious painting in size and scope that Rembrandt had painted up to that time, but it began his downfall among his contemporaries and from then his popularity waned. As his painting got better and better, he got poorer and poorer — so much for the Dutch public of his day and their taste in art!

Rembrandt had a 7th-ray brain and this is demonstrated in the complex composition. It looks entirely naturally done with each figure standing happily and logically in its space; yet the composition is highly contrived and carefully designed.

Probably the outstanding quality of Rembrandt is his ability to confer a sense of unity. There is a picture in London's National Gallery of a woman bathing. It illustrates again, despite the use of a very narrow colour range, his wonderful 4th-ray radiant colour sense — golds, reds, whites and cool flesh colour. Inherent in the pose of the figure is the 2nd-ray modesty of approach, calm harmony with a sweetness of gesture.

There is a beautiful portrait of the Christ by Rembrandt in Munich. It was probably sat for by the man next door who was no nearer to being the Christ than you or I. Yet Rembrandt, with his 2nd-ray soul empathy, was able to confer on him an extraordinary nobility of character and tragic beauty — the kind of thing one would associate with an initiate like the Christ. With the insight of a high initiate himself, Rembrandt is always looking at the world of meaning through his 2nd-ray soul's love, tenderness and patience.

LEONARDO DA VINCI (1452-1519)

Leonardo da Vinci was, by any measurement, an extraordinary man. He was a painter, sculptor, architect, natural scientist, military inventor — the epitome of the Renaissance man. He had an enormous influence on his time. He invented the mortar which is used so extensively in warfare today, and a very nasty catapult. He was engaged by the authorities of Florence to design the fortifications and ensure the freedom of the city state. Needless to say, he had travelled a little way along the initiatory path and was the most advanced of all the painters we know — 4.4 degrees initiate. Five degrees makes you a Master, and so he was all but a Master.

What we are seeing in Leonardo is the detachment of the fourth-degree initiate, who is really totally detached from the world, who is dissecting cadavers to see the formation of the inside of the body for science. He spent hundreds of hours in his cellar cutting up bodies and drawing the results — early anatomical studies are the result of Leonardo's drawings; a horrible pastime, but he liked it.

Actually, he did not come out of our evolution at all. He came from the planet Mercury. He was really a human Avatar and is now no longer in our solar system, but in the system of Sirius. He is now in our terms an eighth-degree initiate, like the Buddha. His ray structure is extraordinary, especially if one remembers that the combination of 4th and 7th rays makes for the highest type of artist:

	Soul	Personality	Mental	Astral	Physical
Rays	4	7	7	4	7
Sub-rays		4	3	4	7

He could be nothing other than the highest type of artist in whose work both colour and form are perfectly realized at the highest level.

Leonardo does not use bright or obvious colours. What one senses in his work is that the pictures are whole, complete. It is not possible to say more than he is saying in each painting. It is as if each one communicates an almost cosmic meaning which is only able to be represented through the radiance of that painting. They take hold of our imagination and impose their extraordinary sensuous but abstract beauty on our minds.

There has to be a reason why *The Mona Lisa* has such a hold on the imagination of countless millions of people in the world, most of whom have seen only reproductions. Why is this so? I suggest that it is our response to the fact that Leonardo is 4.4 degrees initiate, almost a Master. One senses that he is no longer working in the three worlds, physical, astral and mental, in which average humanity lives. His painting represents the beauty of Reality in a spiritual or even a cosmic sense which finds expression through the activity of the 4th and 7th rays — that is, through the relationship between colour and form.

In *The Virgin of the Rocks*, in London and Paris, there is an extraordinary complexity of composition expressing Leonardo's abundance of 7th ray. Only someone with strong 7th-ray influence in his make-up would feel impelled, or have the ability, to carry to such an extent the structure and rhythms creating the forms in space in his painting. It is the 7th-ray ability to design and organize the material which creates such a unity throughout the whole, intricate composition. But Leonardo has too much 4th ray to compose in a hard or dry manner. It is done by chiaroscuro — the relationship of light to dark — and by the manipulation of the edges of each form to overlap, allowing the eye to flow easily from one to another. It creates the sense of totality, of completeness, which is so characteristic of his expression.

RAPHAEL (1483-1520)

Everyone loved Raphael because he had the sweetest nature you can imagine. They called him "The Divine". When we know his ray structure, we can understand why:

	Soul	Personality	Mental	Astral	Physical
Rays	2	4	7	6	7
Sub-rays		6	7	4	2

He was a third-degree initiate, therefore spiritually polarized. He had an oversensitive physical body and did not live very long; he did his whole life work and died by the time he was 37. He was very influenced by Leonardo da Vinci and Michelangelo.

What makes Raphael's work so attractive is the harmony represented in each painting. All movements within the composition have been resolved to create an absolute harmony, a stillness without deadness, a harmony which is somehow buoyant. His portraits are second to none. For example, take his portrait (in London's National Gallery) of Pope Julius II, a tyrant, an absolute rascal and a very clever 3rd-ray type. From Raphael's portrait you might think he was a benign Father Christmas whose grim mouth is only the result of losing his teeth. Raphael may have been sweet-natured but he was not stupid — he simply knew better than to paint everything he saw. However, it is also an expression of his 2nd-ray inclusiveness and goodwill.

The tremendous geometry of the large figure compositions is organized and constructed using his 7th-ray mental and 7th-ray brain. This demonstrates in a wonderful sense of proportion. Everything is done with restraint, without a trace of the exaggeration that came in a later period of Italian art based on his work. It is the balance in his work between colour and form, radiance and structure, atmosphere and architecture that makes him one of the really great painters.

MICHELANGELO (1475-1564)

Michelangelo was mainly a sculptor, but he was also a painter, though he thought that painting was a very inferior art. (That is a glamour shared by many sculptors!) It did not prevent him from being a very remarkable painter indeed.

	Soul	Personality	Mental	Astral	Physical
Rays	1	4	4	6	1
Sub-rays		6	3	6	7

He was 3.3 degrees initiate. He painted figures as pieces of sculpture, as if working from a block of stone. One senses a tremendous rhythmic energy spiralling up and down through the figures. The edges are 'hard', a technique rather liked by the 1st-ray painter, because the hard edge expresses more energy than the soft, blurred nuance. Although the figures are not as realistic as, say, a Rembrandt, they have enormous physical presence, being overlaid with Michelangelo's own powerful personality, infused by his 1st-ray soul. His paintings are abstract ideals in the big, 1st-ray, sense of a symbol — of the Christ or of divinity. It is the broad world view of the 1st ray seen through the eyes of a third-degree initiate. Despite having two 4th rays, Michelangelo's colour is not very characteristic of 4th-ray radiance. It can be a little dry, or pale and sweet, but in some cases can be quite powerful. He is more interested in the form than the colour. However, it is interesting to note that the colour is splendid and decorative in his paintings in the Sistine Chapel, as was revealed by the recent cleaning process. Michelangelo is now on Sirius and is the equivalent (in our solar system) of a seventh-degree initiate.

PAOLO VERONESE (1528-1588)

Paolo Veronese was both a brilliant colourist and a superb organizer of forms, as we can see from his ray structure. He was a third-degree initiate:

	Soul	Personality	Mental	Astral	Physical
Rays	7	4	7	6	7
Sub-rays		7	4	2	3

The two fours provided him with the beautiful, highly characteristic and original, colour quality. He handles colour marvellously, especially colours like rose, gold, blue and flesh. His is the energy of the 7th ray and those who are interested in painting may find inspiration from the colour and organization of all his painting. Clarity, a sense of ease, is always evident in his art. There is breadth and simplicity; also glamorous splendour in the Venetian sense: luxury, ease and grandeur. This comes from his 7th-ray soul and 4/7 personality, and enables him to build those tremendous compositions, like *The Marriage at Cana*, in the Louvre, Paris, with dozens of figures.

Paolo Veronese was a third-degree initiate. He is now a 7th-ray Master and will be very active in the world in the New Age. He will be in charge of, and the inspiration behind, the first 70 or 80 years of the New Age architecture and so will powerfully affect the architecture of the next 150 years or so. He is already drawing up His plans.

EL GRECO (1541-1614)

'El Greco' means 'the Greek' — his real name being Domenicos Theotocopulos, and he signed his pictures thus. He was another third-degree initiate, but with a 1st-ray soul and the following ray structure:

	Soul	Personality	Mental	Astral	Physical
Rays	1	4	7	6	1
Subrays		6	7	6	7

Born in Crete, he went as a young man to Venice to study under Tintoretto, and at first glance some of his early works remind one very much of Tintoretto; certainly he was very much influenced by him during this period. His own innate colour sense came from his 4th- and 6th-ray personality and double 6th-ray astral. This ability was heightened and sharpened and given structure by his experience in Venice under Tintoretto, himself a great colourist. El Greco actually composes with colour, making colour provide the building blocks with which the picture is created. In his later painting, the flamelike forms become the outstanding characteristic, together with an elongation and distortion of the figures to a degree which gives his pictures a Gothic expressiveness and intensity.

The power, vitality, the extraordinary impact of everything he painted is the expression of his 1st-ray soul — the ray of power and purpose. The fiery, flamelike quality is like his signature, his hallmark. It really reflects his knowledge or intuition about the nature of the energy which he embodied. He certainly knew on the soul level that he was a 1st-ray soul and the quality of fire which all his greater pictures explore is the 1st-ray aspect — electrical fire from the Central Spiritual Sun. This can be compared with the work of Raphael and Rembrandt, who demonstrate 2nd-ray fire quality, Solar fire.

El Greco was a great religious painter, expressing genuine religious fervour. This gives his work its ecstatic quality, unlike many painters of the High Renaissance in Italy who were really going through the motions — for example, traditional devotional painters thought it sufficient to show people rolling their eyes to heaven.

It is interesting to consider the influence of a nation's rays on the type of painting being produced. As we have seen, Italy has a 6th-ray soul and 4th-ray personality, and many Italian painters have the same rays. So in Italian painting there is often a measure of play-acting. It can be overblown, the figures and forms are flying too much in the air, or the gestures are too broad. With El Greco, the energy of the 1st and 7th rays are at work, giving his work a rhythmic, linear integration throughout the composition and an absolute seriousness and purpose. He is now a Master, a sixth-degree initiate, working on the inner planes from the Atmic level.

ALBRECHT DÜRER (1471-1528)

Albrecht Dürer was a German painter of the 16th century. He had a 1st-ray soul, and as a 2.4 degree initiate was half way between the second and third initiations, on the verge of spiritual polarization. His ray structure was as follows :

	Soul	Personality	Mental	Astral	Physical
Rays	1	7	7	4	1
Subrays		4	4	6	7

His paintings typically have a hard, linear, wiry quality — the 1st-ray vitality expressed in line. He is not eloquent as a colourist, but he was a great draughtsman and engraver. The technique involves cutting directly into steel, one line engraved at a time, and the result is a hard, tight, physical vitality which you cannot get in any other way. There was no nuance in his drawings but there is an extraordinary realism, coming from his Northern origins. There is always a hint of expressionism, as we have come to call it today, which is seen, for example, in hands being portrayed as slightly tortured in expression. His drawing contains a tension in the lines which gives an unrest, an inner tension. This is the reflection of Dürer's 1st-ray soul powerfully expressing itself through this, as yet not quite soul-infused, individual. Dürer was a brilliant draughtsman and a powerful figure in German art, certainly one of the great influences. He is not everyone's 'cup of tea', I would say, because people are somewhat afraid of the 1st-ray expression in all its manifestations. But in art, in El Greco, in Michelangelo and Dürer, it is remarkable. Dürer is a Master now, on the only sacred 1st-ray planet, Vulcan.

VELASQUEZ (1599-1660)

Velasquez was a 17th century Spanish painter, a 2.4 degree initiate. He is known in the trade as "a painter's painter". He is the kind of painter every painter loves. He is so technically marvellous that the paint looks as if it had never been handled or touched, as if he breathed it on the canvas. His colour is always exquisite as the numerous 4th rays in his make-up ensure: greys, blacks and rose and subtle flesh tints.

	Soul	Personality	Mental	Astral	Physical
Rays	*4*	*7*	*1*	*4*	*7*
Subrays		*6*	*7*	*4*	*3*

The 1st-ray mind gives him his power, his breadth of view, his style, his grandeur, and the 7th subray gives restraint, organizing power, a refined statement. He never overdoes anything, the way an Italian painter might. Double 4 on the astral gives his work its warmth and eloquence, but it is restrained by the 7th-ray personality with its 6th sub-ray. Spain's rays are: 6th ray soul, and 7th ray personality, and of course the rays of a nation always influence the work of an artist whatever their individual rays might be. Velasquez worked in the Court of Spain for most of his life. He had the style and grandeur and restrained beauty of the perfect court painter. He is now a Master on one of the higher spheres of this planet, the 5th sphere, working with the devas — 4th-ray Masters seem often to do that. His aim is to get to Mercury!

For information on the Seven Rays, see the works of Alice Bailey, particularly **Esoteric Psychology Volume One**. *See also chapters on the rays in Benjamin Creme's* **Maitreya's Mission, Volume One** *and* **Maitreya's Mission, Volume Two**. *For an extensive list of the rays of initiates, see the appendix to this book. For the rays of nations, see* **Maitreya's Mission, Volume One**.

COMMENTS ON CERTAIN INDIVIDUALS

Overshadowing

*Re: Krishnamurti's affirmation of the Lord Maitreya's presence in the world. This may come as a surprise to many followers of Krishnamurti's teaching who mistakenly believe that he denied the existence of the Masters and of the Lord Maitreya. This is simply not true. In Mary Lutyens' second book of his biography (**Krishnamurti: The Years of Fulfilment**) on page 207, Mary Zimbalist, after reading the first book (**Krishnamurti: The Years of Awakening**), asked him: " ... why, if the Masters existed, they had spoken then but not now, he suggested that 'There is no need now that the Lord is here'". Anyone who knows the cutting edge of Krishnamurti's teaching will see his statement above as a clear indication of the Lord Maitreya's presence.* (September 1996)

It is possible that Krishnamurti was indeed making a reference to Maitreya's presence but far more likely, I believe, is that he was referring to the presence of Maitreya — the Lord — in so far as Maitreya was *overshadowing Krishnamurti.*

*It has been stated by Mr Creme that J. Krishnamurti took the 4th initiation at the age of 49. He went on to live another 40-odd years, all the while serving humanity, it would seem, through teaching. He is listed as a fourth-degree initiate in **Maitreya's Mission, Volume One**. What happens at the fourth initiation that would preclude any further 'evolution'? Is there some sort of long adjustment period when the soul is absorbed back into the Monad?* (July/August 1996)

Yes. Of course it varies from person to person but there is often a long period of apparent stagnation (of evolutionary impulse) after the climactic experience of the fourth (the Crucifixion) initiation.

What happens during the overshadowing of yourself (Benjamin Creme) at the beginning and end of a meeting? (September 1995)

Some fragment of Maitreya's extraordinary consciousness overshadows — comes into — my consciousness. When the Messages were originally given, Maitreya *thought* the Messages and they automatically entered my mind. At the same time I was very highly magnetized, so I could almost only say what I said and I could not say it in any other way. With the magnetization, my breath was controlled, and the control of the breath controls how you actually speak. Although I was speaking, He was manipulating the breath, so I spoke as I did, with a mantric effect. I gave the physical-plane energy; my etheric energy and my voice allowed Him, at the same time, to impress the same message, the same ideas, on all the planes — for example, on the astral planes, so that they can influence the astral mediums around the world (they do not get it exact, but they get the idea). Thus the world has been prepared in a very definite way about the reality of the Christ's appearance.

My job has been to create the climate of hope, of expectancy, so that Maitreya can enter our lives without infringing free will. For most people, I would say, the truth of what I am saying lies in their experience of the overshadowing. People see me covered with light and actually disappearing during the overshadowing (I don't disappear to myself; I am sitting there absolutely solid, but the light so surrounds me that I am lost in the light). Sometimes people see Maitreya's face appear where my face was, and the room is filled with the light. Only a minuscule quantity of Maitreya's consciousness enters into mine, but it is enough to convince thousands of people all over the world of the reality of this happening. It is a blessing, a spiritual nourishing, which He pours out to the people in the audience. For most people that is what convinces. Anyone can make up a story, but you cannot invent that energy.

My husband and I went with a group to India to see Sathya Sai Baba. One of the group asked about who you (Benjamin Creme) were. Baba replied that we should leave it all to him. We should not be worrying our head about it. Do you know why he replied in such a manner when many of us wanted to know his answer? (May 1993)

I am not at all surprised by Sai Baba's reply. If I may say so, it was occultly correct and just what one would expect. With respect, it is no one's concern (except that of myself and my Master) who or what I am. The information which I make public must be seen and judged, accepted or rejected, on its own merits, and not for any notion of who I am or am not.

Who will continue your work when you will have left this physical body and will not be on Earth any more? (July/August 1996)

I'll be back.

(1) Did Gandhi work consciously with a Master of the Wisdom? (2) Did he know who his Master was? (3) Is he himself now a Master? (4) Has he incarnated again? (April 1995)

(1) No. (2) No. (3) No. (4) No.

Is Jimmy Carter being guided by one of the Masters? (April 1995)

"Guided" is not the word I would use, but he is certainly open to impression. If he lives long enough I believe he will become a member of a "group of wise men" which will function as the future ruling committee of the United States.

Eduard Shevardnadze, the former Soviet Foreign Minister, now a leader in Georgia, has converted to Christianity. Does this have anything to do with Maitreya's appearance in Georgia? (April 1993)

No. Maitreya's appearance in Georgia (Tblisi) was very recent (18 October 1992), while Mr Shevardnadze has been contemplating converting for some two years.

Today's singers from the pop world, actors and actresses from stage and cinema, appeal to the mass of the population all over the world. They must, therefore, have a certain influence on many people. In this case, and considering the times we are now living in, can one see some of them as initiates or advanced disciples? (January/February 1995)

Many are approaching the first initiation and are, therefore, aspirants to discipleship. Some few have taken the first initiation: John Lennon of Beatles fame was, for example, 1.6 degrees initiate.

If I understand you correctly, the Antichrist is a destructive force embodied by Nero and Hitler. Does that mean Hitler himself was directly responsible for what happened in Nazi Germany, or was it just a result of the destructive forces? (January/February 1993)

Hitler was both an agent and responsible. He was obsessed by various members of what are called the Lords of Materiality, which we call the 'forces of evil'. This is a group of 12 highly advanced men — from our point of view they would be Masters except that they have no love in their makeup. They work through those of similar vibration, as do the forces of light, the Hierarchy of Masters.

Hitler was actually a fairly evolved individual, a second-degree initiate; that is, he was two-fifths of the way along the path to becoming a Master. But even when the second initiation is taken, the person is only *potentially* divine. The first initiation that involves the soul is the third. From that point on, the man or woman is truly divine. This is symbolized in the gospel story by the transfiguration of Jesus on the mount. It is true that Hitler was only a second-degree initiate, but so, too, were Mahatma Gandhi, Reich, Freud, Jung, Einstein, Schweitzer, Plato and many other very evolved individuals who have contributed massively to our civilization and culture. Occasionally, however, there is a rotten egg in the basket. Hitler was one of these, a deeply evil personality. Because he was of the second degree, he had power and could be powerfully used, obsessed, by the forces of evil — like vibration attracted like vibration.

The problem for Germany was that Hitler was a medium (Germany is a highly mediumistic country). The Masters use a process of overshadowing which stops just short of obsession, in which the disciple's free will is never infringed, but the forces of materiality obsess right to the point where they completely control the personality. Hitler was controlled in this way. He also patted children on the head, his friends liked him, no doubt, but when the obsession took place, when he was talking to the multitudes, he became a ranting, powerful, obsessed, hollow shell who galvanized Germany, Japan and Italy to link together across the world as the Axis powers. Through that triangle the forces of evil manifested.

So Hitler was involved — as an agent for the forces of evil and also by his own innate evil: it is evil to want to dominate the world for 1,000 years, which is what he envisaged for the Third Reich. Not to mention the gas chambers.

Has the Bishop of Durham (in the UK), who holds what seem to be very heretical views, been impressed by Maitreya? (April 1994)

No. He believed and voiced these beliefs before 1977, when Maitreya came into London. Personally, I do not think he is a heretic or renegade or a bad Christian as he has been accused of being. To my mind, he is a very intelligent man with a better grasp of the Christian realities than any of the more fundamentalist Christian groups. For him, as for me, much of the Gospel teaching is symbolic but we might well differ on exactly which sections and episodes are symbolic and which can be accepted literally.

(1) Was the Danish writer Martinus (1890-1981) overshadowed or inspired by a member of the Hierarchy? (2) If so, by whom? (3) How can the "cosmic consciousness" of Martinus and his "cosmic analyses" be explained, when he was "only" 2.3 degrees initiate? (October 1996)

(1) Yes. (2) The Master Hilarion. (3) He did not have cosmic consciousness. His "cosmic analysis" is explained by the overshadowing.

The performances of illusionist David Copperfield are very spectacular. I am almost convinced that he has full control over his body in the same way as the "mayavirupa" body of Lord Maitreya. (1) Am I correct or is his act only based on tricks? (2) He also seems to control the Law of Gravitation. True or not?

(3) Can you give me his initiate status and ray structure? (January/February 1997)

(1) His act is based on tricks. He is an "illusionist" as you say. (2) True. He has concentrated on this particular ability. (3) No. It would be an infringement of his free will. My Master does not give initiate status or ray structures of living people.

(1) Was Padmasambhava (8th/9th century) an Initiate who just wasn't mentioned in the list of Initiates in **Maitreya's Mission, Volume One**? *If so (2) was he a disciple of Maitreya? (3) What was his ray structure and point of evolution? (4) Where is he now and what is he doing?* (March 1993)

(1) Yes. His rays were given in *Maitreya's Mission, Volume Two.* (2) Yes. (3) Soul 2; personality 4, sub-ray 6; mental body 3, sub-ray 7; astral body 6, sub-ray 6; physical body 7, sub-ray 3. He was 3.0 degrees initiate. (4) He is long since a Master and now works on one of the higher planets of our system.

Could you please say whether Swami Muktananda (1908-1982) and Bhagavan Nityananda (d. 1961) have taken the 5th initiation yet? If they have, will they be part of the group of Masters externalizing with Maitreya? (April 1996)

They are not in incarnation. Initiation can only be taken on the physical plane.

Is the well-known "White Eagle", the spiritual guide of Grace Cooke, a Master of Wisdom? (March 1993)

No. He is 1.5 degrees initiate, is, of course, discarnate, and gives his teaching from the fifth astral plane. It is very heart oriented and pure.

(1) Regarding Bertrand Debruyne, did he really live in the environment of Antwerpen at the turn of the 16th to the 17th centuries, a highly placed clergyman much involved in medical science, physics and geriatrics? (2) If so, would you please give his ray structure and point in evolution, and (3) is it true that the same Bertrand Debruyne is influencing our medicine in this

407

time, particularly promoting the naturopathic forms of it? (December 1994)

(1) Yes. (2) Soul 4; personality 3, sub-ray 7; mental body 4, sub-ray 6; astral body 6, sub-ray 2; physical body 3, sub-ray 7. He was 1.5 degrees initiate. (3) No. He is in incarnation now but is not involved in the medical field.

Books and Messages

I have been helped greatly by reading two books by Murdo Macdonald-Bayne: **Beyond the Himalayas** *and* **The Yoga of Christ**. *(1) Were his teachers in these books (or some of them) Masters? (2) These two books were withdrawn from sale due to a court action brought by Krishnamurti, which baffles me. Could you give the reasons for this action? (3) In* **Divine Healing of Mind and Body**, *by the same author, was he overshadowed by Jesus or Maitreya?* (December 1996)

(1) Yes. (2) The action was brought not by Krishnamurti but by Macdonald-Bayne's family. (3) The Master Jesus.

The Agni Yoga Society recently released two new volumes, **Supermundane, the Inner Life, Volume One** *and* **Volume Two**. *These books are quite different in tone from the earlier series of Agni Yoga books, released between 1924 and 1937. It is our understanding that the earlier books were given telepathically to Helena Roerich by Master Morya and Master Koot Hoomi, and in one instance by Maitreya Himself, to galvanize and inspire the world's disciples in the face of the impending war. These new volumes, though apparently also written in the 1930s, have a much more conversational tone than the ones published at that time. (1) What is the purpose and authorship of the 'Supermundane' books and (2) why have they been released only at this time?* (October 1996)

(1) They were given mainly (though not exclusively) by the Master Koot Hoomi. Their purpose is the same as the other books of the series — enlightenment. (2) It was not the Hierarchical intention that their publication should be held back until now. That is a decision of the Agni Yoga Society.

*Recently I came across a charming book called **The Boy Who Saw True** with an introduction by Cyril Scott. It is the anonymous account of a boy growing up as a clairaudient and clairvoyant in Victorian England. (1) Was the "Elder Brother" Who eventually contacted him a senior disciple, or one of the Masters — perhaps the Master DK or KH? (2) Was this another Hierarchical attempt to inform the general public about Their presence around the turn of the century? (3) Since the boy grew up to be a painter, who died in 1933, are you allowed to give out his name, ray structure and point of evolution?* (January/February 1997)

(1) A senior disciple. (2) Yes. (3) No.

*(1) Is it useful to follow **A Course in Miracles** when you also do Transmission Meditation, and (2) is it useful even if you might not be a first-degree initiate yet?* (December 1995)

(1) Yes. (2) Yes.

*In the book **The Human Aura** by Kuthumi, we read in the glossary: "Kuthumi, head of the Order of the Brothers of the Golden Robe; serving with Jesus in the office of World Teacher: formerly Chohan of the Second Ray." A friend wrote to me that Maitreya was now (since 1956) Lord Divino and had taken the place of the Lord of the World, Sanat Kumara; and that Kuthumi and Jesus were now World Teachers in Maitreya's place. How does this relate to your words: "The Christ (Lord Maitreya), the World Teacher, is now in the world to inaugurate the New Age of Synthesis"? I feel that Maitreya is still the Christ, the World Teacher — but am not too confident in my feelings.* (October 1993)

It is not my practice to discuss the teachings of other groups publicly, but since this directly refers to Maitreya and other Masters I think it necessary in this case.

Of course, the book quoted in no way relates to my statement that the Christ, the Lord Maitreya, is now in the world.

It all depends on whether you accept that the book mentioned is actually written by the Master Koot Hoomi (to give the correct spelling of His name) or not. For my part, it most emphatically is not written by that or any other Master but emanates (as does so much else) from the fifth astral plane (the planes of illusion) through the astral 'channeller' who wrote it down.

Sanat Kumara, the Lord of the World, is the etheric-physical reflection of our Planetary Logos. He has been on Earth for 18.5 million years and will remain, as Lord of the World, for countless millions more — until the end of the 7th and final Round (we are in the middle of the 4th Round).

Exalted as He is: a seventh-degree initiate, a Planetary Life, the Embodiment of the Christ Principle, there is no way in which Maitreya could "take the place" of Sanat Kumara. Nor could the Masters Koot Hoomi and Jesus, singly or together, take Maitreya's place as World Teacher. According to the Master DK (who should know), the Master Koot Hoomi is now in training to become the World Teacher during the Capricornian cycle, some 2,500 years from now. He and the Master Jesus will be among the first group of Maitreya's disciples to make Themselves known after the Day of Declaration.

*In **Las Nuevas Escrituras** (the New Scriptures) **Volume 1**, published by Centro Lusitano de Unificacion Cultural, based in Lisbon, Portugal, it is categorically stated that Master Koot Hoomi gave teachings, coming from the Great White Brotherhood, about the appearance of Maitreya the Christ, saying that early in the morning of 3 June 1985, the full moon of the Christ, His body of manifestation was born. There is therefore a contradiction between the affirmations of the dates for the appearance of the Christ in His mayavirupa: Benjamin Creme — 19 July 1977. Centro Lusitano de Unification Cultural — 3 June 1985. It is said that both these affirmations come from the Great White Brotherhood. How can the Great White Brotherhood of Shamballa give out such visibly different statements?* (July 1994)

I am sure, with a little research, the questioner could find several other "affirmations" about the "birth" of the Christ. A welter of such statements pours daily into the minds of mediums from the astral planes. The fact is, Maitreya was not "born" on 3 June 1985 or at any other time. I have revealed that His body of manifestation is a "mayavirupa" — a self-created body — made, *over several years*, before He emerged from His Himalayan retreat on 8 July 1977. This information does not come from Shamballa (no information comes to humanity from that Centre) but from Hierarchy. The Masters of our Planetary Hierarchy do not give out "such visibly different statements". The difference lies in the levels from which they come. Discrimination is of the essence here.

What connection do you know of between Maitreya and Sananda (who is said to be another form of Jesus on the cosmic realm)? (March 1993)

There is no connection, for the simple reason that "Sananda" does not exist. He is another of the many products of astral imagination which today muddy the waters of new age understanding. The Master Jesus has no "other form on the cosmic realm".

I wonder about Masters like Ramtha saying the Christ will return as a leader of an armada of UFOs when it is already known that Maitreya is in the world. Ramtha speaks of himself as being part of the brotherhood of enlightened souls so therefore he should know about the Christ's activities. (January/February 1993)

It all depends on whether you believe that "Ramtha" is a Master or not. I most certainly do not. Nor do I see him as an "enlightened soul", but as a discarnate entity giving his misinformation (from the fifth astral plane), from the "enlightened" level of a 1.0 degree initiate.

I have seen an advertisement about "OAHSPE, The World's Teacher for the Aquarian Age".

(1) Is this the Antichrist, prophesied by Edgar Cayce?(2) Is this so-called World's Teacher trying to usurp Maitreya's role? (June 1993)

(1) No. The forces of destruction which we term the Antichrist manifested through the Axis Powers in the 1939-45 war, that is through Hitler and his group in Nazi Germany; a group of

militarists in Japan; and a group led by Mussolini in Italy. Their defeat by the Allies represents the defeat of the Antichrist for this time, and in fact makes possible the return of Maitreya and His group of Masters to the everyday world.

(2) Yes. This is only one of many such initiatives coming, through mediums, from the fifth astral plane. Steeped in the illusions of these astral planes, they satisfy the astral aspirations of some, but, increasingly, humanity will be able to discriminate between this type of astral, desire-based 'teaching' and the spiritual teaching of Maitreya and His group. The proof of the pudding ...

(1) Is Vissarion the bringer of the new world religion mentioned by the Master DK as destined to come from Russia? (2) Is he a Master? (3) Is he an advanced disciple? (4) Are his teachings from the astral planes or from higher sources? (5) Is the bringer of the new world religion already active in Russia? (6) Certain books on general spiritual teachings are circulating now in Russia and have also been translated into English — would these teachings be the foundation of the new world religion? (7) Will this task be undertaken by a Master, when the Christ is already known in the world? (8) Are current spiritual teachings circulating in Russia broadly speaking astrally based? (June 1995)

(1) No. (2) No. (3) No. (4) Astral planes. (5) No. (6) No. (7) Yes. (8) Yes. However, this is not confined to Russia but is the case world-wide. The vast majority of people everywhere are astrally polarized and respond more readily to teaching, however distorted and illusory, emanating from the astral planes. The higher teaching, emanating from the Hierarchy of Masters, has a relatively limited audience.

Sai Baba and a few others say that there will be a New Age but there is going to be a great cataclysm before it. (December 1994)

Sai Baba has published a statement completely and categorically denying that He ever made such pronouncements. There are many pronouncements coming through mediums, 'channelled', as they call it, from the astral planes (in particular the fifth astral plane) from various misguided 'guides'; there is no truth in these prognostications, and they should be ignored and given no energy.

They are focused on the astral planes by the forces of materiality precisely to frighten humanity; this mischievous information is deliberately meant to prevent the inauguration of the new structures. If humanity takes all this seriously it becomes afraid, and when it is afraid it creates a thoughtform of catastrophe which can precipitate the very thing of which it is afraid. That is the technique of these 'forces of evil', as we call them — the forces of materiality — to create a thoughtform of violence, destruction and catastrophe.

There *is* catastrophe — it is as if people could not get enough of it, they have to invent it; there are 1,200 million people living in official, absolute poverty: all of that is catastrophe. We are desecrating the planet: burning up the forests on which we rely for the very oxygen that we need to live; despoiling the earth — poisoning it with pesticides, with pollution. With nuclear tests we are creating earthquakes — every underground nuclear explosion is followed inevitably by an earthquake. The nuclear power-stations of the world are pouring into the air thousands of tons of radio-active waste. *All of that is catastrophe* — the *real* catastrophe.

Would it be possible for you to comment on the "pole shift" which, it has been alleged, Sai Baba has said will happen? (November 1995)

Some years ago, Sai Baba issued a statement denying that He had predicted a "pole shift" and subsequent catastrophe, as had been alleged. I know of no reason which would have caused Him to change His views on this and do not believe the current story. People are always citing Sai Baba as confirming their own particular fears or expectations.

At the beginning of November Sai Baba gave an interview to a group of Australians. They reported that He told them several things and that they should make them known. So many rumours come from devotees that I wonder whether your Master confirms these predictions? They were: (1) There will be a world stock-market crash. (2) There will be a shortage of water in the world. (3) There will be worse diseases than AIDS. (4) Do not eat products from New Zealand. (5) Eat mainly green leaf vegetables. (6) Do not eat fish; it is contaminated. (January/February 1996)

(1) Once again, Sai Baba is being used to endorse the prejudices and 'inner information' of groups and individuals. I was sent another report that this same Australian group were told by Sai Baba that the world stock-market crash would take place on 6 or 8 January (1996). Well, Sai Baba did not say that — and it did not happen. Readers of *Share International* will know that Maitreya has predicted a world stock-market crash since 1988, and that some months ago Sai Baba told a Japanese group that it would occur "soon". This is certainly not 'hot' news. (2) People do like to be the carriers of sensational information. There will, indeed, be relatively less water in areas of the world which have seldom been without adequate supplies. However, other areas — today desert or near-desert — will have relatively more water than hitherto. (3) My information is that Sai Baba made no such statement. (4) What Australian prejudice inspires this nonsense? I am informed that Sai Baba made no such statement. (5) It is nutritional common sense to eat enough "greens" — but Sai Baba did not say it. (6) Some fish, around certain polluted shores, are contaminated — as are most agricultural and meat products — but not all fish by any means. Again, Sai Baba made no such reference.

My advice is that people should treat rumours coming from devotees with caution, and use their own discriminating faculties together with large pinches of salt. Poor Sai Baba, the nonsense that is put about in His name.

In the book **When the Sun Speaks**, *the author, Surya Green, has an interview with a person who claims he is Maitreya. Although my intuition says he isn't, he really says the right things. If he is a false Christ, in contradiction to others he has the sympathetic message that the gap between North and South is intolerable,*

414

and that sharing should replace the present financial dictatorship, etc. Is this man really Maitreya? (November 1995)

I have not read the book in question but the author, Surya Green, knows my writings and has attended my lectures. The ideas of sharing and justice, of course, have filtered by now through most societies and groups, and any self-respecting claimant to be "the Christ" would surely have to espouse them. That does not make this gentleman the Christ, however. I have not the slightest doubt that Ms Green has *not* interviewed Maitreya.

In the messages given in Garabandal (northern Spain) mention was made of 'the Warning', and the similarity of the information about Declaration Day is startling. The Garabandal messages speak of a direct intervention by God so that everyone on earth will be given an insight into the state of his/her own soul for between a quarter and a half hour. My main problem is, however, that once again there is also talk of hell and damnation, in short, the wrath of a God of punishment (just like the Fatima and Medjugorje messages). This does not appeal to me (and many others) at all! But still, I am convinced that it was Mary who appeared to those gathered in Garabandal. How can we explain this in terms of what we have been told about Declaration Day? (December 1995)

The Garabandal vision was created by the Master Who was Mary, mother of Jesus, as is the case at Medjugorge and elsewhere. However, no message of any kind was given. The "message" released is the work of the astral imagination of the recipient. Any resemblance to my information about Declaration Day is due to the wide circulation of my information in Spain — but given the usual orthodox Catholic slant of hell and damnation — all astral.

What do you think of mediumistic messages? Do they interfere or help the medium's spiritual development? (December 1995)

Mediums contact the astral planes, usually the fifth, sometimes the sixth. These are the planes of illusion so it follows that whatever proceeds from these planes is, more or less, illusory. This being the case, any long involvement in such activity must interfere with the medium's spiritual development. To my mind, mediumship is an atavistic, backward-looking activity; such people should be aiming for the higher telepathy, stemming from soul contact and polarization.

Can you say whether you have heard of "Ascension" and the "Ascension" process about to occur? If it is imminent, what is the timescale? (January/February 1994)

Several mediums have picked up, from the astral planes (the planes of illusion), the idea that humanity is about to go through a great enlightening experience, a quickening of evolution, to which they have given the term "Ascension".

There are five planetary initiations which complete the experience of this planet. The last, the Resurrection, as symbolized in the Christian Gospel, makes the initiate the Perfected Master. There are four further, Cosmic, initiations which a Master may eventually take. The first of these is the Ascension, which has been taken by relatively few Masters up till now. That experience and achievement, therefore, lies far in the future for the vast majority of humanity today. This is a typical instance of how some esoteric truth or teaching becomes distorted in its "channelled" descent from the astral planes.

I have heard that we are going to be given three opportunities to leave the planet in the next 24 years, while the financial and other changes are going on. Do you know anything about this? (May 1994)

I have heard the same story, and I think it is one huge nonsense. No one leaves the planet except under law, and this is not part of the law. It is certainly not part of the Plan.

(1) I seem to be able to perceive incidents, facts and people, to have a sort of biographical sketch of co-workers, friends and family. This sometimes appears to involve information about them from other, past, lives. Could you please help me to discern — is there any indicator, a certain yardstick — when this is simply an astrally based over-active imagination, or when it might be that I am somehow (how?) picking up information

which might not directly involve the person but be partly and tangentially connected with someone close to them, and when it might be real, an accurate picture? What is this mechanism? Is it a sort of astral clairvoyance? A mixture of that and intuition? Or a kind of intuitive, telepathic sense? (2) a: If one has more (fore)knowledge or intuition of a situation involving others, and they appear oblivious of this, should one tell the person concerned, try to warn them, mention possible consequences, or is this an infringement of their free will to make their own (often huge messes and) mistakes? b: Does more knowledge, possibly a (slightly) higher point of evolution mean that one has greater responsibility? (July/August 1995)

(1) Astral clairvoyance. (2) a: If they appear to be in danger, yes. otherwise, no. b: Yes.

Shall we be moving towards greater contact with people who have passed on? (April 1995)

Yes. There is no doubt at all that the 'web' between the physical plane and the astral planes is becoming thinner all the time. That weakening really began in a major way during the 1914-18 war, with the colossal bombardments and gun shocks, which were then repeated from 1939 to 1945, and again recently in Iraq. All of that breaks the web between the planes, and through that web you get all the 'channelling' which is taking place.

Many people who 'channel' think the information is coming from Masters but it is actually coming (when not from the 'channel's' subconscious) from entities on the astral planes. A growing sensitivity is taking place in humanity which opens many to various levels of these planes — mostly the 5th. Eventually the relationship between those who have passed over and those who are still living on the physical plane will become closer. We will be able to communicate (according to the Master DK through Alice Bailey) not only through mediums but even through animals. We will also be able to communicate through radio — it has already begun to take place.

CHAPTER 6

THE ANTAHKARANA

THE ANTAHKARANA

The following article is an edited version of talks by Benjamin Creme, given during the 1993 Transmission Meditation Conferences in San Francisco, USA, and Kerkrade, the Netherlands.

The science of the antahkarana is probably the most important science of the coming time but this talk will not claim to cover the whole subject of the antahkarana or the science of its use.

This is a science which is, as yet, unknown to humanity but it will be the coming science of mind of the New Age, the science of building the bridge between lower and higher man, and also a number of other bridges: between the members of the human race as a whole; between one Centre — Humanity — and another, Hierarchy; between Hierarchy and Shamballa; between Humanity, through Hierarchy, and Shamballa; and between this planet and other planets, this solar system and other solar systems. All these bridges and connections are the result of the correct use of the science of the antahkarana, which will be the major educational field for humanity in this coming age.

The best way to study the antahkarana is to read the Alice Bailey Teachings, in particular the book *Education in the New Age*, and further references in *The Rays and the Initiations*. You will not get from this talk, or from the Alice Bailey Teachings, the *technique* of the science of the antahkarana. That is something which, as far as humanity as a whole is concerned, lies well in the future. It is a gradual process of enlightenment for humanity, but it will become the major science — the science of evolving as a race and making the inner connections (which of course already exist but which have consciously to be built by the man or woman in incarnation), to weave the thread of return to the source from which we have originally come. It is really the science of the Path of Return.

For long ages, the soul on its own plane looks down at its reflection, the man or woman on the physical plane, and sees no way to interfere with its development. There is very little the soul can do except create a body, give it its various physical, astral and mental make-up, and leave it to get on with the job of evolution.

Eventually, there comes a life — a series of lives in fact — in which the soul sees that its reflection, the man or woman, is beginning to respond to the influence of the energy which connects the soul to its reflection, and the process of 'ensouling' begins.

Each individual is really threefold: the Monad, or spark of God, the impersonal Self which reflects itself on the soul plane as the individualized human soul or ego. The soul, again, reflects itself on the dense physical plane as the man or woman in incarnation.

That is the 'way down', the process by which spirit involves itself in its polar opposite, substance. When the spirit, or life, aspect and the matter aspect come together, a third, the consciousness aspect, is born. The antahkarana is, above all, the thread of consciousness. It is the result of the interaction of the life with the form, with substance, with matter; that produces something entirely different. We call it "consciousness". We can also call it "the Christ Principle". It is the process of evolution itself.

Those who study anthropology, the history of evolution on the physical plane — the evolution of forms — know that in the beginning there were great oceans, teaming with life, nothing on the land, and then gradually some of the more evolved animals — fish, reptiles of all kinds — came on to the land and became the early reptiles and mammals. Gradually, there evolved a pre-human type which eventually became early, animal man, separating itself from the animal kingdom. With the germ of mind — which could become the nucleus of a mental body — at last formed, the human race began. This is denied by Christian fundamentalists and other orthodox religious groups who deny the reality of Darwin's theory of evolution, but esotericists accept it as a more-or-less accurate account of the growth of the form, the evolution of form, on this planet.

We are not concerned with that; we are concerned, as human beings evolving back to our source, with the evolution not of form — which has come more or less to perfection (though there are some minor adjustments and improvements still to be made) but rather with the *evolution of consciousness*. The evolution of consciousness is the basis of how we become aware of ourselves and our environment, and create together the evolution of the human race.

The descent from Monad to soul and from soul to personality has to be re-enacted in reverse order. The threefold man — physical, astral and mental — has to find his way back by a process of at-one-ment, first with the soul and then, through the spiritual triad — the reflection of the Monad — with the Monad itself: the threefold Monadic Being. That return journey, or the process by which that return journey is made, is through the creation, the gradual evolvement and building, of the antahkarana. This is a conscious process and only occurs in stages. As the process downward has been slow, over millions of years, so the process back can be a long, drawn-out process, and for the vast majority of humanity so it is.

We are in the second of a threefold solar system. In other words, this solar system is the second embodiment or manifestation of the great Heavenly Man we call the Solar Logos Who has a Plan for the evolution of all the forms in the solar system.

The first solar system expressed through matter, substance, the quality of active intelligence. It was concerned mainly with the intelligent creation of forms. We are in the second of this threefold expression in which the soul quality — the love or consciousness aspect — of the Logos is in process of being expressed. The Solar Antahkarana is being built by the Solar Logos and by all the forms, whether they know it or not, who have evolved from the first solar system and are now creating the bridge between that system and this one, and, eventually, between this system and the next. The next solar system will be concerned with the Will aspect, the Monadic aspect, of the Solar Logos. When the correct bridge between these three expressions is built, the Solar Antahkarana is in place. This will lead to the culmination of the Plan of our Solar Logos in its threefold expression.

Each solar system creates a body of expression at a higher level than the one before. The first — that to do with form, with substance — is, of course, preparatory to the expression of the soul. It is the soul, in all forms, which incarnates. By descending into form, the soul — actually the Monad, the spirit aspect, through the soul — begins a process of redemption of the soul in form. It begins to spiritualize substance; the underlying purpose of our incarnational experience is, precisely, to spiritualize the substance of this particular solar system. When we have taken the substance — the forms created in the previous solar system — and energized it with the energy of the soul, the consciousness aspect, in this solar system, we will raise it, redeem it, heighten its vibration and bring it up to the level at which the Will, the Purpose aspect of God (in terms of our Solar Logos), can be expressed.

In this present solar system God is Love; Love is the aspect of the soul, Will of the Atmic level of being. In the next solar system God will be Will and Purpose. We are, all of us, as microcosms, evolving in precisely the same way as the macrocosm, our Solar Logos, through its threefold expression, works out its Plan of evolution in every kingdom and in every planet.

In coming into incarnation, therefore, we are doing something quite extraordinary, something far greater than we as individual human beings possibly realize. But as soon as we do realize the interconnectedness of the microcosm with the macrocosm it deepens our sense of purpose — the sense of reality — in life, and it is also a stimulus to concentrate more, and to build a direct line of ascent between this low-level (for that is what it is) expression of Deity and bring it into line with the underlying purpose of Deity for its perfectionment.

The energy of each solar system is raised and becomes the basis for the new system, just as in our incarnational experience every incarnation creates an expression through the vehicles up to a certain vibration. That vibration is held exactly at the point we have reached when we die.

There are three 'permanent atoms' around which the new bodies, physical, astral and mental, are formed. These permanent atoms vibrate at exactly the frequency reached in that particular life, and we can understand, therefore, how the vibrational rate reached is the degree to which we have perfected, or spiritualized, matter. The soul infuses the matter of the three bodies with its energy and in this way salvages, redeems, that matter. It raises their vibration onto an ever-higher level until the point is reached when the soul is reflecting itself, without resistance, directly, through the personality. That is how we *become* divine. We do so by raising the vibrational rate of the substance of these three bodies to a point where the Divine Man, the soul on its own plane, can reflect itself relatively purely through its reflection, the man or woman on the physical plane. That is the evolutionary, the return process; the technique of it is the science of the antahkarana.

Sutratma

There are two major threads which connect the Monad, through the soul, with the man or woman in incarnation. One, the sutratma, the thread of life, is anchored in the heart. It comes directly from the Monad, reflected through the soul, and is fixed in the heart centre at the right-hand side of the body. It is reflected through that etheric centre to the physical heart and into the bloodstream, which, as you know, is the purifying stream which carries the energy of life to every part of the body. While the lifeblood is pumped correctly through the body and is kept free of poisons, the physical body displays all its ability and accuracy of movement and expression. So, too, the connecting body, the astral-emotional body and the mental body are dependent on the life thread, the sutratma, for their existence and correct function.

There is another thread, called, indeed, the antahkarana. This thread is anchored in the centre of the head, and through these two threads the threefold expression — Monad, soul and physical-plane man or woman — live their lives. These two threads *inform* all of these and, in a downward flow, bridge the gaps between, first, Monad and soul, and secondly between soul and its reflection, the man or woman on the physical plane.

Eventually, a third thread is built by the man or woman him/herself through the interaction of soul energy, and eventually, Monadic energy, through the physical apparatus: the thread of creativity. These three threads wound together eventually produce the bridge between the three levels of existence.

The future science of the antahkarana will concern itself with this, the path of return. This will be the New Age education. Individuals will be recognized for what they are, souls in incarnation; their point in evolution and ray structure will be ascertained and known; through this science the gaps between the various levels of our being will be bridged. This is only possible now that the human race has reached the present state and, of course, because of the return to the everyday world of the only people in the world who actually know this science: the Masters.

Since the Masters are returning, this will become an exoteric science. All children, from the earliest age up until 28, will eventually go through this process of education in the science of Life — the science of building the return channel, or pathway.

I would like here to show the inner unity of method and approach of certain terms. The antahkarana is the bridge built — first out of mental matter and later out of light — by the evolving aspirant, disciple and initiate, in turn. Until a certain time, the connection between the man or woman and the soul plane is developed by the control of 'mentation', the energy of the mental body. It brings the mental body under control and the thought-patterns create a bridge. The antahkarana is, therefore, in the first place, a bridge connecting the lower man, the lower mind, with the soul, and then the lower mind, through the soul, with the higher mind which is the lowest aspect of the Spiritual Triad. This is Atma, Buddhi and Manas — the reflection on the soul plane of the threefold Monad, or spark of God.

Path of Return

There are different terms for this and I would like to bring all of these together to show the unity and interconnectedness of these different methods of expressing what is essentially the one process, the return journey: the Path of Return.

The mystic thinks of the Path as the Path to God. He thinks of it generally in terms of his religious or mystical feelings and experiences, his mystical religious beliefs, doctrines, and dogma, his various spiritual practices, the various rituals — all of these to the mystical and devotional type constitute a way of approaching God through belief, a linking in consciousness between the individual man's belief structure (whether that be Christian, Hindu, Buddhist, or whatever) and that which lies behind all creation. The religious person sees that as the Path of Return — and of course that is perfectly true, it is. But not everybody is religious, and the Path of Return, to the esotericist, is a path which, literally, is made by the disciple himself. The disciple makes the Path by *becoming* the Path. It is not something which is already laid down and is whispered into your ear. It is not like that at all. It is the evolutionary process itself. It is that same process which brought the fishes out of the sea onto dry land, from which they evolved into, first, reptiles and then mammals and then the huge variety of animals and eventually, at the peak of that development of form, the human kingdom. Above the human kingdom is the Kingdom of Souls, the kingdom whose nature is *consciousness*. The plane of consciousness is the plane on which the Masters have hitherto worked exclusively. The Path of Return is the Path by which the consciousness of what is and what might be gradually becomes known to the seeker, the evolving individual.

In other words, as you seek, as you aspire, you create before you — as DK says: the "spider creates out of his own being the silken thread" — so, in exactly the same way, the aspirant, the disciple and the initiate are creating before them the Path of Return, the Path which is not yet laid down. It is the path of a growing awareness of what constitutes his/her relationship to the whole. It is a means by which we grasp deeper and deeper realizations and experiences of our connectedness to the whole, to the Macrocosm. This is done by a growing expansion of consciousness.

These expansions of consciousness are marked off on our planet by the five planetary initiations. For the adept there are also four Cosmic initiations. Above these, and on throughout Cosmos, are initiation after initiation upon initiation — on and on eternally, throughout the whole of galactic space. All of that is a process by which, through the building of the antahkarana, our individual relationship to that totality gradually dawns on us.

The antahkarana is not a 'form'. Here you have a form which is called "The Antahkarana", a lithograph made from one of my paintings, and it is a purely formal and symbolic representation of the antahkarana. (See cover of *Maitreya's Mission, Volume Two*.) The Monad reflects itself in the soul as the Spiritual Triad: spiritual Will, spiritual Love-Wisdom and spiritual Intelligence, and these are again reflected in the physical being by the soul. The process by which this takes place is the antahkarana. In this lithograph, the lower shape represents the threefold human being; the white connecting column is the symbolic representation of the threefold thread of the antahkarana; and the pale-yellow shape at the top represents the soul itself.

This lithograph is *not* the antahkarana; the antahkarana is *not* a form. Most people thinking about the antahkarana, because of the nature of the language used, inevitably imagine a bridge. That bridge is built in, first, mental substance and then light, and so they visualize a physical bridge. An artist has to do so, of course; one cannot paint a picture without a form. The artist has to create out of his creative imagination a form which will symbolize a process, but the form is not the process, it is simply a means of expressing the idea of the process.

Anyone who does Transmission Meditation knows about alignment. When that alignment is perfect, symbolically speaking there is a column of light above the head of the meditators. In that light there are three threads, strands, of energy. That is the form, but it is not the antahkarana. We must realize that the form and the idea of a bridge, the idea of a column of light, the idea of some actual form in substance, is only a way of stating something else. What we are really talking about is *awareness*.

Awareness, in a sense, is a vague, generalized way of talking about the process of return. We return through a gradual expansion of conscious awareness, through the conscious building of the antahkarana. This is created firstly in mental matter, between the personality and the soul, and then by the initiate — who has already contacted and come into a close at-one-ment with the soul — in light, between the soul and the Monad, the highest aspect of our threefold being. Then the connectedness eventually is direct between the Monad — the divine being, identical with God, the reflection of our Planetary Logos — and the man or woman on the physical plane. By this process our Planetary Logos works out His Plan of evolution through the human kingdom, and of course in the same way the Solar Logos is working out His greater and vaster Plan through all beings on all planets in this, the second, solar system. This process will be completed in the third solar system, in which the Monadic aspect — the Will, the Purpose, the essential Love of God — will come to its final expression and fulfilment.

Each of us, right now, is engaged in creating the antahkarana. Another term for the antahkarana, besides the bridge of light, is *Self-realization*, which is what Maitreya calls it: "I have come to teach the art of Self-realization," He said. The art of Self-realization is the science of the antahkarana: they are one and the same.

Maitreya has said that the simplest, most direct path is to practise three things: *Honesty of mind; sincerity of spirit*; *and detachment*. These three bring about Self-realization, and they do so by enabling the man or woman to create the antahkarana. For the vast majority of people in the world this is a process which goes on, up till a certain time, quite unconsciously. Most unevolved individuals are connected only by the sutratma, the life thread, coming from the Monad through the soul and anchored in the heart. Average humanity are connected also by the thread of consciousness, the antahkarana, and as the person evolves through the building of the first stage of the antahkarana

427

— that between the lower man and the soul — the energies of the soul become available to him or her.

Then the creative process begins. This stimulates the mind and the creative imagination, and a life of creativity and of service ensues. Creativity and service are one and the same; service is the life of the soul creatively expressed on the physical plane. This, then, dominates more and more in the life of the individual, and so we get the creation of culture. It is not by accident that the culture of any nation is created by the disciples and the initiates of that nation; they are the ones who have already built the first stage of the connecting link, the bridge, between themselves and their soul.

The initiate, having achieved an integration of the three lower vehicles, physical, astral and mental — that is, having brought them to a point of synchronous vibration, takes the third initiation; the soul, henceforward, controls and dominates its vehicle, which is now negative in relation to the purpose of the soul. The divine man or woman displays his or her divinity on the physical plane in a life of service and creativity. The third-degree and the fourth-degree initiate is usually in incarnation for only one or two lives, depending on astrological factors. But having taken thousands of lives to the first initiation, and perhaps five or six to the second, the third is taken very quickly, and the fourth very quickly after that, probably in the next life. Therefore, by the time a person has reached the state of true creativity, is more or less soul-infused and expressing the purpose of the soul, he or she does not have long in which to do this; only three or four lives at the most. Then, as a Master, the whole of this existence is dedicated to the service of the Plan.

Of course, the more one evolves the more one knows. The more one knows, the greater the responsibility of service, and the greater the opportunity for service. The Masters can serve because They *know*. Our service is limited, not only because of lack of desire or energy, but because we do not know enough; we can serve in a rather limited way because our consciousness is limited. The more conscious one is, or the higher the level of consciousness, the greater the number of threads of consciousness extending outwards to the world, the greater awareness there will be of the nature of reality. These are the antahkarana, which is not simply a column of light but threads of awareness spreading outwards from the individual into every sphere of his environment. These threads of awareness multiply endlessly, until, in the Master, they make for omniscience: nothing can happen anywhere of which He is unaware. In this way we reveal the mind of God, become instruments in the furthering of the Plan held in the mind of God. That, really, is the basis of initiation.

When you know consciously, through the building of the antahkarana, how to link the different levels of expression — Monadic with soul, soul with the physical (on the downward path) — when you know this science because you have done it, and done it consciously, when you are a *Master*, you can use this science to create the mayavirupa, the self-created body.

The mayavirupa reverses the process of the antahkarana. It is the result of the ability to create a body because you know the connecting links between the form. A God-realized Master experiences Himself as God in this physical body. For us that physical body is the closest, most important, aspect, whereas for the Master it is only a transitory aspect of the whole. From His God-realized state, the Master can go backwards down the bridge, the antahkarana, can repeat the process and bring together, therefore, matter of the mental, the astral-emotional and the etheric physical plane, and precipitate His consciousness into that. That is the secret behind the creation of the mayavirupa.

The new world religion, when developed, is really the creation of the 'racial' antahkarana. Maitreya has said the He has not come to build a new religion, to create followers, and so on. This is true. Nevertheless there will be what we have to call, for want of another name, a new world 'religion', but it will be the science of which I am speaking.

The new world religion will be a conscious approach by the human race to the Creator, that which stands behind creation — which, of course, is also ourselves, the essential part of ourselves as the Monad. This will be done through the creation of the racial, group, antahkarana. The growing experience of aspirants and disciples of working in groups is a preparatory step towards this great racial grouping, to the creation of the 'world' antahkarana. Eventually the antahkarana links not only peoples, but planets and solar systems. This is the essential nature of Being throughout Cosmos. All that is higher reflects itself through a lower vehicle. This threefold expression is to be found throughout Cosmos.

At our human level, we experience it consciously, because, as souls, we are the "Sons of Mind". Through the expression of the soul, the consciousness aspect, that awareness takes place by which the racial antahkarana can be built. As a Being, as a race, as one big grouping of all peoples, all religions, all types and points of evolution, there will be eventually a conscious approach to Deity, especially at the Three Spiritual Festivals in April, May and June and also at the nine other full-moons. This will constitute "the new world religion", or the technique of the new world religion, in which invocation will replace the present process of worship. We can see therefore that it will be a very scientific religion — it will be very difficult to distinguish between what we call science, religion and education.

This is also the education of the New Age. Children will be trained in the creation of the antahkarana. The science of the antahkarana will be taught — in so far as it can be taught, because it is an experiential thing — to those ready to receive the tuition. Of course, that does not mean all children, but for those more advanced aspirants, for those who are preparing for initiation, this will become the norm. No initiation is possible for anyone without the building of the antahkarana. Indeed, it is precisely the building of the antahkarana, the link between the lower man and the soul, which makes initiation possible. Eventually, the link between the integrated lower man and the soul makes possible the higher initiations in which the at-one-ment is with the Spiritual Triad, and, through that, with the Monad. Then the process is complete; the Godlike man, the God-realized or Self-realized man, has achieved: he is a Master.

The antahkarana is not only the bridge between the different fragments of ourselves, it is the bridge between the worlds: planetary, systemic, and galactic.

The key to the formation of the mayavirupa is found in the right comprehension of the creation of the antahkarana. It is important to remember that as these bridges are built the vitalizing process goes on. It is not simply a question of building a bridge; it is through that bridge that the stimulus from the higher levels takes place.

Three Sciences

Three major sciences will dominate in the New Age: the science of the antahkarana, the science of meditation and the science of service. The science of service utilizes the creativity which is achieved through the building of the antahkarana, and the science of meditation, of course, is a preliminary process leading to, and essential to, the creation of the antahkarana through *its* science. So the science of the antahkarana is very broad indeed, including that of meditation and of service.

The vitalizing agency is, first of all, the soul. The soul opens up on the personality level the Knowledge petals in the crown chakra and vitalizes them; this stimulates the thought processes and galvanizes the man or woman to further creation of the bridge, the antahkarana, between itself and the soul. Soul at-one-ment gradually takes place, and when this has gone a certain distance initiation leads to the opening of the Love petals, and eventually, as a man or woman approaches the third initiation and that is taken, the opening up of the inner three petals which enclose the "jewel", the "jewel in the heart of the lotus", which is the Will aspect.

The Monad reflects more and more in the man or woman on the physical plane, dominating, therefore, the life of that individual. In this process, what was simply emotional aspiration gradually transforms itself into the Monadic will: the purpose of the life is known. This leads to lives of true value on the physical plane, no time is wasted, the individual knows his or her purpose in life and gets on with it without the wastage of time and wrong thought, wrong action, and delays which occur lower down the line. He discovers the value, uses and purposes of the creative imagination. This is all that remains to him eventually of the intensely active astral life lived for so many lives. The astral body becomes a mechanism of transformation — desire transformed into aspiration, aspiration into a growing and expressive intuitive faculty.

The intuitive faculty emerges when true soul contact is achieved, when the bridge between the personality and the soul is of such a constancy and intensity that what was simply emotional aspiration is transformed into a direct linking with the higher aspect of which it is a reflection, the Buddhic aspect of the Spiritual Triad. Our astral-emotional body, in terms of evolutionary purpose, is meant to be, and eventually becomes, simply a still, reflecting vehicle for *Buddhi*. Buddhi is true intuition. It is essentially group consciousness; intuition is another name for group consciousness. It is the Buddhic, the Love-Wisdom, aspect of the Spiritual Triad. Buddhi eventually reflects itself directly through the astral mechanism as intuition: we know, because we know, because we know. There is no thinking about it; it is a direct, spontaneous response to Buddhi, using the purified astral nature as the medium for that intuitive response. The antahkarana produces this, inevitably.

There is a relationship between the science of the antahkarana and Transmission Meditation. Transmission Meditation is a fusion of two Yogas: Karma Yoga — the Yoga of Service — and Laya Yoga — the Yoga of the Chakras, the energies. Essentially, the antahkarana is concerned with the force centres, the chakras, because it is through the scientific manipulation of the energies in the chakras, the correct stimulation of these chakras, that the antahkarana is built. One can say that the science of the antahkarana is the science of the chakras. The sciences of the future — of the antahkarana, of meditation, and of service — are linked. One leads to the other: correct meditation leads to the building of the antahkarana; correct building of the antahkarana leads to the life of service — *correct* service, directed by soul purpose. The knowledge and creativity of the soul is consciously put at the disposal of the individual who scientifically builds the antahkarana. Since Transmission Meditation is a fusion of Karma Yoga and Laya Yoga, what the Masters are actually doing in the Transmission Groups around the world is creating a group antahkarana. It is being done for us.

The average time of real alignment, and therefore of correct transmitting, in any hour is about three-and-a-half to four minutes. It is only because Transmission Meditation is so potent, so scientific, that it is valuable to do even these three-and-a-half minutes. Because of its extraordinary potency, because of the pure, scientific nature of Transmission Meditation, these three-and-a-half to four minutes have an extraordinary value for the world and an extraordinary value for the people doing it. We are gradually having the antahkarana built for us — it is a gift. The Masters are serving us, spoon-feeding us. The antahkarana is being created at an extraordinary rate; so much so that, if people are around the 1.5 mark — between the first and second initiation — and in reasonable health and youth, it is perfectly possible to take the second initiation in this life; not because of any particular effort being made, either in building the antahkarana or in service to the world, but simply by sitting enough times in Transmission Meditation, keeping the attention at the Ajna centre, for the Masters to help create this channel of light between the different aspects of our being.

This is an extraordinary thing that is happening in the Transmission groups, and it is one of the major reasons why people in these groups make such extraordinary advancement. Those who have been transmitting for the last 10 years, say, are far more advanced than they could possibly have been otherwise. They may not realize it, but the Masters do; They measure and register it, and They know those who are ready, in this incarnation, to take the second initiation (most people doing Transmission Meditation have taken the first). This is only possible because of the exigencies of the time which at the same time presents to the aspirant and the disciple an opportunity for service through Transmission Meditation. It cannot be overemphasized how valuable this is proving.

What is being built in the connecting thread, the channel between the different aspects of oneself, is a Path of Return to the Source, the Monad. We are the Monad, which reflects through the soul as the physical-plane personality. We are on the Path of Return, redeeming the matter of our various bodies, physical, astral and mental. That redeemed, spiritualized, matter

433

produces, in the next solar system, matter of a higher rate of vibration. And so the evolution of the body of the Planetary Logos proceeds; we are all involved in that individually and for the planet, for the solar system. That is why we are here. As one grows and evolves one deepens one's consciousness of that reality.

The Macrocosm, as we begin to intuit its nature, to experience it through conscious awareness, tells us that that is the reality, and, more and more, we lose the sense of the separate self. It is said: Lose yourself in service. The process by which we do this is the building of the bridge. It results in the creativity of service: creativity is service, service is creativity. It is the nature of the soul in the three worlds to express itself in some form of creative service, and as we do this we lose sense of the separate self. We deepen our experience of the Macrocosm and realize that that and ourselves are one. That is the growing experience of the man or woman who builds the Bridge, who creates that unity with the soul. Then the soul becomes in a singular life a reality. Beyond all controversy, all gainsaying, we know that we are the soul.

It is not simply a theoretical or intellectual idea, we know it as part of our being, and we know eventually that the soul itself is a light within an even greater light, a fire within an even greater fire. That fire has consciousness — that is the nature of the soul, and the person making contact with the soul eventually realizes that it is a fire within a greater consuming fire, which is Deity itself. It says in the Bible: "God is a consuming fire". That is the reality.

The soul is a great, fiery vortex of forces which are reflected on the lower planes as the man or woman in incarnation. That is what we are: a reflection of these fiery forces, and the bridge that we build — the antahkarana — back to the soul and eventually back to the Monad is the path by which these forces become available to us. They stimulate the mind, the intuition and the creative will, and our life as initiates, knowing initiates, in the process of life, takes place.

(*Share International*, January/February 1994)

THE BUILDING OF THE ANTAHKARANA

What is the correct building of the antahkarana? How is it done?
This science is not in the hands of humanity at the present
moment. Maitreya has made it very simple. He has said: "The
Self alone matters; you are that Self, an immortal being. I have
come to teach the art of Self-realization." It is to do with
awareness.

Putting it as simply as probably only He can, Maitreya says
that we identify with the wrong aspect of ourselves. We do not
identify with ourselves as the soul, as the Self, but with our
body; with what He calls the spirit, which is the energy aspect,
the astral, etheric, the "shakti", the energy of the earth itself; and
with the constructions of our mind, our thinking. All of these we
identify with as if they were the Self, yet none of these is the
Self. The Self stands back of them and observes through them.

The soul creates, again and again, a body which gradually,
over eons of time, allows the Self to manifest totally, purely,
unhindered, through its polar opposite, matter. By that point in
time, the matter has been spiritualized, its vibrational rate lifted.
In religious terminology, it has been "redeemed". That is why
the Christ is called the Redeemer, the Holy Redeemer of men. I
do not mean only for Christians. The Christ Principle is the
redeeming principle. It is that principle which in life, in creation,
informs its vehicle with its own consciousness, with the energy
of consciousness, and, therefore, the energy of evolution. It is
that growth of consciousness, that action of evolution upwards,
through a refining of its nature to a higher and higher frequency,
higher and higher vibration, that constitutes evolution itself. This
leads to a gradual expansion of knowledge of what is and what
might be; it is creative. This is the essence of the soul's nature:
creativity itself.

Creation by its very nature presupposes that it is unfinished.
Creation is movement, but the Self behind creation does not
move. It is changeless, without movement, without any kind of
reflex, simply observing creation. Before creation, there is the
"Supreme Being" of the Self. Creation is the "becoming", as
Maitreya puts it, the "becoming" of the Self. That "becoming" is

the movement of life, the movement of creation, the discovery of what might be.

It is not a question of finding out in life, like a scientist, looking through a microscope and trying to find out how one cell interacts with another and so on. That is valuable on the physical plane, but it is limited. If you think that what you are seeing is all, the totality, you are missing a great movement and mystery. That is the problem for most scientists today. They are looking only at the physical plane surface of life. It is enormously valuable, do not misunderstand me; what they do is of tremendous benefit to health, the overcoming of disease, the understanding of the nature of the physical plane. But in terms of consciousness, in terms of the action of life itself in creation, it tells us very little. That is why we are ignorant. Given the nature of our science, we should be enormously endowed. In a way we are, but only in a very limited way. It is the lower concrete mind which is endowed. But without it we would not have the action of the higher mind. The higher mind can not function before the lower mind. Everything in its time.

You need meditation to bring you into contact with the soul and therefore with the consciousness of the soul. Meditation by its very nature starts the process of the building of the antahkarana.

How is the antahkarana constructed — of thoughtforms? Or how much does thought play in the building of the antahkarana?
Very much. The first span of the antahkarana is built by the energy of mind. It is precisely by the use of mind and the creative imagination that the first part of the antahkarana comes into being. The second part, from the soul to the Monad, is built in light; so first of all it is by thought, then in light — controlled thought, and experienced light.

Is the building of the antahkarana and the raising of the Kundalini the same process?
No, not at all.

What does the personal meditation have to do with the building of the antahkarana?

An enormous amount. In the personal meditation you are gradually aligning yourself with the soul and experiencing the reality of the Self.

The personal meditation directly strengthens the link between the personality and the soul. It aligns you with the soul, invoking soul energy. When you do the personal meditation, you automatically invoke and experience the soul; it becomes a reality. Every time that you do it, soul awareness is growing in you, becoming more and more powerful.

The soul is the intermediary between the Self and the individual. The meditation, if correctly used and assiduously practised, creates an unbroken link. The antahkarana is not a form, a bridge, a shape in a painting. It is awareness. When you do the personal meditation, you are becoming aware of who you are. This awareness grows until you *become* what you are. You are creating the path before you, building the antahkarana step by step before you. It is unfolding every time you do the personal meditation and Transmission Meditation. The combination of these two activities — meditation and service — builds the path of return.

Looking at lithographs of your other paintings helps me — 'The Flaming Diamond' etc. Does looking at 'The Antahkarana' lithograph help build my antahkarana?

Just looking at it does not, but you can use the antahkarana as a personal meditation and visualize it if you understand the symbolism of the picture. The picture is a symbol, not the antahkarana itself. The antahkarana is a bridge of *awareness* created by thought (and eventually by light) which forms a communicational link between the three aspects of our being — the Monad, the soul and the personality. What you see on a picture, or what you might visualize, is simply a symbol for something, in this case for the created antahkarana. If you understand that, and how the antahkarana is built, and visualize it as that symbol, it can help you in the focus needed in building the antahkarana.

437

That is why ideas are presented to you, for example in the Alice Bailey and Theosophical works: to give you an image, an idea, and therefore the beginning of consciousness of the evolutionary process. Esotericism is the science of that process, and inevitably — because it is presenting ideas which are abstract to the lower concrete mind — it has to use it to demonstrate the meaning which underlies the symbol. It is the meaning which is the important thing; the antahkarana, when the link is made with the soul, gives you an entry into the world of meaning.

These 'meanings' are the 'beingness' of the subtler states of being, of the soul-plane, and eventually of the Monadic plane. The symbol itself can only represent that to you in a form which 'stands for' that in your consciousness. Understanding the symbol is very important, if it is potent and correct. The awareness of the meaning of the symbol can add credibility to your endeavour to build the antahkarana; that is certainly true. Some people have been given it as a personal meditation as part of their evolutionary process.

What is the difference between a symbol and a sign?

A symbol can be a sign but a sign is not necessarily a symbol. Many artists create signs, and we call them loosely 'signs and/or symbols'. You can create a sign which is also a symbol, which stands for not just a form but for the meaning behind that form, while a sign simply stands for a form, it is an abbreviated way of showing a form — this is what Chinese characters do: you draw a certain shape and everyone knows that means a house; it is the sign for a house but it is not the symbol for a house. All great art is symbolic in its nature. I do not mean that behind every picture there is a story — the Victorian idea that "every picture tells a story" I think is erroneous — but every picture, whether it tells a story or does not tell a story, however abstract it may be, will be either a sign or a symbol, or both. A sign may be immediately identifiable — examples are the various transportation signs on the highway which are instantly and internationally recognizable— but not symbols.

This (picture of the antahkarana) is a symbol for something that exists in reality, it is a part of reality when it is built because it is built in energy. The 'sign' we have been talking about is not built in energy; it is a sign standing for some form, or some idea in transportation and so on.

What effect does praying have on the antahkarana?
Praying is the result of the emotional aspiration which underlies the sense in every individual that they are divine, that outside themselves, above, beyond, outside their own lower-mind consciousness, there is a greater Source of Consciousness, and of Knowledge and Love and Intelligence. Praying — like the saying of *The Lord's Prayer* — is a recognition of this fact. It is an expression of emotional aspiration, and as such it will certainly have an effect on the beginning of the building of the antahkarana, but the antahkarana itself is pre-eminently a bridge built of thought, and by thought. It has to be done consciously by the man or woman in incarnation; it is essentially the result of the mind being able to visualize and create the bridge. The bridge between the personality and the soul is made by thought, and that between the soul and the Monad in light-substance. But that light-substance is still matter, from the Cosmic point of view.

Praying has an effect, but only in the beginning process. Emotional aspiration has to become the focused, one-pointed activity of the mind. That activity, in building the antahkarana, becomes infused eventually with soul energy and through the soul with abstract, higher mind, the Manasic level of the Spiritual Triad, which is the reflection in the soul of the threefold Monad.

I am thinking about the New Age Prayer — is this an aspect of the antahkarana?
No. The antahkarana, when fully built, will give you the kind of awareness of the Monad which is affirmed in the New Age Prayer. The New Age Prayer is a way of affirming what exists. The antahkarana is deliberately built by the man or woman in incarnation to bridge the gaps in consciousness between the

Monad and its reflection, the soul, and between the soul and the physical personality. These are three distinct phases of expressions of life and have to be reconnected: that is the Path of Return. The New Age Prayer is not the Path of Return but an affirmation that one is the Self, the goal at the end of the Path.

The Monad exists as a reality, so does the soul, so does the man or woman on the physical plane, but from the personality's point of view, for the most part, the other realities are unknown. The antahkarana is the means by which you gain awareness of the connectedness; that is why it is the Path of Return. The affirmations, mantrams, prayers, meditations, and so on are all part of that process.

Can you describe how the activity of service accelerates the building of the antahkarana? How does aspiration and visualization accelerate the building of the antahkarana?

They are part of the science. The aspiration becomes something much more powerful than that; the visualization eventualizes in the building of the antahkarana, but these are simply part of the technique. The activity of service, as I said, is a direct result of the contact with the soul, and is one of the three sciences of the coming time.

What is really going to happen is that humanity will discover that it is a soul, that we are really souls in incarnation. Jesus taught this, but no one remembers it, not even the Christians think about it, except, 'When you die you meet your soul'. No one thinks of the soul actually taking form on the physical plane; this is the new experience for humanity, that every one eventually will realize that we are souls.

The Law of Incarnation, the Law of Rebirth, will be taught in a scientific manner and every one will accept it, just as today we accept all sorts of things which 200 years ago we would not accept. That being so, service as an activity of the soul is an obvious reflection of that soul's activity, and service will be built into the mechanism of life. What we do will be seen to be done as service, and not as a personality demonstration for its own sake. That is where the difference between inner and outer considering comes in.

How does a Master build the mayavirupa?

The ability to build the mayavirupa is dependent upon the knowledge of the science of return. The science of return is the building of the antahkarana. To manifest in the mayavirupa, you must know the Path of Return, you must have done it. As you do it, you have not only the control, you have the powers which come to you on all planes. The powers are a result of knowledge of how the whole mechanism of life works at its different levels. When you go backwards through the levels, you have the knowledge to create the mayavirupa. You can be anywhere you like, by thought.

Does the ray structure, in particular the soul ray and mental ray, qualify the building of the antahkarana?

Because there are seven rays, and therefore seven different types of men and women, there are seven different ways of seeing reality. The soul ray does not change, but all the other rays change or may change from life to life. When people talk about a 1, 3, 5, 7 person or a 2, 4, 6 person, that is a very simplistic and superficial way of describing the person, because everyone, throughout their incarnation experience, has gone through all the rays many, many times, although there are certain rays, like the 1st and the 5th, which are not given until a certain point is reached.

The rays produce a particular method of work; they inform or qualify the building of the antahkarana by the way the person thinks, by the type of mentation they have. A 2nd-ray mental will work very differently from a 1st- or a 5th-ray mental, for example. The 3rd-ray mental will work differently from a 7th- or 4th-ray mental, and so on. The ray colouring the body, and therefore the brain, in this particular life will qualify the way in which you approach the building of the antahkarana. It will not affect the nature of the antahkarana itself.

Do the devas also build an antahkarana?

No, they do not. They work in a completely different way. The antahkarana is built consciously through meditation, through an action of the human mind, using mental energy. The devas do not do that but work in matter, in form. Their evolution proceeds through a growing awareness of the nature of reality, of life as it exists now. We grow in awareness through an understanding of the creative principle. For us, it is not simply a question of understanding what is, but of understanding what is and what might be. It is a creative activity, entirely different from that of the devic evolution.

THE SOUL

Is the soul aware of the Monad?

The Monad is aware of the soul and the soul is aware of the Monad. The soul cyclically turns its attention, and transmits its energy, to its reflection, the man or woman on the physical plane. At other times it turns its attention to that of which *it* is a reflection — the Monad. This goes on all the time while on the physical plane there is a growing awareness of this relationship to the soul.

Once that relationship becomes powerfully constant in our experience, we realize that even that is not the end, that there is above the soul something even higher, a light which is even brighter and clearer and more resplendent. That eventually reveals itself as the Monad, and at the third initiation the energy of the Monad — which is the Will aspect — begins to influence the activity of the individual. From then on, the threads of connectedness between himself and the environment — and by environment I mean everything, not just trees and houses; I mean individuals, groups, the whole world in all its ramifications, all that we contact, whether it is close or far away, grow in every direction.

The evidence of this is that the disciple is the man or woman who has control of his environment while the initiate can be recognized not just by that but by his service to the world. So you move from your own individual environment to the world, and eventually relate to the whole world. That is what the Masters and the higher initiates do. They relate to the world, their threads of connectedness stretch out further and further in every direction. They *are* threads because they are threads of energy — there is not anything else but energy. Every time we make a statement about a form we are really talking about a symbol for energy of one kind or another.

(1) If we won't know our purpose until we know we are a soul, what is the purpose of the soul? (2) Does each soul have a different purpose? (November 1996)

(1) Usually, the soul incarnates with three aims or purposes for that life, one of which is always the creation of right relationships. In the case of working disciples, the soul may present a fourth purpose of specific service. (2) Yes.

As I understand it, everyone comes into incarnation with four soul purposes — one of which is always the creation of right relationships. Regarding the other three purposes, would they typically be as general as "creating right relationships" (ie making known the presence of the Christ in the world, or becoming an artist), or would they be more specific, like developing the quality of courage, of steadfastness, for example? (January/February 1993)

They would be more specific, like becoming an artist (that is very specific) or developing certain qualities or overcoming others, like greed, gluttony, avarice, criticism, fear etc.

I read that the soul is both perfect and yet also continues to evolve, to be enriched through its vehicle's incarnational experience. (1) Could you say something more about Atma and Jiva; is it the experience of Jiva (soul in incarnation, Becoming) which adds to the quality of Atma (soul beyond and outside incarnation, Being)? (2) Why is it the soul which involves itself in matter, rather than the Monad, which must also have consciousness and be a repository of experience? (July/August 1995)

(1) Yes. It adds the quality of individuality, differentiation. (2) The soul is the "Divine Intermediary" between spirit and matter (Monad and personality) because it is individualized. The Monad does involve itself through the agency of its reflection, the soul, until the soul aspect occultly raises the personality to its own level. Then the relationship is direct between Monad and personality.

Could you explain the balance between the individual right to soul-development and the fact that we are one of another? (November 1995)

Two things are involved here. There is the individual who is an evolving unit of the human kingdom, and there is humanity which *is* the human kingdom. The problem, up until now, is that individuals have not seen themselves as part of the whole, but as separate, cut-off individual agents in a world based on competition, satisfaction of greed and so on. The altruism of the soul has hardly manifested through the individual, except in more evolved people who have come in to serve. Only the more developed units of humanity have been able to manifest soul quality. Today is a time in which humanity is faced with calamity unless we can do this. Unless we can manifest, *as a whole*, the soul quality of altruism — the sense that we are all part of one group — then we will destroy the world. It is a spiritual crisis which we are undergoing and that crisis is focused today through the political and economic fields: we share, and live together in peace — or we die together. Maitreya has come now to inspire us to share and prosper; He is in no doubt that we shall share and evolve, manifesting our innate soul qualities which make us One.

Why does the soul incarnate in the first place?
The soul comes into incarnation because it is serving the plan of evolution. It is an intermediary. The soul knows its purpose: to reflect the Monad through the threefold Spiritual Triad — atma, the will aspect, buddhi, the love/wisdom aspect, and manas the intelligence aspect. The interaction of these three produces the motivation for the life. As the antahkarana is built, higher and higher, not as a form but as an abstract state of awareness, the more these three aspects can be used by the man or woman. The manasic aspect is the first that can be used — the person becomes more usefully intelligent. They can use the intelligence factor to direct and shape their lives constructively, creatively, using intelligently the energy of creativity coming from the soul. When you make contact with the soul a creative life is inevitable; it could not be otherwise.

*Is that why the great artists are listed as high initiates in the Initiates List published in your books **Maitreya's Mission. Volume One** and **Maitreya's Mission, Volume Two**?*

Exactly. The culture is always created by the initiates of the nations. The civilization is the result of the dissemination of knowledge, buddhi, or love/wisdom, and the dynamic, atmic will which sets the whole thing in motion and directs it as to purpose. Hence you get a civilization with a particular quality, a particular group of ideas which make it recognizable as a whole. We can say it lasted from this date to that.

The different civilizations back through history have been created, in the first place through the culture, by the initiates of the time.

Would you say that we as human beings are the cells or the corpuscles of the great energy of love in humanity? (July/August 1993)

That is one way, a material, scientific way, of putting it.

If you can think of humanity as soul, there is only one soul, which humanity shares. On the soul plane there is no separation whatsoever, but one great Oversoul. Our souls are individualized aspects of that Oversoul, and it is the individualized soul which incarnates again and again. You could say that individual souls are 'molecules' of that Being, whose nature is love, but I am talking about 'Beingness' rather than 'corporateness'.

Can a soul be destroyed? (January/February 1993)

No. At the fourth initiation the soul is reabsorbed into the Monad, or Divine Spark, but it cannot be destroyed.

What about the increasing number of souls entering the Earth plane. Where do they come from? (January/February 1995)

According to the Ageless Wisdom teachings, there are 60 billion human Monads, or sparks of God, 5.6 billion, only, of which are in incarnation. When not in incarnation these Monads exist in a state of constant bliss, in a level of consciousness called Devachan — equatable to the Christian idea of heaven, until the time comes for their incarnation. The increasing number relates only to the fact that, increasingly, more and more bodies are being created on the Earth plane. This magnetically calls in souls who might not otherwise be prepared to incarnate at this time.

(1) What is the difference between "lost" souls and "earth-bound" souls? (2) This question results from an experience during my reincarnation-therapy. After 12 days of fasting I experienced that my body had 'shrunk', went through the spine of a corpse of a mortally injured patient (I was on duty as a nurse in Belgium in 1972) and that it left the corpse through the fingers. The therapist called this a "soul-liberation" of an earth-bound soul and stated that this soul, having used my body as a medium, could now ascend and reincarnate. Could this be true? (April 1993)

(1) A "lost soul" is someone who, in incarnation, has lost all connection with, and is cut off from, their soul. This would normally result in a life of great evil and destruction. An example of such a person is Adolf Hitler. Untold ages in 'purgatory' then ensues until karma allows a further incarnational experience.

An "earth-bound" soul is someone who, because of intense attachment to a particular house or area, remains tied to the earth on death and 'haunts' the house or area as a 'ghost'. This may also be the result of sudden and (usually) violent death or traumatic experience when the individual remains unaware of having made the transition.

(2) I am afraid the "reincarnation-therapist" was talking nonsense. The experience was purely the result of an over-active astral imagination — not to be wondered at after 12 days of fasting!

You have explained that twin souls reunite at the Monadic level. Do they each retain their separate identity when this occurs, or do they merge again as one Self? (October 1994)

They merge in the one Self.

German scientists at the Technical University in Berlin claim they have proved the existence of the human soul, which they *believe is a form of energy. Weighing 200 terminally ill patients immediately before death and again immediately afterwards, Dr Becker Mertens and his team discovered that the weight loss in each case was identical — 1/3,000th of an ounce. They say they took into consideration other factors such as air leaving the lungs. (Source: Letter to German scientific journal **Horizon**). (1) Are the scientists going along the right lines? (2) Does this really prove the existence of the soul? (3) What does the weight loss consist of?* (November 1993)

(1) No, except in so far as they are interested in trying to prove that the human soul exists. (2) No, they have not proved the reality of the soul but only that there is a weight loss of the body on death. (3) This is due to the reabsorption by the soul of the various ultra-fine nerve gases by which means the soul animates and influences the nervous system during incarnation. The scientists have actually "proved" the existence of these gases.

Can you give some explanation about "Soul Retrieval" which is becoming very popular in some "New Age" circles? A person can supposedly "lose" parts of his/her soul through a traumatic experience or drugs, etc, and through this process they can be brought back together! The soul, I believe, is complete on its level so how can this be? (November 1993)

The soul is, indeed, complete, inviolable and indestructible on its plane. You cannot ever "lose a part" of your soul. You can only be more or less cut off from your soul's influence, certainly by some trauma or drug abuse. Perhaps this is what is really meant. A trauma is a psychological state and concerns only the mind's experience.

Alice Bailey founded the Lucifer Trust, which she later changed to the Lucis Trust — what did she mean by 'Lucifer'? (April 1995)

Lucifer is the name of a great Angel, not an upstart in heaven who revolted against God and was put down into the nether regions as the Devil. That is a complete misinterpretation. Lucifer means light, and comes from the Latin *lux, lucis*, meaning light. It is the name of the Angel Who ensouls the human kingdom; every person, therefore, is a fragment of Lucifer. According to the esoteric teaching, the human souls individualized 18½ million years ago. Lucifer, the Oversoul, diversified itself, and each fragment became individualized.

These individualized human souls descended from the soul plane into incarnation. The 'fall' of Adam and Eve from paradise is the symbolic representation of this event; it has nothing to do with the Devil or with Lucifer as an evil entity, but with the divine nature of humanity itself as souls.

GROUP ANTAHKARANA

Could you enlarge on the relationship between the antahkarana on the group level and the individual level? How does the vertical aspect of the antahkarana, between soul and personality, relate to the horizontal, the threads connecting to the different fields in life? What is that connection? How does it work?

The closer you are to the soul, the more you identify with the soul. The more the soul is acting in the life of the individual, the greater the threads of consciousness which they are sending out from the centre to the periphery. These spread out in every direction.

The disciple is recognized by his control over his environment. By environment, I do not mean just the air, water, and earth. I mean their general environment. Their ability to work correctly, to make a living, to look after their family, to bring up their children, to work in correct, harmless relationship with other people — all of that is the environment. These are the marks of the true disciple who has control of all these aspects of life, the main one being that of interrelationship — the more correctly that person relates to husband, wife, children, friends, society, and the world at large.

The initiate is recognized by the scope of his or her work, the impact of his or her consciousness. When I say initiate, I mean a third-degree initiate, because that is what the Masters mean by initiate. The initiate is the person who not only has that kind of control, but also has an impact on the life of his or her time. The degree of that initiate awareness is measured by the scope of their creative activity — the impact that it has — and occasionally for harm — on a wide scale.

These are the threads of consciousness which the initiate puts out. As he or she becomes more and more imbued with the nature and energy of the soul, becomes more and more ensouled, those threads go out in every direction. The impact of that life is greater and greater. This is why the major figures of life have always been initiates. They set down the thoughtform, the consciousness, of the time. They are the great thinkers, preachers, teachers, musicians, artists, philosophers, leaders, inventors, scientists — great, creative beings because they are soul infused.

The greater the degree of soul infusion, the greater the number of threads which will go out to the world — and the greater the magnetic impact of that life on his or her time. The initiate has the ability to work and organize his life, but on a wide scale, even a world scale — Abraham Lincoln, for example. Abraham Lincoln epitomized initiate consciousness and set it down in words which embody the aspiration of a nation. In a sense, they have become the aspiration of the entire world, which is coloured by the consciousness of Abraham Lincoln whether they have heard of him or not. That is what I mean by putting out threads of consciousness in all directions. The activity of such an individual impinges on more and more people. Lives are changed by coming into contact with such a person, or with his creations and activities. That is the mark of the initiate. That is what I mean by the horizontal threads connecting the different fields in life.

Does the world-wide communication network which enables us to be aware of other people and their problems represent the beginning of the building of the world antahkarana?

Yes. It is the outer expression of an inner awareness. That communication system is bringing humanity together in a very real sense, as part of this gradual awareness, because the antahkarana is really a state of awareness. It is an awareness of the interconnectedness of all life, all aspects of life, of all beings as part of one whole. That is a most important and essential part, because the outer mechanisms reflect the inner reality.

Will the coming into the world of the Masters affect the building of the racial antahkarana?

Of course. If the racial antahkarana is to be built at all, it can only be built consciously. And it can only become conscious if the teaching is given. The teaching will be given by the Masters and Their disciples. It does not mean, necessarily, that the Masters will say every word on every radio programme about the antahkarana, but a body of teaching will be given which will suffice for those ready for that teaching, as has always been the case. It is not different, only that it will be exoteric rather than esoteric. No information, teaching, or knowledge has ever been withheld from humanity if humanity has been ready for it. Wherever there have been groups or individuals ready for the teaching, that teaching has been given. The fact that the teaching has not permeated into all groups is simply because they have not been ready.

How many people today read the Alice Bailey books, for example? Very, very few in relation to the numbers of humanity. How many people read the Agni Yoga teachings or the writings of Blavatsky? A tiny minority. The vast majority of people are not ready for it. You cannot absorb what you are not ready for in terms of consciousness. Like attracts like. Where the consciousness is open and permeable by truth, the truth is given. That truth of course is always relative.

People imagine that when they have the Alice Bailey teachings they have the last word on the subject. Not at all. The Master DK who gave them says that they will last for disciples at the present time, and for those coming into incarnation over the next years up until about half way through the next century. By that time, all that is so difficult and esoteric will become much more exoteric because the Hierarchy of Masters will be working in the world. People will see Them, and Their disciples will be given the task of disseminating that which can be absorbed.

The teaching of the nature of the antahkarana, the function of the antahkarana, the mode of employing and creating it, will be made known. It will be given step by step as groups equip themselves for its use. (The key words here are "as groups *equip themselves*".) The practice of Transmission Meditation is a gift because this group has — created by the Masters for it — a method which is really the method of building the antahkarana. It is done for you.

There are those who think: "I wish he would bring out a booklet and tell us exactly how we do the thing. I want to master this. Why doesn't he produce a book, or at least a booklet?" I can give you a lot of reasons why I do not produce a book or booklet. The main reason is that people do not equip themselves for the information. As soon as humanity is equipped to receive the information, it will be given. It always is. It is a law; the demand produces the supply.

There are some terms, perhaps a question of semantics, such as "racial", in "a racial approach to Deity", and "white" as in "Great White Brotherhood", that could cause discomfort. Please explain how these terms relate with the oneness of humanity.

To me that is just silly — I am sorry to say this, but that is how it seems to me. By a "racial approach to Deity" I do not mean an Asiatic, a Western, a white or a black or a yellow race — I do not mean race in that sense. When I say "racial" I mean *the human race*: humanity as one group, which it is, whatever the colour.

Are we going to get rid of the colours white, red, yellow, blue, green, black? — are we never to say white or black? This is a nonsense. This is taking racial disharmony to a point of total nonsense, it seems to me. Of course there is racial disharmony; it is built on colour and prejudice, but colour prejudice and prejudice of all kinds is going to go out of the window very soon. It will disappear in the new awareness which is going to come to humanity. I mean the experience of finding out who we are and that we are Sons of God. An entirely new awareness is going to be ours in relation to each other, and colour is something which eventually we just will not see. There will continue to be white men, black men and yellow men and reddish and brown men but it will not make one iota of difference. There will not be colour prejudice — and the prejudice of colour prejudice, if you know what I mean. This is a demonstration of colour prejudice; even to voice it is an expression of colour prejudice, even though it is about colour prejudice. If you do not see the difference there is no difference, there is simply *variety*. That is the important thing — let us have all the variety we can in the world but see the underlying unity. That makes for tolerance and a richer life — and the ending of such daft questions!

You said that buddhi is really group consciousness. Can you say how buddhi is group consciousness, how the energy of love/wisdom is group consciousness?

This is awakened when the love petals in the crown chakra are opened. The soul is then strongly influential and it changes the nature of consciousness. By this time, a person has lost his sense of being a separate self.

Most people have the sense that they are separate, the personality, Mr or Mrs whoever. They recognize themselves by what they see in the mirror and take that to be the Self, which is not the case. They take this image to be a separate person, and they are very aware of themselves.

Everyone is very self-conscious. You only have to look around to see that this is the case. Everyone is at the centre of the universe. The universe is revolving around us, and we are in the centre, the important point in life.

Essentially, we feel, what matters is ourselves: are we getting enough to eat, enough sex, enough adulation, kindness, respect? Everyone wants respect. Everyone has to treat us with respect, love, affection, kindness. They have to show they love us, to recognize that we are at the centre of the universe, and as such are due all of this respect, kindness, and love.

Other people are here to satisfy our needs, as we see them. For the most part, they are not our needs but our wants. They are certainly our wants, and that is the trouble. This gives us the sense of being alone and separate and, as it were, in competition, at war with the world to get what we want out of it: what is wrong with other people is that they do not automatically see this, do not see that they are agents for our desires. We all know this; this is everyone's experience.

As we evolve, as the soul knocks on the door for the millionth time, it says: it is not like that. You are not at the centre of the universe. You do not exist as a separate being. Only I, the soul, exist. I know that I am not separate. One day the message from the soul gets through, that this is not real. The sense of being at the centre of the universe gradually erodes, it fades. The underlying truth is that the soul exists, and the man or woman is simply a reflection, an agency. This personality with all its hopes, dreams, desires and needs is simply a dream, a fiction, a creation on the physical plane for a certain time. From one moment to the other it is never the same, is changing all the time. It is even getting old, which is seen as tragic, especially when it is actually happening. The thought about it is crippling enough for most people.

The reality is that as the soul informs its vehicle and the person loses something of this sense of separateness, the important things in life change. What was important becomes unimportant, ceases to have that intensity of need and begins to fade. Other things rise in importance, like service. Service is impersonal and rises up when the personal goes.

When the individual becomes so attuned to the soul, and the soul is beginning to manifest through the individual, the shift takes place from the personal to the impersonal, from the astral/emotional to the heart. The heart is always impersonal. It feels as if it is personal, and it is moved by personal experiences, but it is essentially impersonal. The emotions, on the other hand, are always totally personal, to do with desire. These desires might be high-minded, but they are still desires.

The change takes place through a growing awareness of the nature of the soul and therefore the nature of life. The soul is the means by which life demonstrates itself in the world. It is an agency, just as the physical body with its astral and mental makeup is an agency. The reality is the life. This life pours through all the different forms. One of these forms is the soul. Another of the forms, the reflection of the soul, is the man or woman in incarnation.

As Maitreya says: "The Self alone matters". The Self is the life. The Self alone matters, you are that Self, an immortal being. Our problem is that we do not know it. We identify with that which is not the immortal being and so we suffer. All the suffering, all the pain, all the tyranny of the present is the result of this wrong identification. The path backwards is the creation of the linking bridge, the antahkarana. Maitreya would say, very simply: Practise three things: honesty of mind, sincerity of spirit, and detachment. As you create the antahkarana, these three are automatically being expressed. As you practise them you are automatically creating the antahkarana. The building of the racial antahkarana is the result of the gradual realization by humanity that it is the soul, that it is the Self, and that that is informing this experience we call life. But it is life itself playing through all the forms that gives it reality, dynamism, the need to express.

What is intuition? You said intuition is group consciousness. Could you explain that?

Group consciousness is the realization that we are not separate — and not only the realization but the manifestation of the fact that we are not separate. It results from the awareness of buddhi, love/wisdom. If there is no awareness, there is no life. You cannot say you have life if you are not aware of the life. What you are unaware of does not exist for you; it only exists through the experience we call awareness. This is why there is so much confusion in the occult, esoteric highways and byways, of what is real, where the truth lies. What should I not read? What is a good group? What is a bad group? What should I believe? People ask all these questions because they do not allow their awareness to function. If you allow the intuition to function (it stems from the heart at the right hand side of the chest), it never lies, never gives you a wrong notion, a wrong idea, a wrong choice because it is the anchorage of the soul in the etheric physical body. That being so, all these questions of what is a good way or a bad way can be answered by the opening up of the intuition.

The intuition is knowing. It is not thinking, working out, mentation, but direct, straight knowledge. You know because you know because you know — directly, without even thinking about it. You do not have to think it out, deduce. At the buddhic level, where the Masters function, the link is automatic, contact immediate, because there is only group consciousness. The consciousness of buddhi is group consciousness; the individual, separate self has disappeared from the scene.

If you were to ask a Master what He thinks about this or that, He would not say 'I'. He does not have the word for 'I', because He does not have the concept of 'I'.

The first thought, the first word by which you can express your sense of separation is by saying 'I'. As soon as you say: 'I', you mean that there is that which is not me. But in reality, for the soul, there is not that sense of separation. Functioning as souls, as of course the Masters are, They do not have that sense of 'I' — they have group consciousness. Eventually, the race as a whole will function in this way. Of course, there are not many today with that kind of consciousness, but in the future this will become the reality.

You have said that when the astral body is purified it becomes a mirror for the buddhic level of consciousness. What is the difference between intuition, direct knowledge, that I relate to the higher mental, and the impression that is given from the buddhic level on the astral body? (June 1995)

Technically speaking, intuition — straight-knowledge — proceeds from the buddhic level, not the manasic or higher mental. It is the result of what the Masters call "loving understanding" or wisdom, a fusion of knowledge and love. They know it as "Pure Reason".

THREADS

You said that primitive, unevolved peoples have only the sutratma, the life thread, and that average humanity has both the sutratma and the consciousness thread. Could you explain further about this?

By primitive peoples, I do not mean any particular race or colour. I mean people who in terms of consciousness are still very much at the Atlantean stage of development. They have physical consciousness, and a large degree of astral consciousness, but only a very minimal degree of mental consciousness. There are not too many people in the world like that, but there are some. They are to be found in very primitive societies, like Papua and the Amazon forests. They are not primitive because they have not had the benefits of modern civilization. They are primitive because of the limited nature of the consciousness. Their focus of consciousness is almost exclusively on the physical and emotional/astral planes. Average humanity, on the other hand — the bulk of all others in every country without exception — have the thread of consciousness anchored in the head as well as the thread of life anchored in the heart. These two threads are in place. Average humanity does not have the creative thread to any extent at all. The creative thread is built by the man or woman himself in the actual process of life.

Where is the creative thread anchored in the human being? Is it in the ajna centre?

No, it is anchored in the throat; the chakra connected with the thread of creativity is the throat. Eventually, you will find there is a technique or process of linking between the twofold head centre (the head centre links the ajna and crown as the head centre), the throat centre, and the heart centre. These three centres form a triangle and through that triangle the activity of the developed disciple takes place. That builds, in the first place, the link with the soul, the first span of the bridge of the antahkarana, in mentation. It is done by conscious visualization, conscious, aware, mental activity, and the use of the creative imagination. The second part, the link to the Monad, the divine spark of God, in light, is created by the soul itself — because the person is by then soul-infused.

By the time the fourth initiation is taken, the person is totally soul-infused. Three-quarters of his or her body is now light. The cells are radiating energy which is no longer atomic, but subatomic. The person is ready for the fifth initiation, in due course, when the whole process is perfected. Having acted as the Divine Intermediary between the Monad and the man or woman in incarnation for thousands of incarnations, the soul is no longer needed as a separate entity. The soul was needed to step down the qualities of the Monad — spiritual will, love/wisdom or buddhi, and spiritual intelligence, manas (manas literally means mind). The manasic level is the first to be contacted, being the lowest, the closest to the physical plane. Buddhi, the love/wisdom aspect, is the next. In the chakra at the top of the head there are three groups of petals, one inside the other. The outer, knowledge petals are the first to open. This releases the energy of manas. Then the love/wisdom petals open, releasing the energy of Buddhi. Lastly, the Will or Purpose, Atma, of the innermost petals is released to galvanize and direct the life of the disciple.

Does the third thread, that anchoring in the throat, exist all the time?
No. That is created and anchored in the throat through the actual creative activity of the individual, having built the first span of the bridge between the personality and the soul.

Does that correspond to the second initiation?
No, not necessarily. It would be the result of soul contact, which leads to the first initiation. Between the first initiation and the second you would expect to see a greater and greater ability to serve meaningfully in the world. By the time the second initiation is taken, the service will be so soul-orientated that it will be more and more altruistic and effective, so the *quality* of the service will increase.

The second-degree initiate will work increasingly with the abstract level of thought, as he reaches up through the antahkarana to the soul and the Spiritual Triad. Although a person up to that point might deal with abstract thought (they might be philosophers, for example) it will be at a lesser degree of abstraction and less accurately reflect the inner reality. The "genius" is the man or woman who has such a close moment-to-moment contact with his or her soul that the abstract level of thought, and the true meaning and beauty and light of the inner reality, is reflected spontaneously in his or her work on the physical plane. We say they are "inspired".

Could you explain what you mean by "threads" in contacting our environment; how are they extended?
The word "thread" is, again, simply a symbol to describe an invisible energetic outreach to the environment. A thread is a stream of energy, and all activity is the result of the expression of energy, of force, at some level.

We describe as energy that which we receive, and force as that energy converted by the one who received it and extended out to the world. So the outgoing energy is force. These threads are threads of force which relate the individual who has constructed the antahkarana to the outer world. These many threads, related to the central threefold thread of the antahkarana, become extended in every direction. Every one, having reached that point, is extending their range of awarenesses. What we are talking about all the time is not really the building of a bridge like the Golden Gate or any other bridge; that is only a symbol for what we are really doing which is connecting different levels, since there is a gap in consciousness between the levels.

The aim of evolution is to create continuity of consciousness. When the bridge is properly built, there is such continuity of consciousness, not only between sleep and waking but between one life and another. That gap is bridged so that the man eventually, having constructed the bridge between himself and his higher Self, the soul, and through the soul with the Monad, the essential Deity, knows without any shadow of doubt that he is a living God. That is the result of the creation of the bridge, but the bridge is not the thing, the *awareness* is the thing.

Are there chakras above the head? Could you say something more about this? (May 1995)

The chakras exist in etheric matter and therefore within the aura. The depiction of chakras above the head, often found in Indian Yoga manuals, for example, refer to the spiritual levels of the soul: Manas, Buddhi and Atma.

I understand we are not using part of our brain — will more of it become usable in the future? (December 1994)

There are a number of force centres in the brain which for the vast majority of people are as yet quiescent. Through the evolutionary process these force centres open the way to the higher reaches of the mental plane. There are four mental planes (just as the physical plane is actually seven planes though we think of it as one plane). As, eventually, more and more people see the etheric planes — some already do — they will become a reality and humanity will accept that they exist. There are many centres in the brain of etheric substance which are totally unknown but which gradually unfold and awaken the person to the higher mental planes. In time, we shall use all four of the mental planes, and, higher still, the three spiritual planes: the Manasic, the Buddhic and the Atmic, which are reflections of the spiritual Will, Love and Intelligence of the Spark of God. The way is through meditation and through service to the world.

Do we have an 8th major chakra and, if yes, what is its function? (December 1996)

No.

CREATIVITY AND SERVICE

What do you mean by creativity?

Creativity is the essential expression of the Will and Love of Deity. As you know, there are two threads laid down from the very beginning — the sutratma, the Thread of Life which comes from the Monad and is anchored in the heart; and the antahkarana, the Thread of Consciousness, which comes from the soul and is anchored in the head. The activity of the Monad wills life into being. That is itself a creative act, and when life makes contact with and unites with its polar opposite — substance, the energy of matter — consciousness is created; that is the first creative act. The life stands behind the form, but the substance which creates form, until it unites with life, is itself without expression. When life and form come together, there is consciousness, what we call the Christ Principle. The Christ Principle is the creative process from the interaction of life and form — the result is creativity: it is the essential nature of Divinity.

It is a fundamental occult axiom that "as above so below"; the microcosm exactly mirrors the Macrocosm, and as soon as the man or woman on the physical plane controls the thought processes and therefore the energies of the chakras, the essential creativity of the soul begins to reflect itself in the outer plane.

This creativity can be of many kinds — one of them is service. Creativity is service; service is creativity. They are one and the same, the nature of the soul. The life thread is anchored in the heart, the consciousness thread in the head, and when these two together create the link with the soul, the creativity thread is also formed. When it is strengthened and evolved to a sufficient degree, it is anchored in the throat. Then the head, the heart and the throat together are the centres for the reception of energy from the soul. This leads inevitably to a greater and greater creativity on the part of the individual. This can take any form. Service must, inevitably, be one of these forms. If an artist makes paintings, if a man creates a new political-economic structure, that is creativity and it is also service. You cannot draw a line and say that is service but not creative, or that is creative but not service. All that flows from the soul is both creative and service, because the nature of the soul is creative- and service-oriented.

You say creativity is service, service is creativity. Please explain what the connection is.

Service and creativity are one and the same because they come from the same source — the soul. The nature of the soul is to serve and be creative because the nature of Deity is creativity.

Nothing remains the same. If nothing remains the same, there has to be a creative act which creates the change, which sets the energies in motion, which brings the stimulus of new and higher energies from a higher source — in the case of a planet from its sun, in the case of a sun from a higher solar system, and so on throughout cosmos. Every entity ensouling every vehicle, whether a planet or human body, is receiving energy from above, transmitting energy downwards to a lower entity, who then likewise transmits it downwards. There is thus a constant downward flow of higher energies which creates stimulus.

That stimulus is like winding up a clock. The tension grows — we call it spiritual tension because we are dealing with spiritual energies — and it tightens and tightens the spring of that clock until it is so tense that movement is inevitable. In the case of the clock, it turns the hands. In the case of the life of an individual, it stimulates creativity. The person begins to create in whatever manner that might be. When the soul is invoked, the energy of the soul creates the tension in the spring of your life which sets you on the creative path. The closer you are to the soul, the greater the intensity of that creativity and service. This is how service and creativity are the same; they are both the expression of the soul. There could not be one without the other.

The science of service is a new concept to me. Could you talk more about it.

Service is a necessary and inevitable result of soul-contact — as soon as you make contact with the soul you desire to serve, and the science of service is the science of knowing how best, how most effectively, objectively to serve: what, knowing your point

463

in evolution and your ray-structure, is the best line, the line of least resistance (or in an occasional life it might be the line of most resistance, deliberately chosen).

The Masters will be in the world, They will train Their disciples in this science, and people will go to schools and colleges — the whole of the educational programmes of the world will be completely changed. The present educational systems are not only elementary, they are bad; they really teach wrong relationships: they teach people to be nationals of particular nations, to be intolerant of other nations. One of the first educational needs is to teach children to see themselves as part of a whole, of one great human race made up of different nations, colours, backgrounds, religions, but all with the same Divinity and all treading the same path back to the Source.

Will the knowing of our ray structure and point of evolution help us to know our field of service?

Yes, indeed; if you know your ray structure you will have an insight into your own personal ring-pass-not. You will know that if you do not have certain rays in your makeup it is unlikely that the qualities of these rays will be in the present equipment. That is not to say that you will not have had them in previous lives; the soul rings the changes on all the rays during its incarnational sequence, but inevitably, as ray-qualities are built in, they become less dominant than the ones given in this particular life — these are the ones on which you are working.

The major rays are the ones which the soul hopes in this particular life will "shine through". That is that the virtues of the ray should shine through and become apparent and reflect the quality of the soul ray, whatever it happens to be. The personality ray is conditioned by the physical ray, the way the brain works and by its astral nature; the more polarized astrally the person is the more that is the case. The more mentally polarized, the more the personality is conditioned by the ray of the mental body, and the more spiritually polarized the person is, the more the personality is conditioned not only by these three but by the quality of the soul.

Eventually the quality of the soul is the dominating characteristic of the personality, which retains its own personal ray. The soul ray does not obliterate but conditions the expression of the personality ray.

If you have a 3rd- or 1st-ray personality or mental equipment, then the area of politics, economics and administration would be helped with these rays, and/or the 7th ray. If you are on the 2-4-6 line there are other things at which you would be much more likely to be useful; every ray has its own particular type of service, and all rays should serve. There are seven different ways to serve the world, one might say, although of course they interact and overlap.

The rays are very important in recognizing where and how you should serve. This group is specifically connected with, attracted to, the work of the Reappearance of the Christ and the Externalization of the Hierarchy. It does not matter what ray you have, that can be your task: the working with and making known the information about the Reappearance and the gradual emergence of the Masters on to the dense physical plane. That is the task of everybody in all these groups around the world; no matter what other activity they might be connected with or interested in, that is their primary task, that is why they have come into incarnation. They have come in at this time and gravitate to this message and these ideas specifically because they are needed to do so.

*In **Maitreya's Mission, Volume Two,** page 413, you point out that the list of ray structures of initiates in **Maitreya's Mission, Volume One**, contains practically no 3rd-ray souls above the level of the third initiation, which for a 3rd-ray soul is said to be the most difficult initiation to take. How does a 3rd-ray soul progress after the second initiation (if at all!) Does it need many more lives to take the third initiation than other rays?* (March 1996)

The 3rd ray governs the creation of form. The problem for the 3rd-ray type is its relative difficulty in recognizing the importance of the Life within the form. The third initiation demonstrates union with the soul — the source of Life within the form — and is therefore more of an obstacle than for other rays. It does usually take the third-ray soul more lives to achieve. However, once the inner realization of the Life aspect as paramount is achieved, the 3rd-ray type usually advances faster than others.

Benjamin Creme quite often talks about "mental polarization". What is this exactly? (May 1996)

Evolution proceeds by a shifting (upwards) of the focus of consciousness of any individual or race.

The first race, the Lemurian, had the goal of perfecting physical-plane consciousness. All humanity has long since achieved this — no one today is polarized on the physical plane. Atlantean man's goal was the perfecting of astral/emotional-plane consciousness. So well was this achieved that the majority of humanity today are still polarized on the astral plane.

Mental polarization begins about half-way between the first and second planetary initiations (what I call around 1.5-1.6) and is succeeded by spiritual polarization which begins around 2.5-2.6. That demonstrates as a close interrelation between the soul and its reflection, the man or woman in the three worlds, physical, astral and mental.

Please address the question of considering and consideration among co-workers.

There are two kinds of considering, inner considering and outer considering. We are all good at inner considering; all of us consider ourselves all the time — to everything that happens we ask ourselves: how is this going to affect me? Will this action make me feel comfortable or uncomfortable? How can I get my desire? How can I get this without seeming to get it? How can I be first? How can I get to the top of the queue, the line? If I do that it will tire me, so I won't bother to do it. I'd like to help this person, but I don't feel like it, so I'll ignore them today. All of that is inner considering, and everyone does it all the time.

The problem for humanity is that the way of evolution is through self-sacrifice. People hate the word 'self-sacrifice', and so they do not do it, but if we do not sacrifice we do not evolve

— it is as simple as that. Every one wants to evolve but no one wants to sacrifice themselves in doing so. What are we sacrificing? We sacrifice the lower for the higher: selfish, personality, desire principle for the awareness, the altruism — the forgivingness — of the soul. Self-sacrifice and forgivingness are one and the same: what we forgive we do through self-sacrifice. This is the gradual erosion of the thought that we are the centre of the universe. Inner consideration, which goes on all the time in everyone, is the result of the idea that we are at the centre of the universe, that the universe revolves around us, and that it is there, really, for us, so that we can pick out of it what we feel we want, must have, even if it is only momentarily. That is the common experience; it is called selfishness, egotism, looking after 'number one'.

Outer considering is looking at other people and seeing what they want and, even if it is not what we might want, considering their needs, their work, their time and energy. We all inflict our own desires on the energy systems of others and we do not consider, actually respect, other people's time and energy. These are two great areas in which people inflict themselves on each other.

Where is the will aspect of the Monad reflected on a lower level?
Through the 6th ray. The desire principle is the will aspect in its lower aspect. The first aspect is the life aspect. On the higher level, that is will, purpose. On the lower, in its negative aspect, it is simply desire; it is the desire principle of *life in form.*

It is the nature of the form to desire; it is not the will that desires. The will expresses purpose. But the desire principle desires this, wants that. It responds to the lure of possession. It is the lure of possession which keeps people ignorant, enthralled to that which it possesses. No progress can be made while that is the ruling principle.

Gradually, through life, through the pain and suffering of life, that selfish desire principle is changed into service. That which is wanted for the sensed separate self changes through the influence of the soul, which is selfless. The soul knows only altruistic, impersonal service. Gradually that quality informs the individual

467

and the person is no longer dominated by the desire principle. It gradually erodes and changes to aspiration — first of all emotional aspiration and then gradually to right meditation, right service, through the building of the antahkarana and the contacting, the fusing thereby, of the soul.

Meditation is the beginning. It creates the link, begins the process of linking the person to the soul. Through that first link, gradually at-one-ment, the fusing of the individual with the soul, takes place. Aspiration itself changes into indomitable will, the will of the known purpose that then dominates the life. Once the will petals are opened (the inner petals of which there are three in the "heart of the lotus") and the "jewel" is revealed, the purpose of the Monad for its expression through that individual, now soul-infused, can be demonstrated. Then you get the totally willed, purposed life of the higher initiates. That is what lies ahead for all.

What is the connection between the antahkarana and continuity of consciousness?

Continuity of consciousness depends on the creation of the antahkarana to bring it into being. Without the antahkarana, there can be no continuity of consciousness. Continuity of consciousness exists when there is no gap in consciousness from the waking state to the sleep state and back into the waking state. If the person, a thinking, conscious entity, goes to sleep and continues that state of awareness, and brings its experiences in sleep back onto the physical plane, that is called continuity of consciousness.

There is a further, more developed aspect of this, which is continuity of consciousness between one life and the next; you die consciously. Out of the body you remain totally conscious of who and what you are, what you have done, and what your purpose is. You reincarnate with full consciousness of having lived before and what you did. Continuity of consciousness in this sense is much rarer than that between the waking and sleep states. Eventually, with the building of the antahkarana, that too is developed, and then no time is wasted.

Time is wasted through lack of knowledge which is the result of the non-continuity of consciousness. We are conscious for a bit, and then we forget. We go to sleep, or we die, and we waste time remembering what we were aware of before we went to sleep or in our previous life. Much time and energy is wasted without continuity of consciousness. But when there is such consciousness, it is obvious, the path can be faster, very speedy and direct. If the person is at all disciplined, enormous evolution can take place in a very short time.

What would you say is the purpose behind creation?
There is only one purpose that we can know about in the whole of cosmos — the service of cosmos by cosmos. If it is true to say that we are God, there is no such thing as God out there and us here. God is a state of Being, a state of consciousness. When you have that state of consciousness, you know that you are God. When you do not have that consciousness, you can be told that you are God but you do not experience it. When you experience it, when you know it, you can put it into effect.

The first and foremost way to express that experience is through service. That is why there is this planet Earth, why there is a solar system, a universe. Think of the size of the Milky Way, our own galaxy, with its billions of solar systems, one tiny little corner of the universe. Think of this solar system, with its various planets — some more, some less evolved. Think of our own Earth, with the myriad creatures and individuals on it. All of that is the body of expression of an entity, a Being with consciousness. These are the outer forms of a great entity who is carrying out experiments. The experiments are Earth, Jupiter, Venus, Mars, etc. These are experiments of an entity, the Logos, impelled into creative manifestation by the desire to serve.

That entity is not separate from you and me. It is an aspect of the whole — a more advanced part of the whole than you and me but we are also parts of that same form. If there is a God which created all things, there can not be anything else. There can only be God. In the return journey, in the building of the antahkarana, that is the realization.

You spoke about the education for the New Age based on the science of the antahkarana. In which way could we support the children today?

There is no way you can introduce the children of today to the building of the antahkarana. Just love them and let them be. The time will come when their point in evolution and ray structure will be known. When we speak of children, we are not speaking of very young children. We are referring to children and young adults between the ages of 15 and 28. The building of the antahkarana is a conscious, mental process. That means that children have to be at a certain age before they could even begin to do it. Fifteen is the earliest at which they could start consciously using mentation to the extent of building the antahkarana. (There are exceptions where more advanced souls are concerned.)

The initiates will begin the process of creating the new educational concepts, the building of the antahkarana. This is over a period of time, obviously.

As part of the education in the New Age, how will young people's rays and points in evolution be ascertained and known, and who will teach them the science of the antahkarana? (January/February 1994)

The answer is that the Masters will be in the world and They will train Their disciples to ascertain personal ray-structures. People will have children to provide bodies for souls coming into incarnation, and the knowledge of ray-structure, the point in evolution, and the building of the antahkarana will be learned scientifically.

Why do you focus on the technical aspects and concepts of the science of the antahkarana from the Master DK so much when it seems so much easier to understand Maitreya's concepts about Self Realization?

Half of you will, I think, go home and say: "It was interesting in a way, but he didn't really tell us all that much about the antahkarana. He didn't tell us how to do it. He didn't go into technical details. That's what we need, techniques. Just give us the techniques and we will do it. Why does he say these abstract, non-technical things, these vague concepts, and so on."

The other half will say: "Why did he focus so much on the technical aspects, all these technical concepts of science and such? My mind doesn't run to science. Maitreya put it much more simply; the path of Self-realization."

I am sure both these attitudes exist, and if they do, and in that proportion, I must be getting it about right. I try to bridge them, to say that both are valid. There are many different paths. All paths you could call the building of the antahkarana. I try to link them together and show the interchangability of the language. Each of these concepts is expressed by language which we mistake for the thing. That is not the antahkarana.

The antahkarana is the awareness of what is and what might be. That is what life is about. The creation of the antahkarana is a way in which we build the bridge back to becoming what we are, but in full consciousness.

CHAPTER 7

TRANSMISSION MEDITATION

WHAT IS TRANSMISSION MEDITATION?

This article is an edited version of a talk given by Benjamin Creme at a public Transmission Meditation in Tokyo, May 1996.

Why do we meditate?

What is the purpose of meditation? All of us, without exception, are souls in incarnation. The true purpose of meditation of any kind is to bring the individual into contact with his or her soul. Meditation is a method, more or less scientific, depending on the meditation, of bringing about soul contact and eventually total union with the soul.

Through long, repeated incarnations the soul pays very little attention to its reflection, the man or woman on the physical plane, because they can respond very little to soul energies. Eventually, by dint of long experience on the physical plane, the soul sees in its reflection the readiness for response to its stimulus and impression. The soul then brings the person into meditation of some kind. The first time this occurs, it might be a very fleeting experience, but eventually, perhaps two or three lives later, a great deal of time and attention is given by the person to the practice of meditation. In this way, the soul begins to 'grip' its vehicle — stimulate, impress, and seek to bring the man or woman into a closer relationship to the long-held purpose of the soul.

The more the person meditates, the more energy is received from the soul, and the more the transformation of the individual's relation to the soul takes place. It is necessary to remember in talking about the soul and its vehicle, the man or woman, that the relationship is internal. The soul is not 'speaking' to the individual; the soul is impressing it with intention and releasing to it its spiritual energy. As soon as a degree of contact with the soul is made, the person begins to desire to serve the world in some way. The purpose of the soul is to serve; that is why it comes into incarnation. With the continuance of meditation, and a closer alignment with the soul, the desire to serve eventually becomes very strong.

Individuals have free will. They may or may not serve as they wish. If a person meditates, receives energy from the soul, but does not serve, the energy may create a block, a stasis, and all kinds of difficulties can arise. If, on the other hand, the person takes up the opportunity presented by the soul to serve the world, and does so to the best of his/her ability, things will tend to go well in his/her life: the purpose of the soul is being served. The person becomes more and more impersonal in relation to the world, and so their own personal problems begin to fade into the background. He or she is usually healthier, happier, and therefore more balanced.

Many people today take up meditation, desire to serve, but find they have very little time and energy left over from their everyday life — looking after a family, the pressure of modern work conditions, and so on. The stress of modern life makes it quite difficult for people to serve in a meaningful way. There are many thousands of modern disciples or aspirants to discipleship who would serve if they could find a mode of service which would allow them the time to do the service, and also to care for their families, do their jobs, and take part in modern life. For just such people, Transmission Meditation has been created. Transmission Meditation is primarily a powerful service to the world, which at the same time is a very powerful, dynamic form of personal development of consciousness.

Working in co-operation with the Masters

The Masters of our Spiritual Hierarchy are the custodians of all the spiritual energies entering the planet. A large part of Their work consists in scientifically distributing these energies in the way needed to carry out the Plan of evolution, of which They are also the custodians. The Masters receive energies from cosmic, solar, and extra-planetary levels, and if They were to send them directly into the world as They receive them, for the most part the energies would be too high in vibration; they would simply bounce off the majority of humanity.

Transmission Meditation has been developed to create groups to act as a sub-station for Hierarchy, through which the energies can be sent and transformed, stepped down to a level where they can be absorbed and used by humanity. This also allows the disciples or aspirants to move away from a simple relationship to their own soul to a relationship to the Kingdom of Souls, the esoteric or Spiritual Hierarchy of the world. The Hierarchy of Masters are in the process of returning to the everyday world and large numbers of Them will be living openly among us. Their aim is to work in open, conscious relationship with humanity. In doing Transmission Meditation, we have an opportunity to begin the process of conscious co-operation with the Masters.

Transmission Meditation is very simple and easy to do, because the real work is done for us by the Masters. There are seven force centres, or chakras, in the spine, from the base to the top of the head, through which energy can be sent and distributed. A person's aura is the sum-total of all the energies gathered into and around that person, through the chakras. No matter where these energies originate, they come into the individual through the chakras in the etheric physical body.

In Transmission Meditation, the Masters send energies through the chakras at a particular potency that the individual can support. The energies are automatically stepped down, transformed, and distributed, not by the individual but by the Masters, to wherever they are needed in the world. The chakras used are usually the heart, throat, and the two head chakras — one between the eyebrows and one at the top of the head. The people in the groups are asked not to attempt to send the energy to any particular country, group, or individual who, they think, might benefit from it. Only the Masters know this very complex and exact science of planetary energy distribution. The groups need only hold their attention at the ajna centre, the centre between the eyebrows. The Masters do all the rest of the work.

There are groups all over the world who see it as their task to distribute spiritual energy. They sit down, link together, and send the energy, but it is totally unscientific. The energy is usually their own soul energy, if it is not simply astral energy. It has no *scientific* value in terms of the Masters' plans for the world.

These people would do better by joining or forming a Transmission Meditation group and have really useful energy of the right potency, the right kind and vibration, sent through them by the Masters.

Yoga of the New Age

Transmission Meditation is really a combination of two yogas: Karma Yoga — the yoga of service, and Laya Yoga — the yoga of the chakras, the energies. This is the true yoga of the coming age. By taking part in Transmission Meditation, your evolution is propelled forward at an extraordinary rate, because of the potency of the spiritual energies sent through the chakras. The energies galvanize and activate the chakras as they pass through them. The Masters register the point in evolution of any individual by looking at the state of the chakras.

To take part in Transmission Meditation, you only have to hold your attention at the ajna centre. In practice you will find that the attention will not stay there. It will keep dropping to its usual level somewhere around the solar plexus. As soon as the attention drops and you become aware of that, you have to bring it back to the ajna centre. This is done by thinking, inwardly, the mantram OM. As soon as you think OM, you find that your attention automatically comes back to the ajna centre. While your attention is held at the ajna centre, a connection, or alignment is formed between the physical brain and the soul. The energies do not come from your soul. They come from the Masters, from the Kingdom of Souls. But they proceed from the soul level. While the alignment between the physical brain and the soul is kept, you are in the Transmission. As soon as your attention drops from the ajna centre, you are no longer taking part. As you think OM, the attention rises again, you are aligned. The process is one of being aligned, for a moment not aligned, and then, once again, aligned, back and forth.

The energies are invoked by the group saying the Great Invocation aloud. Members of Transmission groups learn by heart the Great Invocation, which has been translated into many languages. It was used by Maitreya for the first time in June 1945, as a result of His decision to come into the world. The saying of the Great Invocation forms a conduit between the group and the Masters of the Hierarchy, and through that conduit the energies are sent.

The easiest way to do Transmission Meditation is to join an already-existing group. If there is no group in your area within a reasonable distance, you can form your own group by joining with two other people. More people are more useful, but a basic group of three is a practical working group. If you have one group of three people, you have one triangle. The energy is triangulated, which potentizes it. If you have one more person, you have four triangles, which potentizes it more. If you have one more person, five, you have ten triangles — and so on, in arithmetical progression. The more people, the more triangles, the more powerful is the group. It is so powerful that in one year of correct, sustained Transmission Meditation you can make the same kind of advance as in 10, 15, or even 20 years of ordinary meditation. But the true, fundamental purpose of Transmission Meditation is service to the world. The world needs these energies from the Masters at the level that they can be absorbed and used. These are the energies that transform life on the planet.

Maitreya's experiment

When I am present, the meditation takes a somewhat different form, in that I am overshadowed by Maitreya during the entire Transmission. In this way, the energy of Maitreya flows from me to the group, so it becomes a kind of group overshadowing. The energies are distributed around the group, and so it is a tremendous spiritual potentization, a nourishing, of the group.

One of Maitreya's many functions is to act as "the nourisher of the little ones". The "little ones" are not little children, but grown-up men and women who have taken the first two of the five initiations which make one a Master. To the Masters, the second-degree initiates are still "little ones", "Babes in Christ".

The "little ones" are being prepared, stimulated, by Maitreya, to take the third initiation, which from the point of view of the Masters is the first true soul initiation. To illustrate what "little ones" are like, look at the back of *Maitreya's Mission, Volumes One* and *Two,* and you will see in the list of initiates people like

Einstein, Gandhi, Schweitzer, Reich, Jung, Freud, Picasso, Matisse, Cézanne, Schubert, Verdi — people of real impact in the world.

By overshadowing me, as I move around the world visiting the various groups, Maitreya is seeing if He can provide for those in the Transmission Meditation groups who have not necessarily taken the first, let alone the second, initiation, the same kind of spiritual nourishment which up until now has only been possible for those who had taken the second initiation. I am told that the experiment is working out rather well, and a great spiritual stimulus is being given to the groups all over the world.

ALIGNMENT

Editor's note: The questions printed in this chapter are from various sources including the Transmission Meditation Network Conferences in 1990, 1993, and 1994, and are supplemental to the previously published books on Transmission. Readers who are new to Transmission Meditation are recommended to read, in particular, *Transmission: A Meditation for the New Age* by Benjamin Creme for a better understanding of this subject as a whole.

This section focuses on how to maintain the alignment between the physical brain and the soul, a prerequisite for proper Transmission of spiritual energies.

Maintaining Alignment

We have been doing Transmission Meditation for quite some time now, but it seems we have not been able to do it correctly (ie be aligned). Have we not been really serving through Transmission Meditation?

I know people who are very happy and proud to be in a Transmission Meditation group. They talk about it, tell their friends about it, and sometimes write to me about it. Then I find out that they are doing perhaps an hour, or even half an hour, a week. Before they start, they have, perhaps, a study group, do exercises, hold healing sessions, etc. After it, they have cake, coffee, and chat with their friends. In between they put in half an hour or an hour of Transmission Meditation and, in so doing, they think they are serving the Plan. It is really a major glamour. If you are actually aligned for perhaps five minutes in an hour (the average), it is really not very much. Five minutes per hour once a week is hardly serving the Plan of evolution. It is pretending to serve the Plan of evolution. I say this with feeling because I know that many people attend Transmission Meditation in a very casual way: not even every week, perhaps once every two, three, or four weeks. Still, they think of themselves as doing Transmission Meditation. That is their service activity, once a week, or once a month for an hour or a couple of hours at the most, in which they might be aligned, and therefore actually transmitting, for five minutes.

I make a big point of this because it is very important to realize that if you are not aligned, you are not transmitting. The energies proceed from the soul level and you have to be aligned with your soul. That is why you have to hold the attention at the ajna centre. If you do not do that, but look around, or think about what you had for dinner and how it is sitting heavily in your stomach, then most likely you are not aligned at all. Most people have very poor attention and therefore very poor alignment. Having said all that, the saving grace, however, is that Transmission Meditation is so powerful, so scientific, that even these few minutes are more valuable in terms of service and personal growth than anything else you might do.

The Japanese groups, I have to say, have a completely different attitude to Transmission Meditation and to service in general. It is probably due to the 6th-ray soul of Japan and the long tradition which the Japanese have in relation to meditation. They take to Transmission Meditation like ducks to water, as we say. They love it, are good at it, and they hold the world's record for alignment during Transmission and therefore for actually transmitting. The average alignment time in the world is around five or six minutes. There are some, of course, who do very much more. There are people in Japan who do 55 minutes in an hour, and most will be aligned for 10 minutes in an hour. The average in Japan is around 15 to 20 minutes per hour. That is real transmitting.

How can one be sure of true alignment?
There is one way to be sure of true alignment. That is to become mentally polarized. If you are not mentally polarized, you will find it more difficult to maintain alignment. True alignment is the result of a constant polarization and focus on the mental plane or higher.

Humanity is going through a process of gradually lifting its seat of consciousness, the general level where its consciousness acts, from the astral to the mental planes. For six million years, during the first, Lemurian, race, the consciousness of humanity was focused on the physical plane. There is no one in the world today who has only physical plane consciousness. We have awareness on that plane, so it has reality for us, but it is not the seat of our consciousness.

For the bulk of humanity, the seat of consciousness has moved up to the astral plane. This shift of focus was achieved by man during the Atlantean root race, which lasted 12 million years. It took, therefore, a long time for Atlantean man to perfect the astral vehicle, which he did to such good effect that the majority of people today are still polarized on the astral plane. The astral is the most powerful body of the average individual.

We are members of the fifth, or Aryan, root race (which has nothing to do with Hitler's idea of Aryan). We have as an evolutionary goal the perfecting of the mental vehicle, which results when a person has consciousness on all four of the mental planes (there are four sub-planes of the mental as there are seven sub-planes of the astral). When you have achieved polarization on these and have lifted your consciousness up to the causal plane (the highest sub-plane of the mental plane), you have the beginning of spiritual polarization.

In terms of initiation, astral polarization, and therefore astral focus of consciousness, continues until half-way between the first and second initiations — what I call 1.5. For convenience, my Master and I have agreed upon this definition of exactitude in talking about a person's point in evolution. You get a very fine gradation of degree, which means level of consciousness, if you do it that way.

At around 1.5, the shift from astral to mental polarization begins to take place. If you are 1.5, you will probably still be astrally polarized, although from time to time there will be a degree of mental polarization. An oscillation between astral and mental takes place for quite a long time until 1.6. Then you can say that person is mentally polarized, even if only at the beginning of mental polarization. It may be interesting to note that the majority of our present world leaders are around 1.6, so they have the beginnings of mental polarization. They are obviously advanced members of humanity, but from the point of view of the Masters, they are still in the elementary stages of discipleship.

At 1.6 you can begin to function in the world in an altogether more powerful way. As soon as you achieve mental polarization, as soon as you can work on the mental plane intelligently, your influence, power, and input into the world are increased, as the Master DK put it, a hundredfold. Such is the difference between astral and mental polarization that moving from 1.5 to 1.6 gives you a hundredfold more power, influence, and effect in the world — so powerful is the mental plane compared with the astral.

Mental polarization continues until half-way between the second and third initiations. At that point the polarization shifts from the mental plane to the soul level, and the alignment is complete. It may oscillate for some time, but eventually there is steady spiritual polarization. The person is then aligned automatically all the time. There is no effort made to hold the alignment. We do not make any effort to have consciousness on the physical or astral plane; it is natural for us. It is only when it comes to the mental plane that many people have a problem. The spiritual plane for most people is only an idea, something they might touch on in a meditation, but not much more than that.

How can you be sure of true alignment? Become mentally polarized and eventually, of course, spiritually polarized — in other words, become initiate.

How can we recognize that we are actually aligned during a Transmission? How do we know?

It may be that some people cannot know. The person who is very astrally polarized, whose emotional body is highly excited and therefore disruptive of their focus, will most likely not have the attention to discover what alignment is. Alignment between the personality and the soul takes place when you can hold your attention at the ajna centre between the eyebrows. This is the directing centre. Eventually it becomes the synthesis for all the centres below it.

If you are still very astrally polarized, you may not have much attention. The recognition of alignment, and practically everything else in development of any kind, is to do with attention. If you do not have the attention, you do not learn much. If you are teaching a child and the child does not pay attention, he does not learn. You only learn that to which you give your attention. If you want to learn very well, to make the utmost use of the time and energy you give to any job, do it with full, total attention to the exclusion of everything else, totally concentrated and attending to what you are doing.

When someone is talking to you and you really want to know what they are saying (and are not just being polite and thinking your own thoughts), you have to give them attention. When you give them attention, you hear — and usually remember. Likewise, you can recognize the chakras, you can feel whether you are aligned or not, only when you pay attention to what is happening. During a Transmission Meditation, the energies from Hierarchy are going through the various chakras. If your attention is held at the ajna centre, an alignment is automatically created between the physical brain and the soul, using the channel of light we call the antahkarana.

You would not be doing Transmission Meditation if you had not done some form of meditation before this life. All of you have done much meditation in previous lives, perhaps the last four or five, in which you formed, to a considerable degree of efficiency, the antahkarana. That channel is made of energy and connects the soul and the brain of the man or woman. Through it, the alignment between soul and brain is maintained. As soon as you put your attention on the ajna centre, you activate that channel. If you do not pay attention to what is happening to you, you do not become aware. The whole of life, you will find, the whole of development, is a process by which you gradually become aware of more and more. It is a gradual perfecting of an instrument of awareness. In Transmission Meditation, it is an instrument through which the energies are sent out to the world. In the same way, it is an instrument by which the Self can demonstrate Itself, manifest on the physical plane, because that is the nature of the service taking place through the soul. The soul acts in service to the Self. The personality eventually has to act in service to the soul.

Is alignment the same thing as the antahkarana? (January/ February 1994)

There cannot be the building of the antahkarana without alignment, but it would not be true to say that alignment is the same thing as the antahkarana. The antahkarana is more than alignment, although not different from it. Alignment between the physical brain and soul is the fundamental first step towards the building of the antahkarana. There cannot be that building without alignment. When the alignment is held, and is natural and present every day, you can be sure that the antahkarana is in place. Then you will have access to the soul; your intuition will function.

Are there some basic rules for alignment and for knowing when you are aligned, or does it vary according to the rays, body sensitivity, etc?

It certainly varies according to bodily sensitivity. There are some physical bodies seemingly made of wood or stone, quite insensitive to the energies flowing through the etheric body.

Not everyone knows they have an etheric body. They have heard that everyone has an etheric body, but as far as their experience goes, they are not aware of it. This is very much a matter of the physical, not mental or personality, ray. It can be partly (but only partly) to do with actual level of evolution. In groups like these, that is not usually the case because everyone is around the same level, more or less. It is largely that they have this wooden- or mineral-type body which makes them literally insensitive to their physical experience and therefore it does not register in the brain. There is some dichotomy between their physical sensation and the ability of the computer system which is their brain to register it. It does not mean they are less evolved.

Are there some basic rules for alignment? The first rule is to pay attention. Make the concentrated effort of holding the attention at the ajna centre. It does not happen by itself. If you have the will to perform well in Transmission Meditation, and to become a better instrument for the Masters in this way, you have to implement your will. Make the necessary effort. Practise. Hold the attention at the ajna centre. Practise holding it there all the time during the day. And do not keep interrupting and distracting your attention; a positive mental focus is required.

During Transmission Meditation, should we pay attention to the energies coming into the body, feeling the physical plane, or should we just focus on the ajna centre and not bother about sensing the energies in the physical body?

It depends on the type of body you have. Some people have a very strong experience of the energies on the physical plane, in the etheric body. There are those who experience the energies in one way or another, but who say they don't actually feel them, in the physical sense of the word. It would be useless to tell these people to concentrate on the energies on the physical plane, because they don't experience the energies there. If you do experience the energies on the physical plane, clearly and strongly, and your attention is focused on the ajna centre, I don't see how you cannot be aware of them, even without focusing on them.

For myself, I am totally aware of the experience on the physical plane, in the etheric chakras, of the different energies as they come in. I differentiate between one and another, or what the particular blend is. I am overshadowed by Maitreya, and He is releasing the energy of the Cosmic Triangle. He brings it down the planes, and then takes it up the planes. Perhaps the Avatar of Synthesis will be at a certain level, the Spirit of Peace at another level, the Buddha at another level. Maitreya takes the energies up and down, and I watch this taking place. I am not saying that therefore everybody should watch, but if you do watch what your etheric body is experiencing, you can in time begin to differentiate between the different types of energy, each of which is unique. At the beginning of Transmission, I mention the energies as they come in, whether the Cosmic Triangle or the ray energies, so that people can learn to distinguish between one and another. On the other hand, it is perfectly possible for people to transmit efficiently without recognizing one energy from another.

During Transmission Meditation I sometimes cannot feel the ajna centre, even though my mind is still and I feel my attention is in the right neighbourhood. Does this mean (1) I am definitely not aligned, or (2) could I still be aligned but just insensitive to the etheric body?

(1) No, not necessarily. (2) Yes.

I do not know if I am aligned in a Transmission Meditation. Somehow it seems I am not, except for a few minutes in an hour. What is missing?

What is missing is attention. And awareness. Pay attention to what is actually happening, to what you are experiencing as the energies are sent, with your attention held at the ajna centre.

You will become aware of activity in this chakra. You may become aware of activity in other chakras, too, of a vibration of energy, a kind of pressure as the energies flow through the chakras. Every time you take part in a Transmission, the chakras are expanded more than they were before. The energies stimulate the chakras' activity and radiate out to the world, and you should try to become aware of that energy actually flowing through the chakra.

When you are not aligned, when your attention drops, as it inevitably does, you may go on feeling energy and think you are still aligned. But 99 times out of 100 you are simply feeling the residual vibration of the energy after it has passed through the chakra. While you are aligned, there is a dynamic movement through the chakra, but as soon as you stop being aligned, the energy is no longer being sent through you. The energy comes from the soul plane, but if you are not in touch with the soul plane through the alignment, you cannot be receiving the energy.

You have to recognize that this is so by paying attention. Recognize the difference between a dynamic flow of energy through the chakra and simply a residual vibration which exists after the energy has passed through.

Are you saying that we have to become sensitive to the etheric body to recognize if we are aligned with our soul and properly transmitting?

That is a prerequisite. The dense physical comes from the etheric physical which underlies it. The chakras exist not in the dense but in the etheric physical.

Therefore, if you want to become aware of the chakras, and so become more sensitive to the coming and going of energies and of different types of energy — because they all feel different — you have to become aware of the etheric body.

If we are not aware of the chakras during a Transmission, is it likely that we are not properly transmitting?

You can recognize when you are aligned and properly transmitting if you are experiencing the flow of energy through the chakra. You actually feel the pulse of energy. If you are not aware of the chakra, it is possible that you are not actually aligned and not transmitting. You may find that your attention is down at the solar plexus. Many people do not feel this chakra either, but since most people are astrally polarized, it is the regular seat of their consciousness and therefore attention, so they do not even need to feel it. But you can learn to feel this (solar plexus) chakra too.

It is a very powerful chakra, a distributing centre, and you can absorb energy from the sun through it and charge yourself every day. You can close it (and so not waste your energy), work with it scientifically. When you are aware of the chakra, you will find that you can open and close it at will, but you have to become aware of it first of all as a functioning unit in your etheric body. Then it will obey your will; whatever you tell it to do, it will do.

You have said you can still feel a sensation in the ajna centre even though your attention has dropped. It is sort of an after-feeling. How do you differentiate between the two, and how long can that after-feeling go on and can you still be transmitting?

Where are your eyes looking? Your eyes will either be looking through the chakra, in which case you are aligned there, or they will not. There is a kind of negativity which comes in when you focus on the solar plexus. Now I am focusing on the solar plexus, but I am doing it from the ajna. Just watch what is happening. Now I am deliberately experiencing the solar plexus, but you will see that I am doing it from the ajna. It is a conscious intent.

That is different from literally dropping the attention to the solar plexus. You can do anything you like from the ajna centre, if you are focused here. But I am talking about literally dropping the attention and settling into an astral negativity. You can tell if you are focused at the ajna or solar plexus centre. It is a feeling. You can just feel it. Your sensation is in one or the other.

At the Self-Realization Fellowship, they have a picture of Babaji. His eyes are upward almost to the point that they disappear. Is he doing the same thing that we are being asked to do?
If you met Babaji, His eyes would not be up there. He would look normally at you and say: "How do you do?" That is just how He is seen in meditation. His attention is up here, at the top of the head.

Anyone who meditates on the head chakra, the crown, has to turn their eyes upward. But when you do Transmission Meditation, you put your attention on the ajna centre, between the eyebrows. It is not very high up. And you can learn to just hold it there indefinitely. Or you can turn it even higher, but you do not need to do that.

One year I tried literally to look up inwardly with my eyes, and it really had a bad consequence with my physical eyes. It could be a bad thing to do in my case, putting the thinking there ...
The thinking is the important thing, not the turning up of the eyes. All you need to do is hold the attention up. That should not be a strain. If you do it in a rigid way, the eyeballs hurt. But if you do it in a relaxed manner, they pull themselves up and it is held. I think you must have been very rigid.

Is it OK to meditate with your eyes open?
I personally do not recommend it. It is difficult enough to meditate with your eyes shut, without trying to do it with your eyes open. With your eyes open, you are taking in all the experiences that come in through the eyes — all the sensations of light, movement, people, grass, whatever is around you. Meditation is the turning in from that. It is turning towards the soul. If you can shut out all the environment, first of all, it makes

the contact with the soul that much easier. That is why you shut your eyes.

Muktananda talked about seeing a blue pearl at the ajna centre when you are aligned. The Sufis talk about seeing a black light.

It is not necessary. You can add all sorts of possibilities. Many teachers have, from their teacher, traditions to make it easier. But you do not have to see anything to hold your attention here. It is simply a turning up of the attention. You do not have to visualize the chakra. You can if you wish. You can visualize a crystal ball, a black light, a pearl, or whatever. This is only a help to visualize the chakra. But in Transmission Meditation, all the work is done for you. We are not invoking the soul. The work is being done by the Masters, who are pouring the energy through the chakra. All you have to do is hold the attention to allow them to do it. You do not even have to visualize the chakra or anything in the chakra. These are two different functions. They are not doing Transmission Meditation. They are teaching their disciples to contact the soul, which is not what we are about. We are using the chakras in the correct way that the Masters can send Their energies through us. That simply involves the focus — that is all.

After 15 years of doing Transmission Meditation, I find it frustrating to realize that I can only concentrate for a few seconds at a time before my mind wanders. (1) Am I wasting the Masters' time as well as my own? (2) Is this an American problem? (I am an American). Why is it so hard to concentrate for longer periods of time? (April 1996)

(1) You are certainly not wasting the Masters' or your own time. The question is not so much to do with concentration or "wandering mind" as with alignment. The function of the (lower) mind is to think, and *if you are aligned* — the attention focused at the ajna centre (between the eyebrows) — it does not matter if the mind "wanders". The key is not to *follow* the thoughts and they soon slow or stop. Also, time passes very quickly during Transmission Meditation so it is likely that you are aligned for longer than you realize. (2) I have found American transmitters to be rather below average in alignment time. The best are the

Japanese, probably as a result of a long tradition of meditation. I do believe that the American emphasis on competition from an early age is highly detrimental to the inner focus needed for meditation. This is further exacerbated by the constant breaking of attention by adverts which characterizes commercial television.

However, having said all that, it should be understood that Transmission Meditation is so scientific and powerful in the hands of the Masters that every second of alignment allows the distribution of powerful forces into the world. These seconds added together enable the Transmitter to engage in service of real value.

If we are only aligned two or three minutes per hour in Transmission, and if people are aligned at different times, do we ever actually have a triangle formed?

You are very pessimistic. You would be surprised. The alignments do synchronize — for a few minutes on and off — enough to make it more than worthwhile to do. This is the point. They are so potent, these energies, that it is the most important thing you could be doing.

Is it possible to ruminate in your head and think that you are focused on the ajna centre?

It is not only possible, it happens all the time. That is why some people do three or four minutes of real Transmission in the hour. Thinking they are focused on the ajna centre, they are in fact ruminating. Rumination and reverie are astral activities. Reverie is one of the main obstacles to correct Transmission, to any kind of meditation for that matter. A great many people mistake reverie for meditation, and believe that the astral imaginings which they experience in that state are promptings from the soul or messages from Masters or even Archangels, while they are only subconscious musings.

Reverie, rumination, going through those satisfying imaginary experiences, inhibits correct thinking. More and more, the race has to learn to use the mental body, of which we have barely scratched the surface. Therefore, it is essential to lift your consciousness out of the astral morass into the light of the mind through which the soul can work. Bring your mind, and the will behind it, to bear on these astral, glamorous imaginings and reveries and dry them up at the source.

Can you define exactly the mental activity we can and can't have during Transmission? Are there symbols we can visualize or focus on?

There are certainly no symbols you should visualize or focus on. The mental activity you can have during Transmission is any level that does not interfere with your alignment. You will have found, no doubt, that any level at all interferes with your alignment. Ideally, you should be so constantly aligned that you can talk, write, whatever, and still continue in an absolute alignment. It should become as instinctual, as self-maintaining as that.

Since few have that kind of focus, you have to limit the activity of the mental body. That happens automatically when you hold your attention at the ajna centre. If you think OM, there is not much else you can think at the same time. If you think OM, you will find that immediately all the thinking that you were doing before subsides. Your attention is aligned, until you lose it and the whole thing starts up again: the monkey mind becomes active and your attention drops again. When you recognize that, sound OM and you will find that for a time, perhaps seconds or minutes, you are suddenly in another tranquil, more blissful state in which there is no mental activity. It is not necessary to get rid of all mental activity in order to be aligned, but for most people mental activity is a hindrance to alignment.

Is the building of the antahkarana of a Transmission group dependent upon simultaneity of alignment periods of the group members? Do the group members have to be aligned simultaneously for the antahkarana of a Transmission group to be built? (January/February 1994)

If it were so dependent, it would never be built! It is not something which comes and goes, although I did illustrate it as if

491

it were. Once the antahkarana is built, it is built. It is a continuous process, an awareness. I know in the beginning the alignment is not always there. During a Transmission, people are aligned on average for three or four minutes in the hour. The rest of the time is spent either sleeping or ruminating. The consciousness is nowhere. That has nothing to do with meditation, let alone with Transmission Meditation. But for the three or four minutes in which the average person is aligned, the whole process is so powerful, so scientific, it is enormously beneficial. But it does not have to be simultaneous, because it never happens simultaneously.

Does it really make a difference to centre our attention between the eyebrows during Transmission Meditation (in regard to building the antahkarana)? (January/February 1994)

If it did not, do you think we would say so? You are told to focus your attention between the eyebrows, and that is what to do. This chakra is the focus eventually of the energies of all the chakras below it; all the energies are synthesized in this chakra. Then that chakra links with the chakra at the top of the head, and eventually with the throat, and these three eventually receive and distribute the energy from the Monad, the soul and the etheric body, which is the distributor of all these energies through the mechanism.

Why is it necessary to keep the attention on the crown chakra during the overshadowing of yourself by Maitreya? (January/February 1994)

Because this allows Maitreya to nourish, spiritually, the group. The energy goes straight into the lotus at the top of the head. It is held there and then reflected downwards and sent out through the heart and throat centres to the world. He distributes it in that way. It nourishes the Knowledge petals, the Love petals and the inner, Will, petals of the crown chakra and they vibrate and heighten in their activity every time the overshadowing takes place. At the same time Maitreya distributes the energy downwards through the ajna, the throat and the heart centres (a certain amount of it, depending on the individual) to the world.

So it is both a nourishing process and a scientific distribution of the energy as would be normal in a Transmission Meditation.

During the overshadowing you are focusing on the crown chakra, but my attention seemed to be coming back to my ajna centre because it seemed stronger . . .

No, it just dropped, because it is harder to hold it at the top of the head.

Are there safety considerations for holding the attention at the crown chakra?

Yes, there are. It is safe to hold the attention at the ajna centre. This should eventually become the normal place for your attention. This is the directing centre from which all action is taken. The holding of the attention at the top of the head is only to be done during the overshadowing when I am present. It is not safe for most people to hold their attention at the top of the head. Because they have been doing it when I am here, does not mean they should go on doing it. The ajna centre is the safe centre.

Why is it dangerous to put your attention on the head centre when it is not an overshadowing? (January/February 1994)

It is not dangerous for every individual, but for most individuals it is. Because I am not always there to say for whom it would be or would not be dangerous, a broad general rule is given to hold the attention at the ajna centre.

How can I deal with physical discomfort during a Transmission?

Find a comfortable, upright chair and use a cushion if necessary. If you are really aligned, you will not be too aware of your physical sensations. You will feel as if your body has disappeared. You will almost stop breathing. You will find, when you do Transmission correctly, that there are long periods when you do not seem to breathe. The breathing is so slight, so imperceptible, just enough to keep the body going. Then suddenly, involuntarily, you take a big breath of air.

People indulge in all manner of distractions in Transmission, which they think do not matter. They do, unless you have constant, unbroken alignment between your soul and physical brain. You would not then have to sit still, focused, paying tremendous attention. It would be automatic. Until you have that, it matters. You must take it seriously. You must pay attention and concentrate. If you do not concentrate, you cannot pay attention. If you do not pay attention, you will be unaware of what is happening, except that you are uncomfortable.

The thing is to learn to concentrate, to become aware, to achieve that focus of attention which becomes automatic and takes place whether or not you are making any effort at all, or are comfortable or not.

Is it a good idea to interrupt a transmission, to walk around, to try to help the alignment, and then continue?

People cannot keep aligned for long when they are sitting still trying to keep aligned. Do you think if they get up, walk around, have a drink, a little chat, write a word to their friends, do a few handstands, that somehow that will help their alignment? If you interrupt your concentration and attention that much, is it likely that it will help you to align better? Of course not.

Is it OK during Transmission Meditation to use visualization or the creative imagination in attempts at keeping one's attention at the ajna centre — for example, imagining a light at the centre, or something else?

It is OK to do this but it should not be necessary, and too much effort to do so might well interfere with the alignment between brain and soul which must be maintained.

During Transmission Meditation, is it helpful, or even appropriate, to visualize connecting the ajna chakra with the crown chakra?

No. It is interesting how people dislike simplicity, and always try to make simple methods complicated. Transmission Meditation has been formulated by a Master who, I think, has to be trusted to know best how it should be performed. Please — keep it simple, as presented, without visualization.

It seems that so many of us are so powerfully focused in the solar plexus that we have a difficulty bringing the attention up and holding it at the ajna centre. I am wondering, other than in the meditation, just during the course of the day, doing the things that we do, whether making a conscious effort to work at holding the attention at the ajna centre can help over the long term in being able to hold the attention there?

You have to learn to work from the ajna. Most people work from the solar plexus. It is a question of polarization. If you are under 1.5 to 1.6, you are astrally polarized. That means the seat of your consciousness is the astral plane. This conditions everything you do.

If you are mentally polarized, that will condition the physical reaction. If you tell your body to get on with it and sit still, it will do it. You will forget about it, and it will do its work and sit there; the muscles will hold you upright. But if you fall on the astral nature, which longs for comfort — it is the astral desire that responds to the body's need for comfort, not being in pain or stiff or whatever — then you are in trouble. That is why people cannot sit still. In the USA, and it is obviously going to happen in Japan and elsewhere, one of the main killers of this inner stillness, ability to concentrate, is commercial television. The attention span of anyone, from childhood onwards, is minimal. It is cut up into little segments. Whatever they are watching, in a few minutes suddenly comes a commercial. There is a jingle and fast-moving talk, and so on, and their attention is completely shattered. Then after five minutes, they are brought back to the continuation of the story. Then they are engrossed again, their astral nature is satisfied. But this continual shift and change in focus in commercial television is, I think, a great destroyer of concentration. Do not watch commercial television, and keep your attention at the ajna centre at all times.

To "Think" OM during Transmission

I cannot really understand what it means to think OM during Transmission in order to hold my attention on the ajna centre. Do you see the OM?

You do not see the OM, you think OM. It is the thought, the sound of the OM on the mental plane that you use, not seeing it as OM written. It is the sound of the OM, although you are not making a sound. But on the mental plane you are making a sound.

Think the sound of OM?
Think OM. Just like you think any thought. Think the OM thought, not written OM, but thought OM.

Maybe the question is, should OM be generalized in your skull or localized at the centre where you want your attention to go?
It should be in the mind, wherever your thought activity is, which will be your brain. You think OM. You say your name is John. Think John. Or Alice. Or Vera. It is a thought like any other thought.

But . . . if we just think the word, like thinking "book" . . .
You do not think it differently, but the word itself is different, that is the point. The OM is the great mantram.

There must be a way of thinking the word where you hear the sound in a better way than we're doing ...
You do not hear it, you think it. Hearing and thinking are two different things. You can do it fast or slow, but it is thought; it is not different from any other thought, except in its reverberation in the mind. That is what brings your attention to the ajna centre. It is the vibration. If you say "OM" aloud, that vibrates at a certain level. If you say it under your breath (silently), at another. If you think it, that is the highest.

Does the ability to tune into the inner sound inside one's head, the inner OM, have anything to do with overshadowing?
No.

How do you reconcile the OM and the breath?
You do not use the OM in relation to the breath at all. You simply think OM. You can think OM any time, whether you are

breathing or not breathing. It is not a question of "with the outbreath" or "with the inbreath"; it is simply when you realize that your attention is no longer at the ajna centre that you think OM. The reverberation on the mental plane of the OM brings your attention back to the ajna centre.

Do you send out the OM?

You do not send it out. You think it. It is much simpler than people imagine. You should not do any breathing exercise at all. You simply let the breath follow its own rhythm, and it will get slower and slower until it almost disappears. As it slows, you will find your thoughts slow down. When you are really focused, when your breath is still — just the minimum to keep the body going — there is no thought. You go beyond thought.

Breath and Thought

(1) During Transmission Meditation, when one is concentrating on the ajna centre, is it good to breathe at a certain rhythm? (2) By doing so, can you concentrate better?

(1) During Transmission Meditation it is best not to try to regulate or even be aware of the breathing at all. In practice, if the attention is truly held at the ajna centre, it will be found that the breathing practically stops for quite long periods and restarts with a sudden gasp. It should, in any case, be light, high in the chest, and silent. Do not do breathing exercises. (2) No, you are simply concentrating on the breathing.

When the breathing slows down there is suddenly a feeling of panic, of slight suffocation ...

If your breathing slows down so much, there will come a point when you will have to take a breath. But there should be no panic. Do not be afraid. Just take a breath. It is easy! You do not have to remind yourself. The slowing down is instinctual, you do not govern that, nor do you govern when you take a breath; your body will tell you. It has its own intelligence. It knows when it needs some oxygen, and then it will take a breath. Forget about the breathing.

Does your breath slow down because your focus is going away from breathing to this focus that you are holding?

As you focus on the ajna centre your mental activity slows down. It can speed up, I know. But if you do it correctly you will find fewer and fewer thoughts arising in the mind. As the thoughts slow down, the breathing slows down, and vice versa.

That is why one of the main yogic exercises in controlling thought is to control the breath, because thought and breath come from the same source. If you really focus on the ajna centre and hold it there with the OM for long periods, you find there will be no thought, and therefore no breath. Then you will take a breath and start thinking. You sound the OM again and the whole process repeats.

What source do thought and breath come from?

Find that source. Watch the thought of 'I'. With every thought that arises in the mind, ask yourself: "Who thought that?" You will say: "I thought it." Take it back: Who am I? Trace this sense of 'I' and you will find that as you do this, as you go back and back to the source of 'I', your thoughts will slow and also the breath. You will find that both are coming from the same source. Experience for yourself where they come from.

Is this related to what Maitreya says: When there is a space between the breathing and thinking, "There I am."

Yes. That is why He can make use of that space. The point is that what we call breath is the pulse of the universe. The whole of creation is breathing, and we are not separate from that. Our breath is the breath, at this level, of that great pulsation which created all that we can see. That great outbreathing created the universe, all creation. There was not anything, and then there was everything. Then there is the inbreathing, in which all returns to its source. You have the outward movement of creation, and the return movement, involution and evolution. Our breath is intimately related to that breath.

What I am talking about is finding the source of the breath, the source of the 'I' thought, the primal thought. Before the 'I' thought, you are. But as soon as you think 'I', you separate yourself from who you are. Find out who you are, who has the 'I' thought. Who is thinking this 'I'?

Get the sense of that as the Self, and you will find that what we call breathing, this activity that connects us with the universe, and the thought of 'I', come from the same source. There is creation. You are either that, or that which is bringing it into manifestation. Go beyond the 'I' thought. Go beyond the breathing and you will find yourself as the Self, which is beyond creation — that which caused breath in the first place, that which breathed out. When you stop the outbreathing and the inbreathing, there is only cause. You are that cause. Experience it.

ADDITIONAL QUESTIONS ON TRANSMISSION

Do the blessings (during Transmission) go on transforming us even if we are asleep? (January/February 1994)

Yes, the blessings are transforming the person. They emerge from the soul-plane and are given to the souls of the individuals: that is what alignment is about; that is why, during Transmission Meditation, you have to stay aligned. The physical brain has to have the one-pointed and solid connection and alignment with the soul, otherwise that aspect of the communicating channel is missing.

Many people, even if they are not asleep, ruminate; they are in a kind of 'astral daze' for much of the Transmission. That is why the average Transmission time is three-and-a-half minutes rather than 60 minutes per hour. If the alignment were constant the true Transmission time would be 60 minutes in the hour. It is very important, therefore, that you keep that alignment. The person involved receives the blessing; the person is the soul. We are souls, we have to get used to thinking of ourselves as souls —the soul in incarnation is the true man. This personality, with its threefold body, is simply a mechanism, a vehicle, for the true man or woman who is the soul, and it is the soul which receives the blessing. That blessing, of course, has an effect on the vehicles, stimulating the substance of the physical, the astral and the mental bodies, but the actual blessing is for the evolving Son of God in incarnation.

What is the difference between the overshadowing of Maitreya during Transmission Meditation, the Christ Principle, and the phase during Transmission when you say: "This is the true Spirit of the Christ"? (January/February 1994)

When I say: "This is the true Spirit of the Christ," it is to let you know that during the phase that follows Maitreya is releasing specifically what we call the Christ Principle, the energy of consciousness itself. That is the energy He embodies. We call it love, and it flows very potently during that phase. It flows at other times during the Transmission, perhaps most of the time, but because it is mixed in with other energies you do not recognize it. During that phase, He releases it purely. That is why for many people this is the most magical, wonderful part of a Transmission. They feel that wonderful energy of love; they are bathed in it. It is powerful, magnetic. You can bathe in it, feel it all around you; you are floating in a sea of love, which it is. It is a wonderful experience. That is the energy of consciousness.

On the Day of Declaration, that energy will pour out in tremendous potency through the hearts of everybody in the world. Maitreya has said: "It will be as if I embrace the whole world. People will feel it even physically." That is why we say "Love makes the world go round".

Love literally makes the world go around because it is the energy of evolution. Without that energy, there would be no evolution. There would not be the longing, the aspiration, the aiming higher, to what? Why does humanity know that it evolves? Why does humanity aspire to what we call betterment? Why do we do it? Not because churches tell us, but because our soul tells us — as soon as we make any degree of conscious contact with the soul.

Is it almost as valuable to try to do Transmission Meditation alone? Can you actually attract the attention of the Masters? Will it work?

It can. If you use the Great Invocation, the energy will flow. It will not be the same thing, because you do not have the triangle. The triangle potentizes all the energy and is safer; more energy can safely be sent through a group of people who are formed into triangles, than through the same number of separate individuals.

As the mind tends to become rather lulled while one is digesting a meal, eating prior to meditation is not recommended. (1) Would this be the case in relation to taking part in Transmission Meditation? (2) If so, how long prior to sitting ought one to have completed a meal? Or does it not matter at all? (September 1996)

(1) Yes; too heavy a meal dulls the awareness and mental focus necessary in Transmission Meditation. (2) Each person digests at a different speed so definite figures are not possible. I would

suggest at least an hour's interval before the Transmission as reasonable and a light meal as desirable.

Often, during Transmission Meditation, I see very bright, luminous colours, usually blue or purple, sometimes gold. Could you please say what this signifies? (September 1996)
They are visual manifestations of the energies transmitted during the Meditation.

If, during Transmission Meditation, one regularly experiences strong and uncomfortable emotions, is it better to discontinue Transmission for a period of time, until perhaps the feelings subside somewhat, or try to continue on as best as possible in the midst of the emotions? Is the stimulation of strong emotions common in Transmission Meditation? (March 1996)
Try to continue until emotional balance is regained. When properly conducted, that is with the attention focused at the ajna centre (between the eyebrows), the upsurge of strong emotion should be rare.

(1) Mr Creme has said that people who are psychologically unstable would be well advised not to take part in Transmission Meditation. Could you please explain why this is so? (2) If such a person wants to be useful or to try some form of meditation what advice could Mr Creme offer? (May 1995)
(1) Transmission Meditation is very powerful and might over-stimulate. (2) There are many other ways to serve.

(1) As a schizophrenic patient I have come into contact with your work. My question is whether it would be beneficial for me to join a Transmission Meditation group? (2) I would like to find some form of service to be of some use to society as a whole. I am on medication to control my condition. Have you any general advice for people suffering from similar psychological conditions? (June 1995)
(1) No. It could be over-stimulating and create problems. (2) Find some more *exoteric* field of service in which powerful

energies are not involved. For example Oxfam, Greenpeace, Friends of the Earth, etc, etc.

In Transmission Meditation, instead of verbal instructions by one person during the meditation, is it acceptable to ring a bell to refocus the attention? (March 1995)

If it is acceptable to those present it is acceptable, but to my mind it is not a very good idea. The verbal reminder to keep the focus at the ajna centre works because of the specific reference to the centre. There is no such association with a bell sound. I believe people would quickly become used to the bell and ignore it — or even not hear it.

You claim that Transmission Meditation is so extraordinary that, over and above its value as a field of service, its "secondary" effects are so powerful for those who practise it as to accelerate their development perhaps 10 times faster than any other form of personal meditation. (1) How is it that you are alone in presenting this form of meditation? (2) Why do great spiritual beings like Sai Baba, Premananda and others not recommend it? (3) Why is it that even Maitreya, in the Messages given through you, does not speak about it? (November 1996)

(1) Transmission Meditation is a Hierarchical endeavour, presented to disciples and aspirants as a potent field of service by my Master, through me. Its presentation is part, therefore, of my *own* service activity. (2) That it is not expressly recommended by Sai Baba or Swami Premananda is beside the point — They do not recommend people to read Krishnamurti, practise Kriya Yoga, or read Alice Bailey. That is not Their task. As a matter of fact, Transmission Meditation is the only meditation (other than His own) allowed by Sai Baba to be practised in His ashram. (3) Nowhere, in the 140 Messages given publicly through me, does Maitreya mention meditation at all. It is not His major concern.

*I read you to say, somewhere, that Transmission Meditation is a form of Kriya Yoga. This, you may know, is an ancient technique revived by Babaji, and brought to the West (and East) by Yogananda, author of **Autobiography of a Yogi**. Yogananda* *says that Babaji allowed him to give the formerly restricted technique to "all who humbly ask for your help". But, a publisher's note says (p. 366): "Babaji ... nevertheless required of Lahiri Mahasaya and all descendants of his spiritual line (the Self-Realization Fellowship and Yogoda Satsanga Society of India line of Gurus) that they impose on any who sought initiation a period of preliminary spiritual training." Is the SRF-YSS form a more potent form of Kriya Yoga than Transmission Meditation, or is this note mistaken?* (July/August 1993)

No, the publisher's note is not mistaken but neither is the SRF-YSS form of Kriya more potent than Transmission Meditation. On the contrary, done by the same person, Transmission Meditation is much more potent than Kriya because, for those performing this service, the real 'work' is done by the Masters, and is, therefore, totally scientific and energetically correct. Their energies are cosmic, solar and planetary and not simply that of the individual's soul. The point is that, on the whole, people do not do consistent Transmission Meditation until they have reached a certain evolutionary point and are responding to soul impulse — a proof that they have done the necessary preliminary training and preparation — perhaps even in a previous life.

Yogananda's teachings involve Raja Yoga and Kriya Yoga. He said his teachings, as handed down from Babaji, would be the religion of the world. You have said that Transmission Meditation is a combination of Karma Yoga (service) and Laya Yoga (of the chakras). How will these two 'systems' blend in the future? Also, please explain Laya Yoga. (September 1993)

Laya Yoga is the yoga of the energies and of the chakras which receive and distribute the energies. Kriya is a specialized form of Laya Yoga. Transmission Meditation is a form of Kriya Yoga but the 'work' and practice is done for the practitioner by the Masters Who send the energies. The two methods are completely compatible; the difference is that Transmission Meditation is an act of service for the world. This 'allows' the Masters to oversee the occult meditation of those taking part. In the future, I would expect more and more Kriya students to take part — as service

— in Transmission Meditation, which, furthermore, is a group activity.

I've been doing Zen practice (hara-focus) most of my adult life, and Transmission Meditation (ajna-focus) for a dozen years. I believe you said that full-time ajna-focus is the method for making/maintaining soul-contact. Does this mean one ought to give up zazen and full-time zen practice in favour of the ajna-focus if one hopes to evolve into stabilized soul-contact? (January/February 1995)

In general, yes, although much depends on the individual. Any meditation is a method, more or less scientific, depending on the meditation, of making and deepening soul contact. For most aspirants and disciples of today, however, the ajna focus is the prescribed one. This creates an alignment between the personality and the soul essential to the ultimate at-one-ment of these two aspects of ourselves. Eventually, the ajna centre acts as the synthesizer of the energies of all the centres below it.

(1) In what way are 24-hour Transmission Meditations different from ordinary, regular Transmissions? (2) Is it not better to really concentrate and transmit well for, say 10 hours, five hours, three hours, with 10 or 20 people than 24 hours with, at times, only three people?

(1) They are much longer! Also, they are infrequent, perhaps three times, only, a year, at the major Spring Festivals of Easter, Wesak and of Humanity. (2) The answer here is a qualified yes. The three Spring Festivals, however, provide a unique opportunity for groups around the world to establish together a potent rhythm. Throughout 24 hours, Hierarchy can link all working groups together into the global network of light which They are constantly creating and potentizing. There is also a powerful psychological factor involved, namely the added stimulus to aspiration and service which the celebration of these Festivals promotes.

*In **Share International** you speak about the "Christ Festival" at the full moon in Gemini, but by Alice Bailey this festival is called* the "Festival of Good Will" or the "Festival of Humanity." In *The Externalisation of the Hierarchy,* the Easter Festival is called the Christ Festival. So, is **Share International** mistaken? (May 1994)

The festival at the full moon in Gemini (usually in June) is indeed called the "Festival of Good Will" or the "Festival of Humanity". It is also called the "Christ Festival", when the Christ stands *as the Representative of humanity*, as 'the eldest in a great family of brothers'. The great Festival of the East is the "Wesak Festival", the festival of the Buddha, Who approaches humanity more closely at the full moon in Taurus (usually in May).

TRANSMISSION AND
THE REAPPEARANCE WORK

Is Transmission Meditation still important at this time? (October 1994)

Transmission Meditation is important at all times. It is the most important service activity, of major potency and scientific effectiveness, which can be done by disciples with the minimum expenditure of time and energy.

Is Transmission Meditation a priority in the reappearance work?

It is a priority, but not the only priority. The value of Transmission Meditation is that it provides disciples with a field of service second to none in its impact in the world. At the same time, it provides a well, a great reservoir of energy and power from which you can draw at any time. That sustains you. In my experience, the best, the most active, groups, the most effective, have a good, strong Transmission Meditation activity at their base. At the same time, as a field of service, it burns up much of the burden of karma which holds people back. The main hindrance to evolution is karma. Anything which takes the weight of karma from your back should be welcomed, however difficult it is. Obstacles are (karmic) opportunities to overcome and rid yourself of the weight of karma, to resolve it and move forward quickly. Transmission Meditation is the priority in the work of the Transmission Meditation groups. But the first priority is the Reappearance work, making known the fact of the Reappearance.

People often ask me how far we should go in diluting our work for the Reappearance by joining with other groups, doing other kinds of work, getting involved in feeding the hungry, and so on. There are a great many groups serving the cause of hunger, many groups concerned with poverty, many powerful, and more or less effective, agencies at work world-wide.

However, no one in the world except this group is engaged in the work of announcing Maitreya's presence — believing that He is in the world and acting towards that end. There are many

507

groups doing Hierarchical work, who do not believe for a moment that Hierarchy is being externalized and that the Christ is in the world. They work in a different way, subjectively, with less intensity perhaps, and less in response to what is actually happening now. They are doing a more academic type of esoteric work, disseminating information, talking about the various so-called esoteric schools.

They all stem from the same Hierarchical source. They all receive, more or less, Hierarchical energy. The differences in their expression are simply the differences in personality emphasis or ray expression. But we are the only group who, in a very conscious way, is deliberately making known the fact of the Christ's presence in the world.

Other groups, and there are many in all fields — political, economic, social, religious, and so on — are doing the work of preparation. They do not call it that, because they do not know that is what it is. They are doing this work in an unconscious way — preparing the world, making the changes which make it possible for the Hierarchy to emerge.

How far should you engage in other work? That is up to you. If you take my advice, do not dilute your time and energy too much. You cannot do everything. You cannot change the world individually or as a group, and certainly not overnight. Do what you know to do, which is the work of the reappearance.

That is why you are here. If this group were formed simply to talk about the starving millions, to work with Oxfam or whatever, well, there are marvellous things you could do in many different lines of service now being tackled by many people. But tell me where else there is a group doing what we are doing. That being so, it is common sense to give this work of the Reappearance your major time, energy, and effort.

(1) I think there was no need for you to announce the idea of the Day of Declaration, because for those who do Transmission Meditation Maitreya's emergence does not have much importance. Our purpose should be simply to continue and spread selfless service as transmitters of light to humanity. The announcement of the idea of Declaration instils a sense of expectation in the mind of

the transmitter and can lead to the danger of expecting Maitreya unconsciously. Then the work of Transmission, which should be selfless service, will become not for humanity but for oneself and could destroy the purity of the Transmission. (2) Or was this (announcement) done to test transmitters?

I am afraid the questioner has totally misunderstood the purpose behind my work of announcing Maitreya's presence and emergence, and the relation of Transmission Meditation to that event and after.

(1) It is precisely to create the sense of expectation on the widest possible scale that I lecture and write. Far from being a danger to transmitters, this expectation, the more conscious the better, should provide a powerful launching-pad for service, Transmission Meditation, and/or other forms. My task is to inform everyone who will listen, not only those doing Transmission Meditation, about the Day of Declaration, and I really do not see how this information interferes with anyone's selfless service to humanity. Those doing Transmission Meditation should not see themselves as an élite group somehow separate from humanity as a whole. I believe that everyone needs Maitreya's guidance and teaching, that His emergence is important to us all. Nothing can destroy the purity of the Transmission except the emotional glamours and separative tendencies of those taking part. (2) It goes without saying that my announcement of Maitreya's emergence is done with total seriousness of purpose and not to test anyone at all.

After the Day of Declaration, what will be the practical benefit of Transmission Meditation work in the short term?

Transmission Meditation is not simply a way of distributing energies to bring about the Declaration of the Christ. It is a long-term process by which Hierarchical energies can be made available to the mass of humanity at a level that can be absorbed and used. It is also a process which will bring those involved in its practice to the Gates of Initiation. It is a way of co-operating with the Masters of the Hierarchy in serving the world and, at the same time, a yoga of self-development of enormous practical benefit to those taking part in it.

ON MEDITATION IN GENERAL

Why is meditation so important? (April 1994)

The soul is the reality, not the man or woman. The physical plane is real from its own angle, but from the angle of the soul it is not real, it is relative. Our problem is that we take it as the whole while it is only a relative part of a much greater whole. The part cannot see the whole but the whole sees the part — and the different parts. From the point of view of the soul, its effort in incarnating again and again is to create a series of bodies which will gradually build this bridge and unify what was fragmented. The involutionary process into matter is reversed and the spiritualizing of matter takes place.

We spiritualize matter through our own bodies. The soul creates a series of bodies, each incarnation at a higher turn of the spiral, a higher vibrational rate (if all goes well) until we have a body through which the soul can express itself without too much limitation, and eventually without any limitation.

Meditation is the process which sets this in motion. That is why, in every religion and training, at the basis of all paths of ascent, is meditation of one kind or another. It may not be Transmission Meditation, or the various meditations you have come to know or read about; but some form of meditation, an alignment with the soul and its nature, must take place, because it is the soul who has incarnated. The soul cannot be avoided or bypassed. *The soul is the reality*. That reality has to be recognized, and the method by which it is recognized is through the creating of the bridge, the path of return. We do it one step at a time.

It is not a path that you get on and try to stay on, however narrow it may be. The path is created step by step by the individual through their activity in life. It is not a separate part of what we call life; it is what life is about. That is why we are in life. People tend to think that there is the path, there is meditation, there is service, spiritual paths that you can take — and then there is life: eating, shopping, having a haircut, and so on. There is a separation in people's minds between what we call life and what we call the Path, the spiritual life. They are not

510

different or separate. The only way you can live the spiritual life is in life.

(1) Is personal meditation essential for making spiritual progress? (2) Is it important to do it at the same time every day? (May 1995)

(1) Personal meditation is not essential for making spiritual progress, but it is very useful. It is one way, among others, to make progress. (2) It is not essential but very beneficial if it can be achieved. The mind and body react to the regular rhythm thus set up and become predisposed to the inward focus necessary for the meditation. It is also easier to maintain a rhythm which is regular.

If you are in a triangle with someone who dies, should you continue with them or find another person for the triangle? (April 1996)

Find another person and allow the deceased member to continue on his/her way released from all earthly ties.

Is it necessary to have an everyday spiritual practice? (December 1995)

It depends very much on the individual and also on his/her point in evolution. For most aspirants and disciples, some form of meditation and certainly some field of service is usually necessary.

How can we know if it is our soul or a Master who makes contact with our minds? (December 1995)

It is really a question of experience and discrimination. Contact with a Master is relatively rare, and, when real, leaves the disciple in no doubt of its reality and source. The soul may impress its reflection's mind without any special experience being involved.

(1) If one is meditating and there are no thoughts, is one on the egoic plane? (2) If not, on what plane is one? (September 1996)

(1) Not necessarily, it depends on the stage of evolution. (2) It could be on one or other astral or mental plane. The absence of thoughts is no guarantee or indicator of egoic focus.

Could you please explain the difference between the terms "Blessing" and "Overshadowing". I had always thought the processes to be entirely different but was puzzled to hear the terms being used interchangeably recently. (July/August 1993)

Both involve an outflow of energy from a higher source, but a blessing does not necessarily involve overshadowing where the consciousness (some part) of a higher Being "overshadows" or enters into that of the recipient. In Spiritualism, on a lower level, a medium in trance is said to be "overshadowed" by an astral entity who takes over the astral and physical vehicles of the medium. This is never the case where the Masters of Wisdom are concerned — Their "overshadowing" takes place on the soul level.

Are the ashrams "linked" — all meditators creating one huge force for good? (November 1996)

Theoretically, yes, but in practice very many "meditators" lack the discipline and scientific method which would make their practice potent. It is also a mistake to imagine that the ashrams of the Masters are concerned only with meditation. Every department of human activity is covered by Hierarchy.

What is kundalini? (April 1993)

The kundalini is the fiery energy coiled at the chakra at the base of the spine. Kundalini is gradually awakened, and spirals up through the chakras as the chakras above it are prepared to receive it. When it reaches the chakra at the top of the head and unites with it a great awakening takes place. It can be (sometimes is) artificially awakened by certain yogic breathing exercises but this is a highly dangerous thing to do. It can end in death and very often causes lunacy because you can pump up the kundalini before the chakras above it are prepared for its reception. There are groups, especially in India, who practise kundalini yoga but, as Maitreya says, it does not lead to salvation. That is a glamour, a side-track.

If kundalini rises, is this an initiation or enlightenment? Are you changed after this has happened?

It depends on the situation. Many people practise some form of kundalini-yoga and deliberately arouse the kundalini energy, dormant at the base of the spine. This is extremely dangerous unless done under the surpervision of an advanced initiate teacher. The fact that the fire of kundalini can be so roused does not constitute either initiation or enlightenment – it could lead to madness if the chakras are not prepared in advance to receive it. In the normal course of life, kundalini is rising all the time but in small, controlled amounts, thus safely. The regulated life of service is the best guarantee of safe kundalini control. When it is scientifically guided through the chakras, prepared in the correct sequence, there will eventuate a degree of enlightenment and, if the person is ready, initiation.

Some believe that the practice of asanas in Hatha Yoga is potentially dangerous due to crystallization of the subtler bodies and sudden changes in the glands, nervous system and blood. What is your view on this matter? Should one avoid the practice? (June 1995)

Hatha Yoga is tremendously old — the most ancient of all Yogas. For modern disciples (after the first initiation has been taken) it represents a lower (and potentially more dangerous) path. This is especially true for disciples in occidental bodies.

(1) Should people in Transmission Meditation groups avoid Hatha Yoga, asanas and other breathing exercises? (2) Should "working on the chakras" or "balancing the chakras" be avoided? (May 1995)

(1) Generally speaking, yes. (2) Preferably, yes.

CHAPTER 8

THE ART OF WAITING

A NEW AGE CONCEPT OF TIME

by the Master —, through Benjamin Creme

A much needed change in the life of humanity will come about when the concept of Time has undergone a transformation. Today most people think of Time as an ongoing process, linking moments of action, whereas, in truth, Time is not a process but a state of mind. When we see this, we will transform our lives and enter into an altogether closer understanding of reality; a wonderful new freedom will become man's, and, no longer dogged by the limitation of Time, he will soar into his birthright.

How is this to be achieved? At present most of us are confined within the rigid framework of our daily activities: the means of living has to be earned, decisions have to be taken in relation to others' needs, a constant battle goes on against the clock and the remorseless 'passage of time'. There is little hope within our present modes of living of any fundamental shift in our understanding of Time. Now, for the first time in history, the possibility arises for a completely new experience of that phenomenon, and social transformation is the key to this desirable happening. When humanity is One, in fact and in truth, Time will disappear. When man approaches life from the inner, creative standpoint, Time will lose its hold over our minds and thus free us from its tyranny. All of this requires a new assessment of man's place in the Universe and the establishment of a truer rapport with the Source of our Being.

It has become customary to speak of Time as a passage of a sequence of events. A new and more correct view of Time becomes possible when man takes the steps to align himself with his higher Self. This achieved, the way is open for a truer understanding of cyclic activity and non-activity, and thus of Time.

Such a correct understanding is inherent in a correct relationship to our fellow men, for only when the sense of separateness no longer exists can a true realization of cyclic activity come about. A new world order, political and economic, is the essential prerequisite for this truer vision, for the required sense of Oneness can be achieved only when harmony and justice prevail. What this means in practical terms is the creation of structures — political and economic and social — which will bring men together and create the sense of Oneness on all planes and in every field. When men see this, they will take the measures to implement the necessary changes and pave the way for the establishment of correct human relations. From that new relationship between men will emerge the conditions on which a new sense of Time depends.

From the Master's viewpoint, Time exists only in the sense of cyclic waves of activity, followed by non-activity, repeated infinitely. He is completely unconditioned by Time as sensed in the three worlds of human experience, and must make constant adjustments when dealing with His disciples, for instance, in order to accommodate His meaning and intentions to the state of consciousness of those still ensnared by Time.

Already, signs are appearing that men's minds are beginning to realize the inadequacy of their approach to Time, and it will not be long before an intellectual appreciation of this fact becomes more general. Inherent in many of the discoveries of present-day science is the assumption that Time is dual, and, more and more, this will condition men's perception of reality; but only as the result of man's direct awareness of himself as part of an integral Whole will a true realization of Time be his. When man creates around himself the forms and structures, based on unity and brotherhood, essential for that integration to take place, he will stand on the threshold of an entirely new experience of reality from which will flow a steady stream of creativity unlike aught seen before in this world.

(Share International, January 1982*)*

THE ART OF WAITING

The following article is an edited version of a talk given by Benjamin Creme at the 1996 Transmission Meditation Conferences in San Francisco, USA, and Kerkrade, the Netherlands.

Most of the people involved in the work for the Reappearance of the Christ and the Masters of Wisdom have been living for many years under the (false) impression that they have been waiting for something. They have been waiting — some patiently, some very impatiently — for Maitreya's emergence into the open. There has been hardly a phone call to me from a person in one of the groups which did not end with the inevitable words: "Ben, is there any news, anything new? Can you tell us anything about what is happening?"

It is as if I were sitting at a ticker-tape machine, with Hierarchy and all the denizens of the angelic worlds communicating to me the latest news. This goes on all the time, week after week, month after month, year after year, representing for all these people their sense of waiting, impatience, of wanting to know the latest "news".

How could it be news if there is no such thing as news? If there is no such thing as time, there is no such thing as news. News belongs to time. And if time does not exist, news does not exist. The ticker-tape machine is simply the last, the most moronic, expression of our enthralment by time.

If you think about it, it does not take too much of a leap of the imagination to see that time actually does not exist. It is an illusion. And yet we order, we live, our lives in relation to this total illusion: that time is a process of events marked off by the hours and minutes. We think of history, pre-history, and the time yet to come. We are afraid of it. We look ahead and say: "I am going to get old, tired, I am going to die; I cannot, dare not, think of that moment in time, hopefully not tomorrow or next week or next year, not for many, many years to come." People live out the whole of their lives dominated by the concept of the past and the future, so that almost no one to any great extent lives in the present moment.

Everyone, almost without exception, thinks of life as the past and the future. We regret the past and are afraid of the future. Children look forward to being older, brighter, cleverer and stronger, and for them that is the future. But they do not think of it in terms of time. They think of it simply in terms of their new responsibility — the strength, vision, courage, and opportunities that being older will present to them.

Children are notorious for having no sense of time at all. That is why they are practically the only truly alive exponents of the human experiment — because they are not conditioned by time. Everyone else, short of Masters and high initiates, is dominated by the total illusion that time exists. Therefore, we are either regretting something or waiting for something. We are regretting all the years, and all the days in those years, when we did not put into effect all our potential — our work for the Reappearance of the Christ, or whatever it happens to be. We wish we had worked earlier and harder. We wish we had really taken that opportunity and not missed it, not been afraid, tired, or too timid really to do anything special.

Some are counting the days and weeks until Maitreya comes forward, when they can turn to everyone to whom they have vaguely mentioned it and say: "You see, I was right. Time always tells. Time proves that I am right, that I did not waste those hours, days and years of work for this endless 'myth' of the Reappearance of the Christ in the world." The experience of many people in this work, demonstrated by what they say to me on the telephone, or what they write and say to each other, and the rumours which circulate around all the groups, is that they are waiting, waiting, waiting.

Is there some way in which we can look at this idea of time, adjust our relationship to this waiting, and turn the waiting into an art, an experience — hopefully, a vivid, living, useful experience? Some people are already doing that. But a lot of people in the groups around the world are simply waiting. Their energy is running out, their patience, their hope, is running out, their dedication and conviction are running out. This is mainly because their interest is based primarily on an emotional response to the idea, and there is a limit to the amount of astral energy that they can make available to sustain and uphold their commitment to that idea. So they get impatient, and say: "Any news? Any news? Anything happening?"

It is no accident that the very first article that the Master wrote for *Share International*, in January 1982, is called 'A New Age Concept of Time'. The Masters never do anything, however slight, however trivial it might appear, which does not have an underlying purpose. They never waste an opportunity to serve the Plan, to aid a disciple in some way, to enlighten where They can. Everything They do is done with a purpose which, instantaneously, They can realize as They are asked a request.

Every month I say: "Could you please give me the article for the magazine?" Sometimes, on rare occasions, the Master will say: "No, I have no ideas. Ask Me tomorrow, or leave it until Friday." He knows I am so lazy that I would rather leave it until Friday, so He is doing me a good turn. You cannot 'kid' a Master. There is no way I can ask my Master for the article in a frame of mind in which I am hoping He will say: "Not just now," and He does not know that. Every nuance of my thought is as open as a book to Him. I should say: "Do you mind if we leave it until Friday because I am so tired, I am not in the mood." But He knows; He will say: "No, I am busy. Let us leave it until Friday," or "I have no idea. I have not an idea in My head." He must have lots of ideas. This has gone on for years and years; we are now half way through Volume 15 of *Share International*. Every month for 14½ years the Master has been thinking up ideas for the article and dictating them to me. Hopefully this will still go on. I sometimes think that sooner or later He will run out of ideas, but so far it has never happened. I am always amazed with what comes up. Sometimes the ideas are repeated from another angle, so He is broadening our consciousness, enlarging it all the time. But I am certain it is no accident the very first article is about time, or the absence, the illusion, of time: a new-age concept of time.

It is also, I am certain, no accident, the very first time I was overshadowed by Maitreya, in March 1959 (soon after the initial contact with my Master) — when He told me He was coming into the world in about 20 years and that I would have a role to play in His coming if I accepted it — that, at the same time, He gave me the most extraordinary experience: a vision of precisely how the Masters see reality in the complete absence of time.

I was given a vision in which I was inside a brilliant sphere of white light. The right-hand side of this sphere (there were no sides, but it felt like the right-hand side) showed in full colour, though there was a faint veil over the whole succession of scenes, all the events of the world which we call history, like the death of the Queen of England, the battle of so and so. I saw all of that but it was still taking place, layer upon layer of active, moving, coloured events.

At the same time on the left-hand side, without turning my head and without losing the awareness of the events of what we call the past, I was given a view, in colour, a panorama of the events which were going to take place, which we call the future — but which were *simultaneously* taking place. As I watched what looked like the past, I was also watching what looked like the future. I saw myself. I saw people I knew. I saw events connected with the Reappearance. All these things were shown to me. I was totally aware of these events taking place at the same time. There was no sense of past or future. There were simply the events which we call the past and those which we call the future taking place simultaneously. It was an all-around vision and I was in the middle, experiencing it, feeling it. It was like cinema only more real. Even the most horrific battles did not give me any kind of emotion; I simply saw them as events which were happening, and, likewise, in the future. I was seeing that in the only time which exists, which is Now. And it is everlasting. There is no past, there is no future, there is only Now.

That is how the Master, any Master, experiences what we call reality. We, on the other hand, have a confused idea of time. It begins at a certain time in our infancy when we are told it is time to go to bed. "Time to go to bed? What does that have to do with it? I am not tired, Mummy." You only go to bed when you are tired, and you do not even wait to go to bed. Any child in his prime can fall asleep, one moment to the next (like some people I know in Transmission Meditation!). It is a sudden, total, all-embracing experience. And yet as soon as that routine of sleep occurs, and the alarm goes off, it is time to wake. Whether or not we are in the most wonderful experience of soul contact, we are awakened because it is time. If you have ever been in a hospital, you will know what I mean — six o'clock wake up, cup of tea. The nurses are there; they have to do a job so they wake you up.

Illusion

From infancy we become conditioned, and in the deepest sense enthralled, by the illusion that time exists. We make it not only exist, but practically the most important thing that does exist. We govern our lives completely by that illusion. We find waiting difficult because we are conditioned by this factor of time and therefore the expectations which that sets up.

Of course, as we live our lives in relation to other people, earning a living, taking trains, buses and planes, we create the conditions in which time is very important. If you turn up at the airport half an hour after your plane has gone, you have missed it. We regulate our lives in order to conform to that which we take to be the most important thing in life. If, on the other hand, you are a creative person — I mean that in the broadest sense — if your thought processes are creative, emanating from the soul which has no sense of time (the soul is completely outside time), and no doubt if you are a writer, poet, artist, musician, or scientist involved in profoundly engrossing work, anybody who loves work, who can be totally engrossed hour upon hour in that work, you know that what I am saying is true: time no longer exists. It is no factor in the creative process.

The experience of work, and the concentration of all your attention in that work, removes from you, for the period of the work, the illusion which you normally have that time exists. This is why, if you are a creative person, really engrossed in that creativity, you can start work at 9am, and by 4.30pm realize you have had no breakfast or lunch. None of that matters. Breakfast 'time' came and went. Lunch 'time' came and went for most people. But you did not even realize that you had not got dressed yet. You are still in your dressing gown. You have not shaved, or

521

washed, you have not eaten, and it does not matter. This is the kind of attention and concentration which only comes to those who can really immerse themselves in creative work at an intensity where time disappears completely from their consciousness. That is the true state of life. That creative, non-conditioned-by-time awareness is the only true, free, creative condition that exists.

My Master recently wrote about this idea of time and timelessness, and our obsession with time. The article shows how the Masters look at it. It is in the July/August 1996 edition of *Share International*, and is called 'The Perennial Choice'.

He says: *"With impatience do many await this time (the time for the coming out of Maitreya, the choice that lies before humanity, the inspiration and teaching of Maitreya, all of that), knowing little of the many factors, cosmic and other, which must be balanced by Maitreya to fulfil the law. Nothing may be done which infringes the free will of men; naught but the Law, and an understanding of the times, can influence the judgement of Maitreya on the moment of His public appearance. Of one thing you may be assured: not one moment's delay will be countenanced by Maitreya which would, otherwise, allow His open mission of service to begin. He alone is the arbiter of that moment. Await, and trust, His judgement.*

"That judgement rests on knowledge unknown to men. A cosmic grasp alone permits its correct assessment. Even so, Maitreya must make weighty decisions on slender — and changing — data. A fine line, indeed, divides the necessary and the possible.

"Trust then the skill in action of the Lord of Love. Chafe not at the seeming delay of His appearance — in the all-embracing Now no such delay exists."

That is the reality. I do not remember exactly now, but I have no doubt in that vision which Maitreya gave me in March 1959 of the timelessness of all reality, in the 'events-to-come' column, the 'future' column, I saw Maitreya emerged. It was so many years ago that I have forgotten the precise images, but I did see people I recognized, and, almost certainly, Maitreya, the

Masters, the populace gathered together, huge crowds of people full of hope and gratitude: tremendous fervour. All of that I saw.

There is a wonderful quotation from the Agni Yoga teachings: "If you love work, understand it as a substitute for time." That is precisely what work is. If you love work, in the sense of dedicating your time and energy to a creative process of whatever kind, it becomes a substitute for time. Time disappears in that state of creativity.

It was said of Rembrandt, a third-degree initiate and a great artist, that he would not allow an interruption of his work, and therefore of his concentration, even if the King were knocking at the door. He would never allow any kind of interruption in his working time, because he knew that, as soon as the interruption took place, he would be brought back into time. Time is the opposite, the denial, of that creative rhythm which is work. If you love work, therefore, consider it as a substitute for time.

If there is no time there is no waiting, there is no delay. Delay does not exist if time does not exist and is only our sense that we are expecting a certain event. We see time as a succession of events marked off by the days, hours and weeks. It is not that at all. Time pertains only to the brain. It is an illusion; a state of mind.

Most people have the state of mind in which time exists. The Masters have a state of mind in which time does not exist. Babies and young children also have a state of mind in which time does not exist. If you say to a child: "No, you can have it tomorrow," he has no idea of tomorrow. But he knows that later on at some point he will get the ice cream, or whatever it was he wanted. A child lives so much outside time that he forgets. If you say to him: "What did you do today?" He will look at you: "What a stupid idea. How could you expect me to tell you what I did today? I can tell you what I am doing now, which is talking to a stupid man." "But what did you do today?" Today does not exist. There is no sense of that time before this moment, or tomorrow, for a child. He has no concept of that. That is why a child seems so caught up, not taking part in these very closely monitored, registered, cut up bits of experience which we call time.

I wondered at the time why my Master began writing for *Share International* in 1982 with 'A New Age Concept of Time'. Now I realize why, to some extent — because of the extraordinary importance for humanity that we should lose this sense of time. We should not limit our consciousness to time consciousness, which is not real.

As soon as you move out of your physical body, time disappears. If you can do it, and you can very easily learn to do it and move in your etheric body, you lose all sense of time. Out of the physical body, time does not exist because time is simply the illusion of the brain. If we were not conditioned by the way we live, we would have no sense of time. We make it necessary to regulate every moment of our day according to a clock. We build social, political, and economic structures which lock us into a time frame.

In this way people can exert power. You cannot exert power over someone who has no concept of time. Obviously, to catch trains and planes, you have to organize yourself in such a way. But outside these necessities, the more you can live without the sense of time, the freer, happier, and probably healthier, you will be.

Rhythm

That first article written for *Share International* has, to my knowledge, until now and certainly by me, been given very little attention. I remember one of our most active workers, now dead, saying at the time: "I do not understand a word of that article. I just do not understand it." I do not know whether you understand it or will come to understand it, but I think this is one of the most important articles that the Master has written.

As soon as we create the structures which demonstrate the true Oneness of humanity, as soon as humanity accepts the teaching, endorses the advice of Maitreya, and creates sharing, justice and peace in the world, there will flow from that a harmony which at the moment is, sadly, totally lacking. It is a harmony between the outer and inner that creates the conditions in which time disappears. That harmony, that freedom, is the creative mind, state of being, and it is to that harmonious state of mind, of being, that every artist, poet, creative person of any kind, seeks the path. If there is a block to creativity, it is because that state of harmony does not exist. There has to be a period of regeneration, of course, of building up the fires of creativity again and again; that is a period of inaction.

As an artist, I am very conscious of this flow, this sequence of creative activity followed by a fallow period of inactivity in which you have to go and look and absorb or do something else. Then it builds up, gradually, without thinking about it, into another creative activity. It takes place as a sequence, a cyclic flow, a rhythm of activity followed by inactivity.

I believe this cyclic activity and inactivity is closely connected with the absence of time. If you are dominated by time, you say you have no time to do your work, no time to create. If you do it, you find you have time to do it. In my experience, dealing with people who are working in a group, nine times out of 10 it is better to give the work to the people who are already doing most of the work. Do not try giving it to someone who is doing nothing or very little. They are doing nothing or very little because they always do nothing or very little. They are people who are blocked, who may have lots of goodwill but do not have the impetus to work for the group.

It is almost a certainty — if you want to get a job done 'on time' and efficiently, give it to somebody who is already doing too much, who is already stretched to what would appear to be the limit, and you will get it done. They are the people who say: "Yes, I will find time for it." The people who are sitting around doing nothing say yes, but it never gets done because these people never do anything. They say: "I do not have the time." It is not that they really do not have the time. They do not do it because their mind is conditioned by time.

It is not time that is lacking; it is impulse that is lacking. They do not have the initiating impulse to do work. If that is not there they do less and less until they are doing nothing at all. Such people are in every group without exception to a greater or lesser degree. Ask the busy person to do a job and you will get it done, because they know how to work without being dominated by time.

One of the major factors concerned in experiencing a delay in waiting for Maitreya is a complete misunderstanding of how the Masters work. I have already explained that the Masters do not work in time. They have to make real adjustments to try to put into a time frame that might be meaningful for us an event which They already see taking place. The Reappearance of the Christ took place before He came down from the Himalayas. Every event which is concerned with the emergence of Maitreya is already happening.

The stock-exchange crash has already taken place. It is happening now because there is only Now. It is not waiting for a time. It is only we who are waiting for that time to precipitate on the physical plane as the event we call the stock-exchange crash. We can accept that the Japanese crash has occurred because we can see it in the Nikkei average, but we cannot accept that the international crash — the American, French and British, etc — has occurred. And yet, to the Masters it is happening now. Their difficulty is in telling us, from our point of view of time, when these events are going to take place.

Events are only events when they happen. When you tell a child it is his birthday, that is an event which certainly has all his attention — the cake, candles and presents. But if you tell him that tomorrow is going to be his birthday, he is intrigued by the idea for five minutes. But he gets busy doing something else and forgets about it until the next day when he sees the cake. If he remembers it the next day, he will set out the candles again, start lighting them just to prolong the experience. He has no sense of time at all.

The events of the world, what we call the past, which are still happening, the future which is happening now, have to precipitate. They are already taking place on the inner planes, on the subtler levels of reality — the crash of a plane, the crash of the stock exchange, a baby being born, a king being assassinated — these have to precipitate on the physical plane before we are aware of them.

How do you think Maitreya can make all these extraordinary forecasts: the end of the Cold War, the unification of Germany, the release of Mandela, and so on. With some of them, He brought them about. He literally inspired Mr Gorbachev to go to the US to make peace and to open up the Soviet Union. And He did personally visit Nelson Mandela and arrange that whole South African transformation. He also brought about the Middle Eastern accord by appearing to Yasser Arafat and to the King of Jordan. But apart from these, it is simply that He *sees* the events. He knows that these events will happen because they are already happening. Inevitably they will precipitate and become reality. The more we realize this, the more we will lose our impatience. We will find an ability to stand, to be there, and simply watch it take place on the outer physical plane, without this constant desire for news, without saying: "When is it going to happen?"

We all say: "Come on, Maitreya!" to speed it up, to get this period of turmoil and chaos over. It will not be over the moment Maitreya appears, but that will go a long way. We have to realize that as far as Maitreya and the Masters are concerned, especially in connection with the open emergence of Maitreya, there are no set dates. The media and everyone else keep asking me when Maitreya is going to appear. What is the date for this or that?

"Windows of opportunity"

As far as Maitreya is concerned, there is no set date, not even to appear on television. There are "windows of opportunity". These windows are constantly changing. They are the result of His understanding of the cosmic energies as they flow. These are positive and negative, and they change all the time. This is the difficulty for Maitreya. With all His insight and wisdom — and two levels of cosmic consciousness — and overshadowed by two colossal Avatars, with the cosmic understanding that that gives Him, He sees the window of opportunity as only a possibility. As soon as it approaches, something else can happen to change the scene again. This occurs over and over again.

He can see there will be a window of opportunity coming up on the horizon, because certain cosmic energies will be flowing and should sustain themselves for some set cycle. But is humanity ready in that window of opportunity? Are the media responsive then? What other factors we cannot even begin to imagine does He have to take into account as making up that window of opportunity? We should rid our minds of this sense of impatience. What is the date for the Day of Declaration? Maitreya, Himself, does not know. I do not mean He has no idea but the Masters do not think in time so it is irrelevant to set a date.

What He sees is a series of windows in which all the forces which make up the statistics whereby He can judge a moment have to be taken into account — all these different things like the state of humanity, what we do for ourselves, and especially the activity of the Lords of Materiality, the forces of chaos, who are not sitting twiddling their thumbs. They are active as never before, because they know their time is over — as soon as Maitreya comes forward, and humanity sees the Masters and begins the process of reconstruction, lifting humanity above the level where they can be influenced. Through their agents: men and women in the world, some of them very well known in the media and other fields; the leaders of certain countries; certain groups of financiers who are set against this happening; various reactionary groups, political and religious, these destructive forces work to prevent the Christ's open appearance.

They know what is happening, they know that it is not good for them and they are resisting it for as long as they possibly can. There are some well known people who are resisting all they can the externalization of the Hierarchy, because for them it is the end of their power. They are men dominated by power. Their main interest is the sustaining of that power over their employees by the thousands, and the minds of people in their millions all over the world. They are power-hungry men whose only real interest in life, apart probably from making money, is to have power over the minds of others and to regulate their ideas in the way they see as right: the old, greedy, selfish, separatist way of the past. In a sense, they cannot help themselves. They are dominated by their nature and their energies, and they put up a great bulwark against this externalization process. It will not work; it is inevitable that it will not work — it is only a question of time.

Field of service

This "window of opportunity" concept is the way the Masters work in every department of life. They do not set for a disciple a certain programme and say: "In three years he or she should reach that point." They see an opportunity to enhance the activity of a given disciple — someone who is promising, who is working in service with some intensity, who is losing the sense of the separative ego, who is becoming more altruistic and living more and more as a soul. They see all this and stimulate that person with Their energy. They present to him or her some field of service — through the soul, or, if possible, more directly. They see this as a window of opportunity which allows Them to do that. To the same person, at an earlier or later stage, it could, perhaps, not be possible. It is not a constant state, because people are not constant.

Everyone is different. Everyone is unique. This is something that humanity will one day grasp. People say it, but few really grasp the truth of this statement. Every single person is, literally, unique; there are no two people alike. There are no clones. (The idea of clones fascinates humanity, but it is the opposite of reality.) People want to be individual but everyone *is* an individual, a unique Being.

All people express their individuality well or badly, but it is their unique way. That being so, they do not respond to the same kind of stimulus in the same way. Some people may respond quickly. If they are presented with a field of service, they may snap it up; act on it and make great progress. Then, perhaps, they may sit back, rest on the progress and stop there, so that another window of opportunity for that person might take years or incarnations. One or two incarnations from now the window might open again and that person can be stimulated to make a further advance. But if the rhythm is not sufficient to keep the momentum going, they may sit on the achievement. It depends partly on the ray structure, and above all on the unique individuality of the person.

The Masters have to take all of this into account. They know that if They provide an opportunity it may or may not be taken up. The same type of opportunity given to two different individuals may produce entirely different results.

Some people think that because we should be aiming at group consciousness we should lose our individuality. That is the worst thing we could do: lose our uniqueness, our individual pattern, our colour. That is given to us; we call it free will. The abuse of our free will causes all the wars, the harm, the terrible lives which millions of people live. The correct use of free will makes for a clearly defined, individual, unique person which is necessary for the evolutionary process. Without that individuality, we have no freedom, no free will, and no possibility of evolution. It is free will which allows us to evolve; it also allows us to do harm. The correct use of free will produces a clear-cut demonstration of the individuality of the soul.

You will notice that the masses of people are very similar. They might be clearly defined physical types but not clearly defined expressions of thought and ideas. As people advance (if you look up in the list of initiates those who were second- and third-degree initiates), you will see that, although they become fewer and fewer, they become more and more clear-cut, more different from each other.

You would never confuse a Rembrandt with a Velasquez. It would not occur to you to do it. I am taking people at about the same point of evolution, living at the same time. You would never confuse Rembrandt with Vermeer, for example. You would never confuse Beethoven with Berlioz. Berlioz went to Beethoven's funeral, so he was not outside the range of his being a contemporary, although he was born later.

The more advanced a person becomes, the more his soul, and therefore the altruistic nature of the soul, demonstrates. At the same time, the more individual that person becomes too. This seems to be a contradiction but it is not. The more advanced the person, the more the soul *is* the person, the more you are really seeing the nature of that person's soul, and the more creative that person becomes; the more creative, the more distinguishable as an individual.

This is why you would never look at a Matisse and think it was a Picasso, or vice versa. They were contemporaries, exactly the same degree in initiation, 2.4 at the end, but each completely distinct and unique in his way of expression. I use painters as an example because it comes easily to me to think of them. The same could be said of scientists or anyone engaged in creative life: the more advanced, the more they are the soul; the more advanced, the more, paradoxically, they are the unique individual. Individuality is not something which should be lost but it should be enhanced and put at the service of the soul.

When this is done on a wide scale, we have a truly creative era, a true culture. We are about to create that kind of civilization. Under the guidance and tutelage of the Masters, humanity will create the outer political, economic, and social conditions that will rid us, eventually, of the dominance of time.

We will create machinery, for example, which will make all the things that today millions drudge to do. Millions of people in thousands of factories all over the world are doing nothing all day long but acting in a machine-like way. When we create machinery which rids us of the need for drudgery, unnecessary work, the leisure thus achieved will enable humanity to demonstrate its true creativity. The sense of being dominated by time will disappear. We will construct our lives in entirely new ways. People will work more and more at home, for example. They will have altogether more recreation. The energy of millions of people which today is inhibited and contained will be released. A tremendous creativity will flow out from humanity all over the world. Think of the potential in the Third World: three-quarters of the world's population but at present contributing a tiny fraction to the creative life of humanity. When they are freed from drudgery, when they can eat and have normal, decent, human lives, you can imagine the outflow of creative power that will be released.

This will give us a tremendous expansion of consciousness. The creation of better and more just outer forms — political, economic and social — is the key to the new awareness in which time no longer exists. Time is only a state of mind.

(*Share International*, January/February 1997)

WINDOWS OF OPPORTUNITY

What factors create windows of opportunity?

I was talking about windows of opportunity as far as Maitreya is concerned in His assessing of the best time to come forward openly in the world, so I can only address that to the extent that we know some of the factors involved.

The major one, I would imagine, would be the cosmic energies flowing at any given time, which are cyclic, which change — I do not know whether it is from day to day but certainly from week to week and month to month. Maitreya has to make His assessments on these cycles. Energies which are conducive to humanity's correct response to His presence, His teaching and so on, would be the most favourable. Others, at other times, would be less so. Obviously He would choose the time when He could be sure that there would be the maximum positive response to whatever He has to say. That is a major factor in creating a window of opportunity.

Another factor is the state of humanity's being, the state of consciousness at any given time as demonstrated by the various events which take place in the world — what we are doing for ourselves: showing an expansion of consciousness if it is of benefit to the world, and contractions of consciousness if it is another war or some major division which is engrossing the hearts and minds of humanity. That is a major factor, the state of mind, the readiness, perceptiveness, openness, of humanity itself.

There is also the activity of the 'dark forces', as we call them, the Lords of Materiality who, you can be sure, never lose an opportunity to prevent this major threat to their continued enthralment of humanity. There is one thing they will not find pleasing: the open demonstration of the Masters in the world, beginning with Maitreya. So that is another factor.

Everything that Hierarchy does — all but the innermost secrets which can be known only to the Masters — can be known by the opposing forces, so it is very difficult for Hierarchy to work with Their groups without 'the other side' having the intelligence of what is planned and what is actually being done, the effects in the world, which (since there is no time) are already happening before we recognize them as having taken place. We only recognize the precipitation of events; we do not recognize that these events are already taking place in the view of the Masters, and also in the view of the dark forces (what shall I call them?), The anti-Masters.

I know that I will never be given by my Master the date of the first appearance of Maitreya on television. Of course, the Day of Declaration will become generally known because it will take place through the media and does not need a special word to me. If my Master gave me the date it would have to pass through the mind-belt. On the mind-belt every thought is, potentially, interceptible, and the Lords of Materiality are as adept as the Masters in intercepting such thoughts. That thought, although given quicker-than-light from my Master's mind to my mind, could be known by the forces who should not know these details because they would inevitably mount an offensive against it. They are not alone. The Masters can cope relatively easily with the dark forces of our planet, however clever they are, and however many hundreds of thousands of people they have on the physical and astral planes to work with and through, but these dark forces are in contact with cosmic forces who are a different kettle of fish altogether.

So when I say the cosmic forces have to be positive, I mean not only the cosmic forces as they are playing through cosmos from various constellations, but which are not at the same time being influenced by certain cosmic groups of evil. The dark forces on this planet receive their energy from the cosmic astral plane, and there are those within our own system who are adept in the handling of these powerful cosmic energies. All of this is relevant in Maitreya's choice of a window of opportunity. It is changing all the time, it is never static. He might say, for example: "That looks wonderful; We will go for September," and by September the whole pattern could have changed and could be just terrible, depending on the changing forces themselves and on the effect of the groups of evil on these cosmic forces. They can manipulate them, too, as can the Masters.

One of the major factors is the state of readiness of humanity, and this is where we come in. Our job has been to create the climate of hope and expectancy which will allow Maitreya to come forward (without infringing our free will) and declare Himself openly in an arena in which at least a major receptivity exists. Millions of people have heard this story; of course, they do not all believe it. Many thousands, perhaps hundreds of thousands, do believe it to some extent. They are open to the possibility, and that is a good thing. There are — I do not know how many — many hundreds or thousands of really committed, active believers. Their task, our task, is to further this openness of humanity to the possibility of Maitreya's appearance. That helps to create this open window which will allow Him to come forward.

Can you say something about coincidences? (January/February 1993)

Nothing happens by itself. Events happen as a result of a focus of thought, and a thought is a thing, as you may know. A thought develops its own energy and brings about, by relationship, events which then become, as it were, coincidences.

An event interacts with another event which interacts with another event which creates, "coincidentally", a further event, and so on. People are reacting all the time to thoughts in the mind-belt. That mind-belt may be filled with ideas from the Masters but also from much lesser initiates or disciples, or just the broad stream of humanity, who are filling the mind-belt with ideas about sharing, justice, feeding the starving millions and so on. Sensitive individuals focus their minds, especially in meditation, and respond to these thoughtforms but do not know where they are coming from. The mind-belt is saturated with thoughtforms. If the energy of a thoughtform and the energy of an individual are vibrating at more or less the same rate then the individual can 'pull in' that thoughtform and respond to it. You would not respond to something that was against your ideas, but to one which was in line with your own thinking. Others are doing the same and then you meet up because you are sharing the same thoughtform. "What a coincidence," you say. It is not chance, there is no such thing as 'chance'. There is such a thing as coincidence but it is because we share a mind-belt from which our minds are fed. We are naturally telepathic. The trick is to filter out the rubbish.

How can we recognize and make use of these windows of opportunity?
We cannot; only a Master can know anything about these windows. What we can do is use our influence in the sense of working as hard as we can to create windows of opportunity on the physical plane. That is the only way in which we can influence this colossal, cosmic event.

I think people in these groups generally forget the enormity of the event that we are dealing with. We look back in history and say: "Well, the Buddha came, and Jesus came, Mohammed came — it's pretty straightforward." It is anything but straightforward. These are momentous times, and only made possible by the terrible events of the two world wars of this century. This century has been the most crucial experience for humanity in the history of the planet, far exceeding the devastation caused in late Atlantean days, the breakup of Atlantis, and so on. Thinking man is altogether different from Atlantean man. The enormity of the forces which we have in our weapons systems today is such that we could create a catastrophe which would dwarf the Atlantean break-up by many times. It would destroy all life on the planet. We have tremendous responsibility, therefore. There has never been a century of such import — for good or ill. With the defeat of the Axis powers in the war from 1939-1945, it has become possible for the first time in nearly 100,000 years for the Masters to come out openly into the world, not only as individuals, but to set in place, gradually, Their ashrams on the outer plane. That is what the externalization of the Hierarchy is really about. This is extraordinary.

This being so, it needs an enormous educational effort by all who know and believe that this is actually taking place to tell it on the widest possible scale, with every ounce of energy that we can give it. It does not matter if you die in the effort (you won't die) but if you were to die it would not matter because this is only one among countless lives — *one which could not be better spent*. You cannot have spent a life better than this life, dedicated to the furtherance of the Plan for the Externalization of the ashrams of the Hierarchy and the presence of the Christ, Maitreya, in the world. That is so big, so important in planetary terms, that I cannot convey its full import. It is of major life-and-death importance for this planet. The more we work and make it known, the more we help to create the window of opportunity, creating one of the major factors — the readiness of humanity for this event. That is the way we can make use of these windows even though we might not recognize them.

What is the right approach of a disciple to the duties of daily work, so he can fulfil them with a rhythm, as Master DK has stated, and at the same time not be caught in the illusion of time?

To set up a rhythm is not to set up a time frame. There is a difference between a rhythm and time.

In your work as a disciple, you should be able to so structure your work that you set up a rhythm. A rhythm creates movement, and movement creates evolution. Evolution cannot proceed in a static condition. It is cyclic — as is everything. There are moments of total inaction, and these moments might be thousands of years long (in our time). Nevertheless, there is a rhythm in all evolution.

Everyone's rhythm is different, because we are unique. A karmic opportunity is presented to a disciple, and he grasps it and does the work. That gives him a movement forward in his evolutionary cycle. If he does not grasp it, he misses that evolutionary opportunity, the karmic opportunity presented, and is in a more inactive state in terms of evolution. He may be very active on the physical plane, but it is not amounting to anything.

If, on the other hand, he does work and sets up a rhythm, that gives an impetus which can carry him forward life after life after life. The problem is that you can make very fast progress and then sit on the progress and do nothing for a few lives. Then you get bored and want to do something more, so you do it in leaps. There is no rhythm in that. The best movement in evolution is that where you set up a rhythm which is within your capacity but is stretching your capacity. You cannot sit back and say: "Oh, I did enough. The last years I have been working so well and hard, I think I can rest a little now" (which means rest on your laurels). Set up a rhythm which is not too outrageous; do not be a fanatic and set yourself an impossible rhythm.

It depends on your rays. If you have much 6th ray, then you are probably setting yourself a totally impossible pace because you will have no sense of proportion. If you are a 4th-ray type, you probably could not even set up a rhythm at all. "Every day? Oh no, not every day." A rhythm is difficult for some people, and only too easy for others.

If you are a 7th-ray type, you might set up a rhythm that is so mechanical it will never alter. This is how the 7th works, like a metronome. The 7th ray's nature is rhythm; it is through rhythm that the ritual is set up which characterizes the activity of the 7th ray. The 7th ray's role is to relate the spiritual ideal to matter. It is the most material, the most practical, of all the rays. Its problem, or rather its limitation, is that it is so involved in matter and rhythm that the organization of that becomes an end in itself. It can be as mechanical as sitting at an assembly line putting in little parts as they pass you.

The goal is to set up a rhythm which is sensible and reasonable, which extends you but which is not beyond your capacity to sustain. Many people can put in a tremendous amount of time, energy and effort for a short period. You want to set up a rhythm that will take you in a *sustained* way through this life, your next life, and so on, so that every experience, every cycle, is contributing to your evolution, having its own part to play, so that you are not wasting incarnations, which we all do. We waste incarnations because we have not set up a rhythm. Even relatively advanced individuals — in human terms — waste whole lives doing practically nothing of importance from the point of view of their evolution. Many lives are wasted in this way.

The value of a life depends on the rhythm set up by the individual in their *consciousness*. I do not mean setting out a plan, writing down: "Monday I do so-and-so, Tuesday so-and-so." That is fine as long as you do not tie yourself down in that way. It is not so much making a plan as in your consciousness responding to the impulses, the stimuli, given by the Masters and by Maitreya, responding to Them in such a way as you make the most use of them.

The Master discusses the illusion of time, but timing seems to be very important and real. It relates to rhythms and cycles in our activities, setting priorities through awareness and detachment. Also in seizing the moment. Please could you comment on this?

I am absolutely in agreement. Time itself is an illusion, but timing is very important. Timing is sensing the window of opportunity. This is not conditioned by time but by the cyclic movement of life itself. That creates the condition in which a window of opportunity opens for that individual, a karmic opportunity, an opportunity in which his astrological relationships will provide him with a field of energies, a sudden influx of energies, which, if acted upon, will carry him forward — and if not acted upon will be lost.

Shakespeare said: "There comes a tide in the affairs of men which, if taken at the flood, moves on to fortune." Shakespeare was initiate. He knew all about this, and throughout his works are the answers. The aim is to recognize the window of opportunity, to be so skilled and so in the rhythm of your work, that when it opens, you are there. If there is no rhythm, you could be asleep. If you set a rhythm and never sleep — I do not mean never go to sleep in bed — but if you are not mentally asleep, and do not turn off your consciousness, if you keep your consciousness alive and aware all the time, then when the window of opportunity comes you recognize it because you are in that rhythm. If you are not in the rhythm, you could miss it. This is the importance of rhythm, which of course has nothing to do with time. It is to do with awareness, a rhythmic awareness of setting, not goals, but a pattern of action, so you are always ready, "brush in hand".

Has consensus in group work to do with oneness? If it has, could it be a way for us to deal with becoming aware of timelessness?

Yes — if you had group consciousness. Group work is activity towards eventual group consciousness, which is the consciousness that the Masters have. They have no separate consciousness of 'I'. They lost it long ago. When They lost the sense of the separate self They lost the sense of 'I'.

The little baby has no sense of 'I'. The trouble begins, the problems in life, when they have the first sense of 'I'; the 'I' thought is the first thought. Everything is then related to that 'I': "I want, I need..." It is how we go through life, demanding for 'I'. We all do it. This is just what we believe life to be.

The Master does not do this; He knows who He is, which is the Self. He has no sense of any separateness at all. So His consciousness is that of the group. All the Masters are in constant telepathic awareness of each other. They can, of course, block out whatever They do not need to be conscious of. But any Master can tune into, respond to, be aware of, the thought of any Master moment to moment, just as an on-going process. They work as a group with group consciousness.

Group work prepares the disciples of the world for the same kind of group consciousness. It is group consciousness that produces consensus. Consensus is not a majority decision but is arrived at through group awareness, the intuitive, mental awareness of all the people, in time, and as a result of discussion, coming to a mutual conclusion that this is the decision to take. They do not take it by asking: "How many think this? How many think that? The ayes have it." It is a growing awareness of groups who work together, whose minds can relate to each other and despite all the differences arrive at a consensus that such-and-such is the way to act.

It takes a long time but it is a process which leads eventually to group initiation. It is a *sine qua non* that if you do not have group consciousness you will not have group initiation. This is why the constant reading and studying of Rule Eleven, as given in the Alice Bailey books, especially the four requirements of Rule Eleven, are necessary for all people working in the group. They are the essential first steps towards the creation of group consciousness. That is the path to group initiation. The Plan of Hierarchy is for the eventual realization of a group initiatory process in the outer physical world. That is a possibility now for the first time.

THE SENSE OF TIMELESSNESS

Are there ways to implement a sense of timelessness in the world of time?

There are ways, but it is difficult. Time is a very real factor in the lives of most people who are dominated by it, necessarily, in our particular social system. The political, economic, religious, social, and cultural system that we have created and call 20th-century civilization is dominated — harmfully — by time. As soon as, for example, Mr Ford began to make his mystical creation, the motor car, on the assembly line, he fitted millions of people into a notch called time. There is little hope for somebody who has been working on an assembly line for 20 or 30 years ever to get outside the false experience that time exists. He clocks in and out, and every few seconds a part comes to him. This is true if you are making radios, computers, television sets, cars, or whatever is made on the assembly line.

The assembly line process totally conditions its workers to an experience of time — and not even as other people might experience time. If you are a factory worker on an assembly line, you know time as no one else does — especially if you are on piece rates. You know that if you cannot get through a certain number of pieces in a given time you are going to lose money or your job.

The inexorable focus on earning a living is behind this terrible domination by time. For factory workers, it is not just the unbelievable boredom of doing the same action over and over again, which the assembly line creates. It is also the breaking up of your life's experience, your moment-to-moment awareness, into little lozenges related to that object. That creates an inner tension and a negation of life which most of us do not know unless we work in factories on an assembly line basis.

More and more, this kind of total automation is taking place. That means the automization and mechanization of humanity. If the ideal is to replace humanity by true automation using robots, that is a different story. That frees humanity for the gift of leisure, the exploration of our own true creative nature. But unfortunately, when that happens today, it happens in the context of a market forces economy and commercialization. The tendency is always to replace men by machines. But then the men are unemployed. They are no better off; in a certain sense they are worse off than they were before, because no one has education for leisure. And that leisure is pretty well unpaid, or very poorly paid on welfare. If you are made redundant today, you know about it because of the daily changing economic climate.

The shared experience of the group was that when we worked, the waiting stopped.

Precisely. "If you love work, then understand it as a substitute for time." Work and time are two opposites in human consciousness. When you are working with full concentrated attention, with all your faculties focused on it and not with one eye on the clock, you do not go through these pressures of time, this tremendous wear and tear on the nervous system. On the contrary, the concentration, and the inspiration that goes with the concentration, comes from the soul. Where the soul is involved, soul energy is involved. The more soul energy is flowing into its vehicle through all activity, including 'work', the more the parasympathetic and the less the sympathetic nervous system is governing our actions.

The parasympathetic governs the pleasure principle, and work should be part of the pleasure principle. Unfortunately, for probably the majority of people in the world, it is not. If you are working under the pressure of uncongenial work just 'to make a living', if that is your approach, and it is usually behind the approach to work, because much work is a chore, perhaps over-heavy, boring, tedious, mechanical, it will set up a conflict in you. That conflict invokes the activity of the sympathetic nervous system. This results in a dry mouth, fear, a lack of energy and depletion of the forces of the body. That is why people stand still from fright.

An animal does not experience fear, so it does not, usually, stand still; it runs as fast as it can. There are some animals which have a camouflage system and know that if they stay absolutely still the predator will not see them. There are two approaches to danger, therefore, in the animal kingdom. One is to move fast, get away as fast as possible. The other is not to move, not to breathe, not to flicker an eyelid, but just hope. Both are very effective. They have been evolved to safeguard a particular species. If they did not work, they would not be used; they would gradually die out.

The sense of time automatically produces the notion of the ending of things, including the ending of the tiny self, and therefore time equals fear.

Quite so. The sense of time gives one the sense that life has an end, that all of this experiencing that we do every day, the people we know, the work that we do, our hopes, our ambitions, all of that is temporary, it is going to end. We learn that the human race is living longer. We say: "Thank God for that. My father lived till he was 95. It seems to run in the family. Maybe I'll be lucky like that."

But then there is the other point of view: A woman rang me up the other day and said: "It is my birthday this week." I said: "Congratulations." She said: "No, please, don't congratulate me. I am 90 and I never wanted to be 90. I don't want to be 90! I've got a pain here and a pain there," all the aches and pains. I know another woman in her mid-70s who comes from a line of long-livers, who is determined to smoke and drink herself to death before she, too, joins the over-90s club.

Most people think of life as temporary, because they are conscious only of being a physical-plane personality; they have no sense of themselves as the soul. Theoretically, yes, but it does not really affect their lives. It might teach them to live in what they would call an ethical Christian or Jewish or other way, and that would be a good thing, but the sense of being a divine soul in incarnation is, I think, relatively rare, especially in the West.

A child, for example, does not think about life in that sense. The child says: "What is death?" It sees a bird or fish die; its pet rabbit dies or is eaten by a cat. They know that death exists. But for a child, unless they have a close experience of a brother, sister, mother, father or somebody like that, death has no reality. They do not go around fearing death because they have no sense of time. They do not live for tomorrow, next week, or next year. They live for this moment, whatever it is. All of you who are dealing with young children know this to be the case.

It depends on the age of the person. Usually the older a person becomes, the more they are concerned with the temporariness of life. They can feel time running out. This can start at any age, but at whatever age it starts you get the sense that "I can't do things I used to be able to do. I'm not moving so quickly. I'm a bit out of breath more often. I can hardly get off this chair. I can certainly not tie my shoelaces." All these things show people that they are getting older. As you get older, you sense that time is getting on and you probably have a limited amount of time to live, to be in what people call 'life' in this physical body. People equate the physical body and its movement with life, and that causes a lot of anguish and fear, the major anxieties of old people. Many old people get very, very frightened. Mainly they are frightened of death, or at least of dying.

The fear of dying is one of the greatest fears of life. People are afraid of illness, of being ill, afraid of getting old, and afraid of dying, of death. These are the three major fears shared by all humanity. Some people are not afraid of illness; they have never been ill and they are not afraid of getting ill. But there are people who are totally dominated by the fear of being ill. And there are the professionally-ill people who are always ill because that brings the kind of attention that they did not get from their mother. The sad thing is that you can be afraid of dying, afraid of being ill, and afraid of getting old all at once. These three fears dominate the lives of many people.

It is mainly to do with the notion that time exists. If they knew that out of the physical body they will experience a vividness, an intensity of life, which they have never known on the physical plane, they would not have that fear of being dead. If they knew that illness is part of life and in fact corrects karma, is karmically caused and can lead to even better health, a different approach to being ill would take place — if they realized that, as people say, "you're as old as you feel", that at 19 or 90 we can live as vividly and intensely as at any other time of our lives. It will be different — in type, range and style, but life is life, whatever way we live it.

This fear leads to efforts to survive individually. Therefore time equals fear, separation, competition, 'me' with a small 'm'. One of the central problems that we are dealing with in time is the sense of 'me' as being at the centre of the universe. If we do not have the illusion that we are at the centre of the universe, we experience the universe and other people in an entirely different way, our focus is not always on ourselves. The evolutionary process, *per se*, is the process of moving out of that deeply egotistical, selfish view of life.

For those who sense themselves to be at the centre of the universe, everything they hear, feel, everything they experience, has to go through them. There is no sense of objectivity. There is no 'out there'. There is no 'other'. Everything has to pass through themselves in order to be realized at all. That is a major glamour, one of the most profound and deepest-rooted glamours that we can have, and many people have it. It is the cause of all our anxiety, our conflict, our unhappiness, our inability to live life in a full, adequate and harmless way.

What are some practical steps we might take in our lives that would help free us from the snares of time?

This is something I prefer you to explore for yourself. You must become more creative. When you start a job, forget that it has a time factor unless it really has. If, for example, you have one hour before you have to meet a friend or a doctor, or catch a plane, and you are engaged in a piece of work, set an alarm for one hour and forget about time. Just do that one hour. If, on the other hand, there is no time factor involved, and you are engaged in work for Tara Center or the Reappearance, do it with your total concentration for however many hours it takes. If you do not have any fixed time factor, do not put one in artificially. If you have one because of the general condition of our lives, and you are living in the modern world and have to a degree to conform to its demands, you cannot be free of time. But where you can, develop that habit of working outside time, forget time.

When you are in a Transmission Meditation, for example — as happened last night — you do not get up after an hour when you are beginning to feel a bit sore and stiff and say: "I have done my usual hour, that is all right." This is a unique situation: last night the overshadowing by Maitreya continued from 8pm until 3am, but people were leaving all the time, early and late. There were some people who must have stayed for no more than an hour. That is the misuse of time and *opportunity*. Whenever you enter the Transmission room, you should throw away your watch, put it in your pocket. Time should have no bearing on the life of the disciple in his or her discipleship work. Transmission Meditation is discipleship work. Working for *Share International* is discipleship work. Anything which involves the Reappearance of the Christ, the work of Hierarchy, is discipleship work. In these areas, even if only in these areas, you should not work within the limitations of time. You should do what you are doing for however long it takes, glad to be doing it, glad to be able to spend that time in that work and not look on it as a chore, a drudgery. Then you free yourself bit by bit from this total domination by time.

When I was being trained in the beginning by my Master, we worked together non-stop, 20 hours a day, literally, for months and months on end, and less intensely for several years. (I use these personal stories not to show you how good I am, but to show you how a disciple who has undergone conscious training, who has been with a Master, was handled by the Master.)

From five minutes to seven in the morning until 3am the next day, 20 hours plus five minutes a day, every single day, He and I were in constant communication, His voice louder than any thought that went through my head. He literally worked me day and night for 20 hours plus five minutes, then at 3am He would say: "All right, now you can go to bed." So I would go to bed and sleep. At five minutes to seven the next morning He would tap me on the shoulder and say: "Come on, get up. Let us go to the park. Wrap up, it is cold out there." (He is in the Himalayas; it is cold there.) The whole day would be spent going through a hundred different things, always until 3am. That trained me to make do with four hours a night. Four hours, the Master says, is right, is normal. If people sleep for more than about six hours, they are overdoing it, He says. I am not talking about children. Nobody really needs more than about five-and-a-half to six hours sleep a night. For those who have the right frame of mind, and, I suppose, the right frame of body, four hours is adequate.

How can we learn to lose the sense of past and future?
The imperative is to try not to think ahead of time, not to be *dominated* by the idea of the future, and certainly not to waste time in regretting the past. Most people, at least at times in their lives, regret past events, lost opportunities, times when they did not do what they were really about to do and should have done. They realize now it would have changed their lives. But there is no point in regret. It really is past. It also makes no sense to worry about the future; it has not happened yet. You are only here Now. It is the only moment you are here, right Now, at this moment. This very moment is the only moment that exists. The future is not yet, it is only potential. Whatever that potential is you can have a hand in. You can change the future. You can develop thoughtforms which will even destroy thoughtforms which you have already set in motion. You can be conditioned or not, according to your own frame of mind, you can do it or not do it.

The thing I would suggest is to try to live now and forget everything else, forget about worry: "I wonder how the kids are getting on while I am here. I wonder how they are. Maybe I should not have gone away this weekend." All these kinds of worries and anxieties: "What is my husband up to when I am not there? I would like to know. Maybe I should not have come." All of this goes through people's minds and really takes away the present. There is no present if you are living in the future, worrying about the future, or regretting the past. You only have this moment in time, and you are not to know what will happen in one minute's time. Obviously, just living in this modern world makes you conform to time. It really codes you and so you respond to the needs of a time-dominated life. But it need not be quite so. You must give yourself, every day, an area of time in which you relate simply to your Self. Perhaps when you are doing your meditation, or doing Transmission Meditation. Go in, connect with That which is really you, which is outside time, is not concerned about time, does not know what time is. While you are in that relation to your Self, you are not worried about time, not worried about the future or the past. You simply are happy, peaceful, serene, in this moment Now.

In our listening to our higher Self, does it always give the solution when one has a problem of time to solve?
First of all, what do you mean by "listening to your higher self"? And what do you mean by "a problem of time to solve"? I do not know what is meant here by "a problem of time". If time does not exist, there is no problem of time. If you 'listen' to your higher Self in the sense of being aware of the spiritual movement in your consciousness, which is the movement of the higher self, and obey that as it reflects through the heart, it will solve the problems that really matter in life. On an individual basis, I cannot say, but perhaps what you call a problem may not be a problem.

The big problems of life are the problems of knowing who you are. People do not know who they are. They have no awareness of themselves as a soul. You know you have a higher Self, but 'listen' to it? I do not know what you mean by 'listen'. The higher Self is not something that you listen to. The higher Self *is* you. You are either aware of it or you are not aware of it. While you are aware of it, you are in touch with your higher Self. If you meditate, and say the New Age Prayer, you are inculcating an awareness of the higher Self. The more you do it, the more it becomes a reality. What flows from that through the heart is the way to go. The heart always knows how to act.

What happens during sleep time?
It depends on the level of the sleep. In deep sleep there is no awareness of time at all; one is in touch with the soul. If you are a disciple you are probably doing all sorts of soul-oriented work in relation to your own ashram. If you are not yet on the Path, you are resting and recuperating from the traumas of time-ridden daily life.

547

If you are in light sleep, you are dreaming. If you are dreaming, you are still in that misapprehension that you are living in time. Your dreams take no time to work out. You can do 10 years of dream in a few seconds of outer physical time, because dreams are simply thoughtforms in the mind of the person sleeping. That means timelessness can only be experienced in deep sleep. But you do not know you are experiencing it, because you are unconscious. When you are coming out of deep sleep into light sleep, the dreams come one after the other. It is like going to the cinema. Some are very interesting, some are frightening. They are all thoughtforms of the mind conditioned by time.

It seems that much of our inability to experience timelessness might arise from the sense of competitiveness we have between individuals, groups, and nations. Would you discuss the roots of competition and steps we can take to heal it?

This is an interesting question and largely correct, I would say. Competition is not the root of our domination by time, but it is very closely connected with our sense of time, and the growing domination of our lives by market forces and commercialization. Market forces and commercialization are by their very nature competitive. The theory of market forces is based on the idea of supply and demand. If you organize an economy based on supply and demand, the interrelation between demand and supply will regulate the economic flow and make fair trading and fair economic relationship possible. It is based on a myth, because it presupposes that everybody can take out of the supply the amount equal to their needs, which is not the case.

The major nations, in particular the US, take out of the supply hundreds of times more of every possible commodity than they actually need. That is nothing but greed. If you go into any city in the US, into any big or little store, you will find an infinite variety of objects and food, all kinds of things which have been imported or created here and are now sitting on shelves or in warehouses throughout the country. There are many times more sulphates, copper, iron, zinc — all the metals and chemicals which we know go into the manufacturing of all sorts of weapons and the like. There is an arsenal for a potential army many, many times the strength of the present American army, plus the Russians, Germans, and French. There is a colossal overabundance of things in the US. The same is true of Europe to a somewhat lesser extent, and of Japan, Canada, and Australia. All the G7 nations take out of that supply an amount way above their needs. What is that for but greed? Because they produce a lot, they think that they have the prerogative, the right, to use the vast majority, 83 per cent, of all the resources existing in the world. The demand is way above that of the adequacy of the supply, and therefore those who can make little demand, the Third World countries, have to make do with 17 per cent of the supply.

This is the myth of market forces. It is based on greed, not on any intelligent method of distributing the world's resources. On the contrary, it is based simply on survival of the fittest. The fittest are the big, greedy, powerful nations with the wherewithal to buy in the world's market what they think they need, and what they think they might need. They store for the future like squirrels storing for the winter. America has under the mountains great labyrinths of tunnels stored full of every imaginable world commodity from zinc to bicarbonate of soda. This means that the price of all these commodities is kept artificially at a given level. America largely controls that.

America largely controls the economy of the world. Competition is at the very hub of the American approach to life. This is not alone an American phenomenon, but the world is dominated by major thoughtforms. The major thoughtform of competition comes from the US. It is exemplified in the economy, in films, in every aspect of its industry, in its business methods. Everything is done to maximize profits in the most efficient way. The most efficient way is to get rid of the highest overhead which is always the labour force who produce the particular commodity. They are always the first to be axed in any attempt to put a fine competitive edge on a given product.

That is what competition leads to, inevitably: commercialization. Maitreya calls commercialization more dangerous to the world than an atomic bomb. It is killing life at its source, which is human. It is based on competition and greed. Greed and competition are at the basis of the commercial and social life of America, and therefore, through its influence, of a huge section of the world. Even in the Third World, the most popular films are American. This myth of the value of competition and greed is built into every aspect of the American film industry.

What steps may we take to heal it?
The first step is to reject commercialization, reject market forces as an economic theory. It helps a few at the expense of the many. It makes a few very rich indeed and is beginning to make millionaires in what was the Soviet Union. But if it does not work outside Russia, which manifestly it does not when there are millions of people starving to death, then it will certainly not work inside Russia. Already it is causing social disaster there. Eventually there will be internal wars, as has already started, and things will get worse until they get better. Market forces can create, even in the erstwhile Soviet Union, millionaires overnight. That is what they are meant to do. They are meant to present the opportunity of becoming a millionaire to anybody. Anybody with the greed, the initiative, the competitiveness, the energy, to go out there and grab, take and thrust aside others, can do it; that is the American myth. It is in every American film. The American film truly reflects the American psyche and society. I am overstating it, but broadly speaking that is true. If you add to that the European myth, which is largely the same, the Japanese which is identical, and the G7 nations as a whole, you get the problem of the world. And if we do not reject that whole idea of competition and greed as having any part to play in creating right human relations, we will destroy ourselves, we will never make it.

What new socio-economic climate can we develop that will allow us to experience time differently?
The number one priority is to replace this deeply divisive and cruel economic system with something better. Maitreya has spelled it out many times: the *principle of sharing* is the only one

that will save humanity from self-destruction. The more humanity is conditioned by time, the more it is destroying its own nature, because the creative acts of the soul are coming from a level where time does not exist. If you are totally conditioned by time, you are living in a framework in which your very nature is warped. No matter how 'educated' we are, unless we can change the social structures of our life, we cannot change our awareness of life. An awareness of timelessness is an awareness of what life truly is.

Life has nothing to do with time, but only with cycles of activity followed by cycles of inactivity. It is to do with the great outbreathing and inbreathing of cosmos itself. Cosmos breathes out and the worlds are formed, and all activity within the worlds go forward. When a certain point is reached, cosmos inbreathes again and draws all that back into itself. Then a great outbreathing occurs again and the whole process goes on endlessly, infinitely, for ever and ever. That is the nature of life. It is the nature of cosmic life and it should be the nature of our life. It *is* the nature of our life, but while we are dominated by time, it cannot be demonstrated — hence, the pain, the suffering, unhappiness, the terrible misdeeds of humanity against itself. That violence is born out of a sense of deep grief, frustation and abuse from the earliest times.

Everyone, instinctively, is aware of themselves as a soul. Every child knows itself as a soul. It does not know the name for it, but it knows the feeling, the inner awareness of it. And yet as it grows, it becomes more and more alienated from society. Its soul awareness cannot find expression in today's society, so it turns against itself as a part of society. Crime, violence, and alienation are all the result of this discrepancy between the expectations of the soul, the awareness and expectations of the inner spiritual being, and that which is supplied to it on the outer field by the societies of today. The more powerful societies, like the United States of America, Europe, Canada, Australia and Japan — the G7 economic group — are profoundly at fault here in promoting that state of affairs. They seek to dominate the whole of the world's economy for selfish greed and power. Market forces and competition, on which all of this rests, are nothing more than the expression of greed, and cannot be allowed to dominate in the future.

What can we do to change this? Create conditions in which there is harmony. Harmony is the number one necessity in losing the sense of time. Whether in an individual or a nation, we cannot have an awareness and response to the nature of true time if we are in an inharmonious state. Practically everybody today is in an inharmonious state, because there is total disequilibrium in the world. That is our spiritual crisis. We have to change the world's economic structure — not only because it seems more just to do so since it is profoundly evil and unjust; we have to change it or we will destroy the world. It is as simple as that. We must change it so that humanity can begin to live as we (as souls) intend to live — in a society based on harmony and therefore equilibrium. With that equilibrium comes greater and greater awareness of who and what we really are. That is our crisis, our problem for today — to know who we are.

The Master's article on the concept of time states that the stock-exchange crash will begin to release humanity from the time trap . . .

He did not actually say that specifically about the stock exchange. He talked about the transformation of the world, the sharing of the resources, above all the sense of the one humanity. That is what will free humanity from "the time trap". The sense that we are one, brothers and sisters of one humanity, is the fundamental first step towards losing the sense of time. When you realize that there is no separation, that we are all God's children, you realize that we are all together in a process.

The consciousness of the soul reality removes the sense of time. When you can act and work as a soul 100 per cent of the time, you are a Master. But 90 per cent, 80 per cent, whatever per cent of the time you can so work, you grasp the reality of life. It is that realization which frees you from time. This is the revelation for humanity: being able to act as souls removes the sense of time; realizing that what you are doing is coming from the soul level, and your total attention is focused in that. Whatever you give your attention to, you give your energy to.

Energy follows thought. You have to do your work with the total attention which brings in the faculties of the soul.

We are all at different levels in terms of evolution. All have a different degree of contact with the soul. But whatever the degree, if it is given full scope it produces creativity on the physical plane, even if that person is not what you would call highly evolved.

It does not depend on high evolution to be a soul; everyone *is* a soul. When soul awareness is functioning, when the contact with the soul is reasonably intense, creativity flows from that, and you necessarily have lost the consciousness of time. You cannot be creative and conscious of time at the same time. That is why we have the ability in one hour of intense creativity to do something that makes people say: "Staggering! It's a masterpiece!" — a work of art or music, or a revelation of some scientific formula like $E=mc^2$. How long did that take? The mathematics probably took years. The concept probably took an instantaneous moment, because it is a revelation. That is how the soul works, by inspiration and revelation.

The prevailing concept of time in our civilization is the linear one, which brings about fear — fear of eternal damnation if we do not make good in this life. Emotions like fear keep us caught in time, causing inertia. The way we perceive time differs from culture to culture. As the focus of commercialization becomes stronger within society, we become more bound up in time because "time is money".

Quite right. I am certain that the world today is more dominated by the concept of time than ever before in its history. Humanity has always been caught up in this thraldom, but especially now. This is not, I think, just a question of market forces and commercialization, but also, I believe, the effect of the action of the 5th ray of lower mind, or concrete knowledge, or science.

The last 100 years or so has been a period in which the 5th ray has been given a special, short but very intense cycle, out of its normal "incarnation". It was brought in to stimulate the minds of the 5th sub-race of the 5th root race, that is the European and American nations, to bring our useful, practical technology into the world. We would not have our modern communications, on which the ability of the people to see Maitreya on television depends, if that cycle had not been brought in. It has tremendously stimulated the mental processes of, especially, the 5th-ray mental, and also of the 5th sub-race, as a whole, and brought about our modern technology.

That very technology has probably been one of the greatest factors in this domination of humanity by time. It has made possible the material revolution which is behind commercialization. Commercialization would not be possible without the material revolution.

Our technologies now produce goods at a speed and of a quality which allows the Western nations and Japan to dominate the world. They have created the technology, and they dominate the world through the economic success which follows the technology. The economy of today is regulated by computer. Perhaps 70-80 per cent of the world's goods depend on our technology to create them. That has speeded up the whole process, as well as our sense of time, and created the tensions and pressures under which we live today.

The 5th ray is the ray of concrete knowledge. Its area of activity is the material plane. The concrete world is a relative aspect. It is not the be-all and end-all of life. Unfortunately, through the intense influence of this special 5th-ray stimulus, our science today has created a thoughtform, a pattern of life, an educational system, in which the material plane is seen as the only plane that exists. Every question that arises in our life, it is said, can be answered by science. Every question that arises *can* be answered by science — by the esoteric science, the science of the soul, but not by our technological science.

There is not just one science called technology, there is the science of the soul. The soul is a great scientist. The knowledge of the soul can far outdistance the science of the technological wizardry of the exponents of the 5th ray. This has given humanity a very limited view of life. It has shone a very clear light on one aspect. But it is only one aspect. It is a question of not seeing the wood for the trees. You can see the trees very clearly. But there is a huge forest 'round there that you cannot see with this 5th-ray view of life. Science has opened up, and given great revelations about, the nature of the reality in which we live. But it has also, especially the technological aspect of it, limited humanity to a very material expectation of life.

Time and matter go together. The creation of material objects takes time. They take time to distribute, use, wear, wear out and replace. We produce so much so that nothing need have a very long life. If your mother or grandmother bought an object 70 years ago, you could still use it today. Many homes have an object — a knife or a spoon, for example — which was made 70-80 years ago and is still in perfect working order. An object made today has built-in obsolescence. We could make refrigerators or washing machines that would outlast most people, and yet they do not. They last for five years at the very most and have to be replaced.

This is part of the interrelationship between time, profits and money — the creation of profitable objects which will sell quickly and produce the maximum return for the manufacturers. It is a very short-term view of life but it is the dominating one. That is very much to do with our misinterpretation of the experience we call time. The emphasis on it is a 5th-ray creation. If you go back a couple of centuries, if you could relive them, you would find that people had brutish lives, as people have brutish lives today, but time was not the dominating factor.

How do you see the relation to work — in factories for instance — and the globalization of manufacture?
There are two laws here — the mechanical law and the human law. They should not be interacting. There is a place for mechanics; we call it a robot. Robots could now be doing most of the things that human beings do to produce other mechanical objects, like motor cars, television sets and computers. Human beings should not become, and should not have been allowed to become, mechanical.

Mechanical law is also law. A machine is, in the end, a living thing. You can talk to your motor car and get better results out of it than if you curse it for letting you down. Many people have found that if you believe in your car, or whatever your mechanism, and you are decent to it, look after it, and nourish it with the correct nourishment — oil, petrol and water — it will function well through its own mechanical laws. If it is well made, and you treat it correctly, it will begin to respond to that type of treatment because, as Maitreya says, the atoms of all substance are connected.

This is why, Maitreya says, if there is some criminal act on the part of a government — like the shooting down by a US warship of an Iranian aircraft with 300 people on board — it causes a reaction, in this case several American air crashes. It is the Law of Karma, working out through the interconnectedness of the atoms of the plane shot down and the atomic structure of all planes. It related to America because of the karmic connection; they caused the incident.

It is the interconnectedness of atomic matter that makes a series of apparently random air crashes not random at all. These seemingly natural mechanical failures have their origin in destructive actions by humanity.

Likewise with the weather. We alter the weather patterns by our destructive thoughtforms, so that the devas who work with the laws governing our weather go into disequilibrium. Until we come into equilibrium again, they will remain disordered, and so will the weather.

Humanity will rid itself of a mechanical attitude to life by the realization that we are one, that we are all the same. It is not the case that some people should do office work, and millions should be working in the fields and mines and factories, producing the materials for the people who are running the banks and the stock exchanges. We divide humanity. We mechanize some groups who have to work in factories and become robots, doing the same thing all day long. There are degrees of it, but I am putting it at its most mechanical.

There are millions of women making computers and putting together television sets who repeat the same actions over and over again, day in and day out, throughout the Third World. How did Taiwan and Korea become 'first world' countries? Because the cheap labour of people in the factories was used by the global manufacturers, but the riches and benefits accrue in

New York, London or Paris; the actual work is done for a pittance in Korea or Taiwan. That is global commercialization. That kind of exploitation of millions of people has to stop. The first thing that will stop it is when we realize we are one, and therefore the food, raw materials, energy, and science must be redistributed and not held in the hands of the G7 nations of the world.

It comes back again and again to the central point: the spiritual crisis is that we do not relate to each other in the correct way. We do not know who we are, and we do not know how we should live in relation to each other. Therefore we have produced, and complacently accept, the existence of these deeply divisive ways of living and exploiting of millions of people. When that stops, a new notion of time will come to humanity, because the true, creative aspect of work will come to the fore.

People who have been forced into mechanical thinking and action will probably go on that way for a long time. They will, perhaps, no longer be exploited, but the habits of mind will take a long time to dissipate.

Those who have been deeply, painfully exploited for centuries will want to get their own back. They will want revenge. The peons will want to take the señor and string him up on the nearest tree, because he has kept their families in penury for centuries. It will take all that Maitreya has of skill in action to keep that to the very minimum, to teach forgiveness. People will have to forgive. The Master spells it out in many of His articles. There will be a time for the forgiving of old sins, the forgetting of ancient wrongs. This must take place — otherwise it will be worse than it is now. Maitreya and the Masters have the responsibility to curb this desire for revenge, to fill people with the Christ Principle as a corrective to this, quickly to implement the principle of sharing. Speed will be very important. The principle of sharing must be implemented as the number one priority so that people do not have time and thought for this kind of revenge. They will say: "Let it go. Now we have what we need." It is very important to realize this. Otherwise, people will say: "I thought Maitreya was going to bring peace. Look at it.

The world is worse than it has ever been." This would be the reaction of many people who perhaps do not think too deeply.

THE ILLUSION OF TIME

Is distance an illusion as time is?

Yes. Distance is as non-existent as time. Time and distance are experiences only of the mind. We are all sitting on the point of a pin; the 5.5 billion people in incarnation and the 55 billion out of incarnation are all sitting on the top of this same little pin-point. That is distance. We call it planet Earth, which is the size of a pin so fine you could not see it under a microscope. That is the reality. The whole of cosmos exists on that little point; all the people, all the planets, the whole of the universe, sits on that little pinhead. That is the reality of distance. It does not exist.

If you are a Master, with no confinement to what we call distance, you can go anywhere in the universe. When you have the awareness that comes from close identification with the Self, an awareness of the nature of the Self, you can *think* yourself to any country.

Distance is an idea in the brain brought about by conditioning. A young child has no sense of distance. He does not know he is living in a block of flats in a town which is in a country, which is at one side or the other of an ocean, which is in a planet in a solar system. He has no sense of that. But in his consciousness he can go anywhere he likes. In the Self there is no distance. The Self is behind, beyond, all distance. Distance, like time, is simply an experience of the physical brain, something to which we have become conditioned. Of course, it takes time to go from San Francisco to London or to Tokyo, but that is to do with the solid physical plane and not with time or distance. For a Master, it takes no time at all.

Perhaps Self-realization starts off as a momentary experience, and as one evolves, that experience deepens.

It not only deepens, but it prolongs itself as a moment-to-moment experience. As it deepens, it becomes more solid in our consciousness, so we do not turn our attention away from it so often. It is the natural, given state. Every baby has it, at whatever point in evolution it is. If you could speak to your baby, the baby would tell you about the nature of the Self. When you see it gurgling, it is saying: "Oh, what a happy, blissful thing it is to be a baby. But I wish I were a mummy, big like my mummy, big like my daddy." The baby has all the potential, and it feels all that potential, but it cannot do anything. It can hardly turn itself over, perhaps. It is restricted, a frustration for a baby. When a baby is crying, it is not necessarily because its nappy is wet, or because it is hungry, but because it is saying: "Where are my brushes? I want to get on with my painting. If only I had a canvas and colours, I would show them!"

The baby is aware in a way that we can be aware. We can become aware as a Master is aware, moment-to-moment. There is no sense in Them that is not the Self. That is what He is, and that is what the baby is. But when the sense of the ego comes in, and we see ourselves as being at the centre of the world, then the problem begins — because we can only see the little self, with a small 's', and not the Self with a big 'S'. That is the problem; that is where evolution has to come in.

Surely time does exist on the physical plane and we are just trying to come to terms with that psychologically, so that we learn to live with our consciousness on a higher level more constantly, where time does not exist.

Yes, but it is only relative. The relative is not the whole. Do you want the whole? Do you want to know what existence is, what reality is? Or are you content with just a relative notion of it? Time on the physical plane, distance between objects on the physical plane, are relative notions. In reality they are no more real than the figures on a cinema screen. They are shadows, reflections, of a reality.

Our notion of time itself is wrong. It is not just relative; it is wrong. It does not exist as we think it exists. We know a train is taking off at 6.15 to take you to Amsterdam. So you have to be there at 6.15 as it says on your watch. What you are really doing is agreeing with the person who sets the train-time that you will be there when the train is taking off. It is nothing to do with time itself. The 6.15 is only an arrangement to communicate to you the fact that the train is taking off at that moment in the Now. That is not a moment in time but in the Now. We call that moment "6.15 on a Friday afternoon." But it is not real. It simply allows you to be there at that same moment in the Now. Tomorrow is simply an extension of today. But because it gets dark and then light, we cut it up and call it tomorrow and the next day. But it is all Now.

Time as we understand it is simply a way of allowing us to conduct our life in a way in which we can relate to other people. We can be where a train is taking off in the Now, at a moment we call 6.15, so that we can get on it. If you were not there you could not get on it, 6.15 or not. Call it 20.15 or 9.15; it makes no difference. You can call it any number you like. It just means that at that number, an agreed number, that train will leave for Amsterdam.

If time does not exist, why does the Master always use such words as "soon", "forthwith", "in the near future", and so on, in His articles, in this way enhancing the very notion of time?
On the contrary. The Masters have no sense of time at all. They do not see time except as cyclic activity, followed by non-activity, infinitely repeated. They do not see time as we understand time in our brain, as a process of events following one another in sequence. They have simultaneous awareness of all events as Now. Right now the Day of Declaration is happening. For the Masters, it is happening. The stock-exchange crash is happening. But if the Master is talking to us, people reading these articles, He cannot say: "The stock-exchange crash is happening." They would say: "No, it isn't. The Dow Jones index is as high as it has ever been. What are you talking about?"

When the Master says "soon", "forthwith", or "the near future", He is not trying to confuse you, or build in an idea of time which He knows does not exist. In these articles He is sustaining your motivation, enthusiasm, and commitment to the cause of Maitreya; adding to your awareness of what is actually happening in the world. If He did not say it every month, you would forget about it. You would drift off into sailing up and down the Zuider Zee. You would do all sorts of things that would have nothing to do with the Reappearance. I asked the Master what He meant by "soon". He said: "Up to about 10 years." And forthwith? He said: "Anything up to about a year is forthwith." So forthwith is a shortish soon. Very, very soon.

These expressions are only to give you an indication that the time is becoming very short, that what the Masters already know is happening will precipitate. *It is already there.* They are looking at it; They see it not by looking into a crystal ball, but by Their everyday consciousness. They see it in the way that Maitreya showed it to me. You do not even have to turn your head — there is what we call past and there is what we call future. But it is all actually happening now, because the Now is the only thing that does exist. There is no past, no future. There is precipitation of events, and They already see the events. We do not see the precipitation yet. The Master is not really strengthening our sense of time. On the contrary, He is holding us together. He is holding your enthusiasm, conviction and happiness together.

Can we educate children so that they realize the dual concept of time?

Children today are being taught the reality of the dual concept of time probably more than are their parents. It is becoming part and parcel of our modern science. Scientists today are becoming more aware of this reality — that time is not what they thought it was. Their exploration of the atom, the stars, is making them realize that what they thought was distance probably does not exist; that what they thought was time has to be dual. This is the first step into an awareness of the true non-existence of time as a linear succession of events, which is simply a state of mind.

In your vision of the future, you saw future events as if they had already occurred ...

No. I saw future events as if they were occurring. I saw past events as if they were occurring. They were all simultaneously taking place. In the Now, the everlasting, all embracing Now, there is only activity. It is not as if the past is past and finished with. The past is still happening, the future is already happening.

. . . Does this mean these events are predestined? Do we have free will to change these future events?

There are events which are predestined, what in Agni Yoga are called the "predestined dates". If there is no time, there are no dates. But they are signposts. They are dates in the sense of an event which, inevitably, will take place. Why are they predestined? How can we say that these are predestined? Because it is the Will of the Logos, and, therefore, the Plan of Hierarchy, that these events take place. These are the only totally predestined events. Let us not call them dates, but events. I am not going to quarrel with Agni Yoga and its terminology, but it means events.

If the Logos' plan involves the externalization of the Hierarchy, which indeed it does, that is a predestined event. The only question, over more than 500 years, was when. When would that event precipitate? When would the predestined time, date, or event take place in relation to humanity's state of readiness? It was thought for approximately the last 500 years that it would be 1,200 or 1,300 years in the future before the externalization of the Hierarchy could take place. And yet it is taking place now; it began in 1975. And this, because of another event which made it possible. Even the predestined requires the conditions to allow it to precipitate. That event was the defeat of the Axis powers in the war from 1939 to 1945. This cleared the way for the Reappearance of the Christ Principle, the building principle, and therefore of Maitreya, the Christ. It took Him nine years to come to His decision — from a knowledge of the cosmic dates, the cosmic events, the predestined dates, as Agni Yoga would say.

From His knowledge of the predestined Plan, He knew that sooner or later He would be able to come into the world, and that the Hierarchy would be able to return to the world openly. Those nine years (between 1936 and 1945) were, I suppose, years of profound meditation on all the possibilities, all the varied data He had to take into account. No doubt He asked advice from Beings higher even than He is. Eventually, at the end of the war, He came to His decision and announced it in June 1945. That was a predestined event.

Do you accept the fact that from the human point of view we have free will but from the divine point of view we don't have free will? (January/February 1996)

Even from the divine point of view we have limited free will. Free will is really due to the Law of Cause and Effect, which governs all life on the planet. Every thought and action which we have sets in motion a series of causes. The effects stemming from these causes make our lives, for good or for ill.

Everything that happens to us is the result of our response to outer stimuli. We cannot change the stimuli but we can change our reaction to the stimuli. So the nature of our responses governs the nature of our lives — we are really in charge. In the wider, broader, cosmic sense there is a kind of predestination because there is a Plan. That Plan is not made by narrow mathematicians, but by super-mathematicians, Who allow little gaps in the Plan. These gaps can be filled in by humanity, because it is not a dead, rigid Plan but a creative Plan. We are part of that Plan, so our creative input is also part of the Plan. In that sense we have free will.

As soon as we become Initiate we enter into the mind of the Logos to some degree, and as we progress in the initiatory process so we enter deeper and deeper into the mind of the Logos, and therefore into His Plan of evolution. When we know and understand, we are in control. Consciousness gives us, eventually, control of the events of our lives, and then we really have free will. Until then it is a potential free will but real nevertheless.

In the view of how the Masters see time, do They see the future events as fixed and deterministic or only as multiple, probable events which they can change depending on Their actions in the present?

The Masters see these future events as determined but not fixed. There is a difference. They are predestined if they are Hierarchical. If they are planetary, from the Logos, they are definitely predestined, and will inevitably work out. If they are the actions of humanity then they are determined by those actions but not fixed. They can be changed.

The question asked: "Can the Masters change these depending on Their actions in the present?" It depends not so much on the Masters as on humanity itself. Without infringing our free will the Masters do many things to mitigate the effects of our wrong actions, but not the actions themselves. By inspiring Their disciples in service, they can 'burn up' a lot of the karma which is created by these wrong actions. But in the long run those events will precipitate which our free will determines will precipitate. That is true individually and even more true of humanity as a whole.

The voice of humanity as a whole is very powerful indeed. You would be surprised what a powerful impact comes from the manifestation of our free will on the events of the world. We do tremendous harm through the misuse of our free will. Likewise, we can do tremendous good through its correct use. It is largely in humanity's hands; we have enormous power. Used wisely — and in this way you can see how quickly the world can change under the correct leadership and guidance of Maitreya — we can, if we will, transform the world. In two to three years we can transform the whole world in terms of the economic structure simply by humanity making known to the governments of the world that that is how we want it, what must be. Maitreya showing what must be done. We agree with this. We wish it to be done. The will of the people will prevail in this effort, and in two to three years from the acceptance of Maitreya on a wide scale, the transformations of the initial economic evils will have taken place.

Can the Masters move Their point of presence into the past pictures, thereby effectively moving into the past and changing it?

No, They do not change the past. The Masters simply observe the world. The Self only observes. If you have Self-realization and therefore Self-consciousness, you simply observe. You do not make those changes. You look at life, you see it happening, and you observe it. If you are a Master and you are working with a plan, you bring your part of the plan to bear on the current events. But if these events are in what we would call the past, as far as humanity is concerned, they have already taken place. You are not the same personality as you were in a previous incarnation. In a previous incarnation you were, perhaps, a man, for instance, with a different ray structure. Now perhaps you are a woman. There has been a time lapse in the physical sense, but no time lapse in the eternal sense.

Time is dual, it is relative. It is relatively true that time has passed since the battle of Hastings and the battle of Waterloo. They happened in the past. But if you look at it from the Masters' point of view they are still taking place. They are events which are literally happening because there is no time in which they are settled. It is only in the historical, looking-back sense of relative time that they are over. From the higher plane the physical is only relative, so anything that takes place on it is relative. It does not mean to say that it is not real. This physical body is real, but only relatively so. From the point of view of the soul it is a kind of shadow. It is a vehicle. It is like a shadow thrown upon a screen. You see a shadow of a woman or a man or a motor car on a cinema screen. They are not real, they are just shadows. The physical plane is like that to the Self. It has no substantial reality. It is a reflection of a reflection of a reflection. The Masters do not try to change the past. They are concerned with the events yet to coalesce and precipitate. That concerns Them and They make Their plans accordingly. They see that humanity's free will is driving us inexorably to the edge of a precipice, so They take steps to try to prevent that from precipitation.

According to our group, if time is an illusion, then by necessity it would follow that evolution is an illusion. Could you please comment?

No, it is a false logic. Evolution is not an illusion. Time is the illusion. Evolution does not proceed in time, because time does not exist. But evolution does proceed. The consciousness of the child and the consciousness of the adult are entirely different. The consciousness of a first-degree initiate at such-and-such a time in history, and the consciousness of that same soul in incarnation taking the fifth initiation, is entirely different. There has been evolution.

Evolution necessarily takes place, because it is part of the great outbreathing of the Creator, which creates all that exists. It is the Becoming of the Creator. Under the Law of Cause and Effect, and in relation to the Law of Rebirth, evolution proceeds, not in relation to time as we imagine time but in relation to time in the sense of cyclic unfoldment — cyclic activity followed by cyclic inactivity, followed by cyclic activity; this repeated infinitely, for ever and ever.

The heavens, the solar systems, are bodies or vehicles for the expression of great Consciousnesses. It is these great Consciousnesses which exist. The bodies are more or less temporary manifestations in time and space which allow Consciousness to be creative. It is the creation and the Creator behind the creation which are important, not the distance between one solar system and another. There is no distance between one solar system and another in the consciousness of the One Who made the solar system. If time does not exist, distance does not exist.

The only thing that does exist is Consciousness. That is the secret. It is Consciousness which creates. It is the creation which gives rise to the bodies, the apparatuses, through which that Consciousness can express its awareness. The whole of cosmos can sit on the top of a pin, because there is no distance.

If you look into the atom you see a nucleus surrounded by electrons. You have a little solar system in every atom — the nucleus, and the satellites going round it. This is exactly like the sun with its planets going in the same way. That is the creative nucleus of the whole of creation; that is everywhere. The actual atoms are varied because of the nature of their expression; the atom which makes a rock is different from that which makes part of your nervous system or a solar system. But it is fundamentally the same method by which creation takes place. The whole of what there is is inside one atom. That is what Maitreya means when He says that everything is related. All atoms are related to every other atom. It could not be otherwise, because fundamentally there is only one atom, and that is you.

567

In the whole of creation there exists one Being, the Self. You are that Self. Everyone is the Self. That is all there is. That is true for the solar system, for every individual, for every part of the animal kingdom, the devic evolutions, and so on. That is all that exists. It is a state of consciousness. That is God, the Self, cosmos, every solar system that you could imagine, every universe. All of that is part of your consciousness, your awareness; you are not separate from that consciousness. The only way the solar system is real for you is because you have consciousness. Your awareness is what makes it real. If you do not have the awareness, it is not real. This is not something you work out; it is a revelation.

Our sun is 93 million miles from the earth, and the moon is 240,000 miles from earth. These are measurable distances, but they are unreal; they do not mean anything. God is. That is all that there is. That means that there is no such thing as time. There is no such thing as distance. There is no such thing, fundamentally, as a solar system. I do not mean it is an illusion. Time is the illusion. The solar system is not an illusion, it is a reflection.

When you see the world, the solar system, from the point of view of the Self, it is like cinema. It is a shadow on a screen. It is not real, in the sense that we imagine this to be solid and physical and real. At our lowest physical-plane consciousness, it is solid and physical and real. But from the point of view even of the soul, let alone of that of which the soul is a reflection, it is not real. Nothing is real. All of this apparatus of living is like when you are watching a film. You see there is an office, people writing in the office, and they are quarrelling. They go out, cross the street, get in the car, and there is a car chase. None of that is real; only shadows on a screen. But it looks real, it feels real.

What, then, is evolution?

Evolution is the movement by which life knows and expands itself, becomes aware of itself, and creates further, more involved and creative aspects of itself. Evolution is part of that cosmic process by which everything which we call life finds expression in matter. There is tension between the creative process in matter and that which stands behind, which is not matter. That tension sets in motion the creative process and gives opportunity for what we call God, the Creator, to expand and be creative.

That is what we are doing. We are not different from that. We are God. Quite literally, we are God. There is not anything else to be but God. Everything you see, feel, and experience is an experience, real, relatively speaking, or unreal, relatively speaking, of what we call God, the Creator, the "Lord", as Maitreya calls it. The Self gives the Lord the opportunity to create differentiated fragments which are imbued with every aspect of itself.

The Masters say we can realize the Self in a moment. But we are also taught to see it as an evolutionary process in time. How do we solve this paradox?

The evolutionary process is not a process in time. It is a cyclic process outside of, and nothing to do with, time. It is the cyclic process of life itself, the outbreathing and an inbreathing of cosmos itself. That is not the same as time. Cyclic time is not linear time.

"How do we solve this paradox?" It is not a paradox. It is true that you can realize the Self in a moment, if at the moment before that you were at the point just before Self-realization. In other words, if you are a 4.9 degree initiate, you are almost ready for the fifth initiation. But how do you get to be a 4.9 degree initiate? By being a 4.8, 4.7, 4.6. and so on down the degrees. Or some great gift, some unbelievable grace, has to be given to you so that your consciousness is absolutely and totally altered. It is said that a Master can do that. I do not think it ever occurs. I do not believe that you can be a first-degree initiate one day and the next day a Self-realized Master. My Master says that He has never known such a case. Theoretically it is possible, but it is theory, not life.

It is true that we are the Self. But we do not feel it because we do not have Self-awareness. If we really had full Self-awareness, we would then be well on the way to Self-realization. But we do not, or we have it so intermittently that we cannot say we have it as a moment-to-moment experience. If it is for us a moment-to-moment experience, then we are on the verge of Self-realization.

What, really, is evolution for?

If you have a television or radio, you need an aerial. It has to have an antenna to catch the signal. If you do not have it, all you get are lines on the screen. As soon as you put the antenna up and it is tuned to the station, suddenly you get all the pictures and it makes sense. We are like an aerial, an instrument. We are either finely tuned, not very finely tuned, or hardly tuned at all. We are an instrument by which we experience life, become aware of life. As we tune our instrument, we tune in to more and higher aspects of that life.

Evolution is the process by which we tune the instrument of perception. Our consciousness is relative to the sensitivity of the instrument of perception. The more finely tuned, the more aware the instrument, the greater and deeper will be our perception of reality. It depends absolutely on the instrument of perception.

What exists for us, too, is relative to the quality of our instrument. We are an instrument by which we, as a Being, as a soul in incarnation, can tune into the reality which the soul already knows. We think of it as the brain. It is not the brain. The brain is simply the computer which puts together all the different experiences. All our senses, our bodies, are themselves instruments of receptivity on the physical, etheric physical, astral, mental, and if we are lucky, the spiritual planes. All of these become open to the instrument if it is tuned to relate to them.

In the April 1990 issue of **Share International***, you say: "It is precisely through an expansion of conscious awareness that evolution proceeds. It is the difference in conscious awareness that denotes the difference in radiation and therefore the ability to serve the plan of evolution between a rock, a rose, a man, a Master, a Solar Logos, on into infinity." What does one's radiation have to do with the ability to serve the plan of evolution?* (March 1993)

I should have thought it was rather obvious. It is precisely to the extent of one's radiatory capacity that one can affect and influence events. Radiation (and greater radiation) is the aim of evolution in all the kingdoms, from the radio activity of the mineral to the resplendent aura of a Master, the energetic nucleus of an ashram involving perhaps thousands of disciples. The greater the radiation, therefore, the greater the impact of that life expression in each kingdom and the greater the capacity to serve.

Is evolution something to be pressed forward as quickly as possible, or is it a more placid, everything-in-its-own-time sort of thing? (July 1994)

It depends what level of the planet's evolution one means: the lower, the slower; the higher the faster. In a broad, general, sense it is true to say that evolution proceeds slowly, everything-in-its-own-time. This is true for the material structure of the planet and the mineral kingdom. The vegetable kingdom is responsive to higher and more penetrating energetic stimulus and evolves relatively faster as a result. This is also true of the animal kingdom. The Sons of Mind, the human kingdom, evolve faster still in response to yet higher stimulus and differentiated energies, while the members of the Spiritual Kingdom, the initiates and disciples of the world, can (and are encouraged to do so) speed up their own evolution by service and conscious personal action. It is precisely to speed up the human evolution that initiation was instituted on this planet in early Atlantean times. The faster a disciple evolves, of course, the more and better service he or she can put at the disposal of the evolutionary Plan.

Is it not better to lead the spiritual life in a monastery? (May 1994)

For centuries, monks and nuns have separated themselves from life in monasteries and nunneries. They feel they will be closer to God, that it will be easier to know God without the distractions of 'life'. But they cut off an entire area of life from their experience. They find that the very same problems occur in their little enclosure. People are people whether they are in costumes or not. If everyone dressed the same, the problems would not change. They are the problems of human psychology, human consciousness, human ignorance. This ignorance, lack of knowledge, lack of direct experience of life, is what, for the most part, confuses people. Therefore, they think they have to go into a monastery or nunnery, that life is easier there. In some ways it is easier, in that your life is given a framework which provides a training and discipline. It prepares them to be disciples.

But the real disciple has to do it all for himself. He has, of his own volition, to create the path of return, to build the antahkarana, to make the path step by step. He can do it the religious way or he can do it in the more occult way. He can do it as, for example, Mother Teresa does it — partly religious but mainly through active service in the world.

How can we measure someone's spirituality? (October 1994)

By the altruism or otherwise of their actions. The Masters can calculate the exact point gained in evolution by the degree of light radiation from the chakras. With experience, a disciple can measure, likewise, those less evolved than themselves.

Above the physical plane, do we experience all our incarnations simultaneously? (January/February 1997)

It depends what you mean by "we". As a physical-plane personality, unless you have the total consciousness of yourself as the soul, you do not experience them at all. You experience this one, and only a fragment at a time of this one. Right now is a fragment of what we call time. As I am talking now, it is obvious that this is a moment in time. It is not the whole of time. It is a part of that everlasting Now which has neither beginning nor end. We have just taken a fragment. As soon as you become conscious of yourself talking, listening, whatever it is you are doing, you are aware of yourself for that moment in a fragment of the everlasting Now.

If you have the awareness of the soul, then indeed you experience every incarnation simultaneously. Your soul is experiencing everything that it has known. It does this through the body of the soul, the causal body, which is formed when we first come into incarnation. The causal body is, at first, a very ordinary grey, dull thing. But, through the incarnational experience of the soul, everything that happens in each incarnation is fed back into the causal body — which grows and changes, and becomes a very beautiful, brilliant, glowing object in its own right, sparkling with colour and unbelievably rich because of all the varied incarnations which the soul has had up to this point in time.

The soul is not only planning its next incarnational experience now, it is actually going through it. As far as the soul is concerned, your next incarnation is already taking place because there is only the one time, the one Now, in which all takes place: the past, as we call it, the present as we know it, and the future as we await it. All of that is known simultaneously by the soul. In relation to all that it has experienced and which is available to it, moment to moment in the causal body, it plans and prepares a body, the ray-structure, and so on, of the next incarnational experience in time and space. So indeed the answer is yes, we do experience all our incarnations simultaneously if we are talking about ourselves as the soul. If we talk about ourselves as the personality, it is obviously not the case.

If everything already exists, and is realized in the eternal now, what is the significance of life, the Plan, and the whole of creation?

Indeed. That is what you have to find out. That is why you are here as a tiny fragment of the Creator. You are really asking the questions: "What does God mean? What is His plan? Why did He set in motion this whole creation? What is behind it all? Who made God, and who gave Him the idea in the first place?" These are impossible questions, and you expect me to answer them? A Master could not answer these questions.

If past and future are one, all incarnations of a person live at the same time. But how can we make decisions if the future is already happening? Can I influence my past lives in this life?

You cannot influence your past life in this life, but you can influence your next life in this life. You are making your next life now. Every action, every movement of thought, is creating this life and also your next life. This is karma. Karma is this cyclic movement which creates the conditions of the outer events in our lives. We cannot do anything about the events; they happen. All we can do is control how we respond to these events. We respond to them by identification, or we do not identify. If we do not identify with them, we are free. If we identify with them, we are caught up in them. Then we have pain, suffering, and all the rest.

"How can we make decisions if the future is already happening?" The future only happens when we make the decisions. What we call a decision is the moment that decides the precipitation. There are so many things that can happen, but only one of these is going to precipitate. We decide, if we do such and such an action, that is what precipitates. If we do not do this but do that, then that is what precipitates. It is all there in potential; we have thought it all. But only what we make happen precipitates.

What do we want? We want the brotherhood of man, justice, peace. All of this is possible, depending on what we decide. So far, we have not decided to do it, so it has not precipitated. We have kept it as an ideal on the astral plane. We feel it but we keep it on the astral plane by not making the decisions on the outer physical plane to implement what we have already envisioned.

We have had the vision for centuries: the brotherhood of man, freedom, fraternity, equality. The French Revolution was built on that. The Russian Revolution was based on freedom for man. It is like the American Constitution. If you read the Russian Constitution and the American Constitution, you will find that they are almost the same. Look at the two countries: one with no freedom but a certain degree of justice; one with no justice but a certain degree of freedom. They just take what they want out of the vision.

Likewise, we keep this vision of the brotherhood of man, peace, equality, justice, all the wonderful divine things, but never put it into practice. Why? Why do we wait for Maitreya to show us how to do it? We could do it tomorrow. The world could be changed tomorrow, even before Maitreya appears. As soon as we take the decision to do something, we precipitate what we have envisioned. But if we do not actually act on our will, nothing happens. As Maitreya says: "Nothing happens by itself. Man must act and implement his will."

People are living in this mystical illusion that their vision, their ideals, are actually taking place, being implemented. They are not. Otherwise we would not have the pain, the suffering, the wars and all the rest of it. People have to come into reality — above all, the 6th-ray exponent whose major quality is vision and devotion and the capacity to sacrifice themselves for that vision. But as long as it remains on the astral plane simply as an idea, it may as well not be there. You need the ideal, and eventually the ideal will be implemented, but we have to do it.

How can I know what person or thing I was in my past life? (November 1996)

You were certainly not a *thing*! For most people it is not important to know one's past life or lives. If and when it becomes important the memories will rise spontaneously or steps may be taken to acquaint you with them. We always have enough to learn and do in this life as it is!

You speak of reincarnation. Why does every child in the world have to learn its own language if in a previous life it knew its language? (November 1994)

It did not necessarily know the language of the country into which it is born today — you might have been a Frenchman in your last life and turn up as an Englishman in this one, or vice versa. Almost everyone has forgotten the circumstances of the previous life and enters each new life with a new brain. A child has to learn because its brain is not developed, and so it has to learn the language of the country in which it finds itself. We all have to learn, even if we were born in the same country in a previous life — though it might come a bit easier in that case.

If I knew Maitreya in this life, in my next life will I recognize Him? (March 1995)

I would say that whether or not you would recognize Him would depend at what point in evolution you were. If He is in the world for the next 2,500 years as the World Teacher for the whole of humanity, in a very short period of time — from about three or four years old onwards — you would become aware of Him. You might recognize Him from a previous incarnation, but that would depend on whether you were able to bring over in consciousness your memory from one life to another. This would depend on your point of evolution.

Do you believe we can continue to contribute to the betterment of mankind (all life) after we cease to exist physically? I do. (January/February 1995)

Yes, in so far as our state of consciousness allows.

(1) Is material, physical immortality possible? (2) Am I correct in supposing that it is not only possible but that it has been recorded by history? (3) Is it a sign heralding the Age of Aquarius that more people are now attempting to triumph over death? (March 1996)

(1) To a Master, yes. (2) No. (3) No. It is really to do with a better understanding of Resurrection as an occult experience of perfection which the Masters demonstrate. It does not happen below the fifth initiation.

Is Alice Bailey in incarnation at this time? (July 1994)

No.

Are the souls of the philosophers Jean-Jacques Rousseau and Voltaire in incarnation at this moment? (April 1994)

No.

You say that individuals reincarnate in groups. Can you give a rough idea of the size of these groups? I know they must vary but would it be 100 people, or 1,000s, or 10,000s? (April 1995)

1,000s.

576

On average how many lives do we have to become a Master? (November 1994)

It takes hundreds of thousands of incarnational experiences to come up to the first initiation, the first of five. Usually, it takes an average of seven or eight incarnations between the first and second initiation. Between the second and third the whole process speeds up and the third can be taken in the same life as the second if that is taken early enough; then probably the fourth and fifth in the next two or three lives. So, there are very few lives in the last phase of the initiatory process, but up to the first initiation there are literally hundreds of thousands of incarnations.

Among the many revelations which we are given about the higher reality, there are many points of concordance, but there is one point about which there is complete disagreement: the possible number of incarnations, since this varies from hundreds of thousands to 12 or 13. This last number was indicated by a young doctor (Georges Morrannier, discarnate) who has already dictated seven lives to his mother. My question is: Why does such disagreement exist about the number of times we incarnate? (July 1994)

Because information about reincarnation comes largely from two sources: the Hierarchy of Masters, through disciples like H. P. Blavatsky and Alice Bailey, whose information always stresses the large number (hundreds of thousands) of incarnational experiences necessary to complete the course of evolution on this planet.

The other source of information comes, through mediums, from various levels (usually the fifth) of the astral planes. These are the planes of illusion. As a result, the information from these planes is unsound, and, to my mind, should not be given credibility. However, since there is no agreement that reincarnation *is* the reality of our lives, it is not surprising that there is no uniformity of belief in the possible number of incarnations.

How does the Law of Cause and Effect interact with time?
(January/February 1997)

If there is no time, there is nothing to interact with. The Law of Cause and Effect is the basic law governing all activity in our system. It is generated by the energy of the great cosmic Being who ensouls the sun Sirius. This nearest neighbour of ours, Sirius, is the source of that action (and reaction) which, in our system, works out as the Law of Cause and Effect. It sets that great law in motion. It is essential that everyone should have a clear understanding of what that law is, how it works, and how it affects them and their every action.

The Law of Cause and Effect is part of the great cosmic outflow and returning inflow, outbreathing and inbreathing, that governs all creation. In relation to the Law of Rebirth, it sets in motion the evolution of consciousness. Every action we take, every thought we have, creates a cause or sequence of causes, which make our lives, for good or ill. We are, all of us, creating good and harm and under the impact of this law we reap what we sow. We cannot avoid it; this is the basic, fundamental law governing our lives.

How does it relate to, or interact with, time? It cannot relate to time if there is no such thing as time. However, it interacts with time in the sense of the outbreathing and inbreathing of cosmos — in terms of cycles.

The Masters work, in every respect, in cycles, usually — although it can vary — in roughly 2,000-year cycles. All the plans and preparations which They make ahead of 'time' (actually ahead of certain states of consciousness to be attained by humanity and the lower kingdoms) are laid in accordance with the necessity, as They see it, of different stimuli to be given to men, animals, plants, and so on, to bring about a desired effect — the further working out of the Plan of evolution. That effect will work out, as we would say, "in time". From the Masters' point of view, it would simply enter into a position in an outflow of energy acting cyclically.

In the mineral kingdom, that cycle will be very long indeed. The changes taking place in the mineral world are immeasurably slow, from our point of view. In the vegetable kingdom they speed up but still are very slow. With the animal kingdom, the process of change — that is, the effect on that kingdom of this cyclic outflow — is somewhat speeded up. With the human kingdom, it reaches its acme of speed. You can have a degree of experimentation which is quickly enacted. You can see the results of that in relatively quite small time-frames, speaking from our 'time' point of view.

In a thousand years humanity can make a great evolutionary advance, always in relation to the Law of Cause and Effect. The animal kingdom, undergoing a similar kind of stimulus, will go through a relatively very small amount of that change. The vegetable kingdom even slower, and the mineral kingdom practically not at all. It would probably take millions of years to produce changes in the consciousness of the atoms of the rocks in the world. Nevertheless, every atom is living and conscious, and whether it is a rock or a leaf, a lion or a man, change does take place, evolution does proceed, and this in an active, cyclic unfoldment. It is not to do with what we call time, because time does not actually exist except in our brain.

The interaction of cause and effect is really the response in consciousness to our actions, or inactions, because inaction is also action. If you do not do a thing, it probably has as much consequence as if you do a thing, if you *should* do the thing. For example, if you should turn off the gas but do not do it, the consequences might be tremendous: there could be a huge explosion. On the other hand, if it is a question of killing somebody and you refrain from killing that person, then, of course, the karma involved would be less than if you went ahead and did the deed. It really depends on the purpose and intention behind the deed, the quality of the deed, whether it is creative or destructive.

In the ultimate, last, resort, what we are dealing with is creation, with positive or destructive acts of creation. The Law of Cause and Effect governs the creative act — positive, structured, and meaningful, or else destructive. There are only these two processes. People call it good and evil, constructive and destructive. They are talking about the Law of Cause and Effect.

The Law works out in cycles. If, for example, you kill somebody today, and tomorrow you are killed, you could say it is a quick-acting Law of Karma, of Cause and Effect. The more advanced the person is, the faster is the reaction to their action. That is why if a Master wants to create something, if Sai Baba wants to create vibhuti, or Maitreya wants to create a cross of light, They do not set the thing into motion years, months or weeks ahead. They think it, and instantaneously it is. Because of Their level of evolution, the Law acts very quickly.

There is a story in Yogananda's *Autobiography of a Yogi*, in which a famous yogi in India is given a jug of poisoned drink, a very potent poison, by someone, perhaps to test his point in evolution. He thought: "If he can stand up to this he is a pretty advanced guy!" The yogi did not hesitate. He knew, of course, that it was poisoned. He took it and drank it down. And the other man dropped dead! That is fast-acting karma, Cause and Effect. When you are advanced enough, as that one was, it happens very quickly indeed.

(1) How can we change our karma in order to be freed for greater service? (2) Can it be done through meditation or only through service, or both? (November 1993)

(1) This Law is dynamic and can be changed by our action. A life dedicated to altruistic service will 'burn up' existing karmic patterns and release one from some of the burden of past actions. (2) Meditation, of itself, will not alter karma (unless it is some kind of service-meditation such as Transmission Meditation) but, by aligning the individual with his or her own soul, brings the soul influence to bear on the personality life. If followed correctly, this inevitably drives the individual to some form of service — and thus to resolving past karma. A life consciously lived on the principle of harmlessness and right relationship is the best guarantee of making only 'good' karma.

(1) What kind of karma leads to mental debility, constitutional or acquired, and (2) what are the prospects for the debilitated in their next incarnation? (July 1994)

Some mental debility is the result of accident at birth but this, while not rare, is the minority cause. Most constitutional debility is the result of a conscious decision of the soul to limit its vehicle of expression for one life (or more). This tends to 'burn up' or resolve karma which has held back normal evolution. Such a person may well have been 'treading water', so to speak, making little or no progress for several lives. (2) Once the karmic 'backlog' is resolved, the following incarnation should show a renewed impetus and forward drive.

For years I've carried a donor card. Now, I read (in Mr Creme's books) that organ transplants have a karmic effect on the recipient; I would like to know whether there is any karmic effect on the donor (immediately after death) who must usually be operated on as soon as possible after being declared clinically dead. (July/August 1995)

No, none.

(1) Are animals spiritual beings? (2) Is not killing and eating them the same as murdering fellow human beings? (January/February 1995)

(1) All life is spiritual but the animal kingdom is not individualized as is the human — that is, there is no *individual* animal soul. (2) No. While proper relation to the animal kingdom would preclude their killing and eating, such killing cannot be compared to the murder of a human being — *a soul* in incarnation, and may serve to balance ancient karma between the human and animal kingdoms.

Waiting — and the Reappearance

What gave you the idea to talk about time at this particular conference?

I did not, in the beginning, intend to talk about time. That became a kind of revelation to me as I went on thinking about what I might talk about here. What really sent me on this path is what people have found in waiting. That is why I called it the "art of waiting."

People have been waiting for the emergence of Maitreya since 1982. That was the first window of opportunity which Maitreya saw as possible. I have since come to understand that it was 'a long shot', but a 'possible shot', and my Master said it very nearly came to fruition. He said it was very near indeed, much nearer than those of us engaged in it understood at the time. The media almost did enough. They did very little but almost enough. The effect of the world-wide advertisements, the press conference, the media attention which I had received, especially in this country (the US), for two years before that, had done a great deal of the work. The Master said it was almost on the bull's-eye, but not close enough. He said it would have been very remarkable indeed if it had worked. The Masters try, wherever possible, to further Their plan, even if it seems 'a long shot.' It was so touch-and-go that it was a shot obviously worth taking.

If it had worked, Maitreya would have been out in the world since 1982. The world by now, 14 years later, would probably be transformed, far, far better, especially for those conditioned relentlessly by time in the factories of the world. There might by now be factories altogether differently organized, with very sophisticated robots. In 14 years I can imagine that would be so. We would have different systems of energy creation. The first stages of the Technology of Light would likely be known and used. Or, at the very least, nuclear fusion would have replaced nuclear fission. The climate would be better; the devas would have returned to equilibrium. It would be an easier world in which to live. A growing sense of oneness would pertain; it would be an altogether better world.

582

But what would have happened to you? What would have happened to the groups all over the world who would not have worked for the Reappearance of the Christ for the last 14 years? Some are very recently into it, just babes who are trying their hand at this game of approaching the public with this information. But those of you who have been working, for example, in this country since 1980, in Europe and elsewhere since 1975 or 1976, how different you would be. You would have missed an opportunity for growth, for service, for the development of talents, initiatives, which you did not even know you had. It has been an exemplary lesson in what it is to serve.

In all the groups around the world people are doing jobs which they have never done before. They are not trained for these jobs. That is why they sometimes do them a little short of total professional perfection. But they can do them. They can whip out a press release, a booklet, or even a book, to order. They can do things they never thought of doing. These are talents which you learned over the centuries in different incarnations. Inspired by the idea, you have learned to act and serve in a way, which, I am sure, in 1982 you did not think possible. If I had asked you to make a film of me sitting here talking you would have said no, I have never made a film in my life. How could I possibly do it? Or publish books? We do not know anything about publishing. Or organize a whole nation of Transmission groups, publications, *Share International* magazine on a monthly basis, translated into all these different languages. It is unheard of. There is probably no group in the world, for its size, which has contributed so powerfully, not only to the work of the Reappearance, but in terms of self-help. You have remade yourselves in this work over the years — those of you who have been truly awake. Many of you have worked hard to produce the best that is in you in the various fields — producing books, editing, creating conferences and lecture tours, contacting media and so on.

I would say that probably the greatest experience of your life has been the last 14 years since 1982. If Maitreya had come forward then, you would have been delighted, the world would have been delighted, I would have been delighted. (I would have painted many more pictures than I have had the opportunity to do; I would be more than delighted.) But think what has happened, what you have learned, what you have done, how much that has changed you — which would not have happened if Maitreya had come forward. You would have been inspired. You would have received His energy. You would have thought: "We did it. We really did it." But you would not have had that growth experience. You would not have had the tough, uphill struggle, which I am sure it has been, to make known this very difficult and, for some people, very unattractive, idea of changing the world and the Reappearance of the Christ. This, I would say, is the greatest gift given to you. Maitreya said it in many of the messages: "This is a gift unlike aught given before to the world. Make known My coming. Tell the world I am coming and serve your brothers" — or words to that effect. That is what you have done: you have changed yourself, found talents, opportunities, and qualities in yourself, and therefore have expanded and strengthened your character. Of course, you are all 14 years older but 14 years wiser at the same time.

The art of waiting is a special skill of keeping the emergence of Maitreya in mind without being attached to it. If we are conditioned by the concept of the Day of Declaration — D-Day — in the near future, we decrease our ability to work for the Emergence.

I am not talking about being conditioned. But if you lose sight of the possibility of D-Day, you will probably say: "Well, there is no hurry. Let somebody else do it. I have been working hard for a long time. I deserve a rest." But if you sense that D-Day is just around the corner — let us leave out the question of time — that is a better way to see it. Then you increase the impetus rather than the opposite. That is why the Master talks about the "imminence" and "forthwith" — to give us the sense that it really is just 'round the corner'.

How can we remain committed without having expectations?
You would not be committed if you did not have expectations. But you do not have to identify with those expectations to the

degree that people do. If it is going to condition what you do, there is something at fault there. It should be a natural goal to work in such a way that the Plan, so far as your little bit of it is concerned, is working out at a reasonable pace and rhythm — but without being 'hung up' about a time or the Day of Declaration, that kind of expectation.

Without the excitement of expectation it is difficult to talk about the Reappearance with conviction. How are we to enthuse others without a sense of real expectation?

When you tell people about the Reappearance for the first time it will be a revelation to them anyway. Just to hear about it is a revelation. To know that it is possible for a man to overshadow the minds of all humanity. This gives them His stature as the Christ. And to know that this is a natural part of the human potential, that eventually we will all communicate telepathically, at will, over any distance.

When you explain that, you are actually setting up an expectation, an inspiration, in the mind of the listener. You have to do this without being conditioned by it and attached to it. It is doing the work with fervour, with interest, with power, with fiery ardour, and yet being detached.

When you are detached, you can put every ounce of your energy into it. You can talk on mental and emotional levels. You can raise people up to a real pitch of interest, expectation and exhilaration without being attached to it. It is, simply, using the orator's skill of communication. You can do this at any level, or on all levels. One obviously uses every level if one can. But that does not mean to say that if you are inspiring people on the emotional level, you are doing it from your own emotions. You are doing it from your heart, your mind, your experience, your communicating skills. It is an art. You are using the language of oratory, communication and education, to communicate ideas. These ideas can be conveyed on these different levels of expression, without being attached to the action.

Communicating these ideas can be just like the working of an artist, the writing of a poem, or an article for a magazine. It is the same kind of activity, only in a different medium. You are using the energy from the throat chakra and the heart, your mental ability, your soul. You are tuning into your soul. All of this is invoked while you are talking. All of this is being communicated. This is why you can light up audiences and get people to join groups without asking them specifically to do it. They do it because they are caught up in the inspiration of the ideas. If it is only surface excitement they will not do much with it. But if it goes deeply into the heart, and the heart responds, the soul, through the heart, tells them: "This is true. I must get involved, I must teach, I must spread it."

If we put less focus on the Day of Declaration and more emphasis on the preparation, will this free us from a domination by time?

Yes and no. The Day of Declaration is terribly important. You should not lose sight of it. But you should not live from moment to moment in your own expectation of it. You should use the idea in an educational way, without saying: "I wish it was the Day of Declaration. I cannot wait for the Day of Declaration." It is better to do the work and forget about it, if that is the way you approach it. But you can know it and communicate it, without attachment.

When people around me do not seem receptive to my mentioning Maitreya or Sai Baba, it is hard to know whether to be quiet and discreet or faithfully to 'shout it over the roof-tops' — or something in between. Can you comment please? (June 1993)

The best approach, I believe, is to speak out as much as possible — but with a sense of proportion. Do not ram the information down people's reluctant throats. Where questions are asked and interest is evident, do your best to supply the information. Where the doors are closed, try elsewhere.

Are there any guidelines for groups associated with the Reappearance of the Christ as far as money is concerned? For example, all items are kept as inexpensive as possible because the aim is to disseminate information and not to make a profit. Various Transmission Meditation groups around the world also take it on themselves to collect money to feed and help the homeless in their own countries, raise funds for people in developing countries or in countries struggling with rapid political and economic changes. While such work is much needed, collecting money (as known members of Transmission Meditation groups or co-workers of **Share International** *and Benjamin Creme) could provide fuel for mischievous critics.* (March 1996)

Any collecting of money for social or other aid should be done on an individual basis, not as representing a particular group. If such fund-raising is done the strictest keeping of accounts should be followed.

Krishnamurti said: "My memory is my enemy." How do we overcome our grief, pain, and our fear of our memory of abuse that traps us in time?

If you have a memory like mine you have no problem. This is, perhaps, the one thing I share with Krishnamurti — his lack of memory. My favourite joke in the world (which I never fail to tell) is from my daughter's joke book when she was seven: "Doctor! Doctor! I am losing my memory!" "Oh dear, when did this happen?" "When did what happen?" That is the story of my life. I am losing my memory — daily, hourly. I like to put it down to the fact that I am no longer conditioned by time. Of course that is my illusion. But if you lose your memory you even lose your thought of time; time goes as your memory goes.

Krishnamurti says: "My memory is my enemy." Exactly so. Do you know what your memory is? Your memory is yesterday, the past. While you are thinking about the past you are not living in the Now. If you have studied Krishnamurti, almost the whole of his effort was to show his readers, his listeners, that there is only this moment; there is no time. I am looking at this microphone. If I were Krishnamurti it would be a tree, but with me it is a microphone — different age, different circumstances, different role. I am looking at this microphone, but if I am thinking about yesterday's microphone, or the microphone three weeks ago, or that beautiful microphone they had in the studio, I ignore this quite inelegant but nevertheless useful object. If I am thinking of all the past microphones that I have held, then of course I am not living with this microphone, experiencing it.

Your memory is your enemy because you identify with your memory. I ask you: "Who are you?" and you say: "I am Mrs So-and-so, married with three children." Then you go on and say where you live. It is just a story about your memory. You remember being married. You remember having children. You remember what you had to eat yesterday. It is not interesting. I do not mean you are boring me. I mean it is not meaningful to you. You are not experiencing anything in a living way. You are only thinking back and telling something with which you now identify. If you identify with the past, you cannot be identifying with the Now. That is the point. You cannot do both at the same time. There is only the Now. As soon as you identify with your memory, you cut out the experience of the Now. Get rid of your memory, as I am doing fast, and you experience the Now as you have never done before.

"How do we overcome our grief, pain, and our fears of our memory of abuse that traps us in time?" The way to do it is to give it up; do not identify with it. Ask yourself: "Am I this memory?" Obviously you are not. While you identify with your memory and pain, your grief, with the abuse that is trapping you in time, whatever you identify with, holds you. That is what you are. You are pain, grief, abuse, unhappiness, all of these things.

The way not to experience that pain, grief, unhappiness, is not to identify with it. Identify, rather, with who and what you are. Ask yourself: "Who am I?" But without saying: "I should not feel this pain. I should not feel this grief, this unhappiness and abuse — all the things that pain me." Because as you say it, you are doing it. As long as you are trying to rid yourself of it, or indulging it, experiencing it, going over and over it in your mind and relating to it, you are identifying with it.

Whatever you identify with is what you are. If you identify with the physical body, then to all intents and purposes you are the physical body. That traps the Self in the physical plane and causes all the illness — stomach aches, ulcers, and all the rest, of the physical body. If it is on the emotional plane, then likewise you have all the emotional grief. If it is on the mental plane, if it is all to do with your memory, you trap yourself in your beliefs, your ideologies. You are a Conservative, a Communist, a Democrat, a Christian, or a Hindu. These ideologies are only beliefs. While you identify with them, you are trapped in them. Where you are trapped, you are not living. The Self is life. There is only one life, which we all share. That life takes form; you are part of that form. You are life given a certain form. If you look in the mirror, you might like the form or you might wish it had been a bit different. But that's life.

GLOSSARY OF ESOTERIC TERMS

Age — World cycle, approximately 2,350 to 2,500 years, determined by the relation of the Earth, sun and constellations of the zodiac.

Ageless Wisdom — An ancient body of spiritual teaching underlying all the world's religions as well as all scientific, social and cultural achievements. First made available in writing to the general public in the late 1800s by Helena Petrovna Blavatsky and in this century by Alice Bailey, Helena Roerich, and Benjamin Creme.

Ajna centre — The energy centre (chakra) between the eyebrows. Directing centre of the personality. Its correspondence on the physical level is the pituitary gland.

Antahkarana — An invisible channel of light forming the bridge between the physical brain and the soul, built through meditation and service.

Antichrist — Energy of the Will aspect of God, in its involutionary phase, which destroys the old forms and relationships, for example at the end of an age, to prepare the way for the building forces of the Christ Principle. Manifested in Roman times through the Emperor Nero and in modern times through Hitler and six of his associates.

Aquarius — Astronomically, the age of Aquarius, now commencing and lasting 2,350 to 2,500 years. Esoterically, refers to the Water Carrier, the age of Maitreya, and to the spiritual energy of Aquarius: that of synthesis and brotherhood.

Ashram — A Master's group. In the Spiritual Hierarchy there are 49 ashrams, seven major and 42 subsidiary, each headed by a Master of Wisdom.

Astral body — The emotional vehicle of an individual.

Astral plane — The plane of the emotions, including the polar opposites such as hope and fear, sentimental love and hate, happiness and suffering. The plane of illusion.

Astral Polarization — The focus of consciousness is on the astral plane. The first race, the Lemurian, had the goal of

591

perfecting physical-plane consciousness. Atlantean man's goal was the perfecting of astral/emotional consciousness. The majority of humanity today are still polarized on the astral plane. See also Mental Polarization.

Avatar — A spiritual Being who 'descends' in answer to mankind's call and need. There are human, planetary and cosmic Avatars. The latter would be called 'Divine Incarnations'. Their teaching, correctly apprehended and gradually applied by humanity, expands our understanding and presents the next step forward in humanity's evolutionary development.

Avatar of Synthesis — A great cosmic Being who embodies the energies of Will, Love, Intelligence and another energy for which we have as yet no name. Since the 1940s He has been sending these energies into the world, gradually transforming division into unity.

Buddha — Last Avatar of the age of Aries. Previous World Teacher Who manifested through the Prince Gautama around 500 BC. The Embodiment of Wisdom, He currently acts as the 'Divine Intermediary' between Shamballa and Hierarchy. Buddhists expect their next great teacher under the name Maitreya Buddha.

Buddhi — The universal soul or mind; higher reason; loving understanding; love-wisdom. The energy of love as the Masters experience it.

Buddhic plane — Plane of divine intuition.

Causal body — The vehicle of expression of the soul on the causal plane. The receptacle where consciousness of one's evolutionary point of development is stored.

Causal plane — The third of the four higher mental planes on which the soul dwells.

Chakras — Energy centres (vortices) in the etheric body, related to the spine and the seven most important endocrine glands. Responsible for the co-ordination and vitalization of all the bodies (mental, astral and physical) and their correlation with the soul, the main centre of consciousness. There are seven major chakras and 42 lesser ones.

Christ — A term used to designate the head of the Spiritual Hierarchy; the World Teacher; the Master of all the Masters. The office presently held by the Lord Maitreya.

Christ Consciousness — The energy of the Cosmic Christ, also known as the Christ Principle. Embodied for us by the Christ, it is at present awakening in the hearts of millions of people all over the world. The energy of evolution *per se.*

Day of Declaration — Day on which Maitreya will make Himself known to the world during a world-wide radio and television broadcast. Even those who are not listening or watching will hear His words telepathically in their own language and, at the same time, hundreds of thousands of spontaneous healings will take place throughout the world. Beginning of Maitreya's open mission in the world.

Deva — Angel or celestial being belonging to a kingdom in nature evolving parallel to humanity, and ranging from sub-human elementals to super-human beings on a level with a planetary logos. They are the 'active builders', working intelligently with substance to create all the forms we see, including the mental, emotional and physical bodies of humanity.

Energy — From the esoteric point of view, there is nothing but energy in the whole of the manifested universe. Energy vibrates at various frequencies, and the particular frequency determines the form which the energy will take. Energy can be acted upon and directed by thought.

Esotericism — The philosophy of the evolutionary process both in man and the lower kingdoms in nature. The science of the accumulated wisdom of the ages. Presents a systematic and comprehensive account of the energetic structure of the universe and of man's place within it. Describes the forces and influences that lie behind the phenomenal world. Also, the process of becoming aware of and gradually mastering these forces.

Etheric Body — The energetic counterpart of the physical body, composed of seven major centres (chakras) and 42 minor centres, a network which connects all the centres, and infinitesimally small threads of energy (nadis) which underlie every part of the nervous system. Blockages in the etheric body can result in physical illnesses.

Etheric Planes — Four planes of matter finer than the gaseous-physical. As yet invisible to most people.

Evil — Anything which impedes evolutionary development.

Evolution — The process of spiritualization of matter; the way back to the Source. The casting aside of the veils of delusion and illusion, leading eventually to cosmic consciousness.

Forces of Light (Forces of Evolution) — The Spiritual Hierarchy of our planet. Planetary centre of Love-Wisdom. See also Spiritual Hierarchy.

Forces of Darkness (Forces of Evil, Forces of Materiality) — The involutionary or materialistic forces which uphold the matter aspect of the planet. When they overstep their role and impinge upon the spiritual progress of humanity, they are designated as 'evil'.

Glamour — Illusion on the astral plane. The condition when the mind becomes veiled by emotional impulses generated on astral levels, preventing the mind's eye from clearly distinguishing reality. Examples: fear, self-pity, criticism, suspicion, self-righteousness, over-materiality.

God (see also Logos) — The great Cosmic Being who ensouls this planet, embodying all the Laws and all the energies governed by those Laws, which make up everything that we see and cannot see.

Great Invocation — An ancient formula, translated by Hierarchy for the use of mankind to invoke the energies which will change our world. Translated into many languages, it is used daily by millions of people.

Guru — A spiritual teacher.

Hierarchy — See Spiritual Hierarchy.

Hierophant — The Initiator. Either the Christ, at the first two planetary initiations, or the Lord of the World, at the third and higher initiations.

Illusion — Deception on the mental plane. The soul, using the glamoured mind as its instrument, obtains a distorted picture of the phenomenal world.

Imam Mahdi — The prophet Whose return is awaited by some Islamic sects in order that He can complete the work started by Mohammed.

Incarnation — Manifestation of the soul as a three-fold personality, under the Law of Rebirth.

Initiation — A voluntary process whereby successive and graded stages of unification and at-one-ment take place between the man or woman in incarnation, his/her soul, and the divine Monad or 'spark of God'. Each stage confers on the initiate a deeper understanding of the meaning and purpose of God's Plan, a fuller awareness of his/her part in that Plan, and an increasing ability to work consciously and intelligently towards its fulfilment.

Involution — The process whereby spirit descends into matter, its polar opposite.

Jesus — A Master of Wisdom and disciple of the Christ, Maitreya. Allowed the Christ to work through Him during the period from His baptism through the crucifixion. In the coming time He will play a major role in reinspiring and reorienting the whole field of Christian religion. As the Master Jesus, He works closely with Maitreya, often appearing to people (in disguise).

Karma — Eastern name for the Law of Cause and Effect. The basic Law governing our existence in this solar system. Every thought, every action that we have and make sets into motion a cause. These causes have their effects, which make our lives, for good or ill. Expressed in biblical terms: "As you sow, so shall you reap."; in scientific terms: "For every action there is an equal and opposite reaction."

Krishna — A great Avatar who appeared around 3,000 BC and served as the vehicle of manifestation for the Lord Maitreya during the Age of Aries. By demonstrating the need to control the astral/emotional nature, Krishna opened the door to the second initiation. Hindus expect a new incarnation of Krishna at the end of Kali Yuga, the dark age.

Law of Cause and Effect (Law of Action and Reaction) — See Karma

Law of Rebirth — See Reincarnation.

Logos — God. The Cosmic Being who ensouls a planet (Planetary Logos), a solar system (Solar Logos), a galaxy (Galactic Logos) and so on to infinity.

Lord of the World — See Sanat Kumara.

Maitreya — The World Teacher for the age of Aquarius. The Christ and head of the Spiritual Hierarchy of our planet. The Master of all the Masters.

Man/Woman — The physical manifestation of a spiritual Monad (or Self), which is a single spark of the One Spirit (God).

Manas — Higher mind.

Mantram — Formula or arrangement of words or syllables which, when correctly sounded, invokes energy.

Master Djwhal Khul (D.K.) — One of the Masters of the Wisdom, known as the Tibetan, Who dictated the latest phase of the Ageless Wisdom Teaching through the disciple Alice A. Bailey. He was also responsible for the drawings of the atom, etc. in the books of Helena Blavatsky: *The Secret Doctrine* and *Isis Unveiled*.

Masters of Wisdom — Individuals Who have taken the 5th initiation, having passed through all the experiences that life in this world offers and, in the process, having acquired total mastery over themselves and the laws of nature. Custodians of the Plan of evolution and all the energies entering this planet which bring about the fulfilment of the Plan.

Meditation — Scientific means of contacting one's soul and of eventually becoming at-one with the soul. Also the process of being open to spiritual impression and thus to co-operation with the Spiritual Hierarchy.

Mental body — The vehicle of the personality on the mental planes.

Mental plane — The plane of the mind where the mental processes take place.

Mental polarization — The focus of consciousness on the mental plane. The shifting of consciousness onto the mental plane begins half-way between the first and second planetary initiations.

Monad/Self — Pure Spirit reflecting the triplicity of Deity: (1) Divine Will or Power (the Father); (2) Love-Wisdom (the Son); (3) Active Intelligence (the Holy Spirit). The 'spark of God' resident in every human being.

Occult — Hidden. The hidden science of energy (see Esotericism).

Overshadowing — A voluntary co-operative process in which a Master's consciousness temporarily enters and works through the physical, emotional and mental bodies of a disciple.

Permanent atoms — The three atoms of matter — physical, astral and mental — around which the bodies for a new incarnation are formed. They retain the vibratory rate of the individual at the moment of death, guaranteeing that the energetic evolutionary 'status' thus far achieved will be carried over into successive lives.

Personality — Threefold vehicle of the soul on the physical plane, consisting of a mental, an emotional (astral) and a physical-etheric body.

Physical plane — The lowest vibrational states of substance, including: dense-physical, liquid, gaseous and etheric matter.

Pisces, age of — The stream of energy, coming into our planetary life from the constellation Pisces, has for two thousand years conditioned human experience and civilization. It was inaugurated by Jesus in Palestine and, at its best, produces the qualities of sensitivity and sacrifice. The age of Pisces is ending and the new age of Aquarius has begun.

Plane — A level of manifestation.

Planetary Logos — Divine Being ensouling a planet.

Pralaya — A non-mental, non-astral, non-material state of existence somewhere between death and rebirth, where the life impulse is in abeyance. An experience of perfect peace and unending bliss prior to taking the next incarnation. Corresponds to the Christian idea of paradise.

Rays — The seven streams of universal divine energy, each the expression of a great Life, Whose interaction at every conceivable frequency creates the solar systems, galaxies and universes. Movement of these energies, in spiralling cycles, draws all Being into and out of manifestation, colouring and saturating it with specific qualities and attributes.

Rays of Nations — Each nation is governed by two rays: a soul ray, which is sensed and expressed by the initiates and disciples of the nation, and a personality ray, which is the dominant mass influence and expression. From time to time, through the activities of the initiates and disciples of a country, the soul ray may be given expression and the true quality of the nation can be seen.

Reincarnation (Law of Rebirth) — The process which allows God, through an agent (ourselves) to bring Itself down to Its polar opposite — matter — in order to bring that matter back into Itself, totally imbued with the nature of God. The Law of Karma draws us back into incarnation until gradually, through the evolutionary process, we reveal more truly our innate divinity.

Sanat Kumara — The Lord of the World; the etheric-physical expression of our Planetary Logos Who dwells on Shamballa. A great Being, originally from Venus, Who sacrificed Himself to become the personality vehicle for the ensouling deity of our planet 18.5 million years ago. The nearest aspect of God that we can know.

Self/Monad — The divine spark within every human being.

Self-realization — The process of recognizing and expressing our divine nature.

Shamballa — A centre of energy; the major centre in the planet. It is located above the Gobi Desert on the two highest etheric planes. From it and through it flows the Shamballa Force — the energy of Will or Purpose. It corresponds to the crown centre (chakra).

Solar Logos — Divine Being ensouling our solar system.

Soul (Ego, Higher Self, inner ruler, Christ within, Son of Mind, Solar Angel) — The linking principle between Spirit and matter; between God and His form. Provides consciousness, character and quality to all manifestation in form.

Spirit — As used by Maitreya, a term meaning the sum-total of all the energies — the life force — animating and vitalizing an individual. Also used, more esoterically, to mean the Monad which reflects itself in the soul.

Spirit of Peace or Equilibrium — A cosmic Being who assists the work of Maitreya by overshadowing Him with His energy. He works closely with the Law of Action and Reaction, to transform the present chaotic conditions into the opposite state in exact proportion.

Spiritual — The quality of any activity which drives the human being forward towards some form of development — physical, emotional, intuitional, social — in advance of his present state.

Spiritual Hierarchy (White Brotherhood, Society of Illumined Minds) — The Kingdom of God, the Spiritual Kingdom or the Kingdom of souls, made up of the Masters and initiates of all degrees and whose purpose is to implement the Plan of God. Planetary centre of Love-Wisdom.

Three Spiritual Festivals — Determined by the full moons of Aries, Taurus and Gemini (April, May and June). These festivals, celebrated as the Easter, Wesak and Christ Festivals, will be central to the New World Religion and will constitute, each of them, a great Approach of Deity – the evocation of the Divine Light, Divine Love, and Divine Will, which can then be anchored on the Earth and utilised by man.

Transmission Meditation — A group meditation for the purpose of 'stepping down' (transforming) spiritual energies emanating from the Spiritual Hierarchy of Masters which thus become accessible and useful to the general public. It is the creation of a vortex or pool of higher energy for the benefit of humanity. This is a form of service which is simple to do, and is at the same time a powerful means of personal growth. There are hundreds of Transmission Meditation groups active in many countries around the world.

Triangle — A group of three people who link up each day in thought for a few minutes of creative meditation.

Vehicle — The form by means of which higher beings find expression on the lower planes. The physical, astral and mental bodies, for instance, form the vehicles of the soul on lower levels.

Vibration — Movement of energy. All energy vibrates at its own particular frequency. The evolutionary process proceeds through a heightening of the vibrational rate in response to higher incoming energies.

World Teacher — The head of the Spiritual Hierarchy in any given cycle. The Master of all the Masters. The office held at present by the Lord Maitreya.

Yoga — Union of the lower nature with the higher. Also, different forms and techniques to gain control of the physical, astral or mental bodies.

THE LIST OF INITIATES

THEIR RAYS AND STAGE OF EVOLUTION

A ray is, according to the Master DK, "but a name for a particular force or type of energy, with the emphasis upon the quality which that force exhibits". Rays thus qualify all creation, including the human constitution. Soul, personality, mental body, emotional (astral) body, physical body, all are coloured by one or other of the seven rays. In order to facilitate study and comprehension of the rays, Benjamin Creme's Master has kindly provided, over the years, requested information on the ray structure and point of evolution of well-known individuals, but for reasons of privacy, never of living people. Due to politeness the initiatory degree has been omitted in the case of Avatars.

The figures in parenthesis immediately following the names refer to the initiate's exact point of development attained during that life. For example, if an initiate achieved a level halfway between the first and second initiation, it is indicated as 1.5.

Nine figures follow the parenthesis; the rays relate, in order, to the soul, personality, mental body, astral body and physical body. The upper figures represent major rays; the lower figures represent sub-rays. The soul does not have a sub-ray. When the original list of 580 names was published in *Maitreya's Mission, Volume One*, sub-rays were not given. With the exception of those whose sub-rays have been given since then, these names still do not have sub-rays listed.

Following the rays are the dates of birth and death, the country of origin, and the field of endeavour in which the initiate became known. Many of the people on the list were so versatile that it was virtually impossible to classify them in one category. However, the limits of space available left no option. In a few cases, unfortunately, we were not able to find all relevant data; such omissions are noted by a question mark.

*[This list includes all the names of initiates which were published in **Maitreya's Mission, Volumes One, Two** and **Three**, as well as those published in **Share International** between April 1997 and November 2009.]*

Aalto, Alvar (1.6)	2 4 7 6 3	(1898-1976) Finland
	4 3 4 7	Architect
Abbas I (0.9)	3 1 4 6 3	(1557-1628) Persia
	6 7 6 7	Shah
al-Abbas (0.85)	6 6 3 4 3	(565 - 652) Arabia
	1 7 6 7	Uncle of Mohammed
Abbé Pierre (1.7)	6 3 6 4 3	(1912-2007) France
	4 2 6 7	Priest/Emmaus movement
Abd-el-Kader (1.5)	6 6 3 4 3	(1808-1883) Algeria
	6 7 6 1	Patriot
Abd-el-Karim (1.3)	6 3 4 6 3	(1882-1963) Morocco
	6 7 6 7	Patriot
Abdul-Aziz (1.6)	6 3 4 6 3	(1830-1876) Turkey
	7 6 2 7	Sultan
Abdul-Hamid (1.4)	6 6 4 6 3	(1725-1789) Turkey
	3 7 4 7	First Sultan
Abdullah, Basuki (1.49)	6 4 3 6 7	(1915-1993) Indonesia
	7 7 2 3	Naturalist/painter
Abel, Niel Henrik (1.5)	3 6 3 6 3	(1802-1829) Norway
	3 3 6 3	Mathematician
Adamov, Arthur (1.6)	2 3 5 6 3	(1908-1970) France
		Dramatist
Adams, Michael (1.5)	2 4 3 4 7	(1920-2005) UK
	6 7 2 3	Journalist
Adams, Norman (1.4)	2 4 6 6 3	(1927-2005) UK
	6 4 6 3	Painter
Adamski, George (2.0)	2 4 1 6 7	(1891-1965) USA
	6 4 2 3	Writer/Ufologist
Adenauer, Konrad (1.7)	1 3 1 6 3	(1876-1967) Germany
		Statesman
Adler, Alfred (2.0)	2 1 1 2 7	(1870-1937) Austria
		Psychiatrist
Adler, Jankel (2.0)	2 4 1 6 3	(1895-1949) Poland
	7 4 6 7	Painter
Adler, Larry (1.35)	2 4 3 2 3	(1914-2001) USA
	6 7 6 7	Musician
Aeschylus (1.7)	4 1 3 4 7	(525-456 BC) Greece
		Dramatist
Agrippa, H Cornelius (1.58)	3 4 6 6 7	(1486-1535) Germany
	7 3 6 7	Theologian
Aïvanhov, Mikhaèl (2.4)	3 6 6 2 7	(1900-1986) Bulgaria
	3 5 4 3	Fndr. Fraternité Blanche

Akbar the Great (1.45)	1 1 3 6 3	(1542-1605) India Emperor
Akhnaton (1.5)	2 6 1 6 7	(1372-1354 BC) Egypt Pharaoh
Akiva, Rabbi (1.5)	3 1 3 4 7 4 6 2 3	(2nd cent. AD) Palestine Spiritual leader
Alam, Shah Rukne (2.0)	2 3 4 6 3 2 2 4 7	(11th century) Pakistan Sufi
Alberts, Ton (1.4)	3 4 5 6 7 2 7 2 3	(1927-1999) Netherlands Architect
Alder, Vera Stanley (1.65)	2 4 3 4 3 6 6 6 7	(1898-1984) UK Esotericist/writer
Alexander the Great (1.5)	1 1 3 6 1	(356-323 BC) Macedonia King
Alexander, Rolf (1.8)	2 3 4 6 3 6 7 2 7	(b. 1891) Canada Writer
Alfonso X, The Wise (1.6)	6 6 4 2 7 2 6 4 7	(1221-1284) Spain King
Alfonso XIII (1.4)	6 7 4 6 7 3 6 6 3	(1886-1941) Spain King
Alfred the Great (1.3)	4 7 3 6 7 1 7 6 3	(849-c 900) England King
Ali (1.36) (Son-in-law of Mohammed)	4 4 3 4 3 2 7 6 7	(c 600-661) Arabia 4th Caliph
Allison, Audle (1.3)	2 4 3 4 3 6 7 6 7	(d. 1988) USA Mystic/writer
Altman, Robert (1.45)	3 6 4 6 3 6 6 6 7	(1925-2006) USA Film director
Ambartsumian, Victor (1.7)	4 4 3 4 3 6 7 2 3	(1908-1996) Armenia Astrophysicist
Amte, Baba Devidas (2.0)	2 6 6 6 3 2 4 4 7	(1914-2008) India Social activist
Ananda Mayee Ma	2 2 6 4 3 6 6 6 3	(1896-1982) India Avatar
Anderson, Hans C (1.6)	6 4 2 6 7	(1805-1875) Denmark Writer
Anderson, Lindsay (1.5)	2 4 3 4 7 6 7 6 3	(1922-1994) UK Director
Angeles, Victoria de los (1.4)	2 4 3 2 3 6 7 6 3	(1923-2005) Spain Soprano
Angelico, Fra (2.5)	6 4 6 2 7	(1387-1455) Italy Painter
Anglada, Vicente B. (1.5)	2 4 6 6 3 7 3 2 7	(1915-1988) Spain Esoteric writer
Antoine, Catherine (1.4)	4 6 4 6 7 2 6 6 3	(1850-1940) France Wife of Louis Antoine
Antoine, Louis (1.4)	3 4 3 6 5 6 4 6 7	(1846-1912) France Fndr. Antoiniste movement
Antonioni, Michelangelo (1.3)	4 4 6 6 7 6 3 4 3	(1912-2007) Italy Film director

Apelles (1.6)	2 4 4 6 3	(c 325 BC) Greece Painter
Apollinaire, Guillaume (1.6)	2 3 4 6 7	(1880-1918) France Poet
Apollonius of Tyana (5.0)	6 1 1 2 7	(AD 16-c 97) Greece Philosopher
Aquinas, Thomas (2.0)	6 6 7 2 3	(1225-1274) Italy Theologian/philosopher
Aquino, Benigno S. (1.6)	7 4 6 2 7 7 6 6 3	(1932 –1983) Philippines Politician
Arafat, Yasser (2.4)	6 4 1 6 3 6 4 6 7	(1929-2004) Palestine President
Archimedes (2.2)	5 2 1 2 1	(c 287-212 BC) Greece Mathematician
Aris, Michael V. (1.7)	2 6 6 6 7 6 6 4 3	(1946-1999) England Husband of Aung San Suu Kyi
Aristophanes (1.6)	2 4 1 4 7	(448-385 BC) Greece Comic dramatist
Aristotle (2.4)	7 5 1 6 3	(384-322 BC) Greece Philosopher
Arkwright, Sir Richard (1.6)	2 1 5 4 5	(1732-1792) England Inventor
Armstrong, Louis (0.6)	4 4 7 6 3 4 6 2 3	(1899-1974) USA Jazz musician
Arnold, Matthew (2.2)	2 4 6 4 3	(1822-1888) UK Poet
Aron, Raymond (2.0)	3 7 6 6 3	(1905-1983) France Historian/sociologist
Artaud, Antonin (1.6)	3 4 4 6 3	(1896-1948) France Dramatist
Ashe, Arthur (1.6)	2 4 3 4 3 6 6 2 7	(1943-1993) USA Athlete/political activist
Asimov, Isaac (1.6)	3 4 7 4 3 6 3 6 7	(1920-1992) USA Writer
Asoka (3.0)	2 4 1 4 3 6 6 2 7	(264-223 BC) India Emperor
al-Assad, Hafez (1.5)	7 6 3 6 7 6 6 6 7	(1930-2000) Syria President
Assagioli, Roberto (2.0)	2 2 3 6 3 2 5 6 7	(1888-1974) Italy Psychiatrist
Atatürk, Mustafa Kemal (2.2)	1 1 5 2 7 4 6 2 7	(1881-1938) Turkey Statesman
Atkinson, William Walter (1.5)	3 4 4 6 1 6 7 2 3	(1862-1932) USA Writer
Auger, Arleen (1.3)	2 4 3 6 3 4 5 6 7	(1939-1993) USA Singer
Augstein, Rudolf (1.35)	4 6 7 4 3 6 3 6 3	(1923-2002) Germany Publisher of *Der Spiegel*
Augustine (2.3)	6 6 1 4 7 6 4 6 7	(354-430) Numidia (Algeria) Theologian

Augustus (1.75)	1 1 6 6 1 1 4 6 7	(63 BC-AD 14) Rome Emperor
Aulia, Nizamuddin (3.2)	4 6 2 6 7 3 6 6 3	(1238-1324) India Sufi Saint
Auliya, Qalandar Baba (3.3) (Mohammed Azim Barkhia)	4 7 5 6 7 3 7 6 3	(d. 1979) India Sufi Saint
Aurelius, Marcus (1.4)	2 6 6 2 7 4 7 4 7	(121-180) Rome Emperor
Aurobindo Ghose (3.7)	2 6 1 6 3 6 4 6 7	(1872-1950) India Mystic
Aury, Dominique (1.5) (Anne Desclos)	3 6 3 6 7 6 3 6 3	(1907-1998) France Writer/translator
Austen, Jane (1.75)	2 4 6 6 3	(1775-1817) England Novelist
Baba, Haidakhan (3.0)	2 4 3 2 7 7 6 6 7	(c 1952-1984) India Spiritual teacher
Babbit, Edwin D (1.4)	3 3 4 6 5 6 6 2 3	(1828-1905) USA Colour therapy researcher
Bach, C P E (1.6)	4 4 5 6 3 6 4 6 7	(1714-1780) Germany Composer
Bach, Edward (1.6)	2 4 2 6 3 1 6 6 7	(1886-1936) UK Naturopathic healer
Bach, J S (3.1)	2 4 7 6 3 4 7 6 7	(1685-1750) Germany Composer
Bacon, Francis (1.8)	3 4 3 4 7 4 3 6 3	(1909-1992) UK Painter
Bacon, Francis (3.7)	7 4 4 6 3 4 7 2 7	(1561-1626) England Statesman
Bacon, Roger (2.6)	7 4 1 6 3 6 3 4 7	(c 1214-1292) England Philosopher
Baha'u'llah (3.0)	6 6 6 4 7 6 6 4 7	(1817-1892) Iran Founder Bahaism
Bailey, Alice A (3.2)	2 1 1 2 3 6 4 6 7	(1880-1949) UK Occultist
Bailey, Foster (1.85)	2 2 6 6 3 6 4 2 7	(1887/8-1977) USA Occultist
Baird, John Logie (1.7)	2 5 3 6 7 7 5 6 7	(1888-1946) UK Inventor
Balakirev, Mili A (1.4)	6 6 5 6 7 6 1 6 3	(1836-1910) Russia Composer
Balaquer, Josemaria de (1.55)	6 6 6 2 7 6 7 6 7	(1902-1975) Spain Writer
Ballard, Guy (1.5)	2 5 6 6 7 6 4 6 3	(1878-1939) USA 'I AM' leader/writer
Balzac, Honoré de (2.0)	3 7 6 6 3 4 7 2 7	(1799-1850) France Writer
Bandaranaike, Sirimavo (1.6)	2 4 3 6 3 7 7 2 7	(1916-2000) Sri Lanka Prime Minister (1st female)
Bannink, Willem (1.6)	2 6 4 4 3 2 6 6 3	(1888-1971) Netherlands Theologian/sociologist

Bardon, Franz (1.6)	7 6 4 6 7	(1909-1958) Czechoslovakia
	6 7 2 7	Hermetic occultist
Barnard, Christian (1.5)	2 4 6 6 3	(1922 -2001) South Africa
	6 3 2 7	Heart transplant surgeon
Bartók, Béla (1.8)	2 7 4 4 3	(1881-1945) Hungary
	7 6 4 7	Composer
Basho (1.6)	4 6 6 4 7	(1644-1694) Japan
	3 3 6 3	Haiku poet
Basilides (1.57)	3 4 3 4 3	(fl. c 125 AD) Egypt
	6 7 6 7	Gnostic philosopher
Baudelaire, Charles (1.7)	2 4 1 6 3	(1821-1867) France
	4 7 6 7	Poet
Baum, David (1.5)	2 4 3 4 3	(1940-1999) England
	6 7 6 7	Paediatrician
Bausch, Pina (1.4)	4 4 7 6 7	(1940-2009) Germany
	6 3 2 7	Dancer/choreographer
Beaumarchais, Pierre de (1.7)	2 7 6 2 1	(1732-1799) France
	6 4 6 3	Comic dramatist
Beauvoir, Simone de (1.6)	4 5 6 2 3	(1908-1986) France
	6 2 4 7	Writer
Becket, Thomas à (1.75)	6 2 4 6 3	(1118-1170) England
	6 6 4 7	Archbishop/martyr
Beckett, Samuel (1.6)	2 6 1 4 7	(1906-1990) Ireland
	6 6 4 7	Writer
Beckmann, Max (1.6)	4 4 6 6 7	(1884-1950) Germany
	6 3 6 3	Painter
Bede, the Venerable (2.0)	6 6 2 6 1	(c 673-735) England
	6 4 6 7	Historian/scholar
Beesley, Ronald (1.67)	2 6 3 4 7	(1903-1979) UK
	7 4 2 3	Healer
Beethoven, Ludwig van (3.1)	4 4 1 2 7	(1770-1827) Germany
	4 6 4 7	Composer
Behan, Brendan (1.0)	2 4 1 6 3	(1923-1964) Ireland
	4 6 6 7	Writer
Behn, Aphra (2.0)	2 1 5 2 3	(1640-1689) England
	6 4 2 7	Writer
Belisarius (1.7)	5 1 1 4 3	(505-565) Illyria
	7 6 4 7	General
Bell, Alexander Graham (1.75)	3 2 1 2 3	(1847-1922) UK
	4 7 6 7	Inventor
Bell, Arthur (1.6)	6 4 3 4 3	(20th C.) USA
	6 7 6 7	Fndr. Mankind United
Bellini, Giovanni (3.0)	7 6 1 4 7	(c 1430-1516) Italy
	7 4 2 7	Painter
Bellini, Vincenzo (1.8)	2 2 4 4 3	(1801-1835) Italy
	4 6 6 7	Composer
Bellow, Saul (1.6)	3 4 3 6 3	(1915-2005) Canada
(Solomon Belov)	6 7 6 7	Novelist
Benenson, Peter (1.4)	6 3 4 6 3	(1921-2005) UK
	6 7 6 7	Fndr. Amnesty Intl.

Ben-Gurion, David (1.7)	3 1 1 6 3	(1886-1973) Poland/Israel
	6 6 4 7	Statesman
Benes, Eduard (2.0)	1 6 3 2 1	(1884-1948) Czechoslovakia
	6 6 4 7	Statesman
Bentov, Itzak (1.6)	4 4 3 4 3	(1923-1979) Czechoslovakia
	6 5 4 3	Scientist/mystic
Benz, Karl Friedrich (1.7)	3 1 5 4 3	(1844-1929) Germany
	7 6 4 7	Engineer
Berg, Alban (2.0)	2 4 7 6 7	(1885-1935) Austria
	4 6 4 7	Composer
Bergman, Ingmar (1.6)	4 6 7 6 7	(1918-2007) Sweden
	4 3 4 7	Stage and film director
Bergson, Henri (1.75)	3 1 3 2 3	(1859-1941) France
	1 6 4 7	Philosopher
Berkeley, Lennox (1.55)	2 4 6 2 3	(1903-1989) UK
	4 4 6 3	Composer
Berlin, Isaiah (1.5)	3 4 6 2 3	(1909-1997) UK
	5 1 6 7	Philosopher
Berlioz, Hector (2.3)	4 4 4 4 6 3	(1803-1869) France
	1 4 6 7	Composer
Bernhard (1.3)	3 4 3 4 7	(1911-2004) Germany
	6 7 6 3	Prince consort, the Netherlands
Bernhardt, Oskar Ernst (2.0)	4 7 6 6 3	(1875-1941) Germany
(Abd-ru-shin)	5 2 4 7	Writer
Bernhardt, Sarah (1.65)	2 4 4 6 3	(1844-1923) France
	4 6 2 7	Actress
Bernstein, Elmer (1.25)	4 4 6 4 7	(1922-2004) USA
	4 6 6 3	Composer of film music
Bernstein, Leonard (1.6)	4 4 6 2 3	(1918-1990) USA
	4 4 6 7	Conductor/composer
Besant, Annie (2.15)	7 1 4 6 7	(1847-1933) UK
	7 4 6 7	Theosophist
Bettelheim, Bruno (1.5)	6 4 4 6 7	(1903-1990) Austria/USA
	6 5 6 7	Psychologist
Beuys, Joseph (1.4)	2 4 3 4 7	(1921-1986) Germany
	6 7 6 3	Artist
Bhrikuti, The Green Tara (1.4)	2 4 2 4 3	(640-678) Nepal/Tibet
	6 6 6 3	Nepalese princess
Bhutto, Benazir (1.6)	1 6 3 6 7	(1953-2007) Pakistan
	6 7 6 3	Prime Minister
Bhutto, Zulfikar Ali (2.0)	2 4 3 4 3	(1928-1979) Pakistan
	6 7 6 7	Prime Minister
Biko, Steve (1.4)	2 4 6 4 3	(1946-1977) South Africa
	6 6 6 7	Civil rights leader
Bingen, Hildegard von (1.47)	5 6 4 6 3	(1098-1179) Germany
	3 7 4 7	Musician/healer/abbess
Bion, Wilfred (1.76)	2 7 7 6 7	(1897-1979) UK
	4 4 3 3	Psychoanalyst
Bismarck, Otto von (2.0)	1 1 1 6 3	(1815-1898) Germany
	7 7 6 7	Statesman

607

Bizet, Georges (1.6)	4 4 7 6 7	(1838-1875) France
	3 3 6 3	Composer
Bjornson, Bjornstjeme (1.35)	3 4 3 4 3	(1832-1910) Norway
	6 7 6 7	Writer
Blake, William (2.2)	2 4 1 6 3	(1757-1827) UK
	2 6 6 7	Poet/painter
Blavatsky, H P (4.0)	1 2 1 6 3	(1831-1891) Russia
	7 4 6 7	Occultist
Blériot, Louis (1.6)	3 5 7 2 3	(1872-1936) France
	7 7 6 7	Aviator
Bloch, Ernest (1.7)	2 4 6 4 7	(1880-1959) USA
	4 6 4 7	Composer
Bloch, Ernst (1.5)	2 4 3 4 3	(1885-1977) Germany
	6 6 6 7	Philosopher
Bô Yin Râ (1.55)	4 6 6 6 3	(1876-1943) Germany
(J A Schneiderfranken)	6 6 2 7	Writer/painter
Boadicea (Boudicca) (1.6)	4 1 1 6 3	(1st C. AD) Britain
	1 1 6 7	Warrior-queen
Boal, Augusto (1.0)	6 4 3 6 3	(1931-2009) Brazil
	2 7 2 7	Director, writer, politician
Bogarde, Dirk (1.3)	2 4 3 6 7	(1921-1999) UK
	6 7 6 3	Film actor/Writer
Boger, Cyrus Maxwell (1.55)	4 6 4 6 4	(1861-1935) USA
	3 7 2 7	Homoeopath
Bohm, David (1.6)	2 4 7 4 7	(1917-1992) USA
	6 3 6 3	Physicist
Böhm(i)ker, Hubertine D (1.55)	2 6 4 2 3	(18th C.) Germany
	2 6 6 7	Architect
Boleyn, Anne (1.35)	2 4 3 4 3	(1507-1536) England
	6 7 6 7	Wife of King Henry VIII
Bolivar, Simon (1.7)	1 4 3 4 3	(1783-1830) Venezuela
	6 7 2 7	Independence fighter
Bondi, Herman (1.6)	3 6 1 6 3	(1919-2005) Austria
	4 3 6 3	Mathematician/astronomer
Bonninghausen, Clemens v. (1.5)	4 3 3 4 3	(1785-1864) Germany
	7 6 6 7	Homoeopath
Bongo, Omar (0.8)	3, 6 3 6 7	(1936-2009) Gabon
	6 3 2 3	President
Booth, William (1.65)	2 6 6 2 7	(1829-1912) England
	6 7 4 7	Fndr. Salvation Army
Borges, Jorge Luis (1.5)	3 3 4 6 3	(1899-1986) Argentina
	6 7 2 3	Writer/poet
Borgia, Lucrezia (1.6)	1 4 7 2 5	(1480-1519) Italy
	4 6 6 3	Patron of arts
Bos, Sonia (1.4)	3 6 3 6 3	(1946-2009) Netherlands
	2 6 2 7	Mystic/spiritual teacher
Bosch, Hieronymus (1.8)	6 4 7 6 3	(1450-1516) Netherlands
	6 7 6 7	Painter
Bosco, Don Giovanni (1.7)	1 6 1 2 7	(1815-1888) Italy
	6 6 6 7	Preacher

608

Botha, Louis (1.6)	1 3 1 4 1 7 4 2 1	(1862-1919) South Africa Statesman/soldier
Botha, Pieter Willem (0.7)	3 6 3 6 3 6 6 6 7	(1916–2006) South Africa President
Botticelli, Sandro (2.7)	2 6 7 4 7 6 4 6 7	(1445-1510) Italy Painter
Boulanger, Nadia (1.6)	4 4 7 6 7 6 6 6 7	(1887-1979) France Music instructor
Boyle, Robert (2.4)	1 1 3 2 3 6 5 6 7	(1627-1691) Ireland Physicist/chemist
Bradman, Donald (1.4)	2 4 3 4 3 6 7 6 7	(1908-2001) Australia Cricketer
Brahe, Tycho (1.8)	2 1 7 6 3 4 7 6 7	(1546-1601) Denmark Astronomer
Brahma, Prajapita (1.7)	2 4 6 6 4	(1875-1969) India Fndr. Brahma Kumaris
Brahms, Johannes (2.5)	2 4 4 6 3 7 6 2 7	(1833-1897) Germany Composer
Braille, Louis (1.6)	3 6 3 2 3 5 4 6 7	(1809-1852) France Teacher of the blind
Brancusi, Constantin (1.87)	4 6 7 6 4 6 4 6 7	(1876-1957) Romania Sculptor
Brando, Marlon (1.25)	6 4 6 6 7 6 3 2 3	(1924-2004) USA Film actor
Brandt, Willy (2.97)	2 1 5 2 1 4 7 4 3	(1913-1992) Germany Politician
Brasher, Chris (1.4)	2 4 6 2 3 2 6 6 7	(1928-2003) UK Athlete
Brassens, Georges (1.35)	3 4 3 4 1 2 7 6 3	(1921-1981) France Poet/singer
Brazza, Pietro S. (1.55)	3 3 4 6 7 7 6 2 7	(1852-1905) Italy Explorer/human rights worker
Brecht, Bertolt (1.6)	1 4 1 6 3 4 7 6 7	(1898-1956) Germany Dramatist
Breton, André (1.7)	3 2 1 2 3 4 4 6 7	(1896-1966) France Poet
Brezhnev, Leonid (2.0)	1 7 6 6 7 7 6 6 3	(1906-1982) Russia Politician
Brittain, Vera (1.5)	2 3 5 6 3 4 6 6 7	(1893-1970) UK Writer/pacifist
Britten, Benjamin (1.8)	2 4 4 6 3 4 4 6 7	(1913-1976) UK Composer
Broglie, Louis César (1.6)	1 3 1 4 3 5 5 6 7	(1875-1960) France Physicist
Bronson, Charles (1.3)	2 4 3 4 7 6 7 6 3	(1922-2003) USA Actor
Brontë, Emily (1.4)	2 4 4 6 3 5 6 2 7	(1818-1848) UK Writer
Brougham, Henry (1.7)	1 1 7 2 3 6 6 6 7	(1778-1868) UK Politician

Brouwenstijn, Gré (1.4)	4 4 6 2 7 4 6 6 3	(1915-1999) Netherlands Opera singer
Bruckner, Anton (2.2)	4 6 4 2 3 4 7 6 7	(1824-1896) Austria Composer
Brueghel, Pieter (1.9)	4 4 1 6 7 4 7 6 7	(c 1520-1569) Belgium Painter
Brunel, Isambard Kingdom (1.7)	2 5 1 6 5 7 4 6 7	(1806-1859) UK Engineer
Bruno, Giordano (2.3)	1 1 7 6 7 4 7 2 7	(1548-1600) Italy Philosopher
Brunton, Paul (1.8)	2 4 6 6 7	(1898-1981) UK Spiritual writer
Büchner, Georg (1.6)	4 1 1 4 7 5 6 6 3	(1813-1837) Germany Poet
Buddha, Gautama	2 2 1 2 7 4 1 6 7	(c 563-483 BC) India Avatar
Buffet, Bernard (1.5)	3 4 3 4 7 6 7 2 3	(1928-1999) France Painter
Buñuel, Luis (1.4)	6 6 6 4 7 4 6 6 3	(1900-1983) Spain Film director
Burbank, Luther (1.6)	2 2 4 6 3	(1849-1926) USA Horticulturalist
Burgess, Anthony (1.57)	2 4 3 6 3 6 6 6 7	(1917-1993) UK Writer
Burns, George (1.4)	2 4 3 4 7 6 7 6 3	(1896-1996) USA Actor/comedian
Buson (1.5)	6 4 6 6 3 7 3 6 7	(1716-1783) Japan Haiku poet/painter
Byrd, William (2.0)	4 6 4 6 7	(1543-1623) England Composer
Cabezón, Antonio de (1.4)	4 4 4 6 7 2 7 6 3	(1510-1566) Spain Composer
Caddy, Eileen (1.4)	2 4 3 2 3 6 7 6 7	(1917-2006) England Co-founder of Findhorn
Caddy, Peter (1.5)	2 4 3 4 3 6 7 6 1	(1917-1994) UK Co-founder of Findhorn
Cade, C Maxwell (1.4)	2 5 3 4 7 2 6 6 3	(1918-1985) UK EEG researcher
Caedmon (0.6)	2 4 3 4 7 2 7 6 3	(d. 680) England Herdsman/poet
Caesar, Julius (1.3)	1 3 1 6 3	(c 100-44 BC) Rome Statesman
Cagliostro, Count (3.2)	1 4 7 6 1	(1743-1795) France Occultist
Calderón, Pedro (1.8)	6 4 1 2 1	(1600-1681) Spain Dramatist
Caligula (1.2)	1 6 6 6 1	(AD 12-41) Rome Emperor
Callaghan, James (1.4)	2 4 3 6 3 2 6 2 7	(1912-2005) UK Prime Minister

Callas, Maria (2.0)	3 1 1 4 3	(1923-1977) Greece
		Singer
Calvin, John (1.8)	6 1 6 6 3	(1509-1564) France
		Theologian
Calvin, Melvin (1.6)	3 2 4 2 3	(1911-1997) USA
	6 7 6 7	Scientist/chemist
Campbell, Joseph (1.6)	2 4 3 4 7	(1904-1987) USA
	6 7 2 3	Philosopher/teacher
Camus, Albert (1.6)	3 4 3 4 3	(1913-1960) Algeria/France
		Writer
Canaletto (G A Canal) (1.6)	6 4 7 6 7	(1697-1768) Italy
	3 4 6 7	Painter
Cankar, Ivan (1.4)	6 4 3 4 3	(1876-1918) Slovenia
	6 7 6 7	Poet/writer
Capablanca, José Raúl (2.0)	2 3 7 2 7	(1888-1942) Cuba
		Chess master
Caravaggio, Michelangelo (2.6)	7 1 4 2 1	(1569-1609) Italy
		Painter
Carey, Howard Ray (1.5)	2 7 6 2 3	(1902-1989) USA
	2 7 6 7	Minister/writer
Caritat, Jean Antoine N. (1.8)	3 6 4 4 7	(1743-1794) France
	3 7 6 7	Scientist/politician/journalist
Carlyle, Thomas (1.7)	6 6 1 2 1	(1795-1881) UK
		Writer
Carnegie, Andrew (1.6)	3 3 6 6 3	(1835-1918) Scotland
	6 4 6 7	Industrialist/philanthropist
Cartland, Dame Barbara (1.2)	2 4 2 6 3	(1901-2000) UK
	4 6 6 3	British romantic novelist
Caruso, Enrico (1.2)	2 4 1 4 3	(1873-1921) Italy
		Singer
Carver, George Washington (1.4)	2 3 3 4 3	(1860-1943) USA
	5 5 6 7	Scientist
Casals, Pablo (2.0)	2 4 7 6 3	(1876-1973) Spain
		Musician
Cash, Johnny (1.2)	2 4 6 6 7	(1932-2003) USA
	4 4 4 3	Country singer
Casson, Hugh (1.6)	2 4 3 4 3	(1910-1999) England
	6 7 6 7	Architect/painter
Castaneda, Carlos (1.5)	6 6 4 6 3	(c 1930-1998) Peru/USA
	2 3 2 3	Anthropologist/writer
Castle, Baroness Barbara (1.5)	2 4 3 6 7	(1910-2002) UK
	2 7 6 3	Politician
Catherine of Alexandria (2.6)	6 6 6 6 7	(d. AD 307) Egypt
		Saint/martyr
Catherine the Great (1.6)	1 6 1 4 1	(1729-1796) Russia
		Empress
Caxton, William (1.6)	2 5 1 6 5	(c 1422-1491) England
		Printer
Cayce, Edgar (1.7)	2 2 4 6 7	(1877-1945) USA
		Clairvoyant

Ceausescu, Nicolae (1.5)	7 6 7 6 7	(1918-1989) Romania
	6 4 6 3	Dictator
Celibidache, Sergiu (1.5)	4 4 4 6 7	(1912-1996) Romania
	4 6 6 3	Conductor
Cervantes, Miguel (1.7)	6 4 3 6 7	(1547-1616) Spain
		Writer
Cézanne, Paul (2.6)	3 4 7 6 3	(1839-1906) France
		Painter
Chagall, Marc (1.9)	2 4 4 6 7	(1887-1985) Russia/France
(Moshe Shagal)	7 2 4 3	Painter
Chaitanya (4.5)	2 4 6 4 7	(1486-1534) India
	2 2 6 3	Hindu saint
Chamberlain, Neville (1.6)	3 7 1 6 7	(1869-1940) UK
		Politician
Chandraji, Shri Ram	2 6 6 2 7	(1873-1931) India
of Fatehgarh (1.75)	3 4 6 7	Sahaj Marg meditation
Chandraji, Shri Ram	6 4 3 4 3	(1899-1983) India
of Shahjahanpur (2.6)	6 7 6 7	Sahaj Marg meditation
Chang, Iris Shun-Ru (1.45)	3 6 6 2 3	(1968-2004) USA
	2 3 4 3	Historian
Chaplin, Charles (1.6)	2 4 1 4 4	(1889-1977) UK
		Film actor/director
Charlemagne (2.2)	1 1 1 6 7	(742-814) France
		Holy Roman Emperor
Charles, Ray (1.3)	2 4 6 2 7	(1930-2004) USA
	3 6 6 3	Singer
Charles III of Spain (1.5)	4 6 3 4 7	(1716-1788) Spain
	6 7 6 3	King
Chateaubriand, (1.6)	3 6 1 4 7	(1768-1848) France
François-René de		Writer/politician
Chatwin, Bruce (1.4)	2 4 4 6 7	(1942-1989) England
	6 7 2 3	Writer
Chaucer, Geoffrey (1.6)	2 4 6 2 3	(1342-1400) England
		Poet
Chavez, Cesar (1.5)	2 6 7 2 7	(1927-1993) USA
	3 3 4 3	Labour leader
Chekhov, Anton (1.8)	2 4 2 4 3	(1860-1904) Russia
	3 5 6 7	Writer
Cheong, Ong Teng (1.55)	3 6 4 2 7	(1936-2002) Singapore
	3 6 6 3	President
Cherenzi Lind, Om (2.4)	2 4 6 6 7	(d. mid-20th C.) Cuba
	2 4 6 7	Prince/disciple of KH
Chih-i (2.0)	6 6 7 4 3	(538-597) China
(Zhiyi Chen)	7 4 6 2	Fndr. Buddhism/T'ien-t'ai
Chinmoy, Sri Kumar Ghose (4.0)	2 4 1 6 3	(1931-2007) India
	6 7 2 7	Spiritual teacher
Chirico, Giorgio de (1.6)	4 4 1 6 7	(1888-1978) Greece/Italy
	4 6 6 7	Painter
Chisholm, Shirley (1.4)	2 6 3 2 3	(1924-2005) USA
	4 7 6 7	1st African-Am. Congresswoman

Chopin, Frédéric (2.0)	4 4 1 6 2	(1810-1849) Poland
		Composer
Chou En-lai (2.3)	1 3 1 4 3	(1898-1976) China
(Zhou Enlai)		Politician
Christina (1.5)	2 6 6 4 7	(1626-1689) Sweden
		Queen of Sweden
Christodoulos, Archbishop (1.7)	6 6 6 2 7	(1939-2008) Greece
(Christos Paraskevaidis)	2 3 6 3	Archbishop
Churchill, Clementine (1.5)	2 4 5 4 7	(1885-1977) UK
	6 7 6 3	Wife of Winston Churchill
Churchill, Winston (3.0)	2 1 1 4 1	(1874-1965) UK
	4 6 6 3	Statesman
Cicero, Marcus Tullius (1.7)	3 3 1 4 5	(106-43 BC) Rome
		Orator/statesman
Cimabue, Giovanni (2.35)	6 6 4 6 7	(1240-1302) Italy
	6 4 2 7	Painter
Clark, Alan (1.4)	3 4 7 4 7	(1928-1999) England
	4 3 4 3	Politician/Historian
Clarke, Arthur C (1.6)	2 4 3 4 3	(1917-2008) England
	6 7 6 7	Novelist
Claudel, Camille (1.4)	5 6 4 6 7	(1864-1943) France
	7 3 6 7	Sculptor
Clemenceau, Georges (1.6)	3 1 1 6 7	(1841-1929) France
		Statesman
Cleopatra (1.4)	3 4 3 4 3	(69-30 BC) Egypt
	6 7 6 7	Queen
Clerk Maxwell, James (1.7)	2 1 1 2 5	(1831-1879) Scotland
		Physicist
Clough, Prunella (1.6)	2 4 5 6 7	(1919-1999) UK
	3 7 2 3	Painter
Clymer, Emerson (1.5)	2 7 3 4 3	(1911-1983) USA
	4 6 6 7	Grand Master, Rosae Crucis
Clymer, R Swinburn (1.5)	2 4 3 4 3	(1878-1966) USA
	6 7 6 7	Grand Master, Rosae Crucis
Cockerell, Christopher (1.3)	2 3 4 2 3	(1910-1999) England
	7 6 6 5	Inventor of the hovercraft
Cocteau, Jean (1.7)	3 4 4 2 3	(1889-1963) France
		Poet/playwright/film-maker
Coleridge, Samuel Taylor (1.4)	2 4 3 4 3	(1772-1834) England
	2 6 6 7	Poet
Coll, Francisco (1.3)	2 6 6 6 3	(1926-2000) Puerto Rico
	2 2 2 7	Fndr. Inner Peace Movement
Columbus, Christopher (2.0)	6 6 1 2 3	(1451-1506) Italy
		Explorer
Comte, Auguste (1.7)	3 4 1 6 3	(1798-1857) France
		Philosopher
Confucius (5.0)	3 7 2 6 1	(551-479 BC) China
		Philosopher
Conrad, Joseph (1.75)	4 4 6 6 7	(1857-1924) Poland
	7 4 6 7	Writer

613

Constantine I (the Great) (1.8)	1 6 6 2 7	(c 274-337) Rome
		Emperor
Cook, James (1.7)	3 7 1 6 7	(1728-1779) England
		Explorer
Cook, Robin (1.5)	3 4 7 4 7	(1946-2005) UK
	6 3 4 3	Foreign Minister
Cooke, Alistair (1.5)	2 4 4 2 3	(1908-2004) UK
	2 6 6 7	Journalist
Cookson, Catherine (1.3)	2 6 3 4 3	(1906-2003) England
	3 6 6 7	Novelist
Copernicus, Nicolas (2.3)	2 3 5 2 3	(1473-1543) Poland
		Astronomer
Coram, Thomas (1.45)	2 6 4 6 3	(1668-1751) England
	2 7 2 7	Founder Foundling Hospital
Corneille, Pierre (1.7)	3 2 1 6 3	(1606-1684) France
		Dramatist
Corot, Jean Baptiste (1.8)	3 2 4 6 7	(1796-1875) France
		Painter
Cortés, Hernando (1.7)	6 1 7 6 7	(1485-1547) Spain
		Explorer
Cortot, Alfred (1.6)	4 2 4 2 3	(1877-1962) France
		Musician
Coulson, Robert (1.4)	2 3 4 4 3	(d. 1995) USA
	7 6 6 7	Fndr, F'ship of Contempl. Prayer
Couperin, François (2.3)	4 4 4 6 7	(1668-1733) France
		Composer
Courbet, Gustave (2.0)	3 4 5 6 7	(1819-1877) France
	1 7 6 1	Painter/Realist movement
Cousteau, Jacques (1.56)	3 4 3 4 3	(1910-1997) France
	6 7 6 7	Oceanographer
Coverdale, Miles (1.6)	6 6 7 6 3	(1488-1568) England
		Biblical scholar
Coward, Noel (1.3)	2 4 3 4 3	(1899-1973) UK
		Actor/dramatist
Cramp, Leonard George (1.45)	2 4 3 4 7	(1919-2006) UK
	6 7 6 3	Aerospace engineer/writer
Cromwell, Oliver (2.1)	1 1 6 6 3	(1599-1658) England
		Statesman
Cronkite, Walter (1.3)	3 4 3 6 3	(1916-2009) USA
	6 3 6 7	Broadcast journalist
Crosby, Harry (Bing) (1.4)	2 4 6 6 7	(1904-1977) USA
	4 3 6 7	Singer/actor
Crowley, Aleister (1.6)	6 1 7 6 1	(1875-1947) UK
		Occultist
Cullenberg, Birgit (1.5)	3 4 3 4 7	(1908-1999) Sweden
	3 6 6 3	Dancer/choreographer
Cummings, Edward Estlin (1.35)	6 4 4 6 7	(1894-1962) USA
	3 5 2 7	Poet
Curie, Marie (2.0)	3 3 5 4 7	(1867-1934) Poland
		Physicist/chemist

Curuvija, Slavko (1.6)	6 6 6 6 7 6 4 6 7	(1949-1999) Serbia Newspaper editor
Dae-jung, Kim (0.9)	6 6 3 6 3 6 6 6 3	(1925-2009) South Korean President
Dahl, Johan Christian (1.45)	4 4 3 4 3 6 7 6 7	(1788-1857) Norway Painter
D'Aubuisson, Roberto (1.6)	1 1 6 6 7 6 4 6 3	(1944-1992) El Salvador Politician
Daimler, Gottlieb (1.6)	3 5 1 4 3	(1834-1900) Germany Engineer
Dali, Salvador (1.6)	6 4 6 4 7 4 6 4 7	(1904-1989) Spain Painter
Dalton, John (2.0)	2 5 5 4 3	(1766-1844) England Chemist
Dando, Jill (1.3)	2 4 6 4 3 3 2 6 7	(1961-1999) UK Journalist/broadcaster
Daniel (2.0)	6 6 3 4 3 6 3 6 3	(c 600 BC) Palestine Old Testament prophet
Dante (2.0) (Durante degli Alighieri)	1 4 1 6 7	(1265-1321) Italy Poet
Danton, Georges Jacques (1.7)	3 4 1 6 3	(1759-1794) France Politician
Darius the Great (1.6)	1 1 6 4 7	(548-486 BC) Persia King
Darwin, Charles (2.0)	2 7 5 2 5	(1809-1882) UK Scientist
David (1.7)	6 1 1 6 7	(1090-1059 BC) Israel King
David-Neel, Alexandra (1.7)	4 6 6 4 7 4 6 2 7	(1868-1969) France Mystic/writer
De La Warr, George (1.46)	2 3 4 2 3 5 7 4 7	(1905-1969) UK Radionics researcher
Dearmer, Geoffrey (1.4)	2 4 3 4 7 6 7 6 3	(1893-1996) UK Poet
Debruyne, Bertrand (1.5)	4 3 4 6 3 7 6 2 7	(1600-1700) Belgium Clergyman/scientist
Debussy, Claude (1.7)	3 4 4 6 3	(1862-1918) France Composer
Degas, Edgar (1.75)	3 4 3 4 7 6 7 6 7	(1834-1917) France Painter
Deguchi Nao (1.7)	3 6 6 4 7 4 6 2 7	(1837-1918) Japan Fndr. Omotokyo
Deguchi, Wanisaburo (1.7)	3 6 1 6 7 6 6 6 3	(1871-1948) Japan Omotokyo spiritual teacher
Dekker, Eduard Douwes (1.4) (pen-name Multatuli)	2 3 6 6 7 3 4 2 5	(1820-1887) Netherlands Writer/poet
Delacroix, Eugène (2.3)	3 4 1 4 7 4 7 6 7	(1798-1863) France Painter
Delectorskaya, Lydia (1.6)	6 6 5 2 7 2 7 4 3	(1910-1998) Russia Assistant to Henri Matisse

Demosthenes (1.7)	6 1 3 6 1	(383-322 BC) Greece
		Orator/politician
Denning, Alfred (1.45)	3 4 3 4 7	(1899-1999) England
	6 7 6 3	Judge
Descartes, René (2.3)	5 5 1 4 3	(1596-1650) France
		Philosopher/mathematician
Devi, Phoolan (1.65)	2 4 6 6 3	(1963-2001) India
	6 1 6 7	MP/former 'Bandit Queen'
Dewar, Donald (1.7)	2 6 3 2 7	(1937-2000) UK
	2 7 6 7	Politician
Dewey, John (1.65)	2 6 5 2 3	(1859-1952) USA
	2 6 6 3	Educational reformer
Diaghilev, Sergei (1.6)	4 4 1 6 3	(1872-1929) Russia
		Impresario
Diana (1.5)	2 4 2 6 7	(1961-1997) UK
	6 6 6 3	Princess of Wales
Dick, Philip K (1.6)	2 4 4 6 7	(1928-1982) USA
	6 7 6 4	Writer
Dick-Read, Grantly (1.6)	2 6 4 2 3	(1890-1959) England
		Gynaecologist
Dickens, Charles (1.9)	2 4 2 4 3	(1812-1870) UK
		Writer
Dickinson, Emily (1.8)	2 6 6 4 7	(1830-1886) USA
		Poet
Diderot, Denis (1.7)	3 6 4 2 3	(1713-1784) France
		Writer
Diesel, Rudolf (1.6)	6 7 1 4 5	(1858-1913) Germany
		Engineer
Diogenes (1.6)	1 6 1 4 7	(412-323 BC) Greece
		Philosopher
Disraeli, Benjamin (1.7)	2 3 1 4 7	(1804-1881) UK
		Statesman
Dogen (1.5)	6 1 6 4 7	(1200-1253) Japan
	7 3 2 4	Zen/Soto sect
Doko, Toshio (1.5)	3 3 6 2 3	(1896-1988) Japan
	6 2 6 7	Engineer/philanthropist
Dolto, Francoise (1.58)	5 3 6 6 7	(1908-1988) France
	6 4 2 3	Psychoanalyst
Dönhoff, Countess Marion (1.5)	3 6 6 4 7	(1909-2002) Germany
	2 3 2 7	Journalist
Donizetti, Gaetano (1.8)	4 4 4 2 7	(1797-1848) Italy
		Composer
Donne, John (1.8)	2 4 7 4 3	(1572-1631) England
		Poet
Dostoevsky, Fyodor (2.0)	6 7 4 6 3	(1821-1881) Russia
		Writer
Douglas, Tommy (1.5)	2 2 3 6 3	(1904-1986) Canada
	5 7 6 7	Politician/fndr. Medicare
Douglass, Frederick (1.4)	2 4 3 2 7	(1817-1895) USA
	6 7 6 7	Reformer

Dowland, John (1.5)	2 4 3 4 3 6 7 6 3	(1563-1626) England Musician/composer
Doyle, Arthur Conan (1.7)	2 6 4 6 1	(1859-1930) UK Writer
Drake, Francis (1.7)	1 4 1 6 1	(c 1540-1596) England Admiral
Drees, Willem (1.6)	7 6 7 4 7 4 6 6 7	(1886-1988) Netherlands Politician
Driesch, Hans (1.7)	3 3 7 6 3	(1867-1941) Germany Scientist
Drnovšek, Janez (2.0)	3 5 7 4 7 6 3 6 3	(1950-2008) Slovenia President
Dunant, Henri (1.8)	3 6 1 4 3	(1828-1910) Switzerland Philanthropist/writer
Dunnewolt, Hendrik W (1.6)	3 4 4 6 7 6 6 4 5	(1904-1968) Netherlands Writer/theosophist
Dunstan, Don (1.4)	2 5 3 6 7 6 3 2 7	(1926-1999) Australia Premier of South Australia
Durant, Will (1.4)	2 4 2 6 3 6 6 2 7	(1885-1981) USA Writer
du Pré, Jacqueline (1.5)	2 4 4 6 2 2 6 2 4	(1945-1987) UK Cellist
Dürer, Albrecht (2.4)	1 7 7 4 1 4 4 6 7	(1471-1528) Germany Painter
Durkheim, Emile (1.5)	3 4 6 6 7 7 2 2 3	(1858-1917) France Sociologist
Durrell, Gerald (1.46)	2 4 3 6 3 6 7 4 7	(1925-1995) UK Writer/naturalist
Dvorak, Antonin (2.1)	2 4 7 2 3	(1841-1904) Czechoslovakia Composer
Dyck, Anthony van (2.0)	4 4 7 6 7	(1599-1641) Belgium Painter
Easwaran, Eknath (1.5)	2 2 4 6 3 6 6 6 7	(1911-1999) India Meditation teacher
Eckhart, Meister (2.2)	6 6 1 6 3	(c 1260-1327) Germany Mystic/philosopher
Eddy, Mary Baker (2.0)	2 6 1 6 3	(1821-1910) USA Fndr. Christian Science
Edison, Thomas (1.7)	3 1 1 2 5	(1847-1931) USA Inventor
Edward VIII (1.3)	2 4 3 4 7 6 7 6 3	(1894-1972) UK King
Eeden, Frederik van (1.6)	3 3 1 4 7	(1860-1932) Netherlands Writer
Ehret, Arnold (1.55)	2 6 2 4 7 7 6 6 3	(1866-1922) Germany Writer
Einstein, Albert (2.2)	2 2 4 2 3	(1879-1955) Germany Physicist
Eisai (2.2)	7 4 6 6 7 7 4 6 3	(1141-1215) Japan Zen/Rinzai sect

617

Eisenhower, Dwight (1.5)	3 1 1 2 3	(1890-1969) USA General/president
Elgar, Edward (1.8)	2 4 4 4 3 6 6 2 7	(1857-1934) UK Composer
El Greco (3.0) (Domenikos Theotokopoulos)	1 4 7 6 1 6 7 6 7	(1541-1614) Crete Painter
Elijah (2.5)	2 1 1 6 1	(fl. c 900 BC) Israel Prophet
Eliot, George (1.6)	2 4 1 6 3	(1819-1880) UK Writer
Eliot, T S (2.0)	2 3 1 6 7	(1888-1965) USA/UK Poet
Elizabeth (1.3) (Elizabeth Bowes-Lyon)	2 4 3 6 3 2 7 6 7	(1900 -2002) UK Queen/Queen Mother
Elizabeth I (1.6)	2 3 1 6 7	(1533-1603) England Queen
Ellington, Duke (0.6)	6 7 4 6 7 4 6 4 7	(1899-1974) USA Jazz musician
Emerson, Ralph Waldo (2.2)	2 3 7 6 3	(1803-1882) USA Poet
Engels, Friedrich (1.7)	3 4 7 2 7	(1820-1895) Germany Political philosopher
Enwonwu, Benedict Chuka (1.6)	2 4 3 4 3 4 6 6 7	(1921-1994) Nigeria Sculptor
Epicurus (1.6)	6 4 6 4 3	(c 341-270 BC) Greece Philosopher
Equiano, Olaudah (1.3)	2 5 6 4 3 2 3 6 7	(1750-1797) Nigeria Anti-slavery activist
Erasmus, Desiderius (2.2)	2 2 1 6 3 3 6 2 7	(1466-1536) Netherlands Humanist/scholar
Euclid (2.3)	3 5 3 6 7	(fl. 300 BC) Greece Mathematician
Euripides (1.8)	3 4 1 6 3	(c 480-406 BC) Greece Dramatist
Euwe, Max (2.0)	1 5 3 6 7	(1901-1983) Netherlands Chess master
Ewbank, Inga-Stina (1.56)	2 5 5 6 3 3 3 6 7	(1932-2004) Sweden Teacher/academic
Ezra (2.0)	2 6 5 6 7 2 3 4 5	(5th century BC) Palestine Prophet
Farquhar, George (1.8)	6 4 1 6 7	(1678-1707) Ireland Dramatist
Faulkner, William (1.7)	2 4 2 4 7 6 7 6 7	(1897-1962) USA Novelist/poet
Fauré, Gabriel (1.6)	4 4 3 4 7 6 6 4 3	(1845-1924) France Composer
Fellini, Federico (1.6)	4 4 1 4 1 4 6 4 3	(1920-1993) Italy Film director
Ferdinand II of Aragon (1.7)	3 7 7 6 7	(1452-1516) Spain King

Ferrer, Vicente (1.55)	2 3 2 6 3 7 6 2 3	(1920-2009) Spain Humanist
Ferrier, Kathleen (1.5)	4 4 4 2 7 6 6 4 3	(1912-1953) UK Opera singer
Feuerbach, Anselm (1.5)	2 4 3 4 3 6 7 6 7	(1829-1880) Germany Painter
Feuerbach, Henriette (1.3) (Mother-in-law Anselm F.)	2 6 6 6 3 2 3 6 3	(1812-1892) Germany Publisher
Feuiger, Siegmund (1.5) (Nyanaponika)	3 4 3 2 3 6 6 6 7	(1901-1994) Germany/Sri Lanka Buddhist scholar
Feydeau, Georges (1.7)	4 2 7 2 3	(1862-1921) France Dramatist
Feynman, Richard (1.6)	6 7 4 6 7 3 6 4 3	(1918-1988) USA Physicist
Fichte, Johann Gottlieb (1.7)	2 6 7 6 3	(1762-1814) Germany Philosopher
Firth, Sir Raymond (1.5)	2 4 7 2 7 6 3 6 3	(1901-2002) UK Anthropologist
Fischer, Robert (Bobby) (1.2)	6 3 4 4 3 6 7 6 7	(1943-2008) USA Chess player
Flagstad, Kirsten (1.4)	6 4 4 6 7 4 6 6 5	(1895-1962) Norway Opera singer
Fleming, Alexander (2.0)	2 5 5 2 3	(1881-1955) UK Bacteriologist
Foot, Paul (1.4)	2 4 6 2 7 6 6 6 3	(1938-2004) UK Journalist
Ford, Henry (1.7)	5 7 7 6 3	(1863-1947) USA Engineer
Fortuyn, Pim (0.75)	3 4 1 4 7 4 7 6 7	(1948-2002) Netherlands Sociologist/politician
Foulds, John (1.4)	2 4 4 6 3 6 2 6 7	(1880-1939) UK Composer
Fox, Emmet (1.6)	2 4 3 4 3 6 7 6 7	(1886-1951) USA Scientist/philosopher
Fox, George (1.4)	6 6 6 2 3 6 6 6 7	(1624-1691) England Fndr. Quakerism
Francesca, Piero della (2.7)	7 4 6 6 7 7 6 4 3	(1420-1492) Italy Painter
Francis of Assisi (3.5)	6 6 6 2 3	(1182-1226) Italy Saint
Franco, Francisco (1.7)	1 1 1 6 7	(1892-1975) Spain Dictator/general
Franklin, Benjamin (2.5)	4 5 1 6 3	(1706-1790) USA Statesman/scientist
Frederick II (the Great) (1.7)	5 7 7 2 7	(1712-1786) Germany King
Freud, Anna (1.6)	1 6 1 6 1 6 6 6 7	(1895-1982) Austria Psychoanalyst
Freud, Sigmund (2.0)	2 7 1 6 3 2 5 6 7	(1856-1939) Austria Psychoanalyst

Frink, Elizabeth (1.55)	2 4 3 4 7 6 7 6 7	(1930-1993) UK Sculptor
Frisch, Ragnar A K (0.9)	3 3 6 4 7 4 7 6 7	(1895-1945) Norway Social economist
Froebel, Friedrich (1.6)	2 5 1 4 3	(1782-1852) Germany Educator
Fromm, Erich (1.6)	6 2 4 6 7 4 6 6 3	(1900-1980) USA Psychoanalyst
Fujii, Nittatsu (1.8)	2 4 6 6 7 6 6 2 3	(1885-1985) Japan Buddhism/Nichiren sect
Fuller, Buckminster (2.0)	2 1 7 4 7	(1895-1983) USA Architect/engineer
Galbraith, John Kenneth (1.8)	2 4 3 2 7 7 7 6 3	(1908-2006) Canada Economist/writer
Galdós, Benito Pérez (1.4)	4 4 7 4 3 6 3 6 7	(1843-1920) Spain Writer
Gale, Ernest Frederik (1.5)	2 6 4 6 7 2 6 2 3	(1914-2005) UK Microbiologist
Galilei, Galileo (2.2)	1 4 1 6 5	(1564-1642) Italy Astronomer
Galtieri, Leopoldo (1.25)	6 6 6 6 7 1 1 6 1	(1926-2003) Argentina Soldier/president
Gambetta, Léon Michel (1.6)	3 1 1 4 1	(1838-1882) France Statesman
Gandhi, Indira (2.0)	1 1 7 6 3 1 1 6 3	(1917-1984) India Prime Minister
Gandhi, Mahatma (2.0) (Mohandas K. Gandhi)	2 2 6 2 3 6 6 2 7	(1869-1948) India Political/spiritual leader
Ganj, Baba Farid Shakar (3.0)	4 6 4 6 7 6 2 4 3	(11th century) Pakistan Sufi
Garbo, Greta (1.65)	6 7 7 4 7 4 2 6 3	(1905-1990) Sweden Film actress
Garcia, Jerry (1.2)	3 4 4 6 7 3 6 2 3	(1942-1995) USA Rock musician
Garibaldi, Giuseppe (2.0)	1 4 7 6 3	(1807-1882) Italy Revolutionary
Gaskell, Elizabeth (2.0)	2 2 1 4 6	(1810-1865) UK Writer
Gasset, Jose Ortega y (1.4)	3 6 4 2 7 3 7 6 7	(1883-1955) Spain Philosopher
Gaudí, Antonio (1.5)	4 4 3 6 7 6 7 4 3	(1852-1926) Spain Architect
Gauguin, Paul (2.0)	5 4 1 6 7	(1848-1903) France Painter
Gaulle, Charles de (2.4)	3 1 1 4 1	(1890-1970) France General/statesman
Gauss, Johann Karl F (1.7)	3 4 1 6 3	(1777-1855) Germany Mathematician
Gear, William (1.45)	2 4 7 6 3 3 3 2 7	(1915-1997) UK Painter

Genghis Khan (1.5)	1 7 6 6 1	(1167-1227) Mongolia Conqueror/ruler
Gennes, Pierre-Gilles de (1.5)	2 5 3 4 3 3 7 6 7	(1932-2007) France Physicist
George VI (1.6)	2 4 6 6 7 2 2 4 3	(1895- 1952) UK King
George, Henry (1.7)	3 7 4 2 1 5 6 4 7	(1839-1897) USA Political economist
Gershwin, George (1.6)	2 4 3 6 3	(1898-1937) USA Composer
Giacometti, Alberto (1.6)	4 4 2 6 7 6 6 2 3	(1901-1966) Switzerland Sculptor
Gibbon, Edward (1.6)	2 4 1 2 7	(1737-1794) England Historian
Gielgud, Arthur John (1.5)	2 4 3 4 7 4 7 6 3	(1904-2000) UK British actor
Gilruth, Robert (1.4)	6 3 6 4 7 7 3 6 7	(1914-2000) USA Rocket engineer
Ginsberg, Alan (1.3)	4 4 6 6 3 4 6 6 7	(1926-1997) USA Poet
Giorgione (2.3)	4 4 7 6 2	(c 1478-1511) Italy Painter
Giotto di Bondone (2.4)	6 4 6 2 7 4 6 4 7	(1267-1337) Italy Painter/architect
Giraudoux, Jean (1.7)	2 4 1 6 3	(1882-1944) France Writer/diplomat
Gladstone, William (1.7)	2 6 1 6 3	(1808-1898) UK Statesman
Gluck, Christoph W (1.8)	2 4 4 4 3	(1714-1787) Austria Composer
Gödel, Kurt (2.0)	3 4 5 4 7 6 1 6 3	(1906-1978) Austria Logician
Goel, B S (1.7) (Guruji)	2 3 4 6 3 6 7 2 7	(1935-1998) India Writer/philosopher
Goethe, Johann von (2.2)	2 1 4 4 7	(1749-1832) Germany Poet/writer
Gogh, Vincent van (1.9)	2 6 1 4 7	(1853-1890) Netherlands Painter
Gogol, Nikolai (1.7)	2 4 1 6 7	(1809-1852) Russia Dramatist
Goi, Masahisa (2.1)	4 4 6 6 7 6 3 2 7	(1916-1980) Japan Spiritual teacher, Byakkokai
Goldoni, Carlo (1.7)	2 2 4 6 7	(1707-1793) Italy Dramatist
Goldsmith, Jerry (1.3)	2 4 3 4 3 6 7 6 7	(1929-2004) USA Composer of film music
Goldsmith, Joel (1.6)	2 6 6 6 3 2 6 2 7	(1892-1964) USA Writer/spiritual teacher
Goldsmith, Oliver (1.7)	6 2 6 6 3	(1728-1774) Ireland Writer

Goldszmit, Henryk (2.0)	2 6 3 4 7	(1878-1942) Poland
	4 7 6 3	Writer/educational reformer
Goodwin, Richard (1.47)	2 4 3 4 7	(1913-1996) UK
	6 7 6 3	Economist
Gorbachev, Raisa (1.5)	2 6 4 6 3	(1932-1999) Russia
	3 6 2 3	Academic/sociologist
Gordon, Charles George (1.6)	1 6 1 2 1	(1833-1885) UK
		General
Gould, Glenn (1.6)	2 4 7 6 7	(1932-1982) Canada
	6 3 6 3	Pianist
Gould, Jay (1.55)	2 6 4 2 3	(1941-2002) USA
	2 7 6 3	Palaeontologist
Goya, Francisco José de (2.4)	1 4 1 4 1	(1746-1828) Spain
		Painter
Graham, Katherine (1.5)	2 4 6 4 3	(1917-2001) USA
	3 3 6 7	Publisher
Graham, Martha (1.47)	4 6 3 6 7	(1894-1991) USA
	4 7 6 7	Dancer
Granger, Stewart (1.6)	2 4 1 4 7	(1913-1993) UK
	4 6 6 7	Actor
Grant, James (1.5)	2 4 3 4 7	(1922-1995) USA
	6 7 6 3	UNICEF director
Grapelli, Stéphane (1.2)	2 4 3 4 3	(1908-1997) France
	6 7 6 7	Jazz violinist
Graves, Robert (1.5)	2 4 3 4 7	(1895-1985) England
	6 7 6 3	Poet
Greene, Graham (1.5)	3 4 7 6 3	(1904-1991) UK
	6 6 6 7	Writer
Gregory I (2.0)	1 6 1 6 7	(c 540-604) Rome
		Pope
Gregory, John (1.3)	3 4 4 6 7	(1914-1996) UK
	4 6 2 7	Ballet director/actor/writer
Grieg, Edvard (1.7)	2 4 2 6 3	(1843-1907) Norway
		Composer
Grillparzer, Franz (1.6)	4 4 7 6 7	(1791-1872) Austria
		Poet
Grimond, Jo (1.6)	2 4 3 6 7	(1913-1993) UK
	6 7 4 3	Liberal Party leader
Gröning, Bruno (1.5)	2 6 6 4 3	(1906-1959) Germany
	2 2 2 7	Healer
Gropius, Walter (1.68)	2 4 4 6 7	(1883-1969) Germany
	7 3 2 3	Architect
Grotius, Hugo (2.0)	1 3 1 2 3	(1583-1645) Netherlands
		Jurist/theologian
Grünewald, Mathias (2.6)	4 6 6 4 7	(1470-1528) Germany
	4 1 6 7	Painter
Guevara, Ernesto (Che) (1.7)	7 1 1 2 3	(1928-1967) Argentina
		Revolutionary leader
Guinness, Sir Alec (1.4)	2 4 4 2 3	(1914-2000) UK
	2 6 6 7	Actor

Gurdjieff, Georges I (2.2)	4 4 1 6 3	(1872-1949) Russia
		Occultist/teacher
Gyatso, Thubten (2.3)	6 3 2 2 7	(1876-1933) Tibet
	6 4 6 3	13th Dalai Lama
Gyohki, Boddhisattva (2.0)	6 6 6 6 3	(668-749) Japan
	2 4 6 7	Buddhist priest
Haakon VII (1.3)	6 3 7 6 3	(1872-1957) Norway
	7 3 2 7	King
Habash, George (1.65)	6 6 4 6 3	(1926-2008) Palestine
	3 7 2 7	Political leader/fndr. PFLP
Hacquet, Baltasar (1.6)	3 4 3 6 3	(1739-1815) France
	1 5 6 7	Traveller/scientist/physician
Haffner, Sebastian (1.3)	3 6 4 6 3	(1907-1998) Germany
	3 7 6 7	Journalist/historian
Hafiz (1.5)	6 4 6 6 7	(1320-1389) Persia
	2 3 2 7	Poet/Sufi master
Hahn, Kurt (1.6)	4 6 4 6 3	(1886-1974) Germany
	3 6 6 7	Educator
Hahnemann, Samuel (1.75)	2 6 7 4 7	(1755-1843) Germany
	4 6 6 3	Fndr. modern homoeopathy
Haig, Justin Moreward (2.4)	2 6 4 2 3	(19th-20th cent.) UK
(concealed identity)	2 6 6 7	Cyril Scott's "The Initiate"
Hall, Manly Palmer (1.6)	2 2 6 2 7	(1901-1990) Canada/USA
	6 6 6 7	Philosopher
Hallinan, Hazel Hunkins (2.0)	3 4 1 6 7	(1890-1982) USA
		Suffragette
Hallowes, Odette (1.4)	1 1 3 6 3	(1912-1995) France
	4 7 2 7	Resistance worker/war heroine
Hals, Frans (2.3)	3 4 1 4 3	(c 1580-1666) Netherlands
		Painter
Hamer, Fannie Lou (1.5)	2 4 3 2 3	(1917-1977) USA
	6 6 6 7	Civil rights activist
Hammarskjöld, Dag (2.0)	2 6 1 6 3	(1905-1961) Sweden
		Diplomat
Hamstra, Rinze (1.6)	2 4 3 4 3	(1895-1974) Netherlands
	4 7 6 7	Painter
Hamsum, Knut (1.5)	3 4 6 6 3	(1859-1952) Norway
	2 3 6 7	Writer
Händel, Georg Friedrich (2.5)	4 6 1 4 7	(1685-1759) Germany
		Composer
Hannibal (1.7)	1 1 6 6 3	(247-182 BC) Carthage
		Soldier
Hansen, Lucile Taylor (1.65)	4 6 4 2 3	(1897-1976) USA
	2 7 6 7	Archaeologist/writer
Haq, Mahbub ul (2.0)	4 3 6 4 7	(1915-1993) Pakistan
	4 3 6 3	Politician
Hardie, James Keir (1.7)	2 6 1 2 3	(1856-1915) UK
		Politician
Hariharananda, Swami (1.8)	2 3 2 2 3	(1908-2002) India
	6 4 6 3	Yogi /Spiritual teacher

Haring, Keith (1.4)	2 4 6 4 3 6 3 6 7	(1958-1990) USA Painter
Hariri, Rafik al (1.3)	3 4 3 2 7 6 6 6 7	(1944-2005) Lebanon Prime Minister
Harris, Richard (1.4)	2 4 3 4 7 6 7 6 3	(1930-2002) Ireland Actor
Harrison, George (0.9)	2 4 2 2 7 6 6 4 3	(1943-2001) England Musician
Harrison, John (1.4)	2 3 5 6 7 5 7 2 3	(1693-1776) England Inventor of the chronometer
Harrison, Rex (1.35)	2 4 4 6 7 4 3 6 3	(1908-1990) UK Actor
Haskill, Clara (1.4)	4 4 3 6 7 6 7 2 3	(1895-1960) Switzerland Pianist
Hauptmann, Gerhart (1.6)	2 4 3 6 7	(1862-1946) Germany Dramatist
Haydn, Franz Joseph (2.4)	3 4 4 2 7	(1732-1809) Austria Composer
Hazlitt, William (1.3)	3 4 4 6 7 6 2 6 3	(1778-1830) UK Novelist
Heath, Edward (2.0)	2 3 5 2 3 4 1 6 7	(1916-2005) UK Prime Minister
Hebbel, Friedrich (1.5)	2 4 1 4 7	(1813-1863) Germany Dramatist
Hegel, Georg (2.0)	4 2 5 4 3	(1770-1831) Germany Philosopher
Heidegger, Martin (1.7)	4 3 4 6 7 7 6 2 3	(1889-1976) Germany Philosopher
Heifetz, Jascha (1.5)	3 4 6 6 3 4 3 2 7	(1901-1987) Russia Violinist
Heim, Burkhard (2.0)	3 3 5 4 7 2 7 6 3	(1925-2001) Germany Physicist/logician
Heine, Heinrich (2.0)	4 4 1 2 7	(1797-1856) Germany Poet
Heisenberg, W K (1.6)	2 6 3 4 1	(1901-1976) Germany Physicist
Heller, Joseph (1.45)	2 4 6 4 7 6 2 6 3	(1923-1999) USA Writer
Hemingway, Ernest (1.6)	2 1 1 6 1	(1899-1961) USA Writer
Hendrix, Jimi (1.3)	4 6 3 4 7 4 7 6 7	(1942-1970) USA Rock musician
Henriquez, Fiore de (1.4)	4 4 3 6 7 4 4 2 3	(1921-2004) Italy Sculptor
Henriquez, Raúl S (1.5)	6 4 3 6 7 6 7 6 7	(1907-1999) Chile Archbishop/activist
Henry VIII (1.6)	1 1 1 4 1	(1491-1547) England King
Hepburn, Audrey (1.46)	2 4 4 2 3 6 6 4 7	(1929-1993) Belgium Film actress

Hepburn, Katharine (1.3)	2 4 6 6 7	(1909-2003) USA
	4 2 2 7	Film actress
Heraclitus (2.0)	3 4 1 2 3	(c 535-475 BC) Greece
		Philosopher
Hercules (2.2)	1 6 1 6 1	(c 8000 BC) Greece
		Avatar
Hering, Constantin (1.5)	3 3 4 4 3	(1800-1880) Germany
	6 6 2 7	Homoeopath
Hermans, Toon (1.4)	6 6 6 2 7	(1916-2000) Netherlands
	2 6 4 3	Comedian/painter
Hermes (4.0)	5 1 1 6 3	(c 7000 BC) Greece
		Avatar
Herodotus (1.7)	5 1 7 6 7	(c 485-425 BC) Greece
		Historian
Herriot, James (1.3)	2 4 3 4 3	(1916-1995) England
(James Aldred Wight)	6 7 6 7	Writer
Herschel, William (2.0)	2 2 1 6 1	(1738-1822) England
		Astronomer
Hertz, Heinrich (1.7)	3 7 5 6 3	(1857-1894) Germany
		Physicist
Herzl, Theodor (1.7)	3 7 7 2 3	(1860-1904) Austria
		Zionist leader
Hess, Rudolf (1.35)	1 1 6 6 1	(1894-1987) Germany
	4 1 6 7	Nazi official
Hesse, Hermann (2.1)	4 4 3 6 3	(1877-1962) Germany
	2 6 6 4	Writer
Heston, Charlton (1.3)	2 4 6 4 7	(1923-2008) USA
	4 3 6 1	Actor
Heydrich, Reinhart (1.3)	1 1 1 6 1	(1904-1942) Germany
	6 1 6 7	Nazi politician
Heyerdahl, Thor (1.65)	2 4 1 6 7	(1914-2002) Norway
	6 3 4 7	Anthropologist
Hiawatha (0.9)	6 7 7 6 7	(c 1450) N America
	6 7 2 3	Native American leader
Higashiyama, Kaii (1.35)	2 4 3 4 7	(1908-1999) Japan
	6 7 6 3	Painter
Hillary, Edmund (1.3)	2 6 1 4 7	(1919-2008) New Zealand
	2 6 6 3	Mountaineer/explorer
Hillesum, Etty (1.3)	3 7 6 6 7	(1914-1943) Netherlands
	6 5 6 7	Auschwitz victim/diarist
Himmler, Heinrich (1.4)	6 1 1 6 7	(1900-1945) Germany
	1 6 6 1	Nazi Leader
Hindemith, Paul (1.7)	4 4 1 2 3	(1895-1963) USA
		Composer
Hindenburg, Paul von (1.7)	1 1 1 6 7	(1847-1934) Germany
		General/president
Hippocrates (2.0)	2 4 5 6 7	(c 460-370 BC) Greece
		Physician
Hirohito (1.4)	7 6 6 6 7	(1901-1989) Japan
(Emperor Showa)	2 4 2 3	Emperor

Hiroshige (2.0)	4 4 7 6 7	(1797-1858) Japan Painter
Hitler, Adolf (2.0)	2 4 1 4 3 1 6 6 7	(1889-1945) Austria Dictator
Ho Chi Minh (1.7)	1 5 1 6 3	(1892-1969) Vietnam Chief of state, D R Vietnam
Hodgkin, Dorothy (1.7)	3 4 3 6 3 6 7 4 7	(1910-1994) UK Biochemist
Hodson, Geoffrey (1.6)	2 4 6 6 3	(1892-1983) UK Theosophist
Hoffa, Jimmy (1.2)	3 4 4 6 3 6 6 6 3	(1913-1975) USA Labour leader
Hofmannsthal, Hugo von (1.7)	2 4 6 6 3	(1874-1929) Austria Poet/dramatist
Hofman, Greet (1.5)	2 3 4 6 3 6 7 4 7	(1894-1968) Netherlands Healer
Hogarth, William (1.5)	2 4 6 4 3 3 2 6 7	(1697-1764) England Painter/engraver
Hokusai (2.0)	4 7 7 6 5	(1760-1849) Japan Painter/woodblock artist
Holbein, Hans (2.3)	4 1 4 6 5	(1497-1543) Germany Painter
Holberg, Ludvig (1.5)	3 4 3 4 3 7 2 6 7	(1684-1754) Norway Dramatist
Hollows, Fred (1.7)	2 4 5 4 3 6 6 2 7	(1929-1993) New Zealand Eye surgeon
Holmes, Ernest (1.6)	4 1 6 6 3 6 2 6 7	(1887-1960) USA Founder Religious Science
Homer (1.7)	4 2 6 2 4	(c 8th C. BC) Greece Poet
Hon-ami, Koh-etsu (1.65)	2 7 4 6 3 4 6 6 7	(1558-1637) Japan Tea ceremony master
Hon-ami, Myoshuu (1.47)	2 4 3 2 3 7 6 6 3	(16th century) Japan Mother of Koh-etsu Hon-ami
Honen (2.4)	6 4 6 2 7 6 7 4 7	(1133-1212) Japan Fndr. Buddhism/Jodo sect
Hoover, Herbert (2.0)	2 3 3 1 7	(1874-1964) USA President
Hopkins, Gerard Manley (2.2)	4 6 4 2 7	(1844-1889) UK Poet
Houseman, A.E. (1.5)	2 4 3 4 3 6 7 6 7	(1859-1936) England Poet
Hubbard, L Ron (1.8)	3 7 1 6 3 4 6 4 7	(1911-1986) USA Fndr. Scientology
Huber, Bruno (1.5)	3 5 5 6 3 7 6 6 7	(1930-1999) Switzerland Astrologer
Hughes, Ted (1.4)	2 4 3 4 3 6 7 6 7	(1930-1998) England Poet
Hugo, Victor (2.0)	3 4 5 6 3	(1802-1885) France Writer

Hume, David (1.7)	3 6 1 6 3	(1711-1776) Scotland Philosopher
Humphries, Christmas (1.5)	2 6 4 2 3 2 6 6 7	(1901-1983) England Buddhist writer
Hussein bin Talal (1.6)	2 4 4 6 7 6 6 2 3	(1935-1999) Jordan King
Hussein, Saddam (1.45)	3 6 3 6 3 6 1 6 1	(1937-2003) Iraq Dictator
Huxley, Aldous (1.7)	2 4 4 2 3	(1894-1963) UK Writer
Hypatia (1.6)	2 4 3 4 7 1 1 6 1	(c 370-415) Egypt Philosopher
Ibárruri, Dolores (1.5) (La Passionaria)	6 6 3 6 3 6 3 6 7	(1895-1989) Spain Communist leader/activist
Ibsen, Henrik (2.0)	2 4 1 6 5	(1828-1906) Norway Dramatist
Ike, Taiga (1.4)	2 7 6 6 7 4 2 6 3	(1723-1776) Japan Painter/calligrapher
Indra Devi Mataji (2.4)	2 6 4 6 3 2 6 2 3	(1899-2002) Latvia Yoga teacher
Ingres, Jean Auguste (2.2)	4 7 7 4 7	(1780-1867) France Painter
Ionesco, Eugène (1.6)	2 4 3 4 3 6 7 6 7	(1912-1994) Romania Playwright
Isaiah (2.3)	4 6 3 4 7 6 7 6 3	(8th C. BC) Israel Prophet
Jackson, Mahalia (1.3)	2 4 6 6 3 2 2 4 3	(1911-1972) USA Gospel singer
Jackson, Michael (1.2)	4 4 6 6 7 4 6 6 3	(1958-2009) USA Singer/dancer
Jacob (1.6)	3 6 3 6 7 2 7 6 3	(died c 62 AD) Palestine Brother of Jesus
Jacobs, Aletta (2.0)	5 1 3 6 1	(1849-1929) Netherlands Suffragette
Jafri, Ali Sardar (1.5)	4 6 4 6 7 2 2 4 3	(1914-2000) India Poet
Janakananda, Rajarshi (2.0)	2 6 3 2 7 2 6 2 3	(1892-1955) USA Disciple of Yogananda
Janssen, Horst (1.4)	4 4 6 6 3 2 3 6 3	(1929-1995) Germany Painter
Janssen, Ludo (1.35)	1 4 3 4 3 6 7 6 7	(d. 1994) Belgium Spiritual teacher
Jarry, Alfred (1.6)	3 4 4 6 7	(1873-1907) France Writer
Jaurès, Jean (1.45)	3 4 3 4 3 6 7 6 7	(1859-1914) France Writer/politician
Jefferson, Thomas (2.0)	2 6 1 4 7	(1743-1826) USA President
Jenkins, Roy (1.5)	3 3 3 4 3 4 7 6 7	(1920-2003) Wales Labour politician/writer

Jesus of Nazareth (4.0)	6 1 1 2 1	(24 BC-AD 9) Palestine
	6 7 2 3	Spiritual teacher
Jezebel (1.5)	1 6 3 6 3	(d. 846 BC) Phoenicia
		Princess
Jinarajadasa, C. (1.4)	6 3 4 2 3	(1875-1953) Sri Lanka
	7 6 6 7	President Adyar TS
Jinnah, Mohammed Ali (1.8)	3 1 2 4 7	(1876-1948) Pakistan
		First governor general
Jnana Mata, Sri (2.0)	6 6 6 6 3	(1869-1951) Canada
	2 2 6 7	Disciple of Yogananda
Joan of Arc (3.3)	5 1 3 6 6	(c 1412-1431) France
	7 6 6 7	Soldier/martyr
Johfra (Bosschart) (1.45)	2 6 6 6 3	(1919-1998) Netherlands
(J F G van den Berg)	2 6 4 7	Painter
John (3.0)	6 6 6 6 7	(1896-1966) Russia
(Vladika Maximovitch)	2 2 4 7	Archbishop
John of the Cross (1.6)	6 6 6 4 7	(1542-1591) Spain
	6 4 6 7	Mystic
John the Baptist (3.3)	2 6 1 6 1	(1st C. AD) Palestine
		Prophet
John the Beloved (3.0)	2 2 6 2 1	(1st C. AD) Palestine
		Apostle
John XXIII (2.0)	6 2 4 6 3	(1881-1963) Italy
		Pope
John Paul II. (1.6)	6 6 6 6 7	(1920-2005) Poland
	6 4 6 3	Pope
Johnson, Lyndon B (1.5)	2 4 3 4 7	(1908-1973) USA
	6 7 6 3	President
Johnson, Nkosi (0.8)	2 4 3 2 3	(1989-2001) South Africa
	6 2 6 7	AIDS campaigner
Johnson, Samuel (1.6)	2 1 1 6 7	(1709-1784) England
		Writer
Jones, Charles M. (Chuck) (1.4)	2 4 2 4 3	(1912-2002) USA
	6 6 2 3	Cartoon animator
Jones, Marc Edmond (1.6)	4 6 4 6 7	(1888-1980) USA
	4 7 6 3	Astrologer
Jonson, Ben (2.0)	2 4 1 6 3	(1572-1637) England
		Dramatist
Joseph (2.2)	6 2 3 4 2	(1st C. AD) Palestine
		Father of Jesus
Joseph (1.5)	6 6 3 4 3	(1500 BC?) Palestine
(Son of Jacob)	3 6 6 7	Biblical figure
Joseph II (1.65)	4 6 1 4 7	(1741-1790) Austria
	6 5 4 1	Regent
Joseph of Arimathea (2.0)	2 6 1 2 4	(1st C. AD) Palestine
		Biblical figure
Joshua (2.3)	6 7 6 1 1	(c 1500 BC) Israel
		Leader
Jouvenal, Roland de (1.4)	3 6 6 4 7	(d. 1946) France
	3 3 6 7	Parapsychologist

628

Jovellanos, Gaspar M. de (1.4)	6 3 4 6 3 6 7 2 7	(1744-1811) Spain Statesman/writer
Joyce, James (1.7)	2 4 1 4 3	(1882-1941) Ireland Writer
Judas Iscariot (1.7)	6 6 3 4 3	(1st C. AD) Palestine Disciple
Judge, William Q (2.0)	6 2 1 6 3 3 4 6 7	(1851-1896) USA Theosophist
Juliana (1.35)	2 4 3 2 3 6 7 6 3	(1909-2004) Netherlands Queen
Jung, Carl (2.2)	2 6 4 4 3	(1875-1961) Switzerland Fndr. analytical psychology
Jurriaanse, Aart (1.7)	2 6 5 6 1 2 7 2 5	(1907-2002) South Africa Esoteric writer
Kabir, Sant (4.2)	2 2 4 4 7 6 3 6 3	(1450-1518) India Mystic/poet
Kafka, Franz (1.7)	2 4 4 6 3	(1883-1924) Austria Writer
Kalu Rinpoche (2.35)	6 6 3 2 1 6 4 6 3	(1905-1989) Tibet Buddhist teacher
Kaluza, Theodor (1.5)	3 5 1 4 7	(1885-1945) Germany Physicist
Kane, Sarah (1.5)	2 4 6 6 3 2 2 6 7	(1971-1999) UK Playwright
Kano, Aminu (1.5)	2 6 1 2 3	(1920-1983) Nigeria Revolutionary
Kant, Immanuel (2.2)	6 4 1 2 5	(1724-1804) Germany Philosopher
Kardelj, Edvard (2.5)	7 6 7 6 1	(1910-1979) Yugoslavia Yugoslav leader/diplomat
Kartina, Raden Adjeng (1.3)	4 3 6 4 7 7 3 6 7	(1879-1904) Indonesia Freedom fighter
Kashdan, John (1.45)	2 4 3 4 7 6 7 6 3	(1917-2001) UK Painter/printmaker
Kassab, Fr. Nehmet-Allah (4.0) (El-Hardiny)	3 6 3 4 3 4 7 6 7	(1808-1858) Lebanon Theologian/healer
Kasturi, N (1.55)	4 2 4 6 7 6 6 6 3	(1897-1987) India Sai Baba's interpreter
Kaye, Danny (1.55)	6 4 4 6 7 4 6 4 3	(1913-1987) USA Comic actor
Kazantzakis, Nikos (1.6)	3 4 4 6 3 6 7 6 3	(1883-1957) Greece Writer
Keats, John (1.7)	4 6 2 2 2	(1795-1821) England Poet
Keers, Walter (1.5)	6 6 4 6 7 4 2 2 3	(1923-1985) Netherlands Spiritual teacher
Keller, Helen Adams (1.7)	1 1 4 2 5	(1880-1968) USA Writer/political activist
Kellogg, Frank Billings (2.1)	2 3 1 6 7	(1856-1937) USA Statesman

Kelly, Petra (1.5)	2 4 3 4 7 6 7 6 3	(1947-1992) Germany Fndr. Green Party
Kempis, Thomas à (1.5)	2 6 1 2 3 5 4 6 7	(1380-1471) Netherlands Religious writer
Kennedy, Edward (1.3)	2 4 4 4 7 6 7 6 3	(1932-2009) USA Politician
Kennedy, John F (2.4)	2 1 7 6 1	(1917-1963) USA President
Kennedy, Robert (1.6)	2 6 7 6 7 4 3 4 3	(1925-1968) USA Politician
Kennedy, Jacqueline (1.4)	4 4 2 4 3 6 6 6 7	(1929-1994) USA Wife of J. F. Kennedy
Kenyatta, Jomo (1.5)	2 6 1 2 1	(c 1889-1978) Kenya President
Kepler, Johann (1.7)	3 5 1 2 5	(1571-1630) Germany Astronomer
Kerouac, Jack (1.35)	6 6 7 6 7 6 4 4 3	(1922-1969) USA Writer
Keynes, John Maynard (1.8)	5 2 1 2 3	(1883-1946) UK Economist
Khan, Ali Akbar (2.0)	2 4 4 6 7 6 6 2 3	(1922-2009) India Musician
Khan, Inayat (2.1)	6 2 6 6 3	(1882-1927) India Sufi teacher
Khan, Nuzrat Fatteh Ali (1.6)	4 4 4 2 3 4 6 4 3	(1948-1997) Pakistan Singer/musician
Khayyam, Omar (1.6)	6 4 6 2 7	(c 1050-1123) Persia Astronomer/poet
Khomeini, Ayatollah (1.6)	4 1 6 6 7 6 6 6 7	(1900-1989) Iran Islamic leader
Khrushchev, Nikita (2.0)	1 1 6 2 3	(1894-1971) Russia USSR premier
Khyentse, Dilgo (1.7)	3 4 3 6 3 6 7 6 3	(1910-1991) Tibet Nyingma Tibetan Buddhism
Kierkegaard, Søren A. (2.0)	2 4 6 2 3	(1813-1855) Denmark Philosopher
Kilmer, Alfred Joyce (1.36)	2 4 3 4 3 6 7 6 7	(1886-1918) USA Poet
King, Coretta Scott (1.4)	2 2 4 6 3 6 2 6 3	(1927-2006) USA Civil rights activist
King, George (1.7)	2 6 3 6 7 6 6 6 3	(1919-1997) England Fndr. Aetherius Society
King, Martin Luther (2.0)	2 2 1 6 3 3 4 2 7	(1929-1968) USA Civil rights leader
Kingsley, Mary (2.0)	2 1 7 2 7	(1862-1900) UK Traveller/writer
Kinnersley, David (1.45)	2 6 4 2 3 2 6 6 7	(1926-2004) England Fndr. WaterAid
Kinski, Klaus (1.5)	4 4 6 6 7 3 2 4 3	(1926-1991) Germany Actor

Kipling, Rudyard (1.8)	6 6 4 4 3	(1865-1936) UK Writer
Kirwan, Richard (2.0)	5 5 7 4 3	(1733-1812) Ireland Chemist
Kitasato, Shibasaburo (2.0)	3 5 5 6 7	(1856-1931) Japan Bacteriologist
Kitchener, Horatio H. (1.7)	6 7 1 6 7	(1850-1916) UK Soldier/statesman
Kitt, Eartha (1.2)	2 4 6 4 3 4 3 6 7	(1927-2008) USA Singer/actor
Klee, Paul (2.0)	4 2 4 6 3	(1879-1940) Switzerland Painter
Klein, Jean (1.5)	4 6 4 6 1 2 7 6 5	(1916-1998) Czechoslovakia Spiritual teacher
Klein, Melanie (1.8)	2 1 1 4 3	(1882-1960) Austria Psychoanalyst
Klein, Yves (1.5)	4 4 3 4 3 6 7 6 7	(1928-1962) France Painter
Kleist, Heinrich von (1.6)	2 1 4 6 3	(1777-1811) Germany Dramatist/poet
Klemperer, Otto (1.7)	4 4 1 6 7	(1885-1973) Germany Conductor
Klestil, Thomas (1.4)	2 4 7 6 7 3 3 6 3	(1932-2004) Austria President
Klimt, Gustav (1.5)	2 4 6 6 3 6 2 2 7	(1862-1918) Austria Painter
Klint, Hilma af (0.85)	4 4 3 6 3 6 7 2 7	(1862-1944) Sweden Mystic/painter
Knox, John (2.0)	6 6 1 6 3	(1505-1572) Scotland Reformer
König, Franz (2.0)	3 4 3 4 7 6 7 6 3	(1905-2004) Austria Cardinal
Koestler, Arthur (1.7)	2 4 1 6 3	(1905-1983) UK Writer
Kohmyo (1.6) (Shining Empress)	6 6 6 2 7 2 2 6 3	(701-760) Japan Buddhist empress
Kon, Tokoh (1.7)	4 6 4 6 7 6 7 2 7	(1898-1977) Japan Writer/Buddhist priest
Kooning, Willem De (1.5)	4 4 3 4 3 6 7 6 7	(1904-1997) Netherlands Painter
Kopaniak, Bronislawa (1.5)	3 6 3 6 3 2 7 2 7	(1919-2005) Poland WWII Resistance fighter
Kottnauer, Cenek (1.46)	3 3 4 6 3 6 7 2 7	(1910-1996) Czechoslovakia Chess master/teacher
Kreisky, Bruno (2.0)	3 7 1 6 7 6 4 2 3	(1911-1990) Austria Statesman
Kreisler, Fritz (1.6)	4 2 2 4 3	(1875-1962) Austria Musician
Krishna (5.0)	2 6 4 6 3	(c 3000 BC) India Avatar

631

Krishnamacharya, K. E. (1.7)	4 6 4 6 7	(1926-1984) India
	2 6 6 7	Healer
Krishnamurti (4.0)	2 2 4 6 7	(1895-1986) India
	6 4 2 7	Spiritual teacher
Kruger, Paul (2.0)	1 1 1 6 7	(1825-1904) South Africa
		President
Kubelik, Rafael (1.6)	4 4 3 6 7	(1914-1996) Czechoslovakia
	6 7 2 3	Orchestral conductor
Kubrick, Stanley (1.5)	4 4 3 2 3	(1928-1999) USA
	6 7 4 7	Film director
Kukai (2.0)	2 2 4 6 7	(774-835) Japan
	7 6 6 3	Esoteric Buddhism/Shingon
Kurosawa, Akira (1.7)	4 4 4 6 3	(1910-1998) Japan
	6 4 2 7	Film maker
Labiche, Eugène (1.7)	2 4 3 6 7	(1815-1888) France
		Comic dramatist
Laing, R D (1.3)	6 4 3 4 3	(1927-1989) UK
	3 6 4 3	Psychiatrist
Lamb, Charles (1.7)	2 4 4 6 3	(1775-1834) England
		Writer
Lanyon, Walter C. (1.5)	2 6 6 6 7	(1887-1967) USA
	4 2 6 3	Writer
Lao-tse (4.2)	2 4 4 2 3	(570-490 BC) China
		Philosopher
Laplace, Pierre Simon (2.0)	3 3 1 2 3	(1749-1827) France
		Mathematician/ astronomer
Larkin, Philip (1.4)	2 4 6 4 7	(1922-1985) UK
	6 6 6 3	Poet
Lasso, Orlando di (1.55)	4 4 2 6 7	(1530-1594) Italy
	7 4 2 3	Composer
Latimer, Hugh (1.7)	6 6 6 2 3	(c 1485-1555) England
		Martyr
Laurency, Henry T (1.9)	2 6 4 6 7	(1882-1971) Sweden
(Henrik von Zeipel)	2 6 2 3	Esotericist
Lavoisier, Antoine (1.7)	3 5 5 6 3	(1743-1794) France
		Chemist
Lawrence, D H (1.7)	2 2 4 4 3	(1885-1930) UK
		Writer
Lawrence, T E (1.6)	2 6 6 6 3	(1888-1935) UK
		Soldier
Lazarus (0.9)	4 6 6 6 7	(c AD 6) Palestine
	4 4 2 4	Biblical figure
Leadbeater, C W (2.4)	7 3 5 6 7	(1847-1934) UK
	4 1 6 3	Theosophist
Le Corbusier (2.0)	3 7 7 4 7	(1887-1965) Switzerland
(C-E Jeanneret-Gris)		Architect
Ledger, Heathcliff A. (0.9)	6 4 2 6 7	(1979-2008) Australia
	4 6 2 3	Actor
Lee, Bruce (1.0)	4 6 3 6 3	(1940-1973) USA
	6 4 2 7	Actor/martial artist

Lee, Laurie (1.46)	2 4 3 4 3 6 7 6 7	(1914-1997) UK Writer/poet
Lees, Andrew (1.3)	2 3 2 6 7 6 4 6 3	(1955-1995) UK Environmentalist
Leeuwenhoek, Anton van (1.7)	3 5 5 2 7	(1632-1723) Netherlands Scientist
Leibniz, Gottfried (1.7)	5 7 5 6 1	(1646-1716) Germany Philosopher/mathematician
Lemmon, Jack (1.3)	2 4 3 6 3 6 7 2 7	(1925-2001) USA Film actor
Lenin, Vladimir Ilyich (2.2)	5 7 1 6 3 7 1 6 7	(1870-1924) Russia Soviet leader
Lennon, John (1.6)	3 7 4 4 3	(1940-1980) UK Musician
Lenz, Frederick (1.3) (Rama)	2 3 4 6 3 6 7 6 7	(1950 -1998) USA Spiritual teacher
Leo X (2.0)	6 3 7 6 3	(1475-1521) Italy Pope
Leo, Alan (1.6)	2 4 5 4 7 6 6 6 3	(1861-1917) UK Astrologer
Leonardo da Vinci (4.4)	4 7 7 4 7 4 3 4 7	(1452-1519) Italy Painter
Leslie, Desmond (1.5)	2 7 6 6 7 4 2 4 3	(1921-2001) UK Film maker/writer
Lessing, Gotthold E (1.7)	3 4 4 2 3	(1729-1781) Germany Writer
Lévesque, René (1.6)	4 6 4 4 3 1 6 2 7	(1922-1987) Canada Prime Minister of Québec
Levi, Eliphas (1.8)	6 4 3 6 7 7 5 2 3	(1844-1911) USA Occultist
Lewis, C S (1.7)	2 6 6 6 3	(1898-1963) UK Writer
Lewis, Harvey Spencer (1.6)	4 5 5 6 7 1 3 6 7	(1883-1939) USA Fndr. Rosicrucian Order
Lewis, Ralph M (1.7)	6 4 5 2 7 6 6 4 3	(1904-1987) USA Leader, Rosae Crucis
Lichtenstein, Roy (1.5)	2 4 3 4 7 6 7 6 3	(1923-1997) USA Artist
Lie, Trygve H. (1.5)	2 5 4 6 7 2 7 2 7	(1896-1968) Norway First UN Secretary-General
Lincoln, Abraham (3.3)	1 2 1 2 1 1 4 6 7	(1809-1865) USA President
Lind, Jenny (1.25)	4 4 6 6 7 6 4 2 3	(1820-1887) Sweden Opera singer
Lindgren, Astrid (1.5)	2 4 3 6 7 6 7 2 3	(1908-2002) Sweden Writer
Linnaeus, Carl (1.6)	2 4 3 2 3	(1707-1778) Sweden Botanist
Lippi, Fra Filippo (2.0)	6 7 7 6 7 4 6 6 3	(1406-1469) Italy Painter

Liszt, Franz (2.2)	4 6 3 6 7	(1811-1886) Hungary Composer
Livingstone, David (1.6)	2 6 1 6 7	(1813-1873) UK Explorer/missionary
Lloyd George, David (1.8)	4 6 1 6 3	(1863-1945) Wales Statesman
Locke, John (2.3)	4 7 1 2 7	(1632-1704) England Philosopher
Lodro, Jamyang K. C. (2.0)	3 4 3 4 3 6 7 6 7	(1893-1959) Tibet Buddhist monk/scholar
London, Jack (1.45)	4 4 4 4 7 6 6 6 7	(1876-1916) USA Writer
Long, Barry (1.5)	6 6 4 6 3 2 6 2 3	(1926-2003) Australia Spiritual teacher
Lorber, Jacob (1.4)	3 2 5 6 7 6 4 6 3	(1800-1864) Germany Writer/astral sensitive
Lorca, Federico García (2.3)	7 4 1 6 3	(1899-1936) Spain Poet
Lorentz, Hendrik Antoon (2.2)	3 5 5 6 3	(1853-1928) Netherlands Physicist
Lotto, Lorenzo (2.5)	4 4 6 2 7 4 1 4 3	(1480-1556) Italy Painter
Louis IX (1.6)	2 4 3 4 3 6 7 6 7	(1215-1270) France King
Loyola, Ignatius (1.7)	6 6 1 2 7	(1491-1556) Spain Soldier/ecclesiastic
Lubachivsky, Myroslav (1.6)	2 4 3 2 3 6 7 6 7	(1914-2000) Ukraine Cardinal
Ludwig II (1.3)	4 6 4 6 3 3 7 4 7	(1845-1886) Germany King of Bavaria
Luke (2.4)	6 6 2 6 3	(1st C. AD) Palestine Apostle
Luria Ashkenazi, Itzhak (1.4) (Ha'ari)	3 4 4 6 7 1 6 6 3	(1534-1572) Palestine Founder, Lurian Kabbalah
Lusseyran, Jacques (1.5)	2 6 3 4 3 4 7 6 7	(1924-1971) France Blind hero French Resistance
Luther, Martin (2.3)	6 6 1 2 3	(1483-1546) Germany Religious reformer
Lutyens, Mary (1.4)	2 6 6 6 7 2 2 6 3	(1908-1999) UK Writer/Krishnamurti biographer
Luxemburg, Rosa (1.7)	6 3 1 6 3	(1871-1919) Poland Revolutionary
Lympany, Moura (1.5) (Mary Johnstone)	2 4 1 6 3 6 4 6 7	(1916-2005) UK Pianist
MacArthur, Douglas (1.7)	1 3 1 6 1	(1880-1964) USA General
MacDonald-Bayne, Murdo (2.0)	2 4 3 4 3 6 7 6 7	(1887-1955) UK Writer
Machiavelli, Niccolo (1.6)	3 3 6 6 3	(1469-1527) Italy Statesman

Maeterlinck, Maurice (1.7)	4 4 7 6 3	(1862-1949) Belgium Dramatist
Magellan, Ferdinand (2.0)	1 1 5 6 3	(c 1480-1521) Portugal Navigator
Maharaj, Shivabalayogi (2.0)	6 4 6 6 3 6 6 2 3	(1935-1994) India Yogi
Maharishi Mahesh Yogi (3.2)	6 4 6 6 3 3 2 4 3	(1917-2008) India Fndr. Transcendental Meditation
Mahler, Gustav (1.9)	4 4 4 4 6 3	(1860-1911) Austria Composer
Mailer, Norman (1.3)	3 4 3 6 3 6 7 2 7	(1923-2007) USA Writer
Maimonides (2.3) (Moses ben Maimon)	2 1 1 4 3	(1135-1204) Spain Philosopher
Makarios III, Myriarthes (1.7)	3 3 3 6 7 1 3 6 3	(1913-1977) Cyprus Archbishop/politician
Makeba, Miriam (0.8)	3 4 3 2 7 6 6 4 3	(1932 -2008) South Africa Singer/anti-apartheid activist
Makhlouf, Charbel (4.0)	6 6 4 6 7 2 6 2 7	(1828-1898) Lebanon Hermit
Malcolm X (1.4) (Malcom Little)	4 6 7 6 7 6 6 4 7	(1925-1965) USA Civil rights leader
Mallove, Eugene F. (1.5)	2 4 3 6 7 6 7 2 3	(1947-2004) USA Scientist/cold-fusion advocate
Mani (1.46)	6 6 4 2 3 6 7 6 7	(215-277) Persia Early gnostic teacher
Mann, Thomas (2.0)	4 4 7 2 3	(1875-1955) Germany Writer
Mann-Borgese, Elisabeth (1.6) (daughter of Thomas Mann)	3 4 5 2 3 7 7 6 7	(1918-2002) Germany Maritime environmentalist
Mantegna, Andrea (2.2)	2 4 6 6 1	(1431-1506) Italy Painter
Mao Tse-tung (3.2) (Mao Zedong)	1 1 1 2 1 1 4 6 7	(1893-1976) China Chief of state
Marais, Marin (0.85)	3 4 6 6 3 6 4 2 7	(1656-1728) France Composer/viol player
Marat, Jean Paul (1.7)	3 1 1 6 3	(1743-1793) Switzerland Politician
Marc, Franz (1.5)	2 4 5 4 3 6 7 6 7	(1880-1916) Germany Painter
Marceau, Marcel (1.0)	3 4 3 6 3 4 7 2 7	(1923-2007) France Mime artist
Marcion (1.5)	2 6 7 4 3 4 2 6 7	(84-160) Sinope (Turkey) Gnostic teacher
Marconi, Guglielmo (2.0)	2 3 5 6 3	(1874-1937) Italy Inventor
Margaret Rose (0.9)	2 4 6 2 3 3 6 4 7	(1930-2002) UK Princess/Countess Snowdon
Maria Euthymia (1.5)	2 6 6 6 3 2 2 2 7	(1914-1955) Germany Nun

Maria Lucia, Sister (1.4)	6 6 6 2 3 2 2 6 3	(1907-2005) Portugal Visionary of Fatima
Maria Theresa (1.65)	4 6 1 6 7 6 6 4 7	(1717-1780) Austria Empress
Marini, Marino (1.5)	4 4 7 6 7 6 3 2 3	(1901-1980) Italy Sculptor
Marivaux, Pierre de (1.6)	2 4 6 2 7	(1688-1763) France Comic dramatist
Mark (2.3)	6 4 6 6 3	(1st C. AD) Palestine Apostle
Marley, Robert (Bob) (1.36)	4 6 3 4 3 4 6 6 7	(1945-1981) Jamaica Reggae musician
Marlowe, Christopher (1.8)	2 4 1 4 1 6 5 4 3	(1564-1593) England Playwright
Maroun, Abbud (1.4)	3 4 3 4 3 7 6 6 7	(1886-1962) Lebanon Novelist
Marpa (4.5)	6 4 4 6 3	(11th C. AD) Tibet Yogi
Marshall, George C (1.6)	2 2 4 4 3 6 6 2 3	(1880-1959) USA Statesman (Marshall Plan)
Marshall, Malcolm (0.9)	4 4 7 4 7 4 3 6 3	(1958-1999) Barbados Cricketer
Marshall, Thurgood (1.4)	6 6 4 4 3 6 6 2 3	(1908-1993) USA Supreme Court Justice
Martha (1.6)	6 7 4 6 7 4 6 2 7	(1st C. AD) Palestine Biblical figure
Martí, José (1.5)	6 1 7 2 3 6 3 4 7	(1853-1895) Cuba Poet/essayist/journalist
Martini, Simone (2.5)	6 4 1 2 7 4 6 4 3	(c 1284-1344) Italy Painter
Martinus (2.3)	2 4 1 6 7 3 6 6 7	(1890-1981) Denmark Writer
Marx, Karl (2.2)	6 2 5 6 3 3 7 6 7	(1818-1883) Germany Political philosopher
Mary (2.2)	6 6 2 2 3	(1st C. AD) Palestine Mother of Jesus
Mary Magdalene (0.9)	6 6 6 4 3 6 6 2 7	(1st C. AD) Palestine Biblical figure
Mary of Bethany (0.85)	4 6 6 6 7 2 2 4 3	(1st C. AD) Palestine Biblical figure
Masaccio (2.7)	4 4 7 6 3 1 4 6 7	(1401-1428) Italy Painter
Masina, Giulietta (1.5)	2 4 3 4 3 6 7 6 7	(1920-1994) Italy Film actress
Massoud, Ahmad Shah (1.3)	3 4 1 4 7 6 6 6 3	(1954-2001) Afghanistan Northern Alliance general
Massu, Jaques (1.5)	6 3 6 1 7 7 3 6 7	(1908-2002) France General
Mastroianni, Marcello (1.4)	2 4 3 6 7 4 4 6 3	(1924-1996) Italy Film actor

636

Matisse, Henri (2.4)	3 6 1 4 7	(1869-1954) France
		Painter
Matsushita, Konosuke (1.4)	4 6 4 6 3	(1894-1989) Japan
	2 3 2 7	Ethical industrialist
Matthew (2.4)	6 7 4 6 3	(1st C. AD) Palestine
		Apostle
Maugham, W Somerset (1.7)	2 2 4 2 7	(1874-1965) UK
		Writer
Maupassant, Guy de (2.2)	3 4 4 2 1	(1850-1893) France
		Writer
Mavalankar, Damodar K (1.7)	2 6 3 6 3	(1857-1947?) India
		Theosophist
Maxwell, Robert (1.6)	2 4 1 2 3	(1923-1991) Czechoslovakia/UK
	1 3 6 7	Publisher/politician
Mayakovsky, Vladimir (1.7)	4 4 1 6 7	(1894-1930) Russia
		Poet
McCartney, Linda (1.4)	2 4 3 4 7	(1941-1998) USA
	6 7 6 3	Photographer/singer
McKillop, Mary (1.65)	2 4 2 4 3	(1842-1909) Australia
	6 6 6 7	Nun
McNamara, Robert (1.3)	2 3 3 6 7	(1916-2009) USA
	7 3 6 3	Defense Sec/World Bank president
Medici, Lorenzo de (1.8)	4 1 3 4 3	(1449-1492) Italy
		Florentine ruler
Meher Baba (2.4)	2 3 5 6 7	(1894-1969) India
		Spiritual teacher
Meiji (0.8)	3 4 4 6 7	(1852-1912) Japan
	6 7 6 3	Emperor
Meir, Golda (1.7)	3 1 1 6 3	(1898-1978) Israel
		Prime Minister
Mello, Sergio De (1.5)	2 4 3 6 7	(1948-2003) Brazil
	6 7 2 3	UN diplomat
Melville, Herman (1.6)	6 4 4 6 3	(1819-1891) USA
		Writer
Mendelssohn, Felix (2.4)	4 4 1 6 3	(1809-1847) Germany
	2467	Composer
Mendoza, Lydia (1.45)	2 4 2 2 7	(1916-2007) USA
	6 6 6 3	Singer/songwriter
Menes (1.35)	6 6 3 6 4	(c 3400 BC) Egypt
	4 7 2 7	King
Menon Shri Krishna (1.4)	6 4 3 6 7	(1883-1959) India
(Shri Atmananda)	6 7 6 3	Spiritual teacher
Menuhin, Yehudi (1.6)	2 4 3 4 7	(1916-1999) USA
	6 7 6 3	Violinist
Mercury, Freddie (1.3)	4 4 3 4 3	(1946-1991) UK
(Farrokh Bulsara)	4 7 6 7	Rock musician
Mersenne, Marin (1.6)	6 2 6 6 7	(1588-1648) France
	4 2 2 7	Monk/mathematician/musician
Mesmer, Friedrich (1.6)	3 7 1 6 3	(1734-1815) Austria
		Physician

Messiaen, Olivier (1.76)	4 6 7 6 3	(1908-1992) France
	2 1 6 7	Composer
Metternich (1.6)	1 1 1 6 7	(1773-1859) Austria
		Statesman
Michelangelo (3.3)	1 4 4 6 1	(1475-1564) Italy
	6 3 6 7	Sculptor/painter
Michelsen, Christian (1.5)	3 6 3 6 7	(1857-1925) Norway
	6 3 6 7	Politician/businessman
Mies van der Rohe, Ludwig (1.6)	1 4 6 4 7	(1886-1969) Germany/USA
	7 3 6 3	Architect
Mifune, Toshiro (1.3)	4 6 3 6 7	(1920-1997) Japan
	4 6 2 3	Actor
Milarepa (3.5)	6 4 4 4 3	(1052-1135) Tibet
		Yogi
Milhaud, Darius (1.8)	2 4 4 4 7	(1892-1974) France
		Composer
Miller, Arthur (1.4)	3 4 3 4 3	(1915-2005) USA
	6 7 6 7	Playwright
Milligan, T. A. (Spike) (1.3)	2 4 6 6 3	(1918-2002) UK
	4 2 4 7	Writer/performer
Milton, John (1.8)	2 6 4 6 7	(1608-1674) England
		Poet
Miró, Joán (2.0)	2 2 6 6 3	(1893-1983) Spain
	4 4 2 7	Painter
Mirza Ghulam Ahmad (1.6)	4 6 7 6 3	(1835-1908) India
	4 7 6 7	Fndr. Islamic sect
Misora, Hibari (1.35)	2 4 4 6 7	(1937-1989) Japan
	6 6 6 3	Singer
Mitchison, Naomi (1.5)	2 4 6 4 7	(1897-1999) UK
	3 6 2 3	Writer
Mitterrand, François (1.6)	3 4 3 1 7	(1916-1996) France
	6 7 6 1	President
Miura, Sekizo (1.6)	3 3 2 4 7	(1883-1960) Japan
	7 6 2 3	Theosophist/yogi
Miyazawa, Kenji (2.0)	4 6 4 6 7	(1896-1933) Japan
	2 6 6 3	Writer/poet
Modigliani, Amedeo (1.7)	6 4 4 4 7	(1884-1920) Italy
		Painter/sculptor
Mohammed (3.4)	2 3 1 6 3	(570-632) Arabia
		Prophet/spiritual teacher
Molière (2.2)	3 3 1 6 3	(1622-1673) France
(Jean-Baptiste Poquelin]		Dramatist
Molina, Luis de (2.2)	4 6 7 6 3	(1535-1600) Spain
	6 3 6 3	Jesuit theologian
Molina, Tirso de (1.6)	2 4 3 6 3	(1584-1648) Spain
		Dramatist
Monet, Claude (1.9)	3 4 4 6 3	(1840-1927) France
	7 7 6 7	Painter
Monnier, Pierre (1.3)	3 6 3 6 3	(1891-1914) France
	3 6 2 3	Parapsychologist

Monroe, Marilyn (0.9)	4 4 6 2 3 2 4 4 3	(1926-1962) USA Film actress
Montaigne, Michel de (1.7)	3 6 3 6 5	(1533-1592) France Writer
Montesquieu, Charles de (2.0)	3 6 4 6 3	(1689-1755) France Philosopher
Montessori, Maria (1.65)	6 4 7 4 7 4 7 6 3	(1870-1952) Italy Educator
Monteverdi, Claudio (2.4)	4 4 7 6 7	(1567-1643) Italy Composer
Montezuma II (1.6)	6 1 6 6 3	(1466-1520) Mexico Emperor
Montgomery, Bernard (1.7)	2 7 5 6 7 3 7 4 7	(1887-1976) UK General
Moore, Dudley (0.9)	2 4 6 6 3 4 2 2 7	(1935-2002) England Musician/comedian/film actor
Moore, Henry (1.8)	2 4 7 6 7	(1898-1986) UK Sculptor
More, Thomas (1.5)	4 6 6 6 3 4 4 6 3	(1478-1535) England Statesman/writer
Morrannier, Georges (1.4)	4 6 4 4 7 2 6 6 3	(1945-1973) France Parapsychologist
Morris, Margaret (1.4)	6 6 4 2 3 2 6 6 7	(1949-1996) USA Ascetic
Morrison, James (Jim) (1.4)	6 4 5 2 7 6 7 4 3	(1943-1971) USA Musician/songwriter
Moses (2.3)	6 6 1 4 1	(12th C. BC) Egypt Prophet
Mozart, Constanze (1.55)	4 2 2 6 3 4 6 4 7	(1763-1842) Austria Wife of W.A. Mozart
Mozart, Wolfgang A. (3.0)	4 4 4 4 3 4 7 2 3	(1756-1791) Austria Composer
Mühe, Ulrich (1.35)	2 4 3 2 7 4 4 6 3	(1953-2007) Germany Actor
Muhaiyaddeen, Bawa (3.0)	4 6 4 6 7 6 6 6 7	(d. 1986) Sri Lanka Sufi teacher
Muir, John (1.45)	2 4 3 4 7 6 7 6 3	(1838-1914) Scotland Conservationist
Muktananda (4.0)	4 4 2 4 3 3 3 6 7	(1908-1982) India Spiritual teacher
Munakata, Shiko (1.4)	2 4 4 2 7 2 6 6 4	(1903-1975) Japan Printmaker
Munch, Edvard (1.5)	4 4 4 4 6 3 6 6 2 7	(1863-1944) Norway Painter
Munk, Kaj (1.7)	3 4 6 4 3	(1898-1944) Denmark Dramatist/priest
Munthe, Axel (1.5)	2 5 5 6 7 3 3 2 3	(1857-1949) Sweden Physician/writer
Murillo, Bartolomé (2.2)	4 6 1 6 3	(1618-1682) Spain Painter

Musashi, Miyamoto (0.6)	6 6 1 4 7	(16th-17th C.) Japan
	1 3 6 7	Samurai
Musset, Alfred de (1.7)	3 4 5 6 3	(1810-1857) France
		Poet/dramatist
Mussolini, Benito (2.2)	2 1 1 6 1	(1883-1945) Italy
		Dictator
Naganuma, Myoko (1.4)	2 4 3 6 3	(1889-1957) Japan
	6 7 6 3	Co-fndr. Rissho Koseikai
Nahum, Pedro (1.4)	4 6 4 2 3	(1927-1993) Argentina
	6 6 6 7	Scholar (A. A. B. teachings)
Nanak, Guru (3.0)	6 6 1 2 3	(1469-1538) India
	7 4 6 7	Fndr. Sikhism
Nansen, Fridtjof (1.45)	4 6 3 4 7	(1861-1930) Norway
	6 7 6 7	Polar explorer/humanist
Napoleon I (2.2)	3 1 1 4 5	(1769-1821) Corsica/France
	7 6 2 7	General/emperor
Nasser, Gamal Abdel (1.7)	2 1 1 6 1	(1918-1970) Egypt
		President
Neal, Viola Petitt (1.5)	2 4 7 6 7	(1907-1981) USA
	6 3 6 3	Esoteric researcher/writer
Nehru, Jawaharlal (2.0)	1 2 1 6 3	(1889-1964) India
		Statesman
Neill, A S (1.7)	2 6 1 4 3	(1883-1973) UK
		Educator
Nelson, Horatio (1.6)	1 1 5 2 7	(1758-1805) England
		Naval commander
Nero (1.4)	1 1 4 6 3	(37-68 AD) Rome
		Emperor
Neruda, Pablo (1.45)	2 4 3 4 3	(1906-1973) Chile
	6 7 6 7	Poet
Neumann, Therese (1.67)	6 6 2 6 7	(1898-1962) Germany
	6 4 6 3	Mystic/saint
Newhouse, Mildred 'Flower' (1.4)	2 6 6 2 7	(1909-1994) USA
	2 2 6 3	Mystic
Newman, Barnett (1.7)	4 7 7 6 7	(1905-1970) USA
		Painter/mathematician
Newman, Paul (1.3)	2 4 3 6 3	(1925-2008) USA
	6 7 2 7	Film actor
Newton, Isaac (2.2)	3 3 1 6 5	(1642-1727) England
		Scientist
Nichiren (2.0)	3 6 6 2 7	(1222-1282) Japan
	6 1 2 7	Founder Nichiren Buddhism
Nicholson, Ben (1.7)	2 4 4 6 3	(1894-1982) UK
		Painter
Nidal, Abu (0.75)	6 3 6 6 7	(1937-2002) Palestine
(Sabri Khalil al-Banna)	7 6 6 3	Revolutionary/militant
Niering, William Albert (1.5)	2 6 4 2 7	(1924-1999) USA
	2 7 6 3	Ecologist
Nietzsche, Friedrich (1.9)	1 4 1 6 3	(1844-1900) Germany
		Philosopher

Nightingale, Florence (1.6)	2 2 4 6 6	(1820-1910) UK
		Nurse/hospital reformer
Nijgh, Lennaert (1.35)	2 4 7 6 7	(1954-2002) Netherlands
	6 3 2 3	Writer/lyricist
Nisargaradatta Maharaj (3.5)	2 4 4 4 3	(1897-1981) India
	6 1 6 7	Hindu spiritual teacher
Nityananda, Bhagavan (4.5)	2 6 4 2 7	(c 1900-1961) India
	6 6 2 7	Spiritual teacher
Niwano, Nikkyo (1.5)	4 4 3 6 3	(1906-1999) Japan
	2 6 2 3	Co-fndr. Rissho Koseikai
Nixon, Richard (1.5)	3 4 3 6 7	(1913-1994) USA
	6 3 6 3	President
Nkomo, Joshua (1.6)	3 4 3 4 3	(1917-1999) Zimbawe
	6 7 6 7	Politician/activist
Nkrumah, Kwame (1.3)	3 6 6 6 7	(1909-1972) Ghana
	3 3 4 7	President
Nobel, Alfred (1.7)	2 6 3 6 1	(1833-1896) Sweden
		Inventor/manufacturer
Norgay, Tenzing (1.3)	2 4 6 4 5	(1914-1986) Nepal
	6 3 6 3	Sherpa mountaineer
Norman, Mildred (1.6)	6 6 6 2 7	(1908-1981) USA
	6 6 2 7	"Peace Pilgrim"
Nostradamus (1.7)	3 3 6 6 3	(1503-1566) France
		Astrologer
Nureyev, Rudolf (1.46)	4 4 6 4 7	(1938-1993) Russia
	4 3 6 7	Ballet dancer
Nuth (1.36)	1 6 4 6 3	(c 3000 BC) Egypt
	3 7 2 7	Queen
Nyerere, Julius (1.7)	2 3 4 4 7	(1922-1999) Tanzania
	7 6 2 3	President
Ochoa, Severo (1.5)	7 3 4 2 7	(1905-1993) Spain
	7 6 6 3	Biochemist/Nobel laureate
Oda, Nobunaga (0.7)	6 1 6 4 7	(1534-1582) Japan
	7 6 6 1	Feudal lord
O'Day, Anita (0.9)	2 4 6 6 7	(1919-2006) USA
	4 6 2 3	Jazz singer
Oistrakh, David (1.5)	4 4 3 4 3	(1908-1974) Russia
	6 7 6 7	Violinist
Okada, Yoshikazu (2.1)	6 6 6 4 3	(1901-1974) Japan
	4 3 6 7	Spiritual teacher
Okamoto, Taro (1.4)	4 4 3 6 3	(1914-1998) Japan
	6 6 6 7	Painter
Olcott, H S (2.2)	2 1 7 6 7	(1832-1907) USA
		Theosophist
Olivier, Laurence (1.6)	3 4 3 2 7	(1907-1989) UK
	6 1 4 3	Actor
Omananda, Swami (1.75)	2 6 2 2 7	(1882-1967) UK
(Maud MacCarthy)	6 4 6 3	Companion to 'The Boy'
Omkarananda, Swami (1.6)	2 6 3 6 7	(1930-2000) India
	6 3 4 3	Fndr. Divine Light Center

O'Neill, Eugene (1.6)	2 6 1 4 3	(1888-1953) USA
		Dramatist
Oort, Jan Hendrik (1.8)	3 5 7 4 7	(1900-1992) Netherlands
	6 3 6 7	Astronomer
Oppenheimer, J Robert (2.0)	5 3 7 6 3	(1904-1967) USA
		Physicist
Origen (4.3)	2 1 1 6 7	(185-254) Greece
		Theologian/philosopher
Osborne, Arthur (1.6)	2 2 2 6 3	(1906-1970) UK
	4 6 6 7	Biographer of Ramana Maharshi
Osborne, John (1.4)	2 4 3 4 3	(1929-1994) UK
	6 7 6 7	Playwright
Othman (2.7)	4 4 3 4 7	(?-656) Arabia
(Son-in-law of Mohammed)	6 7 6 3	3rd Caliph
Ouspensky, Peter (2.0)	2 4 6 6 3	(1878-1947) Russia
		Mathematician/esotericist
Ovid (1.7)	1 4 7 6 3	(43 BC-AD 17) Rome
		Poet
Paderewski, Ignace Jan (2.0)	6 4 7 4 7	(1860-1941) Poland
		Musician/statesman
Padmasambhava (3.0)	2 4 3 6 7	(c 8th/9th C. AD) India
	6 7 6 3	Lama
Paganini, Nicolo (1.7)	4 4 1 4 7	(1782-1840) Italy
		Musician
Paine, Tom (1.5)	6 6 6 4 3	(1737-1809) England/USA
	6 6 4 3	Revolutionary/pamphleteer
Palestrina, G P da (2.0)	4 6 4 6 3	(1525-1594) Italy
		Composer
Palme, Olof (2.1)	3 6 7 4 7	(1927-1986) Sweden
	4 4 6 3	Prime Minister
Palmer, D D (1.6)	2 4 4 6 7	(1845-1913) USA
	6 2 2 3	Fndr. chiropractic
Panchen Lama (10th) (1.7)	6 4 4 6 7	(1939-1989) Tibet
(Choekyi Gyaltsen)	6 6 6 3	Religious leader
Panini (1.8)	2 5 5 6 7	(4th C. BC) India
		Sanskrit grammarian
Pankhurst, Emmeline (1.7)	6 6 1 2 3	(1857-1928) UK
		Suffragette
Paracelsus (2.3)	1 4 5 6 7	(1493-1541) Switzerland
	6 4 6 7	Physician
Pareto, Vilfredo (2.0)	2 3 3 6 3	(1848-1923) Italy
		Economist/sociologist
Parker, Charlie (0.6)	6 4 6 6 7	(1920-1955) USA
	2 6 2 7	Jazz musician
Parnell, Charles Stewart (1.7)	6 6 1 4 3	(1846-1891) Ireland
		Politician
Pascal, Blaise (2.4)	5 3 1 2 3	(1623-1662) France
		Scientist
Pasmore, Victor (1.5)	2 4 3 2 3	(1908-1998) England
	6 7 6 7	Painter

642

Pasolini, Pier Paolo (1.53)	4 4 3 4 3 4 6 6 7	(1922-1975) Italy Filmmaker
Pasternak, Boris (1.7)	3 4 3 6 7	(1890-1960) Russia Writer
Pasteur, Louis (2.2)	5 7 7 2 3	(1822-1895) France Chemist
Patanjali (4.3)	2 6 1 4 3	(1st C. BC) India Philosopher
Patrick (2.2)	6 1 4 4 1	(c 385-461) England/Ireland Saint/bishop
Patton, George (1.7)	1 6 1 2 1	(1885-1945) USA General
Paul (3.0)	5 1 1 6 1	(1st C. AD) Tarsus (Turkey) Apostle
Pavarotti, Luciano (1.4)	2 4 7 4 7 4 3 6 3	(1935-2007) Italy Opera singer
Paz, Octavio (1.5)	2 4 3 4 3 6 7 6 7	(1914-1998) Mexico Poet/diplomat
Peale, Norman Vincent (1.55)	2 4 3 2 7 4 6 2 3	(1898-1993) USA Inspirational writer/speaker
Peck, Gregory (0.8)	2 4 2 6 7 6 6 2 3	(1916-2003) USA Film actor
Pericles (1.8)	1 7 1 2 1	(c 495-429 BC) Greece Statesman
Perkins, Charles (0.9)	3 3 4 6 5 6 2 2 3	(1936-2000) Australia Aboriginal campaigner/reformer
Perón, Evita (1.6)	1 3 4 6 3	(1919-1952) Argentina Actress/politician
Perón, Juan (1.7)	1 1 1 6 7	(1895-1974) Argentina Soldier/statesman
Perriand, Charlotte (1.4)	4 4 3 4 3 3 7 6 3	(1903-1999) France Designer
Pestalozzi, Johann (1.7)	2 6 7 6 3	(1746-1827) Switzerland Educator
Peter (3.5)	1 4 1 2 7	(1st C. AD) Palestine Apostle
Peter the Great (1.7)	6 7 1 6 3	(1672-1725) Russia Emperor
Peterson, Oscar (0.8)	2 4 3 6 3 4 7 2 7	(1925-2007) Canada Jazz musician
Petrarch, Francesco (1.7)	2 7 1 4 7 3 6 6 3	(1304-1374) Italy Poet/scholar
Phatak, S R (1.56)	4 3 4 6 3 7 6 2 7	(1896-1981) India Homoeopath
Phidias (2.2)	4 7 7 6 7	(5th C. BC) Greece Sculptor
Picasso, Pablo (2.4)	7 4 1 6 3 6 3 2 7	(1881-1973) Spain Painter
Pietrelcina, Pio da (2.3)	6 2 6 2 3	(1887-1969) Italy Priest/healer

Pilate, Pontius (1.4)	2 6 3 6 7	(b. 26 BC) Rome
	6 3 4 1	Procurator of Judea
Pindar (Pindaros) (1.7)	3 7 7 2 3	(c 522-440 BC) Greece
		Poet
Pisano, Giovanni (1.75)	4 6 3 6 7	(c1250-c1315) Italy
	6 7 6 7	Sculptor
Pisano, Nicola (1.75)	4 4 6 6 7	(c1225-c1284) Italy
	6 6 2 7	Sculptor
Pissarro, Camille (1.7)	6 4 6 4 7	(1830-1903) France
	6 2 4 3	Painter
Pitfield, Thomas Baron (1.6)	2 4 3 4 7	(1903-1999) England
	6 7 6 3	Musician/teacher/craftsman
Pitt, William (the Younger) (2.3)	1 1 1 2 3	(1759-1806) England
		Statesman
Planck, Max (2.2)	2 7 1 4 5	(1858-1947) Germany
		Physicist
Plath, Sylvia (1.3)	2 4 2 4 3	(1932-1963) UK
	6 6 6 7	Poet
Plato (2.4)	2 4 7 6 7	(c 427-347 BC) Greece
		Philosopher
Plotinus (1.6)	3 4 3 6 3	(c 204-270) Egypt
	6 7 4 7	Philosopher
Pollock, Jackson (1.5)	3 4 3 2 3	(1912-1956) USA
	3 6 6 7	Painter
Polo, Marco (1.6)	3 3 6 6 3	(1254-1324) Italy
		Explorer
Poonja, H W L (2.5)	2 4 3 4 3	(1910-1997) India
	6 7 6 7	Disciple of Ramana Maharshi
Popper, Karl (1.5)	3 4 3 4 3	(1902-1994) Austria
	6 7 6 7	Philosopher
Porter, Lord George (2.0)	2 3 4 2 3	(1920-2002) England
	7 7 6 7	Scientist/chemist
Pot, Pol (1.6)	3 6 4 6 7	(1925-1998) Cambodia
	1 6 6 3	Leader of the Khmer Rouge
Potter, Dennis (1.5)	2 4 3 6 3	(1935-1994) UK
	6 7 4 7	Playwright
Pound, Ezra (2.0)	7 1 1 4 7	(1885-1972) USA
		Poet
Poussin, Nicolas (2.4)	7 7 6 4 3	(1594-1665) France
	6 7 4 7	Painter
Powell, Enoch (1.4)	3 6 6 6 3	(1912-1998) UK
	3 6 6 5	Politician
Praag, Henri van (2.0)	3 7 7 2 7	(1916-1988) Netherlands
	5 5 4 7	Parapsychologist
Prabhakaran, Velupillai (1.0)	6 6 3 6 3	(1954-2009), Sri Lanka
	6 6 6 7	Founder, Tamil Tigers
Praxiteles (1.6)	4 4 4 6 1	(4th C. BC) Greece
		Sculptor
Preseren, France (1.4)	6 4 5 6 3	(1800-1849) Slovenia
	6 6 4 7	Poet

Presley, Elvis (0.8)	4 4 1 1 7	(1935-1977) USA
	4 6 6 7	Rock and roll star
Priestley, Joseph (2.0)	3 7 5 6 3	(1733-1804) England
		Churchman/chemist
Prokofiev, Sergei (1.8)	4 7 1 4 3	(1891-1955) Russia
		Composer
Proust, Marcel (1.7)	2 4 4 6 7	(1871-1922) France
		Writer
Puccini, Giacomo (1.7)	4 4 4 6 7	(1858-1924) Italy
		Composer
Purcell, Henry (1.6)	4 4 3 4 7	(1659-1695) England
	6 7 6 3	Composer
Purucker, Gottfried de (1.6)	6 4 6 6 3	(1874-1942) USA
	5 7 4 7	Theosophist
Pushkin, Alexandr (2.0)	4 4 1 6 3	(1799-1837) Russia
		Poet
Pythagoras (2.2)	2 6 5 6 3	(6th C. BC) Greece
		Philosopher/mathematician
Qarni, Ovais (4.0)	6 6 3 2 7	(c 6th C.) Arabia
	6 5 2 3	Disciple of Mohammed
Quanjer, Johan Henri (1.4)	2 6 3 6 7	(1935-2001) South Africa
	1 6 6 3	Editor
Quevedo, Francisco de (1.4)	6 6 4 6 3	(1580-1645) Spain
	3 7 2 3	Writer
Quinn, Anthony (1.46)	3 4 3 4 7	(1915-2001) Mexico
	6 7 6 1	Film actor
Quisling, Vidkun A. L. (1.4)	6 2 4 6 7	(1887-1945) Norway
	7 6 6 7	Politician/traitor
Rabin, Yitzhak (1.6)	3 6 5 6 7	(1922-1995) Israel
	1 6 6 3	Prime Minister
Rachmaninov, Sergey (1.7)	4 4 2 4 3	(1873-1943) Russia
	6 6 6 7	Composer
Racine, Jean (2.2)	3 1 7 4 7	(1639-1699) France
		Poet
Rainier III (1.4)	3 3 1 6 3	(1923-2005) Monaco
	6 7 6 7	Ruler/Prince of Monaco
Rajagopal, D (1.7)	2 2 6 4 3	(1900-1988) India
	4 6 6 7	Krishnamurti associate
Rajneesh (Osho) (2.3)	4 6 2 4 7	(1931-1990) India
(Chandra Mohan Jain)	6 6 4 3	Spiritual teacher
Raleigh, Walter (1.7)	1 4 3 4 7	(1552-1618) England
		Courtier/navigator/writer
Rama (4.0)	1 6 1 2 1	(c 6000 BC) India
		Avatar
Ramacharaka, Yogi (2.6)	2 4 3 4 3	(1799-1893) India
	6 7 6 7	Spiritual teacher
Ramakrishna	2 6 6 4 7	(1836-1886) India
		Avatar
Ramana Maharshi	2 6 4 2 3	(1879-1950) India
	6 6 2 7	Avatar

Rameau, Jean Philippe (2.2)	3 4 4 6 7	(1683-1764) France
		Composer
Ramesses II (2.0)	1 1 7 2 5	(1292-1225 BC) Egypt
		Pharaoh
Randall, Tony (1.4)	2 4 6 6 3	(1920-2004) USA
	4 2 4 7	Actor
Rao, Canchupati V. V. (2.0)	3 6 4 6 3	(1926-1984) India
	6 2 2 7	Yogi
Raphael (3.0)	2 4 7 6 7	(1483-1520) Italy
	6 7 4 2	Painter
Raphael, Sarah Natasha (1.4)	2 4 4 2 7	(1960-2001) UK
	2 6 6 3	Painter
Rasputin, Grigori Y (1.6)	6 6 3 6 7	(c 1871-1916) Russia
		Mystic/monk
Ravel, Maurice (2.0)	4 7 3 4 7	(1875-1937) France
		Composer
Reagan, Ronald (1.4)	2 4 6 6 7	(1911-2004) USA
	4 2 2 3	Actor/President
Redhead, Brian (1.4)	2 4 3 4 3	(1929-1994) UK
	6 7 6 7	Broadcaster
Redon, Odilon (1.5)	4 5 2 4 3	(1840-1916) France
	6 6 4 7	Painter
Reed, John (1.4)	2 4 3 4 3	(1909-1999) UK
	6 7 6 7	Musicologist
Reger, Max (1.7)	2 2 4 4 3	(1873-1916) Germany
		Composer
Reich, Wilhelm (2.0)	2 1 7 6 3	(1897-1957) Austria
		Psychologist
Reinhardt, Django (0.6)	3 4 3 6 3	(1910-1953) Belgium/France
	2 7 6 7	Jazz musician
Reiss, Stephen (1.5)	2 4 3 2 7	(1918-1999) UK
	6 7 6 3	Art administrator/historian
Reisz, Karel (1.4)	4 2 4 6 3	(1926-2003) Czechoslovakia
	4 6 2 7	Film director
Rembrandt (3.0)	2 4 3 4 7	(1606-1669) Netherlands
	6 1 4 3	Painter
Renoir, Auguste (2.0)	4 2 3 2 3	(1841-1919) France
		Painter
Respighi, Ottorino (1.65)	4 4 3 6 3	(1879-1936) Italy
		Composer
Reuther, Walter (1.3)	4 6 3 4 3	(1907-1970) USA
	6 6 4 1	Labour leader
Rhodes, Cecil (1.6)	6 1 7 6 3	(1853-1902) UK
		Statesman
Riabouchinska, Tatiana (1.4)	6 6 6 4 3	(1917-2000) Russia
	4 6 6 7	Ballerina
Richard, Mira (2.6)	4 6 6 4 3	(1878-1973) France
(The Mother)	6 6 2 3	Spiritual teacher
Richards, Vernon (1.4)	4 6 6 6 7	(1915-2001) Italy
(Vero Recchioni)	6 1 2 3	Anarchist

Richardson, Ralph (1.7)	2 4 7 2 3	(1902-1983) UK Actor
Richelieu (1.7)	3 3 1 4 7	(1585-1642) France Cardinal/statesman
Richter, Sviatoslav (1.6)	4 6 4 2 7 3 7 6 3	(1915-1997) Russia Pianist
Rilke, Rainer Maria (1.7)	2 4 4 6 3	(1875-1926) Germany Poet
Rimbaud, Arthur (1.7)	3 4 1 2 3	(1854-1891) France Poet
Riviere, Enrique Pichon (2.0)	6 4 7 4 7 6 5 6 3	(1907-1977) Argentina Psychoanalyst
Rizal, José (1.7)	6 4 3 6 3 6 7 6 3	(1861-1896) Philippines Writer/reformer
Roberts, Estelle (1.2)	2 6 6 6 3 4 4 2 3	(1889-1970) UK Healer/medium
Robeson, Paul (1.6)	2 4 1 6 3	(1898-1976) USA Singer/actor
Robespierre (1.7)	1 3 1 4 3	(1758-1794) France Revolutionary
Robin, Marthe (1.8)	4 6 3 4 3 6 6 2 3	(1902-1981) France Mystic/stigmatist
Robson, Robert (Bobby) (0.85)	5 7 5 6 7 3 7 2 3	(1933-2009) UK Footballer/manager
Roddenberry, Gene (1.35)	2 4 3 4 3 6 7 6 7	(1921-1991) USA Creator of "Star Trek"
Roddick, Anita (0.9)	2 6 2 6 7 6 4 2 3	(1942-2007) UK Fndr. The Body Shop
Rodin, Auguste (1.9)	3 4 4 2 7	(1840-1917) France Sculptor
Rodrigues, Amalia (1.4)	4 6 4 2 7 2 7 4 3	(1920-1999) Portugal Fado singer
Roerich, Helena (4.0)	1 2 1 6 3 6 2 4 7	(1879-1955) Russia Occultist
Roerich, Nicholas (2.1)	7 7 7 6 7 4 1 4 7	(1874-1947) Russia Painter/philosopher
Romero (1.7)	2 2 3 6 1	(1917-1980) El Salvador Bishop/human rights activist
Ronsard, Pierre de (1.6)	2 4 4 6 3	(1524-1585) France Poet
Röntgen, Wilhelm von (1.7)	5 7 5 2 3	(1845-1923) Germany Physicist
Roosevelt, Anna Eleanor (2.0)	7 6 1 2 1	(1884-1962) USA Humanitarian
Roosevelt, Franklin D (2.7)	2 4 1 2 1	(1884-1945) USA President
Roper, Frank (1.5)	2 4 6 6 7 2 2 2 7	(1914-2000) UK Sculptor
Rossini, Gioacchino (1.7)	4 4 6 2 3 4 6 4 3	(1792-1868) Italy Composer

Rostropovich, Mstislav (1.6)	4 4 3 4 3	(1927-2007) Russia
	6 7 6 3	Cellist
Rothko, Mark (1.8)	2 4 4 6 3	(1903-1970) Latvia/USA
		Painter
Rousseau, Jean Jacques (2.2)	2 6 7 4 7	(1712-1778) France
		Philosopher
Rózsa, Miklós (1.3)	4 4 3 4 3	(1907-1995) Hungary
	4 7 6 7	Film composer
Rubens, Peter Paul (3.0)	4 7 1 4 7	(1577-1640) Netherlands
		Painter
Rubinstein, Arthur (1.75)	2 4 4 6 7	(1887-1982) Poland
	4 6 6 7	Pianist
Rudhyar, Dane (1.9)	2 4 4 6 3	(1895-1986) USA
	4 6 6 7	Astrologer/composer
Rulof, Joseph (1.5)	3 6 5 6 7	(1889-1952) Netherlands
	6 7 4 7	Parapsychologist
Rumi, Mevlána Jelaluddin (1.8)	6 4 3 4 7	(1207-1273) Persia
	6 7 6 3	Sufi poet
Runcie, Robert (1.4)	2 4 3 4 3	(1921-2000) England
	6 7 6 7	Archbishop of Canterbury
Russel, Walter (1.6)	4 4 7 6 7	(1871-1963) USA
	6 6 4 7	Sculptor
Russell, Bertrand (1.7)	3 3 1 6 3	(1872-1970) UK
		Philosopher
Russell, Charles Taze (1.6)	6 2 1 6 3	(1852-1916) USA
		Fndr. Jehovah's Witnesses
Rutherford, Ernest (2.0)	2 7 7 2 5	(1871-1937) New Zealand
		Physicist
Ruyter, Michael de (2.0)	1 7 1 6 7	(1607-1676) Netherlands
		Naval leader
Ruzicka, Marla (1.4)	4 4 3 6 3	(1976-2005) USA
	6 7 6 7	Peace activist/ fndr. CIVIC
Ryder, Baroness Sue (1.5)	3 6 4 6 7	(1923-2000) England
	2 6 2 3	Philanthropist
Ryohkan (1.4)	2 6 3 6 7	(1758-1831) Japan
	6 3 6 3	Monk/poet/calligrapher
Sadat, Anwar (1.9)	2 6 6 2 3	(1918-1981) Egypt
		President
Sade, Marquis de (0.75)	3 6 6 1 3	(1740-1814) France
	6 4 1 7	Writer
Sagan, Carl (2.4)	4 6 4 6 3	(1934-1996) USA
	2 6 6 3	Scientist/astronomer
Sai Baba of Shirdi	2 4 1 4 3	(1840-1918) India
	7 4 2 7	Avatar
Saicho (1.9)	6 7 4 6 3	(767-822) Japan
	6 6 4 7	Fndr Buddhism/Tendai sect
Said, Edward W (1.5)	3 6 3 2 7	(1935-2003) Palestine
	6 6 4 3	Political activist/literary critic
Saigo, Takamori (1.5)	6 7 1 6 7	(1827-1877) Japan
	7 7 4 7	Soldier/general

Saigyo (1.6)	4 7 3 2 7 4 6 6 3	(1118-1190) Japan Buddhist priest/poet
Saint-Exupéry, Antoine de (1.5)	1 3 5 6 7 1 4 4 7	(1900-1944) France Writer
Saint-Simon, Claude de (1.7)	7 2 6 6 3	(1760-1825) France Political philosopher
Sakharov, Andrei (2.0)	7 6 5 6 3 4 7 4 7	(1921-1989) Russia Physicist
San Martin, General José de (1.4)	6 4 3 4 7 6 7 6 3	(1778-1850) Argentina Liberator
Sanchez, Celia (1.5)	6 6 4 6 3 6 3 6 7	(c 1920-1980) Cuba F. Castro's confidante
Sand, George (1.6)	2 4 4 6 3	(1804-1876) France Writer
Sankaran, P (1.6)	3 6 7 6 3 2 4 2 7	(1922-1979) India Homoeopath
Sant'Anna Galvao, (2.5) Antonio de	6 6 3 6 7 6 3 6 3	(1739-1822) Brazil Franciscan monk
Sappho (1.6)	4 4 4 6 3	(b. c 650 BC) Greece Poet
Saraswati, Akhandananda (1.7)	6 4 6 6 3 3 2 6 3	(c 1947-1997) India Swami/yoga teacher
Sarkar, P R (2.5) (Shri Anandamurti)	2 4 6 4 3 6 2 4 3	(1921-1990) India Philosopher
Sarraute, Nathalie (1.55)	3 6 6 4 3 3 2 6 7	(1900-1999) France Writer
Sartre, Jean Paul (1.7)	3 2 3 6 3 4 3 6 7	(1905-1980) France Philosopher/writer
Satchidananda, Swami (2.5)	2 4 5 6 3 2 7 2 7	(1912-2002) India Founder Integral Yoga Institute
Satie, Erik (1.5)	3 5 7 2 4	(1866-1925) France Composer
Saunders, Cicely M S (1.5)	2 6 4 4 3 2 6 2 7	(1918-2005) England Fndr. hospice movement
Savimbi, Jonas Malheiro (0.9)	6 6 1 6 1 6 6 6 3	(1934-2002) Angola Nationalist leader
Savonarola, Girolamo (1.7)	6 4 1 6 1	(1452-1498) Italy Religious reformer
Scarlatti, Domenico (2.4)	2 3 4 4 7	(1685-1757) Italy Composer
Scarman, Leslie (1.4)	3 7 4 6 7 3 6 2 3	(1911-2004) England Lawyer
Schiele, Egon (1.4)	2 4 7 6 7 3 6 2 7	(1890-1918) Austria Painter
Schikaneder, Emanuel (1.5)	4 4 6 6 7 4 2 4 3	(1751-1812) Austria Librettist of *Die Zauberflöte*
Schiller, Friedrich von (1.7)	2 4 6 2 7	(1759-1805) Germany Dramatist/poet
Schlesinger, Arthur (1.3)	3 7 6 6 3 3 3 6 3	(1917-2007) USA Historian

Schliemann, Heinrich (1.7)	7 1 7 4 7	(1822-1890) Germany Archaeologist
Schmidt, Annie (1.3)	2 4 5 2 3 2 7 6 7	(1911-1995) Netherlands Writer
Schneider, Romy (1.4)	3 4 6 6 3 2 6 4 3	(1938-1982) Germany Actress
Schönberg, Arnold (1.9)	6 4 1 4 7	(1874-1951) Austria Composer
Schopenhauer, Arthur (2.2)	6 6 1 2 7	(1788-1860) Germany Philosopher
Schubert, Franz Peter (2.4)	4 2 2 4 2 4 7 6 3	(1797-1828) Austria Composer
Schütz, Heinrich (2.0)	4 4 6 6 7 7 2 2 3	(1585-1672) Germany Composer
Schulz, Charles M. (1.4)	2 4 3 4 3 6 7 6 7	(1922-2000) USA Cartoonist
Schumacher, Enril (1.5)	2 4 3 4 7 6 7 6 3	(1912-1999) Germany Painter
Schumann, Robert (2.3)	6 4 4 6 5	(1810-1856) Germany Composer
Schuurman, (1.4) Anna-Maria van	2 4 3 4 3 6 7 6 7	(1607-1678) Netherlands Writer/poet
Schuurman, C J (1.5)	3 6 4 4 7 7 6 6 3	(1889-1979) Netherlands Psychiatrist
Schweitzer, Albert (2.4)	2 2 1 4 3	(1875-1965) Germany/France Humanitarian/organist
Scofield, David Paul (1.5)	2 4 7 6 3 3 4 2 7	(1922-2008) England Actor
Scott, Cyril (1.55)	2 4 3 6 3 6 4 4 7	(1879-1970) UK Composer
Segal, Ronald Michael (1.6)	2 4 3 6 7 6 7 4 3	(1932-2008) South Africa Anti-apartheid activist
Segovia, Andrés (1.7)	6 4 4 2 1 4 1 6 7	(1894-1987) Spain Guitarist
Selassie, Haile (1.6)	4 1 6 6 7 6 1 6 7	(1892-1975) Ethiopia Emperor
Sellers, Peter (1.4)	4 4 6 4 7 6 6 4 7	(1925-1980) UK Actor
Sen, Rikyu (0.8)	4 6 4 4 7 7 6 2 3	(1522-1591) Japan Tea ceremony teacher
Seneca (the Younger) (1.7)	3 7 6 2 7	(c 5 BC-AD 65) Rome Philosopher
Serkin, Rudolph (1.55)	4 4 7 4 3 6 3 6 7	(1903-1991) Germany Pianist
Shackleton, Ernest (1.6)	2 6 3 6 7 2 1 6 3	(1874-1922) Ireland Explorer
Shakespeare, William (3.5)	2 4 1 4 3 7 4 6 7	(1564-1616) England Playwright/poet
Shankaracharya	2 1 1 6 3	(788-820) India Avatar

Shaw, George Bernard (2.0)	2 3 1 2 7	(1856-1950) Ireland
		Dramatist/writer
Shelley, Percy Bysshe (1.8)	2 4 3 6 7	(1792-1822) England
	4 6 2 3	Poet
Sheppard, David (1.5)	2 4 7 2 7	(1929-2005) UK
	6 3 6 3	Bishop/cricket captain
Shiba, Ryotaro (1.6)	4 4 2 4 3	(1923-1996) Japan
	6 6 6 7	Novelist
Shimura, Takashi (1.35)	4 4 6 2 7	(1905-1982) Japan
	6 3 4 3	Actor
Shinran (1.8)	6 6 1 6 3	(1173-1262) Japan
	4 7 6 3	Buddhism/Jodo-shinshu
Shivapuri Baba (2.8)	2 4 4 6 7	(1826-1963) India
	6 4 6 3	Hindu saint
Shohmu (2.0)	6 6 6 2 7	(701-756) Japan
(Saint Emperor)	2 4 2 3	Buddhist Emperor
Short, Renée (1.45)	2 4 3 6 3	(1916-2003) UK
	3 7 2 3	Politician
Shostakovich, Dmitri (2.0)	7 4 4 6 7	(1906-1975) Russia
		Composer
Shotoku-Taishi (2.0)	6 6 5 4 3	(574-622) Japan
	7 4 6 3	Prince/regent
Shriver, Eunice Kennedy (1.25)	4 6 3 6 3	(1921-2009) USA
	6 7 6 3	Philanthropist/Special Olympics
Sibelius, Jean (1.87)	2 4 4 6 7	(1865-1958) Finland
	6 4 6 7	Composer
Sidis, William James (1.7)	4 7 4 6 3	(1898-1944) USA
	4 6 6 7	Scientist
Simenon, Georges (1.57)	3 6 4 2 7	(1903-1989) Belgium
	4 7 6 3	Writer
Simpson, James Young (1.7)	5 1 5 4 3	(1811-1870) UK
		Physician
Sinatra, Frank (0.75)	2 4 6 2 3	(1915-1998) USA
	6 4 6 7	Singer
Singh, Sant Darshan (2.4)	4 2 4 4 3	(1921-1989) Pakistan
	6 7 6 7	Fndr. S. Kirpal Ruhani Mission
Singh, Sant Kirpal (2.4)	6 6 3 4 7	(1894-1974) Pakistan
	4 7 6 3	Fndr. Ruhani Satsang
Singh, Sawan (2.4)	2 3 4 2 3	(1858-1940) India
	6 7 4 7	Radhasoami Satsang
Singha, Shyam (1.65)	2 3 4 6 7	(1920-2000) India
	6 7 2 3	Homoeopath/teacher/healer
Sinnett, Alfred P (2.2)	2 6 1 6 3	(1840-1921) UK
		Theosophist
Siva Yogaswami (1.5)	6 2 5 6 7	(1872-1964) Sri Lanka
	2 3 2 3	Spiritual teacher
Sivananda of Rishikesh (4.0)	2 1 6 4 7	(1887-1963) India
	4 3 2 7	Spiritual teacher
Sivaya Subramuniya Swami (1.5)	6 2 3 6 7	(1947-2001) USA
	6 7 2 3	Saiva Siddhanta leader

651

Skinner, Burrhus Frederic (1.5)	2 6 3 2 3 6 7 6 7	(1904-2001) USA Psychologist/behaviourist
Slovo, Joe (1.47)	3 4 3 4 3 6 7 6 7	(1926-1995) Lithuania Anti-apartheid activist
Smit, Alexander (2.0)	3 4 2 6 7 6 6 6 7	(1948-1998) Netherlands Spiritual teacher
Smith, Adam (1.7)	3 3 5 4 3	(1723-1790) England Economist/philosopher
Smith, John (1.57)	3 4 3 4 3 3 7 6 7	(1938-1994) UK Labour Party leader
Smith, Joseph (1.7)	6 6 6 2 7	(1805-1844) USA Fndr. Mormonism
Smith, Samantha (1.5)	1 4 6 4 7 6 6 2 3	(1972-1985) USA Schoolgirl/diplomat
Smuts, Jan Christiaan (2.0)	2 7 1 6 7	(1870-1950) South Africa Statesman/military leader
Socrates (2.4)	6 2 1 6 3	(c 469-399 BC) Greece Philosopher
Solomon (1.7)	2 1 4 2 3	(1059-1013 BC) Israel King
Sontag, Susan (1.5)	2 7 3 6 7 4 6 2 3	(1933-2004) USA Writer
Soper, Donald (1.5)	6 6 3 4 3 6 3 6 7	(1903-1998) UK Minister/pacifist
Sophocles (1.7)	3 6 1 4 7	(c 496-405 BC) Greece Dramatist
Spalding, Baird (1.6)	2 3 5 6 7	(1857-1953) Scotland Traveller/writer
Spartacus (1.5)	1 1 2 2 1	(d. 71 BC) Thrace Rebel (Greece)
Spencer, Herbert (1.6)	2 4 3 4 3 6 7 6 7	(1820-1903) UK Philosopher/sociologist
Spencer, Kelvin (2.0)	2 3 5 2 7 6 7 6 3	(1898-1993) UK Scientist/environmentalist
Spencer, Minocher K. (1.5)	3 6 6 2 7 2 6 4 3	(1888-1958) India Yogi/writer
Spender, Humphrey (1.4)	2 4 3 6 7 4 3 6 3	(1910-2005) UK Photographer
Spender, Stephen (1.6)	2 4 3 4 7 6 6 6 3	(1909-1995) England Poet
Spinoza, Baruch (2.4)	2 3 3 4 3	(1632-1677) Netherlands Philosopher
Spock, Dr Benjamin (1.5)	2 4 3 4 3 7 5 6 7	(1903-1998) USA Paediatrician/writer
Srong-tsan-gam-po (2.0)	2 6 4 2 7 6 6 2 3	(623-689) Tibet King
Staël, Nicolas de (1.8)	4 4 4 6 7	(1914-1955) Russia/France Painter
Stalin, Joseph (2.0)	1 7 7 2 1	(1879-1953) Georgia Soviet leader

Stein, Edith (1.5)	6 6 3 4 1 6 7 6 6	(1891-1942) Germany Saint/Holocaust victim
Steinbeck, John (1.6)	7 4 4 6 7	(1902-1968) USA Writer
Steiner, Rudolf (2.2)	2 4 1 6 3	(1861-1925) Austria Philosopher/educator
Stepanek, Mattie (1.4)	2 6 3 6 3 2 3 2 3	(1990-2004) USA Poet
Stern, Isaac (1.6)	2 4 3 4 3 6 7 6 7	(1920-2001) Russia Violinist
Stevenson, Adlai (1.6)	2 7 6 2 7 4 6 4 7	(1900-1965) USA Politician
Stockhausen, Karlheinz (1.6)	4 4 7 6 7 7 3 4 3	(1928-2007) Germany Composer
Stradivarius, Antonio (1.65)	2 4 2 4 7	(c 1644-1737) Italy Violin maker
Strauss, David Friedrich (2.0)	6 1 1 2 7	(1808-1874) Germany Theologian
Strauss, Franz Josef (1.65)	1 6 7 6 1 1 6 6 7	(1915-1988) Germany Politician
Strauss, Richard (1.8)	1 6 4 4 7	(1864-1949) Germany Composer
Stravinsky, Igor (2.3)	7 4 1 6 7	(1882-1971) Russia Composer
Strindberg, Johan August (1.7)	4 1 7 4 3	(1849-1912) Sweden Dramatist
Stuyvesant, Peter (1.7)	6 7 7 2 7	(1592-1672) Netherlands Administrator
Subba Row, T (1.7)	2 1 7 6 7	(1856-1890) India Theosophist
Suharto, Muhammed (1.3)	3 6 3 4 3 6 6 6 7	(1921-2008) Indonesia Military leader/President
Sukarno, Achmad (1.7)	6 1 3 4 3	(1902-1970) Indonesia President
Sullivan, Anne M (1.75)	2 2 7 6 3	(1866-1936) USA Teacher
Suzmann, Helen (1.6)	2 6 3 6 7 6 3 4 3	(1917-2009) South Africa Anti-apartheid activist
Suzuki, Daisetsu (1.7)	2 6 1 6 3	(1870-1966) Japan Zen scholar
Sviridov, Georgi (1.5)	6 4 3 6 7 6 6 2 3	(1915-1998) Russia Composer
Svoboda, Ludvik (1.7)	5 6 1 6 3	(1895-1979) Czechoslovakia Statesman
Swedenborg, Emanuel (2.3)	2 4 4 6 3	(1688-1772) Sweden Mystic
Sweelinck, Jan Pieterszoon (1.6)	3 4 3 4 7 2 7 6 3	(1562-1621) Netherlands Composer
Swift, Jonathan (1.7)	6 4 1 4 3	(1667-1745) Ireland Writer

Sylvester, David (1.3)	2 6 6 6 3 3 3 2 5	(1924-2001) UK Art critic/curator
Szalonek, Witold (1.5)	6 6 6 6 7 6 6 6 3	(1927-2001) Poland Composer
Tabriz, Shamsi (1.9)	4 6 4 6 3 3 6 2 7	(d. 1247) Persia Sufi poet
Tagore, Rabindranath (2.2)	2 4 1 4 7	(1861-1941) India Poet/philosopher
Taizé, Brother Roger of (1.5) (Roger Schutz)	6 4 6 6 3 6 6 6 3	(1915-2005) Switzerland Priest
Takahashi, Shinji (2.0)	6 6 7 4 7 6 3 6 7	(1927-1976) Japan Religious leader/ fndr. GLA
Takemitu, Tohru (1.46)	3 4 3 4 2 6 7 2 7	(1930-1996) Japan Composer
Talleyrand, Charles de (1.7)	3 1 3 2 3	(1754-1838) France Statesman
Tallis, Thomas (1.7)	4 6 6 6 3	(c 1505-1585) England Composer
Taniguchi, Masaharu (2.3)	6 7 4 6 3	(1894-1985) Japan Spiritual teacher
Tansley, David V.(1.4)	2 4 3 4 3 6 7 6 7	(c 1934-1988) UK Radionics researcher
Tarkowski (1.5)	3 6 4 6 3 3 7 2 7	(1932-1986) Russia Film director
Tati, Jacques (1.57)	4 4 2 4 7 4 2 6 7	(1907-1982) France Filmmaker/comedian
Taungpulu Sayadaw Phaya (1.7)	2 6 6 4 3 2 6 4 7	(1898-1986) Burma Buddhist teacher
Taylor, A J P (1.4)	2 4 4 6 3 2 7 6 2	(1906-1990) UK Historian
Tchaikovsky, Piotr Ilyich (1.8)	4 4 3 6 7	(1840-1893) Russia Composer
Tebaldi, Renata (1.4)	4 4 6 2 7 4 6 4 3	(1922-2004)Italy Opera singer
Teilhard de Chardin, P (2.35)	2 6 3 2 3	(1881-1955) France Scientist/philosopher
Telemann, Georg (1.9)	3 4 6 4 7 4 6 6 3	(1687-1767) Germany Composer
Tendai (2.0)	6 6 7 4 3	(538-597) China Buddhism/Tendai sect
Tennyson, Alfred (2.0)	6 1 4 4 7	(1809-1892) UK Poet
Teresa of Ávila (3.1)	6 6 3 4 3	(1515-1582) Spain Saint/mystic
Teresa, Mother (1.45) (Agnes Bojaxhiu)	6 6 2 6 3 6 6 6 7	(1910-1997)Albania Nun/humanitarian
Tesla, Nikola (2.0)	2 3 1 6 5 6 4 2 7	(1856-1943) Croatia Inventor
Tezuka, Osamu (1.6)	6 4 4 6 7 4 7 4 3	(1926-1989) Japan Cartoonist

654

Thanh, Au Truong (0.85)	4 6 2 6 3 6 6 2 7	(1925-2009) Vietnam Artist/refugee/politician
Thant, U (1.7)	2 2 1 6 2	(1909-1974) Burma Diplomat
Thaw, John (0.85)	2 4 2 6 7 4 4 2 3	(1942-2002)UK Actor
'The Boy' (4.0) (Name not known)	2 4 2 6 7 2 6 2 3	(c 1910-1956) UK Subject *The Boy and the Brothers*
Thibaud, Jacques (1.6)	2 2 4 4 3	(1880-1953) France Musician
Thomas (2.0)	2 5 3 4 7 6 6 6 3	(d. AD 53) Palestine Apostle
Thomas, Dylan (1.5)	2 4 1 4 3	(1914-1953) Wales Poet
Thomas, Ismay (1.6)	2 4 3 2 3 6 7 6 7	(1920-1995) UK Educator
Thompson, E P (1.5)	2 3 6 4 3 4 1 6 7	(1928-1993) UK Historian/peace activist
Thoreau, Henry (1.6)	2 3 3 6 3	(1817-1862) USA Writer
Thucydides (1.6)	5 3 1 2 7	(c 460-400 BC) Greece Historian
Tiberius (1.3)	3 6 3 6 3 6 3 6 7	(42 BC – AD 37) Rome Emperor
Tinbergen, Jan (1.6)	3 6 4 2 3 6 7 6 7	(1903-1994) Netherlands Mathematician
Tintoretto (2.5)	4 7 1 6 7	(1518-1594) Italy Painter
Tippet, Sir Michael (1.6)	2 4 3 4 3 6 7 6 7	(1905-1998) England Composer
Titian (3.0)	4 4 7 6 7	(c 1490-1576) Italy Painter
Tito, Josip Broz (2.5)	1 1 1 4 1	(1892-1980) Croatia President of Yugoslavia
Tobey, Mark (1.6)	2 4 3 4 3 7 7 6 7	(1890-1976) USA Painter
Tobin, James (1.37)	2 6 3 6 3 3 3 2 7	(1918-2002) USA Economist
Tokugawa, Ieyasu (1.55)	2 1 3 6 7 4 7 6 1	(1542-1616) Japan Shogun
Tolkien, J R R (1.7)	4 6 4 4 3	(1892-1973) South Africa/UK Writer
Tolstoy, Leo (2.2)	2 4 6 6 3	(1828-1910) Russia Writer
Tomlinson, Jane (1.2)	2 4 6 6 3 3 6 2 7	(1964-2007) England Athlete/charity campaigner
Tomonaga, Shin-ichiro (1.7)	4 6 4 6 7 7 3 6 5	(1906-1979) Japan Physicist
Tortelier, Paul (1.57)	2 4 1 6 7 4 7 6 7	(1914-1990) France Cellist/teacher

655

Toscanini, Arturo (2.0)	3 1 4 4 3	(1867-1957) Italy
		Conductor
Toure, Ali Farka (1.2)	2 4 6 6 7	(1939-2006) Mali
	4 4 4 3	Musician/mayor
Toynbee, Philip (1.35)	2 6 6 6 3	(1916-1981) UK
	6 6 4 7	Writer
Tratteli, Trygve (1.46)	6 6 4 6 3	(1910-1984) Norway
	3 7 6 3	Politician
Trevelyan, George (1.5)	2 4 6 4 7	(1906-1996) England
	6 2 2 7	Writer/spiritual teacher
Trotsky, Leon (2.2)	7 1 7 6 3	(1879-1940) Russia
		Revolutionary
Trudeau, Pierre (1.5)	6 4 3 4 7	(1919-2000)Canada
	6 7 6 3	Prime Minister
Trungpa Rinpoche, Chögyam (1.8)	2 4 2 4 7	(1940-1987) Tibet
	6 6 4 3	Buddhist meditation teacher
Tudjman, Franjo (1.5)	3 7 7 6 7	(1922-1999) Croatia
	3 6 6 7	President
Tudor Pole, Wellesley (2.0)	2 7 7 6 3	(1884-1968) UK
		Mystic
Tukey, John (1.4)	7 5 6 4 7	(1915-2000) USA
	2 4 6 3	Mathematician
Tulsidas (2.5)	1 4 7 6 7	(1532-1623) India
	7 3 2 3	Poet
Turner, J M W (2.5)	4 4 1 2 3	(1775-1851) England
		Painter
Tutin, Dorothy (1.4)	2 4 4 2 3	(1930-2001) UK
	2 6 6 7	Actress
Twain, Mark (1.7)	6 2 4 6 7	(1835-1910) USA
		Writer
Tyndale, William (1.7)	6 6 7 6 3	(c 1492-1536) England
		Biblical scholar
Uccello, Paolo (2.6)	2 4 4 6 7	(1396-1475) Italy
		Painter
Ueshiba, Morihei (1.5)	6 6 2 4 3	(1883-1969) Japan
	4 6 6 7	Founder of Aikido
Uglow, Euan (1.4)	6 4 3 6 7	(1932-2000) UK
	6 7 6 3	Artist
Unamuno, Miguel (1.5)	4 4 3 4 3	(1864-1936) Spain
	6 7 6 7	Writer
Unseld, Siegfried (1.4)	3 5 3 4 7	(1924-2002) Germany
	2 6 2 3	Publisher
Ursula (2.5)	6 6 6 6 7	(4th C. AD) Germany
		Saint/martyr
Ustinov, Peter Alexander (1.45)	4 4 2 2 3	(1921-2004) UK
	4 6 6 3	Actor/playwright/film director
Uyl, Joop den (1.6)	3 6 6 6 7	(1919-1987) Netherlands
	4 1 4 3	Politician
Valentinus (1.6)	6 1 3 2 7	(2nd C. AD) Egypt
	6 7 4 3	Gnostic philosopher

Valois, Ninette de (1.4)	2 1 3 6 3	(1898-2001) Ireland
(Edris Stannus)	4 6 2 7	Ballerina
Vance, Cyrus (1.5)	2 3 5 2 7	(1917-2002) USA
	3 7 4 3	Statesman
Van der Post, Laurens (1.6)	2 4 6 4 7	(1906-1996) South Africa
	6 3 6 3	Writer/conservationist
van Doesburg, Theo (1.25)	2 4 5 6 3	(1883-1931) Netherlands
	4 7 2 7	Painter/De Stijl movement
Varah, Edward Chad (1.5)	2 4 3 4 3	(1911-2007) UK
	6 7 6 7	Priest/founder Samaritans
Vaughan Williams, Ralph (1.8)	4 4 4 6 7	(1872-1958) UK
	6 4 4 3	Composer
Veening, Cornelis (1.7)	3 4 2 6 7	(1885-1976) Netherlands
	4 4 6 3	Breath therapist
Velasquez, Diego (2.4)	4 7 1 4 7	(1599-1660) Spain
	6 7 4 3	Painter
Vellacott, Elizabeth Jessie (1.3)	2 4 6 4 3	(1905-2002) UK
	6 2 6 7	Artist
Verdi, Giuseppe (1.9)	4 4 4 6 7	(1813-1901) Italy
		Composer
Verduco, Patricia (1.54)	2 3 4 6 3	(1947-2008) Chile
	7 6 2 7	Activist/writer
Vere, Edmund de (1.4)	2 4 3 4 7	(1550-1604) England
	6 7 6 3	Poet/dramatist
Vermeer, Jan (2.4)	3 7 4 2 7	(1632-1675) Netherlands
	6 4 6 7	Painter
Verne, Jules (1.4)	3 4 3 4 3	(1828-1905) France
	6 7 6 7	Novelist
Veronese, Paolo (3.0)	7 4 7 6 7	(1528-1588) Italy
	7 4 2 3	Painter
Vigeland, Gustav (1.4)	4 4 6 6 3	(1869-1943) Norway
	2 6 2 7	Sculptor
Villa, Pancho (1.7)	1 1 3 6 7	(1877-1923) Mexico
		Revolutionary
Vivaldi, Antonio (2.2)	3 4 3 6 7	(1678-1741) Italy
		Composer
Vivekananda	2 1 1 6 1	(1862-1902) India
		Avatar
Voltaire, François de (2.0)	2 4 1 6 3	(1694-1778) France
		Writer/philospher
Vondel, Joost van den (2.0)	3 1 7 6 5	(1587-1679) Netherlands
		Poet
Vonnegut, Kurt (1.4)	2 4 3 6 7	(1922-2007) USA
	6 7 4 7	Novelist
Vyasa, Veda (4.0)	2 4 3 4 3	(c 300 BC) India
	6 7 6 7	Spiritual teacher
Wagner, Cosima (1.6)	4 6 1 2 7	(1837-1930) Germany
	6 6 2 3	Wife of Richard Wagner
Wagner, Richard (2.4)	1 1 4 4 7	(1813-1883) Germany
		Composer

Wallace, Alfred Russel (1.5)	3 5 7 4 7 6 3 6 3	(1823-1913) UK Naturalist
Wallace, William (1.3)	4 6 3 6 7 6 4 2 1	(1274-1305) Scotland Patriot/leader
Wallenberg, Raoul (1.6)	4 6 4 6 7 3 7 2 3	(1912- c 1947) Sweden Diplomat/humanitarian
Waltari, Mika (1.3)	5 4 5 6 7 6 7 2 3	(1908-1979) Finland Writer
Ward, Barbara (2.0)	3 3 5 6 3	(1914-1981) UK Economist/writer
Warhol, Andy (1.5)	2 4 2 6 3 4 2 6 7	(1928-1987) USA Painter
Washington, Booker T. (1.4)	2 5 3 4 7 2 5 2 7	(1856-1915) USA Activist
Washington, George (2.3)	2 3 1 6 3	(1732-1799) USA Military leader/president
Watt, James (1.7)	2 5 5 4 3	(1736-1819) Scotland Inventor
Watteau, Antoine (1.8)	3 4 7 4 3 7 3 2 7	(1684-1721) France Painter
Waugh, Auberon A. (1.5)	2 4 3 6 7 6 6 6 3	(1939-2001) England Writer
Weber, Max (1.5)	4 6 5 6 3 3 7 2 7	(1864-1920) Germany Sociologist
Webern, Anton von (2.0)	4 7 7 6 3	(1883-1945) Austria Composer
Wei, Wang (1.7)	2 7 2 2 3	(699-759) China Buddhist poet/painter
Weill, Kurt (1.7)	6 4 7 6 7	(1900-1950) Germany Composer
Weiss, Peter (1.6)	2 3 5 6 7	(1916-1982) Germany Dramatist
Weizsäcker, Carl F. von (1.6)	7 3 5 6 7 6 3 6 3	(1912-2007) Germany Philosopher/physicist
Wellington, Duke of (1.7) (Arthur Wellesley)	3 1 1 2 7	(1769-1852) Ireland/UK Soldier/statesman
Wells, H G (1.7)	2 2 1 4 3	(1866-1946) UK Writer
Wells, John (1.45)	2 4 3 4 7 6 7 6 3	(1907-2000) England Painter
Wellstone, Paul (1.5)	2 4 6 4 3 6 2 6 7	(1944 - 2002) USA Politician
Welty, Eudora (1.5)	2 4 3 6 3 6 7 2 7	(1909-2001) USA Writer
Wen Ch'eng (1.4)	2 2 3 4 3 4 7 6 7	(603-656) Tibet White Tara Princess
Weor, Samuel Aun (1.45)	4 6 3 6 3 2 6 6 7	(1917-1977) Mexico Gnostic leader
Wergeland, Henrik A (1.3)	4 4 6 2 3 6 6 6 7	(1808-1845) Norway Poet

Wesley, John (1.6)	6 6 2 6 3	(1703-1791) England
		Fndr. Methodism
Wehle, J R (1.5)	4 4 7 6 3	(1848-1936) Germany
	6 4 2 7	Painter
White, Barry (1.2)	2 4 3 6 7	(1944-2003) USA
(Barrence Carter)	4 7 6 3	Singer/songwriter
White, Patrick (1.55)	1 4 7 6 7	(1912-1990) Australia
	6 3 6 7	Writer
Whitman, Walt (1.7)	3 6 1 4 7	(1819-1891) USA
		Poet
Whittle, Frank (1.5)	2 5 5 4 7	(1906-1996) UK
	4 1 6 3	Inventor
Wilberforce, William (1.7)	3 1 1 6 3	(1759-1833) England
		Political reformer
Wilde, Oscar (1.6)	2 4 6 2 7	(1854-1900) Ireland
	4 6 6 3	Dramatist/novelist/poet
Wilhelmina (1.6)	2 4 4 4 3	(1880-1962) Netherlands
	2 2 6 7	Queen
Williams, William Carlos (1.4)	2 4 3 6 7	(1883-1963) USA
	6 7 6 3	Poet/physician
Williams, Tennessee (1.6)	2 4 6 4 3	(1912-1982) USA
		Dramatist
Wilson, Harold (1.6)	3 4 3 4 3	(1916-1995) UK
	3 7 6 7	Prime Minister
Wilson, Tom Two Bears (0.8)	4 6 4 6 7	(?-1980) USA
	6 4 6 7	Medicine man
Wishart, George (2.0)	1 6 6 6 7	(c 1513-1546) Scotland
		Reformer/martyr
Witt, Jan de (1.7)	3 1 7 6 1	(1625-1672) Netherlands
		Politician
Wittgenstein, Ludwig (1.8)	2 7 6 6 7	(1889-1951) Austria
		Philosopher
Wolkers, Jan Hendrik (1.5)	3 3 7 6 7	(1925-2007) Netherlands
	4 3 2 7	Writer/sculptor/painter
Wolsey, Thomas (1.5)	2 6 3 6 7	(1475-1530) England
	6 7 2 3	Cardinal/Lord Chancellor
Woods, Donald (1.5)	4 2 6 6 3	(1933-2001) South Africa
	4 2 6 7	Anti-apartheid campaigner
Wood, Natalie (1.4)	2 6 4 4 7	(1938-1981) USA
(Natalia Zacharenko)	6 7 6 3	Film actress
Woods, Heather (1.47)	2 4 3 4 3	(1949-1993) England
	6 7 6 7	Mystic/stigmatist
Woolf, Adeline Virginia (1.6)	4 4 7 6 7	(1882-1941) UK
	6 4 4 7	Writer
Wordsworth, William (1.7)	6 6 4 6 7	(1770-1850) England
		Poet
Wragg, Ted (1.5)	2 4 7 6 3	(1938-2005) UK
	6 3 2 7	Educator
Wren, Christopher (1.7)	1 1 4 6 7	(1632-1723) England
		Architect

Wresinski, Joseph (1.6)	2 5 3 6 7 6 4 6 3	(1917-1988) France Humanist
Wright, Frank Lloyd (1.6)	2 4 7 4 7 6 3 4 3	(1869-1959) USA Architect
Wycliffe, John (1.7)	2 6 6 2 3	(c 1329-1384) England Religious reformer
Xerxes (1.7)	1 1 3 6 1	(c 519-465 BC) Persia King
Xiaoping, Deng (2.0)	1 6 4 2 7 6 6 6 3	(1904-1997) China Chief of State
Yassin, Sheikh Ahmed (1.4)	3 6 6 6 7 6 1 6 7	(c 1936-2004) Palestine Fndr. Hamas
Yeats, W B (1.8)	2 4 4 6 3	(1865-1939) Ireland Poet/dramatist
Yeltsin, Boris N. (1.5)	6 6 3 4 3 4 6 6 7	(1931-2007) Russia President
Yochay, Shimon Bar (1.4)	3 6 3 6 7 6 1 6 3	(2nd C. AD) Palestine Founder rabbinic Judaism
Yogananda	2 4 6 6 3	(1893-1952) India Avatar
Yogi, Gururaj Ananda (1.75)	6 6 4 6 7 2 7 6 3	(1932-1988) India Spiritual teacher
Yoshida, Kenkoh (1.6)	3 6 3 6 7 4 7 2 3	(1283-1352) Japan Writer
Yoshida, Shigeru (1.55)	2 7 1 6 7 4 3 4 7	(1878-1967) Japan Statesman
Young, Lester (0.6)	2 4 4 2 3 4 6 4 7	(1909-1959) USA Jazz musician
Young, Michael (1.5)	2 6 3 6 3 2 7 6 7	(1915-2002) UK Sociologist/politician
Yukawa, Hideki (1.6)	7 4 6 6 3 7 5 2 3	(1907-1981) Japan Physicist
Zadkine, Ossip (1.6)	2 4 3 4 3	(1890-1967) Russia Sculptor
Zádor, Eugene (Jenö) (1.4)	4 4 6 2 3 7 2 4 7	(1894-1977) Hungary Composer
Zapata, Emiliano (1.6)	1 1 1 6 3	(c 1877-1919) Mexico Revolutionary
Zappa, Frank (1.4)	2 4 6 2 7 4 6 6 3	(1940-1993) USA Rock musician
Zevi, Bruno (1.6)	5 4 7 2 7 6 3 6 3	(1918-2000) Italy Architectural historian
Ziyang, Zhao (1.6)	6 3 6 4 3 5 3 6 3	(1919-2005) China Political reformer
Zola, Émile (2.3)	3 4 1 4 7	(1840-1902) France Writer
Zoroaster (Zarathustra) (4.5)	4 1 4 6 7	(628-551 BC) Persia Teacher
Zuckerman, Solly (1.55)	2 4 3 4 3 6 7 6 7	(1904-1993) UK Zoologist

Zurbarán, Francisco (2.0)	6 7 7 4 7	(1598-1662) Spain
		Painter
Zwingli, Huldreich (1.7)	6 6 1 2 3	(1484-1531) Switzerland
		Religious reformer

THE GREAT INVOCATION

From the point of Light within the Mind of God
Let light stream forth into the minds of men.
Let Light descend on Earth.

From the point of Love within the Heart of God
Let love stream forth into the hearts of men.
May Christ return to Earth.

From the centre where the Will of God is known
Let purpose guide the little wills of men –
The purpose which the Masters know and serve.

From the centre which we call the race of men
Let the Plan of Love and Light work out
And may it seal the door where evil dwells.

Let Light and Love and Power restore the Plan on Earth.

The Great Invocation, used by the Christ for the first time in June 1945, was released by Him to humanity to enable man himself to invoke the energies which would change our world, and make possible the return of the Christ and Hierarchy. This is not the form of it used by the Christ. He uses an ancient formula, seven mystic phrases long, in an ancient sacerdotal tongue. It has been translated (by Hierarchy) into terms which we can use and understand, and, translated into many languages, is used today in every country in the world.

It can be made even more potent in the form of triangles, as in the Triangles Movement (of the Lucis Trust). If you wish to work in this way, arrange with two friends to use the Invocation, aloud, daily. You need not be in the same town, or country, or say it at the same time of day. Simply say it when convenient for each one, and, linking up mentally with the two other members, visualize a triangle of white light circulating above your heads and see it linked to a network of such triangles, covering the world.

Another way, which can be used in conjunction with the triangle, is the following: When you say the first line: "From the point of Light ...," visualize (or think of, if you cannot visualize Him) the Buddha, the Embodiment of Light or Wisdom on the Planet. Visualize Him sitting in the Lotus posture, saffron robe over one shoulder, hand raised in blessing, and see emanating from the heart centre, the ajna centre (between the eyebrows), and the upraised hand of the Buddha, a brilliant golden light. See this light enter the minds of men everywhere.

When you say the line: "Let Light descend on Earth," visualize the Sun, the physical Sun, and see emanating from it beams of white light. See this light enter and saturate the Earth.

When you say: "From the point of Love ...," visualize the Christ (the Embodiment of Love) however you see Him. A good way is to see Him standing at the head of an inverted Y-shaped table, thus: λ, each arm of the of the same length. (That table exists in the world, and the Christ presides at it.) See Him standing, arms raised in blessing, and see emanating from the heart centre and the upraised hands of the Christ, a brilliant rose-coloured light (not red). Visualize this rose light enter the hearts of men everywhere.

When you say the line: "May Christ return to Earth," remember that this refers to the Hierarchy as a whole and not only to the Christ. He is the heart centre of the Hierarchy, and although He is now among us, the remainder of the Hierarchy (that part of it which will externalize slowly, over the years) still requires to be invoked, the magnetic conduit for Their descent has still to be maintained.

When you say: "From the centre where the Will of God is known ...," which is Shamballa, visualize a great sphere of white light. (You can place it, mentally, in the Gobi desert, where it is, on the two highest of the four etheric planes. One day, when mankind develops etheric vision which it will do in this coming age, this centre will be seen and known, as many other etheric centres will be seen and known.) Streaming from this sphere of brilliant light visualize, again, beams of light entering the world, galvanizing mankind into spiritual action.

Do this with focused thought and intention, your attention fixed on the ajna centre between the eyebrows. In this way you form a telepathic conduit between yourselves and Hierarchy. Through that conduit the energies thus invoked can flow. The Great Invocation is used in this way at the start of every Transmission Meditation. There is nothing better you can do for the world or yourselves, than channel these great spiritual potencies.

PRAYER FOR THE NEW AGE

I am the creator of the universe.
I am the father and mother of the universe.
Everything comes from me.
Everything shall return to me.
Mind, spirit and body are my temples,
For the Self to realize in them
My supreme Being and Becoming.

●

The Prayer for the New Age, given by Maitreya, the World Teacher, is a great mantram or affirmation with an invocative effect. It will be a powerful tool in the recognition by us that man and God are One, that there is no separation. The 'I' is the Divine Principle behind all creation. The Self emanates from, and is identical to, the Divine Principle.

The most effective way to use this mantram is to say or think the words with focused will, while holding the attention at the ajna centre between the eyebrows. When the mind grasps the meaning of the concepts, and simultaneously the will is brought to bear, those concepts will be activated and the mantram will work. If it is said seriously every day, there will grow inside you a realization of your true Self.

REFERENCES CITED BY THE AUTHOR

Bailey, Alice A., *Esoteric Healing* (London: Lucis Press, 1953)
—, *Esoteric Psychology, Volumes I & II* (London: Lucis Press, 1936)
—, *The Destiny of the Nations* (London: Lucis Press, 1949)
—, *The Externalisation of the Hierarchy* (London: Lucis Press, 1955)
—, *The Rays and the Initiations* (London: Lucis Press, 1960)
—, *Treatise on Cosmic Fire* (London: Lucis Press, 1925)

Blavatsky, H.P., *Isis Unveiled, Volumes I & II* (London: Theosophical Publishing House, 1877)
—, *The Secret Doctrine* (London: Theosophical Publishing House, 1888)

Roerich, Helena, *Supermundane – The Inner Life, Volumes I & II* (New York: Agni Yoga Society, 1994)

BOOKS BY BENJAMIN CREME

(Listed in order of publication)

The Reappearance of the Christ and the Masters of Wisdom
In his first book, Benjamin Creme gives the background and pertinent information concerning the emergence of Maitreya (the Christ), as World Teacher for the New Age now dawning. Expected under different names by all religious groups, Maitreya comes to help us create co-operation among the many ideological factions, galvanize world goodwill and sharing, and inspire sweeping political, social, economic and environmental reforms. Benjamin Creme puts the most profound event of the last 2,000 years into its correct historical and esoteric context and describes what effect the World Teacher's presence will have on both the world's institutions and the average person. Through his telepathic contact with a Master of Wisdom, Creme offers insights on such subjects as the soul and reincarnation; fear of death; telepathy; meditation; nuclear energy; ancient civilizations; UFOs; problems of the developing world; a new economic order; the antichrist; and the 'last judgement'.
1st edition 1979. 2nd edition 2007. ISBN: 978-90-71484-32-2, 288pp.

Messages from Maitreya the Christ
During the years of preparation for His emergence, Maitreya gave 140 Messages through Benjamin Creme during public lectures in London from 1977 to 1982. The method used was mental overshadowing and a telepathic rapport thus set up.

Maitreya's Messages of sharing, co-operation and unity inspire readers to spread the news of His reappearance and to work urgently for the rescue of millions suffering from poverty and starvation in a world of plenty. In Message No. 11 Maitreya says: "My Plan is to show you that the way out of your problems is to listen again to the true voice of God within your hearts, to share the produce of this most bountiful of worlds among your brothers and sisters everywhere...." (5 January 1978)

Maitreya's words are a unique source of wisdom, hope and succour at this critical time of world change, and when read aloud these profound yet simple Messages invoke His energy and blessing.

1st edition Vol. I 1981, Vol. II 1986. 2nd, combined, edition 1992, reprinted 2001. ISBN 978-90-71484-22-3, 286pp.

Transmission: A Meditation for the New Age
Transmission Meditation is a form of group meditation for the purpose of 'stepping down' (transforming) spiritual energies which thus become accessible and useful to the general public. It is the creation, in co-operation with the Hierarchy of Masters, of a vortex or pool of higher energy for the benefit of humanity.

Introduced in 1974 by Benjamin Creme, under the direction of his Master, this is a form of service which is simple to do and is at the same time a powerful means of personal growth. The meditation is a combination of two yogas: Karma Yoga (yoga of service) and Laya Yoga (yoga of energy or chakras). It is a service in which we can be involved for the rest of our lives knowing that we are helping the evolution of humanity into, and beyond, the New Age. There are hundreds of Transmission Meditation groups active in many countries around the world.

In this practical and inspiring book Benjamin Creme describes the aims, technique and results of Transmission Meditation, as well as the underlying purpose of the meditation for the development of disciples.

1st edition 1983. 5th edition 2006. ISBN 978-90-71484-35-3, 212pp.

A Master Speaks
Humanity is guided from behind the scenes by a highly evolved and illumined group of men Who have preceded us along the path of evolution. These Masters of Wisdom, as They are called, seldom appear openly, but usually work through Their disciples – men and women who influence society through their work in science, education, art, religion, politics, and in every department of life.

British artist Benjamin Creme is a disciple of a Master with Whom he is in close telepathic contact. Since the launching of Share International, the magazine of which Benjamin Creme is editor, his Master has contributed to every issue an inspiring article on a wide range of subjects: reason and intuition; the new civilization; health and healing; the art of living; the need for synthesis; justice is divine; the Son of Man; human rights; the law of rebirth; the end of hunger; sharing for peace; the rise of people power; the brightest future; co-operation – and many more.

The major purpose of these articles is to draw attention to the needs of the present and the immediate future time, and to give information about the teachings of Maitreya, the Master of all the Masters. This third edition contains all 223 articles from the first 22 volumes of Share International.
1st edition 1985. 3rd expanded edition 2004.
ISBN 978-90-71484-29-2, 452pp.

Maitreya's Mission, Volume One
The first of a trilogy of books which describe the emergence and teachings of Maitreya, the World Teacher. As human consciousness steadily matures, many of the ancient 'mysteries' are now being revealed. This volume can be seen as a guidebook for humanity as it travels on the evolutionary journey. The book's canvas is vast: from the new teachings of the Christ to meditation and karma; from life after death, and reincarnation, to healing and social transformation; from initiation and the role of service to the Seven Rays; from Leonardo da Vinci and Mozart to Sathya Sai Baba. It sets the scene and prepares the way for the work of Maitreya, as World Teacher, and the creation of a new and better life for all. It is a powerful message of hope.
1st edition 1986. 3rd edition 1993, reprinted 2003.
ISBN 978-90-71484-08-7, 419pp.

Maitreya's Mission, Volume Two
This inspiring and heart-warming book offers new hope and guidance to a suffering world on the threshold of a Golden Age. It presents the teachings of Maitreya, the World Teacher, on both

the outer, practical, and inner, spiritual levels; His uniquely accurate forecasts of world events, which have astonished international media; and His miraculous appearances which have brought hope and inspiration to many thousands. It also contains a series of unique interviews with Benjamin Creme's Master which throw new and revealing light on some of the greatest problems facing humanity.

This book covers an enormous range: Maitreya's teachings; the growth of consciousness; new forms of government; commercialization and market forces; the principal of sharing; life in the New Age; schools without walls; the Technology of Light; crop circles; the Self; telepathy; disease and death; energy and thought; Transmission Meditation; the soul's purpose. Also includes transcripts of Benjamin Creme's inspiring talks on 'The Overcoming of Fear' and 'The Call to Service'.

1st edition 1993, reprinted 2004. ISBN 978-90-71484-11-7, 753pp.

The Ageless Wisdom Teaching

An overview of humanity's spiritual legacy, this booklet serves as a concise and easy-to-understand introduction to the Ageless Wisdom Teaching. It explains the basic tenets of esotericism, including: source of the Teaching; the emergence of the World Teacher; rebirth and reincarnation; the Law of Cause and Effect; the Plan of evolution; origin of man; meditation and service; future changes. Also included is an esoteric glossary and a recommended reading list.

1st edition 1996, reprinted 2006. ISBN 978-90-71484-13-1, 76pp.

Maitreya's Mission, Volume Three

Benjamin Creme presents a compelling vision of the future. With Maitreya, the World Teacher, and His disciples the Masters of Wisdom openly offering Their guidance, humanity will create a civilization worthy of its divine potential. Peace will be established; sharing the world's resources the norm; maintaining our environment a top priority. The new education will teach the fact of the soul and the evolution of consciousness. The cities of the world will be transformed into centres of great beauty.

This book offers invaluable wisdom on a vast range of topics. It includes Maitreya's priorities for the future, and interviews with a Master of Wisdom on 'The Challenge of the 21st Century'. It explores karma and reincarnation, the origin of humanity, meditation and service, the Plan of evolution, and other fundamental concepts of the Ageless Wisdom Teachings. It includes a fascinating look from an esoteric, spiritual perspective at ten famous artists – among them da Vinci, Michelangelo and Rembrandt – by Benjamin Creme, himself an artist.

Like the first two volumes of Maitreya's Mission, this work combines profound spiritual truths with practical solutions to today's most vexing problems. It is indeed a message of hope for a humanity ready to "begin the creation of a civilization such as this world has never yet seen".
1st edition 1997. ISBN 978-90-71484-15-57, 705pp.

The Great Approach: New Light and Life for Humanity
This prophetic book addresses the problems of our chaotic world and its gradual change under the influence of a group of perfected men, the Masters of Wisdom, Who, with Their leader Maitreya, the World Teacher, are returning openly to the world for the first time in 98,000 years.

The book covers such topics as: sharing; the USA in a quandary; ethnic conflicts; crime and violence; environment and pollution; genetic engineering; science and religion; the nature of light; health and healing; education; miracles; the soul and incarnation. An extraordinary synthesis of knowledge, it throws a searchlight on the future; with clear vision it predicts our highest achievements of thought to reveal the amazing scientific discoveries which lie ahead. It shows us a world in which war is a thing of the past, and the needs of all are met.
1st edition 2001. ISBN 978-90-71484-23-0, 320pp.

The Art of Co-operation
The Art of Co-operation deals with the most pressing problems of our time, and their solution, from the point of view of the

Ageless Wisdom Teachings that, for millennia, have revealed the forces underlying the outer world. Benjamin Creme brings these teachings up to date, preparing the way for the imminent emergence of Maitreya, the World Teacher, and His group of Masters of Wisdom.

This volume looks at a world locked in ancient competition, trying to solve its problems by old and out-worn methods, while the answer – co-operation – lies in our own hands. It shows the way to a world of justice, freedom and peace through a growing appreciation of the unity underlying all life. Maitreya will inspire in us this growing realization.

Topics include: the necessity of co-operation; the USA and competition; organism versus organization; opportunity for service; fear of loss; karma; love; courage and detachment; overcoming of glamour; how the Masters teach; unity in diversity; consensus; trust.
1st edition 2002. ISBN 978-90-71484-26-1, 235pp.

Maitreya's Teachings: The Laws of Life
We do not have even fragments of the teachings of former World Teachers given prior to certain knowledge of Their existence. We do not have the teachings of a Christ, or a Buddha, or a Krishna, except seen through the eyes of later followers. For the first time we are given the flavour of the thoughts and insights of a Being of immeasurable stature to enable us to understand the path of evolution stretching ahead of us which He has come to outline for us. The impression left in the mind by the Teacher is that the breadth and depth of His knowledge and awareness have no limits; that He is tolerant and wise beyond conception, and of amazing humility.

Few could read from these pages without being changed. To some the extraordinary insights into world events will be of major interest, while to others the laying bare of the secrets of self-realization, the simple description of experienced truth, will be a revelation. To anyone seeking to understand the Laws of Life, these subtle and pregnant insights will take them quickly to the core of Life itself, and provide them with a simple path stretching to the mountain-top. The essential unity of all life is underscored in a clear and meaningful way. Never, it would appear, have the Laws by which we live seemed so natural and so unconstraining.

1st edition, 2005. ISBN 978-90-71484-31-5, 258pp.

The Art of Living: Living Within the Laws of Life

Inspired by the writings of two Masters of Wisdom – the Master Djwhal Khul and, particularly, Benjamin Creme's own Master – Part One of this book considers the experience of living as a form of art, like painting or music. To reach a high level of expression requires both knowledge of and adherence to certain fundamental principles. In the art of life, it is through the understanding of the great Law of Cause and Effect, and the related Law of Rebirth, that we achieve the poised harmlessness that leads to personal happiness, right human relations and the correct path for all humanity on its evolutionary journey.

Parts Two and Three, 'The Pairs of Opposites' and 'Illusion', propose that it is man's unique position in the evolutionary scheme – the meeting point of spirit and matter – that produces his seemingly endless struggle both within himself and in outer living. The means by which he emerges from the fog of illusion, and blends these two aspects of himself into one perfect Whole, is living life itself with growing detachment and objective self-awareness.

1st edition 2006. ISBN 978- 90-71484-37-7, 215pp.

The World Teacher for All Humanity

Maitreya, the World Teacher, stands poised, ready to emerge into full public work. This book presents an overview of this momentous event: the return to the everyday world of Maitreya in July 1977 and the gradual emergence of His group, the Masters of Wisdom; the enormous changes that Maitreya's presence has brought about; and His plans, priorities and recommendations for the immediate future. It discusses in detail the quality and capacity of Maitreya based on a series of articles written by Benjamin Creme's Master – Maitreya as a great spiritual Avatar with immeasurable love, wisdom and power; and, as a friend and brother of humanity who is here to lead the

whole of humanity into the New Age of Aquarius.
1st edition, 2007. ISBN 978-90-71484-39-1, 132pp.

The Awakening of Humanity

A companion volume to The World Teacher for All Humanity, published in 2007, which emphasizes the nature of Maitreya as World Teacher, the Embodiment of Love and Wisdom.

The Awakening of Humanity focuses on the day when Maitreya declares Himself openly as World Teacher for the Age of Aquarius. It describes the process of Maitreya's emergence, the steps leading to the Day of Declaration, and humanity's response to this momentous experience.

Of the Day of Declaration Benjamin Creme's Master says: "Never, before, will men have heard the call to their divinity, the challenge to their presence here on Earth. Each, singly, and solemnly alone, will know for that time the purpose and meaning of their lives, will experience anew the grace of childhood, the purity of aspiration cleansed of self. For these precious minutes, men will know afresh the joy of full participation in the realities of Life, will feel connected one to another, like the memory of a distant past.".
1st edition 2008. ISBN 978-90-71484-41-4, 141pp.

Benjamin Creme's books have been translated and published in Dutch, French, German, Japanese and Spanish by groups responding to this message. Some have also been published in Chinese, Croatian, Finnish, Greek, Hebrew, Italian, Portuguese, Romanian, Russian, Slovenian and Swedish. Further translations are planned. Books, as well as audio and video cassettes, are available from local booksellers.

Share International

A unique magazine featuring each month: up-to-date information about the emergence of Maitreya, the World Teacher; an article from a Master of Wisdom; expansions of the esoteric teachings; Benjamin Creme's answers to a wide variety of topical and esoteric questions; articles by and interviews with people at the forefront of progressive world change; news from UN agencies and reports of positive developments in the transformation of our world.

Share International brings together the two major directions of New Age thinking – the political and the spiritual. It shows the synthesis underlying the political, social, economic and spiritual changes now occurring on a global scale, and seeks to stimulate practical action to rebuild our world along more just and compassionate lines.

Share International covers news, events and comments related to Maitreya's priorities: an adequate supply of the right food, housing and shelter for all, healthcare and education as universal rights, and the maintenance of ecological balance in the world.
ISSN 0169-1341

Versions of *Share International* are available in Dutch, French, German, Japanese, Romanian, Slovenian and Spanish. For subscription information, contact the appropriate office below.

For North, Central and South America,
Australia, New Zealand and the Philippines
Share International
PO Box 971, North Hollywood, CA 91603, USA

For the UK
Share International
PO Box 3677, London NW5 1RU, UK

For the rest of the world
Share International
PO Box 41877, 1009 DB Amsterdam, Holland

Extensive information and excerpts from the magazine are published online at: **www.share-international.org**

INDEX